SunShine and Smoke

Sunshine and Smoke

American Writers and the American Environment

Edited by
David D. Anderson
Michigan State University

J. B. Lippincott Company
Philadelphia • New York • Toronto

*For two whose love of the
Ohio countryside was contagious:
my mother, Nora M. Anderson,
and my father, David J. Anderson;
and for my wife, Pat, with thanks
for her encouragement, interest,
patience, and help.*

Contents

Introduction

On April 22, 1970, the first national environmental teach-in was held on American college and university campuses from coast to coast and beyond. Earth Day was proclaimed, and platoons of speakers deplored or condemned the pollution of the American natural environment in terms ranging from the traditional accents of the Establishment to the emotional and simplistic rhetoric of the New Left. College students held elaborate funeral services for dilapidated jalopies, during which a new social cause, to rank alongside the civil rights and antiwar movements, was proclaimed by a generation of young Americans who are eager to proclaim their dedication to such causes. Then they drove off, a few to participate in demands that American corporations become socially responsible, clean up rather than pollute the atmosphere, and join them in refusing to serve the American war effort in Southeast Asia. The throw-away bottle and the aluminum soft-drink can continued to stand beside the peace symbol as the peculiar insignia of the most affluent generation America has yet produced. As the United States began its third century as a nation, its natural environment continued to deteriorate, and its cities continued to decay, as government and industry responded to the tangible demands of material consumption rather than the demands of idealistic declamations.

Is this picture oversimplified, unjust, and cynical, or does the newly awakened interest in the quality of the American environment begin a social cause that will mark a new birth of individual freedom and dignity, as did the great American social crusades of earlier years and centuries? The evidence is not yet in, nor will it be for years, perhaps for decades. The new American concern with the quality of the environment, popularly a part of the practical application of the science of ecology, may become, as did the abolition movement of the nineteenth century, a struggle carried on over generations, culminating in a final massive effort and the proclamation of a new birth of freedom. Or it may become lost in other causes, a tool to be manipulated for other purposes, as did temperance, antiwar, and other reform movements of the past. Or, reaching what ap-

Introduction

pears to be final success, it may abandon the cause, as did the abolitionists, while greater social evils inexorably emerge.

Whatever the outcome, it will be very much in the American tradition of idealistic reform, and the results will have been foreshadowed by precedents of the past. Americans, from the beginning of settlement, have held before themselves a vision of a perfect society, whether in the traditional sense of a stable, stratified society, as did the cavalier settlers of Virginia, who foresaw a new aristocracy, the Puritans of New England, who sought to establish God's commonwealth upon earth, or countless thousands who simply sought a better life, usually in terms of personal freedom and material well-being. Or perhaps that perfect society was seen in terms of the eighteenth-century vision of an orderly, open society based upon government controlled by the governed and responsive to their needs; or in terms of utopias individually or collectively fulfilling, sought by visionaries among practical Jacksonian politicians and Romantic theorists; or a perfect society based upon technology and industry enslaved rather than men, demanded by the muckrakers, theorists, and reform politicians of industrial America from the Civil War to the present, through a century of crisis and conflict.

Whatever its specifics and its degree of success or failure, the Utopian vision has been part of the American tradition for nearly three centuries, and the sudden ecological awareness of the present generation is very much in that tradition. Americans have always sought and believed in the promise of a better life, often a perfect life. Today's leaders of the crusade against pollution, in the tradition of romantic idealism, proclaim such a vision, even as they, in common with visionaries of the past, emphasize the dangers of dissolution and decay if their warnings are not heeded. Americans have always practiced and accepted the technique of the revivalist preacher at the frontier camp meeting, whether it be concerned with religion or politics, abolitionism or prohibition. There is no reason to expect that the tradition and the techniques of fundamentalism displayed at the national teach-in will not play a major role in the ecological crusade.

Also in the American tradition, perhaps more important than the specific techniques of antipollution campaigns and eminently appropriate and significant in the current concern with the quality and nature of the American environment, is an aspect of the American past virtually ignored by literary historians and critics who have attempted to construct elaborate theories of the nature and course of American literature. This is the fact that concern with the American environment is basic to American literature from the beginning to the present. This aspect of American literature is most revealing, as it makes clear the evolution of American attitudes toward the natural environment, attitudes that at once reveal a basic ambiguity in the American character as they point out qualities that make the current concern with the deterioration of the environment both necessary and possible at the same time. This aspect may also make it possible to predict the outcome of the current concern and crusade.

The fact is that throughout American literary history, from the beginning of what can be broadly called American literature, that is, literature primarily in English about American subject matter by writers closely connected with and vitally concerned with American life, American writers have been concerned to a major extent with the basic concerns of today's ecologists. That is, they have been concerned with the nature and quality of the American environment, particularly as it affects the life and well-being of the individual. In this sense, many American writers, whether of fiction or nonfiction, poetry or prose, can be called environmentalists, and American literature, approached from an environmental point of view, can often tell us more about the nature of America and American life and literature than literary theories or approaches which stress aesthetics, economic or environmental determinism, or organic cyclical rhythms. It is possible to perceive an environmental awareness and analysis that has within it elements of all these other attempts at literary analysis and synthesis, but goes beyond them to acknowledge the preoccupation with coming to know, understand, interpret, mould, and shape the American environment. This attitude, evident from the beginning in writing about America, has become the basic American literary tradition, and just as it reveals much about the American past, as any vital literature must do, it also points its way toward the American future.

First, it is evident that the attitudes and attempts of American writers to know and use the American environment have not been static; that is, they have grown and changed, as has the environment itself. Furthermore, it is evident that American writers in substantial numbers, unlike many of their critics, have never been determinists or pessimists. Instead they have been optimistic in their belief that man can mould the environment to his liking; and in their conviction that the results will be better than the reality of the past, they have shared in America's Utopian vision.

Thus, the earliest American writers were to a great extent responsible for establishing the tradition that endures today among American writers as they examine the environment in its relationship to human beings as individuals and as social animals. As they looked at the American environment, they established an attitude that has gone far beyond literature and has become firmly embedded in the national philosophy and faith. These writers saw an abundant America with potential for providing a good life for all, if, in terms of another traditional American belief, each man were willing to work. The earliest literary vision of America was truly a vision of abundance.

With the establishment of an American society and the emergence of a group of writers consciously seeking an American literary tradition appropriate to the new nation, the vision of abundance did not fade. Rather, in the first half of the nineteenth century, as America began its search for a national identity, the writers saw what the new country with its blessed environment promised, and they attempted to define it in their works. This was the vision of fulfillment, an easy fulfillment based upon a free, open society in a free, open setting. Romantic idealists and Jacksonian democratic activists combined to promise whatever fulfillment the indi-

Introduction

vidual sought, and so persuasive were their voices that words of warning, often combined with visions of tragedy, were ignored or denied.

But Civil War, industrialism, urbanization, and Darwinism became material realities, soon to be reinforced by Marxism and Freudianism, and the result was a realistic tempering that threatened for a time to eradicate the visions that writers of the last years of the nineteenth cenury had begun to question and doubt. The reality they saw and attempted to define was grim, so grim that for some of them there was no hope, but only a maliciously indifferent fate. But such conviction was to be a temporary aberration, as the conviction of abundance remained, reinforced by faith in reform, the same faith that motivated earlier idealists and that continues to motivate them today. From realistic, even naturalistic, writers to muckraking journalists and practical politicians, the vision of reality projected in their work was a vision that pointed out shortcomings in the relationship between the individual American and his environment, both natural and social. Implicit in their vision of reality was the conviction that this reality was only temporary, that the future could be reshaped by men to include the promise of the past. The more optimistic among them asserted that this not only could but would be accomplished by men called to leadership through the process defined by Jefferson more than a century before.

The hope engendered by this vision of reality is still with us as we enter the last years of the twentieth century. Because its promise, the Utopian promise of American tradition, has not yet been realized, the voices of our century and of our day are ambiguous, raising visions of hope and despair, sometimes in the same work. But if the perfect society has not yet emerged, neither has the chaos of those whose vision is despairing, and the evidence of the American past justifies the vision of hope rather than despair. The record is clear, as the writers in this collection make evident; the implications are unmistakable, as American writers of the past, who helped to shape the traditions that dominate the present, seek the reality of the American environment. From their works it may be possible to predict the ultimate outcome of the ecology crusade and the relationship between man and his environment in America of the next century.

The selections in part 1 have been modernized with respect to spelling, capitalization, use of italics, and punctuation, insofar as this was possible without changing the wording of sentences. Words that are no longer in current use have been printed in italics.

The selections in parts 2, 3, and 4 have been printed in their original form, except that obvious typographical errors and misspellings have been corrected, and punctuation has been altered in a few instances where the original was clearly inappropriate and confusing.

Introduction

1

The Vision of Abundance

During the more than three hundred years between the first landfall in the West Indies by Columbus and his polyglot crew and the beginning of the nineteenth century, millions of words were written about the nature of America. For the first two hundred of those years, most of this written matter was essentially reporting back to those who had remained in Europe, and its subject was almost invariably the wonder, the beauty, the richness, and the strangeness of the new continent and its inhabitants. For the next century, during which setlements were consolidated and the impact between European cultural maturity and American wilderness began to produce a society aware of its uniqueness, the writing increasingly reveals an eagerness to record and to interpret phenomena that would stimulate self-study and growth.

In both periods, many of the writers showed an eagerness to describe and to understand the American environment as it related to human beings, at first in relationship to those who represented the vanguard of European culture in its most extensive period of migration, and ultimately as the New World affected those who had come to stay and to build something new out of the old culture and the new land. In their eagerness to describe and interpret, these writers reflected not only the basic convictions of intellectual movements ranging from Renaissance curiosity to Enlightenment virtuosity, but established a tradition of concern with the individual and his environment that has provided a focal point for much American writing from that time to this. The individual and his environment have become the great central theme of American literature. In the development of no national literature has that concern been so great or its effects so obvious. More than any other national literature, American literature grows out of its close relationship with the life of its people and their attempt to subdue a wilderness and erect a society not consciously or deliberately unique, but inevitably so, as isolated colonies became a nation.

The origin of this close relationship between American life and the great theme of its literature becomes evident early in the seventeenth century, when permanent settlements at Jamestown, Virginia, in 1607, and Plymouth, Massachusetts, in 1620, were established. By this time the uniqueness of the English impact upon North America was clear, as it was evident that English colonization rather than Spanish and French exploitation would determine the future. Indeed, there was little choice when it was seen that the area of British interest lacked the gold that enriched the Spanish to the south and the easy access to the interior that marked the French sphere of interest to the north. The British, limited to a coastal plain beyond which were mountains, pressed by their traditions of trade, seafaring, and constant striving for social advancement, inevitably chose to settle, hopefully to prosper.

Thomas Hariot, writing as a result of the attempts by Sir Walter Raleigh's company to establish a colony in what is now North Carolina, tells much the same story as his contemporaries. Among them were the Frenchman Father Hennepin, the Spaniard Coronado, and the Englishman John Smith, and their story is similar to that told by those who were

The Vision of Abundance

to come later in New England and Virginia. Although his purpose was to defend Raleigh's venture against its detractors, primarily those who came to make fortunes quickly, Hariot's account is remarkably restrained. He writes of a country that is rich but not profligate, a country in which Europeans can live and prosper, but a land which places responsibilities upon its colonizers to learn to understand and use the land and its produce. To Hariot, as to his contemporary promoters of colonization and their descendants, the potential for profit and finding a fulfilling existence are virtually beyond measure, and the hazards are few. Although Hariot was not above promising a life in which twenty-four hours of labor would provide enough food for a year, an exaggeration almost unforgivable in one of his scientific interests, he presents a picture very much like that which served as the basis of the dream of generations of immigrants: a land limitless in its potential for providing for man's physical needs while serving to fulfill his vision of a perfect society. At the same time, he wrote the first reasonably accurate account available to curious Englishmen of the land, its produce, and its inhabitants.

By Cotton Mather's time, the problem was not that of rationalizing settlement or encouraging migration, particularly in New England. Rather, by the opening years of the eighteenth century, New England, for generations a homogenous English-speaking Puritan commonwealth implanted on the most inhospitable part of England's North American domain, had grown and prospered materially, had established a theocracy that endured the crisis of the Salem witch trials, and had begun to seek its fortune by exploiting its natural ties to the sea rather than depending upon the uncertainties of a harsh climate and rocky soil. Mather effectively marks the end of the attempts to sell the new country to those reluctant to buy and the beginning of the attempt, in the light of the Age of Reason, to describe the natural phenomena of America accurately and completely.

Thus Mather, one side of him looking backward in time to an age of faith and fear, of explanations in terms of the will of God and the machinations of the devil, exhibits a scientific curiosity at odds with the age of Calvinistic belief in the supernatural and much more in keeping with the slowly emerging rational acceptance of the natural. At the same time, he reveals an aspect of the natural environment of America rarely made public up to that time. Still, the American colonies were appendages of the mother country, objects of mere curiosity to most Englishmen, and Mather's letter to John Woodward gives evidence of a colonial inferiority complex that marked much of the writing about America for the time.

With more than a million colonists in English North America by the middle of the eighteenth century—sure proof of the increasing attraction of the new country for so many—and with the proliferation of towns, settlements, and farms up and down the Atlantic coast, it was evident that in spite of perennial threats from French, Spanish, Indians, and climate, the colonies were not only to endure, but that they were to become increasingly one, as outside pressures and domestic changes brought them slowly together. Strained relations with the mother country, leading to revolution

Introduction

and independence, made them one in political fact, turning the attention of the colonists inward as they became aware of the continent that was theirs by inheritance, conquest, and promise. Concurrently, their attention was pointed and focused by the rationally inquiring mind of the age.

The Enlightenment, in full sway, provided the rationale for virtually every function of political, social, economic, and intellectual man during the second half of the eighteenth century, and the documentation of the American environment accelerated rapidly. It manifested itself in a flood of histories, journals, letters, diaries, and ecological studies, often by men of affairs in other areas who, in the fashion of the eighteenth century, were conscious of their debt to the intellectual inheritance of man.

Consequently, during those years the concern with the American environment, already a tradition, intensified in the production of travel documents and scientific treatises, both concerned with aboriginal and European people, the climate, and the flora and fauna of the continent. In these works, the American vision of the natural environment began to take on the continental aspect that provided much of the depth as well as the breadth of writing in the nineteenth century, at least until the Civil War. Elements that point toward the continental vision are evident in William Byrd's *History of the Dividing Line,* a travel diary based upon his survey trip to delineate the Virginia boundary in 1728 (but not published until 1841), and in Samuel Peters's *General History of Connecticut* (1781). Both documents are typical of their time, as the writers' experiences are filtered through their convictions and prejudices. Thus Byrd's genteel manners and aristocratic pretensions color his views of the less pretentious frontiersman whom he encounters. Peters, a clergyman, a Tory, and a sly wit, combines these qualities with perceptive, accurate observations to produce a natural and social history that often takes on the dimension of fantasy.

Neither man, however, had scientific ambitions, and the documents have an added dimension of liveliness that otherwise would have been missing. However, like most accounts of earlier eras, theirs are not scientifically accurate or wholly trustworthy. But such documents are valuable as social history and as records of men reordering established institutions to fashion new orders more harmoniously attuned to the American environment.

In contrast, William Bartram and Thomas Jefferson are true sons of the Enlightenment, seeking objective, verifiable truth, convinced that somewhere beyond the seeming variety of nature there is the perceptible unity of natural law. Bartram, a naturalist by birth as well as by choice, was at once perhaps the finest scientific observer of natural phenomena of his day and so personally delighted by his observations that he anticipated the romantic involvement of a later day. Jefferson, a man of wide-ranging interests, strove for scientific objectivity, and in his search found natural evidence to support the liberal-agrarian philosophic premises that provided much of the motivation and inspiration for his career as scientist, philosopher, and activist. Both men reflect clearly the century of which they

The Vision of Abundance

were a part as they define and describe the countryside, and both convey the flavor of that time as they go beyond the immediate, Bartram to convey a poetic vision, Jefferson to convey a philosopher's insight. Both men also define a natural way of life in which society will be simple and men will be free.

Hector St. Jean de Crèvecoeur and Alexander Hamilton build on the faith and convictions of the eighteenth-century search for a perfect society as they look at the American environment and project the world as they would like it to be, and both have had lasting effects, the former that of an ideal lost, and the latter that of a reality established. De Crèvecoeur shared the Jeffersonian dream of an agrarian society, characterized by social mobility, closeness to nature, and the wise, benevolent leadership of a natural aristocracy. As did Jefferson, he feared that man massed in cities would prevent the democratic dream from becoming reality; he saw no cities in America, and he provided eloquent testimony that none should come. In Jeffersonian terms he envisioned a free society, unmarked by the serfdom or peasantry of the Old World or the slavery of the New. For de Crèvecoeur, the American reality would be composed of a close relationship and working arrangement between free men and the natural world of which they were a part. In the New World, he was convinced, such an arrangement was not only a possibility; it was, as his own experience gave evidence, a realizable, universally attainable fact.

De Crèvecoeur provided a vision, not of the future reality, but of the future ideal, the dream that generations of Americans were to seek, even as they wrestled with reality. That reality, almost pure vision as America became a nation, was defined by Alexander Hamilton as he sought a future composed not of a simple agrarian society, but of a busy, industrious nation devoted to practical affairs and a national existence characterized by usefulness, practicality, and profit.

For Hamilton, as his *Report on the Subject of Manufactures* makes clear, man's goal must not be to work with nature, but to subdue it and reorder its goods through the application of ingenuity and devices, so that it may be more immediately beneficial to man and ultimately conducive to the good life. Hamilton's vision of the America of the future was ideal, as he foresaw a nation progressing, essentially in statistical terms, but it was a vision that was soon to become a dehumanized reality that neither Hamilton nor his followers, eager to exploit and to grow, could anticipate. Hamilton's vision, like Jefferson's a product of the Enlightenment, was perhaps keener in its insights into the nature of man, as he found simultaneously a new society to be built and an untouched continent to be exploited by aggressively free men. Freed by Hamilton's view of the path to plenty, industrialism was to dominate American society after the defeat of agrarianism and the abolition of slavery in the war that refuted the idyllic myth of the antebellum South.

But when Hamilton made his sound and practical plea, industrialization was still in the future, and its domination was beyond even the wildest vision. Nearer in time and in significance were those who sought

Introduction

to build upon the observations of Bartram and others who saw nature unspoiled and searched for meaning beyond it. The most interesting among them were those who tried to project what they saw in verse, as they attempted to convey a vision they believed to be poetic.

The poetic vision of meaning in the late eighteenth century was not a single vision, however. Phillis Wheatley saw America from the peculiar viewpoint of the African become an American. Timothy Dwight, conservative and conventional, looked to the past for his poetic model and his view of perfection, as did the great Calvinists of the generation before him. His world, the "Flourishing Village" which made up part two of *Greenfield Hill*, is in essence the New England theocratic village, smugly secure in the New England countryside, that supporters of the theocracy sought to establish in their "City upon a Hill," and that later generations believed had existed in the past. For Dwight, however, that reality, continued and expanded, would provide a sound foundation for the American future. Without knowing it, he was prophesying the movement that became known as Manifest Destiny. But Dwight's role as prophet was lost on his generation, and it has been ignored by succeeding generations of critics.

While Dwight's complex vision was conventionally theological and nationalistic, Freneau's poetic vision was more nearly in tune with immediate forces and currents of his time. More genuinely a poet of originality and sensitivity than Dwight, Freneau stands as the founder of a gradually emerging American poetry. A patriot and a nationalist, Freneau was a Jeffersonian and a Deist philosophically. Later he began to tap the newly emerging streams of romanticism and nationalism, fusing in his work a search for uniquely American subject matter in nature and a vision of an ultimate spiritual meaning beyond. His work, from its origins in eighteenth-century philosophy, slowly accelerates the search for meaning that preceded the nineteenth, intellectually and culturally as well as chronologically.

With the close of the eighteenth century, the years of America's colonization and consolidation also ended, and the years of America's search for fulfillment of its ideal began. For more than two hundred years writers of English origin, writing in English about the North American countryside that England had marked out as its own, had attempted to define what they saw, and invariably their vision was one of abundance. As the new nation began to emerge, those writers who had been born Englishmen began to surrender their vantage point and their role to a new generation of writers who were born Americans and who sought a vision of America that was truly American. But the foundations of the new tradition were already firmly established, and the new writers sought their fulfillment in the interrelationship between the individual, newly American and free, and his natural, fruitful, and provocative environment. To a major extent, the very reason for the existence of the new American writers of the nineteenth century, as well as the point of departure for their romantic search, was the existence of the writings that follow, the works of those writers born Englishmen who were responsible for the continuing vision of the American environment as abundant.

The Vision of Abundance

Thomas Hariot:
A Brief and True Report
of the Newfound Land
# of Virginia

Thomas Hariot (1560-1621) is distinguished as
the author of the first English book describing
the Virginia (now North Carolina) countryside
and its flora, fauna, and potential for colonization. A friend and defender of Sir Walter
Raleigh's colonization efforts, Hariot wrote his
pamphlet to encourage colonization and refute
those colonists who had returned to England
in disgust and bitterness.

Since the first undertaking by Sir Walter Raleigh to deal in the action of discovering of that country which is now called and known by the name of Virginia, many voyages having been thither made at sundry times to his great charge, as first in the year 1584, and afterwards in the years 1585, 1586, and now of late this last year of 1587. There have been divers and variable reports with some slanderous and shameful speeches bruited abroad by many that returned from thence. Especially of that discovery which was made by the colony transported by Sir Richard Greinvile in the year 1585, being of all the others the most principal and as yet of most effect, the time of their abode in the country being a whole year, when as in the other voyage before they stayed but six weeks; and the others after were only for supply and transportation, nothing more being discovered than had been before. Which reports have not done a little wrong to many that otherwise would have also favored and adventured in the action, to the honor and benefit of our nation, besides the particular profit and credit which would redound to themselves the dealers therein, as I hope by the sequel of events to the shame of those that have avouched the contrary shall be manifest, if you the adventurers, favorers, and well-willers do but either increase in number, or in opinion continue, or having been doubtful renew your good liking and furtherance to deal therein according to the worthiness thereof already found and as you shall understand hereafter to be requisite. Touching which worthiness, through cause of the diversity of relations and reports, many of your opinions could not be firm, nor the minds of some that are well disposed be settled in any certainty.

I have therefore thought it good, being one that have been in the discovery and in dealing with the natural inhabitants specially employed, and having therefore seen and known more than the ordinary, to impart so much unto you of the fruits of our labors as that you may know how injuriously the enterprise is slandered, and that in public manner at this present chiefly for two respects.

First, that some of you which are yet ignorant or doubtful of the state thereof may see that there is sufficient cause why the chief enterpriser with the favor of her Majesty, notwithstanding such reports, hath not only since continued the action by sending into the country again, and replanting this last year a new colony, but is also ready, according as the times and means will afford, to follow and prosecute the same.

Secondly, that you, seeing and knowing the continuance of the action by the view hereof, you may generally know and learn what the country is and thereupon consider how your dealing therein, if it proceed, may return you profit and gain, be it either by inhabiting and planting or otherwise in furthering thereof.

And lest that the substance of my relation should be doubtful unto you, as of others by reason of their diversity, I will first open the cause in a few words wherefore they are so different, referring myself to your favorable constructions, and to be adjudged of as by good consideration you shall find cause.

Of our company that returned, some for their misdemeanor and ill

Thomas Hariot

dealing in the country have been there worthily punished, who, by reason of their bad natures, have maliciously not only spoken ill of their governors, but for their sakes slandered the country itself. The like also have those done which were of their consort.

Some being ignorant of the state thereof, notwithstanding since their return amongst their friends and acquaintance and also others, especially if they were in company where they might not be gainsaid, would seem to know so much as no men more, and make no men so great travelers as themselves. They stood so much as it may seem upon their credit and reputation that, having been a twelvemonth in the country, it would have been a great disgrace unto them, as they thought, if they could not have said much whether it were true or false. Of which some have spoken of more than ever they saw or otherwise knew to be there; othersome have not been ashamed to make absolute denial of that which, although not by them, yet by others is most certainly and there plentifully known. And othersome make difficulties of those things they have no skill of.

The cause of their ignorance was in that they were of that many that were never out of the island where we were seated, or not far, or at the leastwise in few places else during the time of our abode in the country; or of that many that, after gold and silver was not so soon found, as it was by them looked for, had little or no care of any other thing but to pamper their bellies; or of that many which had little understanding, less discretion, and more tongue than was needful or requisite.

Some also were of a nice bringing up, only in cities or towns, or such as never (as I may say) had seen the world before. Because there were not to be found any English cities, nor such fair houses, nor at their own wish any of their old accustomed dainty food, nor any soft beds of down or feathers, the country was to them miserable, and their reports thereof according.

Because my purpose was but in brief to open the cause of the variety of such speeches, the particularities of them and of many envious, malicious, and slanderous reports and devices else by our own countrymen besides, as trifles that are not worthy of wise men to be thought upon, I mean not to trouble you withal, but will pass to the commodities, the substance of that which I have to make relation of unto you. ....

MERCHANTABLE COMMODITIES

Silk of grass or grass silk. There is a kind of grass in the country upon the blades whereof there groweth very good silk in form of a thin glittering skin to be stript off. It groweth two foot and a half high or better; the blades are about two foot in length and half inch broad. The like groweth in Persia, which is in the selfsame climate as Virginia, of which very many of the silk works that come from thence into Europe are made. Hereof, if it be planted and ordered as in Persia, it cannot in reason be otherwise but that there will rise in short time great profit to the dealers therein, seeing there is so great use and vent thereof as well in our country as elsewhere. And by the means of sowing and planting in good ground,

A Brief and True Report of the Newfound Land of Virginia

it will be far greater, better, and more plentiful than it is. Although notwithstanding there is great store thereof in many places of the country growing naturally and wild. Which also by proof here in England, in making a piece of silk grogram, we found to be excellent good.

Worm silk. In many of our journeys we found silkworms fair and great, as big as our ordinary walnuts. Although it hath not been our hap to have found such plenty as elsewhere to be in the country we have heard of, yet seeing that the country doth naturally breed and nourish them, there is no doubt but if art be added in planting of mulberry trees and others fit for them in commodious places, for their feeding and nourishing, and some of them carefully gathered and husbanded in that sort as by men of skill is known to be necessary, there will rise as great profit in time to the Virginians as thereof doth now to the Persians, Turks, Italians, and Spaniards.

Flax and hemp. The truth is that of hemp and flax there is no great store in any one place together, by reason it is not planted but as the soil doth yield it of itself, and howsoever the leaf and stem, or stalk, do differ from ours, the stuff, by the judgment of men of skill, is altogether as good as ours. And if not, as further proof should find otherwise, we have that experience of the soil as that there cannot be showed any reason to the contrary but that it will grow there excellent well and by planting will be yielded plentifully, seeing there is so much ground whereof some may well be applied to such purposes. What benefit hereof may grow in cordage and linens who cannot easily understand?

Alum. There is a vein of earth along the seacoast for the space of forty or fifty miles, whereof, by the judgment of some that have made trial here in England, is made good alum of that kind which is called *Roche Allum.* The richness of such a commodity is so well known that I need not to say anything thereof. The same earth doth also yield white copperas, *Nitrum,* and *Alumen Plumeum,* but nothing so plentifully as the common alum, which be also of price and profitable.

Wapeih. *Wapeih,* a kind of earth so called by the natural inhabitants, very like to terra sigillata, and having been refined, it hath been found by some of our physicians and surgeons to be of the same kind of virtue and more effectual. The inhabitants use it very much for the cure of sores and wounds; there is in divers places great plenty, and in some places of a blue sort.

Pitch, tar, rosin, and turpentine. There are those kinds of trees which yield them abundantly and great store. In the very same island where we were seated, being fifteen miles of length, and five or six miles in breadth, there are few trees else but of the same kind, the whole island being full.

Sassafras. Sassafras, called by the inhabitants *Winauk,* a kind of wood of most pleasant and sweet smell, and of most rare virtues in physic for the cure of many diseases. It is found by experience to be far better and of more uses than the wood which is called guaiacum, or lignum vitae. For the description, the manner of using, and the manifold virtues thereof,

Thomas Hariot

I refer you to the book of Monardus, translated and entitled in English *The Joyful News from the West Indies.*

Cedar. Cedar, a very sweet wood and fine timber, whereof if nests of chests be there made, or timber thereof fitted for sweet and fine bedsteads, tables, desks, lutes, virginals, and many things else (of which there hath been proof made already) to make up freight with other principal commodities will yield profit.

Wine. There are two kinds of grapes that the soil doth yield naturally; the one is small and sour of the ordinary bigness as ours in England; the other far greater and of himself luscious sweet. When they are planted and husbanded as they ought, a principal commodity of wines by them may be raised.

Oil. There are two sorts of walnuts both holding oil, but the one far more plentiful than the other. When there are mills and other devices for the purpose, a commodity of them may be raised because there are infinite store. There are also three several kinds of berries in the form of oak acorns, which also by the experience and use of the inhabitants we find to yield very good and sweet oil. Furthermore, the bears of the country are commonly very fat, and in some places there are many; their fatness, because it is so liquid, may well be termed oil, and hath many special uses.

Furs. All along the seacoast there are great store of otters, which, being taken by weirs and other engines made for the purpose, will yield good profit. We hope also of marten furs, and make no doubt by the relation of the people but that in some places of the country there are store, although there were but two skins that came to our hands. *Luzarnes* also we have understanding of, although for the time we saw none.

Deer skins. Deer skins dressed after the manner of chamois or undressed are to be had of the natural inhabitants, thousands yearly by way of traffic for trifles, and no more waste or spoil of deer than is and hath been ordinarily in time before.

Civet cats. In our travels, there was found one to have been killed by a savage or inhabitant, and in another place the smell where one or more had lately been before, whereby we gather besides then by the relation of the people that there are some in the country; good profit will rise by them.

Iron. In two places of the country specially, one about fourscore and the other sixscore miles from the fort or place where we dwelt, we found near the waterside the ground to be rocky, which by the trial of a mineral man was found to hold iron richly. It is found in many places of the country else. I know nothing to the contrary but that it may be allowed for a good merchantable commodity, considering there the small charge for the labor and feeding of men, the infinite store of wood, the want of wood and dearness thereof in England, and the necessity of ballasting of ships.

Copper. A hundred and fifty miles into the main in two towns we found with the inhabitants divers small plates of copper that had been made, as we understood, by the inhabitants that dwell farther into the country, where, as they say, are mountains and rivers that yield also white grains of metal, which is to be deemed silver. For confirmation whereof at the time of our first arrival in the country, I saw, with some others with me, two small pieces of silver grossly beaten about the weight of a testone hanging in the ears of a *Wiroans* or chief lord that dwelt about fourscore miles from us, of whom, through enquiry by the number of days and the way, I learned that it had come to his hands from the same place or near where I after understood the copper was made and the white grains of metal found. The aforesaid copper we also found by trial to hold silver.

Pearl. Sometimes in feeding on mussels we found some pearl, but it was our hap to meet with rags, or of a pied color, not having yet discovered those places where we heard of better and more plenty. One of our company, a man of skill in such matters, had gathered together from among the savage people about five thousand, of which number he chose so many as made a fair chain, which for their likeness and uniformity in roundness, orientness, and piedness of many excellent colors, with equality in greatness, were very fair and rare, and had therefore been presented to her Majesty, had we not by casualty and through extremity of a storm lost them with many things else in coming away from the country.

Sweet gums. Sweet gums of divers kinds and many other apothecary drugs of which we will make special mention when we shall receive it from such men of skill in that kind that in taking reasonable pains shall discover them more particularly than we have done and than now I can make relation of for want of the examples I had provided and gathered and are now lost with other things by casualty before mentioned.

Dyes of divers kinds. There is shoemake, well known and used in England for black, the seed of an herb called *Wasewowr*, little small roots called *Chappacor*, and the bark of the tree called by the inhabitants *Tangomockonomindge*, which dyes are for divers sorts of red; their goodness for our English clothes remains yet to be proved. The inhabitants use them only for the dying of hair and coloring of their faces and mantles made of deer skins, and also for the dying of rushes to make artificial works withal in their mats and baskets, having no other thing besides that they account of apt to use them for. If they will not prove merchantable, there is no doubt but the planters there shall find apt uses for them, as also for other colors which we know to be there.

Oade. A thing of so great vent and use amongst English dyers, which cannot be yielded sufficiently in our own country for spare of ground, may be planted in Virginia, there being ground enough. The growth thereof need not to be doubted, when as in the islands of the Azores it groweth plentifully, which is in the same climate. So likewise of madder.

Sugar canes. We carried thither sugar canes to plant, which being not so well preserved as was requisite, and besides the time of the year being past for their setting when we arrived, we could not make that proof of them as we desired. Notwithstanding, seeing that they grow in the same climate, in the south part of Spain and in Barbary, our hope in reason may yet continue. So likewise for oranges and lemons; there may be planted also quinces. Whereby may grow in reasonable time, if the action

Thomas Hariot

be diligently prosecuted, no small commodities in sugar, *Suckets*, and marmalades.

Many other commodities by planting may there also be raised, which I leave to your discreet and gentle considerations, and many also may be there which yet we have not discovered. Two more commodities of great value, one of certainty and the other in hope, not to be planted, but there to be raised and in short time to be provided and prepared, I might have specified. So likewise of those commodities already set down I might have said more, as of the particular places where they are found and best to be planted and prepared, by what means and in what reasonable space of time they might be raised to profit and in what proportion; but because others than well-willers might be therewithal acquainted, not to the good of the action, I have wittingly omitted them, knowing that to those that are well disposed I have uttered, according to my promise and purpose, for this part sufficient.

[1588]

A Brief and True Report of the Newfound Land of Virginia

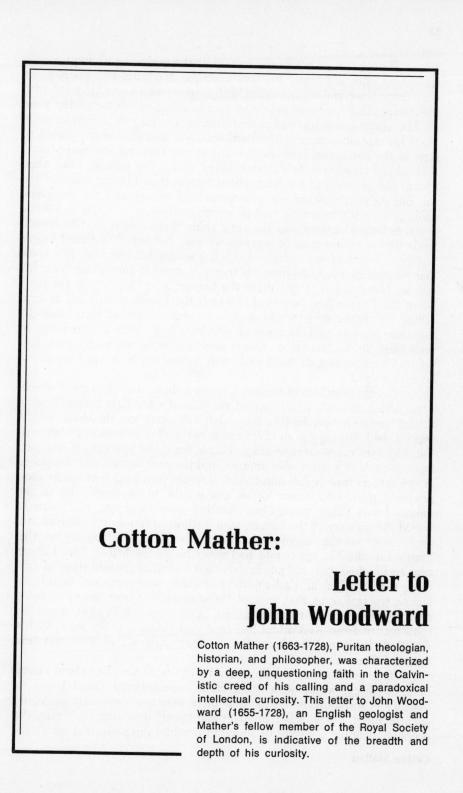

Cotton Mather:

Letter to John Woodward

Cotton Mather (1663-1728), Puritan theologian, historian, and philosopher, was characterized by a deep, unquestioning faith in the Calvinistic creed of his calling and a paradoxical intellectual curiosity. This letter to John Woodward (1655-1728), an English geologist and Mather's fellow member of the Royal Society of London, is indicative of the breadth and depth of his curiosity.

Sir:

Though we are got so far onward at the beginning of another winter, yet we have not forgot the last, which, at the latter end whereof, we were entertained and overwhelmed with a snow, which was attended with some things that were uncommon enough to afford matter for a letter from us. The winter was not so bad as that wherein Tacitus tells us that Corbulo made his expedition against the Parthians. Nor like that which proved so fatal to the beasts and birds in the days of the Emperor Justinian, [nor?] that wherein the very fishes were killed under the freezing sea, when Phocas did as much to the men whom tyrants treat like the fishes of the sea. But the conclusion of our winter was hard enough and was too formidable to be easily forgotten, and of a piece with what you had in Europe a year before. The snow was the chief thing that made it so. For though rarely does a winter pass us wherein we may not say with Pliny, *Ingens Hyeme Nivis apud nos copia*, yet the last winter brought with it a snow that excelled them all. A snow, 'tis true, not equal to that which once fell and lay twenty cubits high, about the beginning of October, in the parts about the Euxine Sea. Nor to that which the French annals tell us kept falling for twenty-nine weeks together. Nor to several mentioned by Boethius, wherein vast numbers of people and of cattle perished; not to those that Strabo finds upon Caucasus and Rhodiginus in Armenia. But yet such an one, and attended with such circumstances, as may deserve to be remembered.

On the twentieth of the last February, there came on a snow which, being added unto what had covered the ground a few days before, made a thicker mantle for our mother than what was usual, and the storm with it was for the following day so violent as to make all communication between the neighbors everywhere to cease. People for some hours could not pass from one side of a street unto another, and the poor women who happened at this critical time to fall into travail were put into hardships which anon produced many odd stories for us. But on the twenty-fourth day of the month comes Pelion upon Ossa. Another snow came on, which almost buried the memory of the former, with a storm so furious that heaven laid an interdict on the religious assemblies throughout the country on this Lord's day, the like whereunto had never been seen before. The Indians near an hundred years old affirm that their fathers never told them of anything that equalled it. Vast numbers of cattle were destroyed in this calamity, whereof some that were of the stronger sort were found standing dead on their legs, as if they had been alive, many weeks after, when the snow melted away. And others had their eyes glazed over the ice at such a rate that, being not far from the sea, they went out of their way and drowned them there.

One gentleman, on whose farms there were now lost above eleven hundred sheep, which with other cattle were interred (shall I say, or *inniv'd*) in the snow, writes me that there were two sheep very singularly circumstanced. For no less than eight and twenty days after the storm, the people pulling out the ruins of above an hundred sheep out of a snowbank

Cotton Mather

which lay sixteen foot high drifted over them, there were two found alive, which had been there all this time and kept themselves alive by eating the wool of their dead companions. When they were taken out, they shed their own fleeces, but soon got into good case again.

Sheep were not the only creatures that lived unaccountably for whole weeks without their usual sustenance, entirely buried in the snow-drifts. The swine had a share with the sheep in strange survivals. A man had a couple of young hogs which he gave over for dead, but on the twenty-seventh day after their burial, they made their way out of a snow-bank, at the bottom of which they found a little tansy to feed upon.

The poultry as unaccountably survived as these. Hens were found alive after seven days; turkeys were found alive after five and twenty days buried in the snow, and at a distance from the ground, and altogether destitute of anything to feed them.

The number of creatures that kept a rigid fast, shut up in snow for several weeks together, and were found alive after all have yielded surprising stories to us.

The wild creatures of the woods (the outgoings of the evening) made their descent, as well as they could in this time of scarcity for them, towards the seaside. A vast multitude of deer, for the same cause taking the same course, and the deep snow spoiling them of their only defense, which is to run, they became such a prey to those devourers that it is thought not one in twenty escaped.

But here again occurred a curiosity.

These carniverous sharpers, and especially the foxes, would make their nocturnal visits to the pens, where the people had their sheep defended from them. The poor ewes big with young were so terrified with the frequent approaches of the foxes, and the terror had such impression on them, that most of the lambs brought forth in the spring following were of Monsieur Reinard's complexion, when the dams were all either white or black.

It was remarkable that immediately after the fall of the snow an infinite multitude of sparrows made their appearance, but then after a short continuance all disappeared.

It is incredible how much damage was done to the orchards, for the snow, freezing to a crust as high as the boughs of the trees, anon split them to pieces. The cattle also, walking on the crusted snow, a dozen foot from the ground, so fed upon the trees as very much to damnify them.

The ocean was in a prodigious ferment, and after it was over, vast heaps of little shells were driven ashore, where they were never seen before. Mighty shoals of porpoises also kept a playday in the disturbed waves of our harbors.

The odd accidents befalling many poor people, whose cottages were totally covered with the snow, and the very tops of their chimneys to be seen, would afford a story, but there not being any relation to philosophy in them, I forbear them. And now, I am *Satis Terris Nivis*. And here is enough of my winter tale. If it serve to no other purpose, yet it will give

Letter to John Woodward

me an opportunity to tell you that nine months ago I did a thousand times wish myself with you in Gresham College, which is never so horribly snowed upon. But instead of so great a satisfaction, all I can attain to is the pleasure of talking with you in this epistolary way and subscribing myself,

Sir, yours with an affection that knows no winter

Cotton Mather

Dr. Woodward

[1717, 1926]

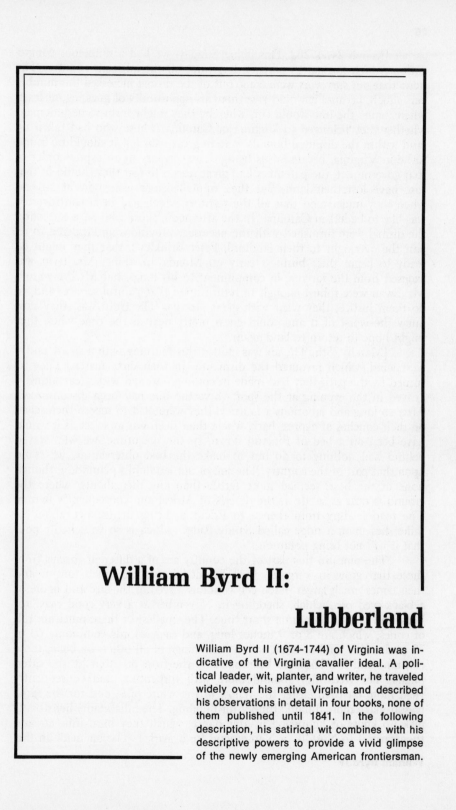

William Byrd II:
Lubberland

William Byrd II (1674-1744) of Virginia was indicative of the Virginia cavalier ideal. A political leader, wit, planter, and writer, he traveled
widely over his native Virginia and described
his observations in detail in four books, none of
them published until 1841. In the following
description, his satirical wit combines with his
descriptive powers to provide a vivid glimpse
of the newly emerging American frontiersman.

[March 24, 1728.] This being Sunday, we had a numerous congregation, which flocked to our quarters from all the adjacent country. The news that our surveyors were come out of the dismal increased the number very much, because it would give them an opportunity of guessing, at least, whereabouts the line would cut, whereby they might form some judgment whether they belonged to Virginia or Carolina. Those who had taken up land within the disputed bounds were in great pain lest it should be found to lie in Virginia, because, this being done contrary to an express order of that government, the patentees had great reason to fear they should in that case have lost their land. But their apprehensions were now at an end when they understood that all the territory which had been controverted was like to be left in Carolina. In the afternoon, those who were to reenter the dismal were furnished with the necessary provisions and ordered to repair the overnight to their landlord, Peter Brinkley's, that they might be ready to begin their business early on Monday morning. Mr. Irvin was excused from the fatigue, in compliment to his lungs, but Mr. Mayo and Mr. Swan were robust enough to return upon that painful service, and, to do them justice, they went with great alacrity. The truth was, they now knew the worst of it and could guess pretty near at the time when they might hope to return to land again.

[March] 25th. The air was chilled this morning with a smart northwest wind, which favoured the dismalites in their dirty march. They returned by the path they had made in coming out, and with great industry arrived in the evening at the spot where the line had been discontinued. After so long and laborious a journey, they were glad to repose themselves on their couches of cypress bark, where their sleep was as sweet as it would have been on a bed of Finland down. In the meantime, we who stayed behind had nothing to do but to make the best observations we could upon that part of the country. The soil of our landlord's plantation, though none of the best, seemed more fertile than any thereabouts, where the ground is near as sandy as the deserts of Africa, and consequently barren. The road leading from thence to Edenton, being in distance about 27 miles, lies upon a ridge called Sandy Ridge, which is so wretchedly poor that it will not bring potatoes.

The pines in this part of the country are of a different species from those that grow in Virginia; their bearded leaves are much longer, and their cones much larger. Each cell contains a seed of the size and figure of a black-eyed pea, which, shedding in November, is a very good mast for hogs, and fattens them in a short time. The smallest of these pines are full of cones, which are 8 or 9 inches long, and each affords commonly 60 or 70 seeds. This kind of mast has the advantage of all other, by being more constant and less liable to be nipped by the frost or eaten by the caterpillars. The trees also abound more with turpentine, and consequently yield more tar than either the yellow or the white pine, and for the same reason make more durable timber for building. The inhabitants hereabouts pick up knots of lightwood in abundance, which they burn into tar and then carry it to Norfolk or Nansemond for a market. The tar made in this

William Byrd II

method is the less valuable because it is said to burn the cordage, though it is full as good for all other uses as that made in Sweden and Muscovy.

Surely there is no place in the world where the inhabitants live with less labor than in North Carolina. It approaches nearer to the description of Lubberland than any other, by the great felicity of the climate, the easiness of raising provisions, and the slothfulness of the people.

Indian corn is of so great increase that a little pains will subsist a very large family with bread, and then they may have meat without any pains at all by the help of the low grounds and the great variety of mast that grows on the highland. The men, for their parts, just like the Indians, impose all the work upon the poor women. They make their wives rise out of their beds early in the morning, at the same time that they lie and snore till the sun has risen one-third of his course and dispersed all the unwholesome damps. Then, after stretching and yawning for half an hour, they light their pipes, and, under the protection of a cloud of smoke, venture out into the open air, though, if it happens to be never so little cold, they quickly return shivering into the chimney corner. When the weather is mild, they stand leaning with both their arms upon the cornfield fence, and gravely consider whether they had best go and take a small heat at the *Hough* but generally find reasons to put it off till another time.

Thus they loiter away their lives, like Solomon's Sluggard, with their arms across, and at the winding up of the year scarcely have bread to eat. To speak the truth, 'tis a thorough aversion to labor that makes people file off to North Carolina, where plenty and a warm sun confirm them in their disposition to laziness for their whole lives.

[March] 26. Since we were like to be confined to this place till the people returned out of the dismal, 'twas agreed that our chaplain might safely take a turn to Edenton to preach the Gospel to the infidels there and christen their children. He was accompanied thither by Mr. Little, one of the Carolina Commissioners, who, to show his regard for the church, offered to treat him on the road with a fricassee of rum. They fried half a dozen rashers of very fat bacon in a pint of rum, both which, being dished up together, served the company at once both for meat and drink. Most of the rum they get in this country comes from New England and is so bad and unwholesome that it is not improperly called "kill-devil." It is distilled there from foreign molasses, which, if skillfully managed, yields near gallon for gallon. Their molasses comes from the same country and has the name of "long sugar" in Carolina, I suppose from the ropiness of it, and serves all the purposes of sugar, both in their eating and drinking.

When they entertain their friends bountifully, they fail not to set before them a capacious bowl of bombo, so called from the admiral of that name. This is a compound of rum and water in equal parts, made palatable with the said long sugar. As good humor begins to flow, and the bowl to ebb, they take care to replenish it with sheer rum, of which there always is a reserve under the table. But such generous doings happen only when that balsam of life is plenty, for they have often such melancholy times that neither landgraves nor cossacks can procure one drop for their wives when

Lubberland

they lie in or are troubled with the colic or vapors. Very few in this country have the industry to plant orchards, which, in a dearth of rum, might supply them with much better liquor. The truth is, there is one inconvenience that easily discourages lazy people from making this improvement: very often, in autumn, when the apples begin to ripen, they are visited with numerous flights of parrakeets that bite all the fruit to pieces in a moment for the sake of the kernels. The havoc they make is sometimes so great that whole orchards are laid waste in spite of all the noises that can be made or mawkins that can be dressed up to fright 'em away. These ravenous birds visit North Carolina only during the warm season, and so soon as the cold begins to come on, retire back towards the sun. They rarely venture so far north as Virginia, except in a very hot summer, when they visit the most southern parts of it. They are very beautiful, but, like some other pretty creatures, are apt to be loud and mischievous.

[March] 27. Betwixt this and Edenton there are many huckleberry slashes, which afford a convenient harbor for wolves and foxes. The first of these wild beasts is not so large and fierce as they are in other countries more northerly. He will not attack a man in the keenest of his hunger, but run away from him as from an animal more mischievous than himself. The foxes are much bolder and will sometimes not only make a stand but likewise assault anyone that would balk them of their prey. The inhabitants hereabouts take the trouble to dig abundance of wolf pits, so deep and perpendicular that when a wolf is once tempted into them, he can no more scramble out again than a husband who has taken the leap can scramble out of matrimony. Most of the houses in this part of the country are log houses, covered with pine or cypress shingles, 3 feet long and one broad. They are hung upon laths with pegs, and their doors, too, turn upon wooden hinges and have wooden locks to secure them, so that the building is finished without nails or other ironwork. They also set up their pales without nails at all, and indeed more securely than those that are nailed. There are 3 rails mortised into the posts, the lowest of which serves as a sill with a groove in the middle big enough to receive the end of the pales; the middle part of the pale rests against the inside of the next rail, and the top of it is brought forward to the outside of the uppermost. Such wreathing of the pales in and out makes them stand firm, and much harder to unfix than when nailed in the ordinary way.

Within 3 or 4 miles of Edenton, the soil appears to be a little more fertile, though it is much cut with slashes, which seem all to have a tendency towards the dismal. This town is situate on the north side of Albemarle Sound, which is thereabout 5 miles over. A dirty slash runs all along the back of it, which in the summer is a foul annoyance and furnishes abundance of that Carolina plague, mosquitoes. There may be 40 or 50 houses, most of them small and built without expense. A citizen here is counted extravagant if he has ambition enough to aspire to a brick chimney. Justice herself is but indifferently lodged, the courthouse having much of the air of a common tobacco house. I believe this is the only metropolis in the Christian or Muhammadan world where there is neither church,

William Byrd II

chapel, mosque, synagogue, or any other place of public worship of any sect or religion whatsoever. What little devotion there may happen to be is much more private than their vices. The people seem easy without a minister, as long as they are exempted from paying him. Sometimes the Society for Propagating the Gospel has had the charity to send over missionaries to this country, but unfortunately the priest has been too lewd for the people, or, which oftener happens, they too lewd for the priest. For these reasons these reverend gentlemen have always left their flocks as arrant heathen as they found them. Thus much, however, may be said for the inhabitants of Edenton, that not a soul has the least taint of hypocrisy or superstition, acting very frankly and aboveboard in all their excesses.

Provisions here are extremely cheap and extremely good, so that people may live plentifully at a trifling expense. Nothing is dear but law, physic, and strong drink, which are all bad in their kind, and the last they get with so much difficulty that they are never guilty of the sin of suffering it to sour upon their hands. Their vanity generally lies not so much in having a handsome dining room as a handsome house of office; in this kind of structure they are really extravagant. They are rarely guilty of flattering or making court to their governors, but treat them with all the excesses of freedom and familiarity. They are of opinion their rulers would be apt to grow insolent if they grew rich, and for that reason take care to keep them poorer and more dependent, if possible, than the saints in New England used to do their governors. They have very little corn, so they are forced to carry on their home traffic with paper money. This is the only cash that will tarry in the country, and for that reason the discount goes on increasing between that and real money, and will do so to the end of the chapter.

[March] 28. Our time passed heavily in our quarters, where we were quite cloyed with the Carolina felicity of having nothing to do. It was really more insupportable than the greatest fatigue, and made us even envy the drudgery of our friends in the dismal. Besides, though the men we had with us were kept in exact discipline, and behaved without reproach, yet our landlord began to be tired of them, fearing they would breed a famine in his family. Indeed, so many keen stomachs made great havoc amongst the beef and bacon which he had laid in for his summer provision; nor could he easily purchase more at that time of the year with the money we paid him, because the people, having no certain market, seldom provide any more of these commodities than will barely supply their own occasions. Besides, the weather was now grown too warm to lay in a fresh stock so late in the spring. These considerations abated somewhat of that cheerfulness with which he bid us welcome in the beginning and made him think the time quite as long as we did until the surveyors returned. While we were thus all hands uneasy, we were comforted with the news that this afternoon the line was finished through the dismal. The messenger told us it had been the hard work of three days to measure the length of only 5 miles and mark the trees as they passed along, and by the most exact survey they found the breadth of the dismal in this place to be completely 15 miles. How wide it may be in other parts, we can give no account, but

Lubberland

believe it grows narrower towards the north; possibly towards Albemarle Sound it may be something broader, where so many rivers issue out of it. All we know for certain is that from the place where the line entered the dismal to where it came out, we found the road round that portion of it belongs to Virginia to be about 65 miles. How great the distance may be from each of these points round that part that falls within the bounds of Carolina, we had no certain information, though 'tis conjectured it cannot be so little as 30 miles. At which rate the whole circuit must be about an hundred. What a mass of mud and dirt is treasured up within this filthy circumference, and what a quantity of water must perpetually drain into it from the rising ground that surrounds it on every side? Without taking the exact level of the dismal, we may be sure that it declines towards the places where the several rivers take their rise, in order to carry off the constant supplies of water. Were it not for such discharges, the whole swamp would long since have been converted into a lake. On the other side this declension must be very gentle, else it would be laid perfectly dry by so many continual drains, whereas, on the contrary, the ground seems everywhere to be thoroughly drenched even in the dryest season of the year. The surveyors concluded this day's work with running 25 chains up into the firm land, where they waited further orders from the commissioners.

[1728, 1841]

William Byrd II

Samuel Peters:

Birds and Frogs

Samuel Peters (1735-1826), ultimately a Tory refugee from America, wrote the *General History of Connecticut* (1781) as an exercise in objective description, barbed humor, and the purging of prejudice. The result is a sort of objectivized fantasy that, based in reality, departs from fact to comment, perceptively if somewhat harshly, on the nature of the American as he confronts the new world at his feet.

BIRDS AND TREE FROGS

The partridges in New England are near as large as a Dorking fowl; the quails, as an English partridge; and the robins twice as big as those in England. The *dewmink*, so named from its articulating those syllables, is black and white, and of the size of an English robin. Its flesh is delicious. The humility is so called because it speaks the word *humility*, and seldom mounts high in the air. Its legs are long enough to enable it to outrun a dog for a little way; its wings long and narrow; body meager, and of the size of a blackbird's; plumage variegated with white, black, blue, and red. It lives on tadpoles, spawn, and worms; has an eye more piercing than the falcon, and the swiftness of an eagle. Hence it can never be shot, for it sees the sparks of fire even before they enkindle the powder, and by the extreme rapidity of its flight gets out of reach in an instant. It is never known to light upon a tree, but is always seen upon the ground or wing. These birds appear in New England in summer only; what becomes of them afterwards is not discovered. They are caught in snares, but can never be tamed.

The whippoorwill has so named itself by its nocturnal songs. It is also called the pope, by reason of its darting with great swiftness from the clouds to the ground, and bawling out *Pope!*, which alarms young people and the fanatics very much, especially as they know it to be an ominous bird. However, it has hitherto proved friendly, always giving travellers and others notice of an approaching storm by saluting them every minute with *Pope! Pope!* It flies only a little before sunset, unless for this purpose of giving notice of a storm. It never deceives the people with false news. If the tempest is to continue long, the augurs appear in flocks, and nothing can be heard but the word *Pope! Pope!* The whippoorwill is about the size of a cuckoo, has a short beak, long and narrow wings, a large head and mouth enormous, yet it is not a bird of prey. Under its throat is a pocket, which it fills with air at pleasure, whereby it sounds forth the fatal words *Pope* in the day and W*hip-ber-I-will* in the night. The superstitious inhabitants would have exorcised this harmless bird long ago as an emissary from Rome and an enemy to the American vine had they not found out that it frequents New England only in the summer and prefers the wilderness to a palace. Nevertheless, many cannot but believe it a spy from some foreign court, an agent of Antichrist, a lover of persecution, and an enemy of Protestants, because it sings of *whipping*, and of the *Pope*, which they think portends misery and a change of religion.

The tree frog cannot be called an insect, a reptile, or one of the winged host. He has four legs, the two foremost short, with claws as sharp as those of a squirrel; the hind legs five inches long, and folding by three joints. His body is about as big as the first joint of a man's thumb. Under his throat is a windbag, which assists him in singing the word *I-sa-ac*, all the night. When it rains and is very dark, he sings the loudest. His voice is not so pleasing as that of a nightingale, but this would be a venial imperfection if he would but keep silence on Saturday nights, and not for-

Samuel Peters

ever prefer *I-sa-ac* to *Abraham* and *Jacob*. He has more elasticity in his long legs than any other creature yet known. By this means he will leap five yards up a tree, fastening himself to it by his forefeet, and in a moment will hop or spring as far as from one tree to another. It is from the singing of the tree frog that the Americans have acquired the name of *Little Isaac*. Indeed, like a certain part of them, the creature appears very devout, noisy, arbitrary, and phlegmatic, and associates with none but what agree with him in his ways.

THE FROGS OF WINDHAM

Windham, the second county in the ancient kingdom of Sassacus, or colony of Saybrook, is hilly, but the soil being rich, has excellent butter, cheese, hemp, wheat, Indian corn, and horses. Its towns are twelve.

Windham resembles Rumford and stands on Winnomantic River. Its meetinghouse is elegant and has a steeple, bell, and clock. Its courthouse is scarcely to be looked upon as an ornament. The township forms four parishes and is ten miles square.

Strangers are very much terrified at the hideous noise made on summer evenings by the vast number of frogs in the brooks and ponds. There are about thirty different voices among them, some of which resemble the bellowing of a bull. The owls and whippoorwills complete the rough concert, which may be heard several miles. Persons accustomed to such serenades are not disturbed by them at their proper stations, but one night, in July, 1758, the frogs of an artificial pond, three miles square, and about five from Windham, finding the water dried up, left the place in a body and marched, or rather hopped, towards Winnomantic River. They were under the necessity of taking the road and going through the town, which they entered about midnight. The bullfrogs were the leaders, and the pipers followed without number. They filled a road 40 yards wide for four miles in length, and were for several hours, in passing through the town, unusually clamorous. The inhabitants were equally perplexed and frightened; some expected to find an army of French and Indians; others feared an earthquake and dissolution of nature. The consternation was universal. Old and young, male and female, fled naked from their beds with worse shriekings than those of the frogs. The event was fatal to several women. The men, after a flight of half a mile, in which they met with many broken shins, finding no enemies in pursuit of them, made a halt and summoned resolution enough to venture back to their wives and children, when they distinctly heard from the enemy's camp these words, "*Wight, Hilderken, Dier, Tete.*" This last they thought meant *treaty*, and plucking up courage, they sent a triumvirate to capitulate with the supposed French and Indians. These three men approached in their shirts and begged to speak with the general, but, it being dark and no answer given, they were sorely agitated for some time betwixt hope and fear; at length, however, they discovered that the dreaded inimical army was an army of thirsty frogs, going to the river for a little water.

Birds and Frogs

Such an incursion was never known before nor since, and yet the people of Windham have been ridiculed for their timidity on this occasion. I verily believe an army under the Duke of Marlborough would, under like circumstances, have acted no better than they did.

In 1768, the inhabitants on Connecticut River were as much alarmed at an army of caterpillars as those of Windham were at the frogs, and no one found reason to jest at their fears. Those worms came in one night and covered the earth on both sides of that river to an extent of three miles in front and two in depth. They marched with great speed and ate up everything green for the space of one hundred miles, in spite of rivers, ditches, fires, and the united efforts of 1,000 men. They were, in general, two inches long, had white bodies covered with thorns, and red throats. When they had finished their work, they went down to the river Connecticut, where they died, poisoning the waters until they were washed into the sea. This calamity was imputed by some to the vast number of trees and logs lying in the creeks, and to the cinders, smoke, and fires made to consume the waste wood for three or four hundred miles up the Connecticut, while others thought it augured future evils similar to those in Egypt. The inhabitants of the Verdmonts would unavoidably have perished by famine in consequence of the devastation of these worms had not a remarkable providence filled the wilderness with wild pigeons, which were killed by sticks as they sat on the branches of trees, in such multitudes that 30,000 people lived on them for three weeks. If a natural cause may be assigned for the coming of the frogs and caterpillars, yet the visit of the pigeons to a wilderness in August has been necessarily ascribed to an interposition of infinite power and goodness. Happy will it be for America if the smiling providence of Heaven produces gratitude, repentance, and obedience amongst her children!

[1781]

Samuel Peters

Thomas Jefferson:
The Foundations of an Agrarian Society

Thomas Jefferson (1743-1826), third president of the United States, author of the Declaration of Independence, and son of the Enlightenment, was characterized by an avid curiosity and a deep faith in the desirability of gathering and publishing scientific data. His *Notes on the State of Virginia* (1787) was a major contribution to American science as well as a significant source of insight into one of the great minds of the Age of Reason.

MOUNTAINS

For the particular geography of our mountains I must refer to Fry and Jefferson's map of Virginia and to Evan's analysis of his map of America for a more philosophical view of them than is to be found in any other work. It is worthy notice that our mountains are not solitary and scattered confusedly over the face of the country, but that they commence at about 150 miles from the seacoast [and] are disposed in ridges one behind another, running nearly parallel with the seacoast, though rather approaching it as they advance northeastwardly. To the southwest, as the tract of country between the seacoast and the Mississippi becomes narrower, the mountains converge into a single ridge, which, as it approaches the Gulf of Mexico, subsides into plain country and gives rise to some of the waters of that gulf, and particularly to a river called the Apalachicola, probably from the Apalachies, an Indian nation formerly residing on it. Hence the mountains giving rise to that river, and seen from its various parts, were called the Appalachian Mountains, being in fact the end or termination only of the great ridges passing through the continent. European geographers, however, extended the name northwardly as far as the mountains extended, some giving it, after their separation into different ridges, to the Blue Ridge, others to the North Mountain, others to the Allegheny, others to the Laurel Ridge, as may be seen in their different maps. But the fact, I believe, is that none of these ridges were ever known by that name to the inhabitants, either native or immigrant, but as they saw them so called in European maps. In the same direction generally are the veins of limestone, coal, and other minerals hitherto discovered, and so range the falls of our great rivers. But the courses of the great rivers are at right angles with these. James and Potomac penetrate through all the ridges of mountains eastward of the Allegheny; that is broken by no watercourse. It is in fact the spine of the country between the Atlantic on one side and the Mississippi and St. Lawrence on the other. The passage of the Potomac through the Blue Ridge is perhaps one of the most stupendous scenes in nature. You stand on a very high point of land. On your right comes up the Shenandoah, having ranged along the foot of the mountain an hundred miles to seek a vent. On your left approaches the Potomac, in quest of a passage also. In the moment of their junction they rush together against the mountain, rend it asunder, and pass off to the sea. The first glance of this scene hurries our senses into the opinion that this earth has been created in time, that the mountains were formed first, that the rivers began to flow afterwards, that in this place particularly they have been dammed up by the Blue Ridge of mountains and have formed an ocean which filled the whole valley, that continuing to rise, they have at length broken over at this spot and have torn the mountain down from its summit to its base. The piles of rock on each hand, but particularly on the Shenandoah, the evident marks of their disrupture and avulsion from their beds by the most powerful agents of nature, corroborate the impression. But the distant finishing which nature has given to the picture is of a very

Thomas Jefferson

different character. It is a true contrast to the foreground. It is as placid and delightful as that is wild and tremendous. For the mountain being cloven asunder, she presents to your eye, through the cleft, a small catch of smooth blue horizon, at an infinite distance in the plain country, inviting you, as it were, from the riot and tumult roaring around, to pass through the breach and participate of the calm below. Here the eye ultimately composes itself, and that way, too, the road happens actually to lead. You cross the Potomac above the junction, pass along its side through the base of the mountain for three miles, its terrible precipices hanging in fragments over you, and within about 20 miles reach Frederic town and the fine country around that. This scene is worth a voyage across the Atlantic. Yet here, as in the neighborhood of the natural bridge, are people who have passed their lives within half a dozen miles and have never been to survey these monuments of a war between rivers and mountains, which must have shaken the earth itself to its center. The height of our mountains has not yet been estimated with any degree of exactness. The Allegheny being the great ridge which divides the waters of the Atlantic from those of the Mississippi, its summit is doubtless more elevated above the ocean than that of any other mountain. But its relative height, compared with the base on which it stands, is not so great as that of some others, the country rising behind the successive ridges like the steps of stairs. The mountains of the Blue Ridge, and of these the Peaks of Otter, are thought to be of a greater height, measured from their base, than any others in our country, and perhaps in North America. From data which may found a tolerable conjecture, we suppose the highest peak to be about 4000 feet perpendicular, which is not a fifth part of the height of the mountains of South America, nor one-third of the height which would be necessary in our latitude to preserve ice in the open air unmelted through the year. The ridge of mountains next beyond the Blue Ridge, called by us the North Mountain, is of the greatest extent, for which reason they were named by the Indians the Endless Mountains.

A substance supposed to be pumice, found floating on the Mississippi, has induced a conjecture that there is a volcano on some of its waters, and as these are mostly known to their sources, except the Missouri, our expectations of verifying the conjecture would, of course, be led to the mountains which divide the waters of the Mexican Gulf from those of the South Sea, but no volcano having ever yet been known at such a distance from the sea, we must rather suppose that this floating substance has been erroneously deemed pumice.

CASCADES
Falling Spring

The only remarkable cascade in this country is that of the Falling Spring in Augusta. It is a water of James River, where it is called Jackson's River, rising in the warm spring mountains about twenty miles southwest of the warm spring, and flowing from that valley. About three-quarters of a mile from its source, it falls over a rock 200 feet into the valley below.

The Foundations of an Agrarian Society

The sheet of water is broken in its breadth by the rock in two or three places, but not at all in its height. Between the sheet and rock, at the bottom, you may walk across dry. This cataract will bear no comparison with that of Niagara as to the quantity of water composing it, the sheet being only 12 or 15 feet wide above and somewhat more spread below, but it is half as high again, the latter being only 156 feet, according to the mensuration made by order of M. Vaudreuil, governor of Canada, and 130 according to a more recent account.

Madison's Cave

In the limestone country, there are many caverns of very considerable extent. The most noted is called Madison's Cave, and is on the north side of the Blue Ridge, near the intersection of the Rockingham and Augusta line with the south fork of the southern river of Shenandoah. It is in a hill of about 200 feet perpendicular height, the ascent of which, on one side, is so steep that you may pitch a biscuit from its summit into the river which washes its base. The entrance of the cave is, in this side, about two-thirds of the way up. It extends into the earth about 300 feet, branching into subordinate caverns, sometimes ascending a little, but more generally descending, and at length terminates, in two different places, at basins of water of unknown extent, and which I should judge to be nearly on a level with the water of the river; however, I do not think they are formed by refluent water from that because they are never turbid, because they do not rise and fall in correspondence with that in times of flood or of drought, and because the water is always cool. It is probably one of the many reservoirs with which the interior parts of the earth are supposed to abound, and which yield supplies to the fountains of water, distinguished from others only by its being accessible. The vault of this cave is of solid limestone, from 20 to 40 or 50 feet high, through which water is continually percolating. This, trickling down the sides of the cave, has incrusted them over in the form of elegant drapery, and, dripping from the top of the valut, generates on that, and on the base below, stalactites of a conical form, some of which have met and formed massive columns.

Another of these caves is near the North Mountain, in the county of Frederick, on the islands of Mr. Zane. The entrance into this is on the top of an extensive ridge. You descend 30 or 40 feet, as into a well, from whence the cave then extends, nearly horizontally, 400 feet into the earth, preserving a breadth of from 20 to 50 feet and a height of from 5 to 12 feet. After entering this cave a few feet, the mercury, which in the open air was at 50°, rose to 57° of Fahrenheit's thermometer, answering to 11° of Reaumur's, and it continued at that to the remotest parts of the cave. The uniform temperature of the cellars of the observatory of Paris, which are 90 feet deep, and of all subterranean cavities of any depth, where no chemical agents may be supposed to produce a factitious heat, has been found to be 10° of Reaumur, equal to 54½° of Fahrenheit. The temperature of the cave above-mentioned so nearly corresponds with this that the difference may be ascribed to a difference of instruments.

Thomas Jefferson

Blowing Cave

At the Panther Gap, in the ridge which divides the waters of the cow and the calf pasture, is what is called the *blowing cave*. It is in the side of a hill, is of about 100 feet diameter, and emits constantly a current of air of such force as to keep the weeds prostrate to the distance of twenty yards before it. This current is strongest in dry, frosty weather, and in long spells of rain weakest. Regular inspirations and expirations of air, by caverns and fissures, have been probably enough accounted for by supposing them combined with intermitting fountains, as they must, of course, inhale air while their reservoirs are emptying themselves and again emit it while they are filling. But a constant issue of air, only varying in its force as the weather is drier or damper, will require a new hypothesis. There is another blowing cave in the Cumberland Mountain, about a mile from where is crosses the Carolina line. All we know of this is that it is not constant, and that a fountain of water issues from it.

Natural Bridge

The *natural bridge*, the most sublime of nature's works, though not comprehended under the present head, must not be pretermitted. It is on the ascent of a hill, which seems to have been cloven through its length by some great convulsion. The fissure, just at the bridge, is, by some admeasurements, 270 feet deep, by others only 205. It is about 45 feet wide at the bottom, and 90 feet at the top; this, of course, determines the length of the bridge and its height from the water. Its breadth in the middle is about 60 feet, but more at the ends, and the thickness of the mass at the summit of the arch, about 40 feet. A part of this thickness is constituted by a coat of earth, which gives growth to many large trees. The residue, with the hill on both sides, is one solid rock of limestone. The arch approaches the semielliptical form, but the larger axis of the ellipsis, which would be the chord of the arch, is many times longer than the semiaxis which gives it's height. Though the sides of this bridge are provided in some parts with a parapet of fixed rocks, yet few men have resolution to walk to them and look over into the abyss. You involuntarily fall on your hands and feet, creep to the parapet, and peep over it. Looking down from this height about a minute gave me a violent headache. This painful sensation is relieved by a short but pleasing view of the Blue Ridge along the fissure downwards, and upwards by that of the Short Hills, which, with the Purgatory Mountain, is a divergence from the North Ridge, and, descending then to the valley below, the sensation becomes delightful in the extreme. It is impossible for the emotions, arising from the sublime, to be felt beyond what they are here: so beautiful an arch, so elevated, so light, and springing, as it were, up to heaven, the rapture of the spectator is really indescribable! The fissure continues deep and narrow, and, following the margin of the stream upwards about three-eighths of a mile, you arrive at a limestone cavern, less remarkable, however, for height and extent than those before described. It's entrance into the hill is but a few feet above the bed of the stream. This bridge is in the county of Rockbridge, to which it has given

The Foundations of an Agrarian Society

name, and affords a public and commodious passage over a valley, which cannot be crossed elsewhere for a considerable distance. The stream passing under it is called Cedar Creek. It is a water of James River, and sufficient in the driest seasons to turn a gristmill, though its fountain is not more than two miles above.

MANUFACTURES

We never had an interior trade of any importance. Our exterior commerce has suffered very much from the beginning of the present contest. During this time we have manufactured within our families the most necessary articles of clothing. Those of cotton will bear some comparison with the same kinds of manufacture in Europe, but those of wool, flax, and hemp are very coarse, unsightly, and unpleasant, and such is our attachment to agriculture, and such our preference for foreign manufactures, that be it wise or unwise, our people will certainly return as soon as they can to the raising [of] raw materials and exchanging them for finer manufactures than they are able to execute themselves.

The political economists of Europe have established it as a principle that every state should endeavour to manufacture for itself, and this principle, like many others, we transfer to America without calculating the difference of circumstance which should often produce a difference of result. In Europe the lands are either cultivated or locked up against the cultivator. Manufacture must therefore be resorted to of necessity, not of choice, to support the surplus of their people. But we have an immensity of land courting the industry of the husbandman. Is it best, then, that all our citizens should be employed in its improvement, or that one-half should be called off from that to exercise manufactures and handicraft arts for the other? Those who labor in the earth are the chosen people of God, if ever he had a chosen people, whose breasts he has made his peculiar deposit for substantial and genuine virtue. It is the focus in which he keeps alive that sacred fire, which otherwise might escape from the face of the earth. Corruption of morals in the mass of cultivators is a phenomenon of which no age nor nation has furnished an example. It is the mark set on those who, not looking up to heaven, to their own soil and industry, as does the husbandman, for their subsistence, depend for it on the casualties and caprice of customers. Dependence begets subservience and venality, suffocates the germ of virtue, and prepares fit tools for the designs of ambition. This, the natural progress and consequence of the arts, has sometimes perhaps been retarded by accidental circumstances, but, generally speaking, the proportion which the aggregate of the other classes of citizens bears in any state to that of its husbandmen is the proportion of its unsound to its healthy parts, and is a good enough barometer whereby to measure its degree of corruption. While we have land to labor, then, let us never wish to see our citizens occupied at a workbench, or twirling a distaff. Carpenters, masons, smiths are wanting in husbandry, but, for the general operations of manufacture, let our workshops remain in Europe. It is better to

Thomas Jefferson

carry provisions and materials to workmen there than bring them to the provisions and materials, and with them their manners and principles. The loss by the transportation of commodities across the Atlantic will be made up in happiness and permanence of government. The mobs of great cities add just so much to the support of pure government as sores do to the strength of the human body. It is the manners and spirit of a people which preserve a republic in vigor. A degeneracy in these is a canker which soon eats to the heart of its laws and constitution.

SUBJECTS OF COMMERCE

Before the present war we exported, *communibus annis*, according to the best information I can get, nearly as follows:

In the year 1758 we exported seventy thousand hogsheads of tobacco, which was the greatest quantity ever produced in this country in one year. But its culture was fast declining at the commencement of this war and that of wheat taking its place, and it must continue to decline on the return of peace. I suspect that the change in the temperature of our climate has become sensible to that plant, which, to be good, requires an extraordinary degree of heat. But it requires still more indispensably an uncommon fertility of soil, and the price which it commands at market will not enable the planter to produce this by manure. Was the supply still to depend on Virginia and Maryland alone, as its culture becomes more difficult, the price would rise, so as to enable the planter to surmount those difficulties and to live. But the western country on the Mississippi and the midlands of Georgia, having fresh and fertile lands in abundance and a hotter sun, will be able to undersell these two states and will oblige them to abandon the raising [of] tobacco altogether. And a happy obligation for them it will be. It is a culture productive of infinite wretchedness. Those employed in it are in a continued state of exertion beyond the powers of nature to support. Little food of any kind is raised by them, so that the men and animals on these farms are badly fed, and the earth is rapidly impoverished. The cultivation of wheat is the reverse in every circumstance. Besides clothing the earth with herbage and preserving its fertility, it feeds the laborers plentifully, requires from them only a moderate toil, except in the season of harvest, raises great numbers of animals for food and service, and diffuses plenty and happiness among the whole. We find it easier to make an hundred bushels of wheat than a thousand-weight of tobacco, and they are worth more when made. The weavil indeed is a formidable obstacle to the cultivation of this grain with us. But principles are already known which must lead to a remedy. Thus a certain degree of heat, to wit, that of the common air in summer, is necessary to hatch the egg. If subterranean granaries, or others, therefore, can be contrived below that temperature, the evil will be cured by cold. A degree of heat beyond that which hatches the egg, we know will kill it. But in aiming at this we easily run into that which produces putrefaction. To produce putrefaction, however, three agents are requisite, heat, moisture, and the

The Foundations of an Agrarian Society

external air. If the absence of any one of these be secured, the other two may safely be admitted. Heat is the one we want. Moisture, then, or external air, must be excluded. The former has been done by exposing the grain in kilns to the action of fire, which produces heat and extracts moisture at the same time; the latter, by putting the grain into hogsheads, covering it with a coat of lime, and heading it up. In this situation its bulk produces a heat sufficient to kill the egg; the moisture is suffered to remain, indeed, but the external air is excluded. A nicer operation yet has been attempted; that is, to produce an intermediate temperature of heat between that which kills the egg and that which produces putrefaction. The threshing [of] the grain as soon as it is cut and laying it in its chaff in large heaps has been found very nearly to hit this temperature, though not perfectly, nor always. The heap generates heat sufficient to kill most of the eggs, whilst the chaff commonly restrains it from rising into putrefaction. But all these methods abridge too much the quantity which the farmer can manage, and enable other countries to undersell him which are not infested with this insect. There is still a desideratum, then, to give with us decisive triumph to this branch of agriculture over that of tobacco. The culture of wheat, by enlarging our pasture, will render the Arabian horse an article of very considerable profit. Experience has shown that ours is the particular climate of America where he may be raised without degeneracy. Southwardly the heat of the sun occasions a deficiency of pasture, and northwardly the winters are too cold for the short and fine hair, the particular sensibility and constitution of that race. Animals transplanted into unfriendly climates either change their nature and acquire new fences against the new difficulties in which they are placed, or they multiply poorly and become extinct. A good foundation is laid for their propagation here by our possessing already great numbers of horses of that blood, and by a decided taste and preference for them established among the people. Their patience of heat without injury, their superior wind, fit them better in this and the more southern climates even for the drudgeries of the plough and wagon. Northwardly they will become an object only to persons of taste and fortune, for the saddle and light carriages. To these, and for these uses, their fleetness and beauty will recommend them. Besides these there will be other valuable substitutes when the cultivation of tobacco shall be discontinued, such as cotton in the eastern parts of the state and hemp and flax in the western.

It is not easy to say what are the articles either of necessity, comfort, or luxury which we cannot raise, and which we therefore shall be under a necessity of importing from abroad, as everything hardier than the olive and as hardy as the fig may be raised here in the open air. Sugar, coffee, and tea, indeed, are not between these limits, and habit having placed them among the necessaries of life with the wealthy part of our citizens, as long as these habits remain, we must go for them to those countries which are able to furnish them.

[1781–1782, 1787]

Thomas Jefferson

William Bartram:
A Southern Journey

William Bartram (1739-1823), a Quaker botanist
and artist of Philadelphia, was content to observe, record, and describe the wonders of
nature, unspoiled by the handiwork of man. His
descriptions of his expeditions to the deep
South foreshadow the romantic view of nature
and the Indians as he saw and portrayed un-
corrupted beauty and nobility in nature and its
children.

Being desirous of continuing my travels and observations higher up the river, and having an invitation from a gentleman who was agent for, and resident at, a large plantation, the property of an English gentleman, about sixty miles higher up, I resolved to pursue my researches to that place, and having engaged in my service a young Indian, nephew to the White Captain, he agreed to assist me in working my vessel up as high as a certain bluff, where I was, by agreement, to land him, on the west, or Indian, shore, whence he designed to go in quest of the camp of the White Trader, his relation.

Provisions and all necessaries being procured, and the morning pleasant, we went on board and stood up the river. We passed for several miles on the left by islands of high swampland, exceedingly fertile, their banks for a good distance from the water much higher than the interior part, and sufficiently so to build upon and be out of the reach of inundations. They consist of a loose black mould, with a mixture of sand, shells, and dissolved vegetables. The opposite Indian coast is a perpendicular bluff, ten or twelve feet high, consisting of a black, sandy earth, mixed with a large proportion of shells, chiefly various species of freshwater *Cochlea* and *Mytuli*. Near the river, on this high shore, grew *Corypha palma, Magnolia grandiflora*, live oak, *Callicarpa, Myrica cerifera, Hybiscus spinifex*, and the beautiful evergreen shrub called wild lime or tallow nut. This last shrub grows six or eight feet high, many erect stems rising from a root; the leaves are lanceolate and entire, two or three inches in length and one in breadth, of a deep green color, and polished; at the foot of each leaf grows a stiff, sharp thorn; the flowers are small and in clusters, of a greenish yellow color, and sweet scented; they are succeeded by a large oval fruit, of the shape and size of an ordinary plumb, of a fine yellow color when ripe; a soft sweet pulp covers a nut which has a thin shell, enclosing a white kernel somewhat of the consistence and taste of the sweet almond, but more oily and very much like hard tallow, which induced by father, when he first observed it, to call it the tallow nut.

At the upper end of this bluff is a fine orange grove. Here my Indian companion requested me to set him on shore, being already tired of rowing under a fervid sun, and having for some time intimated a dislike to his situation; I readily complied with his desire, knowing the impossibility of compelling an Indian against his own inclinations, or even prevailing upon him by reasonable arguments, when labor is in the question; before my vessel reached the shore, he sprang out of her and landed, when uttering a shrill and terrible whoop, he bounded off like a roebuck, and I lost sight of him. I at first apprehended that, as he took his gun with him, he intended to hunt for some game and return to me in the evening. The day being excessively hot and sultry, I concluded to take up my quarters here until next morning.

The Indian not returning this morning, I set sail alone. The coasts on each side had much the same appearance as already described. The palm trees here seem to be of a different species from the cabbage tree; their straight trunks are sixty, eighty, or ninety feet high, with a beautiful

William Bartram

taper of a bright ash color, until within six or seven feet of the top, where it is a fine green color, crowned with an orb of rich green plumed leaves; I have measured the stem of these plumes fifteen feet in length, besides the plume, which is nearly of the same length.

The little lake, which is an expansion of the river, now appeared in view; on the east side are extensive marshes, and on the other high forests and orange groves, and then a bay, lined with vast cypress swamps, both coasts gradually approaching each other, to the opening of the river again, which is in this place about three hundred yards wide; evening now drawing on, I was anxious to reach some high bank of the river, where I intended to lodge, and agreeably to my wishes, I soon after discovered on the west shore a little promontory, at the turning of the river, contracting it here to about one hundred and fifty yards in width. This promontory is a peninsula, containing about three acres of high ground, and is one entire orange grove, with a few live oaks, magnolias, and palms. Upon doubling the point, I arrived at the landing, which is a circular harbor at the foot of the bluff, the top of which is about twelve feet high, and back of it is a large cypress swamp that spreads each way, the right wing forming the west coast of the little lake, and the left stretching up the river many miles and encompassing a vast space of low grassy marshes. From this promontory, looking eastward across the river, we behold a landscape of low country, unparalleled, as I think; on the left is the east coast of the little lake, which I had just passed, and from the orange bluff at the lower end, the high forests begin and increase in breadth from the shore of the lake, making a circular sweep to the right, and contain many hundred thousand acres of meadow, and this grand sweep of high forests encircles, as I apprehend, at least twenty miles of these green fields, interspersed with hommocks or islets of evergreen trees, where the sovereign magnolia and lordly palm stand conspicuous. The islets are high, shelly knolls on the sides of creeks or branches of the river, which wind about and drain off the superabundant waters that cover these meadows during the winter season.

The evening was temperately cool and calm. The crocodiles began to roar and appear in uncommon numbers along the shores and in the river. I fixed my camp in an open plain, near the utmost projection of the promontory, under the shelter of a large live oak, which stood on the highest part of the ground and but a few yards from my boat. From this open, high situation, I had a free prospect of the river, which was a matter of no trivial consideration to me, having good reason to dread the subtle attacks of the alligators, who were crowding about my harbor. Having collected a good quantity of wood for the purpose of keeping up a light and smoke during the night, I began to think of preparing my supper; when, upon examining my stores, I found but a scanty provision, I thereupon determined, as the most expeditious way of supplying my necessities, to take my bob and try for some trout. About one hundred yards above my harbor began a cove or bay of the river, out of which opened a large lagoon. The mouth or entrance from the river to it was narrow, but the waters soon after spread and formed a little lake, extending into the marshes; its entrance and shores within I observed to be verged with floating lawns of the pistia and *Nymphea* and other aquatic plants; these, I knew, were excellent haunts for trout.

The verges and islets of the lagoon were elegantly embellished with flowering plants and shrubs; the laughing coots with wings half spread were tripping over the little coves and hiding themselves in the tufts of grass; young broods of the painted summer teal, skimming the still surface of the waters and following the watchful parent unconscious of danger, were frequently surprised by the voracious trout, and he, in turn, as often by the subtle, greedy alligator. Behold him rushing forth from the flags and reeds. His enormous body swells. His plaited tail, brandished high, floats upon the lake. The waters, like a cataract, descend from his opening jaws. Clouds of smoke issue from his dilated nostrils. The earth trembles with his thunder. When, immediately from the opposite coast of the lagoon, emerges from the deep his rival champion. They suddenly dart upon each other. The boiling surface of the lake marks their rapid course, and a terrific conflict commences. They now sink to the bottom, folded together in horrid wreaths. The water becomes thick and discolored. Again they rise; their jaws clap together, reechoing through the deep surrounding forests. Again they sink, when the contest ends at the muddy bottom of the lake, and the vanquished makes a hazardous escape, hiding himself in the muddy, turbulent waters and sedge on a distant shore. The proud victor, exulting, returns to the place of action. The shores and forests resound his dreadful roar, together with the triumphing shouts of the plaited tribes around, witnesses of the horrid combat.

My apprehensions were highly alarmed after being a spectator of so dreadful a battle; it was obvious that every delay would but tend to increase my dangers and difficulties, as the sun was near setting, and the alligators gathered around my harbor from all quarters; from these considerations I concluded to be expeditious in my trip to the lagoon, in order to take some fish. Not thinking it prudent to take my fusee with me, lest I might lose it overboard in case of a battle, which I had every reason to dread before my return, I therefore furnished myself with a club for my defense, went on board, and penetrating the first line of those which surrounded my harbor, they gave way, but, being pursued by several very large ones, I kept strictly on the watch and paddled with all my might towards the entrance of the lagoon, hoping to be sheltered there from the multitude of my assailants, but ere I had halfway reached the place, I was attacked on all sides, several endeavoring to overset the canoe. My situation now became precarious to the last degree; two very large ones attacked me closely, at the same instant, rushing up with their heads and part of their bodies above the water, roaring terribly and belching floods of water over me. They struck their jaws together so close to my ears as almost to stun me, and I expected every moment to be dragged out of the boat and instantly devoured, but I applied my weapons so effectually about me,

William Bartram

though at random, that I was so successful as to beat them off a little, when, finding that they designed to renew the battle, I made for the shore, as the only means left me for my preservation, for, by keeping close to it, I should have my enemies on one side of me only, whereas I was before surrounded by them, and there was a probability, if pushed to the last extremity, of saving myself by jumping out of the canoe on shore, as it is easy to outwalk them on land, although comparatively as swift as lightning in the water. I found this last expedient alone could fully answer my expectations, for as soon as I gained the shore, they drew off and kept aloof. This was a happy relief, as my confidence was, in some degree, recovered by it. On recollecting myself, I discovered that I had almost reached the entrance of the lagoon, and determined to venture in, if possible, to take a few fish and then return to my harbor while daylight continued, for I could now, with caution and resolution, make my way with safety along shore, and indeed there was no other way to regain my camp without leaving my boat and making my retreat through the marshes and reeds, which, if I could even effect, would have been in a manner throwing myself away, for then there would have been no hopes of ever recovering my bark and returning in safety to any settlements of men. I accordingly proceeded and made good my entrance into the lagoon, though not without opposition from the alligators, who formed a line across the entrance but did not pursue me into it; nor was I molested by any there, though there were some very large ones in a cove at the upper end. I soon caught more trout than I had present occasion for, and the air was too hot and sultry to admit of their being kept for many hours, even though salted or barbecued. I now prepared for my return to camp, which I succeeded in with but little trouble, by keeping close to the shore; yet I was opposed, upon reentering the river out of the lagoon, and pursued near to my landing (though not closely attacked) particularly by an old, daring one, about twelve feet in length, who kept close after me, and when I stepped on shore and turned about, in order to draw up my canoe, he rushed up near my feet and lay there for some time, looking me in the face, his head and shoulders out of water; I resolved he should pay for his temerity, and, having a heavy load in my fusee, I ran to my camp, and, returning with my piece, found him with his foot on the gunwale of the boat, in search of fish; on my coming up he withdrew sullenly and slowly into the water, but soon returned and placed himself in his former position, looking at me and seeming neither fearful nor any way disturbed. I soon dispatched him by lodging the contents of my gun in his head, and then proceeded to cleanse and prepare my fish for supper, and, accordingly, took them out of the boat, laid them down on the sand close to the water, and began to scale them, when, raising my head, I saw before me, through the clear water, the head and shoulders of a very large alligator, moving slowly towards me; I instantly stepped back, when, with a sweep of his tail, he brushed off several of my fish. It was certainly most providential that I looked up at that instant, as the monster would probably, in less than a

A Southern Journey

minute, have seized and dragged me into the river. This incredible bold-ness of the animal disturbed me greatly, supposing there could now be no reasonable safety for me during the night but by keeping continually on the watch; I therefore, as soon as I had prepared the fish, proceeded to secure myself and effects in the best manner I could; in the first place, I hauled my bark upon the shore, almost clear out of the water, to prevent their oversetting or sinking her; after this every movable was taken out and carried to my camp, which was but a few yards off; then, ranging some dry wood in such order as was the most convenient, I cleared the ground round about it, that there might be no impediment in my way, in case of an attack in the night, either from the water or the land, for I discovered by this time that this small isthmus, from its remote situation and fruitful-ness, was resorted to by bears and wolves. Having prepared myself in the best manner I could, I charged my gun and proceeded to reconnoitre my camp and the adjacent grounds, when I discovered that the peninsula and grove, at the distance of about two hundred yards from my encampment, on the land side, were invested by a cypress swamp, covered with water, which below was joined to the shore of the little lake, and above to the marshes surrounding the lagoon, so that I was confined to an islet exceed-ingly circumscribed, and I found there was no other retreat for me, in case of an attack, but by either ascending one of the large oaks or pushing off with my boat.

It was by this time dusk, and the alligators had nearly ceased their roar, when I was again alarmed by a tumultuous noise that seemed to be in my harbor, and therefore engaged my immediate attention. Returning to my camp, I found it undisturbed, and then continued on to the extreme point of the promontory, where I saw a scene, new and surprising, which at first threw my senses into such a tumult that it was some time before I could comprehend what was the matter; however, I soon accounted for the prodigious assemblage of crocodiles at this place, which exceeded every-thing of the kind I had ever heard of.

How shall I express myself so as to convey an adequate idea of it to the reader and at the same time avoid raising suspicions of my want of veracity? Should I say that the river in this place from shore to shore and perhaps near half a mile above and below me appeared to be one solid bank of fish, of various kinds, pushing through this narrow pass of St. Juans into the little lake on their return down the river, and that the alli-gators were in such incredible numbers and so close together from shore to shore that it would have been easy to have walked across on their heads, had the animals been harmless? What expressions can sufficiently declare the shocking scene that for some minutes continued, whilst this mighty army of fish were forcing the pass? During this attempt, thousands, I may say hundreds of thousands of them were caught and swallowed by the devouring alligators. I have seen an alligator take up out of the water sev-eral fish at a time and just squeeze them betwixt his jaws, while the tails of the great trout flapped about his eyes and lips, ere he had swallowed

William Bartram

them. The horrid noise of their closing jaws, their plunging amidst the broken banks of fish and rising with their prey some feet upright above the water, the floods of water and blood rushing out of their mouths, and the clouds of vapor issuing from their wide nostrils were truly frightful. This scene continued at intervals during the night, as the fish came to the pass. After this sight, shocking and tremendous as it was, I found myself somewhat easier and more reconciled to my situation, being convinced that their extraordinary assemblage here was owing to this annual feast of fish, and that they were so well employed in their own element that I had little occasion to fear their paying me a visit.

It being now almost night, I returned to my camp, where I had left my fish broiling and my kettle of rice stewing, and, having with me oil, pepper and salt, and excellent oranges hanging in abundance over my head (a valuable substitute for vinegar), I sat down and regaled myself cheerfully; having finished my repast, I rekindled my fire for light, and whilst I was revising the notes of my past day's journey, I was suddenly roused with a noise behind me toward the mainland; I sprang up on my feet, and, listening, I distinctly heard some creature wading in the water of the isthmus; I seized my gun and went cautiously from my camp, directing my steps towards the noise; when I had advanced about thirty yards, I halted behind a coppice of orange trees and soon perceived two very large bears, which had made their way through the water and had landed in the grove, about one hundred yards distance from me, and were advancing towards me. I waited until they were within thirty yards of me; they there began to snuff and look towards my camp; I snapped my piece, but it flashed, on which they both turned about and galloped off, plunging through the water and swamp, never halting, as I suppose, until they reached fast land, as I could hear them leaping and plunging a long time; they did not presume to return again, nor was I molested by any other creature, except being occasionally awakened by the whooping of owls, screaming of bitterns, or the wood rats running amongst the leaves.

The wood rat is a very curious animal; they are not half the size of the domestic rat, of a dark brown or black color, their tail slender and shorter in proportion and covered thinly with short hair; they are singular with respect to their ingenuity and great labor in the construction of their habitations, which are conical pyramids about three or four feet high, constructed with dry branches, which they collect with great labor and perseverance and pile up without any apparent order; yet they are so interwoven with one another that it would take a bear or wildcat some time to pull one of these castles to pieces and allow the animals sufficient time to secure a retreat with their young.

The noise of the crocodiles kept me awake the greater part of the night, but when I arose in the morning, contrary to my expectations, there was perfect peace; very few of them to be seen, and those were asleep on the shore, yet I was not able to suppress my fears and apprehensions of being attacked by them in future, and, indeed, yesterday's combat with them, notwithstanding I came off in a manner victorious, or at least made a safe retreat, had left sufficient impression on my mind to damp my courage, and it seemed too much for one of my strength, being alone in a very small boat, to encounter such collected danger. To pursue my voyage up the river and be obliged every evening to pass such dangerous defiles appeared to me as perilous as running the gauntlet betwixt two rows of Indians armed with knives and firebrands; I, however, resolved to continue my voyage one day longer, if I possibly could with safety, and then return down the river, should I find the like difficulties to oppose. Accordingly I got everything on board, charged my gun, and set sail cautiously along shore; as I passed by battle lagoon, I began to tremble and keep a good look out, when suddenly a huge alligator rushed out of the reeds and, with a tremendous roar, came up and darted as swift as an arrow under my boat, emerging upright on my lee quarter, with open jaws, and belching water and smoke that fell upon me like rain in a hurricane; I laid soundly about his head with my club and beat him off, and, after plunging and darting about my boat, he went off on a straight line through the water, seemingly with the rapidity of lightning, and entered the cape of the lagoon; I now employed my time to the very best advantage in paddling close along shore, but could not forbear looking now and then behind me, and presently perceived one of them coming up again; the water of the river hereabouts was shoal and very clear; the monster came up with the usual roar and menaces and passed close by the side of my boat, when I could distinctly see a young brood of alligators to the number of one hundred or more following after her in a long train; they kept close together in a column without straggling off to the one side or the other; the young appeared to be of an equal size, about fifteen inches in length, almost black, with pale yellow transverse waved clouds or blotches, much like rattlesnakes in color. I now lost sight of my enemy again.

Still keeping close along shore, on turning a point or projection of the riverbank, at once I beheld a great number of hillocks or small pyramids, resembling haycocks, ranged like an encampment along the banks; they stood fifteen or twenty yards distant from the water, on a high marsh, about four feet perpendicular above the water; I knew them to be the nests of the crocodile, having had a description of them before, and now expected a furious and general attack, as I saw several large crocodiles swimming abreast of these buildings. These nests being so great a curiosity to me, I was determined at all events immediately to land and examine them. Accordingly I ran my bark on shore at one of their landing places, which was a sort of nick or little dock, from which ascended a sloping path or road up to the edge of the meadow, where their nests were; most of them were deserted, and the great, thick, whitish eggshells lay broken and scattred upon the ground round about them.

The nests of hillocks are of the form of an obtuse cone, four feet high and four or five feet in diameter at their bases; they are constructed with mud, grass, and herbage; at first they lay a floor of this kind of tem-

William Bartram

pered mortar upon the ground, upon which they deposit a layer of eggs, and upon this a stratum of mortar seven or eight inches in thickness, and then another layer of eggs, and in this manner one stratum upon another, nearly to the top; I believe they commonly lay from one to two hundred eggs in a nest; these are hatched, I suppose, by the heat of the sun, and perhaps the vegetable substances mixed with the earth, being acted upon by the sun, may cause a small degree of fermentation and so increase the heat in those hillocks. The ground for several acres about these nests showed evident marks of a continual resort of alligators; the grass was everywhere beaten down; hardly a blade or straw was left standing, whereas, all about, at a distance, it was five or six feet high, and as thick as it could grow together. The female, as I imagine, carefully watches her own nest of eggs until they are all hatched, or perhaps while she is attending her own brood, she takes under her care and protection as many as she can get at one time, either from her own particular nest or others, but certain it is that the young are not left to shift for themselves, having had frequent opportunities of seeing the female alligator leading about the shores her train of young ones, just like a hen does her chickens, and she is equally assiduous and courageous in defending the young which are under their care and providing for their subsistence, and when she is basking upon the warm banks with her brood around her, you may hear the young ones continually whining and barking, like young puppies. I believe but few of the brood live to the years of full growth and magnitude, as the old feed on the young as long as they can make prey of them.

The alligator, when full grown, is a very large and terrible creature, and of prodigious strength, activity, and swiftness in the water. I have seen them twenty feet in length, and some are supposed to be twenty-two or twenty-three feet; their body is as large as that of a horse; their shape exactly resembles that of a lizard, except their tail, which is flat or cunei-form, being compressed on each side and gradually diminishing from the abdomen to the extremity, which, with the whole body, is covered with horny plates or *squammae*, impenetrable when on the body of the live animal, even to a rifle ball, except about their head and just behind their fore-legs or arms, where it is said they are only vulnerable. The head of a full-grown one is about three feet, and the mouth opens nearly the same length; the eyes are small in proportion and seem sunk deep in the head, by means of the prominency of the brows; the nostrils are large, inflated and prominent on the top, so that the head in the water resembles, at a distance, a great chunk of wood floating about. Only the upper jaw moves, which they raise almost perpendicular, so as to form a right angle with the lower one. In the forepart of the upper jaw, on each side, just under the nostrils, are two very large, thick, strong teeth or tusks, not very sharp, but rather the shape of a cone; these are as white as the finest polished ivory and are not covered by any skin or lips, and always in sight, which gives the creature a frightful appearance; in the lower jaw are holes opposite to these teeth, to receive them; when they clap their jaws together, it causes

A Southern Journey

a surprising noise, like that which is made by forcing a heavy plank with violence upon the ground, and may be heard at a great distance.

But what is yet more surprising to a stranger is the incredible loud and terrifying roar which they are capable of making, especially in the spring season, their breeding time; it most resembles very heavy distant thunder, not only shaking the air and waters, but causing the earth to tremble, and when hundreds and thousands are roaring at the same time, you can scarcely be persuaded but that the whole globe is violently and dangerously agitated.

An old champion, who is perhaps absolute sovereign of a little lake or lagoon (when fifty less than himself are obliged to content themselves with swelling and roaring in little coves round about) darts forth from the reedy coverts all at once, on the surface of the waters, in a right line, at first seemingly as swift as lightning, but gradually more slowly until he arrives at the center of the lake, when he stops; he now swells himself by drawing in wind and water through his mouth, which causes a loud sonorous rattling in the throat for near a minute, but it is immediately forced out again through his mouth and nostrils, with a loud noise, brandishing his tail in the air, and the vapor ascending from his nostrils like smoke. At other times, when swollen to an extent ready to burst, his head and tail lifted up, he spins or twirls round on the surface of the water. He acts his part like an Indian chief, when rehearsing his feats of war, and then retiring, the exhibition is continued by others who dare to step forth and strive to excel each other to gain the attention of the favorite female.

Having gratified my curiosity at this general breeding place and nursery of crocodiles, I continued my voyage up the river without being greatly disturbed by them; in my way I observed islets or floating fields of the bright green pistia, decorated with other amphibious plants, as *Senecio jacobea, Persicaria amphibia, Coreopsis bidens, Hydrocotyle fluitans,* and many others of less note. . . .

I arrived at Cowe about noon; this settlement is esteemed the capital town; it is situated on the bases of the hills on both sides of the river, near to its bank, and here terminates the great vale of Cowe, exhibiting one of the most charming natural mountainous landscapes perhaps anywhere to be seen; ridges of hills rising grand and sublimely one above and beyond another, some boldly and majestically advancing into the verdant plains, their feet bathed with the silver flood of the Tanase, whilst others far distant, veiled in blue mists, sublimely mount aloft, with yet greater majesty lift up their pompous crests, and overlook vast regions. . . .

Next day after my arrival I crossed the river in a canoe, on a visit to a trader who resided amongst the habitations on the other shore.

After dinner, on his mentioning some curious scenes amongst the hills, some miles distance from the river, we agreed to spend the afternoon in observations on the mountains.

After riding near two miles through Indian plantations of corn, which was well cultivated, kept clean of weeds, and was well advanced,

William Bartram

being near eighteen inches in height, and the beans planted at the corn hills were above ground, we leave the fields on our right, turning towards the mountains and ascending through a delightful green vale or lawn, which conducted us in amongst the pyramidal hills and crossing a brisk flowing creek, meandering through the meads which continued near two miles, dividing and branching in amongst the hills; we then mounted their steep ascents, rising gradually by ridges or steps one above another, frequently crossing narrow, fertile dales as we ascended; the air feels cool and animating, being charged with the fragrant breath of the mountain beauties, the blooming mountain cluster rose, blushing rhododendron, and fair lily of the valley; having now attained the summit of this very elevated ridge, we enjoyed a fine prospect indeed; the enchanting vale of Keowe, perhaps as celebrated for fertility, fruitfulness, and beautiful prospects as the fields of Pharsalia or the vale of Tempe, the town, the elevated peaks of the Jore Mountains, a very distant prospect of the Jore village in a beautiful lawn, lifted up many thousand feet higher than our present situation, besides a view of many other villages and settlements on the sides of the mountains, at various distances and elevations, the silver rivules gliding by them and snow-white cataracts glimmering on the sides of the lofty hills, the bold promontories of the Jore Mountain stepping into the Tanase River, whilst his foaming waters rushed between them.

After viewing this very entertaining scene, we began to descend the mountain on the other side, which exhibited the same order of gradations of ridges and vales as on our ascent, and at length rested on a very expansive, fertile plain, amidst the towering hills, over which we rode a long time, through magnificent high forests, extensive green fields, meadows, and lawns. Here had formerly been a very flourishing settlement, but the Indians deserted it in search of fresh planting land, which they soon found in a rich vale but a few miles distance over a ridge of hills. Soon after entering on these charming, sequestered, prolific fields, we came to a fine little river, which crossing, and riding over fruitful strawberry beds and green lawns, on the sides of a circular ridge of hills in front of us, and going around the bases of this promontory, came to a fine meadow on an arm of the vale, through which meandered a brook, its humid vapors bedewing the fragrant strawberries which hung in heavy red clusters over the grassy verge; we crossed the rivulet, then rising a sloping, green, turfy ascent, alighted on the borders of a grand forest of stately trees, which we penetrated on foot a little distance to a *horse-stamp*, where was a large squadron of those useful creatures, belonging to my friend and companion, the trader, on the sight of whom they assembled together from all quarters; some at a distance saluted him with shrill neighings of gratitude or came prancing up to lick the salt out of his hand, whilst the younger and more timorous came galloping onward, but coyly wheeled off, and, fetching a circuit, stood aloof, but as soon as their lord and master strewed the crystalline salty bait on the hard-beaten ground, they all, old and young, docile and timorous, soon formed themselves in ranks and fell to licking up the delicious morsel.

A Southern Journey

It was a fine sight; more beautiful creatures I never saw; there were of them of all colors, sizes, and dispositions. Every year as they become of age he sends off a troop of them down to Charleston, where they are sold to the highest bidder.

Having paid our attention to this useful part of the creation, who, if they are under our dominion, have consequently a right to our protection and favor, we returned to our trusty servants that were regaling themselves in the exuberant sweet pastures and strawberry fields in sight and mounted again, proceeding on our return to town, continued through part of this high forest skirting on the meadows, began to ascend the hills of a ridge which we were under the necessity of crossing, and, having gained its summit, enjoyed a most enchanting view, a vast expanse of green meadows and strawberry fields, a meandering river gliding through, saluting in its various turnings the swelling, green, turfy knolls, embellished with parterres of flowers and fruitful strawberry beds, flocks of turkeys strolling about them, herds of deer prancing in the meads or bounding over the hills; companies of young, innocent Cherokee virgins, some busily gathering the rich, fragrant fruit, others having already filled their baskets, lay reclined under the shade of floriferous and fragrant native bowers of magnolia, azalea, philadelphus, perfumed calycanthus, sweet yellow jessamine, and cerulean *Glycine frutescens*, disclosing their beauties to the fluttering breeze and bathing their limbs in the cool, fleeting streams, whilst other parties, more gay and libertine, were yet collecting strawberries or wantonly chasing their companions, tantalizing them, staining their lips and cheeks with the rich fruit.

This sylvan scene of primitive innocence was enchanting, and perhaps too enticing for hearty young men long to continue as idle spectators.

In fine, nature prevailing over reason, we wished at least to have a more active part in their delicious sports. Thus precipitately resolving, we cautiously made our approaches, yet undiscovered, almost to the joyous scene of action. Now, although we meant no other than an innocent frolic with this gay assembly of hamadryads, we shall leave it to the person of feeling and sensibility to form an idea to what lengths our passions might have hurried us, thus warmed and excited, had it not been for the vigilance and care of some envious matrons who lay in ambush, and, espying us, gave the alarm, time enough for the nymphs to rally and assemble together; we, however, pursued and gained ground on a group of them who had incautiously strolled to a greater distance from their guardians and, finding their retreat now like to be cut off, took shelter under cover of a little grove, but, on perceiving themselves to be discovered by us, kept their station, peeping through the bushes; when observing our approaches, they confidently discovered themselves and decently advanced to meet us, half unveiling their blooming faces, incarnated with the modest maiden blush, and with native innocence and cheerfulness presented their little baskets, merrily telling us their fruit was ripe and sound.

We accepted a basket, sat down, and regaled ourselves on the delicious fruit, encircled by the whole assembly of the innocently jocose

William Bartram

sylvan nymphs; by this time the several parties under the conduct of the elder matrons had disposed themselves in companies on the green, turfy banks.

My young companion, the trader, by concessions and suitable apologies for the bold intrusion, having compromised the matter with them, engaged them to bring their collections to his house at a stipulated price; we parted friendly.

And now, taking leave of these Elysian fields, we again mounted the hills, which we crossed, and, traversing obliquely their flowery beds, arrived in town in the cool of the evening.

[1774?–1776?, 1791]

Hector St. John de Crèvecoeur: On the Situation, Feelings, and Pleasures of an American Farmer

Hector St. John de Crèvecoeur (1735-1813), an American farmer, social observer, and writer, is best known for his modestly titled but valuable *Letters from an American Farmer* (1782). He attempted to portray America and Americans as he saw them, often expressing views that his liberal faith convinced him would become reality.

As you are the first enlightened European I have ever had the pleasure of being acquainted with, you will not be surprised that I should, according to your earnest desire and my promise, appear anxious of preserving your friendship and correspondence. By your accounts, I observe a material difference subsists between your husbandry, modes, and customs, and ours; everything is local; could we enjoy the advantages of the English farmer, we should be much happier, indeed, but this wish, like many others, implies a contradiction; and could the English farmer have some of those privileges we possess, they would be the first of their class in the world. Good and evil I see is to be found in all societies, and it is in vain to seek for any spot where those ingredients are not mixed. I therefore rest satisfied and thank God that my lot is to be an American farmer, instead of a Russian boor or an Hungarian peasant. I thank you kindly for the idea, however dreadful, which you have given me of their lot and condition; your observations have confirmed me in the justness of my ideas, and I am happier now than I thought myself before. It is strange that misery, when viewed in others, should become to us a sort of real good, though I am far from rejoicing to hear that there are in the world men so thoroughly wretched; they are no doubt as harmless, industrious, and willing to work as we are. Hard is their fate to be thus condemned to a slavery worse than that of our Negroes. Yet when young I entertained some thoughts of selling my farm. I thought it afforded but a dull repetition of the same labors and pleasures. I thought the former tedious and heavy, the latter few and insipid; but when I came to consider myself as divested of my farm, I then found the world so wide, and every place so full, that I began to fear lest there would be no room for me. My farm, my house, my barn presented to my imagination objects from which I adduced quite new ideas; they were more forcible than before. Why should not I find myself happy, said I, where my father was before? He left me no good books, it is true; he gave me no other education than the art of reading and writing; but he left me a good farm, and his experience; he left me free from debts, and no kind of difficulties to struggle with. I married, and this perfectly reconciled me to my situation; my wife rendered my house all at once cheerful and pleasing; it no longer appeared gloomy and solitary as before; when I went to work in my fields, I worked with more alacrity and sprightliness; I felt that I did not work for myself alone, and this encouraged me much. My wife would often come with her knitting in her hand and sit under the shady trees, praising the straightness of my furrows and the docility of my horses; this swelled my heart and made everything light and pleasant, and I regretted that I had not married before. I felt myself happy in my new situation, and where is that station which can confer a more substantial system of felicity than that of an American farmer, possessing freedom of action, freedom of thoughts, ruled by a mode of government which requires but little from us? I owe nothing but a peppercorn to my country, a small tribute to my king, with loyalty and due respect; I know no other landlord than the lord of all land, to whom I owe the most sincere gratitude. My father left me three hundred and seventy-one acres of

Hector St. John de Crèvecoeur

land, forty-seven of which are good timothy meadow, an excellent orchard, a good house, and a substantial barn. It is my duty to think how happy I am that he lived to build and to pay for all these improvements; what are the labors which I have to undergo; what are my fatigues when compared to his, who had everything to do, from the first tree he felled to the finishing of his house? Every year I kill from 1,500 to 2,000 weight of pork, 1,200 of beef, half a dozen of good wethers in harvest; of fowls my wife has always a great stock; what can I wish more? My Negroes are tolerably faithful and healthy; by a long series of industry and honest dealings, my father left behind him the name of a good man; I have but to tread his paths to be happy and a good man like him. I know enough of the law to regulate my little concerns with propriety, nor do I dread its power; these are the grand outlines of my situation, but, as I can feel much more than I am able to express, I hardly know how to proceed. When my first son was born, the whole train of my ideas was suddenly altered; never was there a charm that acted so quickly and powerfully; I ceased to ramble in imagination through the wide world; my excursions since have not exceeded the bounds of my farm, and all my principal pleasures are now centered within its scanty limits, but at the same time there is not an operation belonging to it in which I do not find some food for useful reflections. This is the reason, I suppose, that, when you were here, you used, in your refined style, to denominate me the farmer of feelings; how rude must those feelings be in him who daily holds the axe or the plough; how much more refined, on the contrary, those of the European, whose mind is improved by education, example, books, and by every acquired advantage! Those feelings, however, I will delineate as well as I can, agreeably to your earnest request. When I contemplate my wife, by my fireside, while she either spins, knits, darns, or suckles our child, I cannot describe the various emotions of love, of gratitude, of conscious pride which thrill in my heart and often overflow in involuntary tears. I feel the necessity, the sweet pleasure, of acting my part, the part of an husband and father, with an attention and propriety which may entitle me to my good fortune. It is true these pleasing images vanish with the smoke of my pipe, but though they disappear from my mind, the impression they have made on my heart is indelible. When I play with the infant, my warm imagination runs forward and eagerly anticipates his future temper and constitution. I would willingly open the book of fate and know in which page his destiny is delineated; alas! where is the father who in those moments of paternal ecstasy can delineate one-half of the thoughts which dilate his heart? I am sure I cannot; then again I fear for the health of those who are become so dear to me, and in their sicknesses I severely pay for the joys I experienced while they were well. Whenever I go abroad, it is always involuntary. I never return home without feeling some pleasing emotion, which I often suppress as useless and foolish. The instant I enter on my own land, the bright ideas of property, of exclusive right, of independence exalt my mind. Precious soil, I say to myself, by what singular custom of law is it that thou wast made to constitute the riches of the freeholder? What should

On the Situation, Feelings, and Pleasures of an American Farmer

we American farmers be without the distinct possession of that soil? It feeds, it clothes us; from it we draw even a great exuberancy, our best meat, our richest drink; the very honey of our bees comes from this privileged spot. No wonder we should thus cherish its possession; no wonder that so many Europeans who have never been able to say that such portion of land was theirs cross the Atlantic to realize that happiness. This formerly rude soil has been converted by my father into a pleasant farm, and in return it has established all our rights; on it is founded our rank, our freedom, our power as citizens, our importance as inhabitants of such a district. These images, I must confess, I always behold with pleasure, and extend them as far as my imagination can reach, for this is what may be called the true and the only philosophy of an American farmer. Pray do not laugh in thus seeing an artless countryman tracing himself through the simple modifications of his life; remember that you have required it; therefore with candor, though with diffidence, I endeavour to follow the thread of my feelings, but I cannot tell you all. Often when I plough my low ground, I place my little boy on a chair which screws to the beam of the plough; its motion and that of the horses please him; he is perfectly happy and begins to chat. As I lean over the handle, various are the thoughts which crowd into my mind. I am now doing for him, I say, what my father formerly did for me; may God enable him to live that he may perform the same operations for the same purposes when I am worn out and old! I relieve his mother of some trouble while I have him with me; the odoriferous furrow exhilarates his spirits and seems to do the child a great deal of good, for he looks more blooming since I have adopted that practice; can more pleasure, more dignity be added to that primary occupation? The father thus ploughing with his child, and to feed his family, is inferior only to the emperor of China ploughing as an example to his kingdom. In the evening, when I return home through my low grounds, I am astonished at the myriads of insects which I perceive dancing in the beams of the setting sun. I was before scarcely acquainted with their existence; they are so small that it is difficult to distinguish them; they are carefully improving this short evening space, not daring to expose themselves to the blaze of our meridian sun. I never see an egg brought on my table but I feel penetrated with the wonderful change it would have undergone but for my gluttony; it might have been a gentle, useful hen, leading her chickens with a care and vigilance which speaks shame to many women. A cock perhaps, arrayed with the most majestic plumes, tender to its mate, bold, courageous, endowed with an astonishing instinct, with thoughts, with memory, and every distinguishing characteristic of the reason of man. I never see my trees drop their leaves and their fruit in the autumn and bud again in the spring without wonder; the sagacity of those animals which have long been the tenants of my farm astonish me; some of them seem to surpass even men in memory and sagacity. I could tell you singular instances of that kind. What, then, is this instinct which we so debase, and of which we are taught to entertain so diminutive an idea? My bees, above any other tenants of my farm, attract my attention and respect; I am

Hector St. John de Crèvecoeur

astonished to see that nothing exists but what has its enemy; one species pursues and lives upon the other; unfortunately our kingbirds are the destroyers of those industrious insects; but, on the other hand, these birds preserve our fields from the depredation of crows, which they pursue on the wing with great vigilance and astonishing dexterity. Thus divided by two interested motives, I have long resisted the desire I had to kill them, until last year, when I thought they increased too much, and my indulgence had been carried too far; it was at the time of swarming, when they all came and fixed themselves on the neighboring trees, from whence they catched those that returned loaded from the fields. This made me resolve to kill as many as I could, and I was just ready to fire when a bunch of bees as big as my fist issued from one of the hives, rushed on one of the birds, and probably stung him, for he instantly screamed and flew, not as before, in an irregular manner, but in a direct line. He was followed by the same bold phalanx, at a considerable distance, which, unfortunately becoming too sure of victory, quitted their military array and disbanded themselves. By this inconsiderate step they lost all that aggregate of force which had made the bird fly off. Perceiving their disorder, he immediately returned and snapped as many as he wanted; nay, he had even the impudence to alight on the very twig from which the bees had drove him. I killed him and immediately opened his craw, from which I took 171 bees; I laid them all on a blanket in the sun, and to my great surprise 54 returned to life, licked themselves clean, and joyfully went back to the hive, where they probably informed their companions of such an adventure and escape as I believe had never happened before to American bees! I draw a great fund of pleasure from the quails which inhabit my farm; they abundantly repay me, by their various notes and peculiar tameness, for the inviolable hospitality I constantly show them in the winter. Instead of perfidiously taking advantage of their great and affecting distress, when nature offers nothing but a barren, universal bed of snow, when irresistible necessity forces them to my barn doors, I permit them to feed unmolested, and it is not the least agreeable spectacle which that dreary season presents when I see those beautiful birds, tamed by hunger, intermingling with all my cattle and sheep, seeking in security for the poor, scanty grain which but for them would be useless and lost. Often in the angles of the fences where the motion of the wind prevents the snow from settling, I carry them both chaff and grain, the one to feed them, the other to prevent their tender feet from freezing fast to the earth, as I have frequently observed them to do. I do not know an instance in which the singular barbarity of man is so strongly delineated as in the catching and murthering those harmless birds at that cruel season of the year. Mr. ***, one of the most famous and extraordinary farmers that has ever done honor to the province of Connecticut, by his timely and humane assistance in a hard winter, saved this species from being entirely destroyed. They perished all over the country; none of their delightful whistlings were heard the next spring but upon this gentleman's farm, and to his humanity we owe the continuation of their music. When the severities of that season have

On the Situation, Feelings, and Pleasures of an American Farmer

dispirited all my cattle, no farmer ever attends them with more pleasure than I do; it is one of those duties which is sweetened with the most rational satisfaction. I amuse myself in beholding their different tempers, actions, and the various effects of their instinct now powerfully impelled by the force of hunger. I trace their various inclinations and the different effects of their passions, which are exactly the same as among men; the law is to us precisely what I am in my barnyard, a bridle and check to prevent the strong and greedy from oppressing the timid and weak. Conscious of superiority, they always strive to encroach on their neighbors; unsatisfied with their portion, they eagerly swallow it in order to have an opportunity of taking what is given to others, except they are prevented. Some I chide; others, unmindful of my admonitions, receive some blows. Could victuals thus be given to men without the assistance of any language, I am sure they would not behave better to one another, nor more philosophically than my cattle do. The same spirit prevails in the stable, but there I have to do with more generous animals; there my well-known voice has immediate influence and soon restores peace and tranquillity. Thus by superior knowledge I govern all my cattle, as wise men are obliged to govern fools and the ignorant. A variety of other thoughts crowd on my mind at that peculiar instant, but they all vanish by the time I return home. If in a cold night I swiftly travel in my sledge, carried along at the rate of twelve miles an hour, many are the reflections excited by surrounding circumstances. I ask myself what sort of an agent is that which we call frost? Our minister compares it to needles, the points of which enter our pores. What is become of the heat of the summer; in what part of the world is it that the N.W. keeps these grand magazines of nitre? When I see in the morning a river over which I can travel that in the evening before was liquid, I am astonished indeed! What is become of those million of insects which played in our summer fields, and in our evening meadows; they were so puny and so delicate, the period of their existence was so short, that one cannot help wondering how they could learn, in that short space, the sublime art to hide themselves and their offspring in so perfect a manner as to baffle the rigor of the season and preserve that precious embryo of life, that small portion of ethereal heat, which, if once destroyed, would destroy the species! Whence that irresistible propensity to sleep so common in all those who are severely attacked by the frost. Dreary as this season appears, yet it has, like all others, its miracles; it presents to man a variety of problems which he can never resolve; among the rest, we have here a set of small birds which never appear until the snow falls; contrary to all others, they dwell and appear to delight in that element.

It is my bees, however, which afford me the most pleasing and extensive themes; let me look at them when I will; their government, their industry, their quarrels, their passions always present me with something new, for which reason, when weary with labor, my common place of rest is under my locust tree, close by my beehouse. By their movements I can predict the weather and can tell the day of their swarming, but the most difficult point is, when on the wing, to know whether they want to go to

Hector St. John de Crèvecoeur

the woods or not. If they have previously pitched in some hollow trees, it is not the allurements of salt and water, of fennel, hickory leaves, etc., nor the finest box that can induce them to stay; they will prefer those rude, rough habitations to the best polished mahogany hive. When that is the case with mine, I seldom thwart their inclinations; it is in freedom that they work; were I to confine them, they would dwindle away and quit their labor. In such excursions we only part for a while; I am generally sure to find them again the following fall. This elopement of theirs only adds to my recreations; I know how to deceive even their superlative instinct; nor do I fear losing them, though eighteen miles from my house and lodged in the most lofty trees in the most impervious of our forests. I once took you along with me in one of these rambles, and yet you insist on my repeating the detail of our operations; it brings back into my mind many of the useful and entertaining reflections with which you so happily beguiled our tedious hours.

After I have done sowing, by way of recreation, I prepare for a week's jaunt in the woods, not to hunt either the deer or the bears, as my neighbors do, but to catch the more harmless bees. I cannot boast that this chase is so noble or so famous among men, but I find it less fatiguing and full as profitable, and the last consideration is the only one that moves me. I take with me my dog as a companion, for he is useless as to this game; my gun, for no man you know ought to enter the woods without one; my blanket, some provisions, some wax, vermilion, honey, and a small pocket compass. With these implements I proceed to such woods as are at a considerable distance from any settlements. I carefully examine whether they abound with large trees; if so, I make a small fire on some flat stones in a convenient place; on the fire I put some wax; close by this fire, on another stone, I drop honey in distinct drops, which I surround with small quantities of vermilion, laid on the stone; and then I retire carefully to watch whether any bees appear. If there are any in that neighborhood, I rest assured that the smell of the burnt wax will unavoidably attract them; they will soon find out the honey, for they are fond of preying on that which is not their own; and in their approach they will necessarily tinge themselves with some particles of vermilion, which will adhere long to their bodies. I next fix my compass to find out their course, which they keep invariably straight, when they are returning home loaded. By the assistance of my watch, I observe how long those are returning which are marked with vermilion. Thus possessed of the course, and, in some measure, of the distance, which I can easily guess at, I follow the first and seldom fail of coming to the tree where those republics are lodged. I then mark it, and thus, with patience, I have found out sometimes eleven swarms in a season, and it is inconceivable what a quantity of honey these trees will sometimes afford. It entirely depends on the size of the hollow, as the bees never rest nor swarm till it is all replenished, for, like men, it is only the want of room that induces them to quit the maternal hive. Next I proceed to some of the nearest settlements, where I procure proper assistance to cut down the trees, get all my prey secured, and then return home with

On the Situation, Feelings, and Pleasures of an American Farmer

my prize. The first bees I ever procured were thus found in the woods by mere accident, for at that time I had no kind of skill in this method of tracing them. The body of the tree being perfectly sound, they had lodged themselves in the hollow of one of its principal limbs, which I carefully sawed off and with a good deal of labor and industry brought it home, where I fixed it up again in the same position in which I found it growing. This was in April; I had five swarms that year, and they have been ever since very prosperous. This business generally takes up a week of my time every fall, and to me it is a week of solitary ease and relaxation.

The seed is by that time committed to the ground; there is nothing very material to do at home, and this additional quantity of honey enables me to be more generous to my home bees, and my wife to make a due quantity of mead. The reason, sir, that you found mine better than that of others is that she puts two gallons of brandy in each barrel, which ripens it and takes off that sweet, luscious taste which it is apt to retain a long time. If we find anywhere in the woods (no matter on whose land) what is called a bee tree, we must mark it; in the fall of the year, when we propose to cut it down, our duty is to inform the proprietor of the land, who is entitled to half the contents; if this is not complied with, we are exposed to an action of trespass, as well as he who should go and cut down a bee tree which he had neither found out nor marked.

We have twice a year the pleasure of catching pigeons, whose numbers are sometimes so astonishing as to obscure the sun in their flight. Where is it that they hatch, for such multitudes must require an immense quantity of food? I fancy they breed toward the plains of Ohio and those about Lake Michigan, which abound in wild oats, though I have never killed any that had that grain in their craws. In one of them, last year, I found some undigested rice. Now the nearest rice fields from where I live must be least 560 miles, and either their digestion must be suspended while they are flying, or else they must fly with the celerity of the wind. We catch them with a net extended on the ground, to which they are allured by what we call tame wild pigeons, made blind and fastened to a long string; his short flights and his repeated calls never fail to bring them down. The greatest number I ever catched was fourteen dozen, though much larger quantities have often been trapped. I have frequently seen them at the market so cheap that for a penny you might have as many as you could carry away, and yet from the extreme cheapness you must not conclude that they are but an ordinary food; on the contrary, I think they are excellent. Every farmer has a tame wild pigeon in a cage at his door all the year round in order to be ready whenever the season comes for catching them.

The pleasure I receive from the warblings of the birds in the spring is superior to my poor description, as the continual succession of their tuneful notes is forever new to me. I generally rise from bed about that indistinct interval which, properly speaking, is neither night nor day, for this is the moment of the most universal vocal choir. Who can listen unmoved to the sweet love tales of our robins, told from tree to tree? Or to the

Hector St. John de Crèvecoeur

shrill catbirds? The sublime accents of the thrush from on high always retard my steps, that I may listen to the delicious music. The variegated appearances of the dewdrops, as they hang to the different objects, must present, even to a clownish imagination, the most voluptuous ideas. The astonishing art which all birds display in the construction of their nests, ill provided as we may suppose them with proper tools, their neatness, their convenience, always make me ashamed of the slovenliness of our houses; their love to their dame, their incessant careful attention, and the peculiar songs they address to her while she tediously incubates their eggs remind me of my duty, could I ever forget it. Their affection to their helpless little ones is a lively precept, and, in short, the whole economy of what we proudly call the brute creation is admirable in every circumstance, and vain man, though adorned with the additional gift of reason, might learn from the perfection of instinct how to regulate the follies and how to temper the errors which this second gift often makes him commit. This is a subject on which I have often bestowed the most serious thoughts; I have often blushed within myself and been greatly astonished when I have compared the unerring path they all follow, all just, all proper, all wise, up to the necessary degree of perfection, with the coarse, the imperfect systems of men, not merely as governors and kings, but as masters, as husbands, as fathers, as citizens. But this is a sanctuary in which an ignorant farmer must not presume to enter. If ever man was permitted to receive and enjoy some blessings that might alleviate the many sorrows to which he is exposed, it is certainly in the country, when he attentively considers those ravishing scenes with which he is everywhere surrounded. This is the only time of the year in which I am avaricious of every moment; I therefore lose none that can add to this simple and inoffensive happiness. I roam early throughout all my fields; not the least operation do I perform which is not accompanied with the most pleasing observations; were I to extend them as far as I have carried them, I should become tedious; you would think me guilty of affectation, and I should perhaps represent many things as pleasurable from which you might not perhaps receive the least agreeable emotions. But, believe me, what I write is all true and real.

Some time ago, as I sat smoking a contemplative pipe in my piazza, I saw with amazement a remarkable instance of selfishness displayed in a very small bird, which I had hitherto respected for its inoffensiveness. Three nests were placed almost contiguous to each other in my piazza; that of a swallow was affixed in the corner next to the house; that of a phoebe in the other; a wren possessed a little box which I had made on purpose and hung between. Be not surprised at their tameness; all my family had long been taught to respect them as well as myself. The wren had shown before signs of dislike to the box which I had given it, but I knew not on what account; at last it resolved, small as it was, to drive the swallow from its own habitation, and, to my very great surprise, it succeeded. Impudence often gets the better of modesty, and this exploit was no sooner performed than it removed every material to its own box with the most admirable dexterity; the signs of triumph appeared very visible; it fluttered its wings

On the Situation, Feelings, and Pleasures of an American Farmer

66

with uncommon velocity; a universal joy was perceivable in all its movements. Where did this little bird learn that spirit of injustice? It was not endowed with what we term reason! Here, then, is a proof that both those gifts border very near on one another, for we see the perfection of the one mixing with the errors of the other! The peaceable swallow, like the passive Quaker, meekly sat at a small distance and never offered the least· resistance, but no sooner was the plunder carried away than the injured bird went to work with unabated ardor, and in a few days the depredations were repaired. To prevent, however, a repetition of the same violence, I removed the wren's box to another part of the house.

In the middle of my new parlor I have, you may remember, a curious republic of industrious hornets; their nest hangs to the ceiling by the same twig on which it was so admirably built and contrived in the woods. Its removal did not displease them, for they find in my house plenty of food, and I have left a hole open in one of the panes of the window, which answers all their purposes. By this kind usage they are become quite harmless; they live on the flies, which are very troublesome to us throughout the summer; they are constantly busy in catching them, even on the eyelids of my children. It is surprising how quickly they smear them with a sort of glue, lest they might escape, and, when thus prepared, they carry them to their nests as food for their young ones. These globular nests are most ingeniously divided into many stories, all provided with cells and proper communications. The materials with which this fabric is built they procure from the cottony furze, with which our oak rails are covered; this substance, tempered with glue, produces a sort of pasteboard which is very strong and resists all the inclemencies of the weather. By their assistance, I am but little troubled with flies. All my family are so accustomed to their strong buzzing that no one takes any notice of them, and though they are fierce and vindictive, yet kindness and hospitality has made them useful and harmless.

We have a great variety of wasps; most of them build their nests in mud, which they fix against the shingles of our roofs, as nigh the pitch as they can. These aggregates represent nothing, at first view, but coarse and irregular lumps, but if you break them, you will observe that the inside of them contains a great number of oblong cells, in which they deposit their eggs, and in which they bury themselves in the fall of the year. Thus immured, they securely pass through the severity of that season, and on the return of the sun are enabled to perforate their cells and to open themselves a passage from these recesses into the sunshine. The yellow wasps, which build under ground in our meadows, are much more to be dreaded, for when the mower unwittingly passes his scythe over their holes, they immediately sally forth with a fury and velocity superior even to the strength of man. They make the boldest fly, and the only remedy is to lie down and cover our heads with hay, for it is only at the head they aim their blows; nor is there any possibility of finishing that part of the work until, by means of fire and brimstone, they are all silenced. But though I have been obliged to execute this dreadful sentence in my own defense, I

Hector St. John de Crèvecoeur

have often thought it a great pity, for the sake of a little hay, to lay waste so ingenious a subterranean town, furnished with every conveniency and built with a most surprising mechanism.

I never should have done were I to recount the many objects which involuntarily strike my imagination in the midst of my work and spontaneously afford me the most pleasing relief. These appear insignificant trifles to a person who has traveled through Europe and America and is acquainted with books and with many sciences, but such simple objects of contemplation suffice me, who have no time to bestow on more extensive observations. Happily these require no study; they are obvious; they gild the moments I dedicate to them and enliven the severe labors which I perform. At home my happiness springs from very different objects; the gradual unfolding of my children's reason, the study of their dawning tempers attract all my paternal attention. I have to contrive little punishments for their little faults, small encouragements for their good actions, and a variety of other expedients dictated by various occasions. But these are themes unworthy your perusal, and which ought not to be carried beyond the walls of my house, being domestic mysteries adapted only to the locality of the small sanctuary wherein my family resides. Sometimes I delight in inventing and executing machines which simplify my wife's labor. I have been tolerably successful that way, and these, sir, are the narrow circles within which I constantly revolve, and what can I wish for beyond them? I bless God for all the good he has given me; I envy no man's prosperity, and with no other portion of happiness than that I may live to teach the same philosophy to my children and give each of them a farm, show them how to cultivate it and be like their father, good, substantial, independent American farmers—an appellation which will be the most fortunate one a man of my class can possess, so long as our civil government continues to shed blessings on our husbandry. Adieu.

[1782]

On the Situation, Feelings, and Pleasures of an American Farmer

Alexander Hamilton:
Report on the Subject of Manufactures

Alexander Hamilton (1757-1804), soldier, statesman, economist, and political activist, was one
of the founders of the American economic system, the two-party system, and a stable central
government. Shrewdly realistic, he saw the
course that would lead the new country from
obscurity to greatness. Contrary to Jefferson,
he insisted that the encouragement of manufacturing was essential, and he provided the
rationale for the relationship between government and industry that has dominated conservative American thinking since his time.

The expediency of encouraging manufactures in the United States, which was not long since deemed very questionable, appears at this time to be pretty generally admitted. The embarrassments which have obstructed the progress of our external trade have led to serious reflections on the necessity of enlarging the sphere of our domestic commerce. The restrictive regulations which, in foreign markets, abridge the vent of the increasing surplus of our agricultural produce serve to beget an earnest desire that a more extensive demand for that surplus may be created at home, and the complete success which has rewarded manufacturing enterprise in some valuable branches, conspiring with the promising symptoms which attend some less mature essays in others, justifies a hope that the obstacles to the growth of this species of industry are less formidable than they were apprehended to be, and that it is not difficult to find, in its further extension, a full indemnification for any external disadvantages which are or may be experienced, as well as an accession of resources favorable to national independence and safety. . . .

It may be observed, and the idea is of no inconsiderable weight, that however true it might be that a state which, possessing large tracts of vacant and fertile territory, was at the same time secluded from foreign commerce would find its interest and the interest of agriculture in diverting a part of its population from tillage to manufactures; yet it will not follow that the same is true of a state which, having such vacant and fertile territory, has at the same time ample opportunity of procuring from abroad, on good terms, all the fabrics of which it stands in need for the supply of its inhabitants. The power of doing this at least secures the great advantage of a division of labor, leaving the farmer free to pursue, exclusively, the culture of his land, and enabling him to procure with its products the manufactured supplies requisite either to his wants or to his enjoyments. And though it should be true that in settled countries the diversification of industry is conducive to an increase in the productive powers of labor and to an augmentation of revenue and capital, yet it is scarcely conceivable that there can be anything of so solid and permanent advantage to an uncultivated and unpeopled country as to convert its wastes into cultivated and inhabited districts. If the revenue, in the meantime, should be less, the capital, in the event, must be greater.

To these observations the following appears to be a satisfactory answer:

1st. If the system of perfect liberty to industry and commerce were the prevailing system of nations, the arguments which dissuade a country in the predicament of the United States from the zealous pursuit of manufactures would doubtless have great force. It will not be affirmed that they might not be permitted, with few exceptions, to serve as a rule of national conduct. In such a state of things, each country would have the full benefit of its peculiar advantages to compensate for its deficiencies or disadvantages. If one nation were in a condition to supply manufactured articles on better terms than another, that other might find an abundant indemnification in a superior capacity to furnish the produce of the soil. And a free

Alexander Hamilton

exchange, mutually beneficial, of the commodities which each was able to supply on the best terms might be carried on between them, supporting in full vigor the industry of each. And though the circumstances which have been mentioned, and others which will be unfolded hereafter, render it probable that nations merely agricultural would not enjoy the same degree of opulence in proportion to their numbers as those which united manufactures with agriculture, yet the progressive improvement of the lands of the former might in the end atone for an inferior degree of opulence in the meantime; and in a case in which opposite considerations are pretty equally balanced, the option ought, perhaps, always to be in favor of leaving industry to its own direction.

But the system which has been mentioned is far from characterizing the general policy of nations. The prevalent one has been regulated by an opposite spirit. The consequence of it is that the United States are, to a certain extent, in the situation of a country precluded from foreign commerce. They can, indeed, without difficulty, obtain from abroad the manufactured supplies of which they are in want, but they experience numerous and very injurious impediments to the emission and vent of their own commodities. Nor is this the case in reference to a single foreign nation only. The regulations of several countries with which we have the most extensive intercourse throw serious obstructions in the way of the principal staples of the United States.

In such a position of things, the United States cannot exchange with Europe on equal terms, and the want of reciprocity would render them the victim of a system which would induce them to confine their views to agriculture and refrain from manufactures. A constant and increasing necessity on their part for the commodities of Europe and only a partial and occasional demand for their own, in return, could not but expose them to a state of impoverishment, compared with the opulence to which their political and natural advantages authorize them to aspire.

Remarks of this kind are not made in the spirit of complaint. It is for the nations whose regulations are alluded to to judge for themselves whether by aiming at too much they do not lose more than they gain. It is for the United States to consider by what means they can render themselves least dependent on the combinations, right or wrong, of foreign policy.

It is no small consolation that already the measures which have embarrassed our trade have accelerated internal improvements, which, upon the whole, have bettered our affairs. To diversify and extend these improvements is the surest and safest method of indemnifying ourselves for any inconveniences which those or similar measures have a tendency to beget. If Europe will not take from us the products of our soil upon terms consistent with our interest, the natural remedy is to contract, as fast as possible, our wants of her.

2nd. The conversion of their waste into cultivated lands is certainly a point of great moment in the political calculations of the United States. But the degree in which this may possibly be retarded by the encourage-

Report on the Subject of Manufactures

ment of manufactories does not appear to countervail the powerful inducements to afford that encouragement.

An observation made in another place is of a nature to have great influence upon this question. If it cannot be denied that the interests even of agriculture may be advanced more by having such lands of a state as are occupied under a good cultivation than by having a greater quantity occupied under a much inferior cultivation, and if manufactories, for the reasons assigned, must be admitted to have a tendency to promote a more steady and vigorous cultivation of the lands occupied than would happen without them, it will follow that they are capable of indemnifying a country for a diminution of the progress of new settlements, and may serve to increase both the capital value and the income of its lands, even though they should abridge the number of acres under tillage.

But it does by no means follow that the progress of new settlements would be retarded by the extension of manufactures. The desire of being an independent proprietor of land is founded on such strong principles in the human breast that, where the opportunity of becoming so is as great as it is in the United States, the proportion will be small of those whose situations would otherwise lead to it who would be diverted from it toward manufactures. And it is highly probable, as already intimated, that the accessions of foreigners who, originally drawn over by manufacturing views, would afterward abandon them for agricultural would be more than an equivalent for those of our own citizens who might happen to be detached from them.

The remaining objections to a particular encouragement of manufactures in the United States now require to be examined.

One of these turns on the proposition that industry, if left to itself, will naturally find its way to the most useful and profitable employment. Whence it is inferred that manufactures, without the aid of government, will grow up as soon and as fast as the natural state of things and the interest of the community may require.

Against the solidity of this hypothesis, in the full latitude of the terms, very cogent reasons may be offered. These have relation to the strong influence of habit and the spirit of imitation, the fear of want of success in untried enterprises, the intrinsic difficulties incident to first essays toward a competition with those who have previously attained to perfection in the business to be attempted, the bounties, premiums, and other artificial encouragements with which foreign nations second the exertions of their own citizens in the branches in which they are to be rivaled.

Experience teaches that men are often so much governed by what they are accustomed to see and practice that the simplest and most obvious improvements in the most ordinary occupations are adopted with hesitation, reluctance, and by slow gradations. The spontaneous transition to new pursuits in a community long habituated to different ones may be expected to be attended with proportionately greater difficulty.

When former occupations ceased to yield a profit adequate to the subsistence of their followers, or when there was an absolute deficiency of

Alexander Hamilton

employment in them owing to the superabundance of hands, changes would ensue, but these changes would be likely to be more tardy than might consist with the interest either of individuals or of the society. In many cases they would not happen while a bare support could be insured by an adherence to ancient courses, though a resort to a more profitable employment might be practicable. To produce the desirable changes as early as may be expedient may, therefore, require the incitement and patronage of government.

The apprehension of failing in new attempts is, perhaps, a more serious impediment. There are dispositions apt to be attracted by the mere novelty of an undertaking, but these are not always those best calculated to give it success. To this it is of importance that the confidence of cautious, sagacious capitalists, both citizens and foreigners, should be excited. And to inspire this description of persons with confidence, it is essential that they should be made to see in any project which is new—and for that reason alone, if for no other, precarious—the prospect of such a degree of countenance and support from government as may be capable of overcoming the obstacles inseparable from first experiments.

The superiority antecedently enjoyed by nations who have preoccupied and perfected a branch of industry constitutes a more formidable obstacle than either of those which have been mentioned to the introduction of the same branch into a country in which it did not before exist. To maintain, between the recent establishments of one country and the long-matured establishments of another country, a competition upon equal terms, both as to quality and price, is, in most cases, impracticable. The disparity in the one or in the other or in both must necessarily be so considerable as to forbid a successful rivalship without the extraordinary aid and protection of government.

But the greatest obstacle of all to the successful prosecution of a new branch of industry in a country in which it was before unknown consists, as far as the instances apply, in the bounties, premiums, and other aids which are granted in a variety of cases by the nations in which the establishments to be imitated are previously introduced. It is well known (and particular examples, in the course of this report, will be cited) that certain nations grant bounties on the exportation of particular commodities, to enable their own workmen to undersell and supplant all competitors in the countries to which those commodities are sent. Hence the undertakers of a new manufacture have to contend, not only with the natural disadvantages of a new undertaking, but with the gratuities and remunerations which other governments bestow. To be enabled to contend with success it is evident that the interference and aid of their own government are indispensable. . . .

IRON

The manufactures of this article are entitled to preeminent rank. None are more essential in their kinds, nor so extensive in their use. They constitute, in whole or in part, the implements or the materials, or both, of almost every useful occupation. Their instrumentality is everywhere conspicuous.

It is fortunate for the United States that they have peculiar advantages for deriving the full benefit of this most valuable material, and they have every motive to improve it with systematic care. It is to be found in various parts of the United States in great abundance and of almost every quality, and fuel, the chief instrument in manufacturing it, is both cheap and plenty. This particularly applies to charcoal, but there are productive coal mines already in operation and strong indications that the material is to be found in abundance in a variety of other places.

The inquiries to which the subject of this report has led have been answered with proofs that manufactories of iron, though generally understood to be extensive, are far more so than is commonly supposed. The kinds in which the greatest progress has been made have been mentioned in another place and need not be repeated, but there is little doubt that every other kind, with due cultivation, will rapidly succeed. It is worthy of remark that several of the particular trades of which it is the basis are capable of being carried on without the aid of large capitals.

Ironworks have greatly increased in the United States and are prosecuted with much more advantage than formerly. The average price before the Revolution was about sixty-four dollars per ton; at present it is about eighty—a rise which is chiefly to be attributed to the increase of manufactures of the material.

The still further extension and multiplication of such manufactures will have the double effect of promoting the extraction of the metal itself and of converting it to a greater number of profitable purposes.

Those manufactures, too, unite, in a greater degree than almost any others, the several requisites which have been mentioned as proper to be consulted in the selection of objects.

The only further encouragement of manufactories of this article the propriety of which may be considered as unquestionable seems to be an increase of the duties on foreign rival commodities.

Steel is a branch which has already made considerable progress, and it is ascertained that some new enterprises, on a more extensive scale, have been lately set on foot. The facility of carrying it to an extent which will supply all internal demands and furnish a considerable surplus for exportation cannot be doubted. The duty upon the importation of this article, which is, at present, seventy-five cents per hundredweight, may, it is conceived, be safely and advantageously extended to one hundred cents. It is desirable, by decisive arrangements, to second the efforts which are making in so very valuable a branch.

The United States already, in a great measure, supply themselves with nails and spikes. They are able, and ought certainly, to do it entirely. The first and most laborious operation in this manufacture is performed by water mills, and of the persons afterwards employed, a great proportion are boys, whose early habits of industry are of importance to the commu-

Alexander Hamilton

nity, to the present support of their families, and to their own future comfort. It is not less curious than true that in certain parts of the country the making of nails is an occasional family manufacture.

The expediency of an additional duty on these articles is indicated by an important fact. About one million eight hundred thousand pounds of them were imported into the United States in the course of a year, ending the 30th of September, 1790. A duty of two cents a pound would, it is presumable, speedily put an end to so considerable an importation. And it is, in every view, proper that an end should be put to it.

The manufacture of these articles, like that of some others, suffers from the carelessness and dishonesty of a part of those who carry it on. An inspection in certain cases might tend to correct the evil. It will deserve consideration whether a regulation of this sort cannot be applied, without inconvenience, to the exportation of the articles, either to foreign countries or from one state to another.

The implements of husbandry are made in several states in great abundance. In many places it is done by the common blacksmiths. And there is no doubt that an ample supply for the whole country can, with great ease, be procured among ourselves.

Various kinds of edged tools for the use of mechanics are also made, and a considerable quantity of hollow wares, though the business of castings has not yet attained the perfection which might be wished. It is, however, improving, and as there are respectable capitals, in good hands, embarked in the prosecution of those branches of iron manufacture which are yet in their infancy, they may all be contemplated as objects not difficult to be acquired.

To insure the end it seems equally safe and prudent to extend the duty, ad valorem, upon all manufactures of iron, or of which iron is the article of chief value, to ten percent.

Firearms and other military weapons may, it is conceived, be placed, without inconvenience, in the class of articles rated at fifteen percent. There are already manufactories of these articles, which only require the stimulus of a certain demand to render them adequate to the supply of the United States.

It would also be a material aid to manufactures of this nature, as well as a means of public security, if provisions should be made for an annual purchase of military weapons, of home manufacture, to a certain determinate extent, in order to the formation of arsenals; and to replace, from time to time, such as should be drawn for use, so as to always have in store the quantity of each kind which should be deemed a competent supply.

But it may, hereafter, deserve legislative consideration whether manufactories of all the necessary weapons of war ought not to be established on account of the government itself. Such establishments are agreeable to the usual practice of nations, and that practice seems founded on sufficient reason.

Report on the Subject of Manufactures

There appears to be an improvidence in leaving these essential implements of national defense to the casual speculations of individual adventure—a resource which can less be relied upon in this case than in most others, the articles in question not being objects of ordinary and indispensable private consumption or use. As a general rule, manufactories on the immediate account of government are to be avoided, but this seems to be one of the few exceptions which that rule admits, depending on very special reasons.

Manufactures of steel, generally, or of which steel is the article of chief value, may, with advantage, be placed in the class of goods rated at seven and a half percent. As manufactures of this kind have not yet made any considerable progress, it is a reason for not rating them as high as those of iron, but as this material is the basis of them, and as their extension is not less practicable than important, it is desirable to promote it by a somewhat higher duty than the present.

A question arises how far it might be expedient to permit the importation of iron, in pigs and bars, free from duty. It would certainly be favorable to manufactures of the article, but the doubt is whether it might not interfere with its production.

Two circumstances, however, abate, if they do not remove, apprehension on this score; one is the considerable increase of price which has been already remarked, and which renders it probable that the free admission of foreign iron would not be inconsistent with an adequate profit to the proprietors of ironworks; the other is the augmentation of demand which would be likely to attend the increase of manufactures of the article, in consequence of the additional encouragements proposed to be given. But caution, nevertheless, in a matter of this kind is most advisable. The measure suggested ought, perhaps, rather to be contemplated subject to the lights of further experience than immediately adopted.

FOSSIL COAL

This, as an important instrument of manufactures, may, without impropriety, be mentioned among the subjects of this report.

A copious supply of it would be of great consequence to the iron branch. As an article of household fuel, also, it is an interesting production, the utility of which must increase in proportion to the decrease of wood, by the progress of settlement and cultivation. And its importance to navigation, as an immense article of transportation coastwise, is signally exemplified in Great Britain.

It is known that there are several coal mines in Virginia now worked, and appearances of their existence are familiar in a number of places.

The expediency of a bounty on all this species of coal, of home production, and of premiums on the opening of new mines, under certain qualifications, appears to be worthy of particular examination. The great importance of the article will amply justify a reasonable expense in this way if it shall appear to be necessary to, and shall be thought likely to answer, the end.

Alexander Hamilton

PRINTED BOOKS

The great number of presses disseminated throughout the Union seems to afford an assurance that here is no need of being indebted to foreign countries for the printing of the books which are used in the United States. A duty of ten percent instead of five, which is now charged upon the article, would have a tendency to aid the business internally. . . .

And with regard to books which may be specially imported for the use of particular seminaries of learning and of public libraries, a total exemption from duty would be advisable. . . .

[1791]

Report on the Subject of Manufactures

Timothy Dwight:

The Western World

Timothy Dwight (1752-1817), Calvinist divine, president of Yale College, and Connecticut Wit, wrote *Greenfield Hill* (1794) to amuse and instruct his countrymen, and much of it, in eighteenth-century fashion, is more instructive than amusing. "The Flourishing Village," part 2 of the poem, describes the order and virtue of orthodox New England village life.

Thrice bless'd the life in this glad region spent,
In peace, in competence, and still content;
Where bright, and brighter, all things daily smile,
And rare and scanty flow the streams of ill;
Where undecaying youth sits blooming round,
And spring looks lovely on the happy ground;
Improvement glows along life's cheerful way,
And with soft lustre makes the passage gay.
Thus oft, on yonder sound, when evening gales
Breath'd o'er th' expanse and gently fill'd the sails,
The world was still, the heavens were dress'd in smiles,
And the clear moonbeam tipp'd the distant isles;
On the blue plain a lucid image gave,
And capp'd with silver light each little wave;
The silent splendor, floating at our side,
Mov'd as we mov'd, and wanton'd on the tide,
While shadowy points and havens met the eye,
And the faint-glimmering landmark told us home was nigh.

Age after age the same dull aspect wears;
On the bold mind the weight of system spread
Resistless lies, a cumbrous load of lead;
One beaten course the wheels politic keep,
And slaves of custom lose their woes in sleep;
Stagnant is social life; no bright design
Quickens the sloth or checks the sad decline.
The friend of man casts round a wishful eye,
And hopes, in vain, improving scenes to spy;
Slow o'er his head the dragging moments roll,
And damp each cheerful purpose of the soul.

Thus the bewilder'd traveler, forc'd to roam
Through a lone forest, leaves his friends and home;
Dun evening hangs the sky; the woods around
Join their sad umbrage o'er the russet ground;
At every step new gloom enshrouds the skies;
His path grows doubtful, and his fears arise;
No woodland songstress soothes his mournful way;
No taper gilds the gloom with cheering ray;
On the cold earth he lays his head forlorn,
And watching, looks, and looks, to spy the lingering morn.

And when new regions prompt their feet to roam,
And fix, in untrod fields, another home,
No dreary realms our happy race explore,
Nor mourn their exile from their native shore.
For there no endless frosts the glebe deform,

Timothy Dwight

Nor blows, with icy breath, perpetual storm;
No wrathful suns with sickly splendor glare,
Nor moors, empoison'd, taint the balmy air;
But medial climates change the healthful year;
Pure streamlets wind, and gales of Eden cheer;
In misty pomp the sky-topp'd mountains stand,
And with green bosom humbler hills expand;
With flowery brilliance smiles the woodland glade;
Full teems the soil, and fragrant twines the shade.

There cheaper fields the numerous household charm,
And the glad sire gives every son a farm;
In falling forests, Labor's axe resounds,
Opes the new field, and winds the fence's bounds;
The green wheat sparkles; nods the towering corn;
And meads and pastures lessening wastes adorn.
Where howl'd the forest, herds unnumber'd low;
The fleecy wanderers fear no prowling foe;
The village springs; the humble school aspires;
And the church brightens in the morning fires!
Young Freedom wantons; Art exalts her head;
And infant Science prattles through the shade.
There changing neighbors learn their manners mild,
And toil and prudence dress th' improving wild;
The savage shrinks, nor dares the bliss annoy,
And the glad traveler wonders at the joy.

All hail, thou western world! by heaven design'd,
Th' example bright, to renovate mankind.
Soon shall thy sons across the mainland roam
And claim, on far Pacific shores, their home;
Their rule, religion, manners, arts convey,
And spread their freedom to the Asian sea.
Where erst six thousand suns have roll'd the year,
O'er plains of slaughter and o'er wilds of fear,
Towns, cities, fanes shall lift their towery pride;
The village bloom on every streamlet's side;
Proud Commerce' mole the western surges lave;
The long, white spire lie imag'd on the wave;
O'er morn's pellucid main expand their sails,
And the starr'd ensign court Korean gales.
Then nobler thoughts shall savage trains inform;
Then barbarous passions cease the heart to storm;
No more the captive circling flames devour;
Through the warpath the Indian creep no more;
No midnight scout the slumbering village fire,
Nor the scalp'd infant stain his gasping sire;

The Western World

But peace and truth illume the twilight mind,
The gospel's sunshine, and the purpose kind.
Where marshes teem'd with death shall meads unfold;
Untrodden cliffs resign their stores of gold;
The dance refin'd on Albion's margin move,
And her lone bowers rehearse the tale of love.
Where slept perennial night shall science rise,
And newborn Oxfords cheer the evening skies;
Miltonic strains the Mexic hills prolong,
And Louis murmur to Sicilian song.

Then to new climes the bliss shall trace its way,
And Tartar deserts hail the rising day;
From the long torpor startled China wake;
Her chains of misery rous'd Peruvia break;
Man link to man; with bosom bosom twine;
And one great bond the house of Adam join;
The sacred promise full completion know,
And peace and piety the world o'erflow.

[1787?, 1794]

Timothy Dwight

Philip Freneau:

The Wild Honeysuckle

Philip Freneau (1752-1832), editor, political propagandist, and poet, moved from rationalistic statements to romantic flights in his verse as he spanned revolution and national growth in his lifetime. His dedication to American subject matter as he examined peculiarly American characteristics of the countryside made clear his right to be known as the first truly American poet.

Fair flower, that dost so comely grow,
Hid in this silent, dull retreat,
Untouched thy honied blossoms blow,
Unseen thy little branches greet;
   No roving foot shall crush thee here,
   No busy hand provoke a tear.

By Nature's self in white arrayed,
She bade thee shun the vulgar eye,
And planted here the guardian shade,
And sent soft waters murmuring by;
   Thus quietly thy summer goes,
   Thy days declining to repose.

Smit with those charms, that must decay,
I grieve to see your future doom;
They died—nor were those flowers more gay,
The flowers that did in Eden bloom;
   Unpitying frosts and autumn's power
   Shall leave no vestige of this flower.

From morning suns and evening dews
At first thy little being came;
If nothing once, you nothing lose,
For when you die you are the same;
   The space between is but an hour,
   The frail duration of a flower.

[1786, 1788]

Philip Freneau

Phillis Wheatley:

On Being Brought from Africa to America

Phillis Wheatley (1753?-1784), first black American poet, was brought from Senegal to Boston as a child and educated by her mistress. Formally freed at thirteen, she published her first poem at seventeen. She became known as the "Sable Muse." Her work was in the neoclassic tradition.

'Twas mercy brought me from my pagan land,
Taught my benighted soul to understand
That there's a God, that there's a Saviour too;
Once I redemption neither sought nor knew.
Some view our sable race with scornful eye:
"Their color is a diabolic die."
Remember, Christians, Negroes, black as Cain,
May be refined, and join th' angelic train.

[c. 1775]

Phillis Wheatley

2

The Vision of Fulfillment

The first years of the new American republic and the last years of the eighteenth century were less than satisfying, as rational revolution degenerated into irrational violence abroad, and newly won American freedom began a flirtation with oppression. But by the beginning of the new century the forces demanding that the new country live up to its eighteenth-century libertarian promise had begun to unify behind the leadership of Thomas Jefferson, who in their eyes personified the promise of progress to ultimate perfection.

The election of 1800, termed with some justification the revolution of 1800, reversed the tendencies toward repression and pointed to the path the country was to take for most of the nineteenth century: a period of liberal-supported expansion of the rights, freedoms, and dignity of the individual in American society. It also resulted in increasingly dynamic westward expansion.

The statistics of expansion and growth during the first decades of that century indicate the degree of dynamic change, characterized by increasing use and misuse of the American environment. In 1800 the United States was largely limited to the area east of the Appalachian Mountains, and its transmountain area, extending to the Mississippi and Upper Great Lakes area along an ill-defined, often hostile border, was largely under the domination of the British and the Indians in spite of the outcome of the Revolution. In that year less than five percent of the population lived beyond the mountains.

Three years later, Jefferson arranged the purchase of the Louisiana Territory, not only doubling the size of American territory, but giving substance to the American continental vision and beginning a great age of travel, exploration, and migration. A decade later the Old Northwest was freed of threats from British and Indians by the force of American arms. By 1828 more than a third of the American population lived west of the mountains, many of them in nine new western states carved out of territory that had been wilderness a generation earlier.

During these years, too, America had begun to develop an identity and a philosophy, originating in different geographic areas among members of different economic and social classes, which were mutually reinforcing as they attempted to rationalize and interpret the relationship between the American and the continent before him. The identity, drawn in the image of a hero who had come out of the West to occupy the presidency, was that of an individual who believed that government was his servant and that his destiny was limited only by his ability to subdue the forces of nature and direct them to his own ends. He saw, as part of this identity, that America was a chosen land and its people the chosen people. His creed was expansionist, and he believed with Andrew Jackson in the mission of manifest destiny, "to extend the area of freedom, Christianity, and civilization" to the West. Unspoiled, intuitively wise, self-reliant, he saw himself as part of a cause greater than himself, dedicated to achieving the perfect society, not in some remote time or hereafter, but immediately. Whether he was a frontiersman in fact or not, he was one in spirit.

The Vision of Fulfillment

The philosophy that America began to develop and ultimately came to accept during those years was closely related to the emerging American identity. Growing out of the same soil, it shared the same vision of perfection, attained by similar means. But the perfection it sought was essentially spiritual and romantic rather than material and practical. Growing out of the failure of rationalism to solve man's dilemmas and the search for a new means of doing so, the new philosophy on the highest levels was an attempt to resolve the basic dualism of the universe into ultimate spiritual unity. On the lower levels it sought a way of life that was spiritual, natural, and true. On the highest level it produced transcendentalism, the first attempt to construct a new philosophy suitable for America; on the lower levels it produced the greatest age of reform the world has ever known.

During these years when conservative sentiment had threatened secession and a northeastern confederacy, social and economic life in the new country became increasingly complex. Sectional differences between North and South, East and West, began to sharpen, and although the country was still eighty percent rural, cities were growing and industrialism was becoming more and more important, at first almost unnoticed, along the rapidly flowing waters of New England. But these developments, disturbing notes in a society by common assertion growing better, were largely ignored or denied. The facts of the new nation were filtered through an essentially romantic world view, and accomplishments were measured by a national faith in continued progress and achievable perfectibility. The first half of the nineteenth century was an age of faith, choosing to believe in a new, perfectible, if not yet perfect, relationship between man and his environment.

At the heart of the new national philosophy and the sense of national identity was an awareness of nature, not in the sense of promised abundance, as earlier American writers had seen it, but instead as the source of that promise fulfilled on every level from the most abstractly spiritual to the most immediately practical. The completeness of the faith that man's fullest needs could best be fulfilled by living in harmony and understanding with nature is described in Ralph Waldo Emerson's *Nature* (1836), the document that attempts to point out the way by which man can find the answer to all his problems in a universe clearly, if intuitively, perceived.

Emerson's *Nature* is the single document basic to understanding the transcendentalist attempt to provide answers to all the problems rationalism had ignored or left unsolved. In it, Emerson declares that the ultimate reality, the unity of all things in nature, is spiritual; he insists that intuition is the means whereby that spiritual unity can be found; and he points out that man's responsibility is to understand in himself the manifestation of this spiritual unity, termed by Emerson the Oversoul, and to act in accordance with it.

As a transcendentalist, Emerson attempted to erect a philosophical superstructure that would explain all things in spiritual, intuitional terms. The result is a reflection, on intellectual levels, of beliefs that permeated

Introduction

American society: that the universe and nature are beneficial, provided by God for the fulfillment of all and, in traditional terms, permitting the pursuit of happiness; that all men are good; that evil, if it exists, is inherent in institutions that are correctable if man is determined to do so; that man's will determines whether or not he finds fulfillment. For Emerson the ultimate test of manhood could be met through intuitive self-reliance; to the frontiersman it was found in his brute strength.

If Emerson was the theorist of the transcendental movement, his friend and fellow townsman Henry David Thoreau was certainly the practitioner. Whereas Emerson preached self-reliance, Thoreau went to Walden Pond to live; when Emerson declared for moral responsibility, Thoreau went to jail accepting it. Emerson's nature was usually encountered in repose in his study. Thoreau found his in the berry patches, hills, road and streamsides that he wandered in search of the joy in perception that was a major part of his sense of fulfillment.

"Walking" is typical of Thoreau's encounters with nature, and is also indicative of his perception and insight. Nature, like time, was the stream in which Thoreau went fishing, seeking the reflection of light beyond. Consequently, on one level his work is a record of observation, understanding, and the pleasures of participating in the things of nature. But the transcendental romantic in Thoreau sees these things as symbolic also, and beyond them he sees ultimate truth, as man saunters through nature toward ultimate unity with God.

Regardless of the extent to which other American romantics were convinced that ultimate spiritual truth could be found in nature, there was a common core of conviction that nature was beautiful and that its enjoyment was beneficial. Thus, even Nathaniel Hawthorne, whose vision of reality was clouded by the dark presence of evil, sought natural therapy and fulfillment in nature. His major attempt was at Brook Farm, an institutionalized version of Thoreau's Walden and a failure in its attempts to find fulfillment in a peculiarly naive attempt to commune with man, nature, and God. Hawthorne's more successful attempts were simpler, as he learned the lesson Thoreau, an individual in fact as well as in theory, had known intuitively from the beginning. Hence, Hawthorne's *Notebooks* are full of the kinds of pleasurable moments in nature that his sense of guilt and awareness of evil made scarce in his allegorical fiction.

However, American romantics sought not merely idealistic theory or individualized natural pleasure; they also sought to define in terms reflecting the broad vistas and varied landforms of America the meaning of it all; to attempt, in other words, to incorporate the incredible variety of America in a unified, meaningful vision combining the continental vision, the democratic vision, and the supernatural vision. Walt Whitman dedicated his life to defining the American whole that he saw beyond its diversified parts and segments. His monumental work, the organic poem *Leaves of Grass*, expresses both vision and faith as clearly, completely, and optimistically as the age and his poetic theory demanded.

Less philosophically inclined but no less romantic were those who

The Vision of Fulfillment

sought to experience the grandeur, the wonder, of both the great and spectacular and the small and awe-inspiring in the American scene. Traveling, touring natural wonders, and seeking natural phenomena in their natural setting played a major role in the search for fulfillment in nature. Thus Washington Irving, already a professional and successful man of letters, sought confirmation of the romantic theories to which he subscribed in the wilderness of the West, as did so many others. Abraham Lincoln, a successful prairie lawyer and backwoods politician, came to behold Niagara Falls and departed to ponder; John James Audubon, perhaps subconsciously aware of the fleeting nature of it all, sought to record for all time the beauty of the minute in the vastness of it all; Francis Parkman attempted to fix in prose the wonder of the wilderness. Particularly remarkable in their writings is the record not only of the things in nature, but of their passing—the passenger pigeon and the buffalo at the hands of man, and Niagara as the result of the passage of time and the forces of nature itself.

The search for meaning and consequently for fulfillment manifested itself in another dimension during the first half of the nineteenth century, as an indigenous folklore began to emerge. Based on such realistic incidents as hunting expeditions and roughhouse fights, nomadic wandering and the planting of apple trees on a hardwood frontier, the stories began in fact as they recounted the adventures of Davy Crockett, Mike Fink, Johnny Appleseed, and the Lost Dauphin of France, and quickly took on the depths of myth, the breadth of folklore, and the elevation of the tall tale.

Thomas Bangs Thorpe's "The Big Bear of Arkansas" typifies the latter, as it moves beyond a reality ranging from the mundane to the grim in recreating an extraordinary world inhabited by extraordinary people. The tall tale, the basis of frontier humor and a peculiarly American contribution to literary evolution, has a great many overtones of the world as its participants would have it, as they interpreted their own lives in the image of the life they had created for their hero, Andrew Jackson. More than a yarn, more than entertainment, the tall tale deliberately exaggerates reality, but often the tale ends with the lines between reality and fantasy so thoroughly diffused that the two elements become merged, and the audience, simple or sophisticated, is tempted, if not forced, to believe.

Although Mike Fink had already taken on frontier dimensions by 1828, as Morgan Neville's "The Last of the Boatmen" demonstrates, Fink himself had been but five years in his grave. By that time, however, an even more significant factor in Fink's movement from reality to folklore had taken place. This was the passing of the keelboats and the substitution of steam power for human muscle in moving the freight of mid-America by water. Fink's story, as Neville wrote it in 1828, was not yet the forceful, fast-moving yarn that was to come, but the ingredients were there. The transition from reality to myth had begun, affording a new dimension of the search for fulfillment through the movement beyond objective reality, perhaps a reflection of the search Emerson pursued on a much higher level, resulting in a popular literature wholly American.

Introduction

Conversely, Johnny Appleseed, in reality John or Jonathan Chapman, nurseryman to the midwestern frontier, had not yet become the legendary figure that he was later to be. Not only was he closer in time than Mike Fink, but the fruit of his work was readily discernible—and edible—throughout a wide area. His career had been less remote, and thousands of people still living had seen him, heard him, or given him shelter. Or perhaps more likely is the fact that Chapman's story was so much the essence of frontier romanticism and reality intermixed that it had no need of exaggeration. A Swedenborgian vegetarian and pacifist, so singularly non-boisterous in a boisterous era among men who liked to believe they were larger than life, Chapman was nevertheless an Ohio hero in the War of 1812, feared and respected by the Indians, a carrier of news and messages, and a figure of romance in the midst of frontier reality.

Poets of the age, no less than philosophers and folklorists, contributed to the search for fulfillment and the conviction that it was attainable, as each attempted to probe the natural setting. Like the others of the age, each began in natural reality and sought to press to a meaningful existence beyond. The most widely known and the best loved of a generation of able poets was Henry Wadsworth Longfellow, the deep affection for him resting largely on his ability to recreate simple moments of peace and to evoke the emotions that such moments engender. A gentle man and a true poet, very much in tune with the faith and hope of his age, he reflects the same qualities in ours. In spite of perennial critical condescension there seems no doubt that for most Americans Longfellow was the poet who most nearly tapped the sources of universal truth.

William Cullen Bryant and Henry Timrod are less universally American and more nearly sectional in their immediate appeal, as each has become associated with a regional philosophy and way of life. Actually, they reach across sectional boundaries in their search—Bryant's "To a Waterfowl" and Timrod's "Spring" attempting to define an immortality best seen in nature, also the source of evidence for the cyclical pattern of life.

Almost universally, the American of the first half of the nineteenth century shared the optimism, the faith, and the dream of these writers. As did observers of the American scene in earlier years, they saw a countryside and a continent full of inexhaustible wonders, all of which had been preserved for a virtuous people by a benevolent God. They were to be used and enjoyed, and they ultimately led to unity with Him.

But in the midst of this conviction, elements of doubt, even of fear and uncertainty, began to appear. Thoreau's vague grumblings about the post office and his rejection of the railroad reflect more profound changes beginning to make themselves felt. By the middle of the century evil had become a certainty for such romantics as Nathaniel Hawthorne and Herman Melville, and, as the decade of the 1850s passed, new, dehumanizing forces were becoming visible. Thus Melville's "Tartarus of Maids" reflects not only a measure of impotence in newly emerging institutions, but denies the fulfillment sought by his generation. The destructive effects of exploitative agriculture were becoming evident, to emerge in clear detail and

The Vision of Fulfillment

fearful recognition a generation later, virtually unnoticed by anyone except the sensitive Sidney Lanier. In "Corn" the essence of change from optimism to fear, from near success to futile failure, is defined as only a romantic poet could do it, torn between the vision of fulfillment and the recognition of shortsightedness.

In the background other destructive forces were gathering, often in careful disguise. Abolitionism absorbed the reform energy of its time, and the slavery issue became increasingly agitated as sectional wounds deepened. As the decade neared its close, Charles Darwin in remote England put the final words to a work that was the epitaph of an age. America, on the verge of Civil War and industrialism, failed to grasp the significance of his conclusions.

Introduction

Ralph Waldo Emerson:
Nature

Ralph Waldo Emerson (1803-1882), philosopher of American romanticism and spokesman for transcendentalism, was a poet, essayist, lecturer, and theorist. In each facet of his career, nature, exemplified by the American countryside, provided the solid foundation for his work. It also served as a point of departure, as in *Nature* (1836), for his attempt to define the meaning of man, God, and the universe.

A subtle chain of countless rings
The next unto the farthest brings;
The eye reads omens where it goes,
And speaks all languages the rose;
And, striving to be man, the worm
Mounts through all the spires of form.

INTRODUCTION

Our age is retrospective. It builds the sepulchres of the fathers. It writes biographies, histories, and criticism. The foregoing generations beheld God and nature face to face; we, through their eyes. Why should not we also enjoy an original relation to the universe? Why should not we have a poetry and philosophy of insight and not of tradition, and a religion by revelation to us, and not the history of theirs? Embosomed for a season in nature, whose floods of life stream around and through us, and invite us, by the powers they supply, to action proportioned to nature, why should we grope among the dry bones of the past, or put the living generation into masquerade out of its faded wardrobe? The sun shines to-day also. There is more wool and flax in the fields. There are new lands, new men, new thoughts. Let us demand our own works and laws and worship.

Undoubtedly we have no questions to ask which are unanswerable. We must trust the perfection of the creation so far as to believe that whatever curiosity the order of things has awakened in our minds, the order of things can satisfy. Every man's condition is a solution in hieroglyphic to those inquiries he would put. He acts it as life, before he apprehends it as truth. In like manner, nature is already, in its forms and tendencies, describing its own design. Let us interrogate the great apparition that shines so peacefully around us. Let us inquire, to what end is nature?

All science has one aim, namely, to find a theory of nature. We have theories of races and of functions, but scarcely yet a remote approach to an idea of creation. We are now so far from the road to truth, that religious teachers dispute and hate each other, and speculative men are esteemed unsound and frivolous. But to a sound judgment, the most abstract truth is the most practical. Whenever a true theory appears, it will be its own evidence. Its test is, that it will explain all phenomena. Now many are thought not only unexplained but inexplicable; as language, sleep, madness, dreams, beasts, sex.

Philosophically considered, the universe is composed of Nature and the Soul. Strictly speaking, therefore, all that is separate from us, all which Philosophy distinguishes as the NOT ME, that is, both nature and art, all other men and my own body, must be ranked under this name, NATURE. In enumerating the values of nature and casting up their sum, I shall use the word in both senses;—in its common and in its philosophical import. In inquiries so general as our present one, the inaccuracy is not material; no confusion of thought will occur. *Nature*, in the common sense, refers to essences unchanged by man; space, the air, the river, the leaf. *Art* is applied to the mixture of his will with the same things, as in a house, a

Ralph Waldo Emerson

canal, a statue, a picture. But his operations taken together are so insignificant, a little chipping, baking, patching, and washing, that in an impression so grand as that of the world on the human mind, they do not vary
the result.

I. NATURE

To go into solitude, a man needs to retire as much from his chamber as from society. I am not solitary whilst I read and write, though nobody is with me. But if a man would be alone, let him look at the stars.
The rays that come from those heavenly worlds will separate between him
and what he touches. One might think the atmosphere was made transparent with this design, to give man, in the heavenly bodies, the perpetual
presence of the sublime. Seen in the streets of cities, how great they are! If
the stars should appear one night in a thousand years, how would men
believe and adore; and preserve for many generations the remembrance of
the city of God which had been shown! But every night come out these
envoys of beauty, and light the universe with their admonishing smile.

The stars awaken a certain reverence, because though always present, they are inaccessible; but all natural objects make a kindred impression, when the mind is open to their influence. Nature never wears a mean
appearance. Neither does the wisest man extort her secret, and lose his
curiosity by finding out all her perfection. Nature never became a toy to a
wise spirit. The flowers, the animals, the mountains, reflected the wisdom
of his best hour, as much as they had delighted the simplicity of his childhood.

When we speak of nature in this manner, we have a distinct but
most poetical sense in the mind. We mean the integrity of impression
made by manifold natural objects. It is this which distinguishes the stick
of timber of the wood-cutter from the tree of the poet. The charming landscape which I saw this morning is indubitably made up of some twenty or
thirty farms. Miller owns this field, Locke that, and Manning the woodland beyond. But none of them owns the landscape. There is a property in
the horizon which no man has but he whose eye can integrate all the parts,
that is, the poet. This is the best part of these men's farms, yet to this their
warranty-deeds give no title.

To speak truly, few adult persons can see nature. Most persons do
not see the sun. At least they have a very superficial seeing. The sun illum-
inates only the eye of the man, but shines into the eye and the heart of the
child. The lover of nature is he whose inward and outward senses are still
truly adjusted to each other; who has retained the spirit of infancy even
into the era of manhood. His intercourse with heaven and earth becomes
part of his daily food. In the presence of nature a wild delight runs through
the man, in spite of real sorrows. Nature says,—he is my creature, and
maugre all his impertinent griefs, he shall be glad with me. Not the sun or
the summer alone, but every hour and season yields its tribute of delight;

Nature

for every hour and change corresponds to and authorizes a different state of the mind, from breathless noon to grimmest midnight. Nature is a setting that fits equally well a comic or a mourning piece. In good health, the air is a cordial of incredible virtue. Crossing a bare common, in snow puddles, at twilight, under a clouded sky, without having in my thoughts any occurrence of special good fortune, I have enjoyed a perfect exhilaration. I am glad to the brink of fear. In the woods, too, a man casts off his years, as the snake his slough, and at what period soever of life, is always a child. In the woods is perpetual youth. Within these plantations of God, a decorum and sanctity reign, a perennial festival is dressed, and the guest sees not how he should tire of them in a thousand years. In the woods, we return to reason and faith. There I feel that nothing can befall me in life,—no disgrace, no calamity (leaving me my eyes), which nature cannot repair. Standing on the bare ground,—my head bathed by the blithe air, and uplifted into infinite space,—all mean egotism vanishes. I become a transparent eyeball; I am nothing; I see all; the currents of the Universal Being circulate through me; I am part or parcel of God. The name of the nearest friend sounds then foreign and accidental: to be brothers, to be acquaintances,—master or servant, is then a trifle and a disturbance. I am the lover of uncontained and immortal beauty. In the wilderness, I find something more dear and connate than in streets or villages. In the tranquil landscape, and especially in the distant line of the horizon, man beholds somewhat as beautiful as his own nature.

The greatest delight which the fields and woods minister is the suggestion of an occult relation between man and the vegetable. I am not alone and unacknowledged. They nod to me, and I to them. The waving of the boughs in the storm is new to me and old. It takes me by surprise, and yet is not unknown. Its effect is like that of a higher thought or a better emotion coming over me, when I deemed I was thinking justly or doing right.

Yet it is certain that the power to produce this delight does not reside in nature, but in man, or in a harmony of both. It is necessary to use these pleasures with great temperance. For nature is not always tricked in holiday attire, but the same scene which yesterday breathed perfume and glittered as for the frolic of the nymphs, is overspread with melancholy to-day. Nature always wears the colors of the spirit. To a man laboring under calamity, the heat of his own fire hath sadness in it. Then there is a kind of contempt of the landscape felt by him who has just lost by death a dear friend. The sky is less grand as it shuts down over less worth in the population.

II. COMMODITY

Whoever considers the final cause of the world will discern a multitude of uses that enter as parts into that result. They all admit of being thrown into one of the following classes: Commodity; Beauty; Language; and Discipline.

Ralph Waldo Emerson

Under the general name of commodity, I rank all those advantages which our senses owe to nature. This, of course, is a benefit which is temporary and mediate, not ultimate, like its service to the soul. Yet although low, it is perfect in its kind, and is the only use of nature which all men apprehend. The misery of man appears like childish petulance, when we explore the steady and prodigal provision that has been made for his support and delight on this green ball which floats him through the heavens. What angels invented these splendid ornaments, these rich conveniences, this ocean of air above, this ocean of water beneath, this firmament of earth between? this zodiac of lights, this tent of dropping clouds, this striped coat of climates, this fourfold year? Beasts, fire, water, stones, and corn serve him. The field is at once his floor, his work-yard, his play-ground, his garden, and his bed.

> *More servants wait on man*
> *Than he'll take notice of.*

Nature, in its ministry to man, is not only the material, but is also the process and the result. All the parts incessantly work into each other's hands for the profit of man. The wind sows the seed; the sun evaporates the sea; the wind blows the vapor to the field; the ice, on the other side of the planet, condenses rain on this; the rain feeds the plant; the plant feeds the animal; and thus the endless circulations of the divine charity nourish man.

The useful arts are reproductions or new combinations by the wit of man, of the same natural benefactors. He no longer waits for favoring gales, but by means of steam, he realizes the fable of Æolus's bag, and carries the two and thirty winds in the boiler of his boat. To diminish friction, he paves the road with iron bars, and, mounting a coach with a shipload of men, animals, and merchandise behind him, he darts through the country, from town to town, like an eagle or a swallow through the air. By the aggregate of these aids, how is the face of the world changed, from the era of Noah to that of Napoleon! The private poor man hath cities, ships, canals, bridges, built for him. He goes to the post-office, and the human race run on his errands; to the book-shop, and the human race read and write of all that happens, for him; to the court-house, and nations repair his wrongs. He sets his house upon the road, and the human race go forth every morning, and shovel out the snow, and cut a path for him.

But there is no need of specifying particulars in this class of uses. The catalogue is endless, and the examples so obvious, that I shall leave them to the reader's reflection, with the general remark, that this mercenary benefit is one which has respect to a farther good. A man is fed, not that he may be fed, but that he may work.

III. BEAUTY

A nobler want of man is served by nature, namely, the love of Beauty.

Nature

The ancient Greeks called the world κόσμος, beauty. Such is the constitution of all things, or such the plastic power of the human eye, that the primary forms, as the sky, the mountain, the tree, the animal, give us a delight *in and for themselves*; a pleasure arising from outline, color, motion, and grouping. This seems partly owing to the eye itself. The eye is the best of artists. By the mutual action of its structure and of the laws of light, perspective is produced, which integrates every mass of objects, of what character soever, into a well colored and shaded globe, so that where the particular objects are mean and unaffecting, the landscape which they compose is round and symmetrical. And as the eye is the best composer, so light is the first of painters. There is no object so foul that intense light will not make beautiful. And the stimulus it affords to the sense, and a sort of infinitude which it hath, like space and time, make all matter gay. Even the corpse has its own beauty. But besides this general grace diffused over nature, almost all the individual forms are agreeable to the eye, as is proved by our endless imitations of some of them, as the acorn, the grape, the pine-cone, the wheat-ear, the egg, the wings and forms of most birds, the lion's claw, the serpent, the butterfly, sea-shells, flames, clouds, buds, leaves, and the forms of many trees, as the palm.

For better consideration, we may distribute the aspects of Beauty in a threefold manner.

1. First, the simple perception of natural forms is a delight. The influence of the forms and actions in nature is so needful to man, that, in its lowest functions, it seems to lie on the confines of commodity and beauty. To the body and mind which have been cramped by noxious work or company, nature is medicinal and restores their tone. The tradesman, the attorney comes out of the din and craft of the street and sees the sky and the woods, and is a man again. In their eternal calm, he finds himself. The health of the eye seems to demand a horizon. We are never tired, so long as we can see far enough.

But in other hours, Nature satisfies by its loveliness, and without any mixture of corporeal benefit. I see the spectacle of morning from the hilltop over against my house, from daybreak to sunrise, with emotions which an angel might share. The long slender bars of cloud float like fishes in the sea of crimson light. From the earth, as a shore, I look out into that silent sea. I seem to partake its rapid transformations; the active enchantment reaches my dust, and I dilate and conspire with the morning wind. How does Nature deify us with a few and cheap elements! Give me health and a day, and I will make the pomp of emperors ridiculous. The dawn is my Assyria; the sunset and moonrise my Paphos, and unimaginable realms of faerie; broad noon shall be my England of the senses and the understanding; the night shall be my Germany of mystic philosophy and dreams.

Not less excellent, except for our less susceptibility in the afternoon, was the charm, last evening, of a January sunset. The western clouds divided and subdivided themselves into pink flakes modulated with tints of unspeakable softness, and the air had so much life and sweetness that it was a pain to come within doors. What was it that nature would say? Was

Ralph Waldo Emerson

there no meaning in the live repose of the valley behind the mill, and which Homer or Shakespeare could not re-form for me in words? The leaf-less trees become spires of flame in the sunset, with the blue east for their background, and the stars of the dead calices of flowers, and every withered stem and stubble rimed with frost, contribute something to the mute music.

The inhabitants of cities suppose that the country landscape is pleasant only half the year. I please myself with the graces of the winter scenery, and believe that we are as much touched by it as by the genial influences of summer. To the attentive eye, each moment of the year has its own beauty, and in the same field, it beholds, every hour, a picture which was never seen before, and which shall never be seen again. The heavens change every moment, and reflect their glory or gloom on the plains beneath. The state of the crop in the surrounding farms alters the expression of the earth from week to week. The succession of native plants in the pastures and roadsides, which makes the silent clock by which time tells the summer hours, will make even the divisions of the day sensible to a keen observer. The tribes of birds and insects, like the plants punctual to their time, follow each other, and the year has room for all. By water-courses, the variety is greater. In July, the blue pontederia or pickerel-weed blooms in large beds in the shallow parts of our pleasant river, and swarms with yellow butterflies in continual motion. Art cannot rival this pomp of purple and gold. Indeed the river is a perpetual gala, and boasts each month a new ornament.

But this beauty of Nature which is seen and felt as beauty, is the least part. The shows of day, the dewy morning, the rainbow, mountains, orchards in blossom, stars, moonlight, shadows in still water, and the like, if too eagerly hunted, become shows merely, and mock us with their un-reality. Go out of the house to see the moon, and 'tis mere tinsel; it will not please as when its light shines upon your necessary journey. The beauty that shimmers in the yellow afternoons of October, who ever could clutch it? Go forth to find it, and it is gone; 'tis only a mirage as you look from the windows of diligence.

2. The presence of a higher, namely, of the spiritual element is essential to its perfection. The high and divine beauty which can be loved without effeminacy, is that which is found in combination with the human will. Beauty is the mark God sets upon virtue. Every natural action is graceful. Every heroic act is also decent, and causes the place and the by-standers to shine. We are taught by great actions that the universe is the property of every individual in it. Every rational creature has all nature for his dowry and estate. It is his, if he will. He may divest himself of it; he may creep into a corner, and abdicate his kingdom, as most men do, but he is entitled to the world by his constitution. In proportion to the energy of his thought and will, he takes up the world into himself. "All those things for which men plough, build, or sail, obey virtue;" said Sallust. "The winds and waves," said Gibbon, "are always on the side of the ablest navigators." So are the sun and moon and all the stars of heaven. When a noble act is done,—perchance in a scene of great natural beauty; when

Nature

Leonidas and his three hundred martyrs consume one day in dying, and the sun and moon come each and look at them once in the steep defile of Thermopylæ; when Arnold Winkelried, in the high Alps, under the shadow of the avalanche, gathers in his side a sheaf of Austrian spears to break the line for his comrades; are not these heroes entitled to add the beauty of the scene to the beauty of the deed? When the bark of Columbus nears the shore of America;—before it, the beach lined with savages, fleeing out of all their huts of cane; the sea behind; and the purple mountains of the Indian Archipelago around, can we separate the man from the living picture? Does not the New World clothe his form with her palm-groves and savannahs as fit drapery? Ever does natural beauty steal in like air, and envelope great actions. When Sir Harry Vane was dragged up the Tower-hill, sitting on a sled, to suffer death as the champion of the English laws, one of the multitude cried out to him, "You never sate on so glorious a seat!" Charles II., to intimidate the citizens of London, caused the patriot Lord Russell to be drawn in an open coach through the principal streets of the city on his way to the scaffold. "But," his biographer says, "the multitude imagined they saw liberty and virtue sitting by his side." In private places, among sordid objects, an act of truth or heroism seems at once to draw to itself the sky as its temple, the sun as its candle. Nature stretches out her arms to embrace man, only let his thoughts be of equal greatness. Willingly does she follow his steps with the rose and the violet, and bend her lines of grandeur and grace to the decoration of her darling child. Only let his thoughts be of equal scope, and the frame will suit the picture. A virtuous man is in unison with her works, and makes the central figure of the visible sphere. Homer, Pindar, Socrates, Phocion, associate themselves fitly in our memory with the geography and climate of Greece. The visible heavens and earth sympathize with Jesus. And in common life whosoever has seen a person of powerful character and happy genius, will have remarked how easily he took all things along with him,—the persons, the opinions, and the day, and nature became ancillary to a man.

3. There is still another aspect under which the beauty of the world may be viewed, namely, as it becomes an object of the intellect. Beside the relation of things to virtue, they have a relation to thought. The intellect searches out the absolute order of things as they stand in the mind of God, and without the colors of affection. The intellectual and the active powers seem to succeed each other, and the exclusive activity of the one generates the exclusive activity of the other. There is something unfriendly in each to the other, but they are like the alternate periods of feeding and working in animals; each prepares and will be followed by the other. Therefore does beauty, which, in relation to actions, as we have seen, comes unsought, and comes because it is unsought, remain for the apprehension and pursuit of the intellect; and then again, in its turn, of the active power. Nothing divine dies. All good is eternally reproductive. The beauty of nature re-forms itself in the mind, and not for barren contemplation, but for new creation.

All men are in some degree impressed by the face of the world; some men even to delight. This love of beauty is Taste. Others have the

Ralph Waldo Emerson

same love in such excess, that, not content with admiring, they seek to embody it in new forms. The creation of beauty is Art.

The production of a work of art throws a light upon the mystery of humanity. A work of art is an abstract or epitome of the world. It is the result or expression of nature, in miniature. For although the works of nature are innumerable and all different, the result or the expression of them all is similar and single. Nature is a sea of forms radically alike and even unique. A leaf, a sunbeam, a landscape, the ocean, make an analogous impression on the mind. What is common to them all,—that perfectness and harmony, is beauty. The standard of beauty is the entire circuit of natural forms,—the totality of nature; which the Italians expressed by defining beauty "il più nell' uno." Nothing is quite beautiful alone; nothing but is beautiful in the whole. A single object is only so far beautiful as it suggests this universal grace. The poet, the painter, the sculptor, the musician, the architect, seek each to concentrate this radiance of the world on one point, and each in his several work to satisfy the love of beauty which stimulates him to produce. Thus is Art a nature passed through the alembic of man. Thus in art does Nature work through the will of a man filled with the beauty of her first works.

The world thus exists to the soul to satisfy the desire of beauty. This element I call an ultimate end. No reason can be asked or given why the soul seeks beauty. Beauty, in its largest and profoundest sense, is one expression for the universe. God is the all-fair. Truth, and goodness, and beauty, are but different faces of the same All. But beauty in nature is not ultimate. It is the herald of inward and eternal beauty, and is not alone a solid and satisfactory good. It must stand as a part, and not as yet the last or highest expression of the final cause of Nature.

IV. LANGUAGE

Language is a third use which Nature subserves to man. Nature is the vehicle of thought, and in a simple, double, and threefold degree.

1. Words are signs of natural facts.
2. Particular natural facts are symbols of particular spiritual facts.
3. Nature is the symbol of spirit.

1. Words are signs of natural facts. The use of natural history is to give us aid in supernatural history; the use of the outer creation, to give us language for the beings and changes of the inward creation. Every word which is used to express a moral or intellectual fact, if traced to its root, is found to be borrowed from some material appearance. *Right* means *straight; wrong* means *twisted. Spirit* primarily means *wind; transgression,* the crossing of a *line; supercilious,* the *raising of the eyebrow.* We say the *heart* to express emotion, the *head* to denote thought; and *thought* and *emotion* are words borrowed from sensible things, and now appropriated to spiritual nature. Most of the process by which this transformation is made, is hidden from us in the remote time when language was framed; but the same tendency may be daily observed in children. Children and

savages use only nouns or names of things, which they convert into verbs, and apply to analogous mental acts.

2. But this origin of all words that convey a spiritual import,—so conspicuous a fact in the history of language,—is our least debt to nature. It is not words only that are emblematic; it is things which are emblematic. Every natural fact is a symbol of some spiritual fact. Every appearance in nature corresponds to some state of the mind, and that state of the mind can only be described by presenting that natural appearance as its picture. An enraged man is a lion, a cunning man is a fox, a firm man is a rock, a learned man is a torch. A lamb is innocence; a snake is subtle spite; flowers express to us the delicate affections. Light and darkness are our familiar expression for knowledge and ignorance; and heat for love. Visible distance behind and before us, is respectively our image of memory and hope.

Who looks upon a river in a meditative hour and is not reminded of the flux of all things? Throw a stone into the stream, and the circles that propagate themselves are the beautiful type of all influence. Man is conscious of a universal soul within or behind his individual life, wherein, as in a firmament, the natures of Justice, Truth, Love, Freedom, arise and shine. This universal soul he calls Reason: it is not mine, or thine, or his, but we are its; we are its property and men. And the blue sky in which the private earth is buried, the sky with its eternal calm, and full of everlasting orbs, is the type of Reason. That which intellectually considered we call Reason, considered in relation to nature, we call Spirit. Spirit is the Creator. Spirit hath life in itself. And man in all ages and countries embodies it in his language as the FATHER.

It is easily seen that there is nothing lucky or capricious in these analogies, but that they are constant, and pervade nature. These are not the dreams of a few poets, here and there, but man is an analogist, and studies relations in all objects. He is placed in the centre of beings, and a ray of relation passes from every other being to him. And neither can man be understood without these objects, nor these objects without man. All the facts in natural history taken by themselves, have no value, but are barren, like a single sex. But marry it to human history, and it is full of life. Whole floras, all Linnæus' and Buffon's volumes, are dry catalogues of facts; but the most trivial of these facts, the habit of a plant, the organs, or work, or noise of an insect, applied to the illustration of a fact in intellectual philosophy, or in any way associated to human nature, affects us in the most lively and agreeable manner. The seed of a plant,—to what affecting analogies in the nature of man is that little fruit made use of, in all discourse, up to the voice of Paul, who calls the human corpse a seed,—"It is sown a natural body; it is raised a spiritual body." The motion of the earth round its axis and round the sun, makes the day and the year. These are certain amounts of brute light and heat. But is there no intent of an analogy between man's life and the seasons? And do the seasons gain no grandeur or pathos from that analogy? The instincts of the ant are very unimportant considered as the ant's; but the moment a ray of relation is seen to extend from it to man, and the little drudge is seen to be a moni-

Ralph Waldo Emerson

tor, a little body with a mighty heart, then all its habits, even that said to be recently observed, that it never sleeps, become sublime.

Because of this radical correspondence between visible things and human thoughts, savages, who have only what is necessary, converse in figures. As we go back in history, language becomes more picturesque, until its infancy, when it is all poetry; or all spiritual facts are represented by natural symbols. The same symbols are found to make the original elements of all languages. It has moreover been observed, that the idioms of all languages approach each other in passages of the greatest eloquence and power. And as this is the first language, so is it the last. This immediate dependence of language upon nature, this conversion of an outward phenomenon into a type of somewhat in human life, never loses its power to affect us. It is this which gives that piquancy to the conversation of a strong-natured farmer or backwoodsman, which all men relish.

A man's power to connect his thought with its proper symbol, and so to utter it, depends on the simplicity of his character, that is, upon his love of truth and his desire to communicate it without loss. The corruption of man is followed by the corruption of language. When simplicity of character and the sovereignty of ideas is broken up by the prevalence of secondary desires,—the desire of riches, of pleasure, of power, and of praise, —and duplicity and falsehood take place of simplicity and truth, the power over nature as an interpreter of the will is in a degree lost; new imagery ceases to be created, and old words are perverted to stand for things which are not; a paper currency is employed, when there is no bullion in the vaults. In due time the fraud is manifest, and words lose all power to stimulate the understanding or the affections. Hundreds of writers may be found in every long-civilized nation who for a short time believe and make others believe that they see and utter truths, who do not of themselves clothe one thought in its natural garment, but who feed unconsciously on the language created by the primary writers of the country, those, namely, who hold primarily on nature.

But wise men pierce this rotten diction and fasten words again to visible things; so that picturesque language is at once a commanding certificate that he who employs it is a man in alliance with truth and God. The moment our discourse rises above the ground line of familiar facts and is inflamed with passion or exalted by thought, it clothes itself in images. A man conversing in earnest, if he watch his intellectual processes, will find that a material image more or less luminous arises in his mind, contemporaneous with every thought, which furnishes the vestment of the thought. Hence, good writing and brilliant discourse are perpetual allegories. This imagery is spontaneous. It is the blending of experience with the present action of the mind. It is proper creation. It is the working of the Original Cause through the instruments he has already made.

These facts may suggest the advantage which the country-life possesses, for a powerful mind, over the artificial and curtailed life of cities. We know more from nature than we can at will communicate. Its light flows into the mind evermore, and we forget its presence. The poet, the orator, bred in the woods, whose senses have been nourished by their fair and appeasing changes, year after year, without design and without heed,—shall not lose their lesson altogether, in the roar of cities or the broil of politics. Long hereafter, amidst agitation and terror in national councils,—in the hour of revolution,—these solemn images shall reappear in their morning lustre, as fit symbols and words of the thoughts which the passing events shall awaken. At the call of a noble sentiment, again the woods wave, the pines murmur, the river rolls and shines, and the cattle low upon the mountains, as he saw and heard them in his infancy. And with these forms, the spells of persuasion, the keys of power are put into his hands.

3. We are thus assisted by natural objects in the expression of particular meanings. But how great a language to convey such pepper-corn informations! Did it need such noble races of creatures, this profusion of forms, this host of orbs in heaven, to furnish man with the dictionary and grammar of his municipal speech? Whilst we use this grand cipher to expedite the affairs of our pot and kettle, we feel that we have not yet put it to its use, neither are able. We are like travellers using the cinders of a volcano to roast their eggs. Whilst we see that it always stands ready to clothe what we would say, we cannot avoid the question whether the characters are not significant of themselves. Have mountains, and waves, and skies, no significance but what we consciously give them when we employ them as emblems of our thoughts? The world is emblematic. Parts of speech are metaphors, because the whole of nature is a metaphor of the human mind. The laws of moral nature answer to those of matter as face to face in a glass. "The visible world and the relation of its parts, is the dial plate of the invisible." The axioms of physics translate the laws of ethics. Thus, "the whole is greater than its part;" "reaction is equal to action;" "the smallest weight may be made to lift the greatest, the difference of weight being compensated by time;" and many the like propositions, which have an ethical as well as physical sense. These propositions have a much more extensive and universal sense when applied to human life, than when confined to technical use.

In like manner, the memorable words of history and the proverbs of nations consist usually of a natural fact, selected as a picture or parable of a moral truth. Thus, A rolling stone gathers no moss; A bird in the hand is worth two in the bush; A cripple in the right way will beat a racer in the wrong; Make hay while the sun shines; 'Tis hard to carry a full cup even; Vinegar is the son of wine; The last ounce broke the camel's back; Long-lived trees make roots first;—and the like. In their primary sense these are trivial facts, but we repeat them for the value of their analogical import. What is true of proverbs, is true of all fables, parables, and allegories.

This relation between the mind and matter is not fancied by some poet, but stands in the will of God, and so is free to be known by all men. It appears to men, or it does not appear. When in fortunate hours we ponder this miracle, the wise man doubts if at all other times he is not blind and deaf;

Ralph Waldo Emerson

> *Can such things be,*
> *And overcome us like a summer's cloud,*
> *Without our special wonder?*

for the universe becomes transparent, and the light of higher laws than its own shines through it. It is the standing problem which has exercised the wonder and the study of every fine genius since the world began; from the era of the Egyptians and the Brahmins to that of Pythagoras, of Plato, of Bacon, of Leibnitz, of Swedenborg. There sits the Sphinx at the roadside, and from age to age, as each prophet comes by, he tries his fortune at reading her riddle. There seems to be a necessity in spirit to manifest itself in material forms; and day and night, river and storm, beast and bird, acid and alkali, preëxist in necessary Ideas in the mind of God, and are what they are by virtue of preceding affections in the world of spirit. A Fact is the end or last issue of spirit. The visible creation is the terminus or the circumference of the invisible world. "Material objects," said a French philosopher, "are necessarily kinds of *scoriæ* of the substantial thoughts of the Creator, which must always preserve an exact relation to their first origin; in other words, visible nature must have a spiritual and moral side."

This doctrine is abstruse, and though the images of "garment," "scoriæ," "mirror," etc., may stimulate the fancy, we must summon the aid of subtler and more vital expositors to make it plain. "Every scripture is to be interpreted by the same spirit which gave it forth,"—is the fundamental law of criticism. A life in harmony with Nature, the love of truth and of virtue, will purge the eyes to understand her text. By degrees we may come to know the primitive sense of the permanent objects of nature, so that the world shall be to us an open book, and every form significant of its hidden life and final cause.

A new interest surprises us, whilst, under the view now suggested, we contemplate the fearful extent and multitude of objects; since "every object rightly seen, unlocks a new faculty of the soul." That which was unconscious truth, becomes, when interpreted and defined in an object, a part of the domain of knowledge,—a new weapon in the magazine of power.

V. DISCIPLINE

In view of the significance of nature, we arrive at once at a new fact, that nature is a discipline. This use of the world includes the preceding uses, as parts of itself.

Space, time, society, labor, climate, food, locomotion, the animals, the mechanical forces, give us sincerest lessons, day by day, whose meaning is unlimited. They educate both the Understanding and the Reason. Every property of matter is a school for the understanding,—its solidity or resistance, its inertia, its extension, its figure, its divisibility. The understanding adds, divides, combines, measures, and finds nutriment and room for its activity in this worthy scene. Meantime, Reason transfers all these lessons into its own world of thought, by perceiving the analogy that marries Matter and Mind.

1. Nature is a discipline of the understanding in intellectual truths. Our dealing with sensible objects is a constant exercise in the necessary lessons of difference, of likeness, of order, of being and seeming, of progessive arrangement; of ascent from particular to general; of combination to one end of manifold forces. Proportioned to the importance of the organ to be formed, is the extreme care with which its tuition is provided,—a care pretermitted in no single case. What tedious training, day after day, year after year, never ending, to form the common sense; what continual reproduction of annoyances, inconveniences, dilemmas; what rejoicing over us little men; what disputing of prices, what reckonings of interest,—and all to form the Hand of the mind;— to instruct us that "good thoughts are no better than good dreams, unless they be executed!"

The same good office is performed by Property and its filial systems of debt and credit. Debt, grinding debt, whose iron face the widow, the orphan, and the sons of genius fear and hate;—debt, which consumes so much time, which so cripples and disheartens a great spirit with cares that seem so base, is a preceptor whose lessons cannot be foregone, and is needed most by those who suffer from it most. Moreover, property, which has been well compared to snow,—"if it fall level today, it will be blown into drifts tomorrow,"—is the surface action of internal machinery, like the index on the face of a clock. Whilst now it is the gymnastics of the understanding, it is hiving, in the foresight of the spirit, experience in profounder laws.

The whole character and fortune of the individual are affected by the least inequalities in the culture of the understanding; for example, in the perception of differences. Therefore is Space, and therefore Time, that man may know that things are not huddled and lumped, but sundered and individual. A bell and a plough have each their use, and neither can do the office of the other. Water is good to drink, coal to burn, wool to wear; but wool cannot be drunk, nor water spun, nor coal eaten. The wise man shows his wisdom in separation, in gradation, and his scale of creatures and of merits is as wide as nature. The foolish have no range in their scale, but suppose every man is as every other man. What is not good they call the worst, and what is not hateful they call the best.

In like manner, what good heed Nature forms in us! She pardons no mistakes. Her yea is yea, and her nay, nay.

The first steps in Agriculture, Astronomy, Zoölogy (those first steps which the farmer, the hunter, and the sailor take), teach that Nature's dice are always loaded; that in her heaps and rubbish are concealed sure and useful results.

How calmly and genially the mind apprehends one after another the laws of physics! What noble emotions dilate the mortal as he enters into the councils of the creation, and feels by knowledge the privilege to BE! His insight refines him. The beauty of nature shines in his own breast. Man is greater that he can see this, and the universe less, because Time and Space relations vanish as laws are known.

Here again we are impressed and even daunted by the immense Uni-

Ralph Waldo Emerson

verse to be explored. "What we know is a point to what we do not know." Open any recent journal of science, and weigh the problems suggested concerning Light, Heat, Electricity, Magnetism, Physiology, Geology, and judge whether the interest of natural science is likely to be soon exhausted.

Passing by many particulars of the discipline of nature, we must not omit to specify two.

The exercise of the Will, or the lesson of power, is taught in every event. From the child's successive possession of his several senses up to the hour when he saith, "Thy will be done!" he is learning the secret that he can reduce under his will not only particular events but great classes, nay, the whole series of events, and so conform all facts to his character. Nature is thoroughly mediate. It is made to serve. It receives the dominion of man as meekly as the ass on which the Saviour rode. It offers all its kingdoms to man as the raw material which he may mould into what is useful. Man is never weary of working it up. He forges the subtile and delicate air into wise and melodious words, and gives them wing as angels of persuasion and command. One after another his victorious thought comes up with and reduces all things, until the world becomes at last only a realized will, —the double of the man.

2. Sensible objects conform to the premonitions of Reason and reflect the conscience. All things are moral; and in their boundless changes have an unceasing reference to spiritual nature. Therefore is nature glorious with form, color, and motion; that every globe in the remotest heaven, every chemical change from the rudest crystal up to the laws of life, every change of vegetation from the first principle of growth in the eye of a leaf, to the tropical forest and antediluvian coal-mine, every animal function from the sponge up to Hercules, shall hint or thunder to man the laws of right and wrong, and echo the Ten Commandments. Therefore is Nature ever the ally of Religion: lends all her pomp and riches to the religious sentiment. Prophet and priest, David, Isaiah, Jesus, have drawn deeply from this source. This ethical character so penetrates the bone and marrow of nature, as to seem the end for which it was made. Whatever private purpose is answered by any member or part, this is its public and universal function, and is never omitted. Nothing in nature is exhausted in its first use. When a thing has served an end to the uttermost, it is wholly new for an ulterior service. In God, every end is converted into a new means. Thus the use of commodity, regarded by itself, is mean and squalid. But it is to the mind an education in the doctrine of Use, namely, that a thing is good only so far as it serves; that a conspiring of parts and efforts to the production of an end is essential to any being. The first and gross manifestation of this truth is our inevitable and hated training in values and wants, in corn and meat.

It has already been illustrated, that every natural process is a version of a moral sentence. The moral law lies at the centre of nature and radiates to the circumference. It is the pith and marrow of every substance, every relation, and every process. All things with which we deal, preach to us. What is a farm but a mute gospel? The chaff and the wheat, weeds and plants, blight, rain, insects, sun,—it is a sacred emblem from the first furrow of spring to the last stack which the snow of winter overtakes in the fields. But the sailor, the shepherd, the miner, the merchant, in their several resorts, have each an experience precisely parallel, and leading to the same conclusion: because all organizations are radically alike. Nor can it be doubted that this moral sentiment which thus scents the air, grows in the grain, and impregnates the waters of the world, is caught by man and sinks into his soul. The moral influence of nature upon every individual is that amount of truth which it illustrates to him. Who can estimate this? Who can guess how much firmness the sea-beaten rock has taught the fisherman? how much tranquillity has been reflected to man from the azure sky, over whose unspotted deeps the winds forevermore drive flocks of stormy clouds, and leave no wrinkle or stain? how much industry and providence and affection we have caught from the pantomime of brutes? What a searching preacher of self-command is the varying phenomenon of Health!

Herein is especially apprehended the unity of Nature,—the unity in variety,—which meets us everywhere. All the endless variety of things make an identical impression. Xenophanes complained in his old age, that, look where he would, all things hastened back to Unity. He was weary of seeing the same entity in the tedious variety of forms. The fable of Proteus has a cordial truth. A leaf, a drop, a crystal, a moment of time, is related to the whole, and partakes of the perfection of the whole. Each particle is a microcosm, and faithfully renders the likeness of the world.

Not only resemblances exist in things whose analogy is obvious, as when we detect the type of the human hand in the flipper of the fossil saurus, but also in objects wherein there is great superficial unlikeness. Thus architecture is called "frozen music," by De Staël and Goethe. Vitruvius thought an architect should be a musician. "A Gothic church," said Coleridge, "is a petrified religion." Michael Angelo maintained, that, to an architect, a knowledge of anatomy is essential. In Haydn's oratorios, the notes present to the imagination not only motions, as of the snake, the stag, and the elephant, but colors also; as the green grass. The law of harmonic sound reappears in the harmonic colors. The granite is differenced in its laws only by the more or less of heat from the river that wears it away. The river, as it flows, resembles the air that flows over it; the air resembles the light which traverses it with more subtile currents; the light resembles the heat which rides with it through Space. Each creature is only a modification of the other; the likeness in them is more than the difference, and their radical law is one and the same. A rule of one art, or a law of one organization, holds true throughout nature. So intimate is this Unity, that, it is easily seen, it lies under the undermost garment of Nature, and betrays its source in Universal Spirit. For it pervades Thought also. Every universal truth which we express in words, implies or supposes every other truth. *Omne verum vero consonat.* It is like a great circle on a sphere, comprising all possible circles; which, however, may be drawn and com-

Ralph Waldo Emerson

prise it in like manner. Every such truth is the absolute Ens seen from one side. But it has innumerable sides.

The central Unity is still more conspicuous in actions. Words are finite organs of the infinite mind. They cannot cover the dimensions of what is in truth. They break, chop, and impoverish it. An action is the perfection and publication of thought. A right action seems to fill the eye, and to be related to all nature. "The wise man, in doing one thing, does all; or, in the one thing he does rightly, he sees the likeness of all which is done rightly."

Words and actions are not the attributes of brute nature. They introduce us to the human form, of which all other organizations appear to be degradations. When this appears among so many that surround it, the spirit prefers it to all others. It says, "From such as this have I drawn joy and knowledge; in such as this have I found and beheld myself; I will speak to it; it can speak again; it can yield me thought already formed and alive." In fact, the eye,—the mind,—is always accompanied by these forms, male and female; and these are incomparably the richest informations of the power and order that lie at the heart of things. Unfortunately every one of them bears the marks as of some injury; is marred and superficially defective. Nevertheless, far different from the deaf and dumb nature around them, these all rest like fountain-pipes on the unfathomed sea of thought and virtue whereto they alone, of all organizations, are the entrances.

It were a pleasant inquiry to follow into detail their ministry to our education, but where would it stop? We are associated in adolescent and adult life with some friends, who, like skies and waters, are co-extensive with our idea; who, answering each to a certain affection of the soul, satisfy our desire on that side; whom we lack power to put at such focal distance from us, that we can mend or even analyze them. We cannot choose but love them. When much intercourse with a friend has supplied us with a standard of excellence, and has increased our respect for the resources of God who thus sends a real person to outgo our ideal; when he has, moreover, become an object of thought, and, whilst his character retains all its unconscious effect, is converted in the mind into solid and sweet wisdom,—it is a sign to us that his office is closing, and he is commonly withdrawn from our sight in a short time.

VI. IDEALISM

Thus is the unspeakable but intelligible and practicable meaning of the world conveyed to man, the immortal pupil, in every object of sense. To this one end of Discipline, all parts of nature conspire.

A noble doubt perpetually suggests itself,—whether this end be not the Final Cause of the Universe; and whether nature outwardly exists. It is a sufficient account of that Appearance we call the World, that God will teach a human mind, and so makes it the receiver of a certain number of congruent sensations, which we call sun and moon, man and woman, house and trade. In my utter impotence to test the authenticity of the report of my senses, to know whether the impressions they make on me correspond with outlying objects, what difference does it make, whether Orion is up there in heaven, or some god paints the image in the firmament of the soul? The relations of parts and the end of the whole remaining the same, what is the difference, whether land and sea interact, and worlds revolve and intermingle without number or end,—deep yawning under deep, and galaxy balancing galaxy, throughout absolute space,—or whether, without relations of time and space, the same appearances are inscribed in the constant faith of man? Whether nature enjoy a substantial existence without, or is only in the apocalypse of the mind, it is alike useful and alike venerable to me. Be it what it may, it is ideal to me so long as I cannot try the accuracy of my senses.

The frivolous make themselves merry with the Ideal theory, as if its consequences were burlesque; as if it affected the stability of nature. It surely does not. God never jests with us, and will not compromise the end of nature by permitting any inconsequence in its procession. Any distrust of the permanence of laws would paralyze the faculties of man. Their permanence is sacredly respected, and his faith therein is perfect. The wheels and springs of man are all set to the hypothesis of the permanence of nature. We are not built like a ship to be tossed, but like a house to stand. It is a natural consequence of this structure, that so long as the active powers predominate over the reflective, we resist with indignation any hint that nature is more short-lived or mutable than spirit. The broker, the wheelwright, the carpenter, the tollman, are much displeased at the intimation.

But whilst we acquiesce entirely in the permanence of natural laws, the question of the absolute existence of nature still remains open. It is the uniform effect of culture on the human mind, not to shake our faith in the stability of particular phenomena, as of heat, water, azote; but to lead us to regard nature as phenomenon, not a substance; to attribute necessary existence to spirit; to esteem nature as an accident and an effect.

To the senses and the unrenewed understanding, belongs a sort of instinctive belief in the absolute existence of nature. In their view man and nature are indissolubly joined. Things are ultimates, and they never look beyond their sphere. The presence of Reason mars this faith. The first effort of thought tends to relax this despotism of the senses which binds us to nature as if we were a part of it, and shows us nature aloof, and, as it were, afloat. Until this higher agency intervened, the animal eye sees, with wonderful accuracy, sharp outlines and colored surfaces. When the eye of Reason opens, to outline and surface are at once added grace and expression. These proceed from imagination and affection, and abate somewhat of the angular distinctness of objects. If the Reason be stimulated to more earnest vision, outlines and surfaces becomes transparent, and are no longer seen; causes and spirits are seen through them. The best moments of life are these delicious awakenings of the higher powers, and the reverential withdrawing of nature before its God.

Let us proceed to indicate the effects of culture.

1. Our first institution in the Ideal philosophy is a hint from Nature herself.

Ralph Waldo Emerson

Nature is made to conspire with spirit to emancipate us. Certain mechanical changes, a small alteration in our local position, apprises us of a dualism. We are strangely affected by seeing the shore from a moving ship, from a balloon, or through the tints of an unusual sky. The least change in our point of view gives the whole world a pictorial air. A man who seldom rides, needs only to get into a coach and traverse his own town, to turn the street into a puppet-show. The men, the women,—talking, running, bartering, fighting,—the earnest mechanic, the lounger, the beggar, the boys, the dogs, are unrealized at once, or, at least, wholly detached from all relation to the observer, and seen as apparent, not substantial beings. What new thoughts are suggested by seeing a face of country quite familiar, in the rapid movement of the railroad car! Nay, the most wonted objects, (make a very slight change in the point of vision,) please us most. In a camera obscura, the butcher's cart, and the figure of one of our own family amuse us. So a portait of a well-known face gratifies us. Turn the eyes upside down, by looking at the landscape through your legs, and how agreeable is the picture, though you have seen it any time these twenty years!

In these cases, by mechanical means, is suggested the difference between the observer and the spectacle—between man and nature. Hence arises a pleasure mixed with awe; I may say, a low degree of the sublime is felt, from the fact, probably, that man is hereby apprised that whilst the world is a spectacle, something in himself is stable.

2. In a higher manner the poet communicates the same pleasure. By a few strokes he delineates, as on air, the sun, the mountain, the camp, the city, the hero, the maiden, not different from what we know them, but only lifted from the ground and afloat before the eye. He unfixes the land and the sea, makes them revolve around the axis of his primary thought, and disposes them anew. Possessed himself by a heroic passion, he uses matter as symbols of it. The sensual man conforms thoughts to things; the poet conforms things to his thoughts. The one esteems nature as rooted and fast; the other, as fluid, and impresses his being thereon. To him, the refractory world is ductile and flexible; he invests dust and stones with humanity, and makes them the words of the Reason. The Imagination may be defined to be the use which the Reason makes of the material world. Shakespeare possesses the power of subordinating nature for the purposes of expression, beyond all poets. His imperial muse tosses the creation like a bauble from hand to hand, and uses it to embody any caprice of thought that is uppermost in his mind. The remotest spaces of nature are visited, and the farthest sundered things are brought together, by a subtile spiritual connection. We are made aware that magnitude of material things is relative, and all objects shrink and expand to serve the passion of the poet. Thus in his sonnets, the lays of birds, the scents and dyes of flowers he finds to be the *shadow* of his beloved; time, which keeps her from him, is his *chest*; the suspicion she has awakened, is her *ornament*;

> *The ornament of beauty is Suspect,*
> *A crow which flies in heaven's sweetest air.*

His passion is not the fruit of chance; it swells, as he speaks, to a city, or a state.

> *No, it was builded far from accident;*
> *It suffers not in smiling pomp, nor falls*
> *Under the brow of thralling discontent;*
> *It fears not policy, that heretic,*
> *That works on leases of short numbered hours,*
> *But all alone stands hugely politic.*

In the strength of his constancy, the Pyramids seem to him recent and transitory. The freshness of youth and love dazzles him with its resemblance to morning;

> *Take those lips away*
> *Which so sweetly were forsworn;*
> *And those eyes,—the break of day,*
> *Lights that do mislead the morn.*

The wild beauty of this hyperbole, I may say in passing, it would not be easy to match in literature.

This transfiguration which all material objects undergo through the passion of the poet,—this power which he exerts to dwarf the great, to magnify the small,—might be illustrated by a thousand examples from his Plays. I have before me the Tempest, and will cite only these few lines.

> PROSPERO. *The strong based promontory*
> *Have I made shake, and by the spurs plucked up*
> *The pine and cedar.*

Prospero calls for music to soothe the frantic Alonzo, and his companions;

> *A solemn air, and the best comforter*
> *To an unsettled fancy, cure thy brains*
> *Now useless, boiled within thy skull.*

Again;

> *The charm dissolves apace,*
> *And, as the morning steals upon the night,*
> *Melting the darkness, so their rising senses*
> *Begin to chase the ignorant fumes that mantle*
> *Their clearer reason.*
> *Their understanding*
> *Begins to swell: and the approaching tide*
> *Will shortly fill the reasonable shores*
> *That now lie foul and muddy.*

Ralph Waldo Emerson

The perception of real affinities between events (that is to say, of *ideal* affinities, for those only are real), enables the poet thus to make free with the most imposing forms and phenomena of the world, and to assert the predominance of the soul.

3. Whilst thus the poet animates nature with his own thoughts, he differs from the philosopher only herein, that the one proposes Beauty as his main end; the other Truth. But the philosopher, not less than the poet, postpones the apparent order and relations of things to the empire of thought. "The problem of philosophy," according to Plato, "is, for all that exists conditionally, to find a ground unconditioned and absolute." It proceeds on the faith that a law determines all phenomena, which being known, the phenomena can be predicted. That law, when in the mind, is an idea. Its beauty is infinite. The true philosopher and the true poet are one, and a beauty, which is truth, and a truth, which is beauty, is the aim of both. Is not the charm of one of Plato's or Aristotle's definitions strictly like that of the Antigone of Sophocles? It is, in both cases, that a spiritual life has been imparted to nature; that the solid seeming block of matter has been pervaded and dissolved by a thought; that this feeble human being has penetrated the vast masses of nature with an informing soul, and recognized itself in their harmony, that is, seized their law. In physics, when this is attained, the memory disburthens itself of its cumbrous catalogues of particulars, and carries centuries of observation in a single formula.

Thus even in physics, the material is degraded before the spiritual. The astronomer, the geometer, rely on their irrefragable analysis, and disdain the results of observation. The sublime remark of Euler on his law of arches, "This will be found contrary to all experience, yet is true;" had already transferred nature into the mind, and left matter like an outcast corpse.

4. Intellectual science has been observed to beget invariably a doubt of the existence of matter. Turgot said, "He that has never doubted the existence of matter, may be assured he has no aptitude for metaphysical inquiries." It fastens the attention upon immortal necessary uncreated natures, that is, upon Ideas; and in their presence we feel that the outward circumstance is a dream and a shade. Whilst we wait in this Olympus of gods, we think of nature as an appendix to the soul. We ascend into their region, and know that these are the thoughts of the Supreme Being. "These are they who were set up from everlasting, from the beginning, or ever the earth was. When he prepared the heavens, they were there; when he established the clouds above, when he strengthened the fountains of the deep. Then they were by him, as one brought up with him. Of them took he counsel."

Their influence is proportionate. As objects of science they are accessible to few men. Yet all men are capable of being raised by piety or by passion, into their region. And no man touches these divine natures, without becoming, in some degree, himself divine. Like a new soul, they renew the body. We become physically nimble and lightsome; we tread on air; life is no longer irksome, and we think it will never be so. No man fears age or misfortune or death in their serene company, for he is transported out of the district of change. Whilst we behold unveiled the nature of Justice and Truth, we learn the difference between the absolute and the conditional or relative. We apprehend the absolute. As it were, for the first time, *we exist*. We become immortal, for we learn that time and space are relations of matter; that with a perception of truth or a virtuous will they have no affinity.

5. Finally, religion and ethics, which may be fitly called the practice of ideas, or the introduction of ideas into life, have an analogous effect with all lower culture, in degrading nature and suggesting its dependence on spirit. Ethics and religion differ herein; that the one is the system of human duties commencing from man; the other, from God. Religion includes the personality of God; Ethics does not. They are one to our present design. They both put nature under foot. The first and last lesson of religion is, "The things that are seen, are temporal; the things that are unseen, are eternal." It puts an affront upon nature. It does that for the unschooled, which philosophy does for Berkeley and Viasa. The uniform language that may be heard in the churches of the most ignorant sect is,— "Contemn the unsubstantial shows of the world; they are vanities, dreams, shadows, unrealities; seek the realities of religion." The devotee flouts nature. Some theosophists have arrived at a certain hostility and indignation towards matter, as the Manichean and Plotinus. They distrusted in themselves any looking back to these flesh-pots of Egypt. Plotinus was ashamed of his body. In short, they might all say of matter, what Michael Angelo said of external beauty, "It is the frail and weary weed, in which God dresses the soul which he has called into time."

It appears that motion, poetry, physical and intellectual science, and religion, all tend to affect our convictions of the reality of the external world. But I own there is something ungrateful in expanding too curiously the particulars of the general proposition, that all culture tends to imbue us with idealism. I have no hostility to nature, but a child's love to it. I expand and live in the warm day like corn and melons. Let us speak her fair. I do not wish to fling stones at my beautiful mother, nor soil my gentle nest. I only wish to indicate the true position of nature in regard to man, wherein to establish man all right education tends; as the ground which to attain is the object of human life, that is, of man's connection with nature. Culture inverts the vulgar views of nature, and brings the mind to call that apparent which it uses to call real, and that real which it uses to call visionary. Children, it is true, believe in the external world. The belief that it appears only, is an afterthought, but with culture this faith will as surely arise on the mind as did the first.

The advantage of the ideal theory over the popular faith is this, that it presents the world in precisely that view which is most desirable to the mind. It is, in fact, the view which Reason, both speculative and practical, that is, philosophy and virtue, take. For seen in the light of thought, the world always is phenomenal; and virtue subordinates it to the mind. Idealism sees the world in God. It beholds the whole circle of persons and

Ralph Waldo Emerson

things, of actions and events, of country and religion, not as painfully accumulated, atom after atom, act after act, in an aged creeping Past, but as one vast picture which God paints on the instant eternity for the contemplation of the soul. Therefore the soul holds itself off from a too trivial and microscopic study of the universal tablet. It respects the end too much to immerse itself in the means. It sees something more important in Christianity than the scandals of ecclesiastical history or the niceties of criticism; and, very incurious concerning persons or miracles, and not at all disturbed by chasms of historical evidence, it accepts from God the phenomenon, as it finds it, as the pure and awful form of religion in the world. It is not hot and passionate at the appearance of what it calls its own good or bad fortune, at the union or opposition of other persons. No man is its enemy. It accepts whatsoever befalls, as part of its lesson. It is a watcher more than a doer, and it is a doer, only that it may the better watch.

VII. SPIRIT

It is essential to a true theory of nature and of man, that it should contain somewhat progressive. Uses that are exhausted or that may be, and facts that end in the statement, cannot be all that is true of this brave lodging wherein man is harbored, and wherein all his faculties find appropriate and endless exercise. And all the uses of nature admit of being summed in one, which yields the activity of man an infinite scope. Through all its kingdoms, to the suburbs and outskirts of things, it is faithful to the cause whence it had its origin. It always speaks of Spirit. It suggests the absolute. It is a perpetual effect. It is a great shadow pointing always to the sun behind us.

The aspect of Nature is devout. Like the figure of Jesus, she stands with bended head, and hands folded upon the breast. The happiest man is he who learns from nature the lesson of worship.

Of that ineffable essence which we call Spirit, he that thinks most, will say least. We can foresee God in the coarse, and, as it were, distant phenomena of matter; but when we try to define and describe himself, both language and thought desert us, and we are as helpless as fools and savages. That essence refuses to be recorded in propositions, but when man has worshipped him intellectually, the noblest ministry of nature is to stand as the apparition of God. It is the organ through which the universal spirit speaks to the individual, and strives to lead back the individual to it.

When we consider Spirit, we see that the views already presented do not include the whole circumference of man. We must add some related thoughts.

Three problems are put by nature to the mind: What is matter? Whence is it? and Whereto? The first of these questions only, the ideal theory answers. Idealism saith: matter is a phenomenon, not a substance. Idealism acquaints us with the total disparity between the evidence of our own being and the evidence of the world's being. The one is perfect; the other, incapable of any assurance; the mind is a part of the nature of things; the world is a divine dream, from which we may presently awake to the glories and certainties of day. Idealism is a hypothesis to account for nature by other principles than those of carpentry and chemistry. Yet, if it only deny the existence of matter, it does not satisfy the demands of the spirit. It leaves God out of me. It leaves me in the splendid labyrinth of my perceptions, to wander without end. Then the heart resists it, because it balks the affections in denying substantive being to men and women. Nature is so pervaded with human life that there is something of humanity in all and in every particular. But this theory makes nature foreign to me, and does not account for that consanguinity which we acknowledge to it.

Let it stand then, in the present state of our knowledge, merely as a useful introductory hypothesis, serving to apprise us of the eternal distinction between the soul and the world.

But when, following the invisible steps of thought, we come to inquire, Whence is matter? and Whereto? many truths arise to us out of the recesses of consciousness. We learn that the highest is present to the soul of man; that the dread universal essence, which is not wisdom, or love, or beauty, or power, but all in one, and each entirely, is that for which all things exist, and that by which they are; that spirit creates; that behind nature, throughout nature, spirit is present; one and not compound it does not act upon us from without, that is, in space and time, but spiritually, or through ourselves: therefore, that spirit, that is, the Supreme Being, does not build up nature around us, but puts it forth through us, as the life of the tree puts forth new branches and leaves through the pores of the old. As a plant upon the earth, so a man rests upon the bosom of God; he is nourished by unfailing fountains, and draws at his need inexhaustible power. Who can set bounds to the possibilities of man? Once inhale the upper air, being admitted to behold the absolute natures of justice and truth, and we learn that man has access to the entire mind of the Creator, is himself the creator in the finite. This view, which admonishes me where the sources of wisdom and power lie, and points to virtue as to

The golden key
Which opes the palace of eternity,

carries upon its face the highest certificate of truth, because it animates me to create my own world through the purification of my soul.

The world proceeds from the same spirit as the body of man. It is a remoter and inferior incarnation of God, a projection of God in the unconscious. But it differs from the body in one important respect. It is not, like that, now subjected to the human will. Its serene order is inviolable by us. It is, therefore, to us, the present expositor of the divine mind. It is a fixed point whereby we may measure our departure. As we degenerate, the contrast between us and our house is more evident. We are as much strangers in nature as we are aliens from God. We do not understand the notes of birds. The fox and the deer run away from us; the bear and tiger rend us. We do not know the uses of more than a few plants, as corn and

Ralph Waldo Emerson

the apple, the potato and the vine. Is not the landscape, every glimpse of which hath a grandeur, a face of him? Yet this may show us what discord is between man and nature, for you cannot freely admire a noble landscape if laborers are digging in the field hard by. The poet finds something ridiculous in his delight until he is out of the sight of men.

VIII. PROSPECTS

In inquiries respecting the laws of the world and the frame of things, the highest reason is always the truest. That which seems faintly possible, it is so refined, is often faint and dim because it is deepest seated in the mind among the eternal verities. Empirical science is apt to cloud the sight, and by the very knowledge of functions and processes to bereave the student of the manly contemplation of the whole. The savant becomes unpoetic. But the best read naturalist who lends an entire and devout attention to truth, will see that there remains much to learn of his relation to the world, and that it is not to be learned by any addition or subtraction or other comparison of known quantities, but is arrived at by untaught sallies of the spirit, by a continual self-recovery, and by entire humility. He will perceive that there are far more excellent qualities in the student than preciseness and infallibility; that a guess is often more fruitful than an indisputable affirmation, and that a dream may let us deeper into the secret of nature than a hundred concerted experiments.

For the problems to be solved are precisely those which the physiologist and the naturalist omit to state. It is not so pertinent to man to know all the individuals of the animal kingdom, as it is to know whence and whereto is this tyrannizing unity in his constitution, which evermore separates and classifies things, endeavoring to reduce the most diverse to one form. When I behold a rich landscape, it is less to my purpose to recite correctly the order and superposition of the strata, than to know why all thought of multitude is lost in a tranquil sense of unity. I cannot greatly honor minuteness in details, so long as there is no hint to explain the relation between things and thoughts; no ray upon the *metaphysics* of conchology, of botany, of the arts, to show the relation of the forms of flowers, shells, animals, architecture, to the mind, and build science upon ideas. In a cabinet of natural history, we become sensible of a certain occult recognition and sympathy in regard to the most unwieldy and eccentric forms of beast, fish, and insect. The American who has been confined, in his own country, to the sight of buildings designed after foreign models, is surprised on entering York Minster or St. Peter's at Rome, by the feeling that these structures are imitations also,—faint copies of an invisible archetype. Nor has science sufficient humanity, so long as the naturalist overlooks that wonderful congruity which subsists between man and the world; of which he is lord, not because he is the most subtile inhabitant, but because he is its head and heart, and finds something of himself in every great and small thing, in every mountain stratum, in every new law of color, fact of astronomy, or atmospheric influence which observation or analysis lays open. A perception of this mystery inspires the muse of George Herbert, the beautiful psalmist of the seventeenth century. The following lines are part of his little poem on Man.

> Man is all symmetry,
> Full of proportions, one limb to another,
> And all to all the world besides.
> Each part may call the farthest, brother;
> For head with foot hath private amity,
> And both with moons and tides.
>
> Nothing hath got so far
> But man hath caught and kept it as his prey;
> His eyes dismount the highest star:
> He is in little all the sphere.
> Herbs gladly cure our flesh, because that they
> Find their acquaintance there.
>
> For us, the winds do blow,
> The earth doth rest, heaven move, and fountains flow;
> Nothing we see, but means our good,
> As our delight, or as our treasure;
> The whole is either our cupboard of food,
> Or cabinet of pleasure.
>
> The stars have us to bed:
> Night draws the curtain; which the sun withdraws.
> Music and light attend our head.
> All things unto our flesh are kind,
> In their descent and being; to our mind,
> In their ascent and cause.
>
> More servants wait on man
> Than he'll take notice of. In every path,
> He treads down that which doth befriend him
> When sickness makes him pale and wan.
> Oh mighty love! Man is one world, and hath
> Another to attend him.

The perception of this class of truths makes the attraction which draws men to science, but the end is lost sight of in attention to the means. In view of this half-sight of science, we accept the sentence of Plato, that "poetry comes nearer to vital truth than history." Every surmise and vaticination of the mind is entitled to a certain respect, and we learn to prefer imperfect theories, and sentences which contain glimpses of truth, to digested systems which have no one valuable suggestion. A wise writer will feel that the ends of study and composition are best answered by announcing undiscovered regions of thought, and so communicating, through hope, new activity to the torpid spirit.

I shall therefore conclude this essay with some traditions of man and nature, which a certain poet sang to me; and which, as they have always been in the world, and perhaps reappear to every bard, may be both history and prophecy.

Ralph Waldo Emerson

"The foundations of man are not in matter, but in spirit. But the element of spirit is eternity. To it, therefore, the longest series of events, the oldest chronologies are young and recent. In the cycle of the universal man, from whom the known individuals proceed, centuries are points, and all history is but the epoch of one degradation.

"We distrust and deny inwardly our sympathy with nature. We own and disown our relation to it, by turns. We are like Nebuchadnezzar, dethroned, bereft of reason, and eating grass like an ox. But who can set limits to the remedial force of spirit?

"A man is a god in ruins. When men are innocent, life shall be longer, and shall pass into the immortal as gently as we awake from dreams. Now, the world would be insane and rabid, if these disorganizations should last for hundreds of years. It is kept in check by death and infancy. Infancy is the perpetual Messiah, which comes into the arms of fallen men, and pleads with them to return to paradise.

"Man is the dwarf of himself. Once he was permeated and dissolved by spirit. He filled nature with his overflowing currents. Out of him sprang the sun and moon; from man the sun, from woman the moon. The laws of his mind, the periods of his actions externized themselves into day and night, into the year and the seasons. But, having made for himself this huge shell, his waters retired; he no longer fills the veins and veinlets; he is shrunk to a drop. He sees that the structure still fits him, but fits him colossally. Say, rather, once it fitted him, now it corresponds to him from far and on high. He adores timidly his own work. Now is man the follower of the sun, and woman the follower of the moon. Yet sometimes he starts in his slumber, and wonders at himself and his house, and muses strangely at the resemblance betwixt him and it. He perceives that if his law is still paramount, if still he have elemental power, if his word is sterling yet in nature, it is not conscious power, it is not inferior but superior to his will. It is instinct." Thus my Orphic poet sang.

At present, man applies to nature but half his force. He works on the world with his understanding alone. He lives in it and masters it by a penny-wisdom; and he that works most in it is but a half-man, and whilst his arms are strong and his digestion good, his mind is imbruted, and he is a selfish savage. His relation to nature, his power over it, is through the understanding, as by manure; the economic use of fire, wind, water, and the mariner's needle; steam, coal, chemical agriculture; the repairs of the human body by the dentist and the surgeon. This is such a resumption of power as if a banished king should buy his territories inch by inch, instead of vaulting at once into his throne. Meantime, in the thick darkness, there are not wanting gleams of a better light,—occasional examples of the action of man upon nature with his entire force,—with reason as well as understanding. Such examples are, the traditions of miracles in the earliest antiquity of all nations; the history of Jesus Christ; the achievements of a principle, as in religious and political revolutions, and in the abolition of the slave-trade; the miracles of enthusiasm, as those reported of Swedenborg, Hohenlohe, and the Shakers; many obscure and yet contested facts,

Nature

now arranged under the name of Animal Magnetism; prayer; eloquence; self-healing; and the wisdom of children. These are examples of Reason's momentary grasp of the sceptre; the exertions of a power which exists not in time or space, but an instantaneous instreaming causing power. The difference between the actual and the ideal force of man is happily figured by the schoolmen, in saying, that the knowledge of man is an evening knowledge, *vespertina cognitio*, but that of God is a morning knowledge, *matutina cognitio*.

The problem of restoring to the world original and eternal beauty is solved by the redemption of the soul. The ruin or the blank that we see when we look at nature, is in our own eye. The axis of vision is not coincident with the axis of things, and so they appear not transparent but opaque. The reason why the world lacks unity, and lies broken and in heaps, is because man is disunited with himself. He cannot be a naturalist until he satisfies all the demands of the spirit. Love is as much its demand as perception. Indeed, neither can be perfect without the other. In the uttermost meaning of the words, thought is devout, and devotion is thought. Deep calls unto deep. But in actual life, the marriage is not celebrated. There are innocent men who worship God after the tradition of their fathers, but their sense of duty has not yet extended to the use of all their faculties. And there are patient naturalists, but they freeze their subject under the wintry light of the understanding. Is not prayer also a study of truth,—a sally of the soul into the unfound infinite? No man ever prayed heartily without learning something. But when a faithful thinker, resolute to detach every object from personal relations and see it in the light of thought, shall, at the same time, kindle science with the fire of the holiest affections, then will God go forth anew into the creation.

It will not need, when the mind is prepared for study, to search for objects. The invariable mark of wisdom is to see the miraculous in the common. What is a day? What is a year? What is summer? What is woman? What is a child? What is sleep? To our blindness, these things seem unaffecting. We make fables to hide the baldness of the fact and conform it, as we say, to the higher law of the mind. But when the fact is seen under the light of an idea, the gaudy fable fades and shrivels. We behold the real higher law. To the wise, therefore, a fact is true poetry, and the most beautiful of fables. These wonders are brought to our own door. You also are a man. Man and woman and their social life, poverty, labor, sleep, fear, fortune, are known to you. Learn that none of these things is superficial, but that each phenomenon has its roots in the faculties and affections of the mind. Whilst the abstract question occupies your intellect, nature brings it in the concrete to be solved by your hands. It were a wise inquiry for the closet, to compare, point by point, especially at remarkable crises in life, our daily history with the rise and progress of ideas in the mind.

So shall we come to look at the world with new eyes. It shall answer the endless inquiry of the intellect,—What is truth? and of the affections, —What is good? by yielding itself passive to the educated Will. Then shall come to pass what my poet said: "Nature is not fixed but fluid. Spirit

Ralph Waldo Emerson

alters, moulds, makes it. The immobility or bruteness of nature is the absence of spirit; to pure spirit it is fluid, it is volatile, it is obedient. Every spirit builds itself a house, and beyond its house a world, and beyond its world a heaven. Know then that the world exists for you. For you is the phenomenon perfect. What we are, that only can we see. All that Adam had, all that Cæsar could, you have and can do. Adam called his house, heaven and earth; Cæsar called his house, Rome; you perhaps call yours, a cobbler's trade; a hundred acres of ploughed land; or a scholar's garret. Yet line for line and point for point your dominion is as great as theirs, though without fine names. Build therefore your own world. As fast as you conform your life to the pure idea in your mind, that will unfold its great proportions. A correspondent revolution in things will attend the influx of the spirit. So fast will disagreeable appearances, swine, spiders, snakes, pests, madhouses, prisons, enemies, vanish; they are temporary and shall be no more seen. The sordor and filths of nature, the sun shall dry up and the wind exhale. As when the summer comes from the south the snowbanks melt and the face of the earth becomes green before it, so shall the advancing spirit create its ornaments along its path, and carry with it the beauty it visits and the song which enchants it; it shall draw beautiful faces, warm hearts, wise discourse, and heroic acts, around its way, until evil is no more seen. The kingdom of man over nature, which cometh not with observation,—a dominion such as now is beyond his dream of God,— he shall enter without more wonder than the blind man feels who is gradually restored to perfect sight."

[1836]

Henry David Thoreau:

Walking

Henry David Thoreau (1817-1862), naturalist, poet, essayist, and day laborer, followed Emerson in theory but quickly became his own man as he practiced that theory. His dedication to nature was not abstract, but concrete, as he attempted to forge an entirely natural and practical relationship between himself and the natural world of which he was a part. "Walking" (1862) is in essence a reiteration of the experience defined in *Walden* (1854).

I wish to speak a word for Nature, for absolute freedom and wildness, as contrasted with a freedom and culture merely civil,—to regard man as an inhabitant, or a part and parcel of Nature, rather than a member of society. I wish to make an extreme statement, if so I may make an emphatic one, for there are enough champions of civilization: the minister and the school-committee and every one of you will take care of that.

I have met with but one or two persons in the course of my life who understood the art of Walking, that is, of taking walks,—who had a genius, so to speak, for *sauntering*: which word is beautifully derived "from idle people who roved about the country, in the Middle Ages, and asked charity, under pretense of going *à la Sainte Terre*," to the Holy Land, till the children exclaimed, "There goes a *Sainte-Terrer*," a Saunterer, a Holy-Lander. They who never go to the Holy Land in their walks, as they pretend, are indeed mere idlers and vagabonds; but they who do go there are saunterers in the good sense, such as I mean. Some, however, would derive the word from *sans terre*, without land or home, which, therefore, in the good sense, will mean, having no particular home, but equally at home everywhere. For this is the secret of successful sauntering. He who sits still in a house all the time may be the greatest vagrant of all; but the saunterer, in the good sense, is no more vagrant than the meandering river, which is all the while sedulously seeking the shortest course to the sea. But I prefer the first, which, indeed, is the most probable derivation. For every walk is a sort of crusade, preached by some Peter the Hermit in us, to go forth and reconquer this Holy Land from the hands of the Infidels.

It is true, we are but faint-hearted crusaders, even the walkers, nowadays, who undertake no persevering, never-ending enterprises. Our expeditions are but tours, and come round again at evening to the old hearthside from which we set out. Half the walk is but retracing our steps. We should go forth on the shortest walk, perchance, in the spirit of undying adventure, never to return,—prepared to send back our embalmed hearts only as relics to our desolate kingdoms. If you are ready to leave father and mother, and brother and sister, and wife and child and friends, and never see them again,—if you have paid your debts, and made your will, and settled all your affairs, and are a free man, then you are ready for a walk.

To come down to my own experience, my companion and I, for I sometimes have a companion, take pleasure in fancying ourselves knights of a new, or rather an old, order,—not Equestrians or Chevaliers, not Ritters or Riders, but Walkers, a still more ancient and honorable class, I trust. The chivalric and heroic spirit which once belonged to the Rider seems now to reside in, or perchance to have subsided into, the Walker,—not the Knight, but Walker, Errant. He is a sort of fourth estate, outside of Church and State and People.

We have felt that we almost alone hereabouts practiced this noble art; though, to tell the truth, at least, if their own assertions are to be received, most of my townsmen would fain walk sometimes, as I do, but they cannot. No wealth can buy the requisite leisure, freedom, and independence which are the capital in this profession. It comes only by the

Henry David Thoreau

grace of God. It requires a direct dispensation from Heaven to become a walker. You must be born into the family of the Walkers. *Ambulator nascitur, non fit.* Some of my townsmen, it is true, can remember and have described to me some walks which they took ten years ago, in which they were so blessed as to lose themselves for half an hour in the woods; but I know very well that they have confined themselves to the highway ever since, whatever pretensions they may make to belong to this select class. No doubt they were elevated for a moment as by the reminiscence of a previous state of existence, when even they were foresters and outlaws.

> "When he came to grene wode,
>   In a mery mornynge,
> There he herde the notes small
>   Of byrdes mery syngynge.
>
> "It is ferre gone, sayd Robyn,
>   That I was last here;
> Me lyste a lytell for to shote
>   At the donne dere."

I think that I cannot preserve my health and spirits, unless I spend four hours a day at least,—and it is commonly more than that,—sauntering through the woods and over the hills and fields, absolutely free from all worldly engagements. You may safely say, A penny for your thoughts, or a thousand pounds. When sometimes I am reminded that the mechanics and shopkeepers stay in their shops not only all the forenoon, but all the afternoon too, sitting with crossed legs, so many of them,—as if the legs were made to sit upon, and not to stand or walk upon,—I think that they deserve some credit for not having all committed suicide long ago.

I, who cannot stay in my chamber for a single day without acquiring some rust, and when sometimes I have stolen forth for a walk at the eleventh hour or four o'clock in the afternoon, too late to redeem the day, when the shades of night were already beginning to be mingled with the daylight, have felt as if I had committed some sin to be atoned for,—I confess that I am astonished at the power of endurance, to say nothing of the moral insensibility, of my neighbors who confine themselves to shops and offices the whole day for weeks and months, aye, and years almost together. I know not what manner of stuff they are of,—sitting there now at three o'clock in the afternoon, as if it were three o'clock in the morning. Bonaparte may talk of the three-o'clock-in-the-morning courage, but it is nothing to the courage which can sit down cheerfully at this hour in the afternoon over against one's self whom you have known all the morning, to starve out a garrison to whom you are bound by such strong ties of sympathy. I wonder that about this time, or say between four and five o'clock in the afternoon, too late for the morning papers and too early for the evening ones, there is not a general explosion heard up and down the street, scattering a legion of antiquated and house-bred notions and whims to the four winds for an airing,—and so the evil cure itself.

How womankind, who are confined to the house still more than men, stand it I do not know; but I have ground to suspect that most of

Walking

them do not *stand* it at all. When, early in a summer afternoon, we have been shaking the dust of the village from the skirts of our garments, making haste past those houses with purely Doric or Gothic fronts, which have such an air of repose about them, my companion whispers that probably about these times their occupants are all gone to bed. Then it is that I appreciate the beauty and the glory of architecture, which itself never turns in, but forever stands out and erect, keeping watch over the slumberers.

No doubt temperament, and, above all, age, have a good deal to do with it. As a man grows older, his ability to sit still and follow indoor occupations increases. He grows vespertinal in his habits as the evening of life approaches, till at last he comes forth only just before sundown, and gets all the walk that he requires in half an hour.

But the walking of which I speak has nothing in it akin to taking exercise, as it is called, as the sick take medicine at stated hours,—as the swinging of dumb-bells or chairs; but is itself the enterprise and adventure of the day. If you would get exercise, go in search of the springs of life. Think of a man's swinging dumb-bells for his health, when those springs are bubbling up in far-off pastures unsought by him!

Moreover, you must walk like a camel, which is said to be the only beast which ruminates when walking. When a traveler asked Wordsworth's servant to show him her master's study, she answered, "Here is his library, but his study is out of doors."

Living much out of doors, in the sun and wind, will no doubt produce a certain roughness of character,—will cause a thicker cuticle to grow over some of the finer qualities of our nature, as on the face and hands, or as severe manual labor robs the hands of some of their delicacy of touch. So staying in the house, on the other hand, may produce a softness and smoothness, not to say thinness of skin, accompanied by an increased sensibility to certain impressions. Perhaps we should be more susceptible to some influences important to our intellectual and moral growth, if the sun had shone and the wind blown on us a little less; and no doubt it is a nice matter to proportion rightly the thick and thin skin. But methinks that is a scurf that will fall off fast enough,—that the natural remedy is to be found in the proportion which the night bears to the day, the winter to the summer, thought to experience. There will be so much the more air and sunshine in our thoughts. The callous palms of the laborer are conversant with finer tissues of self-respect and heroism, whose touch thrills the heart, than the languid fingers of idleness. That is mere sentimentality that lies abed by day and thinks itself white, far from the tan and callus of experience.

When we walk, we naturally go to the fields and woods: what would become of us, if we walked only in a garden or a mall? Even some sects of philosophers have felt the necessity of importing the woods to themselves, since they did not go to the woods. "They planted groves and walks of Platanes," where they took *subdiales ambulationes* in porticos open to the air. Of course it is of no use to direct our steps to the woods, if they do not carry us thither. I am alarmed when it happens that I have walked a mile into the woods bodily, without getting there in spirit. In my

Henry David Thoreau

afternoon walk I would fain forget all my morning occupations and my obligations to society. But it sometimes happens that I cannot easily shake off the village. The thought of some work will run in my head and I am not where my body is,—I am out of my senses. In my walks I would fain return to my senses. What business have I in the woods, if I am thinking of something out of the woods? I suspect myself, and cannot help a shudder, when I find myself so implicated even in what are called good works, —for this may sometimes happen.

My vicinity affords many good walks; and though for so many years I have walked almost every day, and sometimes for several days together, I have not yet exhausted them. An absolutely new prospect is a great happiness, and I can still get this any afternoon. Two or three hours' walking will carry me to as strange a country as I expect ever to see. A single farmhouse which I had not seen before is sometimes as good as the dominions of the King of Dahomey. There is in fact a sort of harmony discoverable between the capabilities of the landscape within a circle of ten miles' radius, or the limits of an afternoon walk, and the threescore years and ten of human life. It will never become quite familiar to you.

Nowadays almost all man's improvements, so called, as the building of houses, and the cutting down of the forest and of all large trees, simply deform the landscape, and make it more and more tame and cheap. A people who would begin by burning the fences and let the forest stand! I saw the fences half consumed, their ends lost in the middle of the prairie, and some worldly miser with a surveyor looking after his bounds, while heaven had taken place around him, and he did not see the angels going to and fro, but was looking for an old post-hole in the midst of paradise. I looked again, and saw him standing in the middle of a boggy stygian fen, surrounded by devils, and he had found his bounds without a doubt, three little stones, where a stake had been driven, and looking nearer, I saw that the Prince of Darkness was his surveyor.

I can easily walk ten, fifteen, twenty, any number of miles, commencing at my own door, without going by any house, without crossing a road except where the fox and the mink do: first along by the river, and then the brook, and then the meadow and the woodside. There are square miles in my vicinity which have no inhabitant. From many a hill I can see civilization and the abodes of man afar. The farmers and their works are scarcely more obvious than woodchucks and their burrows. Man and his affairs, church and state and school, trade and commerce, and manufactures and agriculture, even politics, the most alarming of them all,—I am pleased to see how little space they occupy in the landscape. Politics is but a narrow field, and that still narrower highway yonder leads to it. I sometimes direct the traveler thither. If you would go to the political world, follow the great road,—follow that market-man, keep his dust in your eyes, and it will lead you straight to it; for it, too, has its place merely, and does not occupy all space. I pass from it as from a bean-field into the forest, and it is forgotten. In one half-hour I can walk off to some portion of the earth's surface where a man does not stand from one year's end to another,

Walking

and there, consequently, politics are not, for they are but as the cigar-smoke of a man.

The village is the place to which the roads tend, a sort of expansion of the highway, as a lake of a river. It is the body of which roads are the arms and legs,—a trivial or quadrivial place, the thoroughfare and ordinary of travelers. The word is from the Latin *villa*, which together with *via*, a way, or more anciently *ved* and *yella*, Varro derives from *veho*, to carry, because the villa is the place to and from which things are carried. They who got their living by teaming were said *vellaturam facere*. Hence, too, the Latin word *vilis* and our vile; also *villain*. This suggests what kind of degeneracy villagers are liable to. They are wayworn by the travel that goes by and over them, without traveling themselves.

Some do not walk at all; others walk in the highways; a few walk across lots. Roads are made for horses and men of business. I do not travel in them much, comparatively, because I am not in a hurry to get to any tavern or grocery or livery-stable or depot to which they lead. I am a good horse to travel, but not from choice a roadster. The landscape-painter uses the figures of men to mark a road. He would not make that use of my figure. I walk out into a Nature such as the old prophets and poets, Menu, Moses, Homer, Chaucer, walked in. You may name it America, but it is not America; neither Americus Vespucius, nor Columbus, nor the rest were the discoverers of it. There is a truer account of it in mythology than in any history of America, so called, that I have seen.

However, there are a few old roads that may be trodden with profit, as if they led somewhere now that they are nearly discontinued. There is the Old Marlborough Road, which does not go to Marlborough now, methinks, unless that is Marlborough where it carries me. I am the bolder to speak of it here, because I presume that there are one or two such roads in every town.

THE OLD MARLBOROUGH ROAD

Where they once dug for money,
But never found any;
Where sometimes Martial Miles
Singly files,
And Elijah Wood,
I fear for no good:
No other man,
Save Elisha Dugan,—
O man of wild habits,
 Partridges and rabbits,
 Who hast no cares
 Only to set snares
 Who liv'st all alone,
 Close to the bone,
 And where life is sweetest
 Constantly eatest.
When the spring stirs my blood
 With the instinct to travel
 I can get enough gravel
On the Old Marlborough Road.

Henry David Thoreau

Nobody repairs it,
For nobody wears it;
It is a living way,
As the Christians say.
Not many there be
Who enter therein,
Only the guests of the
Irishman Quin.
What is it, what is it,
But a direction out there,
And the bare possibility
Of going somewhere?
Great guide-boards of stone,
But travelers none;
Cenotaphs of the towns
Named on their crowns.
It is worth going to see
Where you *might* be.
What king
Did the thing,
I am still wondering;
Set up how or when,
By what selectmen,
Gourgas or Lee,
Clark or Darby?
They're a great endeavor
To be something forever;
Blank tablets of stone,
Where a traveler might groan,
And in one sentence
Grave all that is known;
Which another might read,
In his extreme need.
I know one or two
Lines that would do,
Literature that might stand
All over the land,
Which a man could remember
Till next December,
And read again in the Spring,
After the thawing.
If with fancy unfurled
You leave your abode,
You may go round the world
By the Old Marlborough Road.

At present, in this vicinity, the best part of the land is not private property; the landscape is not owned, and the walker enjoys comparative freedom. But possibly the day will come when it will be partitioned off into so-called pleasure-grounds, in which a few will take a narrow and exclusive pleasure only,—when fences shall be multipled, and man-traps and other engines invented to confine men to the *public* road, and walking over the surface of God's earth shall be construed to mean trespassing on some gentleman's grounds. To enjoy a thing exclusively is commonly to exclude yourself from the true enjoyment of it. Let us improve our opportunities, then, before the evil days come.

Walking

What is it that makes it so hard sometimes to determine whither we will walk? I believe that there is a subtle magnetism in Nature, which, if we unconsciously yield to it, will direct us aright. It is not indifferent to us which way we walk. There is a right way; but we are very liable from heedlessness and stupidity to take the wrong one. We would fain take that walk, never yet taken by us through this actual world, which is perfectly symbolical of the path which we love to travel in the interior and ideal world; and sometimes, no doubt, we find it difficult to choose our direction, because it does not yet exist distinctly in our idea.

When I go out of the house for a walk, uncertain as yet whither I will bend my steps, and submit myself to my instinct to decide for me, I find, strange and whimsical as it may seem, that I finally and inevitably settle southwest, toward some particular wood or meadow or deserted pasture or hill in that direction. My needle is slow to settle,—varies a few degrees, and does not always point due southwest, it is true, and it has good authority for this variation, but it always settles between west and south-southwest. The future lies that way to me, and the earth seems more unexhausted and richer on that side. The outline which would bound my walks would be, not a circle, but a parabola, or rather like one of those cometary orbits which have been thought to be non-returning curves, in this case opening westward, in which my house occupies the place of the sun. I turn round and round irresolute sometimes for a quarter of an hour, until I decide, for a thousandth time, that I will walk into the southwest or west. Eastward I go only by force; but westward I go free. Thither no business leads me. It is hard for me to believe that I shall find fair landscapes or sufficient wildness and freedom behind the eastern horizon. I am not excited by the prospect of a walk thither; but I believe that the forest which I see in the western horizon stretches uninterruptedly toward the setting sun, and there are no towns nor cities in it of enough consequence to disturb me. Let me live where I will, on this side is the city, on that the wilderness, and ever I am leaving the city more and more, and withdrawing into the wilderness. I should not lay so much stress on this fact, if I did not believe that something like this is the prevailing tendency of my countrymen. I must walk toward Oregon, and not toward Europe. And that way the nation is moving, and I may say that mankind progress from east to west. Within a few years we have witnessed the phenomenon of a southeastward migration, in the settlement of Australia; but this affects us as a retrograde movement, and, judging from the moral and physical character of the first generation of Australians, has not yet proved a successful experiment. The eastern Tartars think that there is nothing west beyond Thibet. "The world ends there," say they; "beyond there is nothing but a shoreless sea." It is unmitigated East where they live.

We go eastward to realize history and study the works of art and literature, retracing the steps of the race; we go westward as into the future, with a spirit of enterprise and adventure. The Atlantic is a Lethean stream, in our passage over which we have had an opportunity to forget the Old World and its institutions. If we do not succeed this time, there

Henry David Thoreau

is perhaps one more chance for the race left before it arrives on the banks of the Styx; and that is in the Lethe of the Pacific, which is three times as wide.

I know not how significant it is, or how far it is an evidence of singularity, that an individual should thus consent in his pettiest walk with the general movement of the race; but I know that something akin to the migratory instinct in birds and quadrupeds,—which, in some instances, is known to have affected the squirrel tribe, impelling them to a general and mysterious movement, in which they were seen, say some, crossing the broadest rivers, each on its particular chip, with its tail raised for a sail, and bridging narrower streams with their dead,—that something like the *furor* which affects the domestic cattle in the spring, and which is referred to a worm in their tails,—affects both nations and individuals, either perennially or from time to time. Not a flock of wild geese cackles over our town, but it to some extent unsettles the value of real estate here, and, if I were a broker, I should probably take that disturbance into account.

> "Than longen folk to gon on pilgrimages,
> And palmeres for to seken strange strondes."

Every sunset which I witness inspires me with the desire to go to a West as distant and as fair as that into which the sun goes down. He appears to migrate westward daily, and tempt us to follow him. He is the Great Western Pioneer whom the nations follow. We dream all night of those mountain-ridges in the horizon, though they may be of vapor only, which were last gilded by his rays. The island of Atlantis, and the islands and gardens of the Hesperides, a sort of terrestrial paradise, appear to have been the Great West of the ancients, enveloped in mystery and poetry. Who has not seen in imagination, when looking into the sunset sky, the gardens of the Hesperides, and the foundation of all those fables?

Columbus felt the westward tendency more strongly than any before. He obeyed it, and found a New World for Castile and Leon. The herd of men in those days scented fresh pastures from afar.

> "And now the sun had stretched out all the hills,
> And now was dropped into the western bay;
> At last *he* rose, and twitched his mantle blue;
> To-morrow to fresh woods and pastures new."

Where on the globe can there be found an area of equal extent with that occupied by the bulk of our States, so fertile and so rich and varied in its productions, and at the same time so habitable by the European, as this is? Michaux, who knew but part of them, says that "the species of large trees are much more numerous in North America than in Europe; in the United States there are more than one hundred and forty species that exceed thirty feet in height; in France there are but thirty that attain this size." Later botanists more than confirm his observations. Humboldt came to America to realize his youthful dreams of a tropical vegetation, and he

Walking

beheld it in its greatest perfection in the primitive forests of the Amazon, the most gigantic wilderness on the earth, which he has so eloquently described. The geographer Guyot, himself a European, goes farther,—farther than I am ready to follow him; yet not when he says: "As the plant is made for the animal, as the vegetable world is made for the animal world, America is made for the man of the Old World. . . . The man of the Old World sets out upon his way. Leaving the highlands of Asia, he descends from station to station towards Europe. Each of his steps is marked by a new civilization superior to the preceding, by a greater power of development. Arrived at the Atlantic, he pauses on the shore of this unknown ocean, the bounds of which he knows not, and turns upon his footprints for an instant." When he has exhausted the rich soil of Europe, and reinvigorated himself, "then recommences his adventurous career westward as in the earliest ages." So far Guyot.

From this western impulse coming in contact with the barrier of the Atlantic sprang the commerce and enterprise of modern times. The younger Michaux, in his "Travels West of the Alleghanies in 1802," says that the common inquiry in the newly settled West was, " 'From what part of the world have you come?' As if these vast and fertile regions would naturally be the place of meeting and common country of all the inhabitants of the globe."

To use an obsolete Latin word, I might say, *Ex Oriente lux; ex Occidente* FRUX. From the East light; from the West fruit.

Sir Francis Head, an English traveler and a Governor-General of Canada, tells us that "in both the northern and southern hemispheres of the New World, Nature has not only outlined her works on a larger scale, but has painted the whole picture with brighter and more costly colors than she used in delineating and in beautifying the Old World. . . . The heavens of America appear infinitely higher, the sky is bluer, the air is fresher, the cold is intenser, the moon looks larger, the stars are brighter, the thunder is louder, the lightning is vivider, the wind is stronger, the rain is heavier, the mountains are higher, the rivers longer, the forests bigger, the plains broader." This statement will do at least to set against Buffon's account of this part of the world and its productions.

Linnæus said long ago, "Nescio quæ facies *læta, glabra* plantis Americanis: I know not what there is of joyous and smooth in the aspect of American plants;" and I think that in this country there are no, or at most very few, *Africanæ bestiæ*, African beasts, as the Romans called them, and that in this respect also it is peculiarly fitted for the habitation of man. We are told that within three miles of the centre of the East-Indian city of Singapore, some of the inhabitants are annually carried off by tigers; but the traveler can lie down in the woods at night almost anywhere in North America without fear of wild beasts.

These are encouraging testimonies. If the moon looks larger here than in Europe, probably the sun looks larger also. If the heavens of America appear infinitely higher, and the stars brighter, I trust that these facts are symbolical of the height to which the philosophy and poetry and re-

Henry David Thoreau

ligion of her inhabitants may one day soar. At length, perchance, the immaterial heaven will appear as much higher to the American mind, and the
intimations that star it as much brighter. For I believe that climate does
thus react on man,—as there is something in the mountain-air that feeds
the spirit and inspires. Will not man grow to greater perfection intellectually as well as physically under these influences? Or is it unimportant
how many foggy days there are in his life? I trust that we shall be more
imaginative, that our thoughts will be clearer, fresher, and more ethereal,
as our sky,—our understanding more comprehensive and broader, like our
plains,—our intellect generally on a grander scale, like our thunder and
lightning, our rivers and mountains and forests,—and our hearts shall even
correspond in breadth and depth and grandeur to our inland seas. Perchance there will appear to the traveler something, he knows not what, of
læta and *glabra*, of joyous and serene, in our very faces. Else to what end
does the world go on, and why was America discovered?

To Americans I hardly need to say,—

"Westward the star of empire takes its way."

As a true patriot, I should be ashamed to think that Adam in paradise was
more favorably situated on the whole than the backwoodsman in this
country.

Our sympathies in Massachusetts are not confined to New England;
though we may be estranged from the South, we sympathize with the
West. There is the home of the younger sons, as among the Scandinavians
they took to the sea for their inheritance. It is too late to be studying
Hebrew; it is more important to understand even the slang of to-day.

Some months ago I went to see a panorama of the Rhine. It was
like a dream of the Middle Ages. I floated down its historic stream in
something more than imagination, under bridges built by the Romans, and
repaired by later heroes, past cities and castles whose very names were
music to my ears, and each of which was the subject of a legend. There
were Ehrenbreitstein and Rolandseck and Coblentz, which I knew only in
history. They were ruins that interested me chiefly. There seemed to come
up from its waters and its vine-clad hills and valleys a hushed music as of
Crusaders departing for the Holy Land. I floated along under the spell of
enchantment, as if I had been transported to an heroic age, and breathed
an atmosphere of chivalry.

Soon after, I went to see a panorama of the Mississippi, and as I
worked my way up the river in the light of to-day, and saw the steamboats
wooding up, counted the rising cities, gazed on the fresh ruins of Nauvoo,
beheld the Indians moving west across the stream, and, as before I had
looked up the Moselle, now looked up the Ohio and the Missouri and
heard the legends of Dubuque and of Wenona's Cliff,—still thinking more
of the future than of the past or present,—I saw that this was a Rhine
stream of a different kind; that the foundations of castles were yet to be
laid, and the famous bridges were yet to be thrown over the river; and I

Walking

felt that *this was the heroic age itself,* though we know it not, for the hero is commonly the simplest and obscurest of men.

The West of which I speak is but another name for the Wild; and what I have been preparing to say is, that in Wildness is the preservation of the World. Every tree sends its fibres forth in search of the Wild. The cities import it at any price. Men plough and sail for it. From the forest and wilderness come the tonics and barks which brace mankind. Our ancestors were savages. The story of Romulus and Remus being suckled by a wolf is not a meaningless fable. The founders of every state which has risen to eminence have drawn their nourishment and vigor from a similar wild source. It was because the children of the Empire were not suckled by the wolf that they were conquered and displaced by the children of the northern forests who were.

I believe in the forest, and in the meadow, and in the night in which the corn grows. We require an infusion of hemlock-spruce or arborvitæ in our tea. There is a difference between eating and drinking for strength and from mere gluttony. The Hottentots eagerly devour the marrow of the koodoo and other antelopes raw, as a matter of course. Some of our Northern Indians eat raw the marrow of the Arctic reindeer, as well as the various other parts, including the summits of the antlers, as long as they are soft. And herein, perchance, they have stolen a march on the cooks of Paris. They get what usually goes to feed the fire. This is probably better than stall-fed beef and slaughter-house pork to make a man of. Give me a wildness whose glance no civilization can endure,—as if we lived on the marrow of koodoos devoured raw.

There are some intervals which border the strain of the wood-thrush, to which I would migrate,—wild lands where no settler has squatted; to which, methinks, I am already acclimated.

The African hunter Cummings tells us that the skin of the eland, as well as that of most other antelopes just killed, emits the most delicious perfume of trees and grass. I would have every man so much like a wild antelope, so much a part and parcel of Nature, that his very person should thus sweetly advertise our senses of his presence, and remind us of those parts of Nature which he most haunts. I feel no disposition to be satirical, when the trapper's coat emits the odor of musquash even; it is a sweeter scent to me than that which commonly exhales from the merchant's or the scholar's garments. When I go into their wardrobes and handle their vestments, I am reminded of no grassy plains and flowery meads which they have frequented, but of dusty merchants' exchanges and libraries rather.

A tanned skin is something more than respectable, and perhaps olive is a fitter color than white for a man,—a denizen of the woods. "The pale white man!" I do not wonder that the African pitied him. Darwin the naturalist says, "A white man bathing by the side of a Tahitian was like a plant bleached by the gardener's art, compared with a fine, dark green one, growing vigorously in the open fields."

Henry David Thoreau

Ben Jonson exclaims,—

"How near to good is what is fair!"

So I would say,—

How near to good is what is *wild*!

Life consists with wildness. The most alive is the wildest. Not yet subdued to man, its presence refreshes him. One who pressed forward incessantly and never rested from his labors, who grew fast and made infinite demands on life, would always find himself in a new country or wilderness, and surrounded by the raw material of life. He would be climbing over the prostrate stems of primitive forest-trees.

Hope and the future for me are not in lawns and cultivated fields, not in towns and cities, but in the impervious and quaking swamps. When, formerly, I have analyzed my partiality for some farm which I had contemplated purchasing, I have frequently found that I was attracted solely by a few square rods of impermeable and unfathomable bog,—a natural sink in one corner of it. That was the jewel which dazzled me. I derive more of my subsistence from the swamps which surround my native town than from the cultivated gardens in the village. There are no richer parterres to my eyes than the dense beds of dwarf andromeda (*Cassandra calyculata*) which cover these tender places on the earth's surface. Botany cannot go farther than tell me the names of the shrubs which grow there, —the high-blueberry, panicled andromeda, lamb-kill, azalea, and rhodora,— all standing in the quaking sphagnum. I often think that I should like to have my house front on this mass of dull red bushes, omitting other flower plots and borders, transplanted spruce and trim box, even graveled walks,— to have this fertile spot under my windows, not a few imported barrow-fulls of soil only to cover the sand which was thrown out in digging the cellar. Why not put my house, my parlor, behind this plot, instead of·behind that meagre assemblage of curiosities, that poor apology for a Nature and Art, which I call my front yard? It is an effort to clear up and·make a decent appearance when the carpenter and mason have departed, though done as much for the passer-by as the dweller within. The most tasteful front-yard fence was never an agreeable object of study to me; the most elaborate ornaments, acorn-tops, or what not, soon wearied and disgusted me. Bring your sills up to the very edge of the swamp, then (though it may not be the best place for a dry cellar), so that there be no access on that side to citizens. Front yards are not made to walk in, but, at most, through, and you could go in the back way.

Yes, though you may think me perverse, if it were proposed to me to dwell in the neighborhood of the most beautiful garden that ever human art contrived, or else of a Dismal Swamp, I should certainly decide for the swamp. How vain, then, have been all your labors, citizens, for me!

My spirits infallibly rise in proportion to the outward dreariness.

Walking

Give me the ocean, the desert, or the wilderness! In the desert, pure air and solitude compensate for want of moisture and fertility. The traveler Burton says of it: "Your *morale* improves; you become frank and cordial, hospitable and single-minded. . . . In the desert, spirituous liquors excite only disgust. There is a keen enjoyment in a mere animal existence." They who have been traveling long on the steppes of Tartary say: "On reëntering cultivated lands, the agitation, perplexity, and turmoil of civilization oppressed and suffocated us; the air seemed to fail us, and we felt every moment as if about to die of asphyxia." When I would recreate myself, I seek the darkest wood, the thickest and most interminable and, to the citizen, most dismal swamp. I enter a swamp as a sacred place,—a *sanctum sanctorum*. There is the strength, the marrow of Nature. The wild-wood covers the virgin-mould,—and the same soil is good for men and for trees. A man's health requires as many acres of meadow to his prospect as his farm does loads of muck. There are the strong meats on which he feeds. A town is saved, not more by the righteous men in it than by the woods and swamps that surround it. A township where one primitive forest waves above while another primitive forest rots below,—such a town is fitted to raise not only corn and potatoes, but poets and philosophers for the coming ages. In such a soil grew Homer and Confucius and the rest, and out of such a wilderness comes the Reformer eating locusts and wild honey.

To preserve wild animals implies generally the creation of a forest for them to dwell in or resort to. So it is with man. A hundred years ago they sold bark in our streets peeled from our own woods. In the very aspect of those primitive and rugged trees there was, methinks, a tanning principle which hardened and consolidated the fibres of men's thoughts. Ah! already I shudder for these comparatively degenerate days of my native village, when you cannot collect a load of bark of good thickness,—and we no longer produce tar and turpentine.

The civilized nations—Greece, Rome, England—have been sustained by the primitive forests which anciently rotted where they stand. They survive as long as the soil is not exhausted. Alas for human culture! little is to be expected of a nation, when the vegetable mould is exhausted, and it is compelled to make manure of the bones of its fathers. There the poet sustains himself merely by his own superfluous fat, and the philosopher comes down on his marrow-bones.

It is said to be the task of the American "to work the virgin soil," and that "agriculture here already assumes proportions unknown everywhere else." I think that the farmer displaces the Indian even because he redeems the meadow, and so makes himself stronger and in some respects more natural. I was surveying for a man the other day a single straight line one hundred and thirty-two rods long, through a swamp, at whose entrance might have been written the words which Dante read over the entrance to the infernal regions,—"Leave all hope, ye that enter,"—that is, of ever getting out again; where at one time I saw my employer actually up to his neck and swimming for his life in his property, though it was still winter. He had another similar swamp which I could not survey at all, because it

Henry David Thoreau

was completely under water, and nevertheless, with regard to a third swamp, which I did *survey* from a distance, he remarked to me, true to his instincts, that he would not part with it for any consideration, on account of the mud which it contained. And that man intends to put a girdling ditch round the whole in the course of forty months, and so redeem it by the magic of his spade. I refer to him only as the type of a class.

The weapons with which we have gained our most important victories, which should be handed down as heirlooms from father to son, are not the sword and the lance, but the bushwhack, the turf-cutter, the spade, and the boghoe, rusted with the blood of many a meadow, and begrimed with the dust of many a hard-fought field. The very winds blew the Indian's corn-field into the meadow, and pointed out the way which he had not the skill to follow. He had no better implement with which to intrench himself in the land than a clam-shell. But the farmer is armed with plough and spade.

In literature it is only the wild that attracts us. Dullness is but another name for tameness. It is the uncivilized free and wild thinking in "Hamlet" and the "Iliad," in all the Scriptures and Mythologies, not learned in the schools, that delights us. As the wild duck is more swift and beautiful than the tame, so is the wild—the mallard—thought, which 'mid falling dews wings its way above the fens. A truly good book is something as natural, and as unexpectedly and unaccountably fair and perfect, as a wild flower discovered on the prairies of the West or in the jungles of the East. Genius is a light which makes the darkness visible, like the lightning's flash, which perchance shatters the temple of knowledge itself,—and not a taper lighted at the hearthstone of the race, which pales before the light of common day.

English literature, from the days of the minstrels to the Lake Poets, —Chaucer and Spenser and Milton, and even Shakespeare, included,— breathes no quite fresh and, in this sense, wild strain. It is an essentially tame and civilized literature, reflecting Greece and Rome. Her wilderness is a greenwood, her wild man a Robin Hood. There is plenty of genial love of Nature, but not so much of Nature herself. Her chronicles inform us when her wild animals, but not when the wild man in her, became extinct.

The science of Humboldt is one thing, poetry is another thing. The poet to-day, notwithstanding all the discoveries of science, and the accumulated learning of mankind, enjoys no advantage over Homer.

Where is the literature which gives expression to Nature? He would be a poet who could impress the winds and streams into his service, to speak for him; who nailed words to their primitive senses, as farmers drive down stakes in the spring, which the frost has heaved; who derived his words as often as he used them,—transplanted them to his page with earth adhering to their roots; whose words were so true and fresh and natural that they would appear to expand like the buds at the approach of spring, though they lay half-smothered between two musty leaves in a library, —ay, to bloom and bear fruit there, after their kind, annually, for the faithful reader, in sympathy with surrounding Nature.

Walking

I do not know of any poetry to quote which adequately expresses this yearning for the Wild. Approached from this side, the best poetry is tame. I do not know where to find in any literature, ancient or modern, any account which contents me of that Nature with which even I am acquainted. You will perceive that I demand something which no Augustan nor Elizabethan age, which no *culture*, in short, can give. Mythology comes nearer to it than anything. How much more fertile a Nature, at least, has Grecian mythology its root in than English literature! Mythology is the crop which the Old World bore before its soil was exhausted, before the fancy and imagination were affected with blight; and which it still bears, wherever its pristine vigor is unabated. All other literatures endure only as the elms which overshadow our houses; but this is like the great dragontree of the Western Isles, as old as mankind, and, whether that does or not, will endure as long; for the decay of other literatures makes the soil in which it thrives.

The West is preparing to add its fables to those of the East. The valleys of the Ganges, the Nile, and the Rhine having yielded their crop, it remains to be seen what the valleys of the Amazon, the Plate, the Orinoco, the St. Lawrence, and the Mississippi will produce. Perchance, when, in the course of ages, American liberty has become a fiction of the past,—as it is to some extent a fiction of the present,—the poets of the world will be inspired by American mythology.

The wildest dreams of wild men, even, are not the less true, though they may not recommend themselves to the sense which is most common among Englishmen and Americans to-day. It is not every truth that recommends itself to the common sense. Nature has a place for the wild clematis as well as for the cabbage. Some expressions of truth are reminiscent,— others merely *sensible*, as the phrase is,—others prophetic. Some forms of disease, even, may prophesy forms of health. The geologist has discovered that the figures of serpents, griffins, flying dragons, and other fanciful embellishments of heraldry, have their prototypes in the forms of fossil species which were extinct before man was created, and hence "indicate a faint and shadowy knowledge of a previous state of organic existence." The Hindoos dreamed that the earth rested on an elephant, and the elephant on a tortoise, and the tortoise on a serpent; and though it may be an unimportant coincidence, it will not be out of place here to state, that a fossile tortoise has lately been discovered in Asia large enough to support an elephant. I confess that I am partial to these wild fancies, which transcend the order of time and development. They are the sublimest recreation of the intellect. The partridge loves peas, but not those that go with her into the pot.

In short, all good things are wild and free. There is something in a strain of music, whether produced by an instrument or by the human voice,—take the sound of a bugle in a summer night, for instance,—which by its wildness, to speak without satire, reminds me of the cries emitted by wild beasts in their native forests. It is so much of their wildness as I can understand. Give me for my friends and neighbors wild men, not tame ones. The wildness of the savage is but a faint symbol of the awful ferity

Henry David Thoreau

with which good men and lovers meet.

I love even to see the domestic animals reassert their native rights,—any evidence that they have not wholly lost their original wild habits and vigor; as when my neighbor's cow breaks out of her pasture early in the spring and boldly swims the river, a cold, gray tide, twenty-five or thirty rods wide, swollen by the melted snow. It is the buffalo crossing the Mississippi. This exploit confers some dignity on the herd in my eyes,—already dignified. The seeds of instinct are preserved under the thick hides of cattle and horses, like seeds in the bowels of the earth, an indefinite period.

Any sportiveness in cattle is unexpected. I saw one day a herd of a dozen bullocks and cows running about and frisking in unwieldy sport, like huge rats, even like kittens. They shook their heads, raised their tails, and rushed up and down a hill, and I perceived by their horns, as well as by their activity, their relation to the deer tribe. But, alas! a sudden loud *Whoa!* would have damped their ardor at once, reduced them from venison to beef, and stiffened their sides and sinews like the locomotive. Who but the Evil One has cried, "Whoa!" to mankind? Indeed, the life of cattle, like that of many men, is but a sort of locomotiveness; they move a side at a time, and man, by his machinery, is meeting the horse and the ox half-way. Whatever part the whip has touched is thenceforth palsied. Who would ever think of a *side* of any of the supple cat tribe, as we speak of a *side* of beef?

I rejoice that horses and steers have to be broken before they can be made the slaves of men, and that men themselves have some wild oats still left to sow before they become submissive members of society. Undoubtedly, all men are not equally fit subjects for civilization; and because the majority, like dogs and sheep, are tame by inherited disposition, this is no reason why the others should have their natures broken that they may be reduced to the same level. Men are in the main alike, but they were made several in order that they might be various. If a low use is to be served, one man will do nearly or quite as well as another; if a high one, individual excellence is to be regarded. Any man can stop a hole to keep the wind away, but no other man could serve so rare a use as the author of this illustration did. Confucius says, "The skins of the tiger and the leopard, when they are tanned, are as the skins of the dog and the sheep tanned." But it is not the part of a true culture to tame tigers, any more than it is to make sheep ferocious; and tanning their skins for shoes is not the best use to which they can be put.

When looking over a list of men's names in a foreign language, as of military officers, or of authors who have written on a particular subject, I am reminded once more that there is nothing in a name. The name Menschikoff, for instance, has nothing in it to my ears more human than a whisker, and it may belong to a rat. As the names of the Poles and Russians are to us, so are ours to them. It is as if they had been named by the child's rigmarole,—*Iery wiery ichery van, tittle-tol-tan*. I see in my mind a herd of wild creatures swarming over the earth, and to each the herdsman has affixed some barbarous sound in his own dialect. The names of men are

Walking

of course as cheap and meaningless as *Bose* and *Tray*, the names of dogs.

Methinks it would be some advantage to philosophy, if men were named merely in the gross, as they are known. It would be necessary only to know the genus and perhaps the race or variety, to know the individual. We are not prepared to believe that every private soldier in a Roman army had a name of his own,—because we have not supposed that he had a character of his own.

At present our only true names are nicknames. I knew a boy who, from his peculiar energy, was called "Buster" by his playmates, and this rightly supplanted his Christian name. Some travelers tell us that an Indian had no name given him at first, but earned it, and his name was his fame; and among some tribes he acquired a new name with every new exploit. It is pitiful when a man bears a name for convenience merely, who has earned neither name nor fame.

I will not allow mere names to make distinctions for me, but still see men in herds for all them. A familiar name cannot make a man less strange to me. It may be given to a savage who retains in secret his own wild title earned in the woods. We have a wild savage in us, and a savage name is perchance somewhere recorded as ours. I see that my neighbor, who bears the familiar epithet William, or Edwin, takes it off with his jacket. It does not adhere to him when asleep or in anger, or aroused by any passion or inspiration. I seem to hear pronounced by some of his kin at such a time his original wild name in some jaw-breaking or else melodious tongue.

Here is this vast, savage, howling mother of ours, Nature, lying all around, with such beauty, and such affection for her children, as the leopard; and yet we are so early weaned from her breast to society, to that culture which is exclusively an interaction of man on man,—a sort of breeding in and in, which produces at most a merely English nobility, a civilization destined to have a speedy limit.

In society, in the best institutions of men, it is easy to detect a certain precocity. When we should still be growing children, we are already little men. Give me a culture which imports much muck from the meadows, and deepens the soil,—not that which trusts to heating manures, and improved implements and modes of culture only!

Many a poor sore-eyed student that I have heard of would grow faster, both intellectually and physically, if, instead of sitting up so very late, he honestly slumbered a fool's allowance.

There may be an excess even of informing light. Niepce, a Frenchman, discovered "actinism," that power in the sun's rays which produces a chemical effect; that granite rocks, and stone structures, and statues of metal, "are all alike destructively acted upon during the hours of sunshine, and, but for provisions of Nature no less wonderful, would soon perish under the delicate touch of the most subtile of the agencies of the universe." But he observed that "those bodies which underwent this change during the daylight possessed the power of restoring themselves to their original conditions during the hours of night, when this excitement was no

Henry David Thoreau

longer influencing them." Hence it has been inferred that "the hours of darkness are as necessary to the inorganic creation as we know night and sleep are to the organic kingdom." Not even does the moon shine every night, but gives place to darkness.

I would not have every man nor every part of a man cultivated, any more than I would have every acre of earth cultivated: part will be tillage, but the greater part will be meadow and forest, not only serving an immediate use, but preparing a mould against a distant future, by the annual decay of the vegetation which it supports.

There are other letters for the child to learn than those which Cadmus invented. The Spaniards have a good term to express this wild and dusky knowledge, *Gramática parda*, tawny grammar, a kind of mother-wit derived from that same leopard to which I have referred.

We have heard of a Society for the Diffusion of Useful Knowledge. It is said that knowledge is power; and the like. Methinks there is equal need of a Society for the Diffusion of Useful Ignorance, what we will call Beautiful Knowledge, a knowledge useful in a higher sense: for what is most of our boasted so-called knowledge but a conceit that we know something, which robs us of the advantage of our actual ignorance? What we call knowledge is often our positive ignorance; ignorance our negative knowledge. By long years of patient industry and reading of the newspapers,—for what are the libraries of science but files of newspapers?—a man accumulates a myriad facts, lays them up in his memory, and then when in some spring of his life he saunters abroad into the Great Fields of thought, he, as it were, goes to grass like a horse and leaves all his harness behind in the stable. I would say to the Society for the Diffusion of Useful Knowledge, sometimes,—Go to grass. You have eaten hay long enough. The spring has come with its green crop. The very cows are driven to their country pastures before the end of May; though I have heard of one unnatural farmer who kept his cow in the barn and fed her on hay all the year round. So, frequently, the Society for the Diffusion of Useful Knowledge treats its cattle.

A man's ignorance sometimes is not only useful, but beautiful,— while his knowledge, so called, is oftentimes worse than useless, besides being ugly. Which is the best man to deal with,—he who knows nothing about a subject, and, what is extremely rare, knows that he knows nothing, or he who really knows something about it, but thinks that he knows all?

My desire for knowledge is intermittent; but my desire to bathe my head in atmospheres unknown to my feet is perennial and constant. The highest that we can attain to is not Knowledge, but Sympathy with Intelligence. I do not know that this higher knowledge amounts to anything more definite than a novel and grand surprise on a sudden revelation of the insufficiency of all that we called Knowledge before,—a discovery that there are more things in heaven and earth than are dreamed of in our philosophy. It is the lighting up of the mist by the sun. Man cannot *know* in any higher sense than this, any more than he can look serenely and with impunity in the face of the sun: 'Ως τί νοῶν, οὐ κεῖνον νοήσεις,—"You will not perceive that, as perceiving a particular thing," say the Chaldean Oracles.

There is something servile in the habit of seeking after a law which we may obey. We may study the laws of matter at and for our convenience, but a successful life knows no law. It is an unfortunate discovery certainly, that of a law which binds us where we did not know before that we were bound. Live free, child of the mist,—and with respect to knowledge we are all children of the mist. The man who takes the liberty to live is superior to all the laws, by virtue of his relation to the law-maker. "That is active duty," says the Vishnu Purana, "which is not for our bondage; that is knowledge which is for our liberation: all other duty is good only unto weariness; all other knowledge is only the cleverness of an artist."

It is remarkable how few events or crises there are in our histories; how little exercised we have been in our minds; how few experiences we have had. I would fain be assured that I am growing apace and rankly, though my very growth disturb this dull equanimity,—though it be with struggle through long, dark, muggy nights or seasons of gloom. It would be well, if all our lives were a divine tragedy even, instead of this trivial comedy or farce. Dante, Bunyan, and others appear to have been exercised in their minds more than we: they were subjected to a kind of culture such as our district schools and colleges do not contemplate. Even Mahomet, though many may scream at his name, had a good deal more to live for, aye, and to die for, than they have commonly.

When, at rare intervals, some thought visits one, as perchance he is walking on a railroad, then indeed the cars go by without his hearing them. But soon, by some inexorable law, our life goes by and the cars return.

> "Gentle breeze, that wanderest unseen,
> And bendest the thistles round Loira of storms,
> Traveler of the windy glens,
> Why hast thou left my ear so soon?"

While almost all men feel an attraction drawing them to society, few are attracted strongly to Nature. In their reaction to Nature men appear to me for the most part, notwithstanding their arts, lower than the animals. It is not often a beautiful relation, as in the case of the animals. How little appreciation of the beauty of the landscape there is among us! We have to be told that the Greeks called the world Κόσμος, Beauty, or Order, but we do not see clearly why they did so, and we esteem it at best only a curious philological fact.

For my part, I feel that with regard to Nature I live a sort of border life, on the confines of a world into which I make occasional and transient forays only, and my patriotism and allegiance to the State into whose territories I seem to retreat are those of a moss-trooper. Unto a life which I call natural I would gladly follow even a will-o'-the-wisp through bogs and sloughs unimaginable, but no moon nor firefly has shown me the causeway to it. Nature is a personality so vast and universal that we have never seen one of her features. The walker in the familiar fields which stretch

Henry David Thoreau

around my native town sometimes finds himself in another land than is described in their owners' deeds, as it were in some far-away field on the confines of the actual Concord, where her jurisdiction ceases, and the idea which the word Concord suggests ceases to be suggested. These farms which I have myself surveyed, these bounds which I have set up, appear dimly still as through a mist; but they have no chemistry to fix them; they fade from the surface of the glass; and the picture which the painter painted stands out dimly from beneath. The world with which we are commonly acquainted leaves no trace, and it will have no anniversary.

I took a walk on Spaulding's Farm the other afternoon. I saw the setting sun lighting up the opposite side of a stately pine wood. Its golden rays straggled into the aisles of the wood as into some noble hall. I was impressed as if some ancient and altogether admirable and shining family had settled there in that part of the land called Concord, unknown to me, —to whom the sun was servant,—who had not gone into society in the village,—who had not been called on. I saw their park, their pleasure-ground, beyond through the wood, in Spaulding's cranberry-meadow. The pines furnished them with gables as they grew. Their house was not obvious to vision; the trees grew through it. I do not know whether I heard the sounds of a suppressed hilarity or not. They seemed to recline on the sunbeams. They have sons and daughters. They are quite well. The farmer's cart-path, which leads directly through their hall, does not in the least put them out, as the muddy bottom of a pool is sometimes seen through the reflected skies. They never heard of Spaulding, and do not know that he is their neighbor,—notwithstanding I heard him whistle as he drove his team through the house. Nothing can equal the serenity of their lives. Their coat of arms is simply a lichen. I saw it painted on the pines and oaks. Their attics were in the tops of the trees. They are of no politics. There was no noise of labor. I did not perceive that they were weaving or spinning. Yet I did detect, when the wind lulled and hearing was done away, the finest imaginable sweet musical hum,—as of a distant hive in May, which perchance was the sound of their thinking. They had no idle thoughts, and no one without could see their work, for their industry was not as in knots and excrescences embayed.

But I find it difficult to remember them. They fade irrevocably out of my mind even now while I speak, and endeavor to recall them and recollect myself. It is only after a long and serious effort to recollect my best thoughts that I become again aware of their cohabitancy. If it were not for such families as this, I think I should move out of Concord.

We are accustomed to say in New England that few and fewer pigeons visit us every year. Our forests furnish no mast for them. So, it would seem, few and fewer thoughts visit each growing man from year to year, for the grove in our minds is laid waste,—sold to feed unnecessary fires of ambition, or sent to mill, and there is scarcely a twig left for them to perch on. They no longer build nor breed with us. In some more genial season, perchance, a faint shadow flits across the landscape of the mind, cast by the *wings* of some thought in its vernal or autumnal migration, but, look-

Walking

ing up, we are unable to detect the substance of the thought itself. Our winged thoughts are turned to poultry. They no longer soar, and they attain only to a Shanghai and Cochin-China grandeur. Those *gra-a-ate thoughts*, those *gra-a-ate men* you hear of!

We hug the earth,—how rarely we mount! Methinks we might elevate ourselves a little more. We might climb a tree, at least. I found my account in climbing a tree once. It was a tall white-pine, on the top of a hill; and though I got well pitched, I was well paid for it, for I discovered new mountains in the horizon which I had never seen before,—so much more of the earth and the heavens. I might have walked about the foot of the tree for three-score years and ten, and yet I certainly should never have seen them. But, above all, I discovered around me,—it was near the end of June,—on the ends of the topmost branches only, a few minute and delicate red cone-like blossoms, the fertile flower of the white pine looking heavenward. I carried straightway to the village the topmost spire, and showed it to stranger jurymen who walked the streets,—for it was court-week,—and the farmers and lumber-dealers and wood-choppers and hunters, and not one had ever seen the like before, but they wondered as at a star dropped down. Tell of ancient architects finishing their works on the tops of columns as perfectly as on the lower and more visible parts! Nature has from the first expanded the minute blossoms of the forest only toward the heavens, above men's heads and unobserved by them. We see only the flowers that are under our feet in the meadows. The pines have developed their delicate blossoms on the highest twigs of the wood every summer for ages, as well over the heads of Nature's red children as of her white ones; yet scarcely a farmer or hunter in the land has ever seen them.

Above all, we cannot afford not to live in the present. He is blessed over all mortals who loses no moment of the passing life in remembering the past. Unless our philosophy hears the cock crow in every barn-yard within our horizon, it is belated. That sound commonly reminds us that we are growing rusty and antique in our employments and habits of thought. His philosophy comes down to a more recent time than ours. There is something suggested by it that is a newer testament,—the gospel according to this moment. He has not fallen astern; he has got up early and kept up early, and to be where he is is to be in season, in the foremost rank of time. It is an expression of the health and soundness of Nature, a brag for all the world,—healthiness as of a spring burst forth, a new fountain of the Muses, to celebrate this last instant of time. Where he lives no fugitive slave laws are passed. Who has not betrayed his master many times since last he heard that note?

The merit of this bird's strain is in its freedom from all plaintiveness. The singer can easily move us to tears or to laughter, but where is he who can excite in us a pure morning joy? When, in doleful dumps, breaking the awful stillness of our wooden sidewalk on a Sunday, or, perchance, a watcher in the house of mourning, I hear a cockerel crow far or near, I think to myself, "There is one of us well, at any rate,"—and with a sudden gush return to my senses.

Henry David Thoreau

We had a remarkable sunset one day last November. I was walking in a meadow, the source of a small brook, when the sun at last, just before setting, after a cold gray day, reached a clear stratum in the horizon, and the softest, brightest morning sunlight fell on the dry grass and on the stems of the trees in the opposite horizon and on the leaves of the shrub-oaks on the hillside, while our shadows stretched long over the meadow eastward, as if we were the only motes in its beams. It was such a light as we could not have imagined a moment before, and the air also was so warm and serene that nothing was wanting to make a paradise of that meadow. When we reflected that this was not a solitary phenomenon, never to happen again, but that it would happen forever and ever an infinite number of evenings, and cheer and reassure the latest child that walked there, it was more glorious still.

The sun sets on some retired meadow, where no house is visible, with all the glory and splendor that it lavishes on cities, and perchance as it has never set before,—where there is but a solitary marsh-hawk to have his wings gilded by it, or only a musquash looks out from his cabin, and there is some little black-veined brook in the midst of the marsh, just beginning to meander, winding slowly round a decaying stump. We walked in so pure and bright a light, gilding the withered grass and leaves, so softly and serenely bright, I thought I had never bathed in such a golden flood, without a ripple or a murmur to it. The west side of every wood and rising ground gleamed like the boundary of Elysium, and the sun on our backs seemed like a gentle herdsman driving us home at evening.

So we saunter toward the Holy Land, till one day the sun shall shine more brightly than ever he has done, shall perchance shine into our minds and hearts, and light up our whole lives with a great awakening light, as warm and serene and golden as on a bankside in autumn.

[1862]

Nathaniel Hawthorne:
The Pleasures of Walking

Nathaniel Hawthorne (1804-1864), writer of novels, short stories, and sketches, saw and defined much of the dark, turbulent, evil, and frightening side of human experience in his work. On occasion, he also saw life as idyllic and nature as fulfilling. His experiences at Brook Farm provide much of the natural foundation for the delightful record that is *The American Notebooks*.

Brook Farm, September 26th.—A walk this morning along the Needham road. A clear, breezy morning, after nearly a week of cloudy and showery weather. The grass is much more fresh and vivid than it was last month, and trees still retain much of their verdure, though here and there is a shrub or a bough arrayed in scarlet and gold. Along the road, in the midst of a beaten track, I saw mushrooms or toadstools which had sprung up probably during the night.

The houses in this vicinity are, many of them, quite antique, with long, sloping roofs, commencing at a few feet from the ground, and ending in a lofty peak. Some of them have huge old elms overshadowing the yard. One may see the family sleigh near the door, it having stood there all through the summer sunshine, and perhaps with weeds sprouting through the crevices of its bottom, the growth of the months since snow departed. Old barns, patched and supported by timbers leaning against the sides, and stained with the excrement of past ages.

In the forenoon I walked along the edge of the meadow towards Cow Island. Large trees, almost a wood, principally of pine with the green pasture-glades intermixed, and cattle feeding. They cease grazing when an intruder appears, and look at him with long and wary observation, then bend their heads to the pasture again. Where the firm ground of the pasture ceases, the meadow begins,—loose, spongy, yielding to the tread, sometimes permitting the foot to sink into black mud, or perhaps over ankles in water. Cattle-paths, somewhat firmer than the general surface, traverse the dense shrubbery which has overgrown the meadow. This shrubbery consists of small birch, elders, maples, and other trees, with here and there white-pines of larger growth. The whole is tangled and wild and thick-set, so that it is necessary to part the nestling stems and branches, and go crashing through. There are creeping plants of various sorts which clamber up the trees; and some of them have changed color in the slight frosts which already have befallen these low grounds, so that one sees a spiral wreath of scarlet leaves twining up to the top of a green tree, intermingling its bright hues with their verdure, as if all were of one piece. Sometimes, instead of scarlet, the spiral wreath is of a golden yellow.

Within the verge of the meadow, mostly near the firm shore of pasture ground, I found several grapevines, hung with an abundance of large purple grapes. The vines had caught hold of maples and alders, and climbed to the summit, curling round about and interwreathing their twisted folds in so intimate a manner that it was not easy to tell the parasite from the supporting tree or shrub. Sometimes the same vine had enveloped several shrubs, and caused a strange, tangled confusion, converting all these poor plants to the purpose of its own support, and hindering their growing to their own benefit and convenience. The broad vine-leaves, some of them yellow or yellowish-tinged, were seen apparently growing on the same stems with the silver-mapled leaves, and those of the other shrubs, thus married against their will by the conjugal twine; and the purple clusters of grapes hung down from above and in the midst, so that one might "gather grapes," if not "of thorns," yet of as alien bushes.

Nathaniel Hawthorne

One vine had ascended almost to the tip of a large white-pine, spreading its leaves and hanging its purple clusters among all its boughs,— still climbing and clambering, as if it would not be content till it had crowned the very summit with a wreath of its own foliage and bunches of grapes. I mounted high into the tree, and ate the fruit there, while the vine wreathed still higher into the depths above my head. The grapes were sour, being not yet fully ripe. Some of them, however, were sweet and pleasant. . . .

October 7th.—Since Saturday last (it being now Thursday), I have been in Boston and Salem, and there has been a violent storm and rain during the whole time. This morning shone as bright as if it meant to make up for all the dismalness of the past days. Our brook, which in the summer was no longer a running stream, but stood in pools along its pebbly course, is now full from one grassy verge to the other, and hurries along with a murmuring rush. It will continue to swell, I suppose, and in the winter and spring it will flood all the broad meadows through which it flows.

I have taken a long walk this forenoon along the Needham road, and across the bridge, thence pursuing a cross-road through the woods, parallel with the river, which I crossed again at Dedham. Most of the road lay through a growth of young oaks principally. They still retain their verdure, though, looking closely in among them, one perceives the broken sunshine falling on a few sere or bright-hued tufts of shrubbery. In low, marshy spots, on the verge of the meadows or along the river-side, there is a much more marked autumnal change. Whole ranges of bushes are there painted with many variegated hues, not of the brightest tint, but of a sober cheerfulness. I suppose this is owing more to the late rains than to the frost; for a heavy rain changes the foliage somewhat at this season. The first marked frost was seen last Saturday morning. Soon after sunrise it lay, white as snow, over all the grass, and on the tops of the fences, and in the yard, on the heap of firewood. On Sunday, I think, there was a fall of snow, which, however, did not lie on the ground a moment.

There is no season when such pleasant and sunny spots may be lighted on, and produce so pleasant an effect on the feelings, as now in October. The sunshine is peculiarly genial; and in sheltered places, as on the side of a bank, or of a barn or house, one becomes acquainted and friendly with the sunshine. It seems to be of a kindly and homely nature. And the green grass, strewn with a few withered leaves, looks the more green and beautiful for them. In summer or spring, Nature is farther from one's sympathies.

October 8th.—Another gloomy day, lowering with portents of rain close at hand. I have walked up into the pastures this morning, and looked about me a little. The woods present a very diversified appearance just now, with perhaps more varieties of tint than they are destined to wear at a somewhat later period. There are some strong yellow hues, and some deep red; there are innumerable shades of green, some few having the depth of summer; others, partially changed towards yellow, look freshly verdant with the delicate tinge of early summer or of May. Then there is the solemn and dark green of the pines. The effect is, that every tree in

The Pleasures of Walking

the wood and every bush among the shrubbery has a separate existence, since, confusedly intermingled, each wears its peculiar color, instead of being lost in the universal emerald of summer. And yet there is a oneness of effect likewise, when we choose to look at a whole sweep of woodland instead of analyzing its component trees. Scattered over the pasture, which the late rains have kept tolerably green, there are spots or islands of dusky red,—a deep, substantial hue, very well fit to be close to the ground,—while the yellow, and light, fantastic shades of green soar upward to the sky. These red spots are the blueberry and whortleberry bushes. The sweet-fern is changed mostly to russet, but still retains its wild and delightful fragrance when pressed in the hand. Wild China asters are scattered about, but beginning to wither. A little while ago, mushrooms or toadstools were very numerous along the wood-paths and by the roadsides, especially after rain. Some were of spotless white, some yellow, and some scarlet. They are always mysteries and objects of interest to me, springing as they do so suddenly from no root or seed, and growing one wonders why. I think, too, that some varieties are pretty objects, little fairy tables, centre-tables, standing on one leg. But their growth appears to be checked now, and they are of a brown tint and decayed.

The farm business to-day is to dig potatoes. I worked a little at it. The process is to grasp all the stems of a hill and pull them up. A great many of the potatoes are thus pulled, clinging to the stems and to one another in curious shapes,—long red things, and little round ones, imbedded in the earth which clings to the roots. These being plucked off, the rest of the potatoes are dug out of the hill with a hoe, the tops being flung into a heap for the cow-yard. On my way home, I paused to inspect the squash-field. Some of the squashes lay in heaps as they were gathered, presenting much variety of shape and hue,—as golden yellow, like great lumps of gold, dark green, striped and variegated; and some were round, and some lay curling their long necks, nestling, as it were, and seeming as if they had life.

In my walk yesterday forenoon I passed an old house which seemed to be quite deserted. It was a two-story, wooden house, dark and weather-beaten. The front windows, some of them, were shattered and open, and others were boarded up. Trees and shrubbery were growing neglected, so as quite to block up the lower part. There was an aged barn near at hand, so ruinous that it had been necessary to prop it up. There were two old carts, both of which had lost a wheel. Everything was in keeping. At first I supposed that there would be no inhabitants in such a dilapidated place; but, passing on, I looked back, and saw a decrepit and infirm old man at the angle of the house, its fit occupant. The grass, however, was very green and beautiful around this dwelling, and, the sunshine falling brightly on it, the whole effect was cheerful and pleasant. It seemed as if the world was so glad that this desolate old place, where there was never to be any more hope and happiness, could not at all lessen the general effect of joy.

I found a small turtle by the roadside, where he had crept to warm himself in the genial sunshine. He had a sable back, and underneath his

Nathaniel Hawthorne

shell was yellow, and at the edges bright scarlet. His head, tail, and claws were striped yellow, black, and red. He withdrew himself as far as he possibly could into his shell, and absolutely refused to peep out, even when I put him into the water. Finally, I threw him into a deep pool and left him. These mailed gentlemen, from the size of a foot or more down to an inch, were very numerous in the spring; and now the smaller kind appear again.

Saturday, October 9th.—Still dismal weather. Our household, being composed in great measure of children and young people, is generally a cheerful one enough, even in gloomy weather. For a week past we have been especially gladdened with a little seamstress from Boston, about seventeen years old; but of such a *petite* figure, that, at first view, one would take her to be hardly in her teens. She is very vivacious and smart, laughing and singing and talking all the time,—talking sensibly; but still, taking the view of matters that a city girl naturally would. If she were larger than she is, and of less pleasing aspect, I think she might be intolerable; but being so small, and with a fair skin, and as healthy as a wildflower, she is really very agreeable; and to look at her face is like being shone upon by a ray of the sun. She never walks, but bounds and dances along, and this motion, in her diminutive person, does not give the idea of violence. It is like a bird, hopping from twig to twig, and chirping merrily all the time. Sometimes she is rather vulgar, but even that works well enough into her character, and accords with it. On continued observation, one discovers that she is not a little girl, but really a little woman, with all the prerogatives and liabilities of a woman. This gives a new aspect to her, while the girlish impression still remains, and is strangely combined with the sense that this frolicsome maiden has the material for the sober bearing of a wife. She romps with the boys, runs races with them in the yard, and up and down the stairs, and is heard scolding laughingly at their rough play. She asks William Allen to place her "on top of that horse," whereupon he puts his large brown hands about her waist, and, swinging her to and fro, lifts her on horseback. William threatens to rivet two horseshoes round her neck, for having clambered, with the other girls and boys, upon a load of hay, whereby the said load lost its balance and slid off the cart. She strings the seed-berries of roses together, making a scarlet necklace of them, which she fastens about her throat. She gathers flowers of everlasting to wear in her bonnet, arranging them with the skill of a dress-maker. In the evening, she sits singing by the hour, with the musical part of the establishment, often breaking into laughter, whereto she is incited by the tricks of the boys. The last thing one hears of her, she is tripping up stairs to bed, talking lightsomely or warbling; and one meets her in the morning, the very image of bright morn itself, smiling briskly at you, so that one takes her for a promise of cheerfulness through the day. Be it said, with all the rest, that there is a perfect maiden modesty in her deportment. She has just gone away, and the last I saw of her was her vivacious face peeping through the curtain of the cariole, and nodding a gay farewell to the family, who were shouting their adieus at the door. With her other merits, she is an excellent daughter, and supports her mother by the labor of her

The Pleasures of Walking

hands. It would be difficult to conceive beforehand how much can be added to the enjoyment of a household by mere sunniness of temper and liveliness of disposition; for her intellect is very ordinary, and she never says anything worth hearing, or even laughing at, in itself. But she herself is an expression well worth studying.

Brook Farm, October 9th.—A walk this afternoon to Cow Island. The clouds had broken away towards noon, and let forth a few sunbeams, and more and more blue sky ventured to appear, till at last it was really warm and sunny,—indeed, rather too warm in the sheltered hollows, though it is delightful to be too warm now, after so much stormy chillness. Oh the beauty of grassy slopes, and the hollow ways of paths winding between hills, and the intervals between the road and wood-lots, where Summer lingers and sits down, strewing dandelions of gold, and blue asters, as her parting gifts and memorials! I went to a grapevine, which I have already visited several times, and found some clusters of grapes still remaining, and now perfectly ripe. Coming within view of the river, I saw several wild ducks under the shadow of the opposite shore, which was high, and covered with a grove of pines. I should not have discovered the ducks had they not risen and skimmed the surface of the glassy stream, breaking its dark water with a bright streak, and, sweeping round, gradually rose high enough to fly away. I likewise started a partridge just within the verge of the woods, and in another place a large squirrel ran across the wood-path from one shelter of trees to the other. Small birds, in flocks, were flitting about the fields, seeking and finding I know not what sort of food. There were little fish, also, darting in shoals through the pools and depths of the brooks, which are now replenished to their brims, and rush towards the river with a swift, amber-colored current.

Cow Island is not an island,—at least, at this season,—though, I believe, in the time of freshets, the marshy Charles floods the meadows all round about it, and extends across its communication with the mainland. The path to it is a very secluded one, threading a wood of pines, and just wide enough to admit the loads of meadow hay which are drawn from the splashy shore of the river. The island has a growth of stately pines, with tall and ponderous stems, standing at distance enough to admit the eye to travel far among them; and, as there is no underbrush, the effect is somewhat like looking among the pillars of a church.

I returned home by the high-road. On my right, separated from the road by a level field, perhaps fifty yards across, was a range of young forest-trees, dressed in their garb of autumnal glory. The sun shone directly upon them; and sunlight is like the breath of life to the pomp of autumn. In its absence, one doubts whether there be any truth in what poets have told about the splendor of an American autumn; but when this charm is added, one feels that the effect is beyond description. As I beheld it to-day, there was nothing dazzling; it was gentle and mild, though brilliant and diversified, and had a most quiet and pensive influence. And yet there were some trees that seemed really made of sunshine, and others were of a sunny red, and the whole picture was painted with but little relief of darksome hues,—

Nathaniel Hawthorne

only a few evergreens. But there was nothing inharmonious; and, on closer examination, it appeared that all the tints had a relationship among themselves. And this, I suppose, is the reason that, while nature seems to scatter them so carelessly, they still never shock the beholder by their contrasts, nor disturb, but only soothe. The brilliant scarlet and the brilliant yellow are different hues of the maple-leaves, and the first changes into the last. I saw one maple-tree, its centre yellow as gold, set in a framework of red. The native poplars have different shades of green, verging towards yellow, and are very cheerful in the sunshine. Most of the oak-leaves have still the deep verdure of summer; but where a change has taken place, it is into a russet-red, warm, but sober. These colors, infinitely varied by the progress which different trees have made in their decay, constitute almost the whole glory of autumnal woods; but it is impossible to conceive how much is done with such scanty materials. In my whole walk I saw only one man, and he was at a distance, in the obscurity of the trees. He had a horse and a wagon, and was getting a load of dry brushwood.

Sunday, October 10th.—I visited my grapevine this afternoon, and ate the last of its clusters. This vine climbs around a young maple-tree, which has now assumed the yellow leaf. The leaves of the vine are more decayed than those of the maple. Thence to Cow Island, a solemn and thoughtful walk. Returned by another path, of the width of a wagon, passing through a grove of hard wood, the lightsome hues of which make the walk more cheerful than among the pines. The roots of oaks emerged from the soil, and contorted themselves across the path. The sunlight, also, broke across in spots, and otherwheres the shadow was deep; but still there was intermingling enough of bright hues to keep off the gloom from the whole path.

Brooks and pools have a peculiar aspect at this season. One knows that the water must be cold, and one shivers a little at the sight of it; and yet the grass about the pool may be of the deepest green, and the sun may be shining into it. The withered leaves which overhanging trees shed upon its surface contribute much to the effect.

Insects have mostly vanished in the fields and woods. I hear locusts yet, singing in the sunny hours, and crickets have not yet finished their song. Once in a while I see a caterpillar,—this afternoon, for instance, a red, hairy one, with black head and tail. They do not appear to be active, and it makes one rather melancholy to look at them.

Tuesday, October 12th.—The cawing of the crow resounds among the woods. A sentinel is aware of your approach a great way off, and gives the alarm to his comrades loudly and eagerly,—Caw, caw, caw! Immediately the whole conclave replies, and you behold them rising above the trees, flapping darkly, and winging their way to deeper solitudes. Sometimes, however, they remain till you come near enough to discern their sable gravity of aspect, each occupying a separate bough, or perhaps the blasted tip-top of a pine. As you approach, one after another, with loud cawing, flaps his wings and throws himself upon the air.

There is hardly a more striking feature in the landscape nowadays

The Pleasures of Walking

than the red patches of blueberry and whortleberry bushes, as seen on a sloping hill-side, like islands among the grass, with trees growing in them; or crowning the summit of a bare, brown hill with their somewhat russet liveliness; or circling round the base of an earth-imbedded rock. At a distance, this hue, clothing spots and patches of the earth, looks more like a picture than anything else,—yet such a picture as I never saw painted.

The oaks are now beginning to look sere, and their leaves have withered borders. It is pleasant to notice the wide circle of greener grass beneath the circumference of an overshadowing oak. Passing an orchard, one hears an uneasy rustling in the trees, and not as if they were struggling with the wind. Scattered about are barrels to contain the gathered apples; and perhaps a great heap of golden or scarlet apples is collected in one place.

Wednesday, October 13th.—A good view, from an upland swell of our pasture, across the valley of the river Charles. There is the meadow, as level as a floor, and carpeted with green, perhaps two miles from the rising ground on this side of the river to that on the opposite side. The stream winds through the midst of the flat space, without any banks at all; for it fills its bed almost to the brim, and bathes the meadow grass on either side. A tuft of shrubbery, at broken intervals, is scattered along its border; and thus it meanders sluggishly along, without other life than what it gains from gleaming in the sun. Now, into the broad, smooth meadow, as into a lake, capes and headlands put themselves forth, and shores of firm woodland border it, covered with variegated foliage, making the contrast so much the stronger of their height and rough outline with the even spread of the plain. And beyond, and far away, rises a long, gradual swell of country, covered with an apparently dense growth of foliage for miles, till the horizon terminates it; and here and there is a house, or perhaps two, among the contiguity of trees. Everywhere the trees wear their autumnal dress, so that the whole landscape is red, russet, orange, and yellow, blending in the distance into a rich tint of brown-orange, or nearly that,—except the green expanse so definitely hemmed in by the higher ground.

I took a long walk this morning, going first nearly to Newton, thence nearly to Brighton, thence to Jamaica Plain, and thence home. It was a fine morning, with a northwest-wind; cool when facing the wind, but warm and most genially pleasant in sheltered spots; and warm enough everywhere while I was in motion. I traversed most of the by-ways which offered themselves to me; and, passing through one in which there was a double line of grass between the wheel-tracks and that of the horses' feet, I came to where had once stood a farmhouse, which appeared to have been recently torn down. Most of the old timber and boards had been carted away; a pile of it, however, remained. The cellar of the house was uncovered, and beside it stood the base and middle height of the chimney. The oven, in which household bread had been baked for daily food, and puddings and cake and jolly pumpkin-pies for festivals, opened its mouth, being deprived of its iron door. The fireplace was close at hand. All round the site of the house was a pleasant, sunny, green space, with old fruit-trees in pretty fair condition, though aged. There was a barn, also aged,

Nathaniel Hawthorne

but in decent repair; and a ruinous shed, on the corner of which was nailed a boy's windmill, where it had probably been turning and clattering for years together, till now it was black with time and weather-stain. It was broken, but still it went round whenever the wind stirred. The spot was entirely secluded, there being no other house within a mile or two.

No language can give an idea of the beauty and glory of the trees, just at this moment. It would be easy, by a process of word-daubing, to set down a confused group of gorgeous colors, like a bunch of tangled skeins of bright silk; but there is nothing of the reality in the glare which would thus be produced. And yet the splendor both of individual clusters and of whose scenes is unsurpassable. The oaks are now far advanced in their change of hue; and, in certain positions relatively to the sun, they light up and gleam with a most magnificent deep gold, varying according as portions of the foliage are in shadow or sunlight. On the sides which receive the direct rays, the effect is altogether rich; and in other points of view it is equally beautiful, if less brilliant. This color of the oak is more superb than the lighter yellow of the maples and walnuts. The whole landscape is now covered with this indescribable pomp; it is discerned on the uplands afar off; and Blue Hill in Milton, at the distance of several miles, actually glistens with rich, dark light,—no, not glistens, nor gleams,—but perhaps to say glows subduedly will be a truer expression for it.

Met few people this morning; a grown girl, in company with a little boy, gathering barberries in a secluded lane; a portly, autumnal gentleman, wrapped in a great-coat, who asked the way to Mr. Joseph Goddard's; and a fish-cart from the city, the driver of which sounded his horn along the lonesome way.

Monday, October 18th.—There has been a succession of days which were cold and bright in the forenoon, and gray, sullen, and chill towards night. The woods have now taken a soberer tint than they wore at my last date. Many of the shrubs which looked brightest a little while ago are now wholly bare of leaves. The oaks have generally a russet-brown shade, although some of them are still green, as are likewise other scattered trees in the forests. The bright yellow and the rich scarlet are no more to be seen. Scarcely any of them will now bear a close examination; for this shows them to be rugged, wilted, and of faded, frost-bitten hue; but at a distance, and in the mass, and enlivened by the sun, they have still somewhat of the varied splendor which distinguished them a week ago. It is wonderful what a difference the sunshine makes; it is like varnish, bringing out the hidden veins in a piece of rich wood. In the cold, gray atmosphere, such as that of most of our afternoons now, the landscape lies dark, —brown, and in a much deeper shadow than if it were clothed in green. But, perchance, a gleam of sun falls on a certain spot of distant shrubbery or woodland, and we see it brighten with many hues, standing forth prominently from the dimness around it. The sunlight gradually spreads, and the whole sombre scene is changed to a motley picture,—the sun bringing out many shades of color, and converting its gloom to an almost laughing cheerfulness. At such times I almost doubt whether the foliage has lost any

The Pleasures of Walking

of its brilliancy. But the clouds intercept the sun again, and lo! old Autumn appears, clad in his cloak of russet-brown.

Beautiful now, while the general landscape lies in shadow, looks the summit of a distant hill (say a mile off), with the sunshine brightening the trees that cover it. It is noticeable that the outlines of hills, and the whole bulk of them at the distance of several miles, become stronger, denser, and more substantial in this autumn atmosphere and in these autumnal tints than in summer. Then they looked blue, misty, and dim. Now they show their great humpbacks more plainly, as if they had drawn nearer to us.

A waste of shrubbery and small trees, such as overruns the borders of the meadows for miles together, looks much more rugged, wild, and savage in its present brown color than when clad in green.

I passed through a very pleasant wood-path yesterday, quite shut in and sheltered by trees that had not thrown off their yellow robes. The sun shone strongly in among them, and quite kindled them; so that the path was brighter for their shade than if it had been quite exposed to the sun.

In the village graveyard, which lies contiguous to the street, I saw a man digging a grave, and one inhabitant after another turned aside from his way to look into the grave and talk with the digger. I heard him laugh, with the traditional mirthfulness of men of that occupation.

In the hollow of the woods, yesterday afternoon, I lay a long while watching a squirrel, who was capering about among the trees over my head (oaks and white-pines, so close together that their branches intermingled). The squirrel seemed not to approve of my presence, for he frequently uttered a sharp, quick, angry noise, like that of a scissors-grinder's wheel. Sometimes I could see him sitting on an impending bough, with his tail over his back, looking down pryingly upon me. It seems to be a natural posture with him, to sit on his hind legs, holding up his fore paws. Anon, with a peculiarly quick start, he would scramble along the branch, and be lost to sight in another part of the tree, whence his shrill chatter would again be heard. Then I would see him rapidly descending the trunk, and running along the ground; and a moment afterwards, casting my eye upward, I beheld him flitting like a bird among the high limbs at the summit, directly above me. Afterwards, he apparently became accustomed to my society, and set about some business of his own. He came down to the ground, took up a piece of a decayed bough (a heavy burden for such a small personage), and, with this in his mouth, again climbed up and passed from the branches of one tree to those of another, and thus onward and onward till he went out of sight. Shortly afterwards he returned for another burden, and this he repeated several times. I suppose he was building a nest,—at least, I know not what else could have been his object. Never was there such an active, cheerful, choleric, continually-in-motion fellow as this little red squirrel, talking to himself, chattering at me, and as sociable in his own person as if he had half a dozen companions, instead of being alone in the lonesome wood. Indeed, he flitted about so quickly, and showed himself in different places so suddenly, that I was in some doubt whether there were not two or three of them.

Nathaniel Hawthorne

I must mention again the very beautiful effect produced by the masses of berry-bushes, lying like scarlet islands in the midst of withered pasture-ground, or crowning the tops of barren hills. Their hue, at a distance, is lustrous scarlet, although it does not look nearly as bright and gorgeous when examined close at hand. But at a proper distance it is a beautiful fringe on Autumn's petticoat.

Friday, October 22d.—A continued succession of unpleasant, Novembery days, and autumn has made rapid progress in the work of decay. It is now somewhat of a rare good fortune to find a verdant, grassy spot, on some slope, or in a dell; and even such seldom-seen oases are bestrewn with dried brown leaves,—which, however, methinks, make the short, fresh grass look greener around them. Dry leaves are now plentiful everywhere, save where there are none but pine-trees. They rustle beneath the tread, and there is nothing more autumnal than that sound. Nevertheless, in a walk this afternoon, I have seen two oaks which retained almost the greenness of summer. They grew close to the huge Pulpit Rock, so that portions of their trunks appeared to grasp the rough surface; and they were rooted beneath it, and, ascending high into the air, overshadowed the gray crag with verdure. Other oaks, here and there, have a few green leaves or boughs among their rustling and rugged shade.

Yet, dreary as the woods are in a bleak, sullen day, there is a very peculiar sense of warmth and a sort of richness of effect in the slope of a bank and in sheltered spots, where bright sunshine falls, and the brown oaken foliage is gladdened by it. There is then a feeling of comfort, and consequently of heart-warmth, which cannot be experienced in summer. . . .

[1841]

The Pleasures of Walking

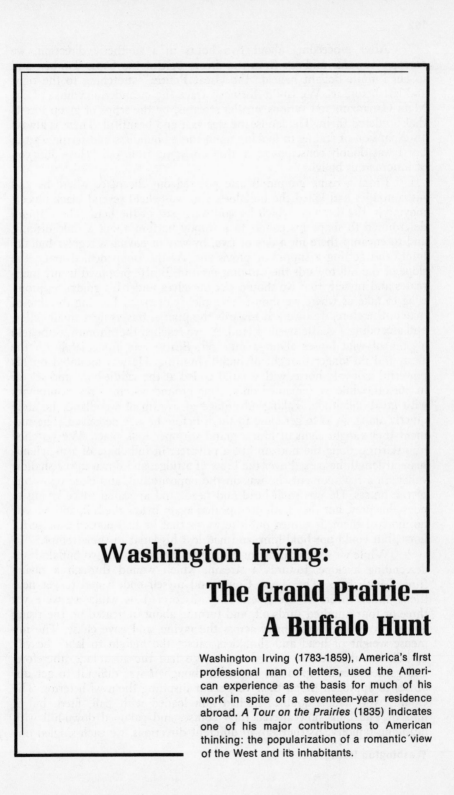

Washington Irving:
The Grand Prairie—
A Buffalo Hunt

Washington Irving (1783-1859), America's first
professional man of letters, used the American experience as the basis for much of his
work in spite of a seventeen-year residence
abroad. *A Tour on the Prairies* (1835) indicates
one of his major contributions to American
thinking: the popularization of a romantic view
of the West and its inhabitants.

After proceeding about two hours in a southerly direction, we emerged towards mid-day from the dreary belt of the Cross Timber, and to our infinite delight beheld "the Great Prairie," stretching to the right and left before us. We could distinctly trace the meandering course of the Main Canadian, and various smaller streams, by the strips of green forests that bordered them. The landscape was vast and beautiful. There is always an expansion of feeling in looking upon these boundless and fertile wastes; but I was doubly conscious of it after emerging from our "close dungeon of innumerous boughs."

From a rising ground Beatte pointed out the place where he and his comrades had killed the buffaloes; and we beheld several black objects moving in the distance, which he said were part of the herd. The Captain determined to shape his course to a woody bottom about a mile distant, and to encamp there for a day or two, by way of having a regular buffalo-hunt, and getting a supply of provisions. As the troop defiled along the slope of the hill towards the camping-ground, Beatte proposed to my mess-mates and myself, that we should put ourselves under his guidance, promising to take us where we should have plenty of sport. Leaving the line of march, therefore, we diverged towards the prairie; traversing a small valley, and ascending a gentle swell of land. As we reached the summit, we beheld a gang of wild horses about a mile off. Beatte was immediately on the alert, and no longer thought of buffalo-hunting. He was mounted on his powerful half-wild horse, with a lariat coiled at the saddle-bow, and set off in pursuit; while we remained on a rising ground watching his manœuvres with great solicitude. Taking advantage of a strip of woodland, he stole quietly along, so as to get close to them before he was perceived. The moment they caught sight of him a grand scamper took place. We watched him skirting along the horizon like a privateer in full chase of a merchant-man; at length he passed over the brow of a ridge, and down into a shallow valley; in a few moments he was on the opposite hill, and close upon one of the horses. He was soon head and head, and appeared to be trying to noose his prey; but they both disappeared again below the hill, and we saw no more of them. It turned out afterwards that he had noosed a powerful horse, but could not hold him, and had lost his lariat in the attempt.

While we were waiting for his return, we perceived two buffalo bulls descending a slope, towards a stream, which wound through a ravine fringed with trees. The young Count and myself endeavored to get near them under covert of the trees. They discovered us while we were yet three or four hundred yards off, and turning about, retreated up the rising ground. We urged our horses across the ravine, and gave chase. The immense weight of head and shoulders causes the buffalo to labor heavily up-hill; but it accelerates his descent. We had the advantage, therefore, and gained rapidly upon the fugitives, though it was difficult to get our horses to approach them, their very scent inspiring them with terror. The Count, who had a double-barrelled gun loaded with ball, fired, but it missed. The bulls now altered their course, and galloped down-hill with headlong rapidity. As they ran in different directions, we each singled one

Washington Irving

and separated. I was provided with a brace of veteran brass-barrelled pistols, which I had borrowed at Fort Gibson, and which had evidently seen some service. Pistols are very effective in buffalo hunting, as the hunter can ride up close to the animal, and fire it while at full speed; whereas the long heavy rifles used on the frontier, cannot be easily managed, nor discharged with accurate aim from horseback. My object, therefore, was to get within pistol-shot of the buffalo. This was no very easy matter. I was well mounted on a horse of excellent speed and bottom, that seemed eager for the chase, and soon overtook the game; but the moment he came nearly parallel, he would keep sheering off, with ears forked and pricked forward, and every symptom of aversion and alarm. It was no wonder. Of all animals, a buffalo, when close pressed by the hunter, has an aspect the most diabolical. His two short black horns curve out of a huge frontlet of shaggy hair; his eyes glow like coals; his mouth is open; his tongue parched and drawn up into a half crescent; his tail is erect, and tufted and whisking about in the air: he is a perfect picture of mingled rage and terror.

It was with difficulty I urged my horse sufficiently near, when, taking aim, to my chagrin both pistols missed fire. Unfortunately the locks of these veteran weapons were so much worn, that in the gallop the priming had been shaken out of the pans. At the snapping of the last pistol I was close upon the buffalo, when, in his despair, he turned round with a sudden snort, and rushed upon me. My horse wheeled about as if on a pivot, made a convulsive spring, and, as I had been leaning on one side with pistol extended, I came near being thrown at the feet of the buffalo.

Three or four bounds of the horse carried us out of the reach of the enemy, who, having merely turned in desperate self-defence, quickly resumed his flight. As soon as I could gather in my panic-stricken horse, and prime the pistols afresh, I again spurred in pursuit of the buffalo, who had slackened his speed to take breath. On my approach he again set off full tilt, heaving himself forward with a heavy rolling gallop, dashing with headlong precipitation through brakes and ravines, while several deer and wolves, startled from their coverts by his thundering career, ran helter-skelter to right and left across the waste.

A gallop across the prairies in pursuit of game is by no means so smooth a career as those may imagine who have only the idea of an open level plain. It is true, the prairies of the hunting-ground are not so much entangled with flowering plants and long herbage as the lower prairies, and are principally covered with short buffalo-grass; but they are diversified by hill and dale, and where most level, are apt to be cut up by deep rifts and ravines, made by torrents after rains; and which, yawning from an even surface, are almost like pitfalls in the way of the hunter, checking him suddenly when in full career, or subjecting him to the risk of limb and life. The plains, too, are beset by burrowing-holes of small animals, in which the horse is apt to sink to the fetlock, and throw both himself and his rider. The late rain had covered some parts of the prairie, where the ground was hard, with a thin sheet of water, through which the horse had to splash his way. In other parts there were innumerable shallow hollows,

The Grand Prairie—A Buffalo Hunt

eight or ten feet in diameter, made by the buffaloes, who wallow in sand and mud like swine. These being filled with water, shone like mirrors, so that the horse was continually leaping over them or springing on one side. We had reached, too, a rough part of the prairie, very much broken and cut up; the buffalo, who was running for life, took no heed to his course, plunging down break-neck ravines, where it was necessary to skirt the borders in search of a safer descent. At length we came to where a winter stream had torn a deep chasm across the whole prairie, leaving open jagged rocks, and forming a long glen bordered by steep crumbling cliffs of mingled stone and clay. Down one of these the buffalo flung himself, half tumbling, half leaping, and then scuttled along the bottom; while I, seeing all further pursuit useless, pulled up, and gazed quietly after him from the border of the cliff, until he disappeared amidst the windings of the ravine.

Nothing now remained but to turn my steed and rejoin my companions. Here at first was some little difficulty. The ardor of the chase had betrayed me into a long, heedless gallop. I now found myself in the midst of a lonely waste, in which the prospect was bounded by undulating swells of land, naked and uniform where, from the deficiency of landmarks and distinct features, an inexperienced man may become bewildered, and lose his way as readily as in the wastes of the ocean. The day, too, was overcast, so that I could not guide myself by the sun; my only mode was to retrace the track my horse had made in coming, though this I would often lose sight of, where the ground was covered with parched herbage.

To one unaccustomed to it, there is something inexpressibly lonely in the solitude of a prairie. The loneliness of a forest seems nothing to it. There the view is shut in by trees, and the imagination is left free to picture some livelier scene beyond. But here we have an immense extent of landscape without a sign of human existence. We have the consciousness of being far, far beyond the bounds of human habitation; we feel as if moving in the midst of a desert world. As my horse lagged slowly back over the scenes of our late scamper, and the delirium of the chase had passed away, I was peculiarly sensible to these circumstances. The silence of the waste was now and then broken by the cry of a distant flock of pelicans, stalking like spectres about a shallow pool; sometimes by the sinister croaking of a raven in the air, while occasionally a scoundrel wolf would scour off from before me, and, having attained a safe distance, would sit down and howl and whine with tones that gave a dreariness to the surrounding solitude.

After pursuing my way for some time, I descried a horseman on the edge of a distant hill, and soon recognized him to be the Count. He had been equally unsuccessful with myself; we were shortly after rejoined by our worthy comrade, the Virtuoso, who, with spectacles on nose, had made two or three ineffectual shots from horseback.

We determined not to seek the camp until we had made one more effort. Casting our eyes about the surrounding waste, we descried a herd of buffalo about two miles distant, scattered apart, and quietly grazing near a small strip of trees and bushes. It required but little stretch of fancy to pic-

Washington Irving

ture them so many cattle grazing on the edge of a common, and that the grove might shelter some lonely farm-house.

We now formed our plant to circumvent the herd, and by getting on the other side of them, to hunt them in the direction where we knew our camp to be situated: otherwise, the pursuit might take us to such a distance as to render it impossible to find our way back before nightfall. Taking a wide circuit, therefore, we moved slowly and cautiously, pausing occasionally when we saw any of the herd desist from grazing. The wind fortunately set from them, otherwise they might have scented us and have taken the alarm. In this way we succeeded in getting round the herd without disturbing it. It consisted of about forty head; bulls, cows, and calves. Separating to some distance from each other, we now approached slowly in a parallel line, hoping by degrees to steal near without exciting attention. They began, however, to move off quietly, stopping at every step or two to graze, when suddenly a bull, that, unobserved by us, had been taking his siesta under a clump of trees to our left, roused himself from his lair, and hastened to join his companions. We were still at a considerable distance, but the game had taken the alarm. We quickened our pace; they broke into a gallop, and now commenced a full chase.

As the ground was level, they shouldered along with great speed, following each other in a line; two or three bulls bringing up the rear, the last of whom, from his enormous size and venerable frontlet, and beard of sunburnt hair, looked like the patriarch of the herd, and as if he might long have reigned the monarch of the prairie.

There is a mixture of the awful and the comic in the look of these huge animals, as they bear their great bulk forwards, with an up and down motion of the unwieldy head and shoulders, their tail cocked up like the cue of Pantaloon in a pantomime, the end whisking about in a fierce yet whimsical style, and their eyes glaring venomously with an expression of fright and fury.

For some time I kept parallel with the line, without being able to force my horse within pistol-shot, so much had he been alarmed by the assault of the buffalo in the preceding chase. At length I succeeded, but was again balked by my pistols missing fire. My companions, whose horses were less fleet and more wayworn, could not overtake the herd; at length Mr. L., who was in the rear of the line, and losing ground, levelled his double-barrelled gun, and fired a long raking shot. It struck a buffalo just above the loins, broke its backbone, and brought it to the ground. He stopped and alighted to dispatch his prey, when, borrowing his gun, which had yet a charge remaining in it, I put my horse to his speed, again overtook the herd which was thundering along, pursued by the Count. With my present weapon there was no need of urging my horse to such close quarters; galloping along parallel, therefore, I singled out a buffalo, and by a fortunate shot brought it down on the spot. The ball had struck a vital part; it could not move from the place where it fell, but lay there struggling in mortal agony, while the rest of the herd kept on their headlong career across the prairie.

The Grand Prairie—A Buffalo Hunt

Dismounting, I now fettered my horse to prevent his straying, and advanced to contemplate my victim. I am nothing of a sportsman; I had been prompted to this unwonted exploit by the magnitude of the game and the excitement of an adventurous chase. Now that the excitement was over, I could not but look with commiseration upon the poor animal that lay struggling and bleeding at my feet. His very size and importance, which had before inspired me with eagerness, now increased my compunction. It seemed as if I had inflicted pain in proportion to the bulk of my victim, and as if there were a hundred-fold greater waste of life than there would have been in the destruction of an animal of inferior size.

To add to these after-qualms of conscience, the poor animal lingered in his agony. He had evidently received a mortal wound, but death might be long in coming. It would not do to leave him here to be torn piecemeal, while yet alive, by the wolves that had already snuffed his blood, and were skulking and howling at a distance, and waiting for my departure; and by the ravens that were flapping about, croaking dismally in the air. It became now an act of mercy to give him his quietus, and put him out of his misery. I primed one of the pistols, therefore, and advanced close up to the buffalo. To inflict a wound thus in cold blood, I found a totally different thing from firing in the heat of the chase. Taking aim, however, just behind the fore-shoulder, my pistol for once proved true; the ball must have passed through the heart, for the animal gave one convulsive throe and expired.

While I stood meditating and moralizing over the wreck I had so wantonly produced, with my horse grazing near me, I was rejoined by my fellow-sportsman the Virtuoso, who, being a man of universal adroitness, and withal more experienced and hardened in the gentle art of "venerie," soon managed to carve out the tongue of the buffalo, and delivered it to me to bear back to the camp as a trophy.

[1835]

Washington Irving

John James Audubon:
Passenger Pigeon

John James Audubon (1785-1851), ornithologist, painter, and nature writer, was the first great American naturalist, and his major works, *The Birds of America* (1827-38), *Ornithological Biography* (1831-39), and *The Viviparous Quadrupeds of North America* (1842-45 and 1846-54), are important milestones in American scientific and intellectual history. Yet all his powers of observation and interpretation could not foresee the fate of the subject of the following essay.

I shall begin my description of the Passenger Pigeon with an account of its flight, because the most important facts connected with its habits relate to its migrations. It migrates for food rather than with a view to escaping the severity of the northern weather, or to seek a southern climate for breeding. Consequently such flights do not take place at any fixed period or season of the year. Indeed it sometimes happens that a continuance of a supply of food in one district will keep these birds away from any other place for years. I know, at least, to a certainty, that in Kentucky they remained for several years constantly, and were nowhere else to be found. They all suddenly disappeared one season when the mast (or acorns, nuts and tree pods) was exhausted, and they did not return for a long period. Similar facts have been observed in other States.

Their great power of flight enables them to survey and pass over an astonishing extent of country in a very short time, as proved by well-known facts. Pigeons have been killed in the neighborhood of New York with their crops full of rice, which they must have collected in the fields of Georgia and Carolina. These districts are the nearest possible for a supply of such food. Their power of digestion is so remarkable that they can entirely assimilate food in twelve hours; therefore, they must have travelled between three and four hundred miles in six hours, showing their speed to be at an average of about one mile a minute. A velocity such as this would enable one of these birds to visit the European continent in less than three days, were it so inclined.

This great power of flight is seconded by as great a power of vision, which enables them to inspect the country below as they travel at that swift rate, and to discover their food with facility. Thus they obtain the object of their journey. I have also proved another point by my observation that they fly high and in an extended front when passing over sterile or poor country. This enables them to survey hundreds of acres at once. On the other hand, when the land is richly covered with food, or the trees abundantly hung with mast, they fly low in order to discover the part most plentifully supplied.

Their body is formed in an elongated oval, which they steer with a long, well-plumed tail and propel with well-set wings, the muscles of which are very large and powerful for the size of the bird. A bird seen gliding through the woods and close to the observer passes like a thought; and the eye tries in vain to see it again, but the bird is gone. It propels itself with extreme rapidity by repeated flapping of the wings, which it brings more or less close to its body, according to the degree of velocity required. Like the domestic Pigeon, it often flies in a circling manner during the love season, supporting itself with both wings elevated at an angle, and keeping them in that position until it is about to alight. Now and then during these circular flights, the tips of the primary quills of each wing are made to strike against each other, producing a smart rap which may be heard thirty or forty yards away. Before alighting, the Wild Pigeon, like the Carolina Parrot and a few other species of birds, breaks the force of its

John James Audubon

flight by repeated flapping, as if apprehensive of injury from too sudden contact with the branch or spot of ground where it intends to settle.

The multitudes of Wild Pigeons in our American woods are astonishing. Indeed, after having viewed them so often and under so many circumstances, I new feel inclined even to pause and reassure myself that what I am going to relate is fact. Yet I have seen it all, and in the company, too, of persons who like myself were struck with amazement.

In the autumn of 1813 I left my house at Henderson on the banks of the Ohio, on my way to Louisville ninety miles distant. In passing over the Kentucky barrens a few miles beyond Hardinsburg, I observed the Passenger Pigeons flying from northeast to southwest in greater numbers than I had ever seen them before, it seemed to me. Feeling an inclination to count the flocks that might pass within the reach of my eye in one hour, I dismounted, seated myself on an eminence, and began to mark a dot with my pencil for every flock that passed. In a short time, finding this task impracticable because the birds were pouring by in countless multitudes, I arose. But before I travelled on, I counted the dots that I had put down and found that one hundred and sixty flocks had been recorded in twenty-one minutes. I met still more, farther on. The air was literally filled with Pigeons, and the noon-day light was obscured as by an eclipse. The dung fell in spots not unlike melting flakes of snow; and the continuous buzz of wings tended to lull my senses.

While waiting for dinner at Young's Inn at the confluence of Salt River with the Ohio, I saw, at my leisure, immense legions still going by. Their front reached far beyond the Ohio on the west, and the beechwood forests directly east of me. Not a single bird alighted, for not a nut or acorn was that year to be seen in the neighborhood. Consequently they were flying so high that different attempts to reach them with a capital rifle proved ineffectual; nor did the reports disturb them in the least. I cannot describe to you the extreme beauty of their aerial evolutions when a Hawk chanced to press upon the rear of a flock. At once, like a torrent, and with a noise like thunder, they rushed in a compact mass, pressing upon each other towards the center. In these almost solid masses they darted forward in undulating and angular lines, descended to the earth and swept close over it with inconceivable velocity. Then they mounted perpendicularly so as to resemble a vast column, and, when high, they were seen wheeling and twisting within their continued lines, which resembled the coils of a gigantic serpent.

Before sunset I reached Louisville, fifty-five miles from Hardinsburg. The Pigeons were still passing in undiminished numbers. They continued to do so for three days in succession. The people were all in arms, and the banks of the Ohio were crowded with men and boys incessantly shooting at the pilgrims, which flew lower as they passed the river. Multitudes were thus destroyed. For a week or more, the population fed on no other flesh than that of Pigeons, and talked of nothing but Pigeons.

It is extremely interesting to see flock after flock performing exactly the same evolutions which a preceding flock has traced in the air. Thus

Passenger Pigeon

should a Hawk charge on a group at a certain point, the angles, curves and undulations described by the birds in their efforts to escape the dreaded talons of the plunderer are undeviatingly followed by the next flock that comes up. Should the bystander happen to witness one of these affrays and be struck with the rapidity and elegance of the motions, and desire to see them repeated, his wishes will be gratified if he but remain in the same place until the next flock of Pigeons comes along.

As soon as the Pigeons discover a sufficiency of food to entice them to alight, they fly around in circles, reviewing the countryside below. During these evolutions the dense mass which they form presents a beautiful spectacle, as it changes its direction, turning from a glistening sheet of azure, as the backs of the birds come simultaneously into view, to a suddenly presented, rich deep purple. After that they pass lower, over the woods, and for a moment are lost among the foliage. Again they emerge and glide aloft. They may now alight, but the next moment take to wing as if suddenly alarmed, the flapping of their wings producing a noise like the roar of distant thunder, as they sweep through the forests to see if danger is near. However, hunger soon brings them to the ground. On alighting they industriously throw aside the withered leaves in quest of the fallen mast. The rear ranks continually rise, passing over the main body and alighting in front, and in such rapid succession that the whole flock seems still on the wing. The quantity of ground swept in this way is astonishing. So completely has it been cleared that the gleaner who might follow in the rear of the flock would find his labor completely lost. While feeding, their avidity is at times so great that, in attempting to swallow a large acorn or nut, they may be seen to gasp for a long while as if in the agonies of suffocation.

When the woods are filled with these Pigeons, they are killed in immense numbers, although no apparent diminution comes of it. About mid-day, after their repast is finished, they settle on the trees to enjoy rest and digest their food. On the ground and on the branches they walk with ease, frequently jerking their beautiful tails and moving their necks backward and forward in the most graceful manner. As the sun begins to sink beneath the horizon, they depart *en masse* for the roosting place which, not infrequently, is hundreds of miles away, a fact ascertained by persons who have kept track of their arrivals and departures.

Let us inspect their place of nightly rendezvous. One of these curious roosting places on the banks of the Green River in Kentucky I repeatedly visited. As always, it was in a part of the forest where the trees were huge and where there was little underbrush. I rode through it for more than forty miles, and on crossing it in different parts I found it rather more than three miles wide on average. My first view of it was at nearly two hours before sunset, about two weeks before the coming of the Pigeons. Few of these birds were then to be seen, but a great gathering of persons with horses and wagons, guns and ammunition had pitched camp on the edge of the forest.

Two farmers from the vicinity of Russellville, more than a hundred

John James Audubon

miles distant, had driven more than three hundred hogs to be fattened on the Pigeons they hoped to slaughter. Here and there, people were busy plucking and salting birds already killed, and they sat amid large piles of them. The dung lay several inches deep, covering the whole roosting place. I noticed that many trees two feet in diameter were broken off at no great distance from the ground; and the branches of many of the largest and tallest had given way. It was as if the forest had been swept by a tornado, proving to me that the number of birds must be immense beyond conception.

As the time of the arrival of the Passenger Pigeons approached, their foes anxiously prepared to receive them. Some persons were ready with iron pots containing sulphur, others with torches of pine knots; many had poles, and the rest, guns. The sun went down, yet not a Pigeon had arrived. However, everything was ready, and all eyes were fixed on the clear sky which could be glimpsed amid the tall tree-tops.

Suddenly a general cry burst forth, "Here they come!" The noise they made, even though still distant, reminded me of a hard gale at sea, passing through the rigging of a close-reefed vessel. As the birds arrived and passed over me, I felt a current of air that surprised me. Thousands of the Pigeons were soon knocked down by the pole-men, while more continued to pour in. The fires were lighted, then a magnificent, wonderful, and almost terrifying sight presented itself. The Pigeons, arriving by the thousands, alighted everywhere, one above another, until solid masses were formed on the branches all around. Here and there the perches gave way with a crash under the weight, and fell to the ground, destroying hundreds of birds beneath, and forcing down the dense groups of them with which every stick was loaded. The scene was one of uproar and confusion. I found it quite useless to speak, or even to shout, to those persons nearest to me. Even the gun reports were seldom heard, and I was made aware of the firing only by seeing the shooters reloading.

No one dared venture nearer the devastation. Meanwhile, the hogs had been penned up. The picking up of the dead and wounded birds was put off till morning. The Pigeons were constantly coming, and it was past midnight before I noticed any decrease in the number of those arriving. The uproar continued the whole night. I was anxious to know how far away the sound could be heard, so I sent off a man used to roaming the forest, who returned in two hours with the information that he had heard it distinctly three miles from the roosting place.

Towards the approach of day, the noise somewhat subsided. Long before I could distinguish them plainly, the Pigeons began to move off in a direction quite different from the one in which they flew when they arrived the evening before. By sunrise all that were able to fly had disappeared. The howling of the wolves now reached our ears, and the foxes, lynxes, cougars, bears, raccoons, opossums and polecats were sneaking off. Eagles and Hawks, accompanied by a crowd of Vultures, took their place and enjoyed their share of the spoils.

Then the authors of all this devastation began to move among the dead, the dying, and the mangled, picking up the Pigeons and piling them

Passenger Pigeon

in heaps. When each man had as many as he could possibly dispose of, the hogs were let loose to feed on the remainder.

Persons unacquainted with these birds might naturally conclude that such dreadful havoc would soon put an end to the species. But I have satisfied myself by long observation that nothing but the gradual diminution of our forests can accomplish their decrease. They not infrequently quadruple their number yearly, and always at least double it. In 1805 I saw schooners loaded with Pigeons caught up the Hudson River, coming into the wharf at New York where the birds sold for a cent apiece. I knew a man in Pennsylvania who caught and killed more than five hundred dozen in a clap-net in one day. Sometimes the net took twenty dozens or more at a single haul. In March, 1830, the Passenger Pigeon was so abundant in the New York markets that piles of them met the eye in every direction. I have seen the Negroes grow weary of killing them as the birds alighted for weeks at a time to drink the water from the pipes at the saltworks of Shawnee Town, on the Tennessee-Kentucky border.

The places they choose for breeding are of interest; though, as I have said, the season varies. Food is most plentiful and most attainable, and water is always at a convenient distance. The tallest trees of the forest are those in which the Pigeons nest. To them countless pairs resort and prepare to fulfil one of the great laws of Nature. At this period the note of the Pigeon is a soft *coo—coo—coo—coo*, much shorter than that of the domestic variety. The common notes resemble *kee—kee—kee—kee*, the first of these being the loudest, and the others gradually diminishing in power. With his tail spread and his wings drooping, the male, whether on the ground or on the branches, follows the female with a pompous demeanor. His body is elevated, his throat swells, his eyes sparkle, as he continues his cooing. Now and then he rises on the wing and flies a few yards towards the fugitive and timorous female. Like the domestic Pigeon and others, they caress each other by billing, an action in which the bill of the one is placed transversely in that of the other. Both birds alternately disgorge the contents of their crops by repeated efforts. After these preliminaries, the Pigeons begin building their nest in peace and harmony, crossing a few dry twigs in the fork of some branches.

Sometimes fifty to a hundred nests may be seen in the same tree. Were I not anxious that you should not feel disposed to refer my account of the Wild Pigeons to the marvelous, however wonderful, I might estimate a much greater number than one hundred.

There are two, broadly elliptical, pure white eggs. The male keeps the female supplied with food during incubation. Indeed the tenderness and affection shown by these birds towards their mates are striking in the highest degree. It is a remarkable fact that each brood hatched usually consists of a male and female.

Here again, the tyrant of creation, man, interferes, disturbing the harmony of this peaceful scene. As the young birds grow up, their enemies, armed with axes, reach the spot and seize and destroy all they can. The trees are felled, and are made to fall in such a way that the cutting of one

John James Audubon

causes the overthrow of another. Or the crash shakes the trees near by so much that the young Pigeons, or squabs, are violently tossed to the ground. In this way immense quantities are destroyed.

The young are fed by the parents as described above. In other words, the old bird puts its bill in the mouth of the young one crosswise, or with the back of the two parts of the bill opposite the young bird's open mouth and disgorges the contents of its crop as food. As soon as the young are able to shift for themselves, they leave their parents and continue apart until they reach maturity. By the end of six months they are capable of reproducing their species.

The flesh of the Wild Pigeon is of a dark color, but affords tolerable eating. That of young birds is much esteemed. The skin is covered with small white filmy scales. The feathers fall off at the least touch, like those of the Carolina Mourning Dove. Like other Pigeons, it immerses its head up to the eyes while drinking.

In March, 1830, I bought about three hundred and fifty of these birds in the New York market at four cents apiece, and carried most of them alive to England. I distributed them among several noblemen, giving some to the Zoological Society also. A curious change of habits has taken place in those which I presented to the Earl of Derby in 1830. That nobleman has assured me that ever since they began breeding in his aviaries near Liverpool they have laid only one egg. My noble friend has raised many and distributed them freely. It is therefore not surprising that some which have escaped confinement have been shot. But that the Passenger Pigeon should have a natural claim to be admitted into the British fauna appears to me very doubtful.

This bird wanders continually in search of food throughout all parts of North America, and is wonderfully abundant at times in particular districts.

[1831–1839]

Passenger Pigeon

Morgan Neville:

The Last of the Boatmen

Morgan Neville (1783-1840), journalist and first
western-born writer of fiction, was the author
of sketches and stories in the western tradition
of the tall tale and the hero larger than life. As
did others of the sort, Neville's works contributed to the spread of frontier folklore. Here
Mike Fink, keelboatman on the rivers, begins to
take on the proportions of the hero of folklore.

I embarked a few years since, at Pittsburgh, for Cincinnati, on board of a steam boat—more with a view of realising the possibility of a speedy return against the current, than in obedience to the call of either business or pleasure. It was a voyage of speculation. I was born on the banks of the Ohio, and the only vessels associated with my early recollections were the canoes of the Indians, which brought to Fort Pitt their annual cargoes of skins and bear's oil. The Flat boat of Kentucky, destined only to float with the current, next appeared; and after many years of interval, the Keel boat of the Ohio, and the Barge of the Mississippi were introduced for the convenience of the infant commerce of the West.

At the period, at which I have dated my trip to Cincinnati, the steam boat had made but few voyages back to Pittsburgh. We were generally skeptics as to its practicability. The mind was not prepared for the change that was about to take place in the West. It is now consummated; and we yet look back with astonishment at the result.

The rudest inhabitant of our forests;—the man whose mind is least of all imbued with a relish for the picturesque—who would gaze with vacant stare at the finest painting—listen with apathy to the softest melody, and turn with indifference from a mere display of ingenious mechanism, is struck with the sublime power and self-moving majesty of a steam boat;—lingers on the shore where it passes—and follows its rapid, and almost magic course with silent admiration. The steam engine in five years has enabled us to anticipate a state of things, which, in the ordinary course of events, it would have required a century to have produced. The art of printing scarcely surpassed it in its beneficial consequences.

In the old world, the places of the greatest interest to the philosophic traveller are ruins, and monuments, that speak of faded splendour, and departed glory. The broken columns of Tadmor—the shapeless ruins of Babylon, are rich in matter for almost endless speculation. Far different is the case in the western regions of America. The stranger views here, with wonder, the rapidity with which cities spring up in forests; and with which barbarism retreats before the approach of art and civilization. The reflection possessing the most intense interest is—not what has been the character of the country, but what shall be her future destiny.

As we coasted along this cheerful scene, one reflection crossed my mind to diminish the pleasure it excited. This was caused by the sight of the ruins of the once splendid mansion of Blennerhassett. I had spent some happy hours here, when it was the favourite residence of taste and hospitality. I had seen it when a lovely and accomplished woman presided—shedding a charm around, which made it as inviting, though not so dangerous, as the island of Calypso;—when its liberal and polished owner made it the resort of every stranger, who had any pretensions to literature or science. I had beheld it again under more inauspicious circumstances:—when its proprietor, in a moment of visionary speculation, had abandoned this earthly paradise to follow an adventurer—himself the dupe of others. A military banditti held possession, acting "by authority." The embellishments of art and taste disappeared beneath the touch of a band of Van-

Morgan Neville

dals, and the beautiful domain which presented the imposing appearance of a palace, and which had cost a fortune in the erection, was changed in one night, into a scene of devastation! The chimneys of the house remained for some years—the insulated monument of the folly of their owner, and pointed out to the stranger the place where once stood the temple of hospitality. Driftwood covered the pleasure grounds; and the massive, cut stone, that formed the columns of the gateway, were scattered more widely than the fragments of the Egyptian Memnon.

When we left Pittsburgh, the season was not far advanced in vegetation. But as we proceeded, the change was more rapid than the difference of latitude justified. I had frequently observed this in former voyages, but it never was so striking, as on the present occasion. The old mode of travelling, in the sluggish flat boat seemed to give time for the change of season; but now a few hours carried us into a different climate. We met spring with all her laughing train of flowers and verdure, rapidly advancing from the south. The buck-eye, cottonwood, and maple, had already assumed, in this region, the rich livery of summer. The thousand varieties of the floral kingdom spread a gay carpet over the luxuriant bottoms on each side of the river. The thick woods resounded with the notes of the feathered tribe —each striving to out-do his neighbor in noise, if not in melody. We had not yet reached the region of paroquets; but the clear toned whistle of the cardinal was heard in every bush; and the cat-bird was endeavouring, with its usual zeal, to rival the powers of the more gifted mocking-bird.

A few hours brought us to one of those stopping points, known by the name of "wooding places." It was situated immediately above Letart's Falls. The boat, obedient to the wheel of the pilot, made a graceful sweep towards the island above the chute, and rounding to, approached the wood pile. As the boat drew near the shore, the escape steam reverberated through the forest and hills, like the chafed bellowing of the caged tiger. The root of a tree, concealed beneath the water, prevented the boat from getting sufficiently near the bank, and it became necessary to use the paddles to take a different position.

"Back out! Mannee—and try it again!" exclaimed a voice from the shore. "Throw your pole wide—and brace off—or you'll run against a snag!"

This was a kind of language long familiar to us on the Ohio. It was a sample of the slang of the keelboatmen.

The speaker was immediately cheered by a dozen of voices from the deck; and I recognized in him the person of an old acquaintance, familiarly known to me from my boyhood. He was leaning carelessly against a large beech; and as his left arm negligently pressed a rifle to his side, presented a figure, that Salvator would have chosen from a million, as a model for his wild and gloomy pencil. His stature was upwards of six feet, his proportions perfectly symmetrical, and exhibiting the evidence of Herculean powers. To a stranger, he would have seemed a complete mulatto. Long exposure to the sun and weather on the lower Ohio and Mississippi had changed his skin; and, but for the fine European cast of his countenance, he might have passed for the principal warrior of some powerful tribe.

The Last of the Boatmen

Although at least fifty years of age, his hair was as black as the wing of the raven. Next to his skin he wore a red flannel shirt, covered by a blue capot, ornamented with white fringe. On his feet were moccasins, and a broad leathern belt, from which hung, suspended in a sheath, a large knife, encircled his waist.

As soon as the steam boat became stationary, the cabin passengers jumped on shore. On ascending the bank, the figure I have just described advanced to offer me his hand.

"How are you, Mike?" said I.

"How goes it?" replied the boatman—grasping my hand with a squeeze, that I can compare to nothing, but that of a blacksmith's vice.

"I am glad to see you, Mannee!"—continued he in his abrupt manner. "I am going to shoot at the tin cup for a quart—off hand—and you must be judge."

I understood Mike at once, and on any other occasion, should have remonstrated, and prevented the daring trial of skill. But I was accompanied by a couple of English tourists, who had scarcely ever been beyond the sound of Bow Bells; and who were travelling post over the United States to make up a book of observations, on our manners and customs. There were, also, among the passengers, a few bloods from Philadelphia and Baltimore, who could conceive of nothing equal to Chestnut or Howard streets; and who expressed great disappointment at not being able to find terrapins and oysters at every village—marvelously lauding the comforts of Rubicum's. My tramontane pride was aroused; and I resolved to give them an opportunity of seeing a Western Lion—for such Mike undoubtedly was—in all his glory. The philanthropist may start, and accuse me of want of humanity. I deny the charge, and refer for apology to one of the best understood principles of human nature.

Mike, followed by several of his crew, led the way to a beech grove, some little distance from the landing. I invited my fellow passengers to witness the scene. On arriving at the spot, a stout bull-headed boatman, dressed in a hunting shirt—but bare-footed—in whom I recognised a younger brother of Mike, drew a line with his toe; and stepping off thirty yards— turned round fronting his brother—took a tin cup, which hung from his belt, and placed it on his head. Although I had seen this feat performed before, I acknowledge, I felt uneasy, whilst this silent preparation was going on. But I had not much time for reflection; for this second Albert exclaimed—

"Blaze away, Mike! and let's have the quart."

My "compagnons de voyage," as soon as they recovered from the first effect of their astonishment, exhibited a disposition to interfere. But Mike, throwing back his left leg, levelled the rifle at the head of his brother. In this horizontal position the weapon remained for some seconds as immoveable, as if the arm which held it, was affected by no pulsation.

"Elevate your piece a little lower, Mike! or you will pay the corn," cried the imperturbable brother.

I know not if the advice was obeyed or not; but the sharp crack of

Morgan Neville

the rifle immediately followed, and the cup flew off thirty or forty yards— rendered unfit for future service. There was a cry of admiration from the strangers, who pressed forward to see, if the fool-hardy boatman was really safe. He remained as immoveable, as if he had been a figure hewn out of stone. He had not even winked, when the ball struck within two inches of his skull.

"Mike has won!" I exclaimed; and my decision was the signal which, according to their rules, permitted him of the target to move from his position. No more sensation was exhibited among the boatmen, than if a common wager had been won. The bet being decided, they hurried back to their boat, giving me and my friends an invitation to partake of "the treat." We declined, and took leave of the thoughtless creatures. In a few minutes afterwards, we observed their "Keel" wheeling into the current,— the gigantic form of Mike, bestriding the large steering oar, and the others arranging themselves in their places in front of the cabin, that extended nearly the whole length of the boat, covering merchandize of immense value. As they left the shore, they gave the Indian yell; and broke out into a sort of unconnected chorus—commencing with—

> "Hard upon the beech oar!—
> She moves too slow!—
> All the way to Shawneetown,
> Long while ago."

In a few moments the boat "took the chute" of Letart's Falls, and disappeared behind the point, with the rapidity of an Arabian courser.

Our travellers returned to the boat, lost in speculation on the scene, and the beings they had just beheld; and, no doubt, the circumstance has been related a thousand times with all the necessary amplifications of finished tourists.

Mike Fink may be viewed, as the correct representative of a class of men now extinct; but who once possessed as marked a character, as that of the Gipsies of England, or the Lazaroni of Naples. The period of their existence was not more than the third of a century. The character was created by the introduction of trade on the Western waters; and ceased with the successful establishment of the steam boat.

There is something inexplicable in the fact, that there could be men found, for ordinary wages, who would abandon the systematic, but not laborious pursuits of agriculture, to follow a life, of all others, except that of the soldier, distinguished by the greatest exposure and privation. The occupation of a boatman was more calculated to destroy the constitution, and to shorten life, than any other business. In ascending the river, it was a continued series of toil, rendered more irksome by the snail like rate, at which they moved. The boat was propelled by poles, against which the shoulder was placed; and the whole strength, and skill of the individual were applied in this manner. As the boatmen moved along the running board, with their heads nearly touching the plank on which they walked, the effect produced on the mind of an observer was similar to that, on be-

The Last of the Boatmen

holding the ox, rocking before an overloaded cart. Their bodies, naked to their waist for the purpose of moving with greater ease, and of enjoying the breeze of the river, were exposed to the burning suns of summer, and to the rains of autumn.—After a hard day's push, they would take their "fillee," or ration of whiskey, and having swallowed a miserable supper of meat half burnt, and of bread half baked, stretch themselves, without covering, on the deck, and slumber till the steersman's call invited them to the morning "fillee." Notwithstanding this, the boatman's life had charms as irresistible, as those presented by the splendid illusion of the stage. Sons abandoned the comfortable farms of their fathers, and apprentices fled from the service of their masters. There was a captivation in the idea of "going down the river;" and the youthful boatman who had "pushed a keel" from New Orleans, felt all the pride of a young merchant, after his first voyage to an English sea port. From an exclusive association together, they had formed a kind of slang peculiar to themselves; and from the constant exercise of wit, with "the squatters" on shore, and crews of other boats, they acquired a quickness, and smartness of vulgar retort, that was quite amusing. The frequent battles they were engaged in with the boatmen of different parts of the river, and with the less civilized inhabitants of the lower Ohio, and Mississippi, invested them with that ferocious reputation, which has made them spoken of throughout Europe.

On board of the boats thus navigated, our merchants entrusted valuable cargoes, without insurance, and with no other guarantee than the receipt of the steersman, who possessed no property but his boat; and the confidence so reposed was seldom abused.

Among these men, Mike Fink stood an acknowledged leader for many years. Endowed by nature with those qualities of intellect, that give the possessor influence, he would have been a conspicuous member of any society, in which his lot might have been cast. An acute observer of human nature has said—"Opportunity alone makes the hero. Change but their situations, and Caesar would have been but the best wrestler on the green." With a figure cast in a mould that added much of the symmetry of an Apollo to the limbs of a Hercules, he possessed gigantic strength; and accustomed from an early period of life to brave the dangers of a frontier life, his character was noted for the most daring intrepidity. At the court of Charlemagne, he might have been a Roland; with the Crusaders, he would have been the favourite of the Knight of the Lion-heart; and in our revolution, he would have ranked with the Morgans and the Putnams of the day. He was the hero of a hundred fights, and the leader in a thousand daring adventures. From Pittsburgh to St. Louis, and New Orleans, his fame was established. Every farmer on the shore kept on good terms with Mike; otherwise, there was no safety for his property. Wherever he was an enemy, like his great prototype, Rob Roy, he levied the contribution of Black Mail for the use of his boat. Often at night, when his tired companions slept, he would take an excursion of five or six miles, and return before morning, rich in spoil. On the Ohio, he was known among his

Morgan Neville

companions by the appellation of the "Snapping Turtle;" and on the Mississippi, he was called "The Snag."

At the early age of seventeen, Mike's character was displayed, by enlisting himself in a corps of Scouts—a body of irregular rangers, which was employed on the North-western frontiers of Pennsylvania, to watch the Indians, and to give notice of any threatened inroad.

At that time, Pittsburgh was on the extreme verge of white population, and the spies, who were constantly employed, generally extended their explorations forty or fifty miles to the west of this post. They went out, singly, lived as did the Indian, and in every respect, became perfectly assimilated in habits, taste, and feeling, with the red men of the desert. A kind of border warfare was kept up, and the scout thought it as praiseworthy to bring in the scalp of a Shawnee, as the skin of a panther. He would remain in the woods for weeks together, using parched corn for bread, and depending on his rifle for his meat—and slept at night in perfect comfort, rolled in his blanket.

In this corps, whilst yet a stripling, Mike acquired a reputation for boldness, and cunning, far beyond his companions. A thousand legends illustrate the fearlessness of his character. There was one, which he told, himself, with much pride, and which made an indelible impression on my boyish memory. He had been out on the hills of Mahoning, when, to use his own words, "he saw signs of Indians being about."—He had discovered the recent print of the moccasin on the grass; and found drops of the fresh blood of a deer on the green bush. He became cautious, skulked for some time in the deepest thickets of hazel and briar, and, for several days, did not discharge his rifle. He subsisted patiently on parched corn and jerk, which he had dried on his first coming into the woods. He gave no alarm to the settlements, because he discovered with perfect certainty, that the enemy consisted of a small hunting party, who were receding from the Alleghany.

As he was creeping along one morning, with the stealthy tread of a cat, his eye fell upon a beautiful buck, browsing on the edge of a barren spot, three hundred yards distant. The temptation was too strong for the woodsman, and he resolved to have a shot at every hazard.—Re-priming his gun, and picking his flint, he made his approaches in the usual noiseless manner. At the moment he reached the spot, from which he meant to take his aim, he observed a large savage, intent upon the same object, advancing from a direction a little different from his own. Mike shrunk behind a tree, with the quickness of thought, and keeping his eye fixed on the hunter, waited the result with patience.—In a few moments, the Indian halted within fifty paces, and levelled his piece at the deer. In the meanwhile, Mike presented his rifle at the body of the savage; and at the moment the smoke issued from the gun of the latter, the bullet of Fink passed through the red man's breast. He uttered a yell, and fell dead at the same instant with the deer. Mike re-loaded his rifle, and remained in his covert for some minutes, to ascertain whether there were more enemies at hand. He then stepped up to the prostrate savage, and having satisfied himself, that life

The Last of the Boatmen

was extinguished, turned his attention to the buck, and took from the carcass those pieces, suited to the process of jerking.

In the meantime, the country was filling up with a white population; and in a few years the red men, with the exception of a few fractions of tribes, gradually receded to the Lakes and beyond the Mississippi. The corps of Scouts was abolished, after having acquired habits, which unfitted them for the pursuits of civilized society. Some incorporated themselves with the Indians; and others, from a strong attachment to their erratic mode of life, joined the boatmen, then just becoming a distinct class. Among these was our hero, Mike Fink, whose talents were soon developed; and for many years, he was as celebrated on the rivers of the West, as he had been in the woods.

I gave to my fellow travellers the substance of the foregoing narrative, as we sat on deck by moonlight, and cut swiftly through the magnificent sheet of water between Letart and the Great Kanhawa. It was one of those beautiful nights, which permitted every thing to be seen with sufficient distinctness to avoid danger,—yet created a certain degree of illusion, that gave reins to the imagination. The outline of the river hills lost all its harshness; and the occasional bark of the house dog from the shore, and the distant scream of the solitary loon, gave increased effect to the scene. It was altogether so delightful, that the hours till morning flew swiftly by, whilst our travellers dwelt with rapture on the surrounding scenery, which shifted every moment like the capricious changes of the kaleidoscope— and listening to tales of border warfare, as they were brought to mind, by passing the places where they happened. The celebrated Hunter's Leap, and the bloody battle of Kanhawa, were not forgotten.

The afternoon of the next day brought us to the beautiful city of Cincinnati, which, in the course of thirty years, has risen from a village of soldiers' huts to a town,—giving promise of future splendour, equal to any on the sea-board.

Some years after the period, at which I have dated my visit to Cincinnati, business called me to New Orleans. On board of the steam boat, on which I had embarked, at Louisville, I recognized, in the person of the pilot, one of those men, who had formerly been a patroon, or keel boat captain. I entered into conversation with him on the subject of his former associates.

"They are scattered in all directions," said he. "A few, who had capacity, have become pilots of steam boats. Many have joined the trading parties that cross the Rocky mountains; and a few have settled down as farmers."

"What has become," I asked, "of my old acquaintance, Mike Fink?"

"Mike was killed in a skrimmage," replied the pilot. "He had refused several good offers on steam boats. He said he could not bear the hissing of steam, and he wanted room to throw his pole. He went to the Missouri, and about a year since he was shooting the tin cup, when he had corned too heavy. He elevated too low, and shot his companion through the head. A friend of the deceased, who was present, suspecting foul play,

Morgan Neville ·

shot Mike through the heart, before he had time to re-load his rifle."
With Mike Fink expired the spirit of the Boatmen.

[1828]

Thomas Bangs Thorpe:
The Big Bear of Arkansas

Thomas Bangs Thorpe (1815-1878), painter, editor, soldier, and writer, drew on the frontier experience of the Old Southwest for the subject matter of *The Mysteries of the Backwoods* (1846) and *The Hive of the Bee Hunter* (1854), collections of sketches in the frontier tall-tale tradition. "The Big Bear of Arkansas" (1841), Thorpe's best work, illustrates the emergence of the tradition as it pits man against his environment.

A steamboat on the Mississippi frequently, in making her regular trips, carries between places varying from one to two thousand miles apart; and as these boats advertise to land passengers and freight at "all intermediate landings," the heterogeneous character of the passengers of one of these up-country boats can scarcely be imagined by one who has never seen it with his own eyes. Starting from New Orleans in one of these boats, you will find yourself associated with men from every state in the Union, and from every portion of the globe; and a man of observation need not lack for amusement or instruction in such a crowd, if he will take the trouble to read the great book of character so favourably opened before him. Here may be seen jostling together the wealthy Southern planter, and the pedlar of tin-ware from New England—the Northern merchant, and the Southern jockey—a venerable bishop, and a desperate gambler,—the land speculator, and the honest farmer—professional men of all creeds and characters—Wolvereens, Suckers, Hoosiers, Buckeyes, and Corn-crackers, beside a "plentiful sprinkling" of the half-horse and half-alligator species of men, who are peculiar to "old Mississippi," and who appear to gain a livelihood simply by going up and down the river. In the pursuit of pleasure or business, I have frequently found myself in such a crowd.

On one occasion, when in New Orleans, I had occasion to take a trip of a few miles up the Mississippi, and I hurried on board the well-known "high-pressure-and-beat-everything" steamboat *Invincible,* just as the last note of the last bell was sounding; and when the confusion and bustle that is natural to a boat's getting under way had subsided, I discovered that I was associated in as heterogeneous a crowd as was ever got together. As my trip was to be of a few hours' duration only, I made no endeavours to become acquainted with my fellow passengers, most of whom would be together many days. Instead of this, I took out of my pocket the "latest paper," and more critically than usual examined its contents; my fellow passengers at the same time disposed themselves in little groups. While I was thus busily employed in reading, and my companions were more busily employed in discussing such subjects as suited their humours best, we were startled most unexpectedly by a loud Indian whoop, uttered in the "social hall," that part of the cabin fitted off for a bar; then was to be heard a loud crowing, which would not have continued to have interested us—such sounds being quite common in that place of spirits— had not the hero of these windy accomplishments stuck his head into the cabin and hallooed out, "Hurra for the Big Bar of Arkansaw!" and then might be heard a confused hum of voices, unintelligible, save in such broken sentences as "horse," "screamer," "lightning is slow" etc. As might have been expected, this continued interruption attracted the attention of every one in the cabin; all conversation dropped, and in the midst of this surprise the "Big Bar" walked into the cabin, took a chair, put his feet on the stove, and looking back over his shoulder, passed the general and familiar salute of "Strangers, how are you?" He then expressed himself as much at home as if he had been at "the Forks of Cypress," and "perhaps a little more so." Some of the company at this familiarity looked a little

Thomas Bangs Thorpe

angry, and some astonished; but in a moment every face was wreathed in a smile. There was something about the intruder that won the heart on sight. He appeared to be a man enjoying perfect health and contentment: his eyes were as sparkling as diamonds, and good-natured to simplicity. Then his perfect confidence in himself was irresistibly droll. "Perhaps," said he, "gentlemen," running on without a person speaking, "perhaps you have been to New Orleans often; I never made *the first visit before,* and I don't intend to make another in a crow's life. I am thrown away in that ar place, and useless, that ar a fact. Some of the gentlemen thar called me *green*—well, perhaps I am, said I, *but.I arn't so at home;* and if I ain't off my trail much, the heads of them perlite chaps themselves wern't much the hardest; for according to my notion, they were real *know-nothings,* green as a pumpkin-vine—couldn't, in farming, I'll bet, raise a crop of turnips; and as for shooting, they'd miss a barn if the door was swinging, and that, too, with the best rifle in the country. And then they talked to me 'bout hunting, and laughed at my calling the principal game in Arkansaw poker, and high-low-jack. 'Perhaps,' said I, 'you prefer chickens and rolette'; at this they laughed harder than ever, and asked me if I lived in the woods, and didn't know what *game* was? At this I rather think I laughed. 'Yes,' I roared, and says, 'Strangers, if you'd asked me *how we got our meat* in Arkansaw, I'd a told you at once, and given you a list of varmints that would make a caravan, beginning with the bar, and ending off with the cat; that's *meat* though, not game.' Game, indeed, that's what city folks call it; and with them it means chippen-birds and shite-pokes; maybe such trash live in my diggens, but I arn't noticed them yet; a bird any way is too trifling. I never did shoot at but one, and I'd never forgiven myself for that, had it weighed less than forty pounds. I wouldn't draw a rifle on any thing less than that; and when I meet with another wild turkey of the same weight I will drap him."

"A wild turkey weighing forty pounds!" exclaimed twenty voices in the cabin at once.

"Yes, strangers, and wasn't it a whopper? You see, the thing was so fat that it couldn't fly far; and when he fell out of the tree, after I shot him, on striking the ground he bust open behind, and the way the pound gobs of tallow rolled out of the opening was perfectly beautiful."

"Where did all that happen?" asked a cynical-looking Hoosier.

"Happen! happened in Arkansaw: where else could it have happened, but in the creation state, the finishing-up country—a state where the *sile* runs down to the centre of the 'arth, and government gives you a title to every inch of it? Then its airs—just breathe them, and they will make you snort like a horse. It's a state without a fault, it is."

"Excepting mosquitoes," cried the Hoosier.

"Well, stranger, except them; for it ar a fact that they are rather *enormous,* and do push themselves in somewhat troublesome. But, stranger, they never stick twice in the same place; and give them a fair chance for a few months, and you will get as much above noticing them as an alligator. They can't hurt my feelings, for they lay under the skin; and I

The Big Bear of Arkansas

never knew but one case of injury resulting from them, and that was to a Yankee; and they take worse to foreigners, anyhow, than they do to natives. But the way they used that fellow up! first they punched him until he swelled up and busted; then he su-per-a-ted, as the doctor called it, until he was as raw as beef; then he took the ager, owing to the warm weather, and finally he took a steamboat and left the country. He was the only man that ever took mosquitoes to heart that I know of. But mosquitoes is natur, and I never find fault with her. If they ar large, Arkansaw is large, her varmints ar large, her trees ar large, her rivers ar large, and a small mosquito would be of no more use in Arkansaw than preaching in a canebrake."

This knock-down argument in favour of big mosquitoes used the Hoosier up, and the logician started on a new track, to explain how numerous bear were in his "diggins," where he represented them to be "about as plenty as blackberries, and a little plentifuler."

Upon the utterance of this assertion, a timid little man near me inquired if the bear in Arkansaw ever attacked the settlers in numbers.

"No," said our hero, warming with the subject, "no, stranger, for you see it ain't the natur of bar to go in droves; but the way they squander about in pairs and single ones is edifying. And then the way I hunt them the old black rascals know the crack of my gun as well as they know a pig's squealing. They grow thin in our parts, it frightens them so, and they do take the noise dreadfully, poor things. That gun of mine is perfect *epidemic among bar*; if not watched closely, it will go off as quick on a warm scent as my dog Bowie-knife will: and then that dog—whew! why the fellow thinks that the world is full of bar, he find them so easy. It's lucky he don't talk as well as think; for with his natural modesty, if he should suddenly learn how much he is acknowledged to be ahead of all other dogs in the universe, he would be astonished to death in two minutes. Strangers, the dog knows a bar's way as well as a horse-jockey knows a woman's; he always barks at the right time, bites at the exact place, and whips without getting a scratch. I never could tell whether he was made expressly to hunt bar, or whether bar was made expressly for him to hunt; any way, I believe they were ordained to go together as naturally as Squire Jones says a man and woman is, when he moralizes in marrying a couple. In fact, Jones once said, said he, 'Marriage according to law is a civil contract of divine origin; it's common to all countries as well as Arkansaw, and people take to it as naturally as Jim Doggett's Bowie-knife takes to bar.'"

"What season of the year do your hunts take place?" inquired a gentlemanly foreigner, who, from some peculiarities of his baggage, I suspected to be an Englishman, on some hunting expedition, probably at the foot of the Rocky Mountains.

"The season for bar hunting, stranger," said the man of Arkansaw, "is generally all the year round, and the hunts take place about as regular. I read in history that varmints have their fat season, and their lean season. That is not the case in Arkansaw, feeding as they do upon the *spontenacious* productions of the sile, they have one continued fat season the year

Thomas Bangs Thorpe

round; though in winter things in this way is rather more greasy than in summer, I must admit. For that reason bar with us run in warm weather, but in winter, they only waddle. Fat, fat! it's an enemy to speed; it tames everything that has plenty of it. I have seen wild turkeys, from its influence, as gentle as chickens. Run a bar in this fat condition, and the way it improves the critter for eating is amazing; it sort of mixes the ile up with the meat, until you can't tell t'other from which. I've done this often. I recollect one perty morning in particular, of putting an old fellow on the stretch, and considering the weight he carried, he run well. But the dogs soon tired him down, and when I came up with him wasn't he in a beautiful sweat—I might say fever; and then to see his tongue sticking out of his mouth a feet, and his sides sinking and opening like bellows, and his cheeks so fat he couldn't look cross. In this fix I blazed at him, and pitch me naked into a briar path if the steam didn't come out of the bullet-hole ten foot in a straight line. The fellow, I reckon, was made on the high-pressure system, and the lead sort of bust his biler."

"That column of steam was rather curious, or else the bear must have been *warm*," observed the foreigner, with a laugh.

"Stranger, as you observe, that bar was WARM, and the blowing off of the steam show'd it, and also how hard the varmint had been run. I have no doubt if he had kept on two miles farther his insides would have been stewed; and I expect to meet with a varmint yet of extra bottom, who will run himself into a skinful of bar's grease: it is possible, much onlikelier things have happened."

"Whereabouts are these bears so abundant?" inquired the foreigner, with increasing interest.

"Why, stranger, they inhabit the neighbourhood of my settlement, one of the prettiest places on old Mississippi—a perfect location, and no mistake; a place that had some defects until the river made the 'cut-off' at 'Shirt-tail bend,' and that remedied the evil, as it brought my cabin on the edge of the river—a great advantage in wet weather, I assure you, as you can now roll a barrel of whiskey into my yard in high water from a boat, as easy as falling off a log. It's a great improvement, as toting it by land in a jug, as I used to do, *evaporated* it too fast, and it became expensive. Just stop with me, stranger, a month or two, or a year if you like, and you will appreciate my place. I can give you plenty to eat; for beside hog and hominy, you can have bar-ham, and bar-sausages, and a mattrass of bar-skins to sleep on, and a wildcatskin, pulled off hull, stuffed with corn-shucks for a pillow. That bed would put you to sleep if you had the rheumatics in every joint in your body. I call that ar bed a *quietus*. Then look at my land—the government ain't got another such a piece to dispose of. Such timber, and such bottom land, why you can't preserve any thing natural you plant in it unless you pick it young, things thar will grow out of shape so quick. I once planted in those diggins a few potatoes and beets; they took a fine start, and after that an ox team couldn't have kept them from growing. About that time I went off to old Kentuck on bisiness, and did not hear from them things in three months, when I accidentally

The Big Bear of Arkansas

stumbled on a fellow who had stopped at my place, with an idea of buying me out. 'How did you like things?' said I. 'Pretty well,' said he; 'the cabin is convenient, and the timber land is good; but that bottom land ain't worth the first red cent.' 'Why?' said I. ''Cause,' said he. ''Cause what?' said I. ''Cause it's full of cedar stumps and Indian mounds,' said he, *and it can't be cleared.* 'Lord,' said I, 'Them ar "cedar stumps" is beets, and them ar "Indian mounds" ar tater hills.' As I expected, the crop was overgrown and useless; the sile is too rich, *and planting in Arkansaw is dangerous.* I had a good-sized sow killed in that same bottom land. The old thief stole an ear of corn, and took it down where she slept at night to eat. Well, she left a grain or two on the ground, and lay down on them; before morning the corn shot up, and the percussion killed her dead. I don't plant any more; natur intended Arkansaw for a hunting ground, and I go according to natur."

The questioner who thus elicited the description of our hero's settlement, seemed to be perfectly satisfied and said no more; but the "Big Bar of Arkansaw" rambled on from one thing to another with a volubility perfectly astonishing, occasionally disputing with those around him, particularly with a "live Sucker" from Illinois, who had the daring to say that our Arkansaw friend's stories "smelt rather tall."

In this manner the evening was spent; but conscious that my own association with so singular a personage would probably end before morning, I asked him if he would not give me a description of some particular bear hunt; adding that I took great interest in such things, though I was no sportsman. The desire seemed to please him, and he squared himself round towards me, saying, that he could give me an idea of a bar hunt that was never beat in this world, or in any other. His manner was so singular, that half of his story consisted in his excellent way of telling it, the great peculiarity of which was the happy manner he had of emphasizing the prominent parts of his conversation. As near as I can recollect, I have italicized them, and given the story in his own words.

"Stranger," said he, "in bar hunts *I am numerous,* and which particular one, as you say, I shall tell, puzzles me. There was the old she devil I shot at the Hurricane last fall—then there was the old hog thief I popped over at the Bloody Crossing, and then—Yes, I have it! I will give you an idea of a hunt, in which the greatest bar was killed that ever lived, *none excepted;* about an old fellow that I hunted more or less for two or three years; and if that ain't a particular bar hunt, I ain't got one to tell. But in the first place, stranger, let me say, I am pleased with you, because you ain't ashamed to gain information by asking, and listening, and that's what I say to Countess's pups every day when I'm home; and I have got great hopes of them ar pups, because they are continually *nosing* about; and though they stick it sometimes in the wrong place, they gain experience any how, and may learn something useful to boot. Well, as I was saying about this big bar, you see when I and some more first settled in our region, we were drivin to hunting naturally; we soon liked it, and after that we found it an easy matter to make the thing our business. One old chap

Thomas Bangs Thorpe

who had pioneered 'afore us, gave us to understand that we had settled in the right place. He dwelt upon its merits until it was affecting, and showed us, to prove his assertions, more marks on the sassafras trees than I ever saw on a tavern door 'lection time. 'Who keeps that ar reckoning?' said I. 'The bar,' said he. 'What for?' said I. 'Can't tell,' said he; 'but so it is; the bar bite the bark and wood too, at the highest point from the ground they can reach, and you can tell, by the marks,' said he, 'the length of the bar to an inch.' 'Enough,' said I; 'I've learned something here a'ready, and I'll put it in practice.'

"Well, stranger, just one month from that time I killed a bar, and told its exact length before I measured it, by those very marks; and when I did that, I swelled up considerable—I've been a prouder man ever since. So I went on, larning something every day, until I was reckoned a buster, and allowed to be decidedly the best bar hunter in my district; and that is a reputation as much harder to earn than to be reckoned first man in Congress, as an iron ramrod is harder than a toadstool. Did the varmints grow over-cunning by being fooled with by green-horn hunters, and by this means get troublesome, they send for me as a matter of course; and thus I do my own hunting, and most of my neighbours'. I walk into the varmints though, and it has become about as much the same to me as drinking. It is told in two sentences—a bar is started, and he is killed. The thing is somewhat monotonous now—I know just how much they will run, where they will tire, how much they will growl, and what a thundering time I will have in getting them home. I could give you this history of the chase with all particulars at the commencement, I know the signs so well—*Stranger, I'm certain*. Once I met with a match though, and I will tell you about it; for a common hunt would not be worth relating.

"On a fine fall day, long time ago, I was trailing about for bar, and what should I see but fresh marks on the sassafras trees, about eight inches above any in the forests that I knew of. Says I, 'them marks is a hoax, or it indicates the d——t bar that was ever grown.' In fact, stranger, I couldn't believe it was real, and I went on. Again I saw the same marks, at the same height, and *I knew the thing lived*. That conviction came home to my soul like an earthquake. Says I, 'here is something a-purpose for me: that bar is mine, or I give up the hunting business.' The very next morning what should I see but a number of buzzards hovering over my cornfield. 'The rascal has been there,' said I, 'for that sign is certain:' and, sure enough, on examining, I found the bones of what had been as beautiful a hog the day before, as was ever raised by a Buckeye. Then I tracked the critter out of the field to the woods, and all the marks he left behind, showed me that he was *the bar*.

"Well, stranger, the first fair chase I ever had with that big critter, I saw him no less than three distinct times at a distance: the dogs run him over eighteen miles and broke down, my horse gave out, and I was as nearly used up as a man can be, made on *my* principle, *which is patent*. Before this adventure, such things were unknown to me as possible; but, strange as it was, that bar got me used to it before I was done with him;

The Big Bear of Arkansas

for he got so at last, that he would leave me on a long chase *quite easy*. How he did it, I never could understand. That a bar runs at all, is puzzling; but how this one could tire down and bust up a pack of hounds and a horse, that were used to overhauling everything they started after in no time, was past my understanding. Well, stranger, that bar finally got so sassy, that he used to help himself to a hog off my premises whenever he wanted one; the buzzards followed after what he left, and so between *bar and buzzard*, I rather think I was *out of pork*.

"Well, missing that bar so often took hold of my vitals, and I wasted away. The thing had been carried too far, and it reduced me in flesh faster than an ager. I would see that bar in every thing I did; *he hunted me*, and that, too, like a devil, which I began to think he was. While in this fix, I made preparations to give him a last brush, and be done with it. Having completed every thing to my satisfaction, I started at sunrise, and to my great joy, I discovered from the way the dogs run, that they were near him; finding his trail was nothing, for that had become as plain to the pack as a turnpike road. On we went, and coming to an open country, what should I see but the bar very leisurely ascending a hill, and the dogs close at his heels, either a match for him in speed, or else he did not care to get out of their way—I don't know which. But wasn't he a beauty, though? I loved him like a brother.

"On he went, until he came to a tree, the limbs of which formed a crotch about six feet from the ground. Into this crotch he got and seated himself, the dogs yelling all around it; and there he sat eyeing them as quiet as a pond in low water. A green-horn friend of mine, in company, reached shooting distance before me, and blazed away, hitting the critter in the centre of his forehead. The bar shook his head as the ball struck it, and then walked down from that tree as gently as a lady would from a carriage. 'Twas a beautiful sight to see him do that—he was in such a rage that he seemed to be as little afraid of the dogs as if they had been sucking pigs; and the dogs warn't slow in making a ring around him at a respectful distance, I tell you; even Bowie-knife, himself, stood off. Then the way his eyes flashed—why the fire of them would have singed a cat's hair; in fact that bar was in a *wrath all over*. Only one pup came near him, and he was brushed out so totally with the bar's left paw, that he entirely disappeared; and that made the old dogs more cautious still. In the meantime, I came up, and taking deliberate aim as a man should do, at his side, just back of his foreleg, *if my gun did not snap*, call me a coward, and I won't take it personal. Yes, stranger, *it snapped*, and I could not find a cap about my person. While in this predicament, I turned round to my fool friend—says I, 'Bill,' says I, 'you're an ass—you're a fool—you might as well have tried to kill that bar by barking the tree under his belly, as to have done it by hitting him in the head. Your shot has made a tiger of him, and blast me, if a dog gets killed or wounded when they come to blows, I will stick my knife into your liver, I will—' my wrath was up. I had lost my caps, my gun had snapped, the fellow with me had fired at the bar's head, and I expected every moment to see him close in with the dogs, and kill a dozen

Thomas Bangs Thorpe

of them at least. In this thing I was mistaken, for the bar leaped over the ring formed by the dogs, and giving a fierce growl, was off—the pack, of course, in full cry after him. The run this time was short, for coming to the edge of a lake the varmint jumped in, and swam to a little island in the lake, which it reached just a moment before the dogs. 'I'll have him now,' said I, for I had found my caps in the *lining of my coat*—so, rolling a log into the lake, I paddled myself across to the island, just as the dogs had cornered the bar in a thicket. I rushed up and fired—at the same time the critter leaped over the dogs and came within three feet of me, running like mad; he jumped into the lake, and tried to mount the log I had just deserted, but every time he got half his body on it, it would roll over and send him under; the dogs, too, got around him, and pulled him about, and finally Bowie-knife clenched with him, and they sunk into the lake together. Stranger, about this time, I was excited, and I stripped off my coat, drew my knife, and intended to have taken a part with Bowie-knife myself, when the bar rose to the surface. But the varmint staid under—Bowie-knife came up alone, more dead than alive, and with the pack came ashore. 'Thank God,' said I, 'the old villain has got his deserts at last.' Determined to have the body, I cut a grape-vine for a rope, and dove down where I could see the bar in the water, fastened my queer rope to his leg, and fished him, with great difficulty, ashore. Stranger, may I be chawed to death by young alligators, if the thing I looked at wasn't a *she bar, and not the old critter after all*. The way matters got mixed on that island was onaccountably curious, and thinking of it made me more than ever convinced that I was hunting the devil himself. I went home that night and took to my bed—the thing was killing me. The entire team of Arkansaw in barhunting, acknowledged himself used up, and the fact sunk into my feelings like a snagged boat will in the Mississippi. I grew as cross as a bar with two cubs and a sore tail. The thing got out 'mong my neighbours, and I was asked how come on that individu-al that never lost a bar when once started? and if that same individ-u-al didn't wear telescopes when he turned a she bar, of ordinary size, into an old he one, a little larger than a horse? 'Perhaps,' said I, 'friends'—getting wrathy—'perhaps you want to call somebody a liar.' 'Oh, no,' said they, 'we only heard such things as being *rather common* of late, but we don't believe one word of it; oh, no,'—and then they would ride off and laugh like so many hyenas over a dead nigger. It was too much, and I determined to catch that bar, go to Texas, or die,—and I made my preparations accordin'. I had the pack shut up and rested. I took my rifle to pieces and iled it. I put caps in every pocket about my person, *for fear of the lining*. I then told my neighbours, that on Monday morning—naming the day—I would start THAT BAR, and bring him home with me, or they might divide my settlement among them, the owner having disappeared. Well, stranger, on the morning previous to the great day of my hunting expedition, I went into the woods near my house, taking my gun and Bowie-knife along, just *from habit*, and there sitting down also from habit, what should I see, getting over my fence, but *the bar!* Yes, the old varmint was within a hundred yards of me, and the way

The Big Bear of Arkansas

he walked *over that fence*—stranger, he loomed up like a *black mist*, he seemed so large, and he walked right towards me. I raised myself, took deliberate aim, and fired. Instantly the varmint wheeled, gave a yell, and *walked through the fence* like a falling tree would through a cobweb. I started after, but was tripped up by my inexpressibles, which either from habit, or the excitement of the moment, were about my heels, and before I had really gathered myself up, I heard the old varmint groaning in a thicket near by, like a thousand sinners, and by the time I reached him he was a corpse. Stranger, it took five niggers and myself to put that carcase on a mule's back, and old long-ears waddled under the load, as if he was foundered in every leg of his body, and with a common whopper of a bar, he would have trotted off, and enjoyed himself. 'Twould astonish you to know how big he was: I made a *bedspread of his skin* and the way it used to cover my bar mattress, and leave several feet on each side to tuck up, would have delighted you. It was in fact a creation bar, and if it had lived in Samson's time, and had met him, in a fair fight, it would have licked him in the twinkling of a dice-box. But, strangers, I never like the way I hunted, and *missed him*. There is something curious about it, I could never understand,—and I never was satisfied at his giving in so easy at last. Perhaps, he had heard of my preparations to hunt him the next day, so he jist come in, like Capt. Scott's coon, to save his wind to grunt with in dying; but that ain't likely. My private opinion is, that that bar was an *unhuntable bar, and died when his time come.*"

When the story was ended, our hero sat some minutes with his auditors in a grave silence; I saw there was a mystery to him connected with the bear whose death he had just related, that had evidently made a strong impression on his mind. It was also evident that there was some superstitious awe connected with the affair,—a feeling common with all "children of the wood," when they meet with any thing out of their everyday experience. He was the first one, however, to break the silence, and jumping up, he asked all present to "liquor" before going to bed,—a thing which he did, with a number of companions, evidently to his heart's content.

Long before day, I was put ashore at my place of destination, and I can only follow with the reader, in imagination, our Arkansas friend, in his adventures at the "Forks of Cypress" on the Mississippi.

[1841]

Thomas Bangs Thorpe

W. D. Haley:

Johnny Appleseed: A Pioneer Hero

W. D. Haley, a nineteenth-century journalist, here contributes to the beginning of one of America's great myths, the story of Johnny Appleseed, as it emerges out of the life of John Chapman (1774-1847), pioneer nurseryman and wanderer in nineteenth-century Pennsylvania, Ohio, and Indiana. Chapman's apple trees, distributed and planted throughout the Midwest, played a substantial part in bringing those areas into cultivation. As a Swedenborgian romantic, Chapman preached a primitive kinship between man and nature.

The "far West" is rapidly becoming only a traditional designation: railroads have destroyed the romance of frontier life, or have surrounded it with so many appliances of civilization that the pioneer character is rapidly becoming mythical. The men and women who obtain their groceries and dry-goods from New York by rail in a few hours have nothing in common with those who, fifty years ago, "packed" salt a hundred miles to make their mush palatable, and could only exchange corn and wheat for molasses and calico by making long and perilous voyages in flat-boats down the Ohio and Mississippi rivers to New Orleans. Two generations of frontier lives have accumulated stores of narrative which, like the small but beautiful tributaries of great rivers, are forgotten in the broad sweep of the larger current of history. The march of Titans sometimes tramples out the memory of smaller but more useful lives, and sensational glare often eclipses more modest but purer lights. This has been the case in the popular demand for the dime novel dilutions of Fenimore Cooper's romances of border life, which have preserved the records of Indian rapine and atrocity as the only memorials of pioneer history. But the early days of Western settlement witnessed sublimer heroisms than those of human torture, and nobler victories than those of the tomahawk and scalping-knife.

Among the heroes of endurance that was voluntary, and of action that was creative and not sanguinary, there was one man whose name, seldom mentioned now save by some of the few surviving pioneers, deserves to be perpetuated.

The first reliable trace of our modest hero finds him in the Territory of Ohio, in 1801, with a horse-load of apple seeds, which he planted in various places on and about the borders of Licking Creek, the first orchard thus originated by him being on the farm of Isaac Stadden, in what is now known as Licking County, in the State of Ohio. During the five succeeding years, although he was undoubtedly following the same strange occupation, we have no authentic account of his movements until we reach a pleasant spring day in 1806, when a pioneer settler in Jefferson County, Ohio, noticed a peculiar craft, with a remarkable occupant and a curious cargo, slowly dropping down with the current of the Ohio River. It was "Johnny Appleseed," by which name Jonathan Chapman was afterward known in every log-cabin from the Ohio River to the Northern lakes, and westward to the prairies of what is now the State of Indiana. With two canoes lashed together he was transporting a load of apple seeds to the Western frontier, for the purpose of creating orchards on the farthest verge of white settlements. With his canoes he passed down the Ohio to Marietta, where he entered the Muskingum, ascending the stream of that river until he reached the mouth of the Walhonding, or White Woman Creek, and still onward, up the Mohican, into the Black Fork, to the head of navigation, in the region now known as Ashland and Richland counties, on the line of the Pittsburg and Fort Wayne Railroad, in Ohio. A long and toilsome voyage it was, as a glance at the map will show, and must have occupied a great deal of time, as the lonely traveler stopped at every inviting spot to plant the seeds and make his infant nurseries. These are

W. D. Haley

the first well-authenticated facts in the history of Jonathan Chapman, whose birth, there is good reason for believing, occurred in Boston, Massachusetts, in 1775. According to this, which was his own statement in one of his less reticent moods, he was, at the time of his appearance on Licking Creek, twenty-six years of age, and whether impelled in his eccentricities by some absolute misery of the heart which could only find relief in incessant motion, or governed by a benevolent monomania, his whole after-life was devoted to the work of planting apple seeds in remote places. The seeds he gathered from the cider-presses of Western Pennsylvania; but his canoe voyage in 1806 appears to have been the only occasion upon which he adopted that method of transporting them, as all his subsequent journeys were made on foot. Having planted his stock of seeds, he would return to Pennsylvania for a fresh supply, and, as sacks made of any less substantial fabric would not endure the hard usage of the long trip through forests dense with underbrush and briers, he provided himself with leathern bags. Securely packed, the seeds were conveyed, sometimes on the back of a horse, and not unfrequently on his own shoulders, either over a part of the old Indian trial that let from Fort Duquesne to Detroit, by way of Fort Sandusky, or over what is styled in the appendix to "Hutchins's History of Boguet's Expedition in 1764" the "second route through the wilderness of Ohio," which would require him to traverse a distance of one hundred and sixty-six miles in a west-northwest direction from Fort Duquesne in order to reach the Black Fork of the Mohican.

This region, although it is now densely populated, still possesses a romantic beauty that railroads and bustling towns can not obliterate—a country of forest-clad hills and green valleys, through which numerous bright streams flow on their way to the Ohio; but when Johnny Appleseed reached some lonely log-cabin he would find himself in a veritable wilderness. The old settlers say that the margins of the streams, near which the first settlements were generally made, were thickly covered with a low, matted growth of small timber, while nearer to the water was a rank mass of long grass, interlaced with morning-glory and wild pea vines, among which funereal willows and clustering alders stood like sentinels on the outpost of civilization. The hills, that rise almost to the dignity of mountains, were crowned with forest trees, and in the coverts were innumerable bears, wolves, deer, and droves of wild hogs, that were as ferocious as any beast of prey. In the grass the massasauga and other venomous reptiles lurked in such numbers that a settler named Chandler has left the fact on record that during the first season of his residence, while mowing a little prairie which formed part of his land, he killed over two hundred black rattlesnakes in an area that would involve an average destruction of one of these reptiles for each rod of land. The frontiers-man, who felt himself sufficiently protected by his rifle against wild beasts and hostile Indians, found it necessary to guard against the attacks of the insidious enemies in the grass by wrapping bandages of dried grass around his buckskin leggings and moccasins; but Johnny would shoulder his bag of apple seeds, and with bare feet penetrate to some remote spot that combined picturesqueness

Johnny Appleseed: A Pioneer Hero

and fertility of soil, and there he would plant his seeds, place a slight in-closure around the place, and leave them to grow until the trees were large enough to be transplanted by the settlers, who, in the mean time, would have made their clearings in the vicinity. The sites chosen by him are, many of them, well known, and are such as an artist or a poet would select —open places on the loamy lands that border the creeks—rich, secluded spots, hemmed in by giant trees, picturesque now, but fifty years ago, with their wild surroundings and the primal silence, they must have been ten-fold more so.

In personal appearance Chapman was a small, wiry man, full of restless activity; he had long dark hair, a scanty beard that was never shaved, and keen black eyes that sparkled with a peculiar brightness. His dress was of the oddest description. Generally, even in the coldest weather, he went barefooted, but sometimes, for his long journeys, he would make himself a rude pair of sandals; at other times he would wear any cast-off foot-covering he chanced to find—a boot on one foot and an old brogan or a moccasin on the other. It appears to have been a matter of conscience with him never to purchase shoes, although he was rarely without money enough to do so. On one occasion, in an unusually cold November, while he was traveling barefooted through mud and snow, a settler who hap-pened to possess a pair of shoes that were too small for his own use forced their acceptance upon Johnny, declaring that it was sinful for a human being to travel with naked feet in such weather. A few days afterward the donor was in the village that has since become the thriving city of Mans-field, and met his beneficiary contentedly plodding along with his feet bare and half frozen. With some degree of anger he inquired for the cause of such foolish conduct, and received for reply that Johnny had overtaken a poor, barefooted family moving Westward, and as they appeared to be in much greater need of clothing than he was, he had given them the shoes. His dress was generally composed of cast-off clothing, that he had taken in payment for apple-trees; and as the pioneers were far less extravagant than their descendants in such matters, the homespun and buckskin garments that they discarded would not be very elegant or serviceable. In his later years, however, he seems to have thought that even this kind of second-hand raiment was too luxurious, as his principal garment was made of a coffee sack, in which he cut holes for his head and arms to pass through, and pronounced it "a very serviceable cloak, and as good clothing as any man need wear." In the matter of head-gear his taste was equally unique; his first experiment was with a tin vessel that served to cook his mush, but this was open to the objection that it did not protect his eyes from the beams of the sun; so he constructed a hat of pasteboard with an immense peak in front, and having thus secured an article that combined usefulness with economy, it became his permanent fashion.

Thus strangely clad, he was perpetually wandering through forests and morasses, and suddenly appearing in white settlements and Indian vil-lages; but there must have been some rare force of gentle goodness dwelling in his looks and breathing in his words, for it is the testimony of all who

W. D. Haley

knew him that, notwithstanding his ridiculous attire, he was always treated with the greatest respect by the rudest frontiers-man, and, what is a better test, the boys of the settlements forbore to jeer at him. With grown-up people and boys he was usually reticent, but manifested great affection for little girls, always having pieces of ribbon and gay calico to give to his little favorites. Many a grandmother in Ohio and Indiana can remember the presents she received when a child from poor homeless Johnny Appleseed. When he consented to eat with any family he would never sit down to the table until he was assured that there was an ample supply for the children; and his sympathy for their youthful troubles and his kindness toward them made him friends among all the juveniles of the borders.

The Indians also treated Johnny with the greatest kindness. By these wild and sanguinary savages he was regarded as a "great medicine man," on account of his strange appearance, eccentric actions, and, especially, the fortitude with which he could endure pain, in proof of which he would often thrust pins and needles into his flesh. His nervous sensibilities really seem to have been less acute than those of ordinary people, for his method of treating the cuts and sores that were the consequences of his barefooted wanderings through briers and thorns was to sear the wound with a red-hot iron, and then cure the burn. During the war of 1812, when the frontier settlers were tortured and slaughtered by the savage allies of Great Britain, Johnny Appleseed continued his wanderings, and was never harmed by the roving bands of hostile Indians. On many occasions the impunity with which he ranged the country enabled him to give the settlers warning of approaching danger in time to allow them to take refuge in their block-houses before the savages could attack them. Our informant refers to one of these instances, when the news of Hull's surrender came like a thunder-bolt upon the frontier. Large bands of Indians and British were destroying every thing before them and murdering defenseless women and children, and even the block-houses were not always a sufficient protection. At this time Johnny traveled day and night, warning the people of the approaching danger. He visited every cabin and delivered this message: "The Spirit of the Lord is upon me, and he hath anointed me to blow the trumpet in the wilderness, and sound an alarm in the forest; for, behold, the tribes of the heathen are round about your doors, and a devouring flame followeth after them." The aged man who narrated this incident said that he could feel even now the thrill that was caused by this prophetic announcement of the wild-looking herald of danger, who aroused the family on a bright moonlight midnight with his piercing voice. Refusing all offers of food and denying himself a moment's rest, he traversed the border day and night until he had warned every settler of the approaching peril.

His diet was as meagre as his clothing. He believed it to be a sin to kill any creature for food, and thought that all that was necessary for human sustenance was produced by the soil. He was also a strenuous opponent of the waste of food, and on one occasion, on approaching a log-cabin, he observed some fragments of bread floating upon the surface

Johnny Appleseed: A Pioneer Hero

of a bucket of slops that was intended for the pigs. He immediately fished them out, and when the housewife expressed her astonishment, he told her that it was an abuse of the gifts of a merciful God to allow the smallest quantity of any thing that was designed to supply the wants of mankind to be diverted from its purpose.

In this instance, as in his whole life, the peculiar religious ideas of Johnny Appleseed were exemplified. He was a most earnest disciple of the faith taught by Emanuel Swedenborg, and himself claimed to have frequent conversations with angels and spirits; two of the latter, of the feminine gender, he asserted, had revealed to him that they were to be his wives in a future state if he abstained from a matrimonial alliance on earth. He entertained a profound reverence for the revelations of the Swedish seer, and always carried a few old volumes with him. These he was very anxious should be read by every one, and he was probably not only the first colporteur in the wilderness of Ohio, but as he had no tract society to furnish him supplies, he certainly devised an original method of multiplying one book into a number. He divided his books into several pieces, leaving a portion at a log-cabin, and on a subsequent visit furnishing another fragment, and continuing this process as diligently as though the work had been published in serial numbers. By this plan he was enabled to furnish reading for several people at the same time, and out of one book; but it must have been a difficult undertaking for some nearly illiterate backwoodsman to endeavor to comprehend Swedenborg by a backward course of reading, when his first installment happened to be the last fraction of the volume. Johnny's faith in Swedenborg's works was so reverential as almost to be superstitious. He was once asked if, in traveling barefooted through forests abounding with venomous reptiles, he was not afraid of being bitten. With his peculiar smile, he drew his book from his bosom, and said, "This book is an infallible protection against all danger here and hereafter."

It was his custom, when he had been welcomed to some hospitable log-house after a weary day of journeying, to lie down on the puncheon floor, and, after inquiring if his auditors would hear "some news right fresh from heaven," produce his few tattered books, among which would be a New Testament, and read and expound until his uncultivated hearers would catch the spirit and glow of his enthusiasm, while they scarcely comprehended his language. A lady who knew him in his later years writes in the following terms of one of these domiciliary readings of poor, self-sacrificing Johnny Appleseed: "We can hear him read now, just as he did that summer day, when we were busy quilting up stairs, and he lay near the door, his voice rising denunciatory and thrilling—strong and loud as the roar of wind and waves, then soft and soothing as the balmy airs that quivered the morning-glory leaves about his gray beard. His was a strange eloquence at times, and he was undoubtedly a man of genius." What a scene is presented to our imagination! The interior of a primitive cabin, the wide, open fire-place, where a few sticks are burning beneath the iron pot in which the evening meal is cooking; around the fireplace the atten-

W. D. Haley

tive group, composed of the sturdy pioneer and his wife and children, listening with a reverential awe to the "news right fresh from heaven;" and reclining on the floor, clad in rags, but with his gray hairs glorified by the beams of the setting sun that flood through the open door and the unchinked logs of the humble building, this poor wanderer, with the gift of genius and eloquence, who believes with the faith of apostles and martyrs that God has appointed him a mission in the wilderness to preach the Gospel of love, and plant apple seeds that shall produce orchards for the benefit of men and women and little children whom he has never seen. If there is a sublimer faith or a more genuine eloquence in richly decorated cathedrals and under brocade vestments, it would be worth a long journey to find it.

Next to his advocacy of his peculiar religious ideas, his enthusiasm for the cultivation of apple-trees in what he termed "the only proper way" —that is, from the seed—was the absorbing object of his life. Upon this, as upon religion, he was eloquent in his appeals. He would describe the growing and ripening fruit as such a rare and beautiful gift of the Almighty with words that became pictures, until his hearers could almost see its manifold forms of beauty present before them. To his eloquence on this subject, as well as to his actual labors in planting nurseries, the country over which he traveled for so many years is largely indebted for its numerous orchards. But he denounced as absolute wickedness all devices of pruning and grafting, and would speak of the act of cutting a tree as if it were a cruelty inflicted upon a sentient being.

Not only is he entitled to the fame of being the earliest colporteur on the frontiers, but in the work of protecting animals from abuse and suffering he preceded, while, in his smaller sphere, he equaled the zeal of the good Mr. Bergh. Whenever Johnny saw an animal abused, or heard of it, he would purchase it and give it to some more humane settler, on condition that it should be kindly treated and properly cared for. It frequently happened that the long journey into the wilderness would cause the new settlers to be encumbered with lame and broken-down horses, that were turned loose to die. In the autumn Johnny would make a diligent search for all such animals, and, gathering them up, he would bargain for their food and shelter until the next spring, when he would lead them away to some good pasture for the summer. If they recovered so as to be capable of working, he would never sell them, but would lend or give them away, stipulating for their good usage. His conception of the absolute sin of inflicting pain or death upon any creature was not limited to the higher forms of animal life, but every thing that had being was to him, in the fact of its life, endowed with so much of the Divine Essence that to wound or destroy it was to inflict an injury upon some atom of Divinity. No Brahmin could be more concerned for the preservation of insect life, and the only occasion on which he destroyed a venomous reptile was a source of long regret, to which he could never refer without manifesting sadness. He had selected a suitable place for planting apple seeds on a small prairie, and in order to prepare the ground he was mowing the long grass, when he

Johnny Appleseed: A Pioneer Hero

was bitten by a rattlesnake. In describing the event he sighed heavily, and said, "Poor fellow, he only just touched me, when I, in the heat of my ungodly passion, put the heel of my scythe in him, and went away. Some time afterward I went back, and there lay the poor fellow dead." Numerous anecdotes bearing upon his respect for every form of life are preserved, and form the staple of pioneer recollections. On one occasion, a cool autumnal night, when Johnny, who always camped out in preference to sleeping in a house, had built a fire near which he intended to pass the night, he noticed that the blaze attracted large numbers of mosquitoes, many of whom flew too near to his fire and were burned. He immediately brought water and quenched the fire, accounting for his conduct afterward by saying, "God forbid that I should build a fire for my comfort which should be the means of destroying any of His creatures!" At another time he removed the fire he had built near a hollow log, and slept on the snow, because he found that the log contained a bear and her cubs, whom, he said, he did not wish to disturb. And this unwillingness to inflict pain or death was equally strong when he was a sufferer by it, as the following will show. Johnny had been assisting some settlers to make a road through the woods, and in the course of their work they accidentally destroyed a hornets' nest. One of the angry insects soon found a lodgment under Johnny's coffee-sack cloak, but although it stung him repeatedly he removed it with the greatest gentleness. The men who were present laughingly asked him why he did not kill it. To which he gravely replied that "It would not be right to kill the poor thing, for it did not intend to hurt me."

Theoretically he was as methodical in matters of business as any merchant. In addition to their picturesqueness, the locations of his nurseries were all fixed with a view to a probable demand for the trees by the time they had attained sufficient growth for transplanting. He would give them away to those who could not pay for them. Generally, however, he sold them for old clothing or a supply of corn meal; but he preferred to receive a note payable at some indefinite period. When this was accomplished he seemed to think that the transaction was completed in a business-like way; but if the giver of the note did not attend to its payment, the holder of it never troubled himself about its collection. His expenses for food and clothing were so very limited that, notwithstanding his freedom from the *auri sacra fames*, he was frequently in possession of more money than he cared to keep, and it was quickly disposed of for wintering infirm horses, or given to some poor family whom the ague had prostrated or the accidents of border life impoverished. In a single instance only he is known to have invested his surplus means in the purchase of land, having received a deed from Alexander Finley, of Mohican Township, Ashland County, Ohio, for a part of the southwest quarter of section twenty-six; but with his customary indifference to matters of value, Johnny failed to record the deed, and lost it. Only a few years ago the property was in litigation.

We must not leave the reader under the impression that this man's life, so full of hardship and perils, was a gloomy or unhappy one. There is an element of human pride in all martyrdom, which, if it does not soften

W. D. Haley

the pains, stimulates the power of endurance. Johnny's life was made serenely happy by the conviction that he was living like the primitive Christians. Nor was he devoid of a keen humor, to which he occasionally gave vent, as the following will show. Toward the latter part of Johnny's career in Ohio an itinerant missionary found his way to the village of Mansfield, and preached to an open-air congregation. The discourse was tediously lengthy, and unnecessarily severe upon the sin of extravagance, which was beginning to manifest itself among the pioneers by an occasional indulgence in the carnal vanities of calico and "store tea." There was a good deal of the Pharisaic leaven in the preacher, who very frequently emphasized his discourse by the inquiry, "Where now is there a man who, like the primitive Christians, is traveling to heaven barefooted and clad in coarse raiment?" When this interrogation had been repeated beyond all reasonable endurance, Johnny rose from the log on which he was reclining, and advancing to the speaker, he placed one of his bare feet upon the stump which served for a pulpit, and pointing to his coffee-sack garment, he quietly said, "Here's your primitive Christian!" The well-clothed missionary hesitated and stammered and dismissed the congregation. His pet antithesis was destroyed by Johnny's personal appearance, which was far more primitive than the preacher cared to copy.

Some of the pioneers were disposed to think that Johnny's humor was the cause of an extensive practical joke; but it is generally conceded now that a wide-spread annoyance was really the result of his belief that the offensively odored weed known in the West as the dog-fennel, but more generally styled the May-weed, possessed valuable antimalarial virtues. He procured some seeds of the plant in Pennsylvania, and sowed them in the vicinity of every house in the region of his travels. The consequence was that successive flourishing crops of the weed spread over the whole country, and caused almost as much trouble as the disease it was intended to ward off; and to this day the dog-fennel, introduced by Johnny Appleseed, is one of the worst grievances of the Ohio farmers.

In 1838—thirty-seven years after his appearance on Licking Creek— Johnny noticed that civilization, wealth, and population were pressing into the wilderness of Ohio. Hitherto he had easily kept just in advance of the wave of settlement; but now towns and churches were making their appearance, and even, at long intervals, the stage-driver's horn broke the silence of the grand old forests, and he felt that his work was done in the region in which he had labored so long. He visited every house, and took a solemn farewell of all the families. The little girls who had been delighted with his gifts of fragments of calico and ribbons had become sober matrons, and the boys who had wondered at his ability to bear the pain caused by running needles into his flesh were heads of families. With parting words of admonition he left them, and turned his steps steadily toward the setting sun.

During the succeeding nine years he pursued his eccentric avocation on the western border of Ohio and in Indiana. In the summer of 1847, when his labors had literally borne fruit over a hundred thousand square

Johnny Appleseed: A Pioneer Hero

miles of territory, at the close of a warm day, after traveling twenty miles, he entered the house of a settler in Allen County, Indiana, and was, as usual, warmly welcomed. He declined to eat with the family, but accepted some bread and milk, which he partook of sitting on the door-step and gazing on the setting sun. Later in the evening he delivered his "news right fresh from heaven" by reading the Beatitudes. Declining other accommodation, he slept, as usual, on the floor, and in the early morning he was found with his features all aglow with a supernal light, and his body so near death that his tongue refused its office. The physician, who was hastily summoned, pronounced him dying, but added that he had never seen a man in so placid a state at the approach of death. At seventy-two years of age, forty-six of which had been devoted to his self-imposed mission, he ripened into death as naturally and beautifully as the seeds of his own planting had grown into fibre and bud and blossom and the matured fruit.

Thus died one of the memorable men of pioneer times, who never inflicted pain or knew an enemy—a man of strange habits, in whom there dwelt a comprehensive love that reached with one hand downward to the lowest forms of life, and with the other upward to the very throne of God. A laboring, self-denying benefactor of his race, homeless, solitary, and ragged, he trod the thorny earth with bare and bleeding feet, intent only upon making the wilderness fruitful. Now "no man knoweth of his sepulchre;" but his deeds will live in the fragrance of the apple blossoms he loved so well, and the story of his life, however crudely narrated, will be a perpetual proof that true heroism, pure benevolence, noble virtues, and deeds that deserve immortality may be found under meanest apparel, and far from gilded halls and towering spires.

[1871]

W. D. Haley

Abraham Lincoln:
Fragment: Niagara Falls

Abraham Lincoln (1809-1865), lawyer, statesman, sixteenth president of the United States,
was only incidentally a writer, but he became a
master of English prose. The following fragment, curiously unfinished, is the result of a
visit to Niagara Falls in 1848. Never made public until after Lincoln's death, it is called by his
secretary-biographers, Nicolay and Hay, "Notes
for a Lecture," but the sentiments reflect Lincoln's psychological reaction as he attempts
to describe his own wonderment rather than to
prepare a carefully contrived lecture.

Niagara Falls! By what mysterious power is it that millions and millions are drawn from all parts of the world to gaze upon Niagara Falls? There is no mystery about the thing itself. Every effect is just such as any intelligent man, knowing the causes, would anticipate, without [seeing] it. If the water moving onward in a great river reaches a point where there is a perpendicular jog, of a hundred feet in descent, in the bottom of the river, —it is plain the water will have a violent and continuous plunge at that point. It is also plain the water, thus plunging, will foam, and roar, and send up a mist, continuously, in which last, during sunshine, there will be perpetual rain-bows. The mere physical of Niagara Falls is only this. Yet this is really a very small part of that world's wonder. Its power to excite reflection and emotion is its great charm. The geologist will demonstrate that the plunge, or fall, was once at Lake Ontario, and has worn its way back to its present position; he will ascertain how *fast* it is wearing now, and so get a basis for determining how *long* it has been wearing back from Lake Ontario, and finally demonstrate by it that this world is at least fourteen thousand years old. A philosopher of a slightly different turn will say Niagara Falls is only the lip of the basin out of which pours all the surplus water which rains down on two or three hundred thousand square miles of the earth's surface. He will estim[ate with] approximate accuracy that five hundred thousand [to]ns of water falls with its full weight a distance of a hundred feet each minute—thus exerting a force equal to the lifting of the same weight, through the same space, in the same time. And then the further reflection comes that this vast amount of water, constantly pouring *down*, is supplied by an equal amount constantly *lifted up*, by the sun; and still he says, "If this much is lifted up, for *this one* space of two or three hundred thousand square miles, an equal amount must be lifted for every other equal space; and he is overwhelmed in the contemplation of the vast power the sun is constantly exerting in [the] quiet, noiseless operation of lifting water *up* to be rained *down* again.

But still there is more. It calls up the indefinite past. When Columbus first sought this continent—when Christ suffered on the cross—when Moses led Israel through the Red Sea—nay, even, when Adam first came from the hand of his Maker—then as now, Niagara was roaring here. The eyes of that species of extinct giants, whose bones fill the mounds of America, have gazed on Niagara, as ours do now. Contemporary with the whole race of men, and older than the first man, Niagara is strong, and fresh to-day as ten thousand years ago. The Mammoth and Mastodon— now so long dead that fragments of their monstrous bones alone testify that they ever lived, have gazed on Niagara. In that long—long time, never still for a single moment. Never dried, never froze, never slept, never rested,

[c. September 25–30, 1848]

Abraham Lincoln

Francis Parkman:

The Buffalo Camp

Francis Parkman (1823-1893), historian and traveler, visited the West to improve his health and study the Indians, living for a time with the Sioux. *The Oregon Trail* (1849) was the first of a long series of studies that grew out of his western experience, and it remains his best-known work. But his research in all of his writing is sound, and his literary style gives an air of immediacy to his material.

No one in the camp was more active than Jim Gurney, and no one half so lazy as Ellis. Between these two there was a great antipathy. Ellis never stirred in the morning until he was compelled, but Jim was always on his feet before daybreak; and this morning as usual the sound of his voice awakened the party.

"Get up, booby! up with you now, you're fit for nothing but eating and sleeping. Stop your grumbling and come out of that buffalo robe, or I'll pull it off for you."

Jim's words were interspersed with numerous expletives, which gave them great additional effect. Ellis drawled out something in a nasal tone from among the folds of his buffalo robe; then slowly disengaged himself, rose into a sitting posture, stretched his long arms, yawned hideously, and, finally raising his tall person erect, stood staring about him to all the four quarters of the horizon. Deslauriers's fire was soon blazing, and the horses and mules, loosened from their pickets, were feeding on the neighboring meadow. When we sat down to breakfast the prairie was still in the dusky light of morning; and as the sun rose we were mounted and on our way again.

"A white buffalo!" exclaimed Munroe.

"I'll have that fellow," said Shaw, "if I run my horse to death after him."

He threw the cover of his gun to Deslauriers and galloped out upon the prairie.

"Stop, Mr. Shaw, stop!" called out Henry Chatillon, "you'll run down your horse for nothing; it's only a white ox."

But Shaw was already out of hearing. The ox, which had no doubt strayed away from some of the government wagon trains, was standing beneath some low hills which bounded the plain in the distance. Not far from him a band of veritable buffalo bulls were grazing; and startled at Shaw's approach, they all broke into a run, and went scrambling up the hillsides to gain the high prairie above. One of them in his haste and terror involved himself in a fatal catastrophe. Along the foot of the hills was a narrow strip of deep marshy soil, into which the bull plunged and hopelessly entangled himself. We all rode to the spot. The huge carcass was half sunk in the mud, which flowed to his very chin, and his shaggy mane was outspread upon the surface. As we came near, the bull began to struggle with convulsive strength; he writhed to and fro, and in the energy of his fright and desperation would lift himself for a moment half out of the slough, while the reluctant mire returned a sucking sound as he strained to drag his limbs from its tenacious depths. We stimulated his exertions by getting behind him and twisting his tail; nothing would do. There was clearly no hope for him. After every effort his heaving sides were more deeply imbedded, and the mire almost overflowed his nostrils; he lay still at length, and looking round at us with a furious eye, seemed to resign himself to his fate. Ellis slowly dismounted, and, leveling his boasted yager, shot the old bull through the heart; then lazily climbed back again to his seat, pluming himself no doubt on having actually killed a buffalo. That

Francis Parkman

day the invincible yager drew blood for the first and last time during the whole journey.

The morning was a bright and gay one, and the air so clear that on the farthest horizon the outline of the pale blue prairie was sharply drawn against the sky. Shaw was in the mood for hunting; he rode in advance of the party, and before long we saw a file of bulls galloping at full speed upon a green swell of the prairie at some distance in front. Shaw came scouring along behind them, arrayed in his red shirt, which looked very well in the distance; he gained fast on the fugitives, and as the foremost bull was disappearing behind the summit of the swell, we saw him in the act of assailing the hindmost; a smoke sprang from the muzzle of his gun and floated away before the wind like a little white cloud; the bull turned upon him, and just then the rising ground concealed them both from view.

We were moving forward until about noon, when we stopped by the side of the Arkansas. At that moment Shaw appeared riding slowly down the side of a distant hill; his horse was tired and jaded, and when he threw his saddle upon the ground, I observed that the tails of two bulls were dangling behind it. No sooner were the horses turned loose to feed than Henry, asking Munroe to go with him, took his rifle and walked quietly away. Shaw, Tête Rouge, and I sat down by the side of the cart to discuss the dinner which Deslauriers placed before us, and we had scarcely finished when we saw Munroe walking towards us along the river bank. Henry, he said, had killed four fat cows, and had sent him back for horses to bring in the meat. Shaw took a horse for himself and another for Henry, and he and Munroe left the camp together. After a short absence all three of them came back, their horses loaded with the choicest parts of the meat. We kept two of the cows for ourselves, and gave the others to Munroe and his companions. Deslauriers seated himself on the grass before the pile of meat, and worked industriously for some time to cut it into thin broad sheets for drying, an art in which he had all the skill of an Indian squaw. Long before night, cords of rawhide were stretched around the camp, and the meat was hung upon them to dry in the sunshine and pure air of the prairie. Our California companies were less successful at the work; but they accomplished it after their own fashion, and their side of the camp was soon garnished in the same manner as our own.

We meant to remain at this place long enough to prepare provisions for our journey to the frontier, which, as we supposed, might occupy about a month. Had the distance been twice as great and the party ten times as large, the rifle of Henry Chatillon would have supplied meat enough for the whole within two days; we were obliged to remain, however, until it should be dry enough for transportation; so we pitched our tent and made other arrangements for a permanent camp. The California men, who had no such shelter, contented themselves with arranging their packs on the grass around their fire. In the meantime we had nothing to do but amuse ourselves. Our tent was within a rod of the river, if the broad sand beds, with a scanty stream of water coursing here and there along their surface, deserve to be dignified with the name of river. The vast flat plains on

The Buffalo Camp

either side were almost on a level with the sand beds, and they were bounded in the distance by low, monotonous hills, parallel to the course of the stream. All was one expanse of grass; there was no wood in view, except some trees and stunted bushes upon two islands which rose from the wet sands of the river. Yet far from being dull and tame, the scene was often a wild and animated one; for twice a day, at sunrise and at noon, the buffalo came issuing from the hills, slowly advancing in their grave processions to drink at the river. All our amusements were to be at their expense. An old buffalo bull is a brute of unparalleled ugliness. At first sight of him every feeling of pity vanishes. The cows are much smaller and of a gentler appearance, as becomes their sex. While in this camp we forbore to attack them, leaving to Henry Chatillon, who could better judge their quality, the task of killing such as we wanted for use; but against the bulls we waged an unrelenting war. Thousands of them might be slaughtered without causing any detriment to the species, for their numbers greatly exceed those of the cows; it is the hides of the latter alone which are used for the purposes of commerce and for making the lodges of the Indians; and the destruction among them is therefore greatly disproportionate.

Our horses were tired, and we now usually hunted on foot. While we were lying on the grass after dinner, smoking, talking, or laughing at Tête Rouge, one of us would look up and observe, far out on the plains beyond the river, certain black objects slowly approaching. He would inhale a parting whiff from the pipe, then rising lazily, take his rifle, which leaned against the cart, throw over his shoulder the strap of his pouch and powderhorn, and with his moccasins in his hand, walk across the sand towards the opposite side of the river. This was very easy; for though the sands were about a quarter of a mile wide, the water was nowhere more than two feet deep. The farther bank was about four or five feet high, and quite perpendicular, being cut away by the water in spring. Tall grass grew along its edge. Putting it aside with his hand, and cautiously looking through it, the hunter can discern the huge shaggy back of the bull slowly swaying to and fro, as, with his clumsy, swinging gait, he advances towards the water. The buffalo have regular paths by which they come down to drink. Seeing at a glance along which of these his intended victim is moving, the hunter crouches under the bank within fifteen or twenty yards, it may be, of the point where the path enters the river. Here he sits down quietly on the sand. Listening intently, he hears the heavy, monotonous tread of the approaching bull. The moment after, he sees a motion among the long weeds and grass just at the spot where the path is channeled through the bank. An enormous black head is thrust out, the horns just visible amid the mass of tangled mane. Half sliding, half plunging, down comes the buffalo upon the river bed below. He steps out in full sight upon the sands. Just before him a runnel of water is gliding, and he bends his head to drink. You may hear the water as it gurgles down his capacious throat. He raises his head, and the drops trickle from his wet beard. He stands with an air

Francis Parkman

of stupid abstraction, unconscious of the lurking danger. Noiselessly the hunter cocks his rifle. As he sits upon the sand, his knee is raised, and his elbow rests upon it, that he may level his heavy weapon with a steadier aim. The stock is at his shoulder; his eye ranges along the barrel. Still he is in no haste to fire. The bull, with slow deliberation, begins his march over the sands to the other side. He advances his foreleg, and exposes to view a small spot, denuded of hair, just behind the point of his shoulder; upon this the hunter brings the sight of his rifle to bear; lightly and delicately his finger presses the hair trigger. The spiteful crack of the rifle responds to his touch, and instantly in the middle of the bare spot appears a small red dot. The buffalo shivers; death has overtaken him, he cannot tell from whence; still he does not fall, but walks heavily forward, as if nothing had happened. Yet before he has gone far out upon the sand, you see him stop; he totters; his knees bend under him, and his head sinks forward to the ground. Then his whole vast bulk sways to one side; he rolls over on the sand, and dies with a scarcely perceptible struggle.

Waylaying the buffalo in this manner, and shooting them as they come to water, is the easiest method of hunting them. They may also be approached by crawling up ravines or behind hills, or even over the open prairie. This is often surprisingly easy; but at other times it requires the utmost skill of the most experienced hunter. Henry Chatillon was a man of extraordinary strength and hardihood; but I have seen him return to camp quite exhausted with his efforts, his limbs scratched and wounded, and his buckskin dress stuck full of the thorns of the prickly-pear, among which he had been crawling. Sometimes he would lie flat upon his face, and drag himself along in this position for many rods together.

On the second day of our stay at this place, Henry went out for an afternoon hunt. Shaw and I remained in camp, until, observing some bulls approaching the water upon the other side of the river, we crossed over to attack them. They were so near, however, that before we could get under cover of the bank our appearance as we walked over the sands alarmed them. Turning round before coming within gunshot, they began to move off to the right in a direction parallel to the river. I climbed up the bank and ran after them. They were walking swiftly, and before I could come within gunshot distance they slowly wheeled about and faced me. Before they had turned far enough to see me I had fallen flat on my face. For a moment they stood and stared at the strange object upon the grass; then turning away, again they walked on as before; and I, rising immediately, ran once more in pursuit. Again they wheeled about, and again I fell prostrate. Repeating this three or four times, I came at length within a hundred yards of the fugitives, and as I saw them turning again, I sat down and leveled my rifle. The one in the center was the largest I had ever seen. I shot him behind the shoulder. His two companions ran off. He attempted to follow, but soon came to a stand, and at length lay down as quietly as an ox chewing the cud. Cautiously approaching him, I saw by his dull and jelly-like eye that he was dead.

When I began the chase, the prairie was almost tenantless; but a

The Buffalo Camp

great multitude of buffalo had suddenly thronged upon it, and looking up I saw within fifty rods a heavy, dark column stretching to the right and left as far as I could see. I walked towards them. My approach did not alarm them in the least. The column itself consisted almost entirely of cows and calves, but a great many old bulls were ranging about the prairie on its flank, and as I drew near they faced towards me with such a grim and ferocious look that I thought it best to proceed no farther. Indeed, I was already within close rifle shot of the column, and I sat down on the ground to watch their movements. Sometimes the whole would stand still, their heads all one way; then they would trot forward, as if by a common impulse, their hoofs and horns clattering together as they moved. I soon began to hear at a distance on the left the sharp reports of a rifle, again and again repeated; and not long after, dull and heavy sounds succeeded, which I recognized as the familiar voice of Shaw's double-barreled gun. When Henry's rifle was at work there was always meat to be brought in. I went back across the river for a horse, and, returning, reached the spot where the hunters were standing. The buffalo were visible on the distant prairie. The living had retreated from the ground, but ten or twelve carcasses were scattered in various directions. Henry, knife in hand, was stooping over a dead cow, cutting away the best and fattest of the meat.

When Shaw left me he had walked down for some distance under the river bank to find another bull. At length he saw the plains covered with the host of buffalo, and soon after heard the crack of Henry's rifle. Ascending the bank, he crawled through the grass, which for a rod or two from the river was very high and rank. He had not crawled far before to his astonishment he saw Henry standing erect upon the prairie, almost surrounded by the buffalo. Henry was in his element. Quite unconscious that anyone was looking at him, he stood at the full height of his tall figure, one hand resting upon his side, and the other arm leaning carelessly on the muzzle of his rifle. His eye was ranging over the singular assemblage around him. Now and then he would select such a cow as suited him, level his rifle, and shoot her dead; then quietly reloading, he would resume his former position. The buffalo seemed no more to regard his presence than if he were one of themselves; the bulls were bellowing and butting at each other, or rolling about in the dust. A group of buffalo would gather about the carcass of a dead cow, snuffing at her wounds; and sometimes they would come behind those that had not yet fallen, and endeavor to push them from the spot. Now and then some old bull would face towards Henry with an air of stupid amazement, but none seemed inclined to attack or fly from him. For some time Shaw lay among the grass, looking in surprise at this extraordinary sight; at length he crawled cautiously forward, and spoke in a low voice to Henry, who told him to rise and come on. Still the buffalo showed no sign of fear; they remained gathered about their dead companions. Henry had already killed as many cows as we wanted for use, and Shaw, kneeling behind one of the carcasses, shot five bulls before the rest thought it necessary to disperse.

Francis Parkman

The frequent stupidity and infatuation of the buffalo seems the more remarkable from the contrast it offers to their wildness and wariness at other times. Henry knew all their peculiarities; he had studied them as a scholar studies his books, and derived quite as much pleasure from the occupation. The buffalo were a kind of companion to him, and, as he said, he never felt alone when they were about him. He took great pride in his skill in hunting. He was one of the most modest of men; yet in the simplicity and frankness of his character, it was clear that he looked upon his preëminence in this respect as a thing too palpable and well established to be disputed. But whatever may have been his estimate of his own skill, it was rather below than above that which others placed upon it. The only time that I ever saw a shade of scorn darken his face was when two volunteer soldiers, who had just killed a buffalo for the first time, undertook to instruct him as to the best method of "approaching." Henry always seemed to think that he had a sort of prescriptive right to the buffalo, and to look upon them as something belonging to himself. Nothing excited his indignation so much as any wanton destruction committed among the cows, and in his view shooting a calf was a cardinal sin.

Henry Chatillon and Tête Rouge were of the same age; that is, about thirty. Henry was twice as large, and about six times as strong as Tête Rouge. Henry's face was roughened by winds and storms; Tête Rouge's was bloated by sherry cobblers and brandy toddy. Henry talked of Indians and buffalo; Tête Rouge of theaters and oyster cellars. Henry had led a life of hardship and privation; Tête Rouge never had a whim which he would not gratify at the first moment he was able. Henry moreover was the most disinterested man I ever saw; while Tête Rouge, though equally good-natured in his way, cared for nobody but himself. Yet we would not have lost him on any account; he served the purpose of a jester in a feudal castle; our camp would have been lifeless without him. For the past week he had fattened in a most amazing manner; and, indeed, this was not at all surprising, since his appetite was inordinate. He was eating from morning till night; half the time he would be at work cooking some private repast for himself, and he paid a visit to the coffee pot eight or ten times a day. His rueful and disconsolate face became jovial and rubicund, his eyes stood out like a lobster's, and his spirits, which before were sunk to the depths of despondency, were now elated in proportion; all day he was singing, whistling, laughing, and telling stories. Being mortally afraid of Jim Gurney, he kept close in the neighborhood of our tent. As he had seen an abundance of low fast life, and had a considerable fund of humor, his anecdotes were extremely amusing, especially since he never hesitated to place himself in a ludicrous point of view, provided he could raise a laugh by doing so. Tête Rouge, however, was sometimes rather troublesome; he had an inveterate habit of pilfering provisions at all times of the day. He set ridicule at defiance, and would never have given over his tricks, even if they had drawn upon him the scorn of the whole party. Now and then, indeed, something worse than laughter fell to his share; on these occasions he would exhibit much con-

The Buffalo Camp

trition, but half an hour after we would generally observe him stealing round to the box at the back of the cart, and slyly making off with the provisions which Deslauriers had laid by for supper. He was fond of smoking; but having no tobacco of his own, we used to provide him with as much as he wanted, a small piece at a time. At first we gave him half a pound together; but this experiment proved an entire failure, for he invariably lost not only the tobacco, but the knife intrusted to him for cutting it, and a few minutes after he would come to us with many apologies and beg for more.

We had been two days at this camp, and some of the meat was nearly fit for transportation, when a storm came suddenly upon us. About sunset the whole sky grew as black as ink, and the long grass at the edge of the river bent and rose mournfully with the first gusts of the approaching hurricane. Munroe and his two companions brought their guns and placed them under cover of our tent. Having no shelter for themselves, they built a fire of driftwood that might have defied a cataract, and, wrapped in their buffalo robes, sat on the ground around it to bide the fury of the storm. Deslauriers ensconced himself under the cover of the cart. Shaw and I, together with Henry and Tête Rouge crowded into the little tent; but first of all the dried meat was piled together, and well protected by buffalo robes pinned firmly to the ground. About nine o'clock the storm broke amid absolute darkness; it blew a gale, and torrents of rain roared over the boundless expanse of open prairie. Our tent was filled with mist and spray beating through the canvas, and saturating everything within. We could only distinguish each other at short intervals by the dazzling flashes of lightning, which displayed the whole waste around us with its momentary glare. We had our fears for the tent; but for an hour or two it stood fast, until at length the cap gave way before a furious blast; the pole tore through the top, and in an instant we were half suffocated by the cold and dripping folds of the canvas, which fell down upon us. Seizing upon our guns, we placed them erect, in order to lift the saturated cloth above our heads. In this agreeable situation, involved among wet blankets and buffalo robes, we spent several hours of the night, during which the storm would not abate for a moment, but pelted down with merciless fury. Before long the water gathered beneath us in a pool two or three inches deep; so that for a considerable part of the night we were partially immersed in a cold bath. In spite of all this, Tête Rouge's flow of spirits did not fail him; he laughed, whistled, and sang in defiance of the storm, and that night paid off the long arrears of ridicule which he owed us. While we lay in silence, enduring the infliction with what philosophy we could muster, Tête Rouge, who was intoxicated with animal spirits, cracked jokes at our expense by the hour together. At about three o'clock in the morning, preferring "the tyranny of the open night" to such a wretched shelter, we crawled out from beneath the fallen canvas. The wind had abated, but the rain fell steadily. The fire of the California men still blazed amid the darkness, and we joined them as they sat around it. We made ready some hot coffee by way of refreshment; but when some

Francis Parkman

of the party sought to replenish their cups, it was found that Tête Rouge, having disposed of his own share, had privately abstracted the coffee pot and drunk the rest of the contents.

In the morning, to our great joy, an unclouded sun rose upon the prairie. We presented a rather laughable appearance, for the cold and clammy buckskin, saturated with water, clung fast to our limbs. The light wind and warm sunshine soon dried it again, and then we were all encased in armor of intolerable stiffness. Roaming all day over the prairie and shooting two or three bulls, were scarcely enough to restore the stiffened leather to its usual pliancy.

Besides Henry Chatillon, Shaw and I were the only hunters in the party. Munroe this morning made an attempt to run a buffalo, but his horse could not come up to the game. Shaw went out with him, and being better mounted, soon found himself in the midst of the herd. Seeing nothing but cows and calves around him, he checked his horse. An old bull came galloping on the open prairie at some distance behind, and turning, Shaw rode across his path, leveling his gun as he passed, and shooting him through the shoulder into the heart.

A great flock of buzzards was usually soaring about a few trees that stood on the island just below our camp. Throughout the whole of yesterday we had noticed an eagle among them; to-day he was still there; and Tête Rouge, declaring that he would kill the bird of America, borrowed Deslauriers's gun and set out on his unpatriotic mission. As might have been expected, the eagle suffered no harm at his hands. He soon returned, saying that he could not find him, but had shot a buzzard instead. Being required to produce the bird in proof of his assertion, he said he believed that he was not quite dead, but he must be hurt, from the swiftness with which he flew off.

"If you want," said Tête Rouge, "I'll go and get one of his feathers; I knocked off plenty of them when I shot him."

Just opposite our camp, was another island covered with bushes, and behind it was a deep pool of water, while two or three considerable streams coursed over the sand not far off. I was bathing at this place in the afternoon when a white wolf, larger than the largest Newfoundland dog, ran out from behind the point of the island, and galloped leisurely over the sand not half a stone's throw distant. I could plainly see his red eyes and the bristles about his snout; he was an ugly scoundrel, with a bushy tail, a large head, and a most repulsive countenance. Having neither rifle to shoot nor stone to pelt him with, I was looking after some missile for his benefit, when the report of a gun came from the camp, and the ball threw up the sand just beyond him; at this he gave a slight jump, and stretched away so swiftly that he soon dwindled into a mere speck on the distant sand beds. The number of carcasses that by this time were lying about the neighboring prairie summoned the wolves from every quarter; the spot where Shaw and Henry had hunted together soon became their favorite resort, for here about a dozen dead buffalo were fermenting under the hot sun. I used often to go over the river and watch them at their

The Buffalo Camp

meal. By lying under the bank it was easy to get a full view of them. There were three different kinds: the white wolves and the gray wolves, both very large, and besides these the small prairie wolves, not much bigger than spaniels. They would howl and fight in a crowd around a single carcass, yet they were so watchful, and their senses so acute, that I never was able to crawl within a fair shooting distance; whenever I attempted it, they would all scatter at once and glide silently away through the tall grass. The air above this spot was always full of turkey buzzards or black vultures; whenever the wolves left a carcass they would descend upon it, and cover it so densely that a rifle bullet shot at random among the gormandizing crowd would generally strike down two or three of them. These birds would often sail by scores just above our camp, their broad black wings seeming half transparent as they expanded them against the bright sky. The wolves and the buzzards thickened about us every hour, and two or three eagles also came to the feast. I killed a bull within rifle shot of the camp; that night the wolves made a fearful howling close at hand, and in the morning the carcass was completely hollowed out by these voracious feeders.

After remaining four days at this camp, we prepared to leave it. We had for our own part about five hundred pounds of dried meat, and the California men had prepared some three hundred more; this consisted of the fattest and choicest parts of eight or nine cows, a small quantity only being taken from each, and the rest abandoned to the wolves. The pack animals were laden, the horses saddled, and the mules harnessed to the cart. Even Tête Rouge was ready at last, and slowly moving from the ground, we resumed our journey eastward. When we had advanced about a mile, Shaw missed a valuable hunting knife, and turned back in search of it, thinking that he had left it at the camp. The day was dark and gloomy. The ashes of the fires were still smoking by the riverside; the grass around them was trampled down by men and horses, and strewn with all the litter of a camp. Our departure had been a gathering signal to the birds and beasts of prey. Scores of wolves were prowling about the smoldering fires, while multitudes were roaming over the neighboring prairie; they all fled as Shaw approached, some running over the sand beds and some over the grassy plains. The vultures in great clouds were soaring overhead, and the dead bull near the camp was completely blackened by the flock that had alighted upon it; they flapped their broad wings, and stretched upwards their crested heads and long skinny necks, fearing to remain, yet reluctant to leave their disgusting feast. As he searched about the fires he saw the wolves seated on the hills waiting for his departure. Having looked in vain for his knife, he mounted again, and left the wolves and the vultures to banquet undisturbed.

[1849]

Francis Parkman

Herman Melville:
The Tartarus of Maids

Herman Melville (1819-1891), one of America's greatest and most powerful novelists, explored the range of human consciousness and the problem of good and evil in a series of allegorical novels, the most complex and skillful of which is *Moby Dick* (1851). Although much of his work, drawing on his own experiences, uses the sea as a microcosm of the universe and a ship as the world, "The Tartarus of Maids" explores in a more limited world the sterility resulting from reverence for the dead past and from acceptance of the mechanical future.

It lies not far from Woedolor Mountain in New England. Turning to the east, right out from among bright farms and sunny meadows, nodding in early June with odorous grasses, you enter ascendingly among bleak hills. These gradually close in upon a dusky pass, which, from the violent Gulf Stream of air unceasingly driving between its cloven walls of haggard rock, as well as from the tradition of a crazy spinster's hut having long ago stood somewhere hereabouts, is called the Mad Maid's Bellows-pipe.

Winding along at the bottom of the gorge is a dangerously narrow wheel-road, occupying the bed of a former torrent. Following this road to its highest point, you stand as within a Dantean gateway. From the steepness of the walls here, their strangely ebon hue, and the sudden contraction of the gorge, this particular point is called the Black Notch. The ravine now expandingly descends into a great, purple, hopper-shaped hollow, far sunk among many Plutonian, shaggy-wooded mountains. By the country people this hollow is called the Devil's Dungeon. Sounds of torrents fall on all sides upon the ear. These rapid waters unite at last in one turbid brick-colored stream, boiling through a flume among enormous boulders. They call this strange-colored torrent Blood River. Gaining a dark precipice it wheels suddenly to the west, and makes one maniac spring of sixty feet into the arms of a stunted wood of gray-haired pines, between which it thence eddies on its further way down to the invisible low lands.

Conspicuously crowning a rocky bluff high to one side, at the cataract's verge, is the ruin of an old saw-mill, built in those primitive times when vast pines and hemlocks superabounded throughout the neighboring region. The black-mossed bulk of those immense, rough-hewn, and spike-knotted logs, here and there tumbled all together, in long abandonment and decay, or left in solitary, perilous projection over the cataract's gloomy brink, impart to this rude wooden ruin not only much of the aspect of one of rough-quarried stone, but also a sort of feudal, Rhineland and Thurmberg look, derived from the pinnacled wildness of the neighboring scenery.

Not far from the bottom of the Dungeon stands a large white-washed building, relieved, like some great whited sepulchre, against the sullen background of mountain side firs, and other hardy evergreens, inaccessibly rising in grim terraces for some two thousand feet.

The building is a paper-mill.

Having embarked on a large scale in the seedsman's business (so extensively and broadcast, indeed, that at length my seeds were distributed through all the Eastern and Northern States, and even fell into the far soil of Missouri and the Carolinas), the demand for paper at my place became so great that the expenditure soon amounted to a most important item in the general account. It need hardly be hinted how paper comes into use with seedsmen, as envelopes. These are mostly made of yellowish paper, folded square; and when filled, are all but flat, and being stamped, and superscribed with the nature of the seeds contained, assume not a little the appearance of business-letters ready for the mail. Of these small enve-

Herman Melville

lopes I used an incredible quantity—several hundreds of thousands in a year. For a time I had purchased my paper from the wholesale dealers in a neighboring town. For economy's sake, and partly for the adventure of the trip, I now resolved to cross the mountains, some sixty miles, and order my future paper at the Devil's Dungeon paper-mill.

The sleighing being uncommonly fine toward the end of January, and promising to hold so for no small period, in spite of the bitter cold I started one gray Friday noon in my pung, well fitted with buffalo and wolf robes; and spending one night on the road, next noon came in sight of Woedolor Mountain.

The far summit fairly smoked with frost; white vapors curled up from its white-wooded top, as from a chimney. The intense congelation made the whole country look like one petrifaction. The steel shoes of my pung craunched and gritted over the vitreous, chippy snow, as if it had been broken glass. The forests here and there skirting the route, feeling the same all-stiffening influence, their inmost fibres penetrated with the cold, strangely groaned—not in the swaying branches merely, but likewise in the vertical trunk—as the fitful gusts remorselessly swept through them. Brittle with excessive frost, many colossal tough-grained maples, snapped in twain like pipestems, cumbered the unfeeling earth.

Flaked all over with frozen sweat, white as a milky ram, his nostrils at each breach sending forth two horn-shaped shoots of heated respiration, Black, my good horse, but six years old, started at a sudden turn, where, right across the track—not ten minutes fallen—an old distorted hemlock lay, darkly undulatory as an anaconda.

Gaining the Bellows-pipe, the violent blast, dead from behind, all but shoved my high-backed pung up-hill. The gust shrieked through the shivered pass, as if laden with lost spirits bound to the unhappy world. Ere gaining the summit, Black, my horse, as if exasperated by the cutting wind, slung out with his strong hind-legs, tore the light pung straight up-hill, and sweeping grazingly through the narrow notch, sped downward madly past the ruined saw-mill. Into the Devil's Dungeon horse and cataract rushed together.

With might and main, quitting my seat and robes, and standing backward, with one foot braced against the dashboard, I rasped and churned the bit, and stopped him just in time to avoid collision, at a turn, with the bleak nozzle of a rock, couchant like a lion in the way—a road-side rock.

At first I could not discover the paper-mill.

The whole hollow gleamed with the white, except, here and there, where a pinnacle of granite showed one windswept angle bare. The mountains stood pinned in shrouds—a pass of Alpine corpses. Where stands the mill? Suddenly a whirring, humming sound broke upon my ear. I looked, and there, like an arrested avalanche, lay the large whitewashed factory. It was subordinately surrounded by a cluster of other and smaller buildings, some of which, from their cheap, blank air, great length, gregarious windows, and comfortless expression, no doubt were boarding-houses of the

The Tartarus of Maids

operatives. A snow-white hamlet amidst the snows. Various rude, irregular squares and courts resulted from the somewhat picturesque clusterings of these buildings, owing to the broken, rocky nature of the ground, which forbade all method in their relative arrangement. Several narrow lanes and alleys, too, partly blocked with snow fallen from the roof, cut up the hamlet in all directions.

When, turning from the traveled highway, jingling with bells of numerous farmers—who, availing themselves of the fine sleighing, were dragging their wood to market—and frequently diversified with swift cutters dashing from inn to inn of the scattered villages—when, I say, turning from that bustling main-road, I by degrees wound into the Mad Maid's Bellows-pipe, and saw the grim Black Notch beyond, then something latent, as well as something obvious in the time and scene, strangely brought back to my mind my first sight of dark and grimy Temple Bar. And when Black, my horse, went darting through the Notch, perilously grazing its rocky wall, I remembered being in a runaway London omnibus, which in much the same sort of style, though by no means at an equal rate, dashed through the ancient arch of Wren. Though the two objects did by no means completely correspond, yet this partial inadequacy but served to tinge the similitude not less with the vividness than the disorder of a dream. So that, when upon reining up at the protruding rock I at last caught sight of the quaint groupings of the factory-buildings and with the traveled highway and the Notch behind, found myself all alone, silently and privily stealing through deep-cloven passages into this sequestered spot, and saw the long, high-gabled main factory edifice, with a rude tower—for hoisting heavy boxes—at one end, standing among its crowded outbuildings and boarding-houses, as the Temple Church amidst the surrounding offices and dormitories, and when the marvelous retirement of this mysterious mountain nook fastened its whole spell upon me, then, what memory lacked, all tributary imagination furnished, and I said to myself, "This is the very counterpart of the Paradise of Bachelors, but snowed upon, and frost-painted to a sepulchre."

Dismounting and warily picking my way down the dangerous declivity—horse and man both sliding now and then upon the icy ledges—at length I drove, or the blast drove me, into the largest square, before one side of the main edifice. Piercingly and shrilly the shotted blast blew by the corner; and redly and demoniacally boiled Blood River at one side. A long wood-pile, of many scores of cords, all glittering in mail of crusted ice, stood crosswise in the square. A row of horse-posts, their north sides plastered with adhesive snow, flanked the factory wall. The bleak frost packed and paved the square as with some ringing metal.

The inverted similitude recurred—"The sweet, tranquil Temple garden, with the Thames bordering its green beds," strangely meditated I.

But where are the gay bachelors?

Then, as I and my horse stood shivering in the wind-spray, a girl ran from a neighboring dormitory door, and throwing her thin apron over her bare head, made for the opposite building.

Herman Melville

"One moment, my girl; is there no shed hereabouts which I may drive into?"

Pausing, she turned upon me a face pale with work and blue with cold; an eye supernatural with unrelated misery.

"Nay," faltered I, "I mistook you. Go on; I want nothing."

Leading my horse close to the door from which she had come, I knocked. Another pale, blue girl appeared, shivering in the doorway as, to prevent the blast, she jealously held the door ajar.

"Nay, I mistake again. In God's name shut the door. But hold, is there no man about?"

That moment a dark-complexioned, well-wrapped personage passed, making for the factory door, and spying him coming, the girl rapidly closed the other one.

"Is there no horse-shed here, sir?"

"Yonder, the wood-shed," he replied, and disappeared inside the factory.

With much ado I managed to wedge in horse and pung between the scattered piles of wood all sawn and split. Then, blanketing my horse, and piling my buffalo on the blanket's top, and tucking in its edges well around the breast-band and breeching, so that the wind might not strip him bare, I tied him fast, and ran lamely for the factory door, stiff with frost, and cumbered with my driver's dreadnaught.

Immediately I found myself standing in a spacious place intolerably lighted by long rows of windows, focusing inward the snowy scene without.

At rows of blank-looking counters sat rows of blank-looking girls, with blank, white folders in their blank hands, all blankly folding blank paper.

In one corner stood some huge frame of ponderous iron, with a vertical thing like a piston periodically rising and falling upon a heavy wooden block. Before it—its tame minister—stood a tall girl, feeding the iron animal with half-quires of rose-hued note-paper which, at every downward dab of the piston-like machine, received in the corner the impress of a wreath of roses. I looked from the rosy paper to the pallid cheek, but said nothing.

Seated before a long apparatus, strung with long, slender strings like any harp, another girl was feeding it with foolscap sheets which, so soon as they curiously traveled from her on the cords, were withdrawn at the opposite end of the machine by a second girl. They came to the first girl blank; they went to the second girl ruled.

I looked upon the first girl's brow, and saw it was young and fair; I looked upon the second girl's brow, and saw it was ruled and wrinkled. Then, as I still looked, the two—for some small variety to the monotony—changed places; and where had stood the young, fair brow, now stood the ruled and wrinkled one.

Perched high upon a narrow platform, and still higher upon a high

The Tartarus of Maids

stool crowning it, sat another figure serving some other iron animal; while below the platform sat her mate in some sort of reciprocal attendance.

Not a syllable was breathed. Nothing was heard but the low, steady overruling hum of the iron animals. The human voice was banished from the spot. Machinery—that vaunted slave of humanity—here stood menially served by human beings, who served mutely and cringingly as the slave serves the Sultan. The girls did not so much seem accessory wheels to the general machinery as mere cogs to the wheels.

All this scene around me was instantaneously taken in at one sweeping glance—even before I had proceeded to unwind the heavy fur tippet from around my neck. But as soon as this fell from me, the dark-complexioned man, standing close by, raised a sudden cry, and seizing my arm, dragged me out into the open air, and without pausing for a word instantly caught up some congealed snow and began rubbing both my cheeks.

"Two white spots like the whites of your eyes," he said; "man, your cheeks are frozen."

"That may well be," muttered I; " 'tis some wonder the frost of the Devil's Dungeon strikes in no deeper. Rub away."

Soon a horrible, tearing pain caught at my reviving cheeks. Two gaunt blood-hounds, one on each side, seemed mumbling them. I seemed Actæon.

Presently, when all was over, I re-entered the factory, made known my business, concluded it satisfactorily, and then begged to be conducted throughout the place to view it.

"Cupid is the boy for that," said the dark-complexioned man. "Cupid!" and by this odd fancy-name calling a dimpled, red-cheeked, spirited-looking, forward little fellow who was rather impudently, I thought, gliding about among the passive-looking girls—like a gold-fish through hueless waves—yet doing nothing in particular that I could see, the man bade him lead the stranger through the edifice.

"Come first and see the water-wheel," said this lively lad, with the air of boyishly-brisk importance.

Quitting the folding-room, we crossed some damp, cold boards, and stood beneath a great wet shed, incessantly showering with foam, like the green barnacled bow of some East Indiaman in a gale. Round and round here went the enormous revolutions of the dark colossal water-wheel, grim with its one immutable purpose.

"This sets our whole machinery a-going, sir; in every part of all these buildings; where the girls work and all."

I looked, and saw that the turbid waters of Blood River had not changed their hue by coming under the use of man.

"You make only blank paper; no printing of any sort, I suppose? All blank paper, don't you?"

"Certainly; what else should a paper-factory make?"

The lad here looked at me as if suspicious of my common-sense.

"Oh, to be sure!" said I, confused and stammering; "it only struck

Herman Melville

me as so strange that red waters should turn out pale chee—paper, I mean."

He took me up a wet and rickety stair to a great light room, furnished with no visible thing but rude, manger-like receptacles running all round its sides; and up to these mangers, like so many mares haltered to the rack, stood rows of girls. Before each was vertically thrust up a long, glittering scythe, immovably fixed at bottom to the manger-edge. The curve of the scythe, and its having no snath to it, made it look exactly like a sword. To and fro, across the sharp edge, the girls forever dragged long strips of rags, washed white, picked from baskets at one side; thus ripping asunder every seam, and converting the tatters almost into lint. The air swam with the fine, poisonous particles, which from all sides darted, subtilely, as motes in sunbeams, into the lungs.

"This is the rag-room," coughed the boy.

"You find it rather stifling here," coughed I in answer; "but the girls don't cough."

"Oh, they are used to it."

"Where do you get such hosts of rags?" picking up a handful from a basket.

"Some from the country round about; some from far over sea—Leghorn and London."

"'Tis not unlikely, then," murmured I, "that among these heaps of rags there may be some old shirts, gathered from the dormitories of the Paradise of Bachelors. But the buttons are all dropped off. Pray, my lad, do you ever find any bachelor's buttons hereabouts?"

"None grow in this part of the country. The Devil's Dungeon is no place for flowers."

"Oh!" you mean the *flowers* so called—the Bachelor's Buttons?"

"And was not that what you asked about? Or did you mean the gold bosom-buttons of our boss, Old Bach, as our whispering girls all call him?"

"The man, then, I saw below is a bachelor, is he?"

"Oh, yes, he's a Bach."

"The edges of those swords, they are turned outward from the girls, if I see right; but their rags and fingers fly so, I can not distinctly see."

"Turned outward."

Yes, murmured I to myself; I see it now; turned outward; and each erected sword is so borne, edge-outward, before each girl. If my reading fails me not, just so, of old, condemned state-prisoners went from the hall of judgment to their doom: an officer before, bearing a sword, its edge turned outward, in significance of their fatal sentence. So, through consumptive pallors of this blank, raggy life, go these white girls to death.

"Those scythes look very sharp," again turning toward the boy.

"Yes; they have to keep them so. Look!"

That moment two of the girls, dropping their rags, plied each a whetstone up and down the swordblade. My unaccustomed blood curdled at the sharp shriek of the tormented steel.

The Tartarus of Maids

Their own executioners; themselves whetting the very swords that slay them, meditated I.

"What makes those girls so sheet-white, my lad?"

"Why"—with a roguish twinkle, pure ignorant drollery, not-knowing heartlessness—"I suppose the handling of such white bits of sheets all the time makes them so sheety."

"Let us leave the rag-room now, my lad."

More tragical and more inscrutably mysterious than any mystic sight, human or machine, throughout the factory, was the strange innocence of cruel-heartedness in this usage-hardened boy.

"And now," said he, cheerily, "I suppose you want to see our great machine, which cost us twelve thousand dollars only last autumn. That's the machine that makes the paper, too. This way, sir."

Following him, I crossed a large, bespattered place, with two great round vats in it, full of a white, wet, woolly-looking stuff, not unlike the albuminous part of an egg, soft-boiled.

"There," said Cupid, tapping the vats carelessly, "these are the first beginnings of the paper, this white pulp you see. Look how it swims bubbling round and round, moved by the paddle here. From hence it pours from both vats into that one common channel yonder, and so goes, mixed up and leisurely, to the great machine. And now for that."

He led me into a room, stifling with a strange, blood-like, abdominal heat, as if here, true enough, were being finally developed the germinous particles lately seen.

Before me, rolled out like some long Eastern manuscript, lay stretched one continuous length of iron framework—multitudinous and mystical, with all sorts of rollers, wheels, and cylinders, in slowly-measured and unceasing motion.

"Here first comes the pulp now," said Cupid, pointing to the nighest end of the machine. "See; first it pours out and spreads itself upon this wide, sloping board; and then—look—slides, thin and quivering, beneath the first roller there. Follow on now, and see it as it slides from under that to the next cylinder. There; see how it has become just a very little less pulpy now. One step more, and it grows still more to some slight consistence. Still another cylinder, and it is so knitted—though as yet mere dragon-fly wing—that it forms an air-bridge here, like a suspended cobweb, between two more separated rollers; and flowing over the last one, and under again, and doubling about there out of sight for a minute among all those mixed cylinders you indistinctly see, it reappears here, looking now at last a little less like pulp and more like paper, but still quite delicate and defective yet awhile. But—a little further onward, sir, if you please—here now, at this further point, it puts on something of a real look, as if it might turn out to be something you might possibly handle in the end. But it's not yet done, sir. Good way to travel yet, and plenty more of cylinders must roll it."

"Bless my soul!" said I, amazed at the elongation, interminable

Herman Melville

convolutions, and deliberate slowness of the machine; "it must take a long time for the pulp to pass from end to end and come out paper."

"Oh! not so long," smiled the precocious lad, with a superior and patronizing air; "only nine minutes. But look; you may try it for yourself. Have you a bit of paper? Ah! here's a bit on the floor. Now mark that with any word you please, and let me dab it on here, and we'll see how long before it comes out at the other end."

"Well, let me see," said I, taking out my pencil; "come, I'll mark it with your name."

Bidding me take out my watch, Cupid adroitly dropped the inscribed slip on an exposed part of the incipient mass.

Instantly my eye marked the second-hand on my dial-plate.

Slowly I followed the slip, inch by inch; sometimes pausing for full half a minute as it disappeared beneath inscrutable groups of the lower cylinders, but only gradually to emerge again; and so, on, and on, and on —inch by inch; now in open sight, sliding along like a freckle on the quivering sheet; and then again wholly vanished; and so, on, and on, and on—inch by inch; all the time the main sheet growing more and more to final firmness—when, suddenly, I saw a sort of paper-fall, not wholly unlike a water-fall; a scissory sound smote my ear, as of some cord being snapped; and down dropped an unfolded sheet of perfect foolscap with my "Cupid" half faded out of it, and still moist and warm.

My travels were at an end, for here was the end of the machine.

"Well, how long was it?" said Cupid.

"Nine minutes to a second," replied I, watch in hand.

"I told you so."

For a moment a curious emotion filled me, not wholly unlike that which one might experience at the fulfillment of some mysterious prophecy. But how absurd, thought I again; the thing is a mere machine, the essence of which is unvarying punctuality and precision.

Previously absorbed by the wheels and cylinders, my attention was now directed to a sad-looking woman standing by.

"That is rather an elderly person so silently tending the machine-end here. She would not seem wholly used to it either."

"Oh," knowingly whispered Cupid, through the din, "she only came last week. She was a nurse formerly. But the business is poor in these parts, and she's left it. But look at the paper she is piling there."

"Aye, foolscap," handling the piles of moist, warm sheets, which continually were being delivered into the woman's waiting hands. "Don't you turn out anything but foolscap at this machine?"

"Oh, sometimes, but not often, we turn out finer work—cream-laid and royal sheets, we call them. But foolscap being in chief demand, we turn out foolscap most."

It was very curious. Looking at that blank paper continually dropping, dropping, dropping, my mind ran on in wonderings of those strange uses to which those thousand sheets eventually would be put. All sorts of writings would be writ on those now vacant things—sermons, lawyers'

The Tartarus of Maids

briefs, physicians' prescriptions, love-letters, marriage certificates, bills of divorce, registers of births, death-warrants, and so on, without end. Then, recurring back to them as they here lay all blank, I could not but bethink me of that celebrated comparison of John Locke, who, in demonstration of his theory that man had no innate ideas, compared the human mind at birth to a sheet of blank paper; something destined to be scribbled on, but what sort of characters no soul might tell.

Pacing slowly to and fro along the involved machine, still humming with its play, I was struck as well by the inevitability as the evolvement-power in all its motions.

"Does that thin cobweb there," said I, pointing to the sheet in its more imperfect stage, "does that never tear or break? It is marvelous fragile, and yet this machine it passes through is so mighty."

"It never is known to tear a hair's point."

"Does it never stop—get clogged?"

"No. It *must* go. The machinery makes it go just *so*; just that very way, and at that very pace you there plainly *see* it go. The pulp can't help going."

Something of awe now stole over me, as I gazed upon this inflexible iron animal. Always, more or less, machinery of this ponderous, elaborate sort strikes, in some moods, strange dread into the human heart, as some living, panting Behemoth might. But what made the thing I saw so specially terrible to me was the metallic necessity, the unbudging fatality which governed it. Though, here and there, I could not follow the thin, gauzy veil of pulp in the course of its more mysterious or entirely invisible advance, yet it was indubitable that, at those points where it eluded me, it still marched on in unvarying docility to the autocratic cunning of the machine. A fascination fastened on me. I stood spell-bound and wandering in my soul. Before my eyes—there, passing in slow procession along the wheeling cylinders, I seemed to see, glued to the pallid incipience of the pulp, the yet more pallid faces of all the pallid girls I had eyed that heavy day. Slowly, mournfully, beseechingly, yet unresistingly, they gleamed along, their agony dimly outlined on the imperfect paper, like the print of the tormented face on the handkerchief of Saint Veronica.

"Halloa! the heat of the room is too much for you," cried Cupid, staring at me.

"No—I am rather chill, if anything."

"Come out, sir—out—out," and, with the protecting air of a careful father, the precocious lad hurried me outside.

In a few moments, feeling revived a little, I went into the folding-room—the first room I had entered, and where the desk for transacting business stood, surrounded by the blank counters and blank girls engaged at them.

"Cupid here has led me a strange tour," said I to the dark-complexioned man before mentioned, whom I had ere this discovered not only to be an old bachelor, but also the principal proprietor. "Your is a most wonderful factory. Your great machine is a miracle of inscrutable intricacy."

Herman Melville

"Yes, all our visitors think it so. But we don't have many. We are in a very out-of-the-way corner here. Few inhabitants, too. Most of our girls come from far-off villages."

"The girls," echoed I, glancing round at their silent forms. "Why is it, sir, that in most factories, female operatives, of whatever age, are indiscriminately called girls, never women?"

"Oh! as to that—why, I suppose, the fact of their being generally unmarried—that's the reason, I should think. But it never struck me before. For our factory here, we will not have married women; they are apt to be off-and-on too much. We want none but steady workers: twelve hours to the day, day after day, through the three hundred and sixty-five days, excepting Sundays, Thanksgiving, and Fast-days. That's our rule. And so, having no married women, what females we have are rightly enough called girls."

"Then these are all maids," said I, while some pained homage to their pale virginity made me involuntarily bow.

"All maids."

Again the strange emotion filled me.

"Your cheeks look whitish yet, sir," said the man, gazing at me narrowly. "You must be careful going home. Do they pain you at all now? It's a bad sign, if they do."

"No doubt, sir," answered I, "when once I have got out of the Devil's Dungeon, I shall feel them mending."

"Ah, yes; the winter air in valleys, or gorges, or any sunken place, is far colder and more bitter than elsewhere. You would hardly believe it now, but it is colder here than at the top of Woedolor Mountain."

"I dare say it is, sir. But time presses me; I must depart."

With that, remuffling myself in dread-naught and tippet, thrusting my hands into my huge seal-skin mittens, I sallied out into the nipping air, and found poor Black, my horse, all cringing and doubled up with the cold.

Soon, wrapped in furs and meditations, I ascended from the Devil's Dungeon.

At the Black Notch I paused, and once more bethought me of Temple Bar. Then, shooting through the pass, all alone with inscrutable nature, I exclaimed—Oh! Paradise of Bachelors! and oh! Tartarus of Maids!

[1855]

The Tartarus of Maids

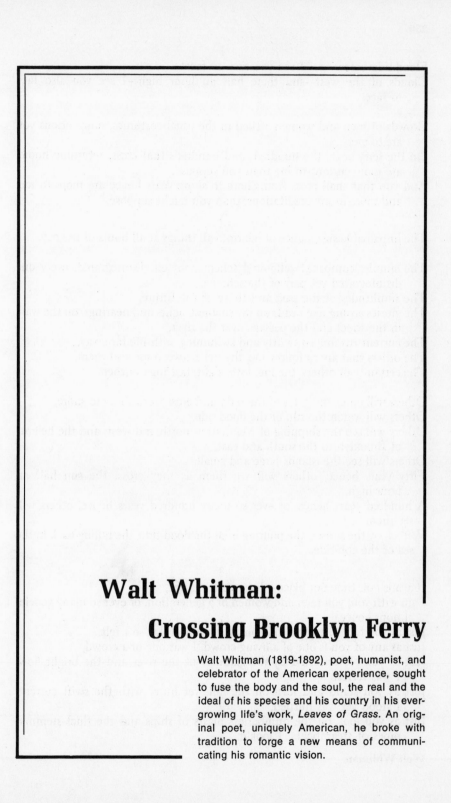

Walt Whitman:
Crossing Brooklyn Ferry

Walt Whitman (1819-1892), poet, humanist, and celebrator of the American experience, sought to fuse the body and the soul, the real and the ideal of his species and his country in his ever-growing life's work, *Leaves of Grass*. An original poet, uniquely American, he broke with tradition to forge a new means of communicating his romantic vision.

1

Flood-tide below me! I see you face to face!
Clouds of the west—sun there half an hour high—I see you also face
to face.

Crowds of men and women attired in the usual costumes, how curious you
are to me!
On the ferry-boats the hundreds and hundreds that cross, returning home,
are more curious to me than you suppose,
And you that shall cross from shore to shore years hence are more to me,
and more in my meditations, than you might suppose.

2

The impalpable sustenance of me from all things at all hours of the day,

The simple, compact, well-join'd scheme, myself disintegrated, every one
disintegrated yet part of the scheme,
The similitudes of the past and those of the future,
The glories strung like beads on my smallest sights and hearings, on the walk
in the street and the passage over the river,
The current rushing so swiftly and swimming with me far away,
The others that are to follow me, the ties between me and them,
The certainty of others, the life, love, sight, hearing of others.

Others will enter the gates of the ferry and cross from shore to shore,
Others will watch the run of the flood-tide,
Others will see the shipping of Manhattan north and west, and the heights
of Brooklyn to the south and east,
Others will see the islands large and small;
Fifty years hence, others will see them as they cross, the sun half an
hour high,
A hundred years hence, or ever so many hundred years hence, others will
see them,
Will enjoy the sunset, the pouring-in of the flood-tide, the falling-back to the
sea of the ebb-tide.

3

It avails not, time nor place—distance avails not,
I am with you, you men and women of a generation, or ever so many genera-
tions hence,
Just as you feel when you look on the river and sky, so I felt,
Just as any of you is one of a living crowd, I was one of a crowd,
Just as you are refresh'd by the gladness of the river and the bright flow,
I was refresh'd,
Just as you stand and lean on the rail, yet hurry with the swift current,
I stood yet was hurried,
Just as you look on the numberless masts of ships and the thick-stemm'd
pipes of steamboats, I look'd.

Walt Whitman

I too many and many a time cross'd the river of old,
Watched the Twelfth-month sea-gulls, saw them high in the air floating
    with motionless wings, oscillating their bodies,
Saw how the glistening yellow lit up parts of their bodies and left the rest
    in strong shadow,
Saw the slow-wheeling circles and the gradual edging toward the south,
Saw the reflection of the summer sky in the water,
Had my eyes dazzled by the shimmering track of beams,
Look'd at the fine centrifugal spokes of light round the shape of my head
    in the sunlit water,
Look'd on the haze on the hills southward and south-westward,
Look'd on the vapor as it flew in fleeces tinged with violet,
Look'd toward the lower bay to notice the vessels arriving,
Saw their approach, saw aboard those that were near me,
Saw the white sails of schooners and sloops, saw the ships at anchor,
The sailors at work in the rigging or out astride the spars,
The round masts, the swinging motion of the hulls, the slender serpentine
    pennants,
The large and small steamers in motion, the pilots in their pilot-houses,
The white wake left by the passage, the quick tremulous whirl of the
    wheels,
The flags of all nations, the falling of them at sunset,
The scallop-edged waves in the twilight, the ladled cups, the frolicsome
    crests and glistening,
The stretch afar growing dimmer and dimmer, the gray walls of the
    granite storehouses by the docks,
On the river the shadowy group, the big steam-tug closely flank'd on each
    side by the barges, the hay-boat, the belated lighter,
On the neighboring shore the fires from the foundry chimneys burning
    high and glaringly into the night,
Casting their flicker of black contrasted with wild red and yellow light over
    the tops of houses, and down into the clefts of streets.

4

These and all else were to me the same as they are to you,
I loved well those cities, loved well the stately and rapid river,
The men and women I saw were all near to me,
Others the same—others who look back on me because I look'd forward
    to them,
(The time will come, though I stop here to-day and to-night.)

5

What is it then between us?
What is the count of the scores or hundreds of years between us?

Whatever it is, it avails not—distance avails not, and place avails not,
I too lived, Brooklyn of ample hills was mine,

Crossing Brooklyn Ferry

I too walk'd the streets of Manhattan island, and bathed in the waters
    around it,
I too felt the curious abrupt questionings stir within me.
In the day among crowds of people sometimes they came upon me,
In my walks home late at night or as I lay in my bed they came upon me,
I too had been struck from the float forever held in solution,
I too had receiv'd identity by my body,
That I was I knew was of my body, and what I should be I knew I should
    be of my body.

6

It is not upon you alone the dark patches fall,
The dark threw its patches down upon me also,
The best I had done seem'd to me blank and suspicious,
My great thoughts as I supposed them, were they not in reality meagre?
Nor is it you alone who know what it is to be evil,
I am he who knew what it was to be evil,
I too knitted the old knot of contrariety,
Blabb'd, blush'd, resented, lied, stole, grudg'd,
Had guile, anger, lust, hot wishes I dared not speak,
Was wayward, vain, greedy, shallow, sly, cowardly, malignant,
The wolf, the snake, the hog, not wanting in me,
The cheating look, the frivolous word, the adulterous wish, not wanting,
Refusals, hates, postponements, meanness, laziness, none of these wanting,
Was one with the rest, the days and haps of the rest,
Was call'd by my nighest name by clear loud voices of young men as they
    saw me approaching or passing,
Felt their arms on my neck as I stood, or the negligent leaning of their
    flesh against me as I sat,
Saw many I loved in the street or ferry-boat or public assembly, yet never
    told them a word,
Lived the same life with the rest, the same old laughing, gnawing, sleeping,
Play'd the part that still looks back on the actor or actress,
The same old role, the role that is what we make it, as great as we like,
Or as small as we like, or both great and small.

7

Closer yet I approach you,
What thought you have of me now, I had as much of you—I laid in my
    stores in advance,
I consider'd long and seriously of you before you were born.

Who was to know what should come home to me?
Who knows but I am enjoying this?
Who knows, for all the distance, but I am as good as looking at you now,
    for all you cannot see me?

Walt Whitman

8

Ah, what can ever be more stately and admirable to me than mast-hemm'd
Manhattan?
River and sunset and scallop-edg'd waves of flood-tide?
The sea-gulls oscillating their bodies, the hay-boat in the twilight, and the
belated lighter?
What gods can exceed these that clasp me by the hand, and with voices
I love call me promptly and loudly by my nighest name as I approach?

What is more subtle than this which ties me to the woman or man that
looks in my face?
Which fuses me into you now, and pours my meaning into you?

We understand then do we not?
What I promis'd without mentioning it, have you not accepted?
What the study could not teach—what the preaching could not accom-
plish is accomplish'd, is it not?

9

Flow on, river! flow with the flood-tide, and ebb with the ebb-tide!
Frolic on, crested and scallop-edg'd waves!
Gorgeous clouds of the sunset! drench with your splendor me, or the men
and women generations after me!
Cross from shore to shore, countless crowds of passengers!
Stand up, tall masts of Mannahatta! stand up, beautiful hills of Brooklyn!
Throb, baffled and curious brain! throw out questions and answers!
Suspend here and everywhere, eternal float of solution!
Gaze, loving and thirsting eyes, in the house or street or public assembly!
Sound out, voices of young men! loudly and musically call me by my
nighest name!
Live, old life! play the part that looks back on the actor or actress!
Play the old role, the role that is great or small according as one makes it!
Consider, you who peruse me, whether I may not in unknown ways be
looking upon you;
Be firm, rail over the river, to support those who lean idly, yet haste with
the hasting current;
Fly on, sea-birds! fly sideways, or wheel in large circles high in the air;
Receive the summer sky, you water, and faithfully hold it till all down-
cast eyes have time to take it from you!
Diverge, fine spokes of light, from the shape of my head, or any one's head,
in the sunlit water!
Come on, ships from the lower bay! pass up or down, white-sail'd
schooners, sloops, lighters!
Flaunt away, flags of all nations! be duly lower'd at sunset!
Burn high your fires, foundry chimneys! cast black shadows at nightfall!
cast red and yellow light over the tops of the houses!
Appearances, now or henceforth, indicate what you are,

Crossing Brooklyn Ferry

You necessary film, continue to envelop the soul,
About by body for me, and your body for you, be hung our divinest aromas,
Thrive, cities—bring your freight, bring your shows, ample and sufficient rivers,

Expand, being than which none else is perhaps more spiritual,
Keep your places, objects than which none else is more lasting.

You have waited, you always wait, you dumb, beautiful ministers,
We receive you with free sense at last, and are insatiate henceforward,
Not you any more shall be able to foil us, or withhold yourselves from us,
We use you, and do not cast you aside—we plant you permanently within us,
We fathom you not—we love you—there is perfection in you also,
You furnish your parts toward eternity,
Great or small, you furnish your parts toward the soul.

[1856, 1881]

Walt Whitman

Henry Wadsworth Longfellow:
Hymn to the Night

Henry Wadsworth Longfellow (1807-1882), America's best-known and best-loved poet, wrote over a wide poetic range, from the sentimental and trivial to the restrained and eloquent. A romantic and an optimist, he found depth and fulfillment in the simple and commonplace, whether in nature or in the closeness of human warmth. At the heart of his faith is a kinship with nature that verges on the mystical.

I heard the trailing garments of the Night
    Sweep through her marble halls!
I saw her sable skirts all fringed with light
    From the celestial walls!

I felt her presence, by its spell of might,
    Stoop o'er me from above;
The calm, majestic presence of the Night,
    As of the one I love.

I heard the sounds of sorrow and delight,
    The manifold, soft chimes,
That fill the haunted chambers of the Night,
    Like some old poet's rhymes.

From the cool cisterns of the midnight air
    My spirit drank repose;
The fountain of perpetual peace flows there,—
    From those deep cisterns flows.

O holy Night! from thee I learn to bear
    What man has borne before!
Thou layest thy finger on the lips of Care,
    And they complain no more.

Peace! Peace! Orestes-like I breathe this prayer!
    Descend with broad-winged flight,

The welcome, the thrice-prayed for, the most fair,
    The best-beloved Night!

[1839]

Henry Wadsworth Longfellow

William Cullen Bryant:
A Forest Hymn

William Cullen Bryant (1794-1878), liberal editor and romantic poet, sought to fuse natural perfection and moral order in verse that manages to evade the didactic. "To a Waterfowl" (1815-18) is perhaps the most nearly perfect romantic statement of the meaning of a thing in nature as a symbol of spiritual truth.

The groves were God's first temples. Ere man learned
To hew the shaft, and lay the architrave,
And spread the roof above them—ere he framed
The lofty vault, to gather and roll back
The sound of anthems; in the darkling wood,
Amid the cool and silence, he knelt down,
And offered to the Mightiest solemn thanks
And supplication. For his simple heart
Might not resist the sacred influences
Which, from the stilly twilight of the place,
And from the gray old trunks that high in heaven
Mingled their mossy boughs, and from the sound
Of the invisible breath that swayed at once
All their green tops, stole over him, and bowed
His spirit with the thought of boundless power
And inaccessible majesty. Ah, why
Should we, in the world's riper years, neglect
God's ancient sanctuaries, and adore
Only among the crowd, and under roofs
That our frail hands have raised? Let me, at least,
Here, in the shadow of this aged wood,
Offer one hymn—thrice happy, if it find
Acceptance in His ear.

Father, thy hand
Hath reared these venerable columns, thou
Didst weave this verdant roof. Thou didst look down
Upon the naked earth, and, forthwith, rose
All these fair ranks of trees. They, in thy sun,
Budded, and shook their green leaves in thy breeze,
And shot toward heaven. The century-living crow
Whose birth was in their tops, grew old and died
Among their branches, till, at last, they stood,
As now they stand, massy, and tall, and dark,
Fit shrine for humble worshipper to hold
Communion with his Maker. These dim vaults,
These winding aisles, of human pomp or pride
Report not. No fantastic carvings show
The boast of our vain race to change the form
Of thy fair works. But thou art here—thou fill'st
The solitude. Thou art in the soft winds
That run along the summit of these trees
In music; thou art in the cooler breath
That from the inmost darkness of the place
Comes, scarcely felt; the barky trunks, the ground,
The fresh moist ground, are all instinct with thee.
Here is continual worship;—Nature, here,

William Cullen Bryant

In the tranquillity that thou dost love,
Enjoys thy presence. Noiselessly, around,
From perch to perch, the solitary bird
Passes; and yon clear spring, that, midst its herbs,
Wells softly forth and wandering steeps the roots
Of half the mighty forest, tells no tale
Of all the good it does. Thou hast not left
Thyself without a witness, in the shades,
Of thy perfections. Grandeur, strength, and grace
Are here to speak of thee. This mighty oak—
By whose immovable stem I stand and seem
Almost annihilated—not a prince,
In all that proud old world beyond the deep,
E'er wore his crown as loftily as he
Wears the green coronal of leaves with which
Thy hand had graced him. Nestled at his root
Is beauty, such as blooms not in the glare
Of the broad sun. That delicate forest flower,
With scented breath and look so like a smile,
Seems, as it issues from the shapeless mould,
An emanation of the indwelling Life.
A visible token of the upholding Love,
That are the soul of this great universe.
      My heart is awed within me when I think
Of the great miracle that still goes on,
In silence, round me—the perpetual work
Of thy creation, finished, yet renewed
Forever. Written on thy works I read
The lesson of thy own eternity.
Lo! all grow old and die—but see again,
How on the faltering footsteps of decay
Youth presses—ever gay and beautiful youth
In all its beautiful forms. These lofty trees
Wave not less proudly that their ancestors
Moulder beneath them. Oh, there is not lost
One of earth's charms: upon her bosom yet,
After the flight of untold centuries,
The freshness of her far beginning lies
And yet shall lie. Life mocks the idle hate
Of his arch-enemy Death—yea, seats himself
Upon the tyrant's throne—the sepulchre,
And of the triumphs of his ghastly foe
Makes his own nourishment. For he came forth
From thine own bosom, and shall have no end.

      There have been holy men who hid themselves
Deep in the woody wilderness, and gave

A Forest Hymn

Their lives to thought and prayer, till they outlived
The generation born with them, nor seemed
Less aged than the hoary trees and rocks
Around them;—and there have been holy men
Who deemed it were not well to pass life thus.
But let me often to these solitudes
Retire, and in thy presence reassure
My feeble virtue. Here its enemies,
The passions, at thy plainer footsteps shrink
And tremble and are still. O God! when thou
Dost scare the world with tempests, set on fire
The heavens with falling thunderbolts, or fill,
With all the waters of the firmament,
The swift dark whirlwind that uproots the woods
And drowns the villages; when, at thy call,
Uprises the great deep and throws himself
Upon the continent, and overwhelms
Its cities—who forgets not, at the sight
Of these tremendous tokens of thy power,
His pride, and lays his strifes and follies by?
Oh, from these sterner aspects of thy face
Spare me and mine, nor let us need the wrath
Of the mad unchained elements to teach
Who rules them. Be it ours to meditate,
In these calm shades, thy milder majesty,
And to the beautiful order of thy works
Learn to conform the order of our lives.

[1825, 1832]

William Cullen Bryant

Henry Timrod:

Spring

Henry Timrod (1828-1867), called "the laureate of the Confederacy," was truly a romantic in spite of some classic restraint in his work. Especially romantic is his subject matter— heroic deeds, brave men, patriotic dedication, and above all a reverence for the real and the symbolic in nature. In "Spring" (1863), he fuses all these elements in a typical near-epic that celebrates the season and his cause.

Spring, with that nameless pathos in the air
Which dwells with all things fair,
Spring, with her golden suns and silver rain,
Is with us once again.

Out in the lonely woods the jasmine burns
Its fragrant lamps, and turns
Into a royal court with green festoons
The banks of dark lagoons.

In the deep heart of every forest tree
The blood is all aglee,
And there's a look about the leafless bowers
As if they dreamed of flowers.

Yet still on every side we trace the hand
Of Winter in the land,
Save where the maple reddens on the lawn,
Flushed by the season's dawn;

Or where, like those strange semblances we find
That age to childhood bind,
The elm puts on, as if in Nature's scorn,
The brown of Autumn corn.

As yet the turf is dark, although you know
That, not a span below,
A thousand germs are groping through the gloom,
And soon will burst their tomb.

Already, here and there, on frailest stems
Appear some azure gems,
Small as might deck, upon a gala day,
The forehead of a fay.

In gardens you may note amid the dearth
The crocus breaking earth;
And near the snowdrop's tender white and green,
The violet in its screen.

But many gleams and shadows need must pass
Along the budding grass,
And weeks go by, before the enamored South
Shall kiss the rose's mouth.

Still there's a sense of blossoms yet unborn
In the sweet airs of morn;

Henry Timrod

One almost looks to see the very street
Grow purple at his feet.

At times a fragrant breeze comes floating by,
And brings, you know not why,
A feeling as when eager crowds await
Before a palace gate

Some wondrous pageant; and you scarce would start,
If from a beech's heart,
A blue-eyed Dryad, stepping forth, should say,
"Behold me! I am May!"

Ah! who would couple thoughts of war and crime
With such a blessèd time!
Who in the west wind's aromatic breath
Could hear the call of Death!

Yet not more surely shall the Spring awake
The voice of wood and brake,
Then she shall rouse, for all her tranquil charms,
A million men to arms.

There shall be deeper hues upon her plains
Than all her sunlit rains,
And every gladdening influence around,
Can summon from the ground.

Oh! standing on this desecrated mould,
Methinks that I behold,
Lifting her bloody daisies up to God,
Spring kneeling on the sod,

And calling, with the voice of all her rills,
Upon the ancient hills
To fall and crush the tyrants and the slaves
Who turn her meads to graves.

[1863]

Spring

Sidney Lanier:

Corn

Sidney Lanier (1842-1881), southern soldier,
musician, and poet, was perceptive in his romanticism, recognizing that pastoral peace and
plenty were often transient or illusory. This recognition is particularly evident in "Corn" (1874),
prophetic in its depiction of the results of a
destructive adherence to agricultural tradition.

To-day the woods are trembling through and through
With shimmering forms, that flash before my view,
Then melt in green as dawn-stars melt in blue.
  The leaves that wave against my cheek caress
  Like women's hands; the embracing boughs express
    A subtlety of mighty tenderness;
  The corpse-depths into little noises start,
  That sound anon like beatings of a heart,
  Anon like talk 'twixt lips not far apart.
  The beech dreams balm, as a dreamer hums a song;
  Through that vague wafture, expirations strong
  Throb from young hickories breathing deep and long
With stress and urgence bold of prisoned spring
      And ecstasy of burgeoning.
  Now, since the dew-plashed road of morn is dry,
  Forth venture odors of more quality
  And heavenlier giving. Like Jove's locks awry,
      Long muscadines
Rich-wreathe the spacious foreheads of great pines,
And breathe ambrosial passion from their vines.
  I pray with mosses, ferns and flowers shy
  That hide like gentle nuns from human eye
  To lift adoring perfumes to the sky.
I hear faint bridal-sighs of brown and green
Dying to silent hints of kisses keen
As far lights fringe into a pleasant sheen.
  I start at fragmentary whispers, blown
  From undertalks of leafy souls unknown,
  Vague purports sweet, of inarticulate tone.
Dreaming of gods, men, nuns and brides, between
Old companies of oaks that inward lean
To join their radiant amplitudes of green
  I slowly move, with ranging looks that pass
  Up from the matted miracles of grass
Into yon veined complex of space
Where sky and leafage interlace
  So close, the heaven of blue is seen
  Inwoven with a heaven of green.

I wander to the zigzag-cornered fence
Where sassafras, intrenched in brambles dense,
Contests with stolid vehemence
  The march of culture, setting limb and thorn
  As pikes against the army of the corn.

There, while I pause, my fieldward-faring eyes
Take harvests, where the stately corn-ranks rise,

Sidney Lanier

Of inward dignities
And large benignities and insights wise,
Graces and modest majesties.
Thus, without theft, I reap another's field;
Thus, without tilth, I house a wondrous yield,
And heap my heart with quintuple crops concealed.

Look, out of line one tall corn-captain stands
Advanced beyond the foremost of his bands,
And waves his blades upon the very edge
And hottest thicket of the battling hedge.
Thou lustrous stalk, that ne'er mayst walk nor talk,
Still shalt thou type the poet-soul sublime
That leads the vanward of his timid time
And sings up cowards with commanding rhyme—
Soul calm, like thee, yet fain, like thee, to grow
By double increment, above, below;
Soul homely, as thou art, yet rich in grace like thee,
Teaching the yeomen selfless chivalry
That moves in gentle curves of courtesy;
Soul filled like thy long veins with sweetness tense,
By every godlike sense
Transmuted from the four wild elements.
Drawn to high plans,
Thou lift'st more stature than a mortal man's,
Yet ever piercest downward in the mould
And keepest hold
Upon the reverend and steadfast earth
That gave thee birth;
Yea, standest smiling in thy future grave,
Serene and brave,
With unremitting breath
Inhaling life from death,
Thine epitaph writ fair in fruitage eloquent,
Thyself thy monument.

As poets should,
Thou hast built up thy hardihood
With universal food,
Drawn in select proportion fair
From honest mould and vagabond air;
From darkness of the dreadful night,
And joyful light;
From antique ashes, whose departed flame
In thee has finer life and longer fame;
From wounds and balms,
From storms and calms,

Corn

From potsherds and dry bones
    And ruin-stones.
Into thy vigorous substance thou hast wrought
Whate'er the hand of Circumstance hath brought;
    Yea, into cool solacing green hast spun
    White radiance hot from out the sun.
So thou dost mutually leaven
Strength of earth with grace of heaven;
    So thou dost marry new and old
    Into a one of higher mould;
    So thou dost reconcile the hot and cold,
        The dark and bright,
And many a heart-perplexing opposite,
            And so,
    Akin by blood to high and low,
Fitly thou playest out thy poet's part,
Richly expending thy much-bruisèd heart
    In equal care to nourish lord in hall
        Or beast in stall:
    Thou took'st from all that thou mightst give to all.

O steadfast dweller on the selfsame spot
Where thou wast born, that still repinest not—
Type of the home-fond heart, the happy lot!—
    Deeply thy mild content rebukes the land
    Whose flimsy homes, built on the shifting sand
Of trade, for ever rise and fall
With alternation whimsical,
    Enduring scarce a day,
    Then swept away
By swift engulfments of incalculable tides
Whereon capricious Commerce rides.
Look, thou substantial spirit of content!
Across this little vale, thy continent,
    To where, beyond the mouldering mill,
    Yon old deserted Georgian hill
Bares to the sun his piteous aged crest
        And seamy breast,
    By restless-hearted children left to lie
    Untended there beneath the heedless sky,
    As barbarous folk expose their old to die.
Upon that generous-rounding side,
        With gullies scarified
    Where keen Neglect his lash hath plied,
Dwelt one I knew of old, who played at toil,
And gave to coquette Cotton soul and soil.
    Scorning the slow reward of patient grain,

Sidney Lanier

He sowed his heart with hopes of swifter gain,
Then sat him down and waited for the rain.
He sailed in borrowed ships of usury—
A foolish Jason on a treacherous sea,
Seeking the Fleece and finding misery.
    Lulled by smooth-rippling loans, in idle trance
    He lay, content that unthrift Circumstance
    Should plough for him the stony field of Chance.
Yea, gathering crops whose worth no man might tell,
He staked his life on games of Buy-and-Sell,
And turned each field into a gambler's hell.
    Aye, as each year began,
    My farmer to the neighboring city ran;
Passed with a mournful anxious face
Into the banker's inner place;
Parleyed, excused, pleaded for longer grace;
    Railed at the drought, the worm, the rust, the grass;
    Protested ne'er again 'twould come to pass;
    With many an *oh* and *if* and *but alas*
Parried or swallowed searching questions rude,
And kissed the dust to soften Dives's mood.
At last, small loans by pledges great renewed,
    He issues smiling from the fatal door,
    And buys with lavish hand his yearly store
    Till his small borrowings will yield no more.
Aye, as each year declined,
With bitter heart and ever-brooding mind
He mourned his fate unkind.
    In dust, in rain, with might and main,
    He nursed his cotton, cursed his grain,
    Fretted for news that made him fret again,
Snatched at each telegram of Future Sale,
And thrilled with Bulls' or Bears' alternate wail—
In hope or fear alike for ever pale.
    And thus from year to year, through hope and fear,
    With many a curse and many a secret tear,
    Striving in vain his cloud of debt to clear,
        At last
He woke to find his foolish dreaming past,
    And all his best-of-life the easy prey
    Of squandering scamps and quacks that lined his way
        With vile array,
From rascal statesman down to petty knave;
Himself, at best, for all his bragging brave,
A gamester's catspaw and a banker's slave.
    Then, worn and gray, and sick with deep unrest,

Corn

He fled away into the oblivious West,
  Unmourned, unblest.

Old hill! old hill! thou gashed and hairy Lear
Whom the divine Cordelia of the year,
E'en pitying Spring, will vainly strive to cheer—
  King, that no subject man nor beast may own,
  Discrowned, undaughtered and alone—
Yet shall the great God turn thy fate,
And bring thee back into thy monarch state
    And majesty immaculate.
  Lo, through hot waverings of the August morn,
  Thou givest from thy vasty sides forlorn
  Visions of golden treasuries of corn—
Ripe largesse lingering for some bolder heart
That manfully shall take thy part,
    And tend thee,
    And defend thee,
With antique sinew and with modern art.

           [1874]

Sidney Lanier

3

The Vision of Reality

In the most simplistic sense, the United States entered the Civil War in 1861 as a nation divided, rural, agricultural, and slave; it emerged four years later united, urban, industrial, and free. In a more profound and realistic sense, the new identity had not yet become fact, but during the four years of war irreversible forces had been unleased and irrevocable commitments made, all of them designed to change the face of America beyond recognition. In this sense, the Civil War marks the watershed of American history—on one side the drying springs of romanticism, on the other the gathering of realistic waters soon to become a flood.

Some changes in American life were immediately discernible. Just as the war had smashed chattel slavery, it had destroyed romanticism and its vision of a fulfillment easily attainable. The vestiges of romanticism that remained were those of a low-level sentimentalism, of which much gradually merged with the myth of a lost but virtuous cause. Local and regional traditions suffered with the destruction of the myth of state sovereignty. Violence, aggressiveness, and exploitation were frankly admitted and admired in American life as the war gave them dignity and virtue. Industries and railroads flourished, legacies of the fact that the Civil War was the first modern technological war. And the bloody shirt became a political weapon, resulting in a long line of Civil War generals, each of whom aspired to the presidency with credentials forged in the campaigns of war rather than on the political stump. The Grand Army of the Republic emerged as an arm of the dominant Republican party; the United Confederate Veterans became its counterpart in the now-solid South. A new political, social, and economic complex had come into being.

The older generation of American writers, those who had attempted to define the fulfilling reality of their age, had by the end of the war largely fallen silent. Hawthorne and Thoreau were dead; Emerson had become repetitive and ill; Melville took refuge in his customhouse, and Longfellow in sentimentality. Southern writers in platoons began the creation of an antebellum myth to match the architecture that had not fallen to Sherman's torch. Virtually no one was left to observe, define, and interpret the new American reality, but a few young men began their apprenticeships.

The new reality that emerged almost unobserved in the decade after the Civil War was compounded of the growth of cities, of industry, and of a new dominant political coalition that replaced the egalitarian tradition that had been shunted aside in the slavery controversy and the war itself. The industrial revolution in America, its effects almost unnoticed except by Melville and southern writers interested in writing apologies for slavery as a "positive good," had laid the foundations for the new American environment during the years between 1820 and 1860. The industrial superstructure with its urban surroundings was erected as a result of the tremendous impetus given industry by the war. Hordes of Europeans, needed as laborers, came to man the factories and live in the cities. They were joined by Americans forced to leave their farms.

The Republican party, without a philosophy since the destruction of slavery but nevertheless the dominant party, turned to the past for

The Vision of Reality

inspiration, to the Whig party out of which many of its founders came, and it turned also to political expediency. By the end of General Grant's second administration, in 1877, the alliance between the Republican party and business was forged so tightly that it was to endure, even under attack, until well into the twentieth century. And as a result of the strange circumstances of the election of 1876, an alliance was made between conservative Republicans and Southern Democrats that was to strengthen the domination of business over the lives of individuals, whose individuality was now threatened and their dignity denied by a new society.

The first group of writers to define the post–Civil War American environment were those whose attempts were rooted in the techniques of the past as they concentrated on exploring regional and local phenomena in literal detail. Called local colorists, they sought to define the uniqueness of the locales of their origins. But they did not share the romantic faith, and they did not find one of their own; consequently, local color's importance was in the direction it pointed out rather than its own accomplishments, and its significance faded.

One writer whose roots were in the local color tradition rose above it to become one of the truly great writers in American literary history. This was Mark Twain, who began with popular humor in *Innocents Abroad* (1869) and concluded with the overwhelming bitterness of the posthumous novel *The Mysterious Stranger* (1916). In all his works, particularly in the most famous, *The Adventures of Tom Sawyer* (1876) and *The Adventures of Huckleberry Finn* (1884), he concerned himself with the nature of the American environment, natural and social, and the impact of both upon man. In *Roughing It* (1872) appears some of his finest writing concerned with the natural environment as it makes its impact upon man; in *The Gilded Age* (1873) with Charles Dudley Warner, he explores the ethics of the new business society; in *Huckleberry Finn* he contrasts natural freedom of life on the river and the unnatural slavery of life in a civilized society.

Mark Twain pointed toward the new attempts to come to grips with the new environment. The attempts became a movement known as realism, with its ethic formulated by William Dean Howells. The goal of realism was definition of the new American society and its newly discovered psychological dimension, but not interpretation. To Howells, realism meant fidelity to the surface appearance and psychological motivation of man's experience, and the realistic ethic led to perceptive observations and ultimately grim conclusions.

Although Howells and his contemporary, Henry James, explored the dimensions of the new reality by pioneering the means of defining it, they did not pursue the subject matter of that reality, the new American environment that had been defined by Mark Twain in *The Gilded Age*. This was left to younger writers, among them Stephen Crane, Frank Norris, Hamlin Garland, and others, each of whom looked carefully at the new environment, recorded what he saw, and drew inevitable conclusions about the impact of that environment upon individual Americans.

Introduction

The reality they perceived was one that had completely rejected the egalitarian dream of fulfillment for all, the dream that had motivated generations of Americans, from philosophers to politicians. The common man had faded into the background during the slavery crisis and the war that he had fought for patriotic and idealistic reasons. Upon his discharge he found that the old frontier mobility that had promised so much to so many had largely disappeared, and in its place the new industries in the growing cities provided a promised livelihood and, for the few who had the ability, a new kind of fulfillment that grew out of material success beyond the dreams of earlier generations.

The price extracted for such fulfillment was extremely high, however, and the economic requirements imposed upon those who sought it were very selective as the new system rejected egalitarianism and supported the growth of a new social and economic elite. With reform energy dissipated and the few remaining movements, such as temperance and women's rights, in the hands of fanatics, there emerged an American creed that rejected the idea of dignity in work. The new creed saw the worker essentially as raw material, and supported a new aristocratic power structure, avowedly still open, as the American ideal insisted it should be, but open only to a few.

The rationale upon which the new elite based its position came to be known, after the words of Andrew Carnegie, one of its most successful believers, as "the Gospel of Wealth," a doctrine that drew its substance from a variety of sources, all selected for what they could offer to support the new elite. From the eighteenth century it drew a variety of ideas, each distorted to its own purposes: from Adam Smith's *The Wealth of Nations* (1776) it took out of context the idea of laissez faire economics; from Thomas Jefferson it accepted the principle of limited government powers; from Alexander Hamilton's *Report on the Subject of Manufactures* it accepted the principles of governmental protection, encouragement, and subsidies for manufacturing. From Darwinism, just making its popular intellectual impact, it took the concept of the survival of the fittest in nature and applied it to the economic realm. Traditional Protestantism contributed the concepts of Christian stewardship and the direct reward of virtue by God, thus providing a major aura of sanctity to bless the logic of accumulating great wealth.

The resulting principles of the Gospel of Wealth insisted first of all that a laissez faire system, combined with the ideals of individualism and government sympathy, would provide freedom and opportunity to the good and the fit in American society. They would then prosper, attaining a position that would enable them to do good to others, thus bringing a perfect society into being. Conversely and ironically, the subscribers to the premises of the Gospel of Wealth insisted that the poor were, in Darwinian terms, unfit, and in Christian terms immoral, lazy, and sinful. In either case, they had been tried and found wanting by the objective standards of God and nature.

The premises of the Gospel of Wealth rationalized but did not hide

The Vision of Reality

the reality of a society in which the rich and powerful subscribed to such premises, and as the new writers of the late nineteenth century pursued the new reality, they saw beyond it. The farmer, the subject of much of the best work of Hamlin Garland and Frank Norris, was the victim of postwar overproduction, high and uneven freight rates, high and expensive interest rates and money supply, and cities populated by hordes too poor to provide markets for food produced and shipped under such expensive, restrictive circumstances. The farmers sought redress within the framework of the system that continued to promise a good life, but with only token success.

In the cities the workers, seen by Stephen Crane, Upton Sinclair, and others, were equally victimized by periods of boom and bust in cyclical regularity, by the competition of cheap child and woman workers, by convictions that unions were un-American, and by a series of strikes that failed as government intervened on the side of business. Consumers of manufactured goods and processed foods, virtually the entire population, were at the mercy of the profit-makers, whose contaminated food, adulterated drugs, and shoddy goods were the result of the principle that the buyer should beware. In the background, forgotten by the party that freed him, the black man was disenfranchised by the 1890s and reduced to a new form of slavery.

Natural America, the land of wonders that had fascinated and pleased the generation of romantics in the years before the Civil War, could still be found and enjoyed, as John Wesley Powell and others discovered. But natural America unspoiled was becoming increasingly difficult to find, as mines, railroads, factories, overgrazing, and unrestricted lumbering, carried on as part of the search for profits, began to denude and pollute the countryside. Powell's Grand Canyon and his Indians were still remote enough to be secure for another generation. However, as in the case of the buffalo, virtually extinct by 1890, and the passenger pigeon, completely extinct a few years later, size and remoteness were no more a sign of permanent security than were the numbers of an earlier day.

Within the context of an environment and a people despoiled by an unrestricted greed, young writers began their search for ultimate meaning as their predecessors did earlier in the century. The technique of realism became the tool by which the search could be carried out; the goal was a natural, inclusive explanation of the phenomena revealed by that tool. The subject matter of the new literature provided the foundation for the new explanations, subject matter so grim that for the people caught up in it, the future seemed hopeless. The despair engendered by the new America was reinforced by the premises of Darwin, expanded from biological theory to social reality. Man was a creature not only of his environment but of the forces of nature. In their pursuit of the realistic ethic they found evidence to substantiate Darwin's premises, particularly as they found and exploited the powerful motivating force of sex, not destroyed as Melville saw it, but brutalized in the New World.

These new writers pursued nature as avidly as did the romantics, but it was a nature of impersonal forces rather than spiritual unity, and the

Introduction

term *naturalist*, applied to the new writers, is perhaps misleading. They pursued nature, but they discovered and defined determinism, a concept that introduces a new definition of man, of nature, and of the relationship between them. For Stephen Crane, the most complete and consistent of the new naturalists or determinists, the implications were clear: in a series of works ranging in subject matter from *Maggie: A Girl of the Streets* of New York to *The Open Boat* adrift in the Gulf Stream and *The Red Badge of Courage* of the Civil War, he proclaimed that the universe consists of natural forces beyond man's comprehension or control. Man is helpless in a world indifferent to him and his individual fate, but because he is weak and helpless, the universe appears hostile.

Frank Norris shared the same view of man's predicament, which he projected in a series of works. The most complex and ambitious of these was *The Octopus*, a novel in which he fuses natural and economic forces into an unwieldy but powerful statement of man's inability to control his destiny. Paradoxically, Norris sought an ultimate good in denying traditional values that interpret good in personal, human terms, seeking it instead in the operation of the natural system itself.

In spite of their assertions that man is helpless and that nothing can be done to alleviate his suffering in a system which is destined to destroy him, these naturalists served an important purpose as social critics, revealing specific abuses that could be eliminated or eased. This was the role Upton Sinclair sought for himself and his fiction, particularly *The Jungle*, in which he attacked the entire exploitative capitalistic system and advocated socialism as the answer to its abuses. Ironically, Sinclair found that he had made a major contribution to legislation designed to clear up the abuses he had pointed out in the meat-packing industry, a major source of a food supply controlled and contaminated by profit-seekers whose helpless city-dwelling victims were horrified by Sinclair's revelations.

These fiction writers, whether conscious social critics or not, prepared the way for another group, less artistic or philosophical but ultimately more successful in bringing about reform in the American environment. Called "muckrakers" by President Theodore Roosevelt, himself a cautious reformer, they were journalists writing for the new mass circulation magazines, who saw their role as exposing the corruption and abuses of a system that had lost sight of its origins, its purposes, or its traditional values and ideals.

Among the muckrakers, the most famous was Lincoln Steffens, whose exposés of the corruption of municipal government, were later gathered in *The Shame of the Cities* (1904). Others among the muckrakers were Ida Tarbell, who shocked a generation with *The History of the Standard Oil Company* (1904) and David Graham Phillips, also a novelist, whose series of articles entitled "The Treason of the Senate" (1906) was largely responsible for the passage of the Seventeenth Amendment to the Constitution, providing for the direct election of United States senators by the people rather than by state legislatures.

Muckrakers tended to specialization, and there was a great deal of

The Vision of Reality

opportunity to expose those who exploited men and nature. Among those who revealed the machinations of direct exploiters, John L. Mathews emphasized the exploitation of water resources.

Social reform was slow in coming, and it was virtually unknown until the forces of protest and reform reiterated the heritage of the American past and insisted that the major political parties accept responsibility for preserving and extending that heritage. By 1896 reform energy captured the Democratic party under the leadership of William Jennings Bryan, and five years later one of the ironic accidents of history placed Theodore Roosevelt, a Progressive and dedicated conservationist, in the White House. As the new century began, it appeared that the political impetus toward reform would be strong enough to rid the nation of abuses and exploitation, particularly as the nation reelected Roosevelt, accepted William Howard Taft upon his recommendation, and finally turned to Woodrow Wilson.

But reform was not to come easily, as a new generation of poets saw more clearly than their contemporary politicians and fellow citizens. While Vachel Lindsay could project an image of a perfect city, he also saw the reality in the broken windows of factory buildings. Edwin Arlington Robinson sought and failed to find an elusive meaning beyond it all for his frustrated people. Paul Laurence Dunbar and W. E. B. Du Bois defined the new reality in ways peculiar to the black man. But Carl Sandburg, a product of the new age, saw clearly one of the fundamental reasons for the elusiveness of perfection or even progress or reform: man is repulsed by corruption, but finds himself simultaneously attracted by it. Easy answers, whether of the idealistic past or the realistic present, were not to be found as easily as optimists, whether Progressives or reformers, seemed to think.

Introduction

Mark Twain:

Lake Tahoe
Mono Lake

Mark Twain (1835-1910), born Samuel Lang-
horne Clemens, an identity virtually lost in that
of his pseudonym, is largely responsible for
the direction that American literature was to
take in the twentieth century. Author of *Huckleberry Finn* (1884), one of America's great novels, he probed the nature of man, and became
increasingly convinced that human nature itself was the source of natural evil. His eye for
nature is shown in the following excerpts from
Roughing It (1872).

LAKE TAHOE

It was the end of August, and the skies were cloudless and the weather superb. In two or three weeks I had grown wonderfully fascinated with the curious new country, and concluded to put off my return to "the States" awhile. I had grown well accustomed to wearing a damaged slouch hat, blue woolen shirt, and pants crammed into boot-tops, and gloried in the absence of coat, vest and braces. I felt rowdyish and "bully," (as the historian Josephus phrases it, in his fine chapter upon the destruction of the Temple). It seemed to me that nothing could be so fine and so romantic. I had become an officer of the government, but that was for mere sublimity. The office was an unique sinecure. I had nothing to do and no salary. I was private Secretary to his majesty the Secretary and there was not yet writing enough for two of us. So Johnny K—— and I devoted our time to amusement. He was the young son of an Ohio nabob and was out there for recreation. He got it. We had heard a world of talk about the marvellous beauty of Lake Tahoe, and finally curiosity drove us thither to see it. Three or four members of the Brigade had been there and located some timber lands on its shores and stored up a quantity of provisions in their camp. We strapped a couple of blankets on our shoulders and took an axe apiece and started—for we intended to take up a wood ranch or so ourselves and become wealthy. We were on foot. The reader will find it advantageous to go horseback. We were told that the distance was eleven miles. We tramped a long time on level ground, and then toiled laboriously up a mountain about a thousand miles high and looked over. No lake there. We descended on the other side, crossed the valley and toiled up another mountain three or four thousand miles high, apparently, and looked over again. No lake yet. We sat down tired and perspiring, and hired a couple of Chinamen to curse those people who had beguiled us. Thus refreshed, we presently resumed the march with renewed vigor and determination. We plodded on, two or three hours longer, and at last the Lake burst upon us— a noble sheet of blue water lifted six thousand three hundred feet above the level of the sea, and walled in by a rim of snow-clad mountain peaks that towered aloft full three thousand feet higher still! It was a vast oval, and one would have to use up eighty or a hundred good miles in traveling around it. As it lay there with the shadows of the mountains brilliantly photographed upon its still surface I thought it must surely be the fairest picture the whole earth affords.

We found the small skiff belonging to the Brigade boys, and without loss of time set out across a deep bend of the lake toward the landmarks that signified the locality of the camp. I got Johnny to row— not because I mind exertion myself, but because it makes me sick to ride backwards when I am at work. But I steered. A three-mile pull brought us to the camp just as the night fell, and we stepped ashore very tired and wolfishly hungry. In a "cache" among the rocks we found the provisions and the cooking utensils, and then, all fatigued as I was, I sat down on a boulder and superintended while Johnny gathered wood and cooked

Mark Twain

supper. Many a man who had gone through what I had, would have wanted to rest.

It was a delicious supper—hot bread, fried bacon, and black coffee. It was a delicious solitude we were in, too. Three miles away was a saw-mill and some workmen, but there were not fifteen other human beings throughout the wide circumference of the lake. As the darkness closed down and the stars came out and spangled the great mirror with jewels, we smoked meditatively in the solemn hush and forgot our troubles and our pains. In due time we spread our blankets in the warm sand between two large boulders and soon fell asleep, careless of the procession of ants that passed in through rents in our clothing and explored our persons. Nothing could disturb the sleep that fettered us, for it had been fairly earned, and if our consciences had any sins on them they had to adjourn court for that night, any way. The wind rose just as we were losing consciousness, and we were lulled to sleep by the beating of the surf upon the shore.

It is always very cold on that lake shore in the night, but we had plenty of blankets and were warm enough. We never moved a muscle all night, but waked at early dawn in the original positions, and got up at once, thoroughly refreshed, free from soreness, and brim full of friskiness. There is no end of wholesome medicine in such an experience. That morning we could have whipped ten such people as we were the day before— sick ones at any rate. But the world is slow, and people will go to "water cures" and "movement cures" and to foreign lands for health. Three months of camp life on Lake Tahoe would restore an Egyptian mummy to his pristine vigor, and give him an appetite like an alligator. I do not mean the oldest and driest mummies, of course, but the fresher ones. The air up there in the clouds is very pure and fine, bracing and delicious. And why shouldn't it be?—it is the same the angels breathe. I think that hardly any amount of fatigue can be gathered together that a man cannot sleep off in one night on the sand by its side. Not under a roof, but under the sky; it seldom or never rains there in the summer time. I know a man who went there to die. But he made a failure of it. He was a skeleton when he came, and could barely stand. He had no appetite, and did nothing but read tracts and reflect on the future. Three months later he was sleeping out of doors regularly, eating all he could hold, three times a day, and chasing game over mountains three thousand feet high for recreation. And he was a skeleton no longer, but weighed part of a ton. This is no fancy sketch, but the truth. His disease was consumption. I confidently commend his experience to other skeletons.

I superintended again, and as soon as we had eaten breakfast we got in the boat and skirted along the lake shore about three miles and disembarked. We liked the appearance of the place, and so we claimed some three hundred acres of it and stuck our "notices" on a tree. It was yellow pine timber land—a dense forest of trees a hundred feet high and from one to five feet through at the butt. It was necessary to fence our property or we could not hold it. That is to say, it was necessary to cut down trees

Lake Tahoe

here and there and make them fall in such a way as to form a sort of enclosure (with pretty wide gaps in it). We cut down three trees apiece, and found it such heart-breaking work that we decided to "rest our case" on those; if they held the property, well and good; if they didn't, let the property spill out through the gaps and go; it was no use to work ourselves to death merely to save a few acres of land. Next day we came back to build a house—for a house was also necessary, in order to hold the property. We decided to build a substantial log-house and excite the envy of the Brigade boys; but by the time we had cut and trimmed the first log it seemed unnecessary to be so elaborate, and so we concluded to build it of saplings. However, two saplings, duly cut and trimmed, compelled recognition of the fact that a still modester architecture would satisfy the law, and so we concluded to build a "brush" house. We devoted the next day to this work, but we did so much "sitting around" and discussing, that by the middle of the afternoon we had achieved only a half-way sort of affair which one of us had to watch while the other cut brush, lest if both turned our backs we might not be able to find it again, it had such a strong family resemblance to the surrounding vegetation. But we were satisfied with it.

We were land owners now, duly seized and possessed, and within the protection of the law. Therefore we decided to take up our residence on our own domain and enjoy that large sense of independence which only such an experience can bring. Late the next afternoon, after a good long rest, we sailed away from the Brigade camp with all the provisions and cooking utensils we could carry off—borrow is the more accurate word—and just as the night was falling we beached the boat at our own landing.

If there is any life that is happier than the life we led on our timber ranch for the next two or three weeks, it must be a sort of life which I have not read of in books or experienced in person. We did not see a human being but ourselves during the time, or hear any sounds but those that were made by the wind and the waves, the sighing of the pines, and now and then the far-off thunder of an avalanche. The forest about us was dense and cool, the sky above us was cloudless and brilliant with sunshine, the broad lake before us was glassy and clear, or rippled and breezy, or black and storm-tossed, according to Nature's mood; and its circling border of mountain domes, clothed with forests, scarred with land-slides, cloven by cañons and valleys, and helmeted with glittering snow, fitly framed and finished the noble picture. The view was always fascinating, bewitching, entrancing. The eye was never tired of gazing, night or day, in calm or storm; it suffered but one grief, and that was that it could not look always, but must close sometimes in sleep.

We slept in the sand close to the water's edge, between two protecting boulders, which took care of the stormy night-winds for us. We never took any paregoric to make us sleep. At the first break of dawn we were always up and running footraces to tone down excess of physical vigor and exuberance of spirits. That is, Johnny was—but I held his hat. While smoking the pipe of peace after breakfast we watched the sentinel peaks

Mark Twain

put on the glory of the sun, and followed the conquering light as it swept down among the shadows, and set the captive crags and forests free. We watched the tinted pictures grow and brighten upon the water till every little detail of forest, precipice and pinnacle was wrought in and finished, and the miracle of the enchanter complete. Then to "business."

That is, drifting around in the boat. We were on the north shore. There, the rocks on the bottom are sometimes gray, sometimes white. This gives the marvelous transparency of the water a fuller advantage than it has elsewhere on the lake. We usually pushed out a hundred yards or so from shore, and then lay down on the thwarts, in the sun, and let the boat drift by the hour whither it would. We seldom talked. It interrupted the Sabbath stillness, and marred the dreams the luxurious rest and indolence brought. The shore all along was indented with deep, curved bays and coves, bordered by narrow sand-beaches; and where the sand ended, the steep mountain-sides rose right up aloft into space—rose up like a vast wall a little out of the perpendicular, and thickly wooded with tall pines.

So singularly clear was the water, that where it was only twenty or thirty feet deep the bottom was so perfectly distinct that the boat seemed floating in the air! Yes, where it was even *eighty* feet deep. Every little pebble was distinct, every speckled trout, every hand's-breadth of sand. Often, as we lay on our faces, a granite boulder, as large as a village church, would start out of the bottom apparently, and seem climbing up rapidly to the surface, till presently it threatened to touch our faces, and we could not resist the impulse to seize an oar and avert the danger. But the boat would float on, and the boulder descend again, and then we could see that when we had been exactly above it, it must still have been twenty or thirty feet below the surface. Down through the transparency of these great depths, the water was not *merely* transparent, but dazzlingly, brilliantly so. All objects seen through it had a bright, strong vividness, not only of outline, but of every minute detail, which they would not have had when seen simply through the same depth of atmosphere. So empty and airy did all spaces seem below us, and so strong was the sense of floating high aloft in mid-nothingness, that we called these boat-excursions "balloon-voyages."

We fished a good deal, but we did not average one fish a week. We could see trout by the thousand winging about in the emptiness under us, or sleeping in shoals on the bottom, but they would not bite—they could see the line too plainly, perhaps. We frequently selected the trout we wanted, and rested the bait patiently and persistently on the end of his nose at a depth of eighty feet, but he would only shake it off with an annoyed manner, and shift his position.

We bathed occasionally, but the water was rather chilly, for all it looked so sunny. Sometimes we rowed out to the "blue water," a mile or two from shore. It was as dead blue as indigo there, because of the immense depth. By official measurement the lake in its centre is one thousand five hundred and twenty-five feet deep!

Sometimes, on lazy afternoons, we lolled on the sand in camp, and

Lake Tahoe

smoked pipes and read some old well-worn novels. At night, by the camp-fire, we played euchre and seven-up to strengthen the mind—and played them with cards so greasy and defaced that only a whole summer's acquaintance with them could enable the student to tell the ace of clubs from the jack of diamonds.

We never slept in our "house." It never occurred to us, for one thing; and besides, it was built to hold the ground, and that was enough. We did not wish to strain it.

By and by our provisions began to run short, and we went back to the old camp and laid in a new supply. We were gone all day, and reached home again about night-fall, pretty tired and hungry. While Johnny was carrying the main bulk of the provisions up to our "house" for future use, I took the loaf of bread, some slices of bacon, and the coffee-pot, ashore, set them down by a tree, lit a fire, and went back to the boat to get the frying-pan. While I was at this, I heard a shout from Johnny, and looking up I saw that my fire was galloping all over the premises!

Johnny was on the other side of it. He had to run through the flames to get to the lake shore, and then we stood helpless and watched the devastation.

The ground was deeply carpeted with dry pine-needles, and the fire touched them off as if they were gunpowder. It was wonderful to see with what fierce speed the tall sheet of flame traveled! My coffee-pot was gone, and everything with it. In a minute and a half the fire seized upon a dense growth of dry manzanita chapparal six or eight feet high, and then the roaring and popping and crackling was something terrific. We were driven to the boat by the intense heat, and there we remained, spellbound.

Within half an hour all before us was a tossing, blinding tempest of flame! It went surging up adjacent ridges—surmounted them and disappeared in the cañons beyond—burst into view upon higher and farther ridges, presently—shed a grander illumination abroad, and dove again—flamed out again, directly, higher and still higher up the mountain-side—threw out skirmishing parties of fire here and there, and sent them trailing their crimson spirals away among remote ramparts and ribs and gorges, till as far as the eye could reach the lofty mountain-fronts were webbed as it were with a tangled network of red lava streams. Away across the water the crags and domes were lit with a ruddy glare, and the firmament above was a reflected hell!

Every feature of the spectacle was repeated in the glowing mirror of the lake! Both pictures were sublime, both were beautiful; but that in the lake had a bewildering richness about it that enchanted the eye and held it with the stronger fascination.

We sat absorbed and motionless through four long hours. We never thought of supper, and never felt fatigue. But at eleven o'clock the conflagration had traveled beyond our range of vision, and then darkness stole down upon the landscape again.

Hunger asserted itself now, but there was nothing to eat. The provisions were all cooked, no doubt, but we did not go to see. We were

Mark Twain

homeless wanderers again, without any property. Our fence was gone, our house burned down; no insurance. Our pine forest was well scorched, the dead trees all burned up, and our broad acres of manzanita swept away. Our blankets were on our usual sand-bed, however, and so we lay down and went to sleep. The next morning we started back to the old camp, but while out a long way from shore, so great a storm came up that we dared not try to land. So I baled out the seas we shipped, and Johnny pulled heavily through the billows till we had reached a point three or four miles beyond the camp. The storm was increasing, and it became evident that it was better to take the hazard of beaching the boat than go down in a hundred fathoms of water; so we ran in, with tall white-caps following, and I sat down in the stern-sheets and pointed her head-on to the shore. The instant the bow struck, a wave came over the stern that washed crew and cargo ashore, and saved a deal of trouble. We shivered in the lee of a boulder all the rest of the day, and froze all the night through. In the morning the tempest had gone down, and we paddled down to the camp without any unnecessary delay. We were so starved that we ate up the rest of the Brigade's provisions, and then set out to Carson to tell them about it and ask their forgiveness. It was accorded, upon payment of damages.

We made many trips to the lake after that, and had many a hair-breadth escape and blood-curdling adventure which will never be recorded in any history.

MONO LAKE

Mono Lake lies in a lifeless, treeless, hideous desert, eight thousand feet above the level of the sea, and is guarded by mountains two thousand feet higher, whose summits are always clothed in clouds. This solemn, silent, sailless sea—this lonely tenant of the loneliest spot on earth—is little graced with the picturesque. It is an unpretending expanse of grayish water, about a hundred miles in circumference, with two islands in its centre, mere upheavals of rent and scorched and blistered lava, snowed over with gray banks and drifts of pumice-stone and ashes, the winding sheet of the dead volcano, whose vast crater the lake has seized upon and occupied.

The lake is two hundred feet deep, and its sluggish waters are so strong with alkali that if you only dip the most hopelessly soiled garment into them once or twice, and wring it out, it will be found as clean as if it had been through the ablest of washerwomen's hands. While we camped there our laundry work was easy. We tied the week's washing astern of our boat, and sailed a quarter of a mile, and the job was complete, all to the wringing out. If we threw the water on our heads and gave them a rub or so, the white lather would pile up three inches high. This water is not good for bruised places and abrasions of the skin. We had a valuable dog. He had raw places on him. He had more raw places on him than sound ones. He was the rawest dog I almost ever saw. He jumped overboard one day to get away from the flies. But it was bad judgment. In his condition, it would have been just as comfortable to jump into the fire. The alkali water nipped him in all the raw places simultaneously, and he struck out for the shore with considerable interest. He yelped and barked and howled as he went—and by the time he got to the shore there was no bark to him—for he had barked the bark all out of his inside, and the alkali water had cleaned the bark all off his outside, and he probably wished he had never embarked in any such enterprise. He ran round and round in a circle, and pawed the earth and clawed the air, and threw double somersaults, sometimes backward and sometimes forward, in the most extraordinary manner. He was not a demonstrative dog, as a general thing, but rather of a grave and serious turn of mind, and I never saw him take so much interest in anything before. He finally struck out over the mountains, at a gait which we estimated at about two hundred and fifty miles an hour, and he is going yet. This was about nine years ago. We look for what is left of him along here every day.

A white man cannot drink the water of Mono Lake, for it is nearly pure lye. It is said that the Indians in the vicinity drink it sometimes, though. It is not improbable, for they are among the purest liars I ever saw. [There will be no additional charge for this joke, except to parties requiring an explanation of it. This joke has received high commendation from some of the ablest minds of the age.]

There are no fish in Mono Lake—no frogs, no snakes, no polliwigs—nothing, in fact, that goes to make life desirable. Millions of wild ducks and sea-gulls swim about the surface, but no living thing exists *under* the surface, except a white feathery sort of worm, one half an inch long, which looks like a bit of white thread frayed out at the sides. If you dip up a gallon of water, you will get about fifteen thousand of these. They give to the water a sort of grayish-white appearance. Then there is a fly, which looks something like our house fly. These settle on the beach to eat the worms that wash ashore—and any time, you can see there a belt of flies an inch deep and six feet wide, and this belt extends clear around the lake—a belt of flies one hundred miles long. If you throw a stone among them, they swarm up so thick that they look dense, like a cloud. You can hold them under water as long as you please—they do not mind it—they are only proud of it. When you let them go, they pop up to the surface as dry as a patent office report, and walk off as unconcernedly as if they had been educated especially with a view to affording instructive entertainment to man in that particular way. Providence leaves nothing to go by chance. All things have their uses and their part and proper place in Nature's economy: the ducks eat the flies—the flies eat the worms—the Indians eat all three—the wild cats eat the Indians—the white folks eat the wild cats—and thus all things are lovely.

Mono Lake is a hundred miles in a straight line from the ocean—and between it and the ocean are one or two ranges of mountains—yet thousands of sea-gulls go there every season to lay their eggs and rear their young. One would as soon expect to find sea-gulls in Kansas. And in this connection let us observe another instance of Nature's wisdom. The islands

Mark Twain

in the lake being merely huge masses of lava, coated over with ashes and pumice-stone, and utterly innocent of vegetation or anything that would burn; and sea-gulls' eggs being entirely useless to anybody unless they be cooked, Nature has provided an unfailing spring of boiling water on the largest island, and you can put your eggs in there, and in four minutes you can boil them as hard as any statement I have made during the past fifteen years. Within ten feet of the boiling spring is a spring of pure cold water, sweet and wholesome. So, in that island you get your board and washing free of charge—and if nature had gone further and furnished a nice American hotel clerk who was crusty and disobliging, and didn't know anything about the time tables, or the railroad routes—or—anything—and was proud of it—I would not wish for a more desirable boarding-house.

Half a dozen little mountain brooks flow into Mono Lake, but *not a stream of any kind flows out of it.* It neither rises nor falls, apparently, and what it does with its surplus water is a dark and bloody mystery.

There are only two seasons in the region round about Mono Lake— and these are, the breaking up of one Winter and the beginning of the next. More than once (in Esmeralda) I have seen a perfectly blistering morning open up with the thermometer at ninety degrees at eight o'clock, and seen the snow fall fourteen inches deep and that same identical thermometer go down to forty-four degrees under shelter, before nine o'clock at night. Under favorable circumstances it snows at least once in every single month in the year, in the little town of Mono. So uncertain is the climate in Summer that a lady who goes out visiting cannot hope to be prepared for all emergencies unless she takes her fan under one arm and her snow shoes under the other. When they have a Fourth of July procession it generally snows on them, and they do say that as a general thing when a man calls for a brandy toddy there, the bar keeper chops it off with a hatchet and wraps it up in a paper, like maple sugar. And it is further reported that the old soakers haven't any teeth—wore them out eating gin cocktails and brandy punches. I do not endorse that statement—I simply give it for what it is worth—and it is worth—well, I should say, millions, to any man who can believe it without straining himself. But I do endorse the snow on the Fourth of July—because I know that to be true.

About seven o'clock one blistering hot morning—for it was now dead summer time—Higbie and I took the boat and started on a voyage of discovery to the two islands. We had often longed to do this, but had been deterred by the fear of storms; for they were frequent, and severe enough to capsize an ordinary row-boat like ours without great difficulty—and once capsized, death would ensue in spite of the bravest swimming, for that venomous water would eat a man's eyes out like fire, and burn him out inside, too, if he shipped a sea. It was called twelve miles, straight out to the islands—a long pull and a warm one—but the morning was so quiet and sunny, and the lake so smooth and glassy and dead, that we could not resist the temptation. So we filled two large tin canteens with water (since we were not acquainted with the locality of the spring said to exist on the large island), and started. Higbie's brawny muscles gave the boat good

Mono Lake

speed, but by the time we reached our destination we judged that we had pulled nearer fifteen miles than twelve.

We landed on the big island and went ashore. We tried the water in the canteens, now, and found that the sun had spoiled it; it was so brackish that we could not drink it; so we poured it out and began a search for the spring—for thirst augments fast as soon as it is apparent that one has no means at hand of quenching it. The island was a long, moderately high hill of ashes—nothing but gray ashes and pumice-stone, in which we sunk to our knees at every step—and all around the top was a forbidding wall of scorched and blasted rocks. When we reached the top and got within the wall, we found simply a shallow, far-reaching basin, carpeted with ashes, and here and there a patch of fine sand. In places, picturesque jets of steam shot up out of crevices, giving evidence that although this ancient crater had gone out of active business, there was still some fire left in its furnaces. Close to one of these jets of steam stood the only tree on the island—a small pine of most graceful shape and most fault-less symmetry; its color was a brilliant green, for the steam drifted unceasingly through its branches and kept them always moist. It contrasted strangely enough, did this vigorous and beautiful outcast, with its dead and dismal surroundings. It was like a cheerful spirit in a mourning household.

We hunted for the spring everywhere, traversing the full length of the island (two or three miles), and crossing it twice—climbing ash-hills patiently, and then sliding down the other side in a sitting posture, plowing up smothering volumes of gray dust. But we found nothing but solitude, ashes and a heart-breaking silence. Finally we noticed that the wind had risen, and we forgot our thirst in a solicitude of greater importance; for, the lake being quiet, we had not taken pains about securing the boat. We hurried back to a point overlooking our landing place, and then—but mere words cannot describe our dismay—the boat was gone! The chances were that there was not another boat on the entire lake. The situation was not comfortable—in truth, to speak plainly, it was frightful. We were prisoners on a desolate island, in aggravating proximity to friends who were for the present helpless to aid us; and what was still more uncomfortable was the reflection that we had neither food nor water. But presently we sighted the boat. It was drifting along, leisurely, about fifty yards from shore, tossing in a foamy sea. It drifted, and continued to drift, but at the same safe distance from land, and we walked along abreast it and waited for fortune to favor us. At the end of an hour it approached a jutting cape, and Higbie ran ahead and posted himself on the utmost verge and prepared for the assault. If we failed there, there was no hope for us. It was driving gradually shoreward all the time, now; but whether it was driving fast enough to make the connection or not was the momentous question. When it got within thirty steps of Higbie I was so excited that I fancied I could hear my own heart beat. When, a little later, it dragged slowly along and seemed about to go by, only one little yard out of reach, it seemed as if my heart stood still; and when it was exactly abreast him and began to widen away, and he still standing like a watching statue, I knew my heart did

Mark Twain

stop. But when he gave a great spring, the next instant, and lit fairly in the stern, I discharged a war-whoop that woke the solitudes!

But it dulled my enthusiasm, presently, when he told me he had not been caring whether the boat came within jumping distance or not, so that it passed within eight or ten yards of him, for he had made up his mind to shut his eyes and mouth and swim that trifling distance. Imbecile that I was, I had not thought of that. It was only a long swim that could be fatal.

The sea was running high and the storm increasing. It was growing late, too—three or four in the afternoon. Whether to venture toward the mainland or not, was a question of some moment. But we were so distressed by thirst that we decided to try it, and so Higbie fell to work and I took the steering-oar. When we had pulled a mile, laboriously, we were evidently in serious peril, for the storm had greatly augmented; the billows ran very high and were capped with foaming crests, the heavens were hung with black, and the wind blew with great fury. We would have gone back, now, but we did not dare to turn the boat around, because as soon as she got in the trough of the sea she would upset, of course. Our only hope lay in keeping her head-on to the seas. It was hard work to do this, she plunged so, and so beat and belabored the billows with her rising and falling bows. Now and then one of Higbie's oars would trip on the top of a wave, and the other one would snatch the boat half around in spite of my cumbersome steering apparatus. We were drenched by the sprays constantly, and the boat occasionally shipped water. By and by, powerful as my comrade was, his great exertions began to tell on him, and he was anxious that I should change places with him till he could rest a little. But I told him this was impossible; for if the steering oar were dropped a moment while we changed, the boat would slue around into the trough of the sea, capsize, and in less than five minutes we would have a hundred gallons of soap-suds in us and be eaten up so quickly that we could not even be present at our own inquest.

But things cannot last always. Just as the darkness shut down we came booming into port, head on. Higbie dropped his oars to hurrah—I dropped mine to help—the sea gave the boat a twist, and over she went!

The agony that alkali water inflicts on bruises, chafes and blistered hands, is unspeakable, and nothing but greasing all over will modify it— but we ate, drank and slept well, that night, notwithstanding.

In speaking of the peculiarities of Mono Lake, I ought to have mentioned that at intervals all around its shores stand picturesque turret-looking masses and clusters of a whitish, coarse-grained rock that resembles inferior mortar dried hard; and if one breaks off fragments of this rock he will find perfectly shaped and thoroughly petrified gulls' eggs deeply imbedded in the mass. How did they get there? I simply state the fact—for it is a fact—and leave the geological reader to crack the nut at his leisure and solve the problem after his own fashion.

At the end of a week we adjourned to the Sierras on a fishing excursion, and spent several days in camp under snowy Castle Peak, and

Mono Lake

fished successfully for trout in a bright, miniature lake whose surface was between ten and eleven thousand feet above the level of the sea; cooling ourselves during the hot August noons by sitting on snow banks ten feet deep, under whose sheltering edges *fine grass and dainty flowers flourished luxuriously;* and at night entertaining ourselves by almost freezing to death. Then we returned to Mono Lake, and finding that the cement excitement was over for the present, packed up and went back to Esmeralda. Mr. Ballou reconnoitred awhile, and not liking the prospect, set out alone for Humboldt.

About this time occurred a little incident which has always had a sort of interest to me, from the fact that it came so near "instigating" my funeral. At a time when an Indian attack had been expected, the citizens hid their gunpowder where it would be safe and yet convenient to hand when wanted. A neighbor of ours hid six cans of rifle powder in the bake-oven of an old discarded cooking stove which stood on the open ground near a frame out-house or shed, and from and after that day never thought of it again. We hired a half-tamed Indian to do some washing for us, and he took up quarters under the shed with his tub. The ancient stove reposed within six feet of him, and before his face. Finally it occurred to him that hot water would be better than cold, and he went out and fired up under that forgotten powder magazine and set on a kettle of water. Then he returned to his tub. I entered the shed presently and threw down some more clothes, and was about to speak to him when the stove blew up with a prodigious crash, and disappeared, leaving not a splinter behind. Fragments of it fell in the streets full two hundred yards away. Nearly a third of the shed roof over our heads was destroyed, and one of the stove lids, after cutting a small stanchion half in two in front of the Indian, whizzed between us and drove partly through the weather-boarding beyond. I was as white as a sheet and as weak as a kitten and speechless. But the Indian betrayed no trepidation, no distress, not even discomfort. He simply stopped washing, leaned forward and surveyed the clean, blank ground a moment, and then remarked:

"Mph! Dam stove heap gone!"—and resumed his scrubbing as placidly as if it were an entirely customary thing for a stove to do. I will explain, that "heap" is "Injun-English" for "very much." The reader will perceive the exhaustive expressiveness of it in the present instance.

[1872]

Mark Twain

John Wesley Powell:
Cliffs and Terraces

John Wesley Powell (1834-1902), geologist, ethnologist, and explorer, led many expeditions into the western mountains and deserts. His major expedition, to conduct a geographical and geological survey of the Colorado River, led to his exploration of the Grand Canyon and to two major books, *Exploration of the Colorado River of the West and Its Tributaries* (1875) and *Canyons of the Colorado* (1895), the latter the source of the following essay.

There is a great group of table-lands constituting a geographic unit which have been named the Terrace Plateaus. They extend from the Paria and Colorado on the east to the Grand Wash and Pine Mountains on the west, and they are bounded on the south by the Grand Canyon of the Colorado, and on the north they divide the waters of the Colorado from the waters of the Sevier, which flows northward and then westward until it is lost in the sands of the Great Desert. It is an irregular system of great plateaus with subordinate mesas and buttes separated by lines of cliffs and dissected by canyons.

In this region all of the features which have been described as found in other portions of the province are grouped except only the cliffs of volcanic ashes, the volcanic cones, and the volcanic domes. The volcanic mountains, cinder cones, and coulées, the majestic plateaus and elaborate mesas, the sculptured buttes and canyon gorges, are all found here, but on a more stupendous scale. The volcanic mountains are higher, the cinder cones are larger, the coulées are more extensive and are often sheets of naked, black rock, the plateaus are more lofty, the cliffs are on a grander scale, the canyons are of profounder depth; and the Grand Canyon of the Colorado, the most stupendous gorge known on the globe, with a great river surging through it, bounds it on the south.

The east-and-west cliffs are escarpments of degradation, the north-and-south cliffs are, in the main, though not always, escarpments of displacement. Let us understand what this means. Over the entire region limestones, shales, and sandstones were deposited through long periods of geologic time to the thickness of many thousands of feet; then the country was upheaved and tilted toward the north; but the Colorado River was flowing when the tilting commenced, and the upheaval was very slow, so that the river cleared away the obstruction to its channel as fast as it was presented, and this is the Grand Canyon.

The rocks above were carried away by rains and rivers, but not evenly all over the country; nor by washing out valleys and leaving hills, but by carving the country into terraces. The upper and later-formed rocks are found far to the north, their edges standing in cliffs; then still earlier rocks are found rising to the southward, until they terminate in cliffs; and then a third series rises to the southward and ends in cliffs, and finally a fourth series, the oldest rocks, terminating in the Grand Canyon wall, which is a line of cliffs. There are in a general way four great lines of cliffs extending from east to west across the district and presenting their faces, or escarpments, southward. If these cliffs are climbed it is found that each plateau or terrace dips gently to the northward until it meets with another line of cliffs, which must be ascended to reach the summit of another plateau. Place a book before you on a table with its front edge toward you, rest another book on the back of this, place a third on the back of the second, and in like manner a fourth on the third. Now the leaves of the books dip from you and the cut edges stand in tiny escarpments facing you. So the rock-formed leaves of these books of geology have the escarpment edges turned southward, while each book itself dips northward, and the crest of

John Wesley Powell

each plateau book is the summit of a line of cliffs. These cliffs of erosion have been described as running from east to west, but they diverge from that course in many ways. First, canyons run from north to south through them, and where these canyons are found deep angles occur; then sharp salients extend from the cliffs on the backs of the lower plateaus. Each great escarpment is made up more or less of minor terraces, or steps; and at the foot of each grand escarpment there is always a great talus, or sloping pile of rocks, and many marvelous buttes stand in front of the cliffs.

But these east-and-west cliffs and the plateaus which they form are divided by north-and-south lines in another manner. The country has been faulted along north-and-south lines or planes. These faults are breaks in the strata varying from 1,000 to 2,000 to 4,000 or 5,000 feet in verticality. On the very eastern margin the rocks are dropped down several thousand feet, or, which means the same thing, the rocks are upheaved on the west side; that is, the beds that were originally horizontal have been differentially displaced, so that on the west side of the fracture the strata are several thousand feet higher than they are on the east side of the fracture. The line of displacement is known as the Echo Cliff Fault. West of this about twenty-five miles, there is another fault with its throw to the east, the upheaved rocks being on the west. This fault varies from 1,500 to 2,500 feet in throw, and extends far to the northward. It is known as the East Kaibab Fault. Still going westward, another fault is found, known as the West Kaibab Fault. Here the throw is on the west side,—that is, the rocks are dropped down to the westward from 1,000 to 2,000 feet. This fault gradually becomes less to the northward and is flexed toward the east until it joins with the East Kaibab Fault. The block between the two faults is the Kaibab Plateau. Going westward from 60 to 70 miles, still another fault is found, known as the Hurricane Ledge Fault. The throw is again on the west side of the fracture and the rocks fall down some thousands of feet. This fault extends far northward into central Utah. To the west 25 or 30 miles is found a fault with the throw still on the west. It has a drop of several thousand feet and extends across the Rio Colorado far to the southwest, probably beyond the Arizona–New Mexico line. It also extends far to the north, until it is buried and lost under the Pine Valley Mountains, which are of volcanic origin.

Now let us see what all this means. In order clearly to understand this explanation the reader is referred to the illustration designated "Section and Bird's-Eye View of the Plateaus North of the Grand Canyon." Starting at the Grand Wash on the west, the Grand Wash Cliffs, formed by the Grand Wash Fault, are scaled; and if we are but a few miles north of the Grand Canyon we are on the Shiwits Plateau. Its western boundary is the Grand Wash Cliffs, its southern boundary is the Grand Canyon, and its northern boundary is a line of cliffs of degradation, which will be described hereafter. Going eastward across the Shiwits Plateau the Hurricane Cliffs are reached, and climbing them we are on the Uinkaret Plateau, which is bounded on the south by the Grand Canyon and on the north by the Vermilion Cliffs, that rise above its northern foot. Still going eastward

Cliffs and Terraces

30 or 40 miles to the brink of the Kanab Canyon, the West Kanab Plateau is crossed, which is bounded by the Toroweap Fault on the west, separating it from the Uinkaret Plateau, and by the Kanab Canyon on the east, with the Grand Canyon on the south and the Vermilion Cliffs on the north. Crossing the Kanab, we are on the East Kanab Plateau, which extends about 30 miles to the foot of the West Kaibab Cliffs, or the escarpment of the West Kaibab Fault. This canyon also has the Grand Canyon on the south and the Vermilion Cliffs on the north. Climbing the West Kaibab Fault, we are on the Kaibab Plateau. Now we have been climbing from west to east, and each ascent has been made at a line of cliffs. Crossing the Kaibab Plateau to the East Kaibab Cliffs; the country falls down once more to the top of Marble Canyon Plateau. Crossing this plateau to the eastward, we at last reach the Echo Cliff Fault, where the rocks fall down on the eastern side once more; but the surface of the country itself does not fall down—the later rocks still remain, and the general level of the country is preserved except in one feature of singular interest and beauty, to describe which a little further explanation is necessary.

I have spoken of these north-and-south faults as if they were fractures; and usually they are fractures, but in some places they are flexures. The Echo Cliffs displacement is a flexure. Just over the zone of flexure a long ridge extends from north to south, known as the Echo Cliffs. It is composed of a comparatively hard and homogeneous sandstone of a later age than the limestones of the Marble Canyon Plateau west of it; but the flexure dips down so as to carry this sandstone which forms the face of the cliff (presented westward) far under the surface, so that on the east side rocks of still later age are found, the drop being several thousand feet. The inclined red sandstone stands in a ridge more than 75 miles in length, with an escarped face presented to the west and a face of inclined rock to the east. The western side is carved into beautiful alcoves and is buttressed with a magnificent talus, and the red sandstone stands in fractured columns of giant size and marvelous beauty. On the east side the declining beds are carved into pockets, which often hold water. This is the region of the Thousand Wells. The foot of the cliffs on the east side is several hundred feet above the foot of the cliffs on the west side. On the west there is a vast limestone stretch, the top of the Marble Canyon Plateau; on the east there are drifting sand-dunes.

The terraced land described has three sets of terraces: one set on the east, great steps to the Kaibab Plateau; another set on the west, from the Great Basin region to the Kaibab Plateau; and a third set from the Grand Canyon northward. There are thus three sets of cliffs: cliffs facing the east, cliffs facing the west, and cliffs facing the south. The north-and-south cliffs are made by faults; the east-and-west cliffs are made by differential degradation.

The stupendous cliffs by which the plateaus are bounded are of indescribable grandeur and beauty. The cliffs bounding the Kaibab Plateau descend on either side, and this is the culminating portion of the region. All the other plateaus are terraces, with cliffs ascending on the one side

John Wesley Powell

and descending on the other. Some of the tables carry dead volcanoes on their backs that are towering mountains, and all of them are dissected by canyons that are gorges of profound depth. But every one of these plateaus has characteristics peculiar to itself and is worthy of its own chapter. On the north there is a pair of plateaus, twins in age, but very distinct in development, the Paunsagunt and Markagunt. They are separated by the Sevier River, which flows northward. Their southern margins constitute the highest steps of the great system of terraces of erosion. This escarpment is known as the Pink Cliffs. Above, pine forests are found; below the cliffs are hills and sand-dunes. The cliffs themselves are bold and often vertical walls of a delicate pink color.

In one of the earlier years of exploration I stood on the summit of the Pink Cliffs of the Paunsagunt Plateau, 9,000 feet above the level of the sea. Below me, to the southwest, I could look off into the canyons of the Virgen River, down into the canyon of the Kanab, and far away into the Grand Canyon of the Colorado. From the lowlands of the Great Basin and from the depths of the Grand Canyon clouds crept up over the cliffs and floated over the landscape below me, concealing the canyons and mantling the mountains and mesas and buttes; still on toward me the clouds rolled, burying the landscape in their progress, until at last the region below was covered by a mantle of storm—a tumultuous sea of rolling clouds, black and angry in parts, white as the foam of cataracts here and there, and everywhere flecked with resplendent sheen. Below me spread a vast ocean of vapor, for I was above the clouds. On descending to the plateau, I found that a great storm had swept the land, and the dry arroyos of the day before were the channels of a thousand streams of tawny water, born of the ocean of vapor which had invaded the land before my vision.

Below the Pink Cliffs another irregular zone of plateaus is found, stretching out to the margin of the Gray Cliffs. The Gray Cliffs are composed of a homogeneous sandstone which in some places weathers gray, but in others is as white as virgin snow. On the top of these cliffs hills and sand-dunes are found, but everywhere on the Gray Cliff margin the rocks are carved in fantastic forms; not in buttes and towers and pinnacles, but in great rounded bosses of rock.

The Virgen River heads back in the Pink Cliffs of the Markagunt Plateau and with its tributaries crosses one of these plateaus above the Gray Cliffs, carving a labyrinth of deep gorges. This is known as the Colob Plateau. Above, there is a vast landscape of naked, white and gray sandstone, billowing in fantastic bosses. On the margins of the canyons these are rounded off into great vertical walls, and at the bottom of every winding canyon a beautiful stream of water is found running over quicksands. Sometimes the streams in their curving have cut under the rocks, and overhanging cliffs of towering altitudes are seen; and somber chambers are found between buttresses that uphold the walls. Among the Indians this is known as the "Rock Rovers' Land," and is peopled by mythic beings of uncanny traits.

Below the Gray Cliffs another zone of plateaus is found, separated

Cliffs and Terraces

by the north-and-south faults and divided from the Colob series by the Gray Cliffs and demarcated from the plateaus to the south by the Vermilion Cliffs. The Vermilion Cliffs that face the south are of surpassing beauty. The rocks are of orange and red above and of chocolate, lavender, gray, and brown tints below. The canyons that cut through the cliffs from north to south are of great diversity and all are of profound interest. In these canyon walls many caves are found, and often the caves contain lakelets and pools of clear water. Canyons and re-entrant angles abound. The faces of the cliffs are terraced and salients project onto the floors below. The outlying buttes are many. Standing away to the south and facing these cliffs when the sun is going down beyond the desert of the Great Basin, shadows are seen to creep into the deep recesses, while the projecting forms are illumined, so that the lights and shadows are in great and sharp contrast; then a million lights seem to glow from a background of black gloom, and a great bank of Tartarean fire stretches across the landscape.

At the foot of the Vermilion Cliffs there is everywhere a zone of vigorous junipers and piñons, for the belt of country is favored with comparatively abundant rain. When the clouds drift over the plateaus below from the south and west and strike the Vermilion Cliffs, they are abruptly lifted 2,000 feet, and to make the climb they must unload their burdens; so that here copious rains are discharged, and by such storms the cliffs are carved and ever from age to age carried back farther to the north. In the Pink Cliffs above and the Gray Cliffs and the Vermilion Cliffs, there are many notches that mark channels running northward which had their sources on these plateaus when they extended farther to the south. The Rio Virgen is the only stream heading in the Pink Cliffs and running into the Colorado which is perennial. The other rivers and creeks carry streams of water in rainy seasons only. When a succession of dry years occurs the canyons coming through the cliffs are choked below, as vast bodies of sand are deposited. But now and then, ten or twenty years apart, great storms or successions of storms come, and the channels are flooded and cut their way again through the drifting sands to solid rock below. Thus the streams below are alternately choked and cleared from period to period.

To the south of the Vermilion Cliffs the last series or zone of plateaus north of the Grand Canyon is found. The summits of these plateaus are of cherty limestone. In the far west we have the Shiwits Plateau covered with sheets of lava and volcanic cones; then climbing the Hurricane Ledge we have the Kanab Plateau, on the southwest portion of which the Uinkaret Mountains stand—a group of dead volcanoes with many black cinder cones scattered about. It is interesting to know how these mountains are formed. The first eruptions of lava were long ago, and they were poured out upon a surface 2,000 feet or more higher than the general surface now found. After the first eruptions of coulées the lands round about were degraded by rains and rivers. Then new eruptions occurred and additional sheets of lava were poured out; but these came not through the first channels, but through later ones formed about the flanks of the elder beds of lava, so that the new sheets are imbricated or shingled over the old

John Wesley Powell

sheets. But the overlap is from below upward. Then the land was further degraded, and a third set of coulées was spread still lower down on the flanks, and on these last coulées the black cinder cones stand. So the foundations of the Uinkaret Mountains are of limestones, and these foundations are covered with sheets of lava overlapping from below upward, and the last coulées are decked with cones.

Still farther east is the Kaibab Plateau, the culminating table-land of the region. It is covered with a beautiful forest, and in the forest charming parks are found. Its southern extremity is a portion of the wall of the Grand Canyon; its western margin is the wall of the West Kaibab Fault; its eastern edge is the wall of the East Kaibab Fault; and its northern point is found where the two faults join. Here antelope feed and many a deer goes bounding over the fallen timber. In winter deep snows lie here, but the plateau has four months of the sweetest summer man has ever known.

On the terraced plateaus three tribes of Indians are found: the Shiwits ("people of the springs"), the Uinkarets ("people of the pine mountains"), and the Unkakaniguts ("people of the red lands," who dwell along the Vermilion Cliffs). They are all Utes and belong to a confederacy with other tribes living farther to the north, in Utah. These people live in shelters made of boughs piled up in circles and covered with juniper bark supported by poles. These little houses are only large enough for half a dozen persons huddling together in sleep. Their aboriginal clothing was very scant, the most important being wildcatskin and wolfskin robes for the men, and rabbitskin robes for the women, though for occasions of festival they had clothing of tanned deer and antelope skins, often decorated with fantastic ornaments of snakeskins, feathers, and the tails of squirrels and chipmunks. A great variety of seeds and roots furnish their food, and on the higher plateaus there is much game, especially deer and antelope. But the whole country abounds with rabbits, which are often killed with arrows and caught in snares. Every year they have great hunts, when scores of rabbits are killed in a single day. It is managed in this way: They make nets of the fiber of the wild flax and of some other plant, the meshes of which are about an inch across. These nets are about three and a half feet in width and hundreds of yards in length. They arrange such a net in a circle, not quite closed, supporting it by stakes and pinning the bottom firmly to the ground. From the opening of the circle they extend net wings, expanding in a broad angle several hundred yards from either side. Then the entire tribe will beat up a great district of country and drive the rabbits toward the nets, and finally into the circular snare, which is quickly closed, when the rabbits are killed with arrows.

A great variety of desert plants furnish them food, as seeds, roots, and stalks. More than fifty varieties of such seed-bearing plants have been collected. The seeds themselves are roasted, ground, and preserved in cakes. The most abundant food of this nature is derived from the sunflower and the nuts of the piñon. They still make stone arrowheads, stone knives, and stone hammers, and kindle fire with the drill. Their medicine men are famous sorcerers. Coughs are caused by invisible winged insects, rheuma-

Cliffs and Terraces

tism by flesh-eating bugs too small to be seen, and the toothache by invisible worms. Their healing art consists in searing and scarifying. Their medicine men take the medicine themselves to produce a state of ecstasy, in which the disease pests are discovered. They also practice dancing about their patients to drive away the evil beings or to avert the effects of sorcery. When a child is bitten by a rattlesnake the snake is caught and brought near to the suffering urchin, and ceremonies are performed, all for the purpose of prevailing upon the snake to take back the evil spirit. They have quite a variety of mythic personages. The chief of these are the Enupits, who are pigmies dwelling about the springs, and the Rock Rovers, who live in the cliffs. Their gods are zoic, and the chief among them are the wolf, the rabbit, the eagle, the jay, the rattlesnake, and the spider. They have no knowledge of the ambient air, but the winds are the breath of beasts living in the four quarters of the earth. Whirlwinds that often blow among the sand-dunes are caused by the dancing of Enupits. The sky is ice, and the rain is caused by the Rainbow God; he abraids the ice of the sky with his scales and the snow falls, and if the weather be warm the ice melts and it is rain. The sun is a poor slave compelled to make the same journey every day since he was conquered by the rabbit. These tribes have a great body of romance, in which the actors are animals, and the knowledge of these stories is the lore of their sages.

Scattered over the plateaus are the ruins of many ancient stone pueblos, not unlike those previously described.

The Kanab River heading in the Pink Cliffs runs directly southward and joins the Colorado in the heart of the Grand Canyon. Its way is through a series of canyons. From one of these it emerges at the foot of the Vermilion Cliffs, and here stood an extensive ruin not many years ago. Some portions of the pueblo were three stories high. The structure was one of the best found in this land of ruins. The Mormon people settling here have used the stones of the old pueblo in building their homes, and now no vestiges of the ancient structure remain. A few miles below the town other ruins were found. They were scattered to Pipe's Springs, a point twenty miles to the westward. Ruins were also discovered up the stream as far as the Pink Cliffs, and eastward along the Vermilion Cliffs nearly to the Colorado River, and out on the margin of the Kanab Plateau. These were all ruins of outlying habitations belonging to the Kanab pueblo. From the study of the existing pueblos found elsewhere and from extensive study of the ruins, it seems that everywhere tribal pueblos were built of considerable dimensions, usually to give shelter to several hundred people. Then the people cultivated the soil by irrigation, and had their gardens and little fields scattered at wide distances about the central pueblo, by little springs and streams and wherever they could control the water with little labor to bring it on the land. At such points stone houses were erected sufficient to accommodate from one to two thousand people, and these were occupied during the season of cultivation and are known as rancherias. So one great tribe had its central pueblo and its outlying rancherias. Sometimes the rancherias were occupied from year to year, especially in time of peace, but

John Wesley Powell

usually they were occupied only during seasons of cultivation. Such groups of ruins and pueblos with accessory rancherias are still inhabited, and have been described as found throughout the Plateau Province except far to the north beyond the Uinta Mountains. A great pueblo once existed in the Uinta Valley on the south side of the mountains. This is the most northern pueblo which has yet been discovered. But the pueblo-building tribes extended beyond the area drained by the Colorado. On the west there was a pueblo in the Great Basin at the site now occupied by Salt Lake City, and several more to the southward, all on waters flowing into the desert. On the east such pueblos were found among mountains at the headwaters of the Arkansas, Platte, and Canadian rivers. The entire area drained by the Rio Grande del Norte was occupied by pueblo tribes, and a number are still inhabited. To the south they extended far beyond the territory of the United States, and the so-called Aztec cities were rather superior pueblos of this character. The known pueblo tribes of the United States belong to several different linguistic stocks. They are far from being one homogeneous people, for they have not only different languages but different religions and worship different gods. These pueblo peoples are in a higher grade of culture than most Indian tribes of the United States. This is exhibited in the slight superiority of their arts, especially in their architecture. It is also noticeable in their mythology and religion. Their gods, the heroes of their myths, are more often personifications of the powers and phenomena of nature, and their religious ceremonies are more elaborate, and their cult societies are highly organized. As they had begun to domesticate animals and to cultivate the soil, so as to obtain a part of their subsistence by agriculture, they had almost accomplished the ascent from savagery to barbarism when first discovered by the invading European. All the Indians of North America were in this state of transition, but the pueblo tribes had more nearly reached the higher goal. . . .

[1895]

Cliffs and Terraces

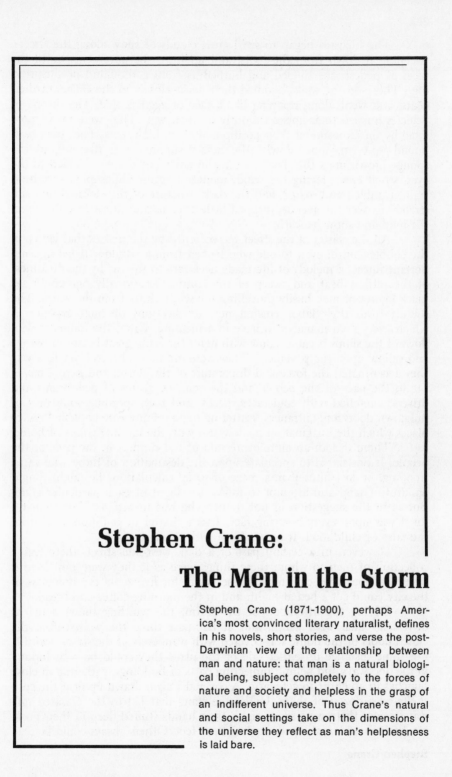

Stephen Crane:
The Men in the Storm

Stephen Crane (1871-1900), perhaps America's most convinced literary naturalist, defines in his novels, short stories, and verse the post-Darwinian view of the relationship between man and nature: that man is a natural biological being, subject completely to the forces of nature and society and helpless in the grasp of an indifferent universe. Thus Crane's natural and social settings take on the dimensions of the universe they reflect as man's helplessness is laid bare.

The blizzard began to swirl great clouds of snow along the streets, sweeping it down from the roofs, and up from the pavements, until the faces of pedestrians tingled and burned as from a thousand needle-prickings. Those on the walks huddled their necks closely in the collars of their coats, and went along stooping like a race of aged people. The drivers of vehicles hurried their horses furiously on their way. They were made more cruel by the exposure of their position, aloft on high seats. The street cars, bound up-town, went slowly, the horses slipping and straining in the spongy brown mass that lay between the rails. The drivers, muffled to the eyes, stood erect, facing the wind, models of grim philosophy. Overhead trains rumbled and roared, and the dark structure of the elevated railroad, stretching over the avenue, dripped little streams and drops of water upon the mud and snow beneath.

All the clatter of the street was softened by the masses that lay upon the cobbles, until, even to one who looked from a window, it became important music, a melody of life made necessary to the ear by the dreariness of the pitiless beat and sweep of the storm. Occasionally one could see black figures of men busily shovelling the white drifts from the walks. The sounds from their labor created new recollections of rural experiences which every man manages to have in a measure. Later, the immense windows of the shops became aglow with light, throwing great beams of orange and yellow upon the pavement. They were infinitely cheerful, yet in a way they accentuated the force and discomfort of the storm, and gave a meaning to the pace of the people and the vehicles, scores of pedestrians and drivers, wretched with cold faces, necks, and feet, speeding for scores of unknown doors and entrances, scattering to an infinite variety of shelters, to places which the imagination made warm with the familiar colors of home.

There was an absolute expression of hot dinners in the pace of the people. If one dared to speculate upon the destination of those who came trooping, he lost himself in a maze of social calculation: he might fling a handful of sand and attempt to follow the flight of each particular grain. But as to the suggestion of hot dinners, he was in firm lines of thought, for it was upon every hurrying face. It is a matter of tradition; it is from the tales of childhood. It comes forth with every storm.

However, in a certain part of a dark west-side street, there was a collection of men to whom these things were as if they were not. In this street was located a charitable house where for five cents the homeless of the city could get a bed at night, and in the morning coffee and bread.

During the afternoon of the storm, the whirling snows acted as drivers, as men with whips, and at half-past three the walk before the closed doors of the house was covered with wanderers of the street, waiting. For some distance on either side of the place they could be seen lurking in the doorways and behind projecting parts of buildings, gathering in close bunches in an effort to get warm. A covered wagon drawn up near the curb sheltered a dozen of them. Under the stairs that led to the elevated railway station, there were six or eight, their hands stuffed deep in their pockets, their shoulders stooped, jiggling their feet. Others always could be seen

Stephen Crane

coming, a strange procession, some slouching along with the characteristic hopeless gait of professional strays, some coming with hesitating steps, wearing the air of men to whom this sort of thing was new.

It was an afternoon of incredible length. The snow, blowing in twisting clouds, sought out the men in their meager hiding-places, and skilfully beat in among them, drenching their persons with showers of fine stinging flakes. They crowded together, muttering, and fumbling in their pockets to get their red inflamed wrists covered by the cloth.

New-comers usually halted at one end of the groups and addressed a question, perhaps much as a matter of form, "Is it open yet?"

Those who had been waiting inclined to take the questioner seriously and became contemptuous. "No; do yeh think we'd be standin' here?"

The gathering swelled in numbers steadily and persistently. One could always see them coming, trudging through the storm.

Finally, the little snow plains in the street began to assume a leaden hue from the shadows of evening. The buildings upreared gloomily save where various windows became brilliant figures of light, that made shimmers and splashes of yellow on the snow. A street lamp on the curb struggled to illuminate, but it was reduced to impotent blindness by the swift gusts of sleet crusting its panes.

In this half-darkness, the men began to come from their shelter-places and to mass in front of the doors of charity. They were of all types, but the nationalities were mostly American, German, and Irish. Many were strong, healthy, clear-skinned fellows, with that stamp of countenance which is not frequently seen upon seekers after charity. There were men of undoubted patience, industry, and temperance, who, in time of ill-fortune, do not habitually turn to rail at the state of society, snarling at the arrogance of the rich, and bemoaning the cowardice of the poor, but who at these times are apt to wear a sudden and singular meekness, as if they saw the world's progress marching from them, and they were trying to perceive where they had failed, what they had lacked, to be thus vanquished in the race. Then there were others, of the shifting Bowery element, who were used to paying ten cents for a place to sleep, but who now came here because it was cheaper.

But they were all mixed in one mass so thoroughly that one could not have discerned the different elements, but for the fact that the laboring men, for the most part, remained silent and impassive in the blizzard, their eyes fixed on the windows of the house, statues of patience.

The sidewalk soon became completely blocked by the bodies of the men. They pressed close to one another like sheep in a winter's gale, keeping one another warm by the heat of their bodies. The snow came upon this compressed group of men until, directly from above, it might have appeared like a heap of snow-covered merchandise, if it were not for the fact that the crowd swayed gently with a unanimous rhythmical motion. It was wonderful to see how the snow lay upon the heads and shoulders of these men, in little ridges an inch thick perhaps in places, the flakes steadily adding drop and drop, precisely as they fall upon the unresisting grass of

The Men in the Storm

the fields. The feet of the men were all wet and cold, and the wish to warm them accounted for the slow, gentle rhythmical motion. Occasionally some man whose ear or nose tingled acutely from the cold winds would wriggle down until his head was protected by the shoulders of his companions.

There was a continuous murmuring discussion as to the probability of the doors being speedily opened. They persistently lifted their eyes toward the windows. One could hear little combats of opinion.

"There's a light in th' winder!"

"Naw; it's a reflection f'm across th' way."

"Well, didn't I see 'em light it?"

"You did?"

"I did!"

"Well, then, that settles it!"

As the time approached when they expected to be allowed to enter, the men crowded to the doors in an unspeakable crush, jamming and wedging in a way that it seemed would crack bones. They surged heavily against the building in a powerful wave of pushing shoulders. Once a rumor flitted among all the tossing heads.

"They can't open th' door! Th' fellers er smack up agin 'em."

Then a dull roar of rage came from the men on the outskirts; but all the time they strained and pushed until it appeared to be impossible for those that they cried out against to do anything but be crushed to pulp.

"Ah, git away f'm th' door!"

"Git outa that!"

"Throw 'em out!"

"Kill 'em!"

"Say, fellers, now, what th' 'ell? G've 'em a chance t' open th' door!"

"Yeh damn pigs, give 'em a chance t' open th' door!"

Men in the outskirts of the crowd occasionally yelled when a boot-heel of one of the trampling feet crushed their freezing extremities.

"Git off me feet, yeh clumsy tarrier!"

"Say, don't stand on me feet! Walk on th' ground!"

A man near the doors suddenly shouted: "O-o-oh! Le' me out—le' me out!" And another, a man of infinite valor, once twisted his head so as to half face those who were pushing behind him. "Quit yer shovin', yeh"— and he delivered a volley of the most powerful and singular invective, straight into the faces of the men behind him. It was as if he was hammering the noses of them with curses of triple brass. His face, red with rage, could be seen, upon it an expression of sublime disregard of consequences. But nobody cared to reply to his imprecations; it was too cold. Many of them snickered, and all continued to push.

In occasional pauses of the crowd's movement the men had opportunities to make jokes; usually grim things, and no doubt very uncouth. Nevertheless, they were notable—one does not expect to find the quality of humor in a heap of old clothes under a snowdrift.

The winds seemed to grow fiercer as time wore on. Some of the gusts of snow that came down on the close collection of heads cut like

Stephen Crane

knives and needles, and the men huddled, and swore, not like dark assassins, but in a sort of American fashion, grimly and desperately, it is true, but yet with a wondrous under-effect, indefinable and mystic, as if there was some kind of humor in this catastrophe, in this situation in a night of snow-laden winds.

Once the window of the huge dry-goods shop across the street furnished material for a few moments of forgetfulness. In the brilliantly lighted space appeared the figure of a man. He was rather stout and very well clothed. His beard was fashioned charmingly after that of the Prince of Wales. He stood in an attitude of magnificent reflection. He slowly stroked his mustache with a certain grandeur of manner, and looked down at the snow-encrusted mob. From below, there was denoted a supreme complacence in him. It seemed that the sight operated inversely, and enabled him to more clearly regard his own delightful environment.

One of the mob chanced to turn his head, and perceived the figure in the window. "Hello, look-it 'is whiskers," he said genially.

Many of the men turned then, and a shout went up. They called to him in all strange keys. They addressed him in every manner, from familiar and cordial greetings to carefully-worded advice concerning changes in his personal appearance. The man presently fled, and the mob chuckled ferociously, like ogres who had just devoured something.

They turned then to serious business. Often they addressed the stolid front of the house.

"Oh, let us in fer Gawd's sake!"

"Let us in, or we'll all drop dead!"

"Say, what's th' use o' keepin' us poor Indians out in th' cold?"

And always some one was saying, "Keep off my feet."

The crushing of the crowd grew terrific toward the last. The men, in keen pain from the blasts, began almost to fight. With the pitiless whirl of snow upon them, the battle for shelter was going to the strong. It became known that the basement door of the foot of a little steep flight of stairs was the one to be opened, and they jostled and heaved in this direction like laboring fiends. One could hear them panting and groaning in their fierce exertion.

Usually some one in the front ranks was protesting to those in the rear— "O-o-ow! Oh, say now, fellers, let up, will yeh? Do yeh wanta kill somebody?"

A policeman arrived and went into the midst of them, scolding and berating, occasionally threatening, but using no force but that of his hands and shoulders against these men who were only struggling to get in out of the storm. His decisive tones rang out sharply— "Stop that pushin' back there! Come, boys, don't push! Stop that! Here you, quit yer shovin'! Cheese that!"

When the door below was opened, a thick stream of men forced a way down the stairs, which were of an extraordinary narrowness, and seemed only wide enough for one at a time. Yet they somehow went down almost three abreast. It was a difficult and painful operation. The crowd

The Men in the Storm

was like a turbulent water forcing itself through one tiny outlet. The men in the rear, excited by the success of the others, made frantic exertions, for it seemed that this large band would more than fill the quarters, and that many would be left upon the pavements. It would be disastrous to be of the last, and accordingly men with the snow biting their faces writhed and twisted with their might. One expected that, from the tremendous pressure, the narrow passage to the basement door would be so choked and clogged with human limbs and bodies that movement would be impossible. Once indeed the crowd was forced to stop, and a cry went along that a man had been injured at the foot of the stairs. But presently the slow movement began again, and the policeman fought at the top of the flight to ease the pressure of those that were going down.

A reddish light from a window fell upon the faces of the men when they, in turn, arrived at the last three steps and were about to enter. One could then note a change of expression that had come over their features. As they stood thus upon the threshold of their hopes, they looked suddenly contented and complacent. The fire had passed from their eyes and the snarl had vanished from their lips. The very force of the crowd in the rear, which had previously vexed them, was regarded from another point of view, for it now made it inevitable that they should go through the little doors into the place that was cheery and warm with light.

The tossing crowd on the sidewalk grew smaller and smaller. The snow beat with merciless persistence upon the bowed heads of those who waited. The wind drove it up from the pavements in frantic forms of winding white, and it seethed in circles about the huddled forms passing in one by one, three by three, out of the storm.

[1898]

Stephen Crane

Frank Norris:

The Sheep

Frank Norris (1870-1902), dedicated literary naturalist and epic novelist, emphasized the creed of the determinists as he depicted in his works the sweep of life forces, the conflicts that permit the fittest to survive, and the bondage of economic and social determinism. Among them are the major works *The Octopus* (1901) and *The Pit* (1903), two volumes of a projected trilogy tracing the growth and consumption of wheat.

Presley climbed to the summit of one of the hills — the highest — that rose out of the cañon, from the crest of which he could see for thirty, fifty, sixty miles down the valley, and, filling his pipe, smoked lazily for upwards of an hour, his head empty of thought, allowing himself to succumb to a pleasant, gentle inanition, a little drowsy, comfortable in his place, prone upon the ground, warmed just enough by such sunlight as filtered through the live-oaks, soothed by the good tobacco and the prolonged murmur of the spring and creek. By degrees, the sense of his own personality became blunted, the little wheels and cogs of thought moved slower and slower; consciousness dwindled to a point, the animal in him stretched itself, purring. A delightful numbness invaded his mind and his body. He was not asleep, he was not awake, stupefied merely, lapsing back to the state of the faun, the satyr.

After a while, rousing himself a little, he shifted his position, and, drawing from the pocket of his shooting coat his little tree-calf edition of the Odyssey, read far into the twenty-first book, where, after the failure of all the suitors to bend Ulysses's bow, it is finally put, with mockery, into his own hands. Abruptly the drama of the story roused him from all his languor. In an instant, he was the poet again, his nerves tingling, alive to every sensation, responsive to every impression. The desire of creation, of composition, grew big within him. Hexameters of his own clamoured, tumultuous, in his brain. Not for a long time had he "felt his poem," as he called this sensation, so poignantly. For an instant he told himself that he actually held it.

It was, no doubt, Vanamee's talk that had stimulated him to this point. The story of the Long Trail, with its desert and mountain, its cliff-dwellers, its Aztec ruins, its colour, movement, and romance, filled his mind with picture after picture. The epic defiled before his vision like.a pageant. Once more, he shot a glance about him, as if in search of the inspiration, and this time he all but found it. He rose to his feet, looking out and off below him.

As from a pinnacle, Presley, from where he now stood, dominated the entire country. The sun had begun to set, everything in the range of his vision was overlaid with a sheen of gold.

First, close at hand, it was the Seed ranch, carpeting the little hollow behind the Mission with a spread of greens, some dark, some vivid, some pale almost to yellowness. Beyond that was the Mission itself, its venerable campanile, in whose arches hung the Spanish King's bells, already glowing ruddy in the sunset. Farther on, he could make out Annixter's ranch house, marked by the skeleton-like tower of the artesian well, and, a little farther to the east, the huddled tiled roofs of Guadalajara. Far to the west and north, he saw Bonneville very plain, and the dome of the courthouse, a purple silhouette against the glare of the sky. Other points detached themselves, swimming in a golden mist, projecting blue shadows far before them; the mammoth live-oak by Hooven's, towering superb and magnificent; the line of eucalyptus trees, behind which he knew was the Los Muertos ranch house — his home; the watering-tank, the great iron-

Frank Norris

hooped tower of wood that stood at the joining of the Lower Road and the County Road; the long wind-break of poplar trees and the white walls of Caraher's saloon on the County Road.

But all this seemed to be only foreground, a mere array of accessories — a mass of irrelevant details. Beyond Annixter's, beyond Guadalajara, beyond the Lower Road, beyond Broderson Creek, on to the south and west, infinite, illimitable, stretching out there under the sheen of the sunset forever and forever, flat, vast, unbroken, a huge scroll, unrolling between the horizons, spread the great stretches of the ranch of Los Muertos, bare of crops, shaved close in the recent harvest. Near at hand were hills, but on that far southern horizon only the curve of the great earth itself checked the view. Adjoining Los Muertos, and widening to the west, opened the Broderson ranch. The Osterman ranch to the northwest carried on the great sweep of landscape; ranch after ranch. Then, as the imagination itself expanded under the stimulus of that measureless range of vision, even those great ranches resolved themselves into mere foreground, mere accessories, irrelevant details. Beyond the fine line of the horizons, over the curve of the globe, the shoulder of the earth, were other ranches, equally vast, and beyond these, others, and beyond these, still others, the immensities multiplying, lengthening out vaster and vaster. The whole gigantic sweep of the San Joaquin expanded, Titanic, before the eye of the mind, flagellated with heat, quivering and shimmering under the sun's red eye. At long intervals, a faint breath of wind out of the south passed slowly over the levels of the baked and empty earth, accentuating the silence, marking off the stillness. It seemed to exhale from the land itself, a prolonged sigh as of deep fatigue. It was the season after the harvest, and the great earth, the mother, after its period of reproduction, its pains of labour, delivered of the fruit of its loins, slept the sleep of exhaustion, the infinite repose of the colossus, benignant, eternal, strong, the nourisher of nations, the feeder of an entire world.

Ha! there it was, his epic, his inspiration, his West, his thundering progression of hexameters. A sudden uplift, a sense of exhilaration, of physical exaltation appeared abruptly to sweep Presley from his feet. As from a point high above the world, he seemed to dominate a universe, a whole order of things. He was dizzied, stunned, stupefied, his morbid super-sensitive mind reeling, drunk with the intoxication of mere immensity. Stupendous ideas for which there were no names drove headlong through his brain. Terrible, formless shapes, vague figures, gigantic, monstrous, distorted, whirled at a gallop through his imagination.

He started homeward, still in his dream, descending from the hill, emerging from the cañon, and took the short cut straight across the Quien Sabe ranch, leaving Guadalajara far to his left. He tramped steadily on through the wheat stubble, walking fast, his head in a whirl.

Never had he so nearly grasped his inspiration as at that moment on the hill-top. Even now, though the sunset was fading, though the wide reach of valley was shut from sight, it still kept him company. Now the details came thronging back — the component parts of his poem, the signs

The Sheep

and symbols of the West. It was there, close at hand, he had been in touch with it all day. It was in the centenarian's vividly coloured reminiscences — De La Cuesta, holding his grant from the Spanish crown, with his power of life and death; the romance of his marriage; the white horse with its pillion of red leather and silver bridle mountings; the bullfights in the Plaza; the gifts of gold dust, and horses and tallow. It was in Vanamee's strange history, the tragedy of his love; Angéle Varian, with her marvellous loveliness; the Egyptian fulness of her lips, the perplexing upward slant of her violet eyes, bizarre, oriental; her white forehead made three-cornered by her plaits of gold hair; the mystery of the Other; her death at the moment of her child's birth. It was in Vanamee's flight into the wilderness; the story of the Long Trail; the sunsets behind the altar-like mesas, the baking desolation of the deserts; the strenuous, fierce life of forgotten towns, down there, far off, lost below the horizons of the southwest; the sonorous music of unfamiliar names — Quijotoa, Uintah, Sonora, Laredo, Uncompahgre. It was in the Mission, with its cracked bells, its decaying walls, its venerable sun dial, its fountain and old garden, and in the Mission Fathers themselves, the priests, the padres, planting the first wheat and oil and wine to produce the elements of the Sacrament — a trinity of great industries, taking their rise in a religious rite.

Abruptly, as if in confirmation, Presley heard the sound of a bell from the direction of the Mission itself. It was the *de Profundis*, a note of the Old World; of the ancient regime, an echo from the hillsides of mediæval Europe, sounding there in this new land, unfamiliar and strange at this end-of-the-century time.

By now, however, it was dark. Presley hurried forward. He came to the line fence of the Quien Sabe ranch. Everything was very still. The stars were all out. There was not a sound other than the *de Profundis*, still sounding from very far away. At long intervals the great earth sighed dreamily in its sleep. All about, the feeling of absolute peace and quiet and security and untroubled happiness and content seemed descending from the stars like a benediction. The beauty of his poem, its idyl, came to him like a caress; that alone had been lacking. It was that, perhaps, which had left it hitherto incomplete. At last he was to grasp his song in all its entity.

But suddenly there was an interruption. Presley had climbed the fence at the limit of the Quien Sabe ranch. Beyond was Los Muertos, but between the two ran the railroad. He had only time to jump back upon the embankment when, with a quivering of all the earth, a locomotive, single, unattached, shot by him with a roar, filling the air with the reek of hot oil, vomiting smoke and sparks; its enormous eye, Cyclopean, red, throwing a glare far in advance, shooting by in a sudden crash of confused thunder; filling the night with the terrific clamour of its iron hoofs.

Abruptly Presley remembered. This must be the crack passenger engine of which Dyke had told him, the one delayed by the accident on the Bakersfield division and for whose passage the track had been opened all the way to Fresno.

Before Presley could recover from the shock of the irruption, while

Frank Norris

the earth was still vibrating, the rails still humming, the engine was far away, flinging the echo of its frantic gallop over all the valley. For a brief instant it roared with a hollow diapason on the Long Trestle over Broderson Creek, then plunged into a cutting farther on, the quivering glare of its fires losing itself in the night, its thunder abruptly diminishing to a subdued and distant humming. All at once this ceased. The engine was gone.

But the moment the noise of the engine lapsed, Presley — about to start forward again — was conscious of a confusion of lamentable sounds that rose into the night from out the engine's wake. Prolonged cries of agony, sobbing wails of infinite pain, heart-rending, pitiful.

The noises came from a little distance. He ran down the track, crossing the culvert, over the irrigating ditch, and at the head of the long reach of track — between the culvert and the Long Trestle — paused abruptly, held immovable at the sight of the ground and rails all about him.

In some way, the herd of sheep — Vanamee's herd — had found a breach in the wire fence by the right of way and had wandered out upon the tracks. A band had been crossing just at the moment of the engine's passage. The pathos of it was beyond expression. It was a slaughter, a massacre of innocents. The iron monster had charged full into the midst, merciless, inexorable. To the right and left, all the width of the right of way, the little bodies had been flung; backs were snapped against the fence posts; brains knocked out. Caught in the barbs of the wire, wedged in, the bodies hung suspended. Under foot it was terrible. The black blood, winking in the starlight, seeped down into the clinkers between the ties with a prolonged sucking murmur.

Presley turned away, horror-struck, sick at heart, overwhelmed with a quick burst of irresistible compassion for this brute agony he could not relieve. The sweetness was gone from the evening, the sense of peace, of security, and placid contentment was stricken from the landscape. The hideous ruin in the engine's path drove all thought of his poem from his mind. The inspiration vanished like a mist. The *de Profundis* had ceased to ring.

He hurried on across the Los Muertos ranch, almost running, even putting his hands over his ears till he was out of hearing distance of that all but human distress. Not until he was beyond earshot did he pause, looking back, listening. The night had shut down again. For a moment the silence was profound, unbroken.

Then, faint and prolonged, across the levels of the ranch, he heard the engine whistling for Bonneville. Again and again, at rapid intervals in its flying course, it whistled for road crossings, for sharp curves, for trestles; ominous notes, hoarse, bellowing, ringing with the accents of menace and defiance; and abruptly Presley saw again, in his imagination, the galloping monster, the terror of steel and steam, with its single eye, Cyclopean, red, shooting from horizon to horizon; but saw it now as the symbol of a vast power, huge, terrible, flinging the echo of its thunder over all the reaches of the valley, leaving blood and destruction in its path, the leviathan, with

The Sheep

tentacles of steel clutching into the soil, the soulless Force, the iron-hearted Power, the monster, the Colossus, the Octopus.

[1901]

Frank Norris

Upton Sinclair:
The Initiation

Upton Sinclair (1878-1968), novelist, socialist,
and prolific propagandist, joined all three roles
in more than one hundred novels. The most
influential, *The Jungle* (1906), is also the best
known of those works that sought to reorder
the values of an industrial society.

They had bought their home. It was hard for them to realize that the wonderful house was theirs to move into whenever they chose. They spent all their time thinking about it, and what they were going to put into it. As their week with Aniele was up in three days, they lost no time in getting ready. They had to make some shift to furnish it, and every instant of their leisure was given to discussing this.

A person who had such a task before him would not need to look very far in Packingtown—he had only to walk up the avenue and read the signs, or get into a street-car, to obtain full information as to pretty much everything a human creature could need. It was quite touching, the zeal of people to see that his health and happiness were provided for. Did the person wish to smoke? There was a little discourse about cigars, showing him exactly why the Thomas Jefferson Five-cent Perfecto was the only cigar worthy of the name. Had he, on the other hand, smoked too much? Here was a remedy for the smoking habit, twenty-five doses for a quarter, and a cure absolutely guaranteed in ten doses. In innumerable ways such as this, the traveller found that somebody had been busied to make smooth his paths through the world, and to let him know what had been done for him. In Packingtown the advertisements had a style all of their own, adapted to the peculiar population. One would be tenderly solicitous. "Is your wife pale?" it would inquire. "Is she discouraged, does she drag herself about the house and find fault with everything? Why do you not tell her to try Dr. Lanahan's Life Preservers?" Another would be jocular in tone, slapping you on the back, so to speak. "Don't be a chump!" it would exclaim. "Go and get the Goliath Bunion Cure." "Get a move on you!" would chime in another. "It's easy, if you wear the Eureka Two-fifty Shoe."

Among these importunate signs was one that had caught the attention of the family by its pictûres. It showed two very pretty little birds building themselves a home; and Marija had asked an acquaintance to read it to her, and told them that it related to the furnishing of a house. "Feather your nest," it ran—and went on to say that it could furnish all the necessary feathers for a four-room nest for the ludicrously small sum of seventy-five dollars. The particularly important thing about this offer was that only a small part of the money need be had at once—the rest one might pay a few dollars every month. Our friends had to have some furniture, there was no getting away from that; but their little fund of money had sunk so low that they could hardly get to sleep at night, and so they fled to this as their deliverance. There was more agony and another paper for Elzbieta to sign, and then one night when Jurgis came home, he was told the breathless tidings that the furniture had arrived and was safely stowed in the house: a parlor set of four pieces, a bedroom set of three pieces, a dining-room table and four chairs, a toilet-set with beautiful pink roses painted all over it, an assortment of crockery, also with pink roses—and so on. One of the plates in the set had been found broken when they unpacked it, and Ona was going to the store the first thing in the morning to make them change it; also they had promised three sauce-pans, and

Upton Sinclair

there had only two come, and did Jurgis think that they were trying to cheat them?

The next day they went to the house; and when the men came from work they ate a few hurried mouthfuls at Aniele's, and then set to work at the task of carrying their belongings to their new home. The distance was in reality over two miles, but Jurgis made two trips that night, each time with a huge pile of mattresses and bedding on his head, with bundles of clothing and bags and things tied up inside. Anywhere else in Chicago he would have stood a good chance of being arrested; but the policemen in Packingtown were apparently used to these informal movings, and contented themselves with a cursory examination now and then. It was quite wonderful to see how fine the house looked, with all the things in it, even by the dim light of a lamp: it was really home, and almost as exciting as the placard had described it. Ona was fairly dancing, and she and Cousin Marija took Jurgis by the arm and escorted him from room to room, sitting in each chair by turns, and then insisting that he should do the same. One chair squeaked with his great weight, and they screamed with fright, and woke the baby and brought everybody running. Altogether it was a great day; and tired as they were, Jurgis and Ona sat up late, contented simply to hold each other and gaze in rapture about the room. They were going to be married as soon as they could get everything settled, and a little spare money put by; and this was to be their home—that little room yonder would be theirs!

It was in truth a never-ending delight, the fixing up of this house. They had no money to spend for the pleasure of spending, but there were a few absolutely necessary things, and the buying of these was a perpetual adventure for Ona. It must always be done at night, so that Jurgis could go along; and even if it were only a pepper-cruet, or half a dozen glasses for ten cents, that was enough for an expedition. On Saturday night they came home with a great basketful of things, and spread them out on the table, while every one stood round, and the children climbed up on the chairs, or howled to be lifted up to see. There were sugar and salt and tea and crackers, and a can of lard and a milk-pail, and a scrubbing-brush, and a pair of shoes for the second oldest boy, and a can of oil, and a tack-hammer, and a pound of nails. These last were to be driven into the walls of the kitchen and the bedrooms, to hang things on; and there was a family discussion as to the place where each one was to be driven. Then Jurgis would try to hammer, and hit his fingers because the hammer was too small, and get mad because Ona had refused to let him pay fifteen cents more and get a bigger hammer; and Ona would be invited to try it herself, and hurt her thumb, and cry out, which necessitated the thumb's being kissed by Jurgis. Finally, after every one had had a try, the nails would be driven, and something hung up. Jurgis had come home with a big packing-box on his head, and he sent Jonas to get another that he had bought. He meant to take one side out of these to-morrow, and put shelves in them, and make them into bureaus and places to keep things for the bed-

The Initiation

rooms. The nest which had been advertised had not included feathers for quite so many birds as there were in this family.

They had, of course, put their dining-table in the kitchen, and the dining-room was used as the bedroom of Teta Elzbieta and five of her children. She and the two youngest slept in the only bed, and the other three had a mattress on the floor. Ona and her cousin dragged a mattress into the parlor and slept at night, and the three men and the oldest boy slept in the other room, having nothing but the very level floor to rest on for the present. Even so, however, they slept soundly—it was necessary for Teta Elzbieta to pound more than once on the door at a quarter past five every morning. She would have ready a great pot full of steaming black coffee, and oatmeal and bread and smoked sausages; and then she would fix them their dinner pails with more thick slices of bread with lard between them—they could not afford butter—and some onions and a piece of cheese, and so they would tramp away to work.

This was the first time in his life that he had ever really worked, it seemed to Jurgis; it was the first time that he had ever had anything to do which took all he had in him. Jurgis had stood with the rest up in the gallery and watched the men on the killing-beds, marvelling at their speed and power as if they had been wonderful machines; it somehow never occurred to one to think of the flesh-and-blood side of it—that is, not until he actually got down into the pit and took off his coat. Then he saw things in a different light, he got at the inside of them. The pace they set here, it was one that called for every faculty of a man—from the instant the first steer fell till the sounding of the noon whistle, and again from half-past twelve till heaven only knew what hour in the late afternoon or evening, there was never one instant's rest for a man, for his hand or his eye or his brain. Jurgis saw how they managed it; there were portions of the work which determined the pace of the rest, and for these they had picked men whom they paid high wages, and whom they changed frequently. You might easily pick out these pace-makers, for they worked under the eye of the bosses, and they worked like men possessed. This was called "speeding up the gang," and if any man could not keep up with the pace, there were hundreds outside begging to try.

Yet Jurgis did not mind it; he rather enjoyed it. It saved him the necessity of flinging his arms about and fidgeting as he did in most work. He would laugh to himself as he ran down the line, darting a glance now and then at the man ahead of him. It was not the pleasantest work one could think of, but it was necessary work; and what more had a man the right to ask than a chance to do something useful, and to get good pay for doing it?

So Jurgis thought, and so he spoke, in his bold, free way; very much to his surprise, he found that it had a tendency to get him into trouble. For most of the men here took a fearfully different view of the thing. He was quite dismayed when he first began to find it out—that most of the men *hated* their work. It seemed strange, it was even terrible, when you came to find out the universality of the sentiment; but it was certainly the fact—

Upton Sinclair

they hated their work. They hated the bosses and they hated the owners; they hated the whole place, the whole neighborhood—even the whole city, with an all-inclusive hatred, bitter and fierce. Women and little children would fall to cursing about it; it was rotten, rotten as hell—everything was rotten. When Jurgis would ask them what they meant, they would begin to get suspicious, and content themselves with saying, "Never mind, you stay here and see for yourself."

One of the first problems that Jurgis ran upon was that of the unions. He had had no experience with unions, and he had to have it explained to him that the men were banded together for the purpose of fighting for their rights. Jurgis asked them what they meant by their rights, a question in which he was quite sincere, for he had not any idea of any rights that he had, except the right to hunt for a job, and do as he was told when he got it. Generally, however, this harmless question would only make his fellow-workingmen lose their tempers and call him a fool. There was a delegate of the butcher-helpers' union who came to see Jurgis to enroll him; and when Jurgis found that this meant that he would have to part with some of his money, he froze up directly, and the delegate, who was an Irishman and only knew a few words of Lithuanian, lost his temper and began to threaten him. In the end Jurgis got into a fine rage, and made it sufficiently plain that it would take more than one Irishman to scare him into a union. Little by little he gathered that the main thing the men wanted was to put a stop to the habit of "speeding-up"; they were trying their best to force a lessening of the pace, for there were some, they said, who could not keep up with it, whom it was killing. But Jurgis had no sympathy with such ideas as this—he could do the work himself, and so could the rest of them, he declared, if they were good for anything. If they couldn't do it, let them go somewhere else. Jurgis had not studied the books, and he would not have known how to pronounce "laissez-faire"; but he had been round the world enough to know that a man has to shift for himself in it, and that if he gets the worst of it, there is nobody to listen to him holler.

Yet there have been known to be philosophers and plain men who swore by Malthus in the books, and would, nevertheless, subscribe to a relief fund in time of a famine. It was the same with Jurgis, who consigned the unfit to destruction, while going about all day sick at heart because of his poor old father, who was wandering somewhere in the yards begging for a chance to earn his bread. Old Antanas had been a worker ever since he was a child; he had run away from home when he was twelve, because his father beat him for trying to learn to read. And he was a faithful man, too; he was a man you might leave alone for a month, if only you had made him understand what you wanted him to do in the meantime. And now here he was, worn out in soul and body, and with no more place in the world than a sick dog. He had his home, as it happened, and some one who would care for him if he never got a job; but his son could not help thinking, suppose this had not been the case. Antanas Rudkus had been into every building in Packingtown by this time, and into nearly every

The Initiation

room; he had stood mornings among the crowd of applicants till the very policemen had come to know his face and to tell him to go home and give it up. He had been likewise to all the stores and saloons for a mile about, begging for some little thing to do; and everywhere they had ordered him out, sometimes with curses, and not once even stopping to ask him a question.

So, after all, there was a crack in the fine structure of Jurgis's faith in things as they are. The crack was wide while Dede Antanas was hunting a job—and it was yet wider when he finally got it. For one evening the old man came home in a great state of excitement, with the tale that he had been approached by a man in one of the corridors of the pickle-rooms of Durham's, and asked what he would pay to get a job. He had not known what to make of this at first; but the man had gone on with matter-of-fact frankness to say that he could get him a job, provided that he were willing to pay one-third of his wages for it. Was he a boss? Antanas had asked; to which the man had replied that that was nobody's business, but that he could do what he said.

Jurgis had made some friends by this time, and he sought one of them and asked what this meant. The friend, who was named Tamoszius Kuszleika, was a sharp little man who folded hides on the killing-beds, and he listened to what Jurgis had to say without seeming at all surprised. They were common enough, he said, such cases of petty graft. It was simply some boss who proposed to add a little to his income. After Jurgis had been there awhile he would know that the plants were simply honey-combed with rottenness of that sort—the bosses grafted off the men, and they grafted off each other; and some day the superintendent would find out about the boss, and then he would graft off the boss. Warming to the subject, Tamoszius went on to explain the situation. Here was Durham's, for instance, owned by a man who was trying to make as much money out of it as he could, and did not care in the least how he did it; and under-neath him, ranged in ranks and grades like an army, were managers and superintendents and foremen, each one driving the man next below him and trying to squeeze out of him as much work as possible. And all the men of the same rank were pitted against each other; the accounts of each were kept separately, and every man lived in terror of losing his job, if another made a better record than he. So from top to bottom the place was simply a seething cauldron of jealousies and hatreds; there was no loyalty or decency anywhere about it, there was no place in it where a man counted for anything against a dollar. And worse than there being no decency, there was not even any honesty. The reason for that? Who could say? It must have been old Durham in the beginning; it was a heritage which the self-made merchant had left to his son, along with his millions.

Jurgis would find out these things for himself, if he stayed there long enough; it was the men who had to do all the dirty jobs, and so there was no deceiving them; and they caught the spirit of the place, and did like all the rest. Jurgis had come there, and thought he was going to make himself useful, and rise and become a skilled man; but he would soon find

Upton Sinclair

out his error—for nobody rose in Packingtown by doing good work. You could lay that down for a rule—if you met a man who was rising in Packingtown, you met a knave. That man who had been sent to Jurgis's father by the boss, *he* would rise; the man who told tales and spied upon his fellows would rise; but the man who minded his own business and did his work—why, they would "speed him up" till they had worn him out, and then they would throw him into the gutter.

Jurgis went home with his head buzzing. Yet he could not bring himself to believe such things—no, it could not be so. Tamoszius was simply another of the grumblers. He was a man who spent all his time fiddling; and he would go to parties at night and not get home till sunrise, and so of course he did not feel like work. Then, too, he was a puny little chap; and so he had been left behind in the race, and that was why he was sore. And yet so many strange things kept coming to Jurgis's notice every day!

He tried to persuade his father to have nothing to do with the offer. But old Antanas had begged until he was worn out, and all his courage was gone; he wanted a job, any sort of a job. So the next day he went and found the man who had spoken to him, and promised to bring him a third of all he earned; and that same day he was put to work in Durham's cellars. It was a "pickle-room," where there was never a dry spot to stand upon, and so he had to take nearly the whole of his first week's earnings to buy him a pair of heavy-soled boots. He was a "squeedgie" man; his job was to go about all day with a long-handled mop, swabbing up the floor. Except that it was damp and dark, it was not an unpleasant job, in summer.

Now Antanas Rudkus was the meekest man that God ever put on earth; and so Jurgis found it a striking confirmation of what the men all said, that his father had been at work only two days before he came home as bitter as any of them, and cursing Durham's with all the power of his soul. For they had set him to cleaning out the traps; and the family sat round and listened in wonder while he told them what that meant. It seemed that he was working in the room where the men prepared the beef for canning, and the beef had lain in vats full of chemicals, and men with great forks speared it out and dumped it into trucks, to be taken to the cooking-room. When they had speared out all they could reach, they emptied the vat on the floor, and then with shovels scraped up the balance and dumped it into the truck. This floor was filthy, yet they set Antanas with his mop slopping the "pickle" into a hole that connected with a sink, where it was caught and used over again forever; and if that were not enough, there was a trap in the pipe, where all the scraps of meat and odds and ends of refuse were caught, and every few days it was the old man's task to clean these out, and shovel their contents into one of the trucks with the rest of the meat!

This was the experience of Antanas; and then there came also Jonas and Marija with tales to tell. Marija was working for one of the independent packers, and was quite beside herself and outrageous with triumph over the sums of money she was making as a painter of cans. But one

The Initiation

day she walked home with a pale-faced little woman who worked opposite to her, Jadvyga Marcinkus by name, and Jadvyga told her how she, Marija, had chanced to get her job. She had taken the place of an Irish woman who had been working in that factory ever since any one could remember, for over fifteen years, so she declared. Mary Dennis was her name, and a long time ago she had been seduced, and had a little boy; he was a cripple, and an epileptic, but still he was all that she had in the world to love, and they had lived in a little room alone somewhere back of Halsted Street, where the Irish were. Mary had had consumption, and all day long you might hear her coughing as she worked; of late she had been going all to pieces, and when Marija came, the "forelady" had suddenly decided to turn her off. The forelady had to come up to a certain standard herself, and could not stop for sick people, Jadvyga explained. The fact that Mary had been there so long had not made any difference to her—it was doubtful if she even knew that, for both the forelady and the superintendent were new people, having only been there two or three years themselves. Jadvyga did not know what had become of the poor creature; she would have gone to see her, but had been sick herself. She had pains in her back all the time, Jadvyga explained, and feared that she had womb trouble. It was not fit work for a woman, handling fourteen-pound cans all day.

It was a striking circumstance that Jonas, too, had gotten his job by the misfortune of some other person. Jonas pushed a truck loaded with hams from the smoke-rooms on to an elevator, and thence to the packing-rooms. The trucks were all of iron, and heavy, and they put about three-score hams on each of them, a load of more than a quarter of a ton. On the uneven floor it was a task for a man to start one of these trucks, unless he was a giant; and when it was once started he naturally tried his best to keep it going. There was always the boss prowling about, and if there was a second's delay he would fall to cursing; Lithuanians and Slovaks and such, who could not understand what was said to them, the bosses were wont to kick about the place like so many dogs. Therefore these trucks went for the most part on the run; and the predecessor of Jonas had been jammed against the wall by one and crushed in a horrible and name-less manner.

All of these were sinister incidents; but they were trifles compared to what Jurgis saw with his own eyes before long. One curious thing he had noticed, the very first day, in his profession of shoveller of guts; which was the sharp trick of the floor-bosses whenever there chanced to come a "slunk" calf. Any man who knows anything about butchering knows that the flesh of a cow that is about to calve, or has just calved, is not fit for food. A good many of these came every day to the packing-houses—and, of course, if they had chosen, it would have been an easy matter for the packers to keep them till they were fit for food. But for the saving of time and fodder, it was the law that cows of that sort came along with the others, and whoever noticed it would tell the boss, and the boss would start up a conversation with the government inspector, and the two would stroll away. So in a trice the carcass of the cow would be cleaned out, and the

Upton Sinclair

entrails would have vanished; it was Jurgis's task to slide them into the trap, calves and all, and on the floor below they took out these "slunk" calves, and butchered them for meat, and even used the skins of them.

One day a man slipped and hurt his leg; and that afternoon, when the last of the cattle had been disposed of, and the men were leaving, Jurgis was ordered to remain and do some special work which this injured man had usually done. It was late, almost dark, and the government inspectors had all gone, and there were only a dozen or two of men on the floor. That day they had killed about four thousand cattle, and these cattle had come in freight trains from far states, and some of them had got hurt. There were some with broken legs, and some with gored sides; there were some that had died, from what cause no one could say; and they were all to be disposed of, here in darkness and silence. "Downers," the men called them; and the packing-house had a special elevator upon which they were raised to the killing-beds, where the gang proceeded to handle them, with an air of businesslike nonchalance which said plainer than any words that it was a matter of everyday routine. It took a couple of hours to get them out of the way, and in the end Jurgis saw them go into the chilling-rooms with the rest of the meat, being carefully scattered here and there so that they could not be identified. When he came home that night he was in a very sombre mood, having begun to see at last how those might be right who had laughed at him for his faith in America.

[1906]

The Initiation

Lincoln Steffens:
Tweed Days in St. Louis

Lincoln Steffens (1866-1936), best known of
the "muckrakers," exposé writers for the new
mass circulation magazines such as *McClure's,*
Collier's, and the *American,* specialized in examining the nature of the great cities that had
risen in America as the nation became increasingly industrialized. A lively writer, he
combined the best of his work in *The Shame*
of the Cities (1904).

St. Louis, the fourth city in size in the United States, is making two announcements to the world: one that it is the worst-governed city in the land; the other that it wishes all men to come there and see it. It isn't our worst-governed city; Philadelphia is that. But St. Louis is worth examining while we have it inside out.

There is a man at work there, one man, working all alone, but he is the Circuit (district or state) Attorney, and he is "doing his duty." That is what thousands of district attorneys and other public officials have promised to do and boasted of doing. This man has a literal sort of mind. He is a thin-lipped, firm-mouthed, dark little man, who never raises his voice, but goes ahead doing, with a smiling eye and a set jaw, the simple thing he said he would do. The politicians and reputable citizens who asked him to run urged him when he declined. When he said that if elected he would have to do his duty, they said, "Of course." So he ran, they supported him, and he was elected. Now some of these politicians are sentenced to the penitentiary, some are in Mexico. The Circuit Attorney, finding that his "duty" was to catch and convict criminals, and that the biggest criminals were some of these same politicians and leading citizens, went after them. It is magnificent, but the politicians declare it isn't politics.

The corruption of St. Louis came from the top. The best citizens—the merchants and big financiers—used to rule the town, and they ruled it well. They set out to outstrip Chicago. The commercial and industrial war between these two cities was at one time a picturesque and dramatic spectacle such as is witnessed only in our country. Businessmen were not mere merchants and the politicians were not mere grafters; the two kinds of citizens got together and wielded the power of banks, railroads, factories, the prestige of the city and the spirit of its citizens to gain business and population. And it was a close race. Chicago, having the start, always led, but St. Louis had pluck, intelligence, and tremendous energy. It pressed Chicago hard. It excelled in a sense of civic beauty and good government; and there are those who think yet it might have won. But a change occurred. Public spirit became private spirit, public enterprise became private greed.

Along about 1890, public franchises and privileges were sought, not only for legitimate profit and common convenience, but for loot. Taking but slight and always selfish interest in the public councils, the big men misused politics. The riffraff, catching the smell of corruption, rushed into the Municipal Assembly, drove out the remaining respectable men, and sold the city—its streets, its wharves, its markets, and all that it had—to the now greedy businessmen and bribers. In other words, when the leading men began to devour their own city, the herd rushed into the trough and fed also.

So gradually has this occurred that these same citizens hardly realize it. Go to St. Louis and you will find the habit of civic pride in them; they still boast. The visitor is told of the wealth of the residents, of the financial strength of the banks, and of the growing importance of the indus-

Lincoln Steffens

tries, yet he sees poorly paved, refuse-burdened streets, and dusty or mud-covered alleys; he passes a' ramshackle firetrap crowded with the sick, and learns that it is the City Hospital; he enters the "Four Courts," and his nostrils are greeted by the odor of formaldehyde used as a disinfectant, and insect powder spread to destroy vermin; he calls at the new City Hall, and finds half the entrance boarded with pine planks to cover up the unfinished interior. Finally, he turns a tap in the hotel, to see liquid mud flow into wash basin or bathtub.

The St. Louis charter vests legislative power of great scope in a Municipal Assembly, which is composed of a Council and a House of Delegates. Here is a description of the latter by one of Mr. Folk's grand juries:

"We have had before us many of those who have been, and most of those who are now, members of the House of Delegates. We found a number of these utterly illiterate and lacking in ordinary intelligence, unable to give a better reason for favoring or opposing a measure than a desire to act with the majority. In some, no trace of mentality or morality could be found; in others, a low order of training appeared, united with base cunning, groveling instincts, and sordid desires. Unqualified to respond to the ordinary requirements of life, they are utterly incapable of comprehending the significance of an ordinance, and are incapacitated, both by nature and training, to be the makers of laws. The choosing of such men to be legislators makes a travesty of justice, sets a premium on incompetency, and deliberately poisons the very source of the law."

These creatures were well organized. They had a "combine"—a legislative institution—which the grand jury described as follows:

"Our investigation, covering more or less fully a period of ten years, shows that, with few exceptions, no ordinance has been passed wherein valuable privileges or franchises are granted until those interested have paid the legislators the money demanded for action in the particular case. Combines in both branches of the Municipal Assembly are formed by members sufficient in number to control legislation. To one member of this combine is delegated the authority to act for the combine, and to receive and to distribute to each member the money agreed upon as the price of his vote in support of, or opposition to, a pending measure. So long has this practice existed that such members have come to regard the receipt of money for action on pending measures as a legitimate perquisite of a legislator."

One legislator consulted a lawyer with the intention of suing a firm to recover an unpaid balance on a fee for the grant of a switchway. Such difficulties rarely occurred, however. In order to insure a regular and indisputable revenue, the combine of each house drew up a schedule of bribery prices for all possible sorts of grants, just such a list as a commercial traveler takes out on the road with him. There was a price for a grain elevator, a price for a short switch; side tracks were charged for by the linear foot, but at rates which varied according to the nature of the ground taken; a street improvement cost so much; wharf space was classified and precisely

Tweed Days in St. Louis

rated. As there was a scale for favorable legislation, so there was one for defeating bills. It made a difference in the price if there was opposition, and it made a difference whether the privilege asked was legitimate or not. But nothing was passed free of charge. Many of the legislators were saloon-keepers—it was in St. Louis that a practical joker nearly emptied the House of Delegates by tipping a boy to rush into a session and call out, "Mister, your saloon is on fire"—but even the saloonkeepers of a neighborhood had to pay to keep in their inconvenient locality a market which public interest would have moved.

From the Assembly, bribery spread into other departments. Men empowered to issue peddlers' licenses and permits to citizens who wished to erect an awning or use a portion of the sidewalk for storage purposes charged an amount in excess of the prices stipulated by law, and pocketed the difference. The city's money was loaned at interest, and the interest was converted into private bank accounts. City carriages were used by the wives and children of city officials. Supplies for public institutions found their way to private tables; one itemized account of food furnished the poorhouse included California jellies, imported cheeses, and French wines! A member of the Assembly caused the incorporation of a grocery company, with his sons and daughters the ostensible stockholders, and succeeded in having his bid for city supplies accepted although the figures were in excess of his competitors'. In return for the favor thus shown, he indorsed a measure to award the contract for city printing to another member, and these two voted aye on a bill granting to a third the exclusive right to furnish city dispensaries with drugs.

Men ran into debt to the extent of thousands of dollars for the sake of election to either branch of the Assembly. One night, on a street car going to the City Hall, a new member remarked that the nickel he handed the conductor was his last. The next day he deposited $5,000 in a savings bank. A member of the House of Delegates admitted to the grand jury that his dividends from the combine netted $25,000 in one year; a council-man stated that he was paid $50,000 for his vote on a single measure.

Bribery was a joke. A newspaper reporter overheard this conversation one evening in the corridor of the City Hall:

"Ah there, my boodler!" said Mr. Delegate.

"Stay there, my grafter!" replied Mr. Councilman. "Can you lend me a hundred for a day or two?"

"Not at present. But I can spare it if the Z—— bill goes through tonight. Meet me at F——'s later."

"All right, my jailbird; I'll be there."

The blackest years were 1898, 1899, and 1900. Foreign corporations came into the city to share in its despoliation, and home industries were driven out by blackmail. Franchises worth millions were granted without one cent of cash to the city, and with provision for only the smallest future payment; several companies which refused to pay blackmail had to leave; citizens were robbed more and more boldly; payrolls were padded with the

Lincoln Steffens

names of nonexistent persons; work on public improvements was neglected, while money for them went to the boodlers.

Some of the newspapers protested, disinterested citizens were alarmed, and the shrewder men gave warnings, but none dared make an effective stand. Behind the corruptionists were men of wealth and social standing, who, because of special privileges granted them, felt bound to support and defend the looters. Independent victims of the far-reaching conspiracy submitted in silence, through fear of injury to their business. Men whose integrity was never questioned, who held high positions of trust, who were church members and teachers of Bible classes, contributed to the support of the dynasty—became blackmailers, in fact—and their excuse was that others did the same, and that if they proved the exception it would work their ruin. The system became loose through license and plenty till it was as wild as that of Tweed in New York.

Then the unexpected happened—an accident. There was no uprising of the people, but they were restive; and the Democratic party leaders, thinking to gain some independent votes, decided to raise the cry "reform" and put up a ticket of candidates different enough from the usual offerings of political parties to give color to their platform. These leaders were not in earnest. There was little difference between the two parties in the city; but the rascals that were in had been getting the greater share of the spoils, and the "outs" wanted more than was given to them. "Boodle" was not the issue, no exposures were made or threatened, and the bosses expected to control their men if elected. Simply as part of the game, the Democrats raised the slogan, "reform" and "no more Ziegenheinism."

Mayor Ziegenhein, called "Uncle Henry," was a "good fellow," "one of the boys," and though it was during his administration that the city grew ripe and went to rot, his opponents talked only of incompetence and neglect, and repeated such stories as that of his famous reply to some citizens who complained because certain street lights were put out: "You have the moon yet—ain't it?"

When somebody mentioned Joseph W. Folk for Circuit Attorney the leaders were ready to accept him. They didn't know much about him. He was a young man from Tennessee; had been president of the Jefferson Club, and arbitrated the railroad strike of 1898. But Folk did not want the place. He was a civil lawyer, had had no practice at the criminal bar, cared little about it, and a lucrative business as counsel for corporations was interesting him. He rejected the invitation. The committee called again and again, urging his duty to his party, and the city, etc.

"Very well," he said, at last, "I will accept the nomination, but if elected I will do my duty. There must be no attempt to influence my actions when I am called upon to punish lawbreakers."

The committeemen took such statements as the conventional platitudes of candidates. They nominated him, the Democratic ticket was elected, and Folk became Circuit Attorney for the Eighth Missouri District.

Three weeks after taking the oath of office his campaign pledges were put to the test. A number of arrests had been made in connection with the recent election, and charges of illegal registration were preferred against men of both parties. Mr. Folk took them up like routine cases of ordinary crime. Political bosses rushed to the rescue. Mr. Folk was reminded of his duty to his party, and told that he was expected to construe the law in such a manner that repeaters and other election criminals who had hoisted democracy's flag and helped elect him might be either discharged or receive the minimum punishment. The nature of the young lawyer's reply can best be inferred from the words of that veteran political leader, Colonel Ed Butler, who, after a visit to Mr. Folk, wrathfully exclaimed, "D——n Joe! He thinks he's the whole thing as Circuit Attorney."

The election cases were passed through the courts with astonishing rapidity; no more mercy was shown Democrats than Republicans, and before winter came a number of ward heelers and old-time party workers were behind the bars in Jefferson City. He next turned his attention to grafters and straw bondsmen with whom the courts were infested, and several of these leeches are in the penitentiary today. The business was broken up because of his activity. But Mr. Folk had made little more than the beginning.

One afternoon, late in January 1903, a newspaper reporter, known as "Red" Galvin, called Mr. Folk's attention to a ten-line newspaper item to the effect that a large sum of money had been placed in a bank for the purpose of bribing certain Assemblymen to secure the passage of a street railroad ordinance. No names were mentioned, but Mr. Galvin surmised that the bill referred to was one introduced on behalf of the Suburban Railway Company. An hour later Mr. Folk sent the names of nearly one hundred persons to the sheriff, with instructions to subpoena them before the grand jury at once. The list included councilmen, members of the House of Delegates, officers and directors of the Suburban Railway, bank presidents and cashiers. In three days the investigation was being pushed with vigor, but St. Louis was laughing at the "huge joke." Such things had been attempted before. The men who had been ordered to appear before the grand jury jested as they chatted in the anterooms, and newspaper accounts of these preliminary examinations were written in the spirit of burlesque.

It has developed since that Circuit Attorney Folk knew nothing, and was not able to learn much more during the first few days; but he says he saw here and there puffs of smoke and he determined to find the fire. It was not an easy job. The first break into such a system is always difficult. Mr. Folk began with nothing but courage and a strong personal conviction. He caused peremptory summonses to be issued, for the immediate attendance in the grand jury room of Charles H. Turner, president of the Suburban Railway, and Philip Stock, a representative of brewers' interests, who, he had reason to believe, was the legislative agent in this deal.

"Gentlemen," said Mr. Folk, "I have secured sufficient evidence to warrant the return of indictments against you for bribery, and I shall prosecute you to the full extent of the law and send you to the penitentiary unless you tell to this grand jury the complete history of the corruptionist

Lincoln Steffens

methods employed by you to secure the passage of Ordinance No. 44. I shall give you three days to consider the matter. At the end of that time, if you have not returned here and given us the information demanded, warrants will be issued for your arrest."

They looked at the audacious young prosecutor and left the Four Courts building without uttering a word. He waited. Two days later, ex-Lieutenant Governor Charles P. Johnson, the veteran criminal lawyer, called, and said that his client, Mr. Stock, was in such poor health that he would be unable to appear before the grand jury.

"I am truly sorry that Mr. Stock is ill," replied Mr. Folk, "for his presence here is imperative, and if he fails to appear he will be arrested before sundown."

That evening a conference was held in Governor Johnson's office, and the next day this story was told in the grand jury room by Charles H. Turner, millionaire president of the Suburban Railway, and corroborated by Philip Stock, man-about-town and a good fellow: the Suburban, anxious to sell out at a large profit to its only competitor, the St. Louis Transit Co., caused to be drafted the measure known as House Bill No. 44. So sweeping were its grants that Mr. Turner, who planned and executed the document, told the directors in his confidence that its enactment into law would enhance the value of the property from three to six million dollars. The bill introduced, Mr. Turner visited Colonel Butler, who had long been known as a legislative agent, and asked his price for securing the passage of the measure. "One hundred and forty-five thousand dollars will be my fee," was the reply. The railway president demurred. He would think the matter over, he said, and he hired a cheaper man, Mr. Stock. Stock conferred with the representative of the combine in the House of Delegates and reported that $75,000 would be necessary in this branch of the Assembly. Mr. Turner presented a note indorsed by two of the directors whom he could trust, and secured a loan from the German American Savings Bank.

Bribe funds in pocket, the legislative agent telephoned John Murrell, at that time a representative of the House combine, to meet him in the office of the Lincoln Trust Company. There the two rented a safe-deposit box. Mr. Stock placed in the drawer the roll of $75,000, and each subscribed to an agreement that the box should not be opened unless both were present. Of course the conditions spread upon the bank's daybook made no reference to the purpose for which this fund had been deposited, but an agreement entered into by Messrs. Stock and Murrell was to the effect that the $75,000 should be given Mr. Murrell as soon as the bill became an ordinance, and by him distributed to the members of the combine. Stock turned to the Council, and upon his report a further sum of $60,000 was secured. These bills were placed in a safe-deposit box of the Mississippi Valley Trust Co., and the man who held the key as representative of the Council combine was Charles H. Kratz.

All seemed well, but a few weeks after placing these funds in escrow, Mr. Stock reported to his employer that there was an unexpected hitch due to the action of Emil Meysenburg, who, as a member of the Council

Tweed Days in St. Louis

Committee on Railroads, was holding up the report on the bill. Mr. Stock said that Mr. Meysenburg held some worthless shares in a defunct corporation and wanted Mr. Stock to purchase this paper at its par value of $9,000. Mr. Turner gave Mr. Stock the money with which to buy the shares.

Thus the passage of House Bill 44 promised to cost the Suburban Railway Co. $144,000, only one thousand dollars less than that originally named by the political boss to whom Mr. Turner had first applied. The bill, however, passed both houses of the Assembly. The sworn servants of the city had done their work and held out their hands for the bribe money.

Then came a court mandate which prevented the Suburban Railway Co. from reaping the benefit of the vote-buying, and Charles H. Turner, angered at the check, issued orders that the money in safe-deposit boxes should not be touched. War was declared between bribe-givers and bribe-takers, and the latter resorted to tactics which they hoped would frighten the Suburban people into submission—such as making enough of the story public to cause rumors of impending prosecution. It was that first item which Mr. Folk saw and acted upon.

When Messrs. Turner and Stock unfolded in the grand jury room the details of their bribery plot, Circuit Attorney Folk found himself in possession of verbal evidence of a great crime; he needed as material exhibits the two large sums of money in safe-deposit vaults of two of the largest banking institutions of the West. Had this money been withdrawn? Could he get it if it was there? Lock-boxes had always been considered sacred and beyond the power of the law to open. "I've always held," said Mr. Folk, "that the fact that a thing never had been done was no reason for thinking it couldn't be done." He decided in this case that the magnitude of the interests involved warranted unusual action, so he selected a committee of grand jurors and visited one of the banks. He told the president, a personal friend, the facts that had come into his possession, and asked permission to search for the fund.

"Impossible," was the reply. "Our rules deny anyone the right."

"Mr. ———," said Mr. Folk, "a crime has been committed, and you hold concealed the principal evidence thereto. In the name of the State of Missouri I demand that you cause the box to be opened. If you refuse, I shall cause a warrant to be issued, charging you as an accessory."

For a minute not a word was spoken by anyone in the room; then the banker said in almost inaudible tones:

"Give me a little time, gentlemen. I must consult with our legal adviser before taking such a step."

"We will wait ten minutes," said the Circuit Attorney. "By that time we must have access to the vault or a warrant will be applied for."

At the expiration of that time a solemn procession wended its way from the president's office to the vaults in the subcellar—the president, the cashier, and the corporation's lawyer, the grand jurors, and the Circuit Attorney. All bent eagerly forward as the key was inserted in the lock. The iron drawer yielded, and a roll of something wrapped in brown paper was brought to light. The Circuit Attorney removed the rubber bands, and

Lincoln Steffens

national bank notes of large denomination spread out flat before them. The money was counted, and the sum was $75,000!

The boodle fund was returned to its repository, officers of the bank were told they would be held responsible for it until the courts could act. The investigators visited the other financial institution. They met with more resistance there. The threat to procure a warrant had no effect until Mr. Folk left the building and set off in the direction of the Four Courts. Then a messenger called him back, and the second box was opened. In this was found $60,000. The chain of evidence was complete.

From that moment events moved rapidly. Charles Kratz and John K. Murrell, alleged representatives of Council and House combines, were arrested on bench warrants and placed under heavy bonds. Kratz was brought into court from a meeting at which plans were being formed for his election to the national Congress. Murrell was taken from his undertaking establishment. Emil Meysenburg, millionaire broker, was seated in his office when a sheriff's deputy entered and read a document that charged him with bribery. The summons reached Henry Nicolaus while he was seated at his desk, and the wealthy brewer was compelled to send for a bondsman to avoid passing a night in jail. The cable flashed the news to Cairo, Egypt, that Ellis Wainwright, many times a millionaire, proprietor of the St. Louis brewery that bears this name, had been indicted. Julius Lehmann, one of the members of the House of Delegates, who had joked while waiting in the grand jury's anteroom, had his laughter cut short by the hand of a deputy sheriff on his shoulder and the words, "You are charged with perjury." He was joined at the bar of the criminal court by Harry Faulkner, another jolly good fellow.

Consternation spread among the boodle gang. Some of the men took night trains for other states and foreign countries; the majority remained and counseled together. Within twenty-four hours after the first indictments were returned, a meeting of bribe-givers and bribe-takers was held in South St. Louis. The total wealth of those in attendance was $30,000,000, and their combined political influence sufficient to carry any municipal election under normal conditions.

This great power was aligned in opposition to one man, who still was alone. It was not until many indictments had been returned that a citizens' committee was formed to furnish funds, and even then most of the contributors concealed their identity. Mr. James L. Blair, the treasurer, testified in court that they were afraid to be known lest "it ruin their business."

At the meeting of corruptionists three courses were decided upon. Political leaders were to work on the Circuit Attorney by promise of future reward, or by threats. Detectives were to ferret out of the young lawyer's past anything that could be used against him. Witnesses would be sent out of town and provided with money to remain away until the adjournment of the grand jury.

Mr. Folk at once felt the pressure, and it was of a character to startle one. Statesmen, lawyers, merchants, clubmen, churchmen—in fact, men prominent in all walks of life—visited him at his office and at his home, and urged that he cease such activity against his fellow townspeople. Political preferment was promised if he would yield; a political grave if he persisted. Threatening letters came, warning him of plots to murder, to disfigure, and to blackguard. Word came from Tennessee that detectives were investigating every act of his life. Mr. Folk told the politicians that he was not seeking political favors, and not looking forward to another office; the others he defied. Meantime he probed the deeper into the municipal sore. With his first successes for prestige and aided by the panic among the boodlers, he soon had them suspicious of one another, exchanging charges of betrayal, and ready to "squeal" or run at the slightest sign of danger. One member of the House of Delegates became so frightened while under the inquisitorial cross-fire that he was seized with a nervous chill; his false teeth fell to the floor, and the rattle so increased his alarm that he rushed from the room without stopping to pick up his teeth, and boarded the next train.

It was not long before Mr. Folk had dug up the intimate history of ten years of corruption, especially of the business of the North and South and the Central Traction franchise grants, the last-named being even more iniquitous than the Suburban.

Early in 1898 a "promoter" rented a bridal suite at the Planters' Hotel, and having stocked the rooms with wines, liquors and cigars until they resembled a candidate's headquarters during a convention, sought introduction to members of the Assembly and to such political bosses as had influence with the city fathers. Two weeks after his arrival the Central Traction bill was introduced "by request" in the Council. The measure was a blanket franchise, granting rights of way which had not been given to old-established companies, and permitting the beneficiaries to parallel any track in the city. It passed both houses despite the protests of every newspaper in the city, save one, and was vetoed by the mayor. The cost to the promoter was $145,000.

Preparations were made to pass the bill over the executive's veto. The bridal suite was restocked, larger sums of money were placed on deposit in the banks, and the services of three legislative agents were engaged. Evidence now in the possession of the St. Louis courts tells in detail the disposition of $250,000 of bribe money. Sworn statements prove that $75,000 was spent in the House of Delegates. The remainder of the $250,-000 was distributed in the Council, whose members, though few in number, appraised their honor at a higher figure on account of their higher positions in the business and social world. Finally, but one vote was needed to complete the necessary two-thirds in the upper Chamber. To secure this a councilman of reputed integrity was paid $50,000 in consideration that he vote aye when the ordinance should come up for final passage. But the promoter did not dare risk all upon the vote of one man, and he made this novel proposition to another honored member, who accepted it:

"You will vote on roll call after Mr. ——. I will place $45,000 in the hands of your son, which amount will become yours, if you have to

Lincoln Steffens

vote for the measure because of Mr. ———'s not keeping his promise. But if he stands out for it you can vote against it, and the money shall revert to me."

On the evening when the bill was read for final passage the City Hall was crowded with ward heelers and lesser politicians. These men had been engaged by the promoter, at five and ten dollars a head, to cheer on the boodling assemblymen. The bill passed the House with a rush, and all crowded into the Council Chamber. While the roll was being called the silence was profound, for all knew that some men in the Chamber whose reputations had been free from blemish were under promise and pay to part with honor that night. When the clerk was two-thirds down the list those who had kept count knew that but one vote was needed. One more name was called. The man addressed turned red, then white, and after a moment's hesitation he whispered "Aye"! The silence was so deathlike that his vote was heard throughout the room, and those near enough heard also the sigh of relief that escaped from the member who could now vote "No" and save his reputation.

The Central Franchise bill was a law, passed over the mayor's veto. The promoter has expended nearly $300,000 in securing the legislation, but within a week he sold his rights of way to "eastern capitalists" for $1,250,-000. The United Railways Company was formed, and without owning an inch of steel rail, or a plank in a car, was able to compel every street railroad in St. Louis, with the exception of the Suburban, to part with stock and right of way and agree to a merger. Out of this grew the St. Louis Transit Company of today.

Several incidents followed this legislative session. After the Assembly had adjourned, a promoter entertained the $50,000 councilman at a downtown restaurant. During the supper the host remarked to his guest, "I wish you would lend me that $50,000 until tomorrow. There are some of the boys outside whom I haven't paid." The money changed hands. The next day, having waited in vain for the promoter, Mr. Councilman armed himself with a revolver and began a search of the hotels. The hunt in St. Louis proved fruitless, and the irate legislator kept on the trail until he came face to face with the lobbyist in the corridor of the Waldorf-Astoria. The New Yorker, seeing the danger, seized the St. Louisan by the arm and said soothingly, "There, there; don't take on so. I was called away suddenly. Come to supper with me; I will give you the money."

The invitation was accepted, and champagne soon was flowing. When the man from the West had become sufficiently maudlin the promoter passed over to him a letter, which he had dictated to a typewriter while away from the table for a few minutes. The statement denied all knowledge of bribery.

"You sign that and I will pay you $5,000. Refuse, and you don't get a cent," said the promoter. The St. Louisan returned home carrying the $5,000, and that was all.

Meanwhile the promoter had not fared so well with other spoilsmen. By the terms of the ante-legislation agreement referred to above, the

Tweed Days in St. Louis

son of one councilman was pledged to return $45,000 if his father was saved the necessity of voting for the bill. The next day the New Yorker sought out this young man and asked for the money.

"I am not going to give it to you," was the cool rejoinder. "My mamma says that it is bribe money and that it would be wrong to give it to either you or father, so I shall keep it myself." And he did. When summoned before the grand jury this young man asked to be relieved from answering questions. "I am afraid I might commit perjury," he said. He was advised to "Tell the truth and there will be no risk."

"It would be all right," said the son, "if Mr. Folk would tell me what the other fellows have testified to. Please have him do that."

Two indictments were found as the result of this Central Traction bill, and bench warrants were served on Robert M. Snyder and George J. Kobusch. The state charged the former with being one of the promoters of the bill, the definite allegation being bribery. Mr. Kobusch, who is president of a street-car manufacturing company, was charged with perjury.

The first case tried was that of Emil Meysenburg, the millionaire who compelled the Suburban people to purchase his worthless stock. He was defended by three attorneys of high repute in criminal jurisprudence, but the young Circuit Attorney proved equal to the emergency, and a conviction was secured. Three years in the penitentiary was the sentence. Charles Kratz, the Congressional candidate, forfeited $40,000 by flight, and John K. Murrell also disappeared. Mr. Folk traced Murrell to Mexico, caused his arrest in Guadalajara, negotiated with the authorities for his surrender, and when this failed, arranged for his return home to confess, and his evidence brought about the indictment, on September 8, of eighteen members of the municipal legislature. The second case was that of Julius Lehmann. Two years at hard labor was the sentence, and the man who had led the jokers in the grand jury anteroom would have fallen when he heard it, had not a friend been standing near.

Besides the convictions of these and other men of good standing in the community, and the flight of many more, partnerships were dissolved, companies had to be reorganized, business houses were closed because their proprietors were absent, but Mr. Folk, deterred as little by success as by failure, moved right on; he was not elated; he was not sorrowful. The man proceeded with his work quickly, surely, smilingly, without fear or pity. The terror spread, and the rout was complete.

When another grand jury was sworn and proceeded to take testimony there were scores of men who threw up their hands and crying "Mea culpa!" begged to be permitted to tell all they knew and not be prosecuted. The inquiry broadened. The son of a former mayor was indicted for misconduct in office while serving as his father's private secretary, and the grand jury recommended that the ex-mayor be sued in the civil courts, to recover interests on public money which he had placed in his own pocket. A true bill fell on a former City Register, and more assemblymen were arrested, charged with making illegal contracts with the city. At last the ax struck upon the trunk of the greatest oak of the forest. Colonel Butler, the

Lincoln Steffens

boss who has controlled elections in St. Louis for many years, the million-aire who had risen from bellows-boy in a blacksmith's shop to be the maker and guide of the governors of Missouri, one of the men who helped nominate and elect Folk—he also was indicted on two counts charged with attempted bribery. That Butler has controlled legislation in St. Louis had long been known. It was generally understood that he owned assemblymen before they ever took the oath of office, and that he did not have to pay for votes. And yet open bribery was the allegation now. Two members of the Board of Health stood ready to swear that he offered them $2,500 for their approval of a garbage contract.

Pitiful? Yes, but typical. Other cities are today in the same condition as St. Louis before Mr. Folk was invited in to see its rottenness. Chicago is cleaning itself up just now, so is Minneapolis, and Pittsburgh recently had a bribery scandal; Boston is at peace, Cincinnati and St. Paul are satisfied, while Philadelphia is happy with the worst government in the world. As for the small towns and the villages, many of these are busy as bees at the loot.

St. Louis, indeed, in its disgrace, has a great advantage. It was exposed late; it has not been reformed and caught again and again, until its citizens are reconciled to corruption. But, best of all, the man who has turned St. Louis inside out, turned it, as it were, upside down, too. In all cities, the better classes—the businessmen—are the sources of corruption; but they are so rarely pursued and caught that we do not fully realize whence the trouble comes. Thus most cities blame the politicians and the ignorant and vicious poor.

Mr. Folk has shown St. Louis that its bankers, brokers, corporation officers—its businessmen—are the sources of evil, so that from the start it will know the municipal problem in its true light. With a tradition for public spirit, it may drop Butler and its runaway bankers, brokers and brewers, and pushing aside the scruples of the hundreds of men down in blue book, and red book, and church register, who are lying hidden behind the statutes of limitations, the city may restore good government. Other-wise the exposures by Mr. Folk will result only in the perfection of the corrupt system. For the corrupt can learn a lesson when the good citizens cannot. The Tweed regime in New York taught Tammany to organize its boodle business: the police exposure taught it to improve its method of collecting blackmail. And both now are almost perfect and safe. The rascals of St. Louis will learn in like manner; they will concentrate the control of their bribery system, excluding from the profit-sharing the great mass of weak rascals, and carrying on the business as a business in the interest of a trustworthy few. District Attorney Jerome cannot catch the Tammany men, and Circuit Attorney Folk will not be able another time to break the St. Louis ring. This is St. Louis' one great chance.

But, for the rest of us, it does not matter about St. Louis any more than it matters about Colonel Butler et al. The point is, that what went on in St. Louis is going on in most of our cities, towns and villages. The problem

Tweed Days in St. Louis

of municipal government in America has not been solved. The people may
be tired of it, but they cannot give it up—not yet.

[1902]

Lincoln Steffens

John L. Mathews:

Mr. Ballinger
and the
National Grab Bag

John L. Mathews (1874-1916), muckraking
journalist, specialized in exposing plunderers
of America's natural resources, particularly
waterpower and mineral resources. Many of
those plunderers, he pointed out, were sworn
to uphold the public interest, and their interpre-
tations of that interest often seemed rather
strange, if not illegal.

Out of the desert of Central Oregon, down from a plateau 3,000 feet above sea level, flows the Des Chutes River, in many ways the most remarkable in America. Seeping out from a soil of volcanic ash, fed by the melting snows of distant mountain tops, it flows almost without variation from January to December. Its flood plane is not more than four feet above its low-water surface. From its head to its mouth it plunges precipitously. There is scarcely a foot along its course where a dam could not be installed for the profitable development of power. In one hundred miles its steady discharge of more than 5,000 second-feet provide for the creation of 1,000,000 electric horsepower—a greater energy than is possessed by any other river of this capacity in the world.

It has, besides this, another potential value for power; for though its banks are precipitous cliffs of basalt and of lava, though it lies sometimes more than a thousand feet below the rim of its gorge, the desert which sweeps away from this canyon to the Cascades on one side and to the John Day Valley and so to Idaho on the other, is a fertile and as ready for irrigation as the rich Horse Heaven country across the Columbia River in the State of Washington.

This Des Chutes River belongs to the people of the State of Oregon. Its banks and the adjacent desert (or such part of it as has not been given away, often on fraudulent land grants) belong to the people of the United States. The people of Oregon, more advanced in the direction of good water laws than the rest of us, and more vitally concerned because of this immense desert which covers the greater part of their map, have adopted a water law, recommended to them by their state engineer. This is the first clause:

"All the waters in the State of Oregon, from whatever source, belong to the public."

They have gone further and have provided that any person developing water power must do so on a limited franchise and pay an annual tax, which may amount to $2 per horsepower per year, the horsepower being defined by its minimum description in water, not by a generous measure in electric current. This amounts to practically $4 on the electric power when it reaches a market.

Under this law the water in the Des Chutes, developed for its power, should return an income of more than $2,000,000 a year to the State of Oregon. But let us consider for a moment its value from another standpoint. In the city of Spokane, Washington, is a typical General Electric power company, which has grabbed without return to state or nation the principal powers and reservoirs of the upper Spokane River. This company was financed by the sale of bonds, as is the common practice with water-power grabbers, and its plant cost about $8,000,000. The company charges the citizens of Spokane $40 for ten-hour power which it could afford to sell for $20. This high price is possible because of the cost of coal in Spokane. On this tremendous charge the Washington Water Power Company pays dividends of seven per cent on its $5,000,000 stock, water and all, interest on its $8,000,000 bonds, and has accumulated a surplus of about $300,000.

John L. Mathews

The only protection against the water-power grabbers which will be continually effective is public ownership. If the people of Oregon developed the Des Chutes they could afford to sell its power to themselves and even to their Washington neighbors for $20 for ten or $30 for twenty-four-hour horsepower, at which rate the river would return the state an income of $30,000,000 yearly, on an investment of probably $125,000,000.

This possible million horsepower represents the equivalent of one-fifth of the total country. It is far more than the State of Oregon will use for many decades. So let us suppose that she develops but half of it and uses part of that half to pump the remaining half of the water up to the desert for irrigation. The pumping would require only a small part of the developed power, so that a large balance could be sold.

The irrigating half of the stream would suffice to water not less than 400,000 acres of the Oregon uplands. Put into the ordinary crops of the northwestern irrigated lands this would produce not less than $80,000,000 annually in crops, and would support in comfort 40,000 families on the irrigated lands besides thousands more in the cities and villages which would grow up in that neighborhood.

I have gone at length into this Des Chutes case and the value of that water to the state through which it flows, because it is a fitting introduction to the story of the acts of Richard A. Ballinger as custodian of the national grab bag. Mr. Ballinger has unloosed the drawstrings of the grab bag just enough to allow the whole Des Chutes River to be pulled out by two of the most earnest grabbers of the Northwest—James J. Hill and the late Edward H. Harriman.

It needs but a glance at the map of Oregon and its neighbors to show one familiar with railway engineering that the Des Chutes Valley has a great value apart from its running water. It is of enormous strategic importance to the railway builders who wish to reach central Oregon. It is of even greater importance to those who wish to secure an economical line with low grades between San Francisco and the northern seaports. Because of this feature it early attracted the attention of Hill and Harriman. The old routes from San Francisco north circle the base of Mount Shasta after a heavy climb in each direction, and make travel and freight hauling slow and costly either way. To lessen this the Harriman lines have been for some years building an easterly division, but even this comes at last to the headwaters of the Willamette River and descends that stream to Portland and the Columbia.

At Portland, Harriman's domain ended and Hill's began. Hill could not cross and pass the rich gateway to western Oregon. Harriman could not advance upon Tacoma and Seattle. A couple of years ago Hill marched down the Columbia Valley with a short route to Portland known as the North Bank road, and in retaliation Harriman forced his way to Puget Sound. The war did not stop there. Balked at Portland, Hill was determined to seek a short cut through the great desert of central Oregon to California. Half a dozen routes were open, but all of them face steep grades and costly railroading except the Des Chutes. By this single river

Mr. Ballinger and the National Grab Bag

it is possible to build a railroad not exceeding 1 per cent in grade (that is, nowhere rising more than one foot in a hundred) from the Columbia to San Francisco. By this entrance, therefore, Hill determined to drive a wedge into the exclusively Harriman territory of central California and bring the southern magnate to terms.

Almost at the same moment Harriman advanced upon the gateway for a route northward toward Puget Sound and the Inland Empire cheaper for hauling than his existing lines. Porter Brothers, railway contractors representing in this deal the Hill interests, and John S. Stevens filed with the Secretary of the Interior a right of way up the Des Chutes. Immediately afterwards Harriman filed another. For many miles their traced railways were on the same side of the river and occupied the same ground. In one important particular they were exactly alike: they occupied the flood plane of the river, or were as slightly above it as circumstances would permit.

At President Roosevelt's instigation Secretary of the Interior Garfield made an investigation and discovered that the proposed railways would ruin the water power of the Des Chutes without any adequate return to the people. He therefore refused to grant the right of way until it should be so resurveyed that the railway tracks would be above the level of the dams and reservoirs necessary to develop the country.

The river banks are steep and high. The work of building a line high up in this canyon would not be vastly greater than building the lower line. Engineers have estimated that $500,000 extra money would carry them at high grade throughout without any extra gradient in the track. I discussed this point with Secretary Ballinger a short time ago, and he placed the cost higher than the estimate of engineers. "A million dollars, perhaps three or four times as much," was the Ballinger statement. On either basis, the amount it would cost the railroads is a bagatelle in comparison with the money loss each year to the State of Oregon.

The railroads refused to spend the money necessary to put their roadbeds higher up, and in this they were penny wise and pound foolish. If the Des Chutes could be developed along the lines I have suggested, the country would fill up with people, and the increased passenger and freight traffic would very soon wipe out the extra cost of construction.

The Hill and Harriman interests played 'possum during the last days of Roosevelt and waited until his successor came into office. That happened on March 4, 1909. Their waiting was well rewarded. Within three weeks after he became Secretary of the Interior, Mr. Ballinger signed and approved the rights-of-way of the rival railway constructors. He approved them notwithstanding the fact that the rights-of-way conflicted with each other, without ruling on which side of the river they should go, without requiring that their conflicting locations be resurveyed. Also, he approved them without taking any measures whatever to preserve to the people of Oregon the enormous public resource contained in the running water. Mr. Ballinger was custodian of the banks of the river. He gave away this valuable property in such wise that its use will wreck the great heritage of the people of Oregon.

John L. Mathews

Meantime, the rival railroads are already engaged in a bitter, costly war. Tens of thousands of dollars have been lavished in counsel fees and court costs. Armies of workmen are deploying along the Des Chutes; I saw them last August engaged at close range in as bitter a fight as their employers, each gang expending more energy in hindering the work of the opponent than in prosecuting its own. Fist fights, battles with stones, these were part of the day's warfare. And in the end, little will be gained. The money that would have been required to elevate the tracks will be spent in warfare. Such is the rule of grab.

Before the invasion of the Des Chutes I called upon Secretary Ballinger in Washington and asked him if it were true that he had granted these permits. He was at first vexed that the matter was out, but quickly recovered himself.

"The permits are not granted, but they will be at once," he said.

"Is any reservation made about water power?" I asked.

"Only that at one point if the government ever desires to put in a dam the railroads must raise their tracks one hundred feet."

"What is your object in giving in to the railroads and letting them destroy this water power?"

Mr. Ballinger is not a large man. He has been questioned and quizzed about his troubles over conservation until he is no longer able to control his temper. He stepped away from his desk and paced rapidly up and down his office.

"See here. You don't understand this thing," he said. "You chaps who are in favor of this conservation program are all wrong. You are hindering the development of the West. These railroads are necessary to the country. And more than that, this whole big domain is a blanket—it is oppressing the people. The thing to do with it—" and here he stopped and faced me. "In my opinion the proper course to take with regard to this domain is to divide it up among the big corporations and the people who know how to make money out of it and let the people at large get the benefit of the circulation of the money."

It becomes necessary to quote this statement of Mr. Ballinger to make clear his position. It is not probable that he is corrupt, in the sense that a direct bribe could induce him to defraud the government. Mr. Ballinger is primarily an attorney who has received his training in representing large business interests, and it is entirely natural that his sympathies should be found on the side of corporations and capitalists when they come into conflict with the interests of the whole people as represented by the government.

It is worth while to examine briefly the history of the Public Domain and see how it came to be transferred into a grab bag and how there grew up men who believe that it is a grab bag to be emptied by everyone fortunate enough to be able to find the opening and insert his hand.

In Revolutionary times several of the colonies laid claim to lands running to the Mississippi, or to the Pacific, over the frontiers of which

Mr. Ballinger and the National Grab Bag

they had waged bitter war with the Indians and the French. All through the Revolution this frontier conflict was continued, and the British lost no opportunity of inciting the redskins to massacre. The heavy loss of life in defending the frontier was common to all. Its continuance appalled the struggling colonies, and the Legislature of Maryland demanded that if these lands were to be secured at the cost of the common blood they should be common lands, belonging to the nation and not to the several states.

Maryland's appeal won her neighbors. Colony after colony relinquished its claims to the country at large, until, when the nation was put upon its feet, there existed a great territory stretching west from the Alleghenies to the Pacific which, except for a number of colonial and royal grants antedating the Revolution, belonged to the nation.

That was the birth of the Public Domain, begot in bloodshed, a perpetual reminder of the hard struggles of our forefathers, a reward for their patriotism and unselfishness.

Then came those vast acquisitions that rounded out the great domain from the Mississippi River to the Pacific Ocean, including the Louisiana Purchase, which took from the treasury of the nation then a larger sum in proportion to its wealth than the whole Panama Canal project is taking from us now.

With this vast domain our nation in its youth started the most amazing campaign of expansion, through home-making, the world has ever seen. All the people of the world were invited to take up the farming land of the great West and become disciples of liberty, freedmen with their own land.

It was this that made America, but it was inevitable that this giving away of a great continent should excite the rapacity, the selfishness of many men who had no need for new homes, but who saw in the untillable areas opportunities for what they grew to call "development." Under the sanction of this phrase great timber grabbers swept away the vast timber lands of Michigan, Wisconsin and Minnesota, often carelessly setting fire to what they did not themselves cut off for lumber. Buying a few thousand acres, unscrupulous operators would use it as a cloak to steal the timber from the adjacent government lands; and so were built up many of the largest fortunes in the world.

What was done by the timber grabbers was done by the coal-mine grabbers, and by the men who fenced the grazing lands. They made tremendous fortunes, and the sight of these aggregations of wealth was welcomed by the pioneers in the West as a sign of development and an indication that they were approaching the civilization of the eastern states.

Able by the use of their money to command the strongest lawyers as well as to dominate socially, these grabbers of the Public Domain were powerful enough to build up not only a long series of court decisions supporting their claims and their actions, but a public opinion which condoned, if it did not defend; which came to regard, as they did, the grabbing of anything from the Public Domain as a process of "development" neces-

John L. Mathews

sary to the prosperity of the new country. To call such affairs stealing would have been cause for ostracism and persecution a decade ago.

From the old-fashioned point of view it is of very little importance whether interior Oregon is ever irrigated, or whether the people of that state save and develop their water power. But it is of supreme importance that two railway magnates who desire to build railways—which will aid in developing the West, will absorb capital, will lead to uncut forests and unopened mines—have every facility to advance without regard to the result upon the public.

However, a revolution in this popular sentiment has taken place and the point of view of yesterday is not that of today. The people are beginning to insist that the laws passed to defend the Public Domain should defend it; should be obeyed; should not be ridden over roughshod, or evaded by clever lawyer tricks. The Domain should not be a grab bag, but a treasure house in which the nation shall hold a vast store of riches to be developed economically for the public's good.

The Secretary of the Interior is custodian of the Public Domain. He is in control of the national grab bag. Therefore, it is of the greatest importance that we study and analyze the acts and the record of the man who holds this important position, so that we may determine whether his point of view is that of the grabbers or of the conservers. Sidelights on the man's business and professional life may help us in reaching a clearer understanding. . . . Let us look at him now in his relation to Alaska, a subject . . . very much connected with the trustification of our national resources.

The present movement in Alaska is the most tremendous attempt yet made by capitalists to obtain a monopolistic control of the natural resources remaining in the United States. Alaska, which we bought for $7,500,000, is the best bargain Uncle Sam's family has ever obtained. Its wealth is beyond computation. In gold a hundred million—two hundred million—no man can estimate it; the value may be two billion dollars. In timber, in agricultural land, in copper, the values run into the hundreds of millions of dollars. In coal the value is uncountable; it probably amounts to billions of dollars. The fisheries, already trustified, the sealeries controlled by Senator Elkins' trust, add to this return for our small investment.

To grab this vast treasure has stirred the pirate blood in many of our money kings till they would make any endeavor, legal or illegal, to obtain it.

The Guggenheims, smelter kings, first set eyes upon Alaska and obtained virtual monopoly of the navigation, railways and provision companies which control and direct the lives of those that work within the borders of the territory. Combining with J. Pierpont Morgan they fought for the copper empire of Alaska and secured such a wealth of deposits through methods we cannot here describe that their resources in Alaska are estimated to be worth $500,000,000. This half a billion dollars has been transferred from the national storehouse to theirs. There has been ro reason for the transfer, save that the Guggenheims are strong,

Mr. Ballinger and the National Grab Bag

powerful grabbers. There has been no recompense to the people other than the government's nominal fees.

The Standard Oil-Amalgamated Copper interests, striving to secure for themselves hundreds of millions of copper in the Copper River country, fought the Guggenheims in Alaska for a long time. Opposing gangs of men hired to build impossible railways across glaciers, over morasses and through narrow gorges of rivers swollen by repeated floods, spent much of their time stalking and shooting their rivals. Often murder was done to advance the fight. At last Big Business triumphed over personal rivalry, and Morgan, Guggenheim, Standard Oil and Amalgamated signed a treaty of peace and directed their united energies toward grabbing everything of value in Alaska.

The cause of much of this trouble was the coal land of the Controller Bay region. Into the Pacific along the southern coast of Alaska flow two big rivers, the Susitna and the Copper, the one into Prince William Sound, the other into Cook Inlet. Just to the east of Cook Inlet is the town of Katalla and the body of water known as Controller Bay. Copper River is the great inlet from the south to central Alaska and the Yukon by river and by rail. At its head it comes close to the Tanana, which flows into the Yukon. A railway runs by a treacherous and difficult route from Katalla and from Cordova up the Copper River to its principal rapids, and above that its glacier-fed waters support steamboat navigation into the richest copper region yet discovered in America. This copper, which "the interests" seek to control, is the key to the prolongation of the Smelter Trust.

To smelt copper are needed two things: water power and coal, principally coal.

Back of Controller Bay, beginning almost at tidewater and extending inward until they are lost beneath the immense ice masses of Bering and Martin's River Glaciers, extend the coal fields. Near the seashore this coal, which crops out upon the surface, is of a soft, bituminous character about the equal of the best Illinois fuel. A little farther back is found an enormous amount of a semibituminous, coking coal, the equal of Pocahontas, George's Creek, or any other first-class coking coal of West Virginia. And beyond this again lies Carbon Mountain, practically a great mountain of the finest anthracite in the world—probably the largest known deposit of this valuable mineral.

The total value of these Controller Bay deposits (and they are but a small part of the total Alaskan coal fields) is beyond calculation. They have never been surveyed. The coal in sight on Carbon Mountain is in four veins reaching to thirty feet in thickness and extending entirely around and through the mountain. What lies beneath the surface no man knows. All this coal is within an hour of the ship side and can be transshipped to San Francisco for less than Colorado coal can climb the first range of mountains.

A vast quantity of this coal is well adapted for use in the vessels of the Pacific Squadron, making these coal lands especially valuable to

John L. Mathews

the government. At present that squadron is supplied with coal from the East.

In 1906, nine hundred mineral claims, aggregating about 150,000 acres, were pending against these Controller Bay deposits. These nine hundred claims are still pending, for President Roosevelt in 1906 withdrew all the coal lands in Alaska from entry. Mr. Ballinger has not yet questioned the President's authority to take this action. Among these claims are included certain groups known as the Greene group, the Alaska Petroleum and Coal Company group, the Alaska Development Company group, the Harriman group and the Cunningham group.

The first group of filings on this Alaskan land—and these are among the nine hundred awaiting patent—were made for the Alaska Development Company of Seattle, in 1902. They were of the worst type of "dummy entries." A contractor and a Katalla saloonkeeper picked the dummies and paid them $100 each to file on the claims and assign them to the Alaska Development Company. Later, when the government detected this fraud, members of the Alaska Development Company refiled on the same claims. These claims are believed to be under option to the firm of MacKenzie and Mann, the Canadian financiers said to represent the Standard Oil group, and owners of the Canadian Northern Railway. Standard Oil interests are involved in the Greene group, controlled by former Mayor Harry White, of Seattle, now of California, and by other Seattle men. The most serious charges made against Secretary Ballinger are in connection with various of these Alaskan coal claims. To understand the situation we need to examine the land laws which govern Alaska.

The general coal land law of 1873 provided that any person or association (the person being a citizen and with the usual qualifications) might enter for an individual 160 acres, or for an association 320 acres of coal lands not otherwise withdrawn or appropriated; and pay for it $10 an acre if it was more than fifteen miles from a railway, $20 if it was nearer. The law, however, does not limit this price, but says "not less than $20."

Another section of the same act provides that when any such association of not less than four persons has expended not less than $5,000 on improvements it may enter 640 acres embracing such improvements. Only one entry is allowed to each citizen and having made one he cannot sell that and make another. In determining disputed titles "continued good faith" is indicated as the proper guide. A "preference right of entry" is given by the improvement work. This is known as the "location," and by the rules the assessment work is required to be actually done to the opening of the mine. The right continues for one year.

In 1900 these laws were extended to Alaska. In 1904 the rules were amended to cover the unsurveyed districts and allow a claimant to lay out forty acres or a multiple of forty acres in a rectangle, with north and south boundaries, and to record and patent it under regulations.

The object of these various laws and regulations is to prevent a trust from securing control of an enormous tract of priceless mineral land

Mr. Ballinger and the National Grab Bag

at ten dollars an acre. The law expressly forbids an agreement among men to patent coal lands for the use of a corporation. Filings made under such an agreement are by that act void. After location and before entry, holders of Alaska claims up to 2,560 acres may combine them for mutual working . . . but no larger amount and no previous agreement is permitted.

In 1907 the Seattle *Star* blazoned forth on its front page an "exposé" of the Alaska Petroleum and Coal Company. This corporation, headed by Clarke Davis (according to the *Star* story—and it has never been gainsaid), a well-known and prosperous citizen of Seattle, had sought for oil in Alaska, and had failed to find it, but had found the now famous coal lands. Then a number of men who had organized the corporation filed, by power of attorney, upon these Alaska coal lands. Each took 160 acres, and all of them transferred their locations to the corporation. Then the corporation issued $5,000,000 of stock in one-dollar shares, basing the value on the ownership of the coal lands. Clarke Davis, said the *Star*, received one million shares for promotion work and for his own coal locations. Other shares were given to organizers of the corporation, and yet others were placed in the hands of men whose influence would be of value to the company. Many treasury shares were sold at prices ranging from seven cents to forty cents per share.

The *Star* created a sensation by announcing that under the law it is impossible to transfer titles to the location before entry, and that if any plan is entered into to do so the entry is refused and the land becomes again part of the Public Domain.

A prospectus was issued by the company and widely circulated through the mails. It stated that the company owned 1,920 acres of valuable coal lands in Alaska. Many people invested in stock. Failing legislation that would make their filings legal and give them title to the coal, the directors were in a dilemma. If they proved their claims and assigned them to the company, after taking oath that they were filing on them for their own use, they would be liable to prosecution by the government. And, on the other hand, if the company failed to get possession of the coal lands its officers might be liable to prosecution for the use they had made of the mails.

Mr. Ballinger was the attorney chosen to relieve this situation and to pilot the Alaska Petroleum and Coal Company through legal obstacles to a clear title. He went to Washington and did all in his power in two directions—one to secure the patenting of the lands in dispute, the other to secure broader laws for the use of corporations in grabbing Alaska.

The firm of Ballinger, Ronald & Battle, of which Mr. Ballinger was the senior partner until he became connected with the public service, is one of the leading legal forces of Seattle. In the Northwest, Ballinger, Ronald & Battle are generally recognized as the legal representatives of Standard Oil in Seattle.

Ballinger adds an agreeable personality to a keen knowledge of the law. He had been Mayor of Seattle and by a war on slot machines had made something of a reputation as a reformer. He had served the

John L. Mathews

government as a lawyer on one or two occasions, and in various ways had attracted the attention of Roosevelt. In March 1907 the President appointed him Commissioner of the General Land Office in Washington. The unpleasant significance of this lies in the fact that Mr. Ballinger was thus in charge of the department which could refuse or consent to patent the Clarke Davis group of coal claims.

He took no action on the claims of his clients while he was Commissioner, but his appearance in Washington was immediately followed by the turning of Roosevelt's attention to the question of Alaska coal lands and a message to Congress asking that corporations be permitted to patent considerably larger areas. Ballinger appeared before the Committee on Public Lands for the House of Representatives, and urged the passage of such an act. In referring to the Clarke Davis situation he stated that to his own knowledge the men concerned had been guilty of merely technical violations of the law.

In the year 1907 a law *was* passed and presented to the President, but it was destined to go no further. While it was pending before President Roosevelt, however, Mr. Ballinger was actively at work for it.

Meetings were held in Seattle at which men prominent in northwestern business and political circles were present. Among others interested in these conferences were former Governor McGraw, of Washington; H. R. Harriman, an officer of the Alaska Petroleum and Coal Company, from whose connection it comes about that these are known as the Harriman claims; John Schram, president of the Washington Trust Company and a trustee of the Alaska Petroleum and Coal Company, and F. F. Evans, a mining broker. Mr. Ballinger was moved to leave his desk in the national capital and go to Seattle and there meet with the conferees. These men used their influence in urging James Garfield, then Secretary of the Interior, to aid in securing the signing of the bill.

Mr. Ballinger's friends in Seattle, and he has many of them, have assured me that they could see nothing improper in his thus pushing the claims of his former clients against the very department of the government with which he was officially connected. Indeed, some of his friends explained his participation to me—and they could see no objection to the situation—by the statement that Mr. Ballinger is, or has been, financially interested in 155,000 shares of the stock of the Alaska Petroleum and Coal Company.

But although the act of 1907 did not get past President Roosevelt, nevertheless, on the twenty-eighth of May 1908, there did go into effect a new law providing that locators who had, in good faith and for their own use, located prior to November 12, 1906, on coal lands in Alaska, might be allowed to combine their holdings to 2,560 acres (four square miles), and work them as a corporation.

This might be read in three ways: it might be construed to admit only those that had entered the lands before planning to combine; it might be construed to admit everybody even if their plan to incorporate were made before location; or it might take a middle course and include

Mr. Ballinger and the National Grab Bag

those that filed in good faith as individuals and then formed a corporation before entering for patent.

"We hoped," says a man very close to Ballinger, "to be able to give the statute the broadest possible interpretation so that all locators would be included. We hoped, in fact, to find in it a new rule for construing more broadly the old 640-acre statute."

In the meantime—in March 1908—Mr. Ballinger had resigned his position as Commissioner of the General Land Office. It may, therefore, have been due to his absence from the scene that this law, which Ballinger had helped to pass, contained a truly Rooseveltian last paragraph so strongly antitrust that the purpose of the law was lost. This paragraph, too long to quote, provides that if by any means whatever, tacitly or directly or in any indirect way or in any manner whatever the lands involved become concerned with, or the property of, or in any way connected with any agreement in restraint of trade or any *corporation* concerned in such an agreement, *the lands shall revert to the United States and the title become void*. It is said that Gifford Pinchot drafted this paragraph. Part of the coal lands lie in the Chugach Forest Reserve—which would give Mr. Pinchot good reason to take an interest in the legislation.

This antitrust paragraph daunted the promoters. Not a single claim has been pressed for entry under this antitrust act and the grabbers are pushing to have it repealed.

In March 1908, then, because his professional and business interests in Seattle demanded his time, Ballinger retired from the Commissionership and went home. He became immediately involved in another group of Alaska claims called the Cunningham group directly concerned with the Morgan-Guggenheim-Standard Oil combination and with the exploiting of Alaska.

Clarence Cunningham, a typical prospector who had tramped all over the Northwest, went up to the Controller Bay region in 1902 when others were hunting for gold, and examined the Carbon Mountain coal. He returned to Washington state, and pressed about among his friends with the news of the value and availability of this deposit and organized a syndicate to grab all they could of it and sell it out to bigger interests.

Into this Cunningham group came a number of men of wealth, and a few others who were acting as dummies. Each of these men gave Cunningham a power of attorney and with this he went to Alaska and filed on thirty-three claims, 5,280 acres of Carbon Mountain and adjacent coal lands, all richly underlaid with the fuel. It is alleged freely that the Cunningham group intended to form a corporation, to which their lands were to be sold, and that the corporation was to pass into the hands of the Guggenheims. But Roosevelt's last paragraph had prevented the execution of such a plan.

With the law against them, the Cunningham claimants turned to Ballinger. They presented to his attention their thirty-three claims, worth many millions of dollars, and sent Mr. Ballinger, who had just resigned

John L. Mathews

the Commissionership, back to Washington to appeal to the Department of the Interior.

There is a law which to the common intellect seems to make that act of Ballinger's illegal. Section 190 of the revised statutes forbids *for two years after he has left the department,* any officer of a governmental department from practicing before that department in behalf of any claim which was pending during his term of office. It is designed to prevent department lawyers from being subsidized by corporations to resign and use their information against the government from which they have obtained it.

The Cunningham claims had been before the Land Office when Mr. Ballinger was Commissioner. Nevertheless, Attorney Ballinger soon appeared before his successor and pleaded to have the Cunningham claims passed to entry and patent. Attorney Ballinger's efforts in this case were not successful.

And then the presidential election came—and a few months later Mr. Ballinger was occupying the position of Secretary of the Interior in Mr. Taft's Cabinet. And very soon after his installation in this honorable and important position he began to undo the work accomplished by Theodore Roosevelt. . . .

Bear distinctly in mind that I charge no corrupt motive in Mr. Ballinger's appearance in official Washington. That is, no corrupt motive in his mind or the President's.

In the Northwest charges are made that connect Postmaster General Frank Hitchcock—in his capacity of manager of the latest Republican national campaign—with the Guggenheim interests in an arrangement to secure the Interior portfolio for Mr. Ballinger. This may be partisan political gossip. It is very easy for interested parties to start such rumors, and very difficult for them to prove them.

Unquestionably Mr. Ballinger has strong political influences back of him. As I have shown, many powerful selfish interests would be more than willing to aid him in any ambition for high government position. But this would not prove that Mr. Ballinger was corrupt. As I have said, his talents as a lawyer have ever been employed by corporations or individuals who believe that the treasures of the Public Domain should become their private property. Mr. Ballinger is undoubtedly sincere and honest in his desires to further what he believes to be the legitimate interests of his clients. His point of view may be old-fashioned, but it is not likely that he can be proved guilty of corrupt acts.

When Mr. Ballinger was still Commissioner of the Land Office this peculiar train of events came to the attention of Louis R. Glavis, a special agent of the Department of the Interior. Glavis is young, enthusiastic, determined to follow the Roosevelt idea of protecting the public lands and of prosecuting graft to the end. His duties were to investigate claims offered for entry at the Government Land Offices. Many such claims are contested by rival applicants; many are fraudulent upon the face of them; and many, like these Cunningham claims, while apparently legal are believed to be really parts of a conspiracy to wrest property illegally from the

Mr. Ballinger and the National Grab Bag

Public Domain. It is the business of special agents to investigate these cases as fully as possible, and for that purpose Mr. Glavis was stationed at Portland, Oregon. From there, about two years ago, he sent a secret service agent named Smith to begin an investigation into the Cunningham claims. Then Glavis followed Smith almost immediately and so far as possible carried on the search for Cunningham evidence personally.

Some time ago the department, through the efforts of Mr. Taft, was awarded an extra appropriation of $1,000,000 to increase its staff and facilitate the movement of some 30,000 claims which had been delayed through the routine of the Land Office. Among these 30,000 claims were the Cunningham entries.

To expedite the work it was necessary to divide Mr. Glavis' district, and he was accordingly relieved of work at Portland and allowed to station himself at Seattle with practically nothing to occupy his attention but the alleged Alaskan coal frauds. He says that he saw a record belonging to Clarence Cunningham containing a list of those concerned in the Cunningham entry; the sums of money each was to receive for his land, when it was turned over to the eventual syndicate; and other evidence of a conspiracy to combine or trustify this big tract. This, with other evidence, was sent to Mr. Taft.

In addition to this evidence of the Cunningham plans, Mr. Glavis, feeling that his investigation was being interfered with, believed that he had stumbled upon evidence which indicated collusion between the officials of his department and the owners of these fraudulent claims, to facilitate the patenting. However, President Taft has made no comment whatever upon the Cunningham cases, but in his reply to Mr. Ballinger concerning the Glavis charges devotes himself to those of official collusion and dismisses them as unworthy of consideration because they are inferential, and because Glavis had not given Mr. Ballinger the inferential benefit of certain modifying circumstances.

President Taft dismissed Mr. Glavis from the government service, and thoroughly "whitewashed" his Secretary of the Interior. The speedy removal of the youthful inspector Glavis from the service emphasized the indorsement. So we have the "Pinchot-Ballinger Controversy." . . .

[1909]

John L. Mathews

Theodore Roosevelt:
The Natural Resources of the Nation

Theodore Roosevelt (1858-1919), writer, soldier, statesman, and twenty-sixth president of the United States, was a dedicated conservationist and reformer as he sought through his Square Deal programs to make government and business more responsive to the public good. Although known as the "trustbuster," his most significant contributions were toward the preservation of natural resources and phenomena.

The first work I took up when I became President was the work of reclamation. Immediately after I had come to Washington, after the assassination of President McKinley, while staying at the house of my sister, Mrs. Cowles, before going into the White House, [Frederick Hayes] Newell and [Gifford] Pinchot called upon me and laid before me their plans for National irrigation of the arid lands of the West, and for the consolidation of the forest work of the Government in the Bureau of Forestry.

At that time a narrowly legalistic point of view toward natural resources obtained in the Departments, and controlled the Governmental administrative machinery. Through the General Land Office and other Government bureaus, the public resources were being handled and disposed of in accordance with the small considerations of petty legal formalities, instead of for the large purposes of constructive development, and the habit of deciding, whenever possible, in favor of private interests against the public welfare was firmly fixed. It was as little customary to favor the bona-fide settler and home builder, as against the strict construction of the law, as it was to use the law in thwarting the operations of the land grabbers. A technical compliance with the letter of the law was all that was required.

The idea that our natural resources were inexhaustible still obtained, and there was as yet no real knowledge of their extent and condition. The relation of the conservation of natural resources to the problems of National welfare and National efficiency had not yet dawned on the public mind. The reclamation of arid public lands in the West was still a matter for private enterprise alone; and our magnificent river system, with its superb possibilities for public usefulness, was dealt with by the National Government not as a unit, but as a disconnected series of pork-barrel problems, whose only real interest was in their effect on the reëlection or defeat of a Congressman here and there—a theory which, I regret to say, still obtains.

The place of the farmer in the National economy was still regarded solely as that of a grower of food to be eaten by others, while the human needs and interests of himself and his wife and children still remained wholly outside the recognition of the Government.

All the forests which belonged to the United States were held and administered in one Department, and all the foresters in Government employ were in another Department. Forests and foresters had nothing whatever to do with each other. The National Forests in the West (then called forest reserves) were wholly inadequate in area to meet the purposes for which they were created, while the need for forest protection in the East had not yet begun to enter the public mind.

Such was the condition of things when Newell and Pinchot called on me. I was a warm believer in reclamation and in forestry, and, after listening to my two guests, I asked them to prepare material on the subject for me to use in my first message to Congress, of December 3, 1901. This message laid the foundation for the development of irrigation and forestry during the next seven and one-half years. It set forth the new attitude

Theodore Roosevelt

toward the natural resources in the words: "The Forest and water problems are perhaps the most vital internal problems of the United States."

On the day the message was read, a committee of Western Senators and Congressmen was organized to prepare a Reclamation Bill in accordance with the recommendations. By far the most effective of the Senators in drafting and pushing the bill, which became known by his name, was Newlands. The draft of the bill was worked over by me and others at several conferences and revised in important particulars; my active interference was necessary to prevent it from being made unworkable by an undue insistence upon States Rights, in accordance with the efforts of Mr. Mondell and other Congressmen, who consistently fought for local and private interests as against the interests of the people as a whole.

On June 17, 1902, the Reclamation Act was passed. It set aside the proceeds of the disposal of public lands for the purpose of reclaiming the waste areas of the arid West by irrigating lands otherwise worthless, and thus creating new homes upon the land. The money so appropriated was to be repaid to the Government by the settlers, and to be used again as a revolving fund continuously available for the work.

The impatience of the Western people to see immediate results from the Reclamation Act was so great that red tape was disregarded, and the work was pushed forward at a rate previously unknown in Government affairs. Later, as in almost all such cases, there followed the criticisms of alleged illegality and haste which are so easy to make after results have been accomplished and the need for the measures without which nothing could have been done has gone by. These criticisms were in character precisely the same as that made about the acquisition of Panama, the settlement of the anthracite coal strike, the suits against the big trusts, the stopping of the panic of 1907 by the action of the Executive concerning the Tennessee Coal and Iron Company; and, in short, about most of the best work done during my administration.

With the Reclamation work, as with much other work under me, the men in charge were given to understand that they must get into the water if they would learn to swim; and, furthermore, they learned to know that if they acted honestly, and boldly and fearlessly accepted responsibility, I would stand by them to the limit. In this, as in every other case, in the end the boldness of the action fully justified itself.

Every item of the whole great plan of Reclamation now in effect was undertaken between 1902 and 1906. By the spring of 1909 the work was an assured success, and the Government had become fully committed to its continuance. The work of Reclamation was at first under the United States Geological Survey, of which Charles D. Walcott was at that time Director. In the spring of 1908 the United States Reclamation Service was established to carry it on, under the direction of Frederick Hayes Newell, to whom the inception of the plan was due. Newell's single-minded devotion to this great task, the constructive imagination which enabled him to conceive it, and the executive power and high character through which he and his assistant, Arthur P. Davis, built up a model service—all these have

The Natural Resources of the Nation

made him a model servant. The final proof of his merit is supplied by the character and records of the men who later assailed him.

Although the gross expenditure under the Reclamation Act is not yet as large as that for the Panama Canal, the engineering obstacles to be overcome have been almost as great, and the political impediments many times greater. The Reclamation work had to be carried on at widely separated points, remote from railroads, under the most difficult pioneer conditions. The twenty-eight projects begun in the years 1902 and 1906 contemplated the irrigation of more than three million acres and the watering of more than thirty thousand farms. Many of the dams required for this huge task are higher than any previously built anywhere in the world. They feed main-line canals over seven thousand miles in total length, and involve minor constructions, such as culverts and bridges, tens of thousands in number.

What the Reclamation Act has done for the country is by no means limited to its material accomplishment. This Act and the results flowing from it have helped powerfully to prove to the Nation that it can handle its own resources and exercise direct and business-like control over them. The population which the Reclamation Act has brought into the arid West, while comparatively small when compared with that in the more closely inhabited East, has been a most effective contribution to the National life, for it has gone far to transform the social aspect of the West, making for the stability of the institutions upon which the welfare of the whole country rests: it has substituted actual homemakers, who have settled on the land with their families, for huge, migatory bands of sheep herded by the hired shepherds of absentee owners. . . .

When I became President, the Bureau of Forestry (since 1905 the United States Forest Service) was a small but growing organization, under Gifford Pinchot, occupied mainly with laying the foundation of American forestry by scientific study of the forests, and with the promotion of forestry on private lands. It contained all the trained foresters in the Government service, but had charge of no public timberland whatsoever. The Government forest reserves of that day were in the care of a Division in the General Land Office, under the management of clerks wholly without knowledge of forestry, few if any of whom had ever seen a foot of the timberlands for which they were responsible. Thus the reserves were neither well protected nor well used. There were no foresters among the men who had charge of the National Forests, and no Government forests in charge of the Government foresters.

In my first message to Congress I strongly recommended the consolidation of the forest work in the hands of the trained men of the Bureau of Forestry. This recommendation was repeated in other messages, but Congress did not give effect to it until three years later. In the meantime, by thorough study of the Western public timberlands, the groundwork was laid for the responsibilities which were to fall upon the Bureau of Forestry when the care of the National Forests came to be transferred to it. It was

Theodore Roosevelt

evident that trained American Foresters would be needed in considerable numbers, and a forest school was established at Yale to supply them.

In 1901, at my suggestion as President, the Secretary of the Interior, Mr. Hitchcock, made a formal request for technical advice from the Bureau of Forestry in handling the National Forests, and an extensive examination of their condition and needs was accordingly taken up. The same year a study was begun of the proposed Appalachian National Forest, the plan of which, already formulated at that time, has since been carried out. A year later experimental planting on the National Forests was also begun, and studies preparatory to the application of practical forestry to the Indian Reservations were undertaken. In 1903, so rapidly did the public work of the Bureau of Forestry increase, that the examination of land for new forest reserves was added to the study of those already created, the forest lands of the various States were studied, and coöperation with several of them in the examination and handling of their forest lands was undertaken. While these practical tasks were pushed forward, a technical knowledge of American Forests was rapidly accumulated. The special knowledge gained was made public in printed bulletins; and at the same time the Bureau undertook, through the newspaper and periodical press, to make all the people of the United States acquainted with the needs and the purposes of practical forestry. It is doubtful whether there has ever been elsewhere under the Government such effective publicity—publicity purely in the interest of the people—at so low a cost. Before the educational work of the Forest Service was stopped by the Taft Administration, it was securing the publication of facts about forestry in fifty million copies of newspapers a month at a total expense of $6000 a year. Not one cent has ever been paid by the Forest Service to any publication of any kind for the printing of this material. It was given out freely, and published without cost because it was news. Without this publicity the Forest Service could not have survived the attacks made upon it by the representatives of the great special interests in Congress; nor could forestry in America have made the rapid progress it has.

The result of all the work outlined above was to bring together in the Bureau of Forestry, by the end of 1904, the only body of forest experts under the Government, and practically all of the first-hand information about the public forests which was then in existence. In 1905, the obvious foolishness of continuing to separate the foresters and the forests, reënforced by the action of the First National Forest Congress, held in Washington, brought about the Act of February 1, 1905, which transferred the National Forests from the care of the Interior Department to the Department of Agriculture, and resulted in the creation of the present United States Forest Service.

The men upon whom the responsibility of handling some sixty million acres of National Forest lands was thus thrown were ready for the work, both in the office and in the field, because they had been preparing for it for more than five years. Without delay they proceeded, under the leadership of Pinchot, to apply to the new work the principles they had already formulated. One of these was to open all the resources of the National Forests to regulated use. Another was that of putting every part of the land to that use in which it would best serve the public. Following this principle, the Act of June 11, 1906, was drawn, and its passage was secured from Congress. This law throws open to settlement all land in the National Forests that is found, on examination, to be chiefly valuable for agriculture. Hitherto all such land had been closed to the settler.

The principles thus formulated and applied may be summed up in the statement that the rights of the public to the natural resources outweigh private rights, and must be given its first consideration. Until that time, in dealing with the National Forests, and the public lands generally, private rights had almost uniformly been allowed to over-balance public rights. The change we made was right, and was vitally necessary; but, of course, it created bitter opposition from private interests.

One of the principles whose application was the source of much hostility was this: It is better for the Government to help a poor man to make a living for his family than to help a rich man make more profit for his company. This principle was too sound to be fought openly. It is the kind of principle to which politicians delight to pay unctuous homage in words. But we translated the words into deeds; and when they found that this was the case, many rich men, especially sheep owners, were stirred to hostility, and they used the Congressmen they controlled to assault us—getting most aid from certain demagogues, who were equally glad improperly to denounce rich men in public and improperly to serve them in private. The Forest Service established and enforced regulations which favored the settler as against the large stock owner; required that necessary reductions in the stock grazed on any National Forest should bear first on the big man, before the few head of the small man, upon which the living of his family depended, were reduced; and made grazing in the National Forests a help, instead of a hindrance, to permanent settlement. As a result, the small settlers and their families became, on the whole, the best friends the Forest Service has; although in places their ignorance was played on by demagogues to influence them against the policy that was primarily for their own interest.

Another principle which led to the bitterest antagonism of all was this—whoever (except a bona-fide settler) takes public property for private profit should pay for what he gets. In the effort to apply this principle, the Forest Service obtained a decision from the Attorney-General that it was legal to make the men who grazed sheep and cattle on the National Forests pay for what they got. Accordingly, in the summer of 1906, for the first time, such a charge was made; and, in the face of the bitterest opposition, it was collected.

Up to the time the National Forests were put under the charge of the Forest Service, the Interior Department had made no effort to establish public regulation and control of water powers. Upon the transfer, the Service immediately began its fight to handle the power resources of the National Forests so as to prevent speculation and monopoly and to yield a

Theodore Roosevelt

fair return to the Government. On May 1, 1906, an Act was passed granting the use of certain power sites in Southern California to the Edison Electric Power Company, which Act, at the suggestion of the Service, limited the period of the permit to forty years, and required the payment of an annual rental by the company, the same conditions which were thereafter adopted by the Service as the basis for all permits for power development. Then began a vigorous fight against the position of the Service by the water-power interests. The right to charge for water-power development was, however, sustained by the Attorney-General.

In 1907, the area of the National Forests was increased by Presidential proclamation more than forty-three million acres; the plant necessary for the full use of the Forests, such as roads, trails, and telephone lines, began to be provided on a large scale; the interchange of field and office men, so as to prevent the antagonism between them, which is so destructive of efficiency in most great businesses, was established as a permanent policy; and the really effective management of the enormous area of the National Forests began to be secured.

With all this activity in the field, the progress of technical forestry and popular education was not neglected. In 1907, for example, sixty-one publications on various phases of forestry, with a total of more than a million copies, were issued, as against three publications, with a total of eighty-two thousand copies, in 1901. By this time, also, the opposition of the servants of the special interests in Congress to the Forest Service had become strongly developed, and more time appeared to be spent in the yearly attacks upon it during the passage of the appropriation bills than on all other Government Bureaus put together. Every year the Forest Service had to fight for its life. . . .

By 1908, the fire prevention work of the Forest Service had become so successful that eighty-six per cent of the fires that did occur were held down to an area of five acres or less, and the timber sales, which yielded $60,000 in 1905, in 1908 produced $850,000. In the same year, in addition to the work of the National Forests, the responsibility for the proper handling of Indian timberlands was laid upon the Forest Service, where it remained with great benefit to the Indians until it was withdrawn, as a part of the attack on the Conservation policy made after I left office.

By March 4, 1909, nearly half a million acres of agricultural land in the National Forests had been opened to settlement under the Act of June 11, 1906. The business management of the Forest Service became so excellent, thanks to the remarkable executive capacity of the Associate Forester, Overton W. Price (removed after I left office), that it was declared by a well-known firm of business organizers to compare favorably with the best managed of the great private corporations, an opinion which was confirmed by the report of a Congressional investigation, and by the report of the Presidential Committee on Department method. The area of the National Forests had increased from 43 to 194 million acres; the force from about 500 to more than 3000. There was saved for public use in the National Forests more Government timberland during the seven and a half years

The Natural Resources of the Nation

prior to March 4, 1909, than during all previous and succeeding years put together.

The idea that the Executive is the steward of the public welfare was first formulated and given practical effect in the Forest Service by its law officer, George Woodruff. The laws were often insufficient, and it became well nigh impossible to get them amended in the public interest when once the representatives of privilege in Congress grasped the fact that I would sign no amendment that contained anything not in the public interest. It was necessary to use what law was already in existence, and then further to supplement it by Executive action. The practice of examining every claim to public land before passing it into private ownership offers a good example of the policy in question. This practice, which has since become general, was first applied in the National Forests. Enormous areas of valuable public timberland were thereby saved from fraudulent acquisition; more than 250,000 acres were thus saved in a single case.

This theory of stewardship in the interest of the public was well illustrated by the establishment of a water-power policy. Until the Forest Service changed the plan, water-powers on the navigable streams, on the public domain, and in the National Forests were given away for nothing, and substantially without question, to whoever asked for them. At last, under the principle that public property should be paid for and should not be permanently granted away when such permanent grant is avoidable, the Forest Service established the policy of regulating the use of power in the National Forests in the public interest and making a charge for value received. This was the beginning of the water-power policy now substantially accepted by the public, and doubtless soon to be enacted into law. But there was at the outset violent opposition to it on the part of the water-power companies, and such representatives of their views in Congress as Messrs. Tawney and Bede.

Many bills were introduced in Congress aimed, in one way or another, at relieving the power companies of control and payment. When these bills reached me I refused to sign them; and the injury to the public interest which would follow their passage was brought sharply to public attention in my message of February 26, 1908. The bills made no further progress.

Under the same principle of stewardship, railroads and other corporations, which applied for and were given rights in the National Forests, were regulated in the use of those rights. In short, the public resources in charge of the Forest Service were handled frankly and openly for the public welfare under the clear-cut and clearly set forth principle that the public rights come first and private interest second.

The natural result of this new attitude was the assertion in every form by the representatives of special interests that the Forest Service was exceeding its legal powers and thwarting the intention of Congress. Suits were begun wherever the chance arose. It is worth recording that, in spite of the novelty and complexity of the legal questions it had to face, no court of last resort has ever decided against the Forest Service. This state-

Theodore Roosevelt

ment includes two unanimous decisions by the Supreme Court of the United States (U. S. *vs.* Grimaud, 220 U. S., 506, and Light *vs.* U. S., 220 U. S., 523).

In its administration of the National Forests, the Forest Service found that valuable coal lands were in danger of passing into private ownership without adequate money return to the Government and without safeguard against monopoly; and that existing legislation was insufficient to prevent this. When this condition was brought to my attention I withdrew from all forms of entry about sixty-eight million acres of coal land in the United States, including Alaska. The refusal of Congress to act in the public interest was solely responsible for keeping these lands from entry.

The Conservation movement was a direct outgrowth of the forest movement. It was nothing more than the application to our other natural resources of the principles which had been worked out in connection with the forests. Without the basis of public sentiment which had been built up for the protection of the forests, and without the example of public foresight in the protection of this, one of the great natural resources, the Conservation movement would have been impossible. The first formal step was the creation of the Inland Waterways Commission, appointed on March 14, 1907. In my letter appointing the Commission, I called attention to the value of our streams as great natural resources, and to the need for a progressive plan for their development and control, and said: "It is not possible to properly frame so large a plan as this for the control of our rivers without taking account of the orderly development of other natural resources. Therefore I ask that the Inland Waterways Commission shall consider the relations of the streams to the use of all the great permanent natural resources and their conservation for the making and maintenance of prosperous homes."

Over a year later, writing on the report of the Commission, I said:

"The preliminary Report of the Inland Waterways Commission was excellent in every way. It outlines a general plan of waterway improvement which when adopted will give assurance that the improvements will yield practical results in the way of increased navigation and water transportation. In every essential feature the plan recommended by the Commission is new. In the principle of coördinating all uses of the waters and treating each waterway system as a unit; in the principle of correlating water traffic with rail and other land traffic; in the principle of expert initiation of projects in accordance with commercial foresight and the needs of a growing country; and in the principle of coöperation between the States and the Federal Government in the administration and use of waterways, etc.; the general plan proposed by the Commission is new, and at the same time sane and simple. The plan deserves unqualified support. I regret that it has not yet been adopted by Congress, but I am confident that ultimately it will be adopted." . . .

The things accomplished that have been enumerated above were of immediate consequence to the economic well-being of our people. In addition certain things were done of which the economic bearing was more remote, but which bore directly upon our welfare, because they add to the beauty of living and therefore to the joy of life. Securing a great artist, Saint-Gaudens, to give us the most beautiful coinage since the decay of Hellenistic Greece was one such act. In this case I had power myself to direct the Mint to employ Saint-Gaudens. The first, and most beautiful, of his coins were issued in thousands before Congress assembled or could intervene; and a great and permanent improvement was made in the beauty of the coinage. In the same way, on the advice and suggestion of Frank Millet, we got some really capital medals by sculptors of the first rank. Similarly, the new buildings in Washington were erected and placed in proper relation to one another, on plans provided by the best architects and landscape architects. I also appointed a Fine Arts Council, an unpaid body of the best architects, painters, and sculptors in the country, to advise the Government as to the erection and decoration of all new buildings. The "pork-barrel" Senators and Congressmen felt for this body an instinctive, and perhaps from their standpoint a natural, hostility; and my successor a couple of months after taking office revoked the appointment and disbanded the Council.

Even more important was the taking of steps to preserve from destruction beautiful and wonderful wild creatures whose existence was threatened by greed and wantonness. During the seven and a half years closing on March 4, 1909, more was accomplished for the protection of wild life in the United States than during all the previous years, excepting only the creation of the Yellowstone National Park. The record includes the creation of five National Parks—Crater Lake, Oregon; Wind Cave, South Dakota; Platt, Oklahoma; Sully Hill, North Dakota, and Mesa Verde, Colorado; four big game refuges in Oklahoma, Arizona, Montana, and Washington; fifty-one bird reservations; and the enactment of laws for the protection of wild life in Alaska, the District of Columbia, and on National bird reserves. These measures may be briefly enumerated as follows:

The enactment of the first game laws for the Territory of Alaska in 1902 and 1908, resulting in the regulation of the export of heads and trophies of big game and puting an end to the slaughter of deer for hides along the southern coast of the Territory.

The securing in 1902 of the first appropriation for the preservation of buffalo and the establishment in the Yellowstone National Park of the first and now the largest herd of buffalo belonging to the Government.

The passage of the Act of January 24, 1905, creating the Wichita Game Preserves, the first of the National game preserves. In 1907, 12,000 acres of this preserve were inclosed with a woven wire fence for the reception of the herd of fifteen buffalo donated by the New York Zoölogical Society.

The passage of the Act of June 29, 1906, providing for the establishment of the Grand Cañon Game Preserve of Arizona, now comprising 1,492,928 acres.

The passage of the National Monuments Act of June 8, 1906, under which a number of objects of scientific interest have been preserved for all

Theodore Roosevelt

time. Among the Monuments created are Muir Woods, Pinnacles National Monument in California and the Mount Olympus National Monument, Washington, which form important refuges for game.

The passage of the Act of June 30, 1906, regulating shooting in the District of Columbia and making three-fourths of the environs of the National Capital within the District in effect a National Refuge.

The passage of the Act of May 23, 1908, providing for the establishment of the National Bison Range in Montana. This range comprises about 18,000 acres of land formerly in the Flathead Indian Reservation, on which is now established a herd of eighty buffalo, a nucleus of which was donated to the Government by the American Bison Society.

The issue of the Order protecting birds on the Niobrara Military Reservation, Nebraska, in 1908, making this entire reservation in effect a bird reservation.

The establishment by Executive Order between March 14, 1903, and March 4, 1909, of fifty-one National Bird Reservations distributed in seventeen States and Territories from Porto Rico to Hawaii and Alaska. The creation of these reservations at once placed the United States in the front rank in the world work of bird protection. Among these reservations are the celebrated Pelican Island rookery in Indian River, Florida; The Mosquito Inlet Reservation, Florida, the northernmost home of the manatee; the extensive marshes bordering Klamath and Malheur Lakes in Oregon, formerly the scene of slaughter of ducks for market and ruthless destruction of plume birds for the millinery trade; the Tortugas Key, Florida, where, in connection with the Carnegie Institute, experiments have been made on the homing instinct of birds; and the great bird colonies on Laysan and sister islets in Hawaii, some of the greatest colonies of sea birds in the world.

[1913]

Edwin Arlington Robinson:

Sonnet

Edwin Arlington Robinson (1869-1935), considered in the 1920s America's greatest living poet, was avowedly modern in tone. Firmly rooted in objective reality, he rarely becomes obscure, emphasizing instead the fleeting, unhappy nature of man's life.

Oh for a poet—for a beacon bright
To rift this changeless glimmer of dead gray;
To spirit back the Muses, long astray,
And flush Parnassus with a newer light;
To put these little sonnet-men to flight
Who fashion, in a shrewd mechanic way,
Songs without souls, that flicker for a day,
To vanish in irrevocable night.

What does it mean, this barren age of ours?
Here are the men, the women, and the flowers,
The seasons, and the sunset, as before.
What does it mean? Shall there not one arise
To wrench one banner from the western skies,
And mark it with his name forevermore?

[1897]

Edwin Arlington Robinson

Vachel Lindsay:
A Gospel of Beauty

Factory Windows Are Always Broken

Vachel Lindsay (1879-1931), visionary poet, mystic, and reformer, distinguished clearly between the American ideal and its reality, but he saw no reason that would prevent men from making the ideal real. He insisted this achievement could come about only through man's determination to resist and defeat corruption.

A GOSPEL OF BEAUTY

I. The Proud Farmer

[In memory of E. S. Frazee, Rush County, Indiana.]

Into the acres of the newborn state
He poured his strength, and plowed his ancient name,
And, when the traders followed him, he stood
Towering above their furtive souls and tame.

That brow without a stain, that fearless eye
Oft left the passing stranger wondering
To find such knighthood in the sprawling land,
To see a democrat well-nigh a king.

He lived with liberal hand, with guests from far,
With talk and joke and fellowship to spare,—
Watching the wide world's life from sun to sun,
Lining his walls with books from everywhere.

He read by night, he built his world by day.
The farm and house of God to him were one.
For forty years he preached and plowed and wrought—
A statesman in the fields, who bent to none.

His plowmen-neighbors were as lords to him.
His was an ironside, democratic pride.
He served a rigid Christ, but served him well—
And, for a lifetime, saved the countryside.

Here lie the dead, who gave the church their best
Under his fiery preaching of the word.
They sleep with him beneath the ragged grass . . .
The village withers, by his voice unstirred.

And tho' his tribe be scattered to the wind
From the Atlantic to the China sea,
Yet do they think of that bright lamp he burned
Of family worth and proud integrity.

And many a sturdy grandchild hears his name
In reverence spoken, till he feels akin
To all the lion-eyed who built the world—
And lion-dreams begin to burn within.

Vachel Lindsay

II. The Illinois Village

O you who lose the art of hope,
Whose temples seem to shrine a lie,
Whose sidewalks are but stones of fear,
Who weep that Liberty must die,
Turn to the little prairie towns,
Your higher hope shall yet begin.
On every side awaits you there
Some gate where glory enters in.
Yet when I see the flocks of girls,
Watching the Sunday train go thro'
(As tho' the whole wide world went by)
With eyes that long to travel too,
I sigh, despite my soul made glad
By cloudy dresses and brown hair,
Sigh for the sweet life wrenched and torn
By thundering commerce, fierce and bare.
Nymphs of the wheat these girls should be:
Kings of the grove, their lovers strong.
Why are they not inspired, aflame?
This beauty calls for valiant song—
For men to carve these fairy-forms
And faces in a fountain-frieze;
Dancers that own immortal hours;
Painters that work upon their knees;
Maids, lovers, friends, so deep in life,
So deep in love and poet's deeds,
The railroad is a thing disowned,
The city but a field of weeds.

Who can pass a village church
By night in these clean prairie lands
Without a touch of Spirit-power?
So white and fixed and cool it stands—
A thing from some strange fairy-town,
A pious amaranthine flower,
Unsullied by the winds, as pure
As jade or marble, wrought this hour:—
Rural in form, foursquare and plain,
And yet our sister, the new moon,
Makes it a praying wizard's dream.
The trees that watch at dusty noon
Breaking its sharpest lines, veil not
The whiteness it reflects from God,
Flashing like Spring on many an eye,
Making clean flesh, that once was clod.

A Gospel of Beauty

Who can pass a district school
Without the hope that there may wait
Some baby-heart the books shall flame
With zeal to make his playmates great,
To make the whole wide village gleam
A strangely carved celestial gem,
Eternal in its beauty-light,
The Artist's town of Bethlehem!

Let not our town be large, remembering
That little Athens was the Muses' home,
That Oxford rules the heart of London still,
That Florence gave the Renaissance to Rome.

Record it for the grandson of your son—
A city is not builded in a day:
Our little town cannot complete her soul
Till countless generations pass away.

Now let each child be joined as to a church
To her perpetual hopes, each man ordained:
Let every street be made a reverent aisle
Where Music grows and Beauty is unchained.

Let Science and Machinery and Trade
Be slaves of her, and make her all in all,
Building against our blatant, restless time
An unseen, skilful, medieval wall.

Let every citizen be rich toward God.
Let Christ the beggar, teach divinity.
Let no man rule who holds his money dear.
Let this, our city, be our luxury.

We should build parks that students from afar
Would choose to starve in, rather than go home,
Fair little squares, with Phidian ornament,
Food for the spirit, milk and honeycomb.

Songs shall be sung by us in that good day,
Songs we have written, blood within the rhyme
Beating, as when Old England still was glad,—
The purple, rich Elizabethan time.

Say, is my prophecy too fair and far?
I only know, unless her faith be high,
The soul of this, our Nineveh, is doomed,
Our little Babylon will surely die.

Vachel Lindsay

Some city on the breast of Illinois
No wiser and no better at the start
By faith shall rise redeemed, by faith shall rise
Bearing the western glory in her heart.

The genius of the Maple, Elm and Oak,
The secret hidden in each grain of corn,
The glory that the prairie angels sing
At night when sons of Life and Love are born,

Born but to struggle, squalid and alone,
Broken and wandering in their early years.
When will they make our dusty streets their goal,
Within our attics hide their sacred tears?

When will they start our vulgar blood athrill
With living language, words that set us free?
When will they make a path of beauty clear
Between our riches and our liberty?

We must have many Lincoln-hearted men.
A city is not builded in a day.
And they must do their work, and come and go
While countless generations pass away.

[1908?]

FACTORY WINDOWS ARE ALWAYS BROKEN

Factory windows are always broken.
Somebody's always throwing bricks,
Somebody's always heaving cinders,
Playing ugly Yahoo tricks.

Factory windows are always broken.
Other windows are let alone.
No one throws through the chapel-window
The bitter, snarling, derisive stone.

Factory windows are always broken.
Something or other is going wrong.
Something is rotten—I think, in Denmark.
End of the factory-window song.

[1914]

Carl Sandburg:

Chicago

Carl Sandburg (1878-1967), historian, biographer of Lincoln, folk singer, and poet, firmly rooted in the American experience and language, was simultaneously fascinated and repulsed by the phenomena of the new mass industrial age. His poem "Chicago" (1914) captures that attitude in a dissonant reflection of the city that inspired it.

Hog Butcher for the World,
Tool Maker, Stacker of Wheat,
Player with Railroads and the Nation's Freight Handler;
Stormy, husky, brawling,
City of the Big Shoulders:

They tell me you are wicked and I believe them, for I have seen your
painted women under the gas lamps luring the farm boys.
And they tell me you are crooked and I answer: Yes, it is true I have
seen the gunman kill and go free to kill again.
And they tell me you are brutal and my reply is: On the faces of women
and children I have seen the marks of wanton hunger.
And having answered so I turn once more to those who sneer at this my
city, and I give them back the sneer and say to them:

Come and show me another city with lifted head singing so proud to be
alive and coarse and strong and cunning.
Flinging magnetic curses amid the toil of piling job on job, here is a tall
bold slugger set vivid against the little soft cities;
Fierce as a dog with tongue lapping for action, cunning as a savage pitted
against the wilderness,
Bareheaded,
Shoveling,
Wrecking,
Planning,
Building, breaking, rebuilding,
Under the smoke, dust all over his mouth, laughing with white teeth,
Under the terrible burden of destiny laughing as a young man laughs,
Laughing even as an ignorant fighter laughs who has never lost a battle,
Bragging and laughing that under his wrist is the pulse, and under his
ribs the heart of the people,
Laughing!
Laughing the stormy, husky, brawling laughter of Youth, half-naked,
sweating, proud to be Hog Butcher, Tool Maker, Stacker of Wheat,
Player with Railroads and Freight Handler to the Nation.

[1916]

Carl Sandburg

W. E. B. Du Bois:

The Song of the Smoke

William Edward Burghardt Du Bois (1868-1963), intellectual and father of various black intellectual, scholarly, and militant movements, made his best-known contributions as a historian and professor. His classic work is *Souls of Black Folk* (1903). A Marxist, he died in Ghana.

I am the smoke king,
I am black.
I am swinging in the sky.
I am ringing worlds on high:
I am the thought of the throbbing mills,
I am the soul toil kills,
I am the ripple of trading rills,

Up I'm curling from the sod,
I am whirling home to God.
I am the smoke king,
I am black.

I am the smoke king,
I am black.
I am wreathing broken hearts,
I am sheathing devils' darts;
Dark inspiration of iron times,
Wedding the toil of toiling climes
Shedding the blood of bloodless crimes.

Down I lower in the blue,
Up I tower toward the true,
I am the smoke king,
I am black.

I am the smoke king,
I am black.

I am darkening with song,
I am hearkening to wrong;
I will be black as blackness can,
The blacker the mantle the mightier the man,
My purpl'ing midnights no day dawn may ban.

I am carving God in night,
I am painting hell in white.
I am the smoke king,
I am black.

I am the smoke king,
I am black.

I am cursing ruddy morn,
I am nursing hearts unborn;
Souls unto me are as mists in the night,

W. E. B. Du Bois

I whiten my blackmen, I beckon my white,
What's the hue of a hide to a man in his might!

Sweet Christ, pity toiling lands!
Hail to the smoke king,
Hail to the black!

[1899]

The Song of the Smoke

Paul Laurence Dunbar:
To the Miami

Paul Laurence Dunbar (1872-1906), popular, prolific, and famous black poet, published four novels, four collections of short stories, and six volumes of poetry. Equally adept at formal and colloquial writing, he wrote verse in both styles. His best poetry appears in *Lyrics of Lowly Life* (1896).

Kiss me, Miami, thou most constant one!
   I love thee more for that thou changest not.
When Winter comes with frigid blast,
Or when the blithesome Spring is past
   And Summer's here with sunshine hot,
Or in sere Autumn, thou hast still the pow'r
To charm alike, whate'er the hour.

Kiss me, Miami, with thy dewy lips;
   Throbs fast my heart e'en as thine own breast beats.
My soul doth rise as rise thy waves,
As each on each the dark shore laves
   And breaks in ripples and retreats.
There is a poem in thine every phase;
Thou still hast sung through all thy days.

Tell me, Miami, how it was with thee
   When years ago Tecumseh in his prime
His birch boat o'er thy waters sent,
And pitched upon thy banks his tent.
   In that long-gone, poetic time,
Did some bronze bard thy flowing stream sit by
And sing thy praises, e'en as I?

Did some bronze lover 'neath this dark old tree
   Whisper of love unto his Indian maid?
And didst thou list his murmurs deep,
And in thy bosom safely keep
   The many raging vows they said?
Or didst thou tell to fish and frog and bird
The raptured scenes that there occurred?

But, O dear stream, what volumes thou couldst tell
   To all who know thy language as I do,
Of life and love and jealous hate!
But now to tattle were too late,—
   Thou who hast ever been so true.
Tell not to every passing idler here
All those sweet tales that reached thine ear.

But, silent stream, speak out and tell me this:
   I say that men and things are still the same;
Were men as bold to do and dare?
Were women then as true and fair?
   Did poets seek celestial flame,
The hero die to gain a laureled brow,
And women suffer, then as now?

[c. 1905]

Paul Laurence Dunbar

4

Visions of Hope and Despair

With the opening of the twentieth century, America became, however reluctantly, an empire and a world power. During the last years of the nineteenth century, the United States had acquired the Hawaiian Islands, the Philippines, and various other Pacific islands, making it a major Pacific power with colonies on the shores of Asia; and it had acquired Puerto Rico and in practice controlled Cuba, thus reaching into the Caribbean. In a few years it was destined to control the Isthmus of Panama and construct a canal between the Atlantic and the Pacific, a task and a dream that had frustrated earlier empires.

With the rise of empire, American industrial development increased under the protection of the McKinley Tariff, until it was essentially ready to compete in foreign markets while its home markets remained secure. Theodore Roosevelt's administrations were significant for their emphasis on belated but important measures of conservation, of government reform, particularly in the cities, and of increased emphasis upon protection for the consumer of foods and drugs in interestate commerce. They were also years of nationalistic pride and of industrial growth, in spite of the panic of 1907, further evidence of the need for reform.

Nevertheless, America's fascination with empire quickly faded; Cuba became at least nominally free; and prolonged attempts at "pacification" of the Philippines led to plans for their ultimate independence. Never before had a new empire begun to dismantle itself even before it had savored its winning. However, the emphasis upon America's heritage of the past, including the eighteenth-century concepts of natural rights and human equality and the nineteenth-century egalitarian spirit, made clear to sensitive Americans that manifest destiny and natural pride, however appealing, had no place in the policies of a country that still professed to believe in its idealistic heritage. Nationalistic pride continued, and Roosevelt's concept of America as a world power became a cornerstone of his philosophy of government. But the majority of Americans, for more than a century distrustful of the foreign entanglements against which George Washington had warned and conscious of the unfinished domestic reforms, chose to turn their backs on the logical results of Roosevelt's dream of the twentieth century as an American one.

His battles with traditional Republican leadership won, and the party firmly in his control, Roosevelt chose his heir, William Howard Taft, as a caretaker and went abroad, confident that his carefully controlled progressivism would continue to prevail. But with Roosevelt out of the country and the resurgence of the Republican regulars and Democratic midterm gains, reform began to give way to political expediency and traditional alliances. By 1912, when Roosevelt sought to reassert his control of the party and replace Taft as its candidate, it was too late, and the Progressive party was formed under Roosevelt's personal guidance.

The three-way election of 1912 was to be the last for twenty years in which reform was a major issue. With the Republicans split, historical precedent indicated a Democratic victory, and the nomination, with the support of William Jennings Bryan, went to Woodrow Wilson, scholar

The Vision of Hope and Despair

and governor of New Jersey. Wilson's election on a reform platform that he had begun to call the "New Freedom" indicated that major American concern would once more be domestic, with the focal point of Wilson's attention the means whereby the new industrial-urban environment might be brought under control by a powerful government for the benefit of all Americans.

Wilson's plans were ambitious, starting with governmental control of the financial structure of the country and extending to the improvement of working conditions in factories and mines. His purpose, made clear in an extended analogy, was to construct a new American society in which the new industrialism would be forced to mesh with traditional American values of democracy, liberty, and equality, working as a perfectly functioning machine that would produce freedom for all. Traditional American values were sound, he insisted, but the means of preserving and protecting them, defined by Jefferson in an agricultural society more than a century before, were no longer workable. It was his goal to construct new means to curb private and corporate power and to spread the benefits of industrialism.

Wilson's program, considered dangerously radical not only by conservatives but also by Theodore Roosevelt, never had a fair opportunity to succeed. By the fall of 1914 Europe was at war. In spite of American neutrality, this danger, together with continued unrest in Mexico, made it clear that whether America chose to remain aloof or not, the outcome would be the same. As a major power, it could not withdraw from its international ventures, and ultimately it would be forced into conflict with one or more belligerents. By 1916, in spite of Wilson's reelection slogan, "He kept us out of war," we had already invaded Mexico to punish Pancho Villa's irregulars, and the threat of conflict with Germany at sea was potentially explosive.

Although America's neutrality was more apparent than real, and Wilson's attention was primarily devoted to the international situation, the election of 1916 became another battle of progressives, with Charles Evans Hughes the Republican candidate. Wilson was narrowly reelected, and although he reemphasized his concern with domestic problems and neutrality, little more than a month after his inauguration he asked Congress for a declaration of war against Germany. Once more America had acknowledged its role as a world power, and in so doing brought the end of attempts to reform the American environment for that time. The progressive spirit had prevailed for a generation; it was to spend the next decade in retreat before national crisis and popular demand once more made it a political issue.

Wilsonian international idealism went the way of reform, followed by Harding complacency and corruption, Coolidge indifference, and Hoover despair. The seriousness of the economic collapse after the stock market crash of 1929 was an abrupt awakening, accompanied by belated recognition of the price America had paid in depleted resources and displaced human lives. This intensified the suffering of the times, suffering that had to be alleviated immediately, even before economic reconstruction could begin. Basic to action was identifying the abuses of the age, which had gone unnoticed and untreated for a generation that was the period of the greatest prosperity that America had ever known, ostensibly for everyone, but actually for a few.

The nature of the neglect of the environment, the continued despoiling of a continent, largely through greed, but also because of ignorance and obstinance, was made clear on the most obvious level by Sherwood Anderson. In the previous decade, in *Windy McPherson's Son* (1916), *Winesburg, Ohio* (1919), *Poor White* (1920), and other works, he had defined the price paid in human terms for progress and the domination of material values. In "I'll Say We've Done Well" he examined his native state of Ohio, depicting in microcosm the debasement of the nation.

Anderson's tone was ironic, and it indicated agreement with Sinclair Lewis and others of his contemporaries that there was little to be done about the blight of the countryside except to watch it grow. With government pledged to business values during much of the decade in which he wrote, he was right. But in 1932 the depression brought a change at the polls and in the guiding philosophy of the nation in many ways as revolutionary as that of 1800. At the heart of that change was a determination to act, to apply intelligence to obvious problems, and to try to resolve them, if not in one way, then in another. The revolution of 1932 did not bring about a new idealism, but it introduced pragmatism as a major force in American political life for the first time.

Although Franklin Roosevelt was elected on a conventional platform, his attitude toward the relationship between government and the environment had been made clear during his tenure as governor of New York. In essence a continuation of Woodrow Wilson's New Freedom, his concept of government planning, applied to land utilization for the public benefit, was to provide the theoretical foundations for the New Deal and for such specific conservation programs as the Civilian Conservation Corps and the Tennessee Valley Authority. To reinforce the capabilities of his administration for such change, he brought to his cabinet men who reflected his views, among them Henry A. Wallace, the most rational, dedicated, and experimental of America's secretaries of agriculture.

But concern for the countryside and for the people who live in it was not merely a major interest of political leaders during the 1930s; writers of fiction continued American involvement with the nature of the environment, rediscovering both the mystic experience and the harsh reality of man in nature. Thomas Wolfe's attempt to recreate the subjective American experience in a series of sprawling novels permitted a resurgence of emotional identification with America virtually unknown since Walt Whitman, as he fused man and nature, time and technology, in works of vital feeling and energy that recreate a romantic microcosm.

Out of a series of novels styled "proletarian" because they accepted the dictates of Marxian criticism and attempted to project Marxian realism and social consciousness out of the failure of the American system, few

The Vision of Hope and Despair

survive. Each of the survivors rises above the dogmatic limitations of the movement. The greatest of these and the most eloquent human document of the decade of the depression as well as the most profound statement of hope growing from despair was John Steinbeck's *The Grapes of Wrath*. An epic work, it records the abuse of land and of men and defines what is ultimately man's only hope for survival in the face of a dehumanized system afraid of a people driven by hunger and pride.

Optimism in the face of despair and the search for identity and fulfillment within the context of an urban technological society, defined by Steinbeck and Wolfe, were characteristic of many writers' concern as the depression of the thirties faded under the impetus of pragmatic experiment and war. At the same time, the new optimism, a low-level post-Darwinian romanticism, continued, as the reform impulse faded in World War II, prosperity, international responsibilities, and a cold war that sometimes became hot, as in Korea and Vietnam. Sherwood Anderson's disgust with the despoliation of Ohio a decade before gave way to hope during the depression as he toured the South and the Upper Midwest gathering data for *Puzzled America*. Particularly impressing to him as indications of progress and promise for the future were the Civilian Conservation Corps camps and the uplifting of an entire region through the Tennessee Valley Authority.

Donald Culross Peattie suggests in *A Prairie Grove* that the passage of time, the cycles of nature, and the migrations of living things are not, as the earlier naturalists would have it, a sign of human helplessness; they are instead symbols of hope, of permanence even in change. The passing of the passenger pigeon, regretful though it is as a sign of man's greed, is nevertheless indicative of the nature of that cycle. Consequently, man, who populates and cherishes the earth, is acting not in accordance with some obscure morality, but with the forces that join nature and man together.

But hope lies not only in the fact of natural change itself, nor does it lie alone in the objective, rational planning of governmental agencies. Rather, man's hope for a meaningful relationship with a healthy natural environment lies in joining the two—natural acceptance and intelligent direction—in a new partnership. This was the conclusion of a good many writers, many of whom joined in a return to the farm movement as profound in its way in the 1930s and 1940s as the flight to Paris had been for writers of the twenties. Sherwood Anderson had marked the way by fleeing to a Virginia farm in the 1920s; Charles Allen Smart moved to a farm in the hills of southern Ohio in the thirties and produced the best-selling *R.F.D.* (1938). Louis Bromfield, perhaps the most famous and successful of them all, in writing and in farming, moved to rural Ohio when World War II drove him from rural France. One of the most promising writers of the 1920s, his fiction fell into critical disfavor in the thirties, but he wrote a series of first-rate books based on his agricultural theories and experience in the forties and fifties. "The Cycle of a Farm Pond" is typical not only of his writing in that genre, but of his favorite

Introduction

theory—that man must learn to live within the laws of nature if he and his species are to survive on an abused planet.

Joseph Wood Krutch was, like many of the others—except Bromfield, who considered himself a dirt farmer—a naturalist by avocation rather than profession, although he became a fine, perceptive nature writer. His wide-ranging work shows, no less truly than the romantics of an earlier century, the affinity that Americans, and particularly American writers, have for nature, although he deprecates the idea himself. Nevertheless he recognizes, perhaps more clearly than others, the sense of incompleteness that afflicts modern man in the artificial environment that has come to dominate his life. Although he asserts that salvation lies in the study of politics, sociology, and economics, he makes clear that fulfillment comes when man finds wonder and inspiration in the natural world of which he is a part.

Nevertheless Krutch anticipates a major emphasis of the ecological movement of the 1970s as he insists that man cannot save himself from his artificial environment, but that he must find salvation within it, as Woodrow Wilson had asserted a half-century before. A generation of Americans since World War II has attempted to be of but not in modern civilization as they fled to the suburbs, to find there a plethora of blessings and frustrations. Works ranging from Richard Yates's excellent novel *Revolutionary Road* to sociological studies such as Maurice Stein's "Suburbia—A Walk on the Mild Side" have attempted to define this new environmental phenomenon, with varying degrees of precision, objectivity, and success. They are, however, convinced that the suburb is a significant part of contemporary American reality. Praised and condemned, loved and hated, it is here to stay.

As a technique, the sociological-psychological approach to studying the modern environment, whether in fact or fiction, is the most significant development in analyses of the 1960s. As in the biological studies of Rachel Carson and other gifted nature writers, this approach uses the method if not the mechanisms of science. At the same time, in spite of the publicity reaped by those who have elected to drop out of modern American society, particularly by living in rural, often isolated communes, the majority of American writers today are convinced that man must find whatever fulfillment he can within the confines of mass technological society. They are almost invariably convinced also that that environment can be made rewarding.

Many of them, such as Norman Mailer, choose to live in the cities, and Mailer himself was a candidate for mayor of New York City. Nevertheless, dehumanization, lack of imagination, and intellectual stagnation are as much aspects of urban blight and decay as the more publicized ghettos, as Mailer points out in his comments on the new architecture of the cities. The cities, he makes clear, are worthy of man's highest talents, but they have not received that attention.

But the sixties did not merely continue and intensify the American writer's concern with his environment; instead, they introduced a note of

The Vision of Hope and Despair

apprehension, an awareness of the imminence of natural disaster if man did not reverse what seemed to be an insane determination to destroy his environment. Rachel Carson in *Silent Spring* (1962) defined what might come about and cited evidence to support her fears; Lynn White, Jr., explored the origin of the threat in the nature of man and his cultural heritage in "The Historical Roots of our Ecologic Crisis" (1967); and Paul R. Ehrlich projected present patterns of behavior into future reality in "Eco-Catastrophe!" (1969), the ultimate warning in tones that have been responsible for the present state of alarm and resolutions to stave off disaster through intelligent action.

The alarms, the fears, and the sense of despair engendered by the imminent death of Lake Erie and the poisoning of the atmosphere, combined with the decay of the cities and the sterility of the suburbs, whether projected by the mass media or by contemporary writers, have been examined and defined by America's modern poets almost unnoticed by most of their contemporaries. Robert Frost's awareness that man must find his destiny and fulfillment in the reality of earth, T. S. Eliot's vision of man's end decades before Carson's; Hart Crane's vision of a river that is pristine America, and Robinson Jeffers's view of man's irrational pollution echo what is and what might be. From them it is possible to see the lines that lead directly to contemporary concerns with the reality of the present: Denise Levertov's "Merritt Parkway," Lawrence Ferlinghetti's "A Coney Island of the Mind"; Allen Ginsberg's "A Supermarket in California"; Galway Kinnell's "The River That Is East"; and LeRoi Jones's "A Contract for the Destruction and Rebuilding of Paterson." Somewhere in the works of these American poets, attuned as they must be, in Walt Whitman's terms, to the nature of America, there is the answer to contemporary crisis. And the prognosis is uncertain as they define America's reality in terms of the environment that is and will be. In so doing, they are, as Emerson insisted, writing the books for tomorrow.

Franklin D. Roosevelt:

State Planning for Land Utilization

Franklin Delano Roosevelt (1882-1945), progressive statesman and thirty-second president
of the United States, presided over the nation
during its most severe depression and most destructive war. A pragmatist who sought reform
rather than revolution, he contributed much to
the conservation of American natural resources
through specific legislation and as an adjunct
of attempts to end the depression.

I wish to cite the example of an economic plan which has been put into effect and which is still in its experimental stages, yet is not only without detriment to any class of citizen or interest but is certainly and positively proving itself more and more valuable to a very considerable mass of the population of this country. Thirteen millon men and women are involved in it and I feel sure great many millions more will be in the future. I refer to the state planning of the use of land for industry and agriculture in the State of New York, a plan which I confidently feel will prove practicable to the nation as a whole.

The problem arises out of the dislocation of a proper balance between urban and rural life. A phrase that covers all its aspects is "Land Utilization and State Planning."

Land utilization involves more than a mere determining of what each and every acre of land can be used for, or what crops it can best grow. That is the first step; but having made that determination, we arrive at once at the larger problem of getting men, women and children—in other words, population—to go along with a program and carry it out.

It is not enough to pass resolutions that land must, or should, be used for some specific purpose. Government itself must take steps with the approval of the governed to see that plans become realities.

This, it is true, involves such mighty factors as the supply and not the over-supply of agricultural products; it involves making farm life far more attractive both socially and economically than it is today; it involves the possibilities of creating a new classification of our population.

We know from figures of a century ago that seventy-five percent of the population lived on farms and twenty-five percent in cities. Today the figures are exactly reversed. A generation ago there was much talk of a back-to-the-farm movement. It is my thought that this slogan is outworn. Hitherto, we have spoken of two types of living and only two—urban and rural. I believe we can look forward to three rather than two types in the future, for there is a definite place for an intermediate type between the urban and the rural, namely, a rural-industrial group.

I can best illustrate the beginnings of the working out of the problem by reviewing briefly what has been begun in the State of New York during the past three years toward planning for a better use of our agricultural, industrial and human resources.

The State of New York has definitely undertaken this as a governmental responsibility. Realizing that the maladjustment of the relationship between rural and city life had reached alarming proportions, the State Administration undertook a study of the agricultural situation with the immediate purpose of relieving impossible and unfair economic conditions on the farms of the State. The broader ultimate purpose was to formulate a well thought out and scientific plan for developing a permanent agriculture.

The immediate situation was met by the enactment of several types of laws that resulted in the relief of farms from an uneven tax burden and

Franklin D. Roosevelt

made a net saving to agriculture of approximately twenty-four million dollars a year.

First, the State developed additional State aid for rural education, especially in the communities which are so sparsely settled that one-room schools predominate. This State aid gave the smaller rural schools the same advantages already enjoyed by the schools in the larger communities.

Second, a fair equalization of State aid to towns for the maintenance of dirt roads was accomplished by putting it on the basis of mileage rather than of assessed valuation.

Third, through a gasoline tax, additional aid was given to the counties for the development of a definite system of farm-to-market roads.

Fourth, the State embarked on a definite program of securing cheaper electricity for the agricultural communities. It proposes to harness the St. Lawrence River as part of this program, and the electricity developed is by the new law intended primarily for the farmer, the household user, and the small industrialist or store-keeper rather than for large industrial plants.

This was the program to relieve immediate needs.

In all this work, it is worth recording that not only the immediate program but also the long-time planning was worked out in a wholly nonpartisan manner. It received the benefits of study by the Legislature and legislative commissions. Much of the program was worked out by the Governor's Agricultural Advisory Commission. This Commission consisted of representatives of great farm organizations such as the Grange, the Farm and Home Bureau, Master Farmers, the Dairymen's League, the G.F.L., members of the Legislature, representatives of State Colleges and various departments of the State government. It received the hearty cooperation of the Mayors' Conference, and that of business men who were willing to give thought to the future of the State and the nation.

The program for the future was worked out upon that common sense basis which must be the core of every economic plan that will come up for consideration. Details cannot be brushed aside for they all dovetail into the larger ultimate picture.

We knew that out of the thirty million acres in the State, three million were in cities, villages, residential areas; five million were in mountains and forests, and by the way, of this five million the State itself had about two million acres in the great Catskill and Adirondack preserves; four million acres were once farmed but now abandoned, leaving a total of eighteen million acres for agriculture, divided into one hundred and sixty thousand farms.

The first definite step was to start a survey of the entire State. This involved a study of all the physical factors both above and below the surface of the soil, and a study of economic and social factors. The study was divided into six important sections. The soil was analyzed. The climate was determined—that is, the length of growing season between killing frosts, and the amount of annual rainfall. The present use of the land was surveyed—whether forest, swamp or improved, in pasture, in hay or in

State Planning for Land Utilization

annual crops, and what crops. Those who lived on this land were investigated—who owned it and how he used it—that is, whether to make his livelihood out of it or to occupy it only as a house while working away from the farm in the city or elsewhere. A more specific census of those who lived on this land was made; whether they were old people who had always been there, or new people who had recently come; whether Americans or foreigners; whether the young people were staying on the land or leaving it; whether the cultivation of the farm was supporting the farmer in accordance with an American standard of living. Finally, the measure of the contribution that each farm was making to the food supply of the nation was gauged.

It seemed most desirable to make this survey so detailed that it would give separate data for each ten acre square. Already one county has thus been surveyed and we expect to cover the entire eighteen million acres within the next ten years or less.

The survey is being made on the assumption that good economics require the use of good materials. For example, fifty years ago, the State of New York every year mined thousands of tons of iron ore and turned it into iron and steel. The discovery and the development of the vast fields of a more economical grade of iron ore in Minnesota and the other sections of the country forced the closing of the New York State iron mines. The raw materials did not meet the economic standard. By the same token it may have been profitable when land was first cleared to farm this land, but today, with the tremendous competition of good land in this country and in other parts of the world it has become uneconomical to use land which does not produce good crops.

Therefore, we proposed to find out what every part of the State is capable of producing.

From the survey already made we have come to the belief that a certain percentage of the farm land in the State now under cultivation ought to be abandoned for agricultural purposes. It is possible that the percentage will run as high as somewhere between twenty and twenty-five percent.

We are faced with a situation of farmers attempting to farm under conditions where it is impossible to maintain an American standard of living. They are slowly breaking their hearts, their health and their pocketbooks against a stone wall of impossibilities and yet they produce enough farm products to add to the national surplus; furthermore their products are of such low quality that they injure the reputation and usefulness of the better class of farm products of the State which are produced, packed, and shipped along modern economic lines.

If this is true in the State of New York, it is, I am convinced, equally true of practically every other state east of the Mississippi and of at least some of the states west of the Mississippi.

What then are we to do with this sub-marginal land that exists in every state, which ought to be withdrawn from agriculture? Here we have a definite program. First, we are finding out what it can best be used for.

Franklin D. Roosevelt

At the present time it seems clear that the greater part of it can be put into a different type of crop—one which will take many years to harvest but one which, as the years go by, will, without question, be profitable and at the same time economically necessary—the growing of crops of trees.

This we are starting by a new law providing for the purchase and reforestation of these lands in a manner approved by the State, part of the cost being borne by the county and part by the State. Furthermore, a Constitutional Amendment was voted by the people of the State, providing for appropriations of twenty million dollars over an eleven-year period to make possible the purchase and reforestation of over one million acres of land, which is better suited for forestry than for agriculture.

We visualized also the very definite fact that the use of this submarginal agricultural land for forestry will, in the long run, pay for itself (we will get that twenty million dollars back many times over) and will, from the very start, begin to yield dividends in the form of savings from waste.

For instance, the farms to be abandoned will eliminate the necessity of maintaining thousands of miles of dirt roads leading to these farms, the maintenance cost of which averages one hundred dollars a mile a year. The reforestation of these farms will eliminate the need of providing thousands of miles of electric light and telephone lines reaching out into uneconomical territory. The reforestation of these farms will eliminate the upkeep of many small scattered one-room schools which cost approximately fourteen hundred dollars each per year to the State government.

This is why we are confident that over a period of years this State planning will more than pay for itself in a financial saving to the population as a whole.

Modern society moves at such an intense pace that greater recreation periods are necessary, and at the same time our efficiency, state and national, in production is such that more time can be used for recreation. This is increasingly evident this particular year. By reforestation the land can be turned into a great State resource which will yield dividends at once. As one small detail of this plan, the Conservation Commissioner was able to throw open for hunting and fishing the twenty-five thousand acres recently purchased. He will do the same with additional reforestation areas when they are purchased.

These reforested areas are largely at the higher elevations at the headwaters of streams. Reforestation will regulate stream flow, aid in preventing floods and provide a more even supply of pure water for villages and cities.

What will be done for the population now residing on these submarginal lands? First, most of the comparatively small number of people on these farms which are to be abandoned will be absorbed into the better farming areas of the State. Second, we are continuing the idea of the State-wide plan by studying the whole future population trend; here is where there is a definite connection between the rural dweller and the popula-

State Planning for Land Utilization

tion engaged in industry, between the rural dweller and the city dweller, between the farmer and the people engaged in industry.

Experiments have already been made in some states looking to a closer relationship between industry and agriculture. These take two forms —first, what may be called the bringing of rural life to industry; second, the bringing of industry to agriculture by the establishment of small industrial plants in areas which are now wholly given over to farming.

In this particular connection the State of Vermont, through a splendid commission, seems to be taking the lead in seeking to bring industry to the agricultural regions.

For example, in a valley in Vermont a wood-turning factory for the making of knobs for the lids of kettles has already been so successful that the trend of the rural population to the city has been definitely stopped and the population of the valley finds that it can profitably engage in agriculture during the summer with a definite wage-earning capacity in the local factory during the winter months.

Another example is that of one of the larger shoe manufacturers established in a New York village. Many of the workers live in this village and many others live in the open country within a radius of ten miles or more.

As a nation we have only begun to scratch the surface along these lines and the possibility of diversifying our industrial life by sending a fair proportion of it into the rural districts. Cheap electric power, good roads and automobiles make such a rural-industrial development possible. Without question there are many industries which can succeed just as well, if not better, by bringing them to rural communities. At the same time these communities will be given higher annual income capacity. We will be restoring the balance.

Through such state planning as I have just outlined many of the problems of transportation, of over-crowded cities, of high cost of living, of better health for the race, of a better balance for the population as a whole, can be solved by the states themselves during the coming generation.

These experiments should and will be worked out in accordance with conditions which vary greatly in different sections of the country. I have said "by the states themselves" because some of the state methods of approaching the problem may not be economically sound in the light of future experiences, whereas others may point the way toward a definite national solution of the problems.

I remember that many years ago when James Bryce was Ambassador from England in Washington he said: "The American form of government will go on and live long after most of the other forms of government have fallen or been changed, and the reason is this: In other nations of the world when a new problem comes up it must be tested in a national laboratory, and a solution of the problem must be worked out, and when it is worked out that solution must be applied to the nation as a whole. Sometimes it may be the correct solution and other times it may be the wrong solution. But you in the United States have forty-eight laboratories and

Franklin D. Roosevelt

when new problems arise you can work out forty-eight different solutions to meet the problem. Out of these forty-eight experimental laboratories, some of the solutions may not prove sound or acceptable, but out of this experimentation history shows you have found at least some remedies which can be made so successful that they will become national in their application."

In state economic planning the state needs the sympathetic cooperation of the national government, if as only an information-gathering body. The national government can and should act as a clearing-house for all of the Governors to work through. I am very confident that during the next few years state after state will realize, as has New York, that it is a definite responsibility of government to reach out for new solutions for the new problems. In the long run state and national planning is an essential to the future prosperity, happiness and the very existence of the American people.

[1933]

State Planning for Land Utilization

Henry A. Wallace:
Putting Our Lands in Order

Henry A. Wallace (1888-1965), political leader, social idealist, and agricultural administrator, entered public life in the latter capacity as secretary of agriculture under Franklin D. Roosevelt. Later vice-president under Roosevelt (1941-1945) and then Progressive party candidate for the presidency in 1948, he maintained his faith that problems in the natural world could best be met by rational planning.

The Chinese are the greatest individualists on earth. They cut their forests, silted up their streams, and destroyed millions of acres of their land by erosion gullies. Thus, they became increasingly subject to flood and drought. Their soil, exposed without cover to high winds, blew around in raging dust storms. The Chinaman's individualistic treatment of the land has exposed the Chinese again and again to famine.

They have been there a long time. Destructive as they have been, we in the United States, during the past mere 150 years, have handled our land in a way that indicates even more destructive possibilities. Over large areas we are even worse than the Chinese, because we made no real effort to restore to the soil the fertility which has been removed.

We have permitted the livestock men of the West to overgraze the public domain and so expose it to wind and water erosion. Much of the grass land of the great plains has been plowed, exposed, and allowed to blow away. Timber land under private ownership has been destructively logged off, without proper provision for leaving seed trees. All of this has been careless, thoughtless, wanton and to the disadvantage of nearly every one, immediately and in the future.

Early in the century, the conscience of our people began to awaken, under the leadership of Gifford Pinchot and Theodore Roosevelt. One hundred and sixty million acres of western public land were withdrawn from entry and set aside as great national forests. Places of great scenic beauty were set aside as National Parks. More recently we have appropriated money year by year to buy new land to incorporate in the national forests.

There are now 230 million acres of land in private ownership which are in serious danger of being exploited in ways harmful to the public welfare, and which should be purchased as rapidly as possible. During the 22 years of the Weeks' Forest Purchase Act, previous to this Administration, a total of 4,700,000 acres of forest land had been acquired. During the first year and a half of this Administration, this 22-year total has been slightly exceeded, and if this rate of acquisition is continued, the forest resources of the United States will be under adequate supervision and the headquarters of streams will be protected from erosion and unduly rapid run-off within twenty years.

Under the leadership of Franklin Roosevelt, the whole land problem has received an emphasis such as it never had before. As a young man, he was a close student of the Pinchot conservation policies, and he set out thousands of trees on his own farm. As Governor of New York, he had inaugurated a policy of buying poor land and reforesting it. As President, he soon saw the foolishness of spending millions in public works money to irrigate new land while at the same time, the AAA was taking land out of use. His suggested solution was to unify the program by allocating money to buy sub-marginal land to off-set the new irrigated land. To carry out this policy, 25 million dollars were allocated by Public Works in 1934 to buy poor land.

In the meantime, as a result of the AAA taking out of use 40,000,000

Henry A. Wallace

acres of crop land on 3,000,000 different farms, there was growing interest in a more permanent solution. Sensible business men said, "Let's buy these surplus acres and have done with it instead of renting them year after year." Economists pointed out that it would be much sounder to take out of use the 70,000,000 poorest acres of crop land concentrated in the sub-marginal areas than 40,000,000 average acres on 3,000,000 farms scattered all over the United States. The best farmers on good land had adopted rotations and reduced their percentage of land in a cash crop like corn and cotton to 20 per cent but were getting yields twice that of their neighbors. Poor farmers on poor land without rotation sometimes had 60 per cent or more of their land in cash crops and were getting yields only half as great as their neighbors, or one-fourth as great as the good farmers. From the standpoint of pure mathematics, and of getting as much as possible out of our farm labor, it would seem that we should not take any of our good land out of use, but should confine our attention to buying poor land.

Unfortunately, from the standpoint of meeting the agricultural emergency at any time in the next five years, the proposal to buy poor land is not as practical as it sounds. In the first place, people living on the poorest land do not sell much. If we bought the 100 million poorest acres of farm land, we probably would not cut the crop output of the United States as much as 5 per cent. Moreover, the people who sell their poor land will often buy better land, and that leads to the application of more labor to the better land of the United States.

In the second place, the purchase of sub-marginal lands must of necessity be slow, partly to protect the government from the standpoint of reasonable price and good title, and partly to protect the human rights of the people living on the poor land. Franklin Roosevelt, working out the New York land problem as Governor of New York, solved the human side of the problem by giving a life estate in the property under consideration to old couples who were so fond of a particular spot that they did not want to move. Human rights must be conserved, and the government must not be cheated. Of necessity, then, the land program will develop so slowly that it will not greatly help the agricultural emergency at any time in the next five years.

Nevertheless government land purchase of poor and eroded land should be pushed with all possible speed. Human beings are ruining land, and bad land is ruining human beings, especially children. There are certain poor land regions so remote that it is impossible to maintain decent schools, roads and churches. It would be economy not to permit such areas to be settled except perhaps by childless adults who do not expect ever to lead civilized lives. Some areas are so unproductive that they will actually produce more food per acre if returned to natural game cover and re-stocked with wild life.

The human waste on poor land is even more appalling than the soil waste. The Federal Emergency Relief has approached the land problem from the standpoint of farmers now on relief. Several hundred thousand of these have been trying to accomplish the impossible, but they didn't

Putting Our Lands in Order

know it until their endurance was sapped, and their case made plainly hopeless by the depression. With these families, the smaller part of the problem is buying the miserable land where they have been trying to make a living. The difficult thing is to find a new and better place for them to go—a place that will not mean that the government, in placing them there, is simply subsidising trouble for someone else. While no hard and fast rule can be drawn, it would seem that in the eastern half of the United States, the ideal location for many of these poor land farmers who are now on relief would be on self-subsistence homesteads where part of the family can work in industry. This may also be the destiny of some of the unemployed in our cities. It costs only one-third as much to take care of a farm family on relief as a city family, and if the Federal Relief has to support several million families for several years, it will try to make the money go as far as possible by getting several hundred thousand of them out on the land, establishing them in part-time farming and part-time industry.

This trend is a matter of grave concern to established industry and agriculture. We in the AAA will of course insist that these government financed people do not produce farm products for sale. Industry will probably insist that they do not produce industrial products for sale. But industry can not solve the problem this easily, because ultimately industry through the income tax has to foot the government relief bill.

The 10 million unemployed plus the 5 million living on land which can never be farmed are a continuing menace to the established industry and agriculture of the United States. To solve it means decentralized industrial planning relative to land. If the heads of our two hundred leading corporations were to take into account the full significance of paved roads, autos, trucks, high line electricity, and the increased happiness of human beings close to the land, might they not enthusiastically start a decentralized, industrial, self-subsistence homestead program on a scale which would jerk us out of the depression for years to come?

If industry does not seize this opportunity, its only effective defense against serious trouble will be such a revival in business that two-thirds of the unemployed will be put to work again at their accustomed places in the big cities. It would seem high time for those big industries which are truly conservative and interested in their long-time welfare to begin to do a little real planning about the unemployment problem. Agriculture should be in on this, because the wrong kind of decentralization would increase the burden of agriculture.

Land planning is no longer an academic question. A wise use of our land is intimately related to future of industry and the unemployed. So long as there are more than five million unemployed in the United States, there will be a steady and irresistible push toward the lower living costs of open country. Nearly half of the unemployed are under thirty years of age. The larger part of them have at least high school education and many have college diplomas. They are well equipped in mind and body and can see no good reason why it is so hard for them to find jobs.

As I have indicated, there is some danger that these younger unem-

Henry A. Wallace

ployed, joining hands with farmers who have been in the most serious trouble, and with certain other underprivileged groups, will push the nation so far to the left that we will be headed toward the land of nightmare, even as the unemployed youths have succumbed to misguided leadership in certain foreign countries. This group, by asking more relief year after year than the Government can afford, can eventually bring on an uncontrolled inflation. To avoid this disaster, it will be necessary to get more and more of our people thinking seriously about that continuously balanced harmonious relationship which I call the Land of Tomorrow. The industries of the country must be brought definitely face to face with their responsibility for these unemployed. If they dodge, it will be the duty of the Government to go ahead with its own method of rehabilitation and build out of the unemployed a self-subsistence system of exchange cooperatives which are outside the capitalistic system.

The repeated droughts of the last five years demand special attention to another critical maladjustment. During the last 70 years several generations of suckers have been enticed by real estate men to the western great plains in years of good rainfall, only to be burned out later. This sort of robbery should not be perpetrated. No state can build a permanent prosperity on the falsehoods of realtors and promoters. Wisconsin has recognized this by adopting a zoning law which divides the state in such way as definitely limits the field of these predators. Their game can be rather definitely limited to areas where a man has at least a gambling chance to make a living at farming.

Persons deeply interested in ducks, pheasants, deer, fish and other forms of game, and who lament the passing of these native species, want the government to acquire the poorer types of land, especially low-land pastures and meadows near streams and lakes, for game refuges. By planting the right kind of shrubs and grasses and protecting nestlings from pasturing and mowing, we can work wonders in restoring wild life over considerable areas unfit to farm.

In the eastern half of the United States, we need national recreational parks fifteen or twenty miles from the larger cities. These parks might well be located where most of the land is so rough that farmers there are making a miserable living now.

Because of white encroachments, many of the Indian reservations are now terribly short of land. An increase in Indian population has contributed to this jamming-in of too many Indians on too little land. Indians are already subsistence farmers. To transfer to certain of their land-hungry tribes the sub-marginal land of the neighborhood, would seem to be both fair and wise.

Other poor land might well be turned over to the Erosion Service to see what can be done to restore it. If nothing else can be done with it, it can be put into long-time use under the Forest Service, the National Parks Service, or restored to the Public Domain.

Certain large areas of the great plains now plowed, should be put down to grass again. Some of these regrassed areas might be grazed by cattle,

Putting Our Lands in Order

under controlled conditions. Other areas of regrassed land might be best restored to wild life, including antelope, deer and buffalo.

But these are fragments. Fortunately the whole land question will probably be debated at length in 1935. In June of 1934, President Roosevelt appointed a special natural resources committee—the Secretary of the Interior, Secretary of War, Secretary of Agriculture, Secretary of Labor, Frederick Delano, Wesley C. Mitchell, Charles Merriam, and Harry Hopkins.

Frederick Delano, serving as chairman of a special advisory committee of this board, has prepared a report which will be submitted to Congress when it meets in January of 1935.

When this report is submitted we shall have had the benefit of some of the preliminary experience gained by spending a part of the 25 million dollars for purchase of sub-marginal land. We shall know more definitely the nature of the obstacles and how fast we can go.

The Federal Emergency Relief Administration has been discovering more definitely the areas where the farm people have the lowest standards of living and where it is impossible, one year after another, to make enough out of the soil to raise the children decently. Already the FERA has had some experience with buying out farmers in western South Dakota, and in providing them a better farm opportunity in eastern South Dakota. The money for purchasing the land in eastern South Dakota has come in considerable measure from the Farm Credit Administration, but a part of the money has also been furnished by the FERA, on the theory that such expenditure would reduce the relief load next year, and for years to come.

In the past, our land policies have often contradicted and cancelled each other. The government had no agency to unify such policies. Both the land and its people have suffered.

This year we are really beginning to build on the foundation nobly laid by the forest acquisition policy of Theodore Roosevelt and Gifford Pinchot. The report submitted by the natural resources committee to Congress in January of 1935 will, in all probability, if the Congress and the American people are willing, furnish the blueprint for putting our lands in order. In many parts of our social structure the blueprint method of approach is not advisable, but land is so fundamental and precious a heritage, that we should outline a policy to continue over many administrations, and stick to it for the sake of our children and their great grandchildren. The alternative is to maim and misuse our basic heritage, as have the Chinese.

[1934]

Henry A. Wallace

Thomas Wolfe:

The Train in the Night

Thomas Wolfe (1900-1938), novelist who sought
to re-create the myth of America in broad,
sweeping works that grew out of his own experience, deals with the peculiar combination of
human life and the social and natural phenomena of the nation. Here, in his description of an
overnight train ride, he reaches out to grasp the
meaning of the countryside through which the
train passes.

The journey from the mountain town of Altamont to the tower-masted island of Manhattan is not, as journeys are conceived in America, a long one. The distance is somewhat more than 700 miles, the time required to make the journey a little more than twenty hours. But so relative are the qualities of space and time, and so complex and multiple their shifting images, that in the brief passage of this journey one may live a life, share instantly in 10,000,000 other ones, and see pass before his eyes the infinite panorama of shifting images that make a nation's history.

First of all, the physical changes and transitions of the journey are strange and wonderful enough. In the afternoon one gets on the train and with a sense of disbelief and wonder sees the familiar faces, shapes, and structures of his native town recede out of the last fierce clasp of life and vision. Then, all through the waning afternoon, the train is toiling down around the mountain curves and passes. The great shapes of the hills, embrowned and glowing with the molten hues of autumn, are all about him: the towering summits, wild and lonely, full of joy and strangeness and their haunting premonitions of oncoming winter soar above him, the gulches, gorges, gaps, and wild ravines, fall sheer and suddenly away with a dizzy terrifying steepness, and all the time the great train toils slowly down from the mountain summits with the sinuous turnings of an enormous snake. And from the very toiling slowness of the train, together with the terrific stillness and nearness of the marvellous hills, a relation is established, an emotion evoked, which it is impossible to define, but which, in all its strange and poignant mingling of wild sorrow and joy, grief for the world that one is losing, swelling triumph at the thought of the strange new world that one will find, is instantly familiar, and has been felt by every one.

The train toils slowly round the mountain grades, the short and powerful blasts of its squat funnel sound harsh and metallic against the sides of rocky cuts. One looks out the window and sees cut, bank, and gorge slide slowly past, the old rock wet and gleaming with the water of some buried mountain spring. The train goes slowly over the perilous and dizzy height of a wooden trestle; far below, the traveller can see and hear the clean foaming clamours of rock-bright mountain water; beside the track, before his little hut, a switchman stands looking at the train with the slow wondering gaze of the mountaineer. The little shack in which he lives is stuck to the very edge of the track above the steep and perilous ravine. His wife, a slattern with a hank of tight-drawn hair, a snuff-stick in her mouth, and the same gaunt, slow wondering stare her husband has, stands in the doorway of the shack, holding a dirty little baby in her arms.

It is all so strange, so near, so far, so terrible, beautiful, and instantly familiar, that it seems to the traveller that he must have known these people for ever, that he must now stretch forth his hand to them from the windows and the rich and sumptuous luxury of the Pullman car, that he must speak to them. And it seems to him that all the strange and bitter miracle of life—how, why, or in what way, he does not know—is in that instant greeting and farewell; for once seen, and lost the moment that he

Thomas Wolfe

sees it, it is his for ever and he can never forget it. And then the slow toiling train has passed these lives and faces and is gone, and there is something in his heart he cannot say.

At length the train has breached the last great wall of the soaring ranges, has made its slow and sinuous descent around the powerful bends and cork-screws of the shining rails (which now he sees above him seven times) and towards dark, the lowland country has been reached. The sun goes down behind the train a tremendous globe of orange and pollen, the soaring ranges melt swiftly into shapes of smoky and enchanted purple, night comes—great-starred and velvet-breasted night—and now the train takes up its level pounding rhythm across the piedmont swell and convolution of the mighty State.

Towards nine o'clock at night there is a pause to switch cars and change engines at a junction town. The traveller, with the same feeling of wild unrest, wonder, nameless excitement and wordless expectancy, leaves the train, walks back and forth upon the platform, rushes into the little station luncheon room or out into the streets to buy cigarettes, a sandwich—really just to feel this moment's contact with another town. He sees vast flares and steamings of gigantic locomotives on the rails, the seamed, blackened, lonely faces of the engineers in the cabs of their great engines, and a little later he is rushing again across the rude, mysterious visage of the powerful, dark, and lonely earth of old Catawba.

Toward midnight there is another pause at a larger town—the last stop in Catawba—again the feeling of wild unrest and nameless joy and sorrow. The traveller gets out, walks up and down the platform, sees the vast slow flare and steaming of the mighty engine, rushes into the station, and looks into the faces of all the people passing with the same sense of instant familiarity, greeting, and farewell,—that lonely, strange, and poignantly wordless feeling that Americans know so well. Then he is in the Pullman again, the last outposts of the town have slipped away from him and the great train which all through the afternoon has travelled eastward from the mountains half across the mighty State, is now for the first time pointed northward, worldward, towards the secret borders of Virginia, towards the great world cities of his hope, the fable of his childhood legendry, and the wild and secret hunger of his heart, his spirit and his life.

Already the little town from which he came in the great hills, the faces of his kinsmen and his friends, their most familiar voices, the shapes of things he knew seem far and strange as dreams, lost at the bottom of the million-visaged sea-depth of dark time, the strange and bitter miracle of life. He cannot think that he has ever lived there in the far lost hills, or ever left them, and all his life seems stranger than the dream of time, and the great train moves on across the immense and lonely visage of America, making its great monotone that is the sound of silence and for ever. And in the train, and in ten thousand little towns, the sleepers sleep upon the earth.

Then bitter sorrow, loneliness and joy come swelling to his throat—quenchless hunger rises from the adyts of his life and conquers him, and

The Train in the Night

with wild wordless fury horsed upon his life, he comes at length, in dark mid-watches of the night, up to the borders of the old earth of Virginia.

Who has seen fury riding in the mountains? Who has known fury striding in the storm? Who has been mad with fury in his youth, given no rest or peace or certitude by fury, driven on across the earth by fury, until the great vine of the heart was broke, the sinews wrenched, the little tenement of bone, blood, marrow, brain, and feeling in which great fury raged, was twisted, wrung, depleted, worn out, and exhausted by the fury which it could not lose or put away? Who has known fury, how it came?

How have we breathed him, drunk him, eaten fury to the core, until we have him in us now and cannot lose him anywhere we go? It is a strange and subtle worm that will be for ever feeding at our heart. It is a madness working in our brain, a hunger growing from the food it feeds upon, a devil moving in the conduits of our blood, it is a spirit wild and dark and uncontrollable for ever swelling in our soul, and it is in the saddle now, horsed upon our lives, rowelling the spurs of its insatiate desire into our naked and defenceless sides, our owner, master, and the mad and cruel tyrant who goads us on for ever down the blind and brutal tunnel of kaleidoscopic days at the end of which is nothing but the blind mouth of the pit and darkness and no more.

Then, then, will fury leave us, he will cease from those red channels of our life he has so often run, another sort of worm will work at the great vine, whereat he fed. Then, then, indeed, he must give over, fold his camp, retreat; there is no place for madness in a dead man's brain, no place for hunger in a dead man's flesh, and in a dead man's heart there is a place for no desire.

At what place of velvet-breasted night long, long ago, and in what leafy darkened street of mountain summer, hearing the footsteps of approaching lovers in the night, the man's voice, low, hushed, casual, confiding, suddenly the low rich welling of a woman's laughter, tender and sensual in the dark, going, receding, fading, and then the million-noted silence of the night again? In what ancient light of fading day in a late summer; what wordless passion then of sorrow, joy, and ecstasy—was he betrayed to fury when it came?

Or in the black dark of some forgotten winter's morning, child of the storm and brother to the dark, alone and wild and secret in the night as he leaned down against the wind's strong wall towards Niggertown, blocking his folded papers as he went, and shooting them terrifically in the wind's wild blast against the shack-walls of the jungle-sleeping blacks, himself alone awake, wild, secret, free and stormy as the wild wind's blast, giving it howl for howl and yell for yell, with madness, and a demon's savage and exultant joy, up-welling in his throat! Oh, was he then, on such a night, betrayed to fury—was it then, on such a night, that fury came?

He never knew; it may have been a rock, a stone, a leaf, the moths of golden light as warm and moving in a place of magic green, it may have been the storm-wind howling in the barren trees, the ancient fading light

Thomas Wolfe

of day in some forgotten summer, the huge unfolding mystery of undulant, oncoming night.

Oh, it might have been all this in the April and moist lilac darkness of some forgotten morning as he saw the clean line of the East cleave into morning at the mountain's ridge. It may have been the first light, bird-song, an end to labour and the sweet ache and pure fatigue of the lightened shoulder as he came home at morning hearing the single lonely hoof, the jinking bottles, and the wheel upon the street again, and smelled the early morning breakfast smells, the smoking wheat cakes, and the pungent sausages, the steaks, biscuits, grits, and fried green apples, and the brains and eggs. It may have been the coil of pungent smoke upcurling from his father's chimney, the clean sweet gardens and the peach-bloom, apples, crinkled lettuce wet with dew, bloom and cherry bloom down-drifting in their magic snow within his father's orchard, and his father's giant figure awake now and astir, and moving in his house!

Oh, ever to wake at morning knowing he was there! To feel the fire-full chimney-throat roar up a-tremble with the blast of his terrific fires, to hear the first fire crackling in the kitchen range, to hear the sounds of morning in the house, the smells of breakfast and the feeling of security never to be changed! Oh, to hear him prowling like a wakened lion below, the stertorous hoarse frenzy of his furious breath; to hear the ominous muttering mounting to faint howls as with infuriated relish he prepared the roaring invective of the morning's tirade, to hear him muttering as the coal went rattling out upon the fire, to hear him growling as savagely the flame shot up the trembling chimney-throat, to hear him muttering back and forth now like a raging beast, finally to hear his giant stride racing through the house prepared now, storming to the charge, and the well-remembered howl of his awakened fury as springing to the door-way of the back-room stairs he flung it open, yelling at them to awake.

Was it in such a way, one time as he awoke, and heard below his father's lion-ramp of morning that fury came? He never knew, no more than one could weave the great web of his life back through the brutal chaos of ten thousand furious days, unwind the great vexed pattern of his life to silence, peace, and certitude in the magic land of new beginnings, no return.

He never knew if fury had lain dormant all those years, had worked secret, silent, like a madness in the blood. But later it would seem to him that fury had first filled his life, exploded, conquered, and possessed him, that he first felt it, saw it, knew the dark illimitable madness of its power, one night years later on a train across Virginia.

It was a little before midnight when the youth entered the smoking room of the Pullman where, despite the lateness of the hour, several men still sat. At just this moment the train had entered the State of Virginia, although, of course, none of the men who sat there talking knew this.

It is true that some of them might have known, had their interest and attention been directed toward this geographic fact, had they been looking for it. Just at this moment, indeed, as the train, scarcely slackening its

The Train in the Night

speed, was running through the last of the Catawba towns, one of the men glanced up suddenly from the conversation in which he and the others were earnestly engaged, which was exclusively concerned with the fascinating, ever-mounting prices of their property and the tempting profits undoubtedly to be derived from real-estate speculation in their native town. He had looked up quickly, casually, and absently, with that staggering indifference of prosperous men who have been so far, so often, on such splendid trains, that a trip across the continent at night toward the terrific city is no longer a grand adventure of their lives, but just a thing of custom, need, and even weariness, and who, therefore, rarely look out of windows any more:

"What is this?" he said quickly. "Oh, Maysville, probably. Yes, I guess this must be Maysville," and had then returned vigorously from his brief inspection of the continent of night, a few lights, and a little town, to the enticing topic which had for several hours absorbed the interests of the group.

Nor was there any good reason why this traveller who had glanced so swiftly and indifferently from the window of the train should feel any greater interest than he showed. Certainly the briefest and most casual inspection would have convinced the observer that, in Baedeker's celebrated phrase, there was "little here that need detain the tourist." What the man saw in the few seconds of his observation was the quiet, dusty and sparsely lighted street of a little town in the upper South. The street was shaded by large trees and there were some level lawns, more trees, and some white frame-houses with spacious porches, gables, occasionally the wooden magnificence of Georgian columns.

On everything—trees, houses, foliage, yards, and street—there was a curious loneliness of departure and October, an attentive almost mournful waiting. And yet this dark and dusty street of the tall trees left a haunting, curiously pleasant feeling of strangeness and familiarity. One viewed it with a queer sudden ache in the heart, a feeling of friendship and farewell, and this feeling was probably intensified by the swift and powerful movement of the train which seemed to slide past the town almost noiselessly, its wheels turning without friction, sound, or vibrancy on the pressed steel ribbons of the rails, giving to a traveller, and particularly to a youth who was going into the secret North for the first time, a feeling of illimitable and exultant power, evoking for him the huge mystery of the night and darkness, and the image of ten thousand lonely little towns like this across the continent.

Then the train slides by the darkened vacant-looking little station and for a moment one has a glimpse of the town's chief square and business centre. And as he sees it he is filled again with the same feeling of loneliness, instant familiarity, and departure. The square is one of those anomalous, shabby-ornate, inept, and pitifully pretentious places that one finds in little towns like these. But once seen, if only for this fraction of a moment, from the windows of a train, the memory of it will haunt one for ever after.

Thomas Wolfe

And this haunting and lonely memory is due probably to the combination of two things: the ghastly imitation of swarming life and metropolitan gaiety in the scene, and the almost total absence of life itself. The impression one gets, in fact, from that brief vision is one of frozen cataleptic silence in a world from which all life has recently been extinguished by some appalling catastrophe. The lights burn, the electric signs wink and flash, the place is still horribly intact in all its bleak prognathous newness, but all the people are dead, gone, vanished. The place is a tomb of frozen silence, as terrifying in its empty bleakness as those advertising backdrops one saw formerly in theatres, where the splendid buildings, stores, and shops of a great street are painted in the richest and most flattering colours, and where there is no sign of life whatever.

So was it here, save that here the illusion of the dead world gained a hideous physical reality by its stark, staring, nakedly concrete dimensions.

All this the boy had seen, or rather sensed, in the wink of an eye, a moment's vision of a dusty little street, a fleeting glimpse of a silent little square, a few hard lights, and then the darkness of the earth again—these half-splintered glimpses were all the boy could really see in the eye-wink that it took the train to pass the town. And yet, all these fragmentary things belonged so completely to all the life of little towns which he had known, that it was not as if he had seen only a few splintered images, but rather as if the whole nocturnal picture of the town was instantly whole and living in his mind.

Beyond the station, parked in a line against the curb, is a row of empty motor cars, and he knows instantly that they have been left there by the patrons of he little moving-picture theatre which explodes out of the cataleptic silence of the left-hand side of the square into a blaze of hard white and flaming posters which seem to cover the entire façade. Even here, no movement of life is visible, but one who has lived and known towns like these feels for the first time an emotion of warmth and life as he looks at the gaudy, blazing bill-beplastered silence of that front.

For suddenly he seems to see the bluish blaze of carbon light that comes from the small slit-like vent-hole cut into the wall and can hear again—one of the loneliest and most haunting of all sounds—the rapid shuttering sound of the projection camera late at night, a sound lonely, hurried, unforgettable, coming out into those cataleptic squares of silence in the little towns—as if the operator is fairly racing through the last performance of the night like a weary and exhausted creature whose stale, over-driven life can find no joy in what is giving so much joy to others, and who is pressing desperately ahead toward the merciful rewards of food, sleep, and oblivion which are already almost in his grasp.

And as he remembers this, he also suddenly sees and knows the people in the theatre, and in that instant greets them, feels his lonely kinship with them, with the whole family of the earth, and says farewell. Small, dark, lonely, silent, thirsty, and insatiate, the people of the little town are gathered there in that one small cell of radiance, warmth, and joy. There for a little space they are united by the magic spell the theatre casts upon

The Train in the Night

them. They are all dark and silent leaning forward like a single mind and congeries of life, and yet they are all separate too.

Yes, lonely, silent, for a moment beautiful, he knows the people of the town are there, lifting the small white petals of their faces, thirsty and insatiate, to that magic screen: now they laugh exultantly as their hero triumphs, weep quietly as the mother dies, the little boys cheer wildly as the rascal gets his due—they are all there in darkness, under immense immortal skies of time, small nameless creatures in a lost town on the mighty continent, and for an instant we have seen them, known them, said farewell.

Around the four sides of the square at even intervals, the new standards of the five-bulbed lamps cast down implacably upon those cataleptic pavements the cataleptic silence of their hard white light. And this, he knows, is called "the Great White Way," of which the town is proud. Somehow the ghastly, lifeless silence of that little square is imaged nowhere else so cruelly as in the harsh, white silence of these lights. For they evoke terribly, as nothing else can do, the ghastly vacancy of light without life. And poignantly, pitifully, and unutterably their harsh, white silence evokes the moth-like hunger of the American for hard, brilliant, blazing incandescence.

It is as if there may be in his soul the horror of the ancient darkness, the terror of the old immortal silences, which will not down and must be heard. It is as if he feels again the ancient fear of—what? Of the wilderness, the wet and lidless eye of shame and desolation feeding always on unhoused and naked sides. It is as if he fears the brutal revelation of his loss and loneliness, the furious, irremediable confusion of his huge unrest, his desperate and unceasing flight from the immense and timeless skies that bend above him, the huge, doorless and unmeasured vacancies of distance, on which he lives, on which, as helpless as a leaf upon a hurricane, he is driven on for ever, and on which he cannot pause, which he cannot fence, wall, conquer, make his own.

Then the train, running always with its smooth, powerful, almost noiseless movement, has left the station and the square behind it. The last outposts of the town appear and vanish in patterns of small, lonely light, and there is nothing but huge and secret night before us, the lonely, everlasting earth, and presently Virginia.

And surely, now, there is little more to be seen. Surely, now, there is almost nothing that by day would be worthy of more than a glance from those great travellers who have ranged the earth, and known all its wild and stormy seas, and seen its rarest glories. And by night, now, there is nothing, nothing by night but darkness and a space we call Virginia through which the huge projectile of the train is hurtling onward in the dark.

Field and fold and gulch and hill and hollow, forest and stream and bridge and bank and cut, the huge earth, the rude earth, the wild, formless, infinitely various, most familiar, ever-haunting earth, the grand and casual earth that is so brown, so harsh, so dusty, so familiar, the strange and

Thomas Wolfe

homely earth wrought in our blood, our brain, our heart, the earth that can never be forgotten or described, is flowing by us, by us, by us in the night.

What is it that we know so well and cannot speak? What is it that we want to say and cannot tell? What is it that keeps swelling in our hearts its grand and solemn music, that is aching in our throats, that is pulsing like a strange wild grape through all the conduits of our blood, that maddens us with its exultant and intolerable joy and that leaves us tongueless, wordless, maddened by our fury to the end?

We do not know. All that we know is that we lack a tongue that could reveal, a language that could perfectly express the wild joy swelling to a music in our heart, the wild pain welling to a strong ache in our throat, the wild cry mounting to a madness in our brain, the thing, the word, the joy we know so well, and cannot speak! All that we know is that the little stations whip by in the night, the straggling little towns whip by with all that is casual, rude, familiar, ugly, and unutterable. All that we know is that the earth is flowing by us in the darkness, and that this is the way the world goes—with a field and a wood and a field! And of the huge and secret earth all we know is that we feel with all our life its texture with our foot upon it.

All that we know is that having everything we yet hold nothing, that feeling the wild song of this great earth upwelling in us we have no words to give it utterance. All that we know is that here the passionate enigma of our lives is so bitterly expressed, the furious hunger that so haunts and hurts Americans so desperately felt—that being rich, we all are yet so poor, that having an incalculable wealth we have no way of spending it, that feeling an illimitable power we yet have found no way of using it.

Therefore we hurtle onward in the dark across Virginia, we hurtle onward in the darkness down a million roads, we hurtle onward driven by our hunger down the blind and brutal tunnel of ten thousand furious and kaleidoscopic days, the victims of the cruel impulse of a million chance and fleeting moments, without a wall at which to thrust the shoulder of our strength, a roof to hide us in our nakedness, a place to build in, or a door.

[1935]

The Train in the Night

Sherwood Anderson:
I'll Say We've Done Well
The TVA

Sherwood Anderson (1876-1941), novelist, short-story writer, and conscious man of letters, was, through his influence on Ernest Hemingway and William Faulkner, important in marking out the stylistic and linguistic path that modern American literature has taken. Much of his literary and emotional energy was expended in attacking the exploiters of man and nature who had despoiled twentieth-century America.

I am compelled to write of the State of Ohio reminiscently and from flashing impressions got during these last ten years, although I was born there, spent my young manhood within its borders, and later went back and spent another five or six years as a manufacturer in the State. And so I have always thought of myself as an Ohioan and no doubt shall always remain, inside myself, an Ohioan.

Very well, then, it is my State and there are a thousand things within it I love and as many things I do not like much at all. And I dare say I might have some difficulty setting down just the things about Ohio that I most dislike were it not for the fact that what I am to write is to appear in *The Nation*, and *The Nation*, being—well, anyway, what they call broad-minded, cannot well refuse room to my particular form of broadening out, as it were.

Ohio is a big State. It is strong. It is the State of Harding and McKinley. I am told that my own father once played in the Silver Cornet Band at Caledonia, Ohio. Warren G. might have remembered him as Teddy, sometimes called Major Anderson. He ran a small harness shop at Caledonia. Just why he was called Major I never knew. Perhaps because his people came from the South. Anyway, I ought to have got a job at Washington. Everyone else from that county did.

And now Ohio has got very big and very strong and its Youngstown, Cincinnati, Akron, Cleveland, Toledo, and perhaps a dozen other prosperous industrial cities, can put themselves forward as being as ugly, as noisy, as dirty, and as careless in their civic spirit as any American industrial cities anywhere. "Come you men of 'these States,'" as old Walt Whitman was so fond of saying, in his windier moods, trot out your cities. Have you a city that smells worse than Akron, that is a worse junk-heap of ugliness than Youngstown, that is more smugly self-satisfied than Cleveland, or that has missed as unbelievably great an opportunity to be one of the lovely cities of the world as has the city of Cincinnati? I'll warrant you have not. In this modern pushing American civilization of ours you other States have nothing on our Ohio. Credit where credit is due, citizens. I claim that we Ohio men have taken as lovely a land as ever lay outdoors and that we have, in our towns and cities, put the old stamp of ourselves on it for keeps.

Of course, you understand, that to do this we have had to work. Take, for example, a city like Cincinnati. There it sits on its hills, the lovely southern Ohio and northern Kentucky hills, and a poet coming there might have gone into the neighboring hills and looked down on the site of the great city; well, what I say is that such a poet might have dreamed of a white and golden city nestling there with the beautiful Ohio at its feet. And that city might, you understand, have crept off into the green hills, that the poet might have compared to the breasts of goddesses, and in the morning when the sun came out and the men, women, and children of the city came out of their houses and looking abroad over the sweet land of Ohio———

But pshaw, let's cut that bunk.

We Ohioans tackled the job and we put the kibosh on that poet tribe

Sherwood Anderson

for keeps. If you don't believe it, go down and look at our city of Cincinnati now. We have done something against great odds down there. First, we had to lick the poet out of our own hearts and then we had to lick nature herself, but we did it. Today our river front in Cincinnati is as mean looking a place as the lake front in Chicago or Cleveland, and you please bear in mind that down there in Cincinnati we had less money to work with than they did up in Chicago or even in Cleveland.

Well, we did it. We have ripped up those hills and cut out all that breasts-of-goddesses stuff and we've got a whanging big Rotary Club and a few years ago we won the World Series, or bought it, and we've got some nice rotten old boats in the river and some old sheds on the waterfront where, but for us, there might not have been anything but water.

And now let's move about the State a little while I point out to you a few more things we have done. Of course we haven't any Henry Ford over there; but just bear in mind that John D. Rockefeller and Mark Hanna and Harvey Firestone and Willys up at Toledo and a lot of other live ones are Ohio men and what I claim is—they have done well.

Look at what we had to buck up against. You go back into American history a little and you'll see for yourself what I mean. Do you remember when La Salle was working his way westward, up there in Canada, and he kept hearing about a country to the south and a river called the Ohio? The rest of his crowd didn't want to go down that way and so, being a modest man and not wanting to set himself up against public opinion, he pretended to be down of a bad sickness. So the rest of the lot, priests and Indians and others, went on out west and he just took a couple of years off and cut out southward alone, with a few Indians. And even afoot and through the thick woods a man can cover quite a considerable amount of territory in two years. My notion is he probably saw it all.

I remember that an old man I knew when I was a boy told me about seeing the Ohio River in the early days, when the rolling hills along its banks were still covered with great trees, and what he said I can't remember exactly, but anyway, he gave me the impression of a sweet, clear and majestic stream, in which a man could swim and see the sand of the bottom far below, through the sparkling water. The impression I got from the old man was of boys swimming on their backs, white clouds floating overhead, the hills running away and the branches of trees tossed by the wind like the waves of a vast green sea.

It may be that La Salle went there and did that. It wouldn't surprise me if some such scandal should creep out about him. And then, maybe, after he got down to where Louisville, Kentucky, now stands, and he found he couldn't get any further with his boats because of the falls in the river—or pretended he couldn't because he was so stuck on the fine Ohio country up above—it may be, I say, that he turned back and went northward along eastern Ohio and into a land of even more majestic hills and finer forests and got finally into that country of soft-stepping little hills, up there facing Lake Erie.

I say maybe he did and I have my own reasons. You see this fellow

I'll Say We've Done Well

La Salle wasn't much of a one to talk. He didn't advertise very well. What I mean is he was an uncommunicative man. But you go look him up in the books and you will see that later he was always being condemned, after that trip, and that he was always afterward accused of being a visionary and a dreamer.

From all I've ever been able to hear about Ohio, as it was before we white men and New Englanders got in there and went to work, the land might have done that to La Salle, and for that matter to our own sons too, if we, God-fearing men, hadn't got in there just when we did, and rolled up our sleeves and got right down to the business of making a good, up-and-coming, Middle-Western American State out of it. And, thank goodness, we had the old pep in us to do it. We original northern Ohio men were mostly New Englanders and we came out of cold, stony New England and over the rocky hills of northern New York State to get into Ohio.

I suppose the hardship we endured before we got to Ohio was what helped us to bang right ahead and cut down trees and build railroads and whang the Indians over the heads with our picks and shovels and put up churches and later start the Anti-saloon League and all the other splendid things we have done. I'll tell you what the country makes no mistake when it comes to our State for Presidents. We train our sons up right over there.

Why, I can remember myself, when I was a boy, and how I once got out of a job and went one fall with a string of race horses all over our State. I found out then what La Salle was up against when our State was what you might call new, in a way of speaking. Why, I got as dreamy and mopy, drifting along through the beautiful Ohio country that fall, as any no-account you ever saw. I fooled along until I got fired. That's how I came out.

Then, of course, I had to go into the cities and get a job in a factory and the better way of life got in its chance at me, so that for years I had as good a bringing up and knew as much about hustling and pushing myself forward and advertising and not getting dreamy or visionary as any American there is. What I mean is that if I have slipped any since I do not blame the modern Ohio people for it. It's my own fault. You can't blame a town like Toledo or Cleveland or Akron or any of our up-and-coming Ohio cities if a man turns out to be a bum American and doesn't care about driving a motor at fifty miles an hour or doesn't go to the movies much evenings.

What I mean to say is that this business of writing up the States in the pages of The Nation is, I'll bet anything, going to turn out just as I expected. There'll be a lot of knocking, that's what I'll bet. But I'm not going to do that. I live in Chicago now and our motto out here is, "Put away your hammer and get our your horn." Mayor Thompson of Chicago got that up. And, anyway, I think it is pretty much all silliness, this knocking and this carping criticism of everything American and splendid

Sherwood Anderson

I hear going on nowadays. I'm that way myself sometimes and I'm ashamed of it.

The trouble with me is that I once had a perfectly good little factory over in Ohio, and there was a nice ash-heap in a vacant lot beside it, and it was on a nice stream, and I dumped stuff out of my factory and killed the fish in it and spoiled it just splendid for a while. What I think now is that I would have been all right and a good man too, but on summer afternoons I got to moping about the Ohio hills alone, instead of going over to the Elks Club and playing pool where I might have got in with some of the boys and picked up some good points. There were a lot of good bang-up Ohio pushers over in that Ohio town I had my factory in and I neglected them. So, of course, I went broke and I'll admit I've been rather a sorehead ever since. But when I come down to admit the honest truth I'll have to say it wasn't Ohio's fault at all.

Why, do you know, I've had times when I thought I'd like to see that strip of country we call Ohio, just as that Frenchman La Salle must have seen it. What I mean is with nothing over there but the dear green hills and the clear sweet rivers and nobody around but a few Indians and all the whites and the splendid modern cities all gone to—I won't say where because it's a thought I don't have very often and I'm ashamed of it.

What I suppose gets me yet is what got me when I stayed away from the Elks Club and went walking in the hills when I was trying to be a manufacturer, and what got me fired when I was a race-track swipe. I get to thinking of what that darned old man once told me. I'll bet he was a Bolshevik. What he told me set me dreaming about swimming in clear streams, and seeing white cities sitting on hills, and of other cities up along the northern end of my State, facing Lake Erie, where in the evening canoes and maybe even gondolas would drift in and out of the lake and among the stone houses, whose color was slowly changing and growing richer with the passage of time.

But, as I say, that's all poet stuff and bunk. Having such pipe dreams is just what put the old kibosh on my factory, I'll bet anything. What I think is that a man should be glad it's getting harder and harder for any of our sons to make the same mistakes I did. For, as I figure it out, things are going just splendidly over in Ohio now. Why, nearly every town is a factory town now and some of them have got streets in them that would make New York or London or Chicago sit up and take notice. What I mean is, almost as many people to every square foot of ground and just as jammed up and dirty and smoky.

To be sure, the job isn't all done yet. There are lots of places where you can still see the green hills and every once in a while a citizen of a city like Cleveland, for example, gets a kind of accidental glimpse at the lake, but even in a big town like Chicago, where they have a lot of money and a large police force, a thing like that will happen now and then. You can't do everything all at once. But things are getting better all the time. A little more push, a little more old zip and go, and a man over in Ohio can lead a decent life.

I'll Say We've Done Well

He can get up in the morning and go through a street where all the houses are nicely blacked up with coal soot, and into a factory where all he has to do all day long is to drill a hole in a piece of iron. It's fine the way Ford and Willys and all such fellows have made factory work so nice. Nowadays all you have to do, if you live in an up-to-date Ohio town, is to make, say, twenty-three million holes in pieces of iron, all just alike, in a lifetime. Isn't that fine? And at night a fellow can go home thanking God, and he can walk right past the finest cinder piles and places where they dump old tin cans and everything without paying a cent.

And so I don't see why what such cities as Cleveland and Cincinnati have done to knock dreaminess and natural beauty of scene galley-west can't be done also by all the smaller towns and cities pretty fast now. What I'm sure is they can do it if the old New England stock hasn't worn out and if they keep out foreign influences all they can. And even the farmers can make their places out in the country look more modern and like the slums of a good live city like Chicago or Cleveland if they'll only pep up and work a little harder this fall when the crops are laid by.

And so, as far as I can see, what I say is, Ohio is O.K.

[1922]

THE TVA

There is the Tennessee River. It starts up in the Blue Ridge country. Little rivers come racing down, the Clinch, the Holston, and others. The Tennessee is a hill-country river, working its way down valleys, under big hills, little hills, now creeping west, now south, now north—Virginia, West Virginia, Kentucky, Tennessee, down into northern Alabama. The hill country of north Georgia is in the TVA sphere of influence. That is what this TVA thing is, "a sphere of influence."

It is something to dream and hope for, this land drained by the Tennessee. There are a few rich valleys, growing blue grass. There are mountain ranges. Once all these mountains and hills were covered with magnificent forests. It was one of the two Morgans who are in charge of this vast enterprise with David Lilienthal, H. A. Morgan, the land man, the folk man of the project, who talked to me of that. He was president of the University of Tennessee before he got into this thing and he is a land-man.

He talked for an hour and I got a sharp sense of the land-loving man. There was the story of how the hill lands had been robbed. No use blaming any one. The big timber men came to denude the hills. Then the little ones with the "peckerwood" mills came to clean up.

The farmers were left on the hills. Traditions grew up about these people. John Fox wrote of them in The Trail of the Lonesome Pine. Not so good. Jeeter, of Erskine Caldwell's Tobacco Road, is nearer the real thing. They were of the feud country, a pretty romantic lot, in books and stories. In real life they were something else—in real life it was a pitiful rather than a romantic story.

Sherwood Anderson

It was the story of a people clinging, year after year, to little hill-side farms. Every year they got poorer and poorer. Some of these men went out of their hills to the coal mines and later to the factory towns that had come into the hills, but many came back. There is the love of his own country in the hill man. He does not want to leave the hills.

The depression brought the hill men back faster. I went into little upland valleys where a farm of thirty or forty acres might once have sustained one family. (It would have been poor enough fare—hard enough living for the one family.)

But now, often, on such a farm I found three or four families. Sons had come back to their mountain fathers, bringing wives, bringing children. They had built little huts—often without windows.

"At least here, on my father's land, a little corn can be raised. There will be a cabin floor to sleep on at night. It is less terrible than walking among the out-of-works, in some industrial town."

There is a story of an Englishman coming into the hill country, going among the hill men. The Englishman was stunned.

"These hill men are English," he said. "I don't like it."

"You don't like what?"

"I don't like their failing; I don't like to think of Englishmen as failures in a new land."

It is a land of tall, straight men—the kind of stock out of which came Daniel Boone, Andrew Jackson, Andrew Johnson. They have fine looking children, these men. The children fade young. The women fade young.

There is bad diet. No money. The soil gets thinner and thinner with every passing year. Most of this hill land should go back into forest. Every rain that washes down the hillsides takes more of the soil away.

Suppose you put the hills back into forest, what are you to do with these people? Are you to herd them down into industrial cities, where there are already too many men out of work, living on charity?

You have to think of the fact that what we call the modern world has pretty much gone on past these people, as it has gone completely past the tenant farmers, farther South. There are these mountaineers, millions of them scattered over a vast territory, touching several states. These are not the foreigners of whom we Americans can say so glibly—"If they do not like it here, let them go back where they came from." These men are from the oldest American stock we have. It is the kind of stock out of which came Abraham Lincoln. Robert Lincoln, his father, and Nancy Hanks, his mother, were poor whites of the hills.

And there is all this other stuff about us of which we Americans are so proud, our well-equipped houses, motor cars, bathrooms, warm clothes—what we call our American standard of living. All these things not touching these mountain people.

They are clinging to their hills in one of the most beautiful lands in the world.

"Can we take what they and their hills already have—adding

The TVA

nothing—find the riches in their hills—and give these men modern life? If this modern mechanical life is any good, it should be good for these people."

There is wealth in the land on which these people have tried to live. It is a new kind of wealth, the wealth of the modern man, of the modern world. It is wealth in the form of energy.

Power—the coinage of the modern world!

There is plenty of power—the private companies have only got a little of it so far—flowing silently away, along the Tennessee, along the rivers that come down out of the hills to make the Tennessee.

Long ago, I'm told, army engineers went through these hills. They drew up a kind of plan, having in mind the use of all this wasted power in case of war, power to be harnessed, to make munitions, to kill men.

There came the World War and the building of the Wilson Dam at Muscle Shoals. That is where the Tennessee, in its wanderings, dips down into northern Alabama, thrusts down into the land of cotton. It is something to be seen. All good Americans should go and see it. If the Russians had it there would be parades, special editions of illustrated magazines got out and distributed by the government.

There it is, however, completely magnificent. You go down, by elevator, some ten stories, under the earth, under the roaring river, and walk out into great light clean rooms. There is a song, the song of the great motors. You are stirred. Something in you—the mechanically-minded American in you, begins to sing. Everything is so huge, so suggestive of power and at the same time so delicate. You walk about muttering.

"No wonder the Russians wanted our engineers," you say to yourself.

The great motors sing on, each motor as large as a city room. There is a proud kind of rebirth of Americanism in you.

"Some of our boys did this," you say to yourself, throwing out your chest.

The Wilson Dam never was made to impound much water. The idea was to take the power directly out of the swirl of water rushing down over the shoals.

But sometimes it doesn't rush. Dry seasons come, far up-river and in the little rivers. The forest-denuded hills do not hold back the water after rains. Every time you build another dam up-river you get power out of the new dam and you increase the power at Muscles Shoals. They are building two dams now, each to make a great lake, the Joe Wheeler, some twenty-five miles above the Wilson, and the Norris, far up-river, a day's drive, near Knoxville. They will both make great lakes, the shore line of the Norris to be some nine hundred miles, it to be at places two hundred feet deep.

Power stored to make a steady stream of power—power from the Wilson being used to build the Joe Wheeler and the Norris—the river being made to harness itself. There is a new kind of poetry in that thought.

These, the first of perhaps a dozen dams to be built along one

Sherwood Anderson

river—power aplenty for great stretches of country far outside the sphere
of influence of the present TVA.

The power to be used, to give an opportunity to small industries,
reduce the power costs in towns over a wide country, make electrical power
available in homes where it cannot now be used—the money coming in to
go back into the country out of which the power came————

Denuded hills to be reforested, soil washing stopped.

This soil washing, going on in every denuded hill country, filling
your lakes with mud after you build your dams, utterly destroying, making
a barren waste of wide stretches of country. It's hard to dramatize the
slow, steady year-after-year eating away of soil richness. Whole lands have
been destroyed by it, made into deserts. The government foresters, working
with the CCC boys, are like wronged children in their eagerness to make
their work understood. "Tell them about it. Please tell them," they keep
saying. They follow you around eagerly. "You are a writer. Can't you tell
them? Can't you make them understand that we are builders? These CCC
camps. We are taking these city kids and making builders of them. The
boys in the camps begin to understand. Please make every one understand."

Engineers and foresters going at night, after the day's work, to
country towns in the district, to country school houses, lecturing, explain-
ing. I found in these men working on the TVA something I have been
hungry to find, men working at work they love, not thinking of money or
promotion, happy men, laughing men. They think they are saving something. They think they are making something.

I went into the TVA accompanied by a friend, a business man who
lives in Chicago. Formerly he was a college professor. Once he wrote a
beautiful novel that got little or no attention. He was poor and went
into business. He succeeded.

But like a good many American business men, he wasn't very happy
in his success. When the New Deal was announced he went in for it, head
over heels.

He was strong for the NRA, but recently he has been skeptical. I
had written him, telling him that I was going to look at the TVA and he
wanted to go along. We met in Knoxville and spent most of the first
night in a hotel room, talking.

He was discouraged.

"It isn't going to work," he said. He was speaking of the NRA.
"They are trying to fix prices now. The small man is doomed." He is him-
self not one of the small men. "You can't stop the chisellers. You can't.
You can't."

We went to look at the TVA. We did look. We listened. We went
down among the workers on the dams. We went into power houses, visited
men in their offices. Sometimes we were accompanied by enthusiasts,
engineers, foresters, and others, and often we were alone. We had our
own car.

We kept talking. We kept looking. A change came over my friend.

The TVA

"So this is the South," he said.

He had the Northern man's point of view. To the Southerner the South is the deep South. He began talking of the TVA as the South's opportunity. In spite of the fact that my friend was once a college professor he is an educated man. He knows his American history.

"Look what we Northerners did to the South," he kept saying as his enthusiasm grew. "And now this."

We took our look at the TVA, the immediate sphere of influence, and pushed on down into the deep South. We got into the back country, going by back roads.

Men were plowing in the Southern fields. There was the thing, always a new wonder to the city man, the patience of men with the earth, the way they cling to it. We were in a poor district. They are not hard to find in the back country of the deep South. There were these miles of back roads, deeply rutted, even dangerous, bridges fallen into decay.

"It is a kind of inferno," my friend kept saying. We had just left the land of new hope, men busy, the strikingly charming government-built town of Norris, at Norris Dam, going up, men laughing at their work———

Memory in us both of a lunch had with a dozen foresters in a town in the heart of the TVA—the town setting on land that would presently be a lake bottom—the laughter in the room, the anxiety of the men that their story be told straight———

"Don't talk too big. Don't promise too much. We may be stopped."

That against the land of desolation, of no hope—the poor farmers, getting poorer every year. The cotton allotment in the South wasn't going to be of much help to the people along the road we had got into. It would go to the land owners and not one out of ten of the little farmers, white or black, along the road we travelled would own the land he was plowing———

Poor little unpainted cabins half fallen down. Pale women with tired eyes. Undernourished children playing in bare yards before the cabins.

"There are too many of these."

We had got into an argument. My friend had lived his boyhood on an Iowa farm.

"You have places as bad as this in your Chicago," I said, not wanting him to think all American misery was in the South.

"I know, but not on the land! In the end, everything comes back to the land."

"The people who cannot love the land on which they live are a lost people."

"Is it right that all America should try this experiment in the South," he said. There were the one-mule farmers patiently plowing the land beside the road.

"It is wonderful the way man goes on. In spite of defeat he goes on," my friend said.

Two old men came out of a strip of pine woods. They were tooth-

Sherwood Anderson

less, bent old men, Southerners, poor whites, going along the road in silence. We passed them.

My friend leaned out of the car. He was excited.

"Hey!" he called.

The two old men stopped and stared at us. I stopped the car. My friend hesitated.

"Drive on," he said. He turned to me and laughed. "I wanted to tell them something. I can't," he said. "It would sound too silly."

"What?" I said.

"Something new in American life is begun back there, and it mustn't be stopped," he said. I thought it was the feeling, alive in him, as it is still curiously alive in so many Americans, alive in spite of greed, chiseling, desire for fake money, bigness. The feeling of men for men—desire to some day work for others. The TVA may be a beginning.

[1935]

Donald Culross Peattie:
The Buffalo
The Passenger Pigeons

Donald Culross Peattie (1898-1964), author and
botanist, is largely responsible for the popularization of natural science in recent years. In
all his works intimate and perceptive detail is
joined with reverence and affection for his subject matter. *A Prairie Grove* (1938), his best-
known work, recreates the natural setting of
the American past as it focuses that past upon
the reality of the present.

THE BUFFALO

No one will ever know within two or three million the numbers of the bison horde. When the creature was going, stumbling toward extinction, there were censuses.

You come on phrases, from Texas, from Wyoming, serious estimates: "About a million"; "only half a million now"; "twenty-five thousand." The greatest North American animal of historic times, it stamped from the eastern forests to the Rockies, it wandered north in summer up to Athabaska and struggled through the drifts with the norther at its hindquarters into Texas. When the bison went on the march to the salt licks of Kentucky, to the watering holes of the great plains, it traveled sometimes in single file. So the buffalo trails were made. These were the first roads that ever crossed the continent. The Indians walked in these trails too, as a goshawk will stalk down a rabbit's runway through the brush. The white man followed in the buffalo way, and they called it "the buffalo trace," "the Kentucky road," "the Governor's trace." Cutting through the tedium of rectilinear Chicago today runs the slanting Vincennes road; here the buffalo came from Indiana to the prairies. They were monarchs once, thundering along the routes where now the trucks and busses rattle on the metaled highways.

All but two of the continents have had their buffalo or their wild oxen, and there are most of them in Asia. In the rice fields of India plod the water buffalo, subdued to the will of the children that tend them. The cliff paintings of the European New Stone Age show impounded herds of long-horned cattle, and there is a memory in Russia and the marshlands of Lithuania of the aurochs that stood as tall as the American bison. But it had not the mighty chest of our plains monarch. For the bison, like the lion, was a king in front; he had the eye of wrath, the snort of scorn, the collar of kingship; only in the hinder quarters did he betray how he too was mortal flesh. At the height of the hump a bull stood six feet, a cow a foot less. A full-grown master of the herd would measure nine feet from the muzzle to the rump. When he stamped, he could throw the weight of a thousand pounds upon whatever lay beneath his feet. The horns of the bison curved upward, fit for battle. Among the American fossil species there are some whose horns stand out at right angles, and others with drooping horns. Only the one combative, prolific, indomitable sort survived the glaciers.

The last of the buffalo were wary, but the great original horde relied upon the might and the temper and the collective will of the mob which, be it buffaloes or ants or angry men, leaves the individual slight choice and a drunken insensibility to details and warnings. Perhaps there were many herds, or perhaps, biologically speaking, it was one great population. Where it went, grinding the grass with the many million molars and covering the land with the returned fertility of its great flaps, the horse-flies swarmed and gorged themselves; the cowbirds walked among the great beasts, sat on them and ate their ticks and lived themselves in polyg-

Donald Culross Peattie

amous, helpful, jackal plenty. The wolves hung on the flanks of the herd, gray flickering cowardice emboldened by hunger. A strong cow defending her calf would stamp them out like tongues of prairie flame; a bull would toss them gored from his horns into their own ranks to be devoured. One of the old cattle could stand them off for a day; in the end they got him, and the hungry waves closed over him.

Wherever the herd turned they had the Indians upon their trail. The Crees and the Arickarees, the Mandans and Kansas, the Ioways and Osages lived by the buffalo. They lusted for him as the wolves did, but with that strange human element in lust called loved. They worshiped what they killed; they feasted on his flesh and they wore his horns because it gave them stature. Of his bones they made their ladles and bodkins; they used his sinews for thread and his dung for fire. Their wigwams were of buffalo hide, so were their boats and robes and moccasins and belts. Even the Illinois learned from the Sioux to make a shield of buffalo leather, and the Illinois women spun the buffalo wool, sometimes as fine as silk, for gowns sewn with roebuck sinews, for garters, belts, and dyed scarves. The buffalo meant abundance, warmth, excitement, and when they came it was as if earth had suddenly flung open the woolly sack of plenty and given wealth and purpose. They put the manhood into man, they gave him his way of life; they were what he could win by bravery. His art and his songs, his prayers and his dances exulted in the perilous opportunity that thundered on him in a golden pillar of dust.

Trampling eastward from the western droughts, from the harrying of the mounted Sioux, came the buffalo to the prairie seas about my island grove. They had the wind against them, and they could not smell the Illinois encampment, but they saw the woods and they flanked away to southward. In the shadows of the trees Nikanapi held the young men back. He did not want the wary cows started with a premature attack. And a buffalo surround was a half religious matter, not to be entered on without some thoughts and reverence for this fellow creature who was friend and enemy. It gave the chief the opportunity he never neglected for oratory and the bestowing of advice. So he told them all what they all knew already, but being ceremonious animals, they liked to hear it again.

The attack was planned like a battle, and the first war party was sent behind the groves and in the concealing marshes far ahead to start the prairie fire. On the flank of the herd the village waited, hidden, watching the great straggling defile till the center with the calves went by, and in the rear, ready with fire, the most skilful of the hunters crept, covered with wolfskins, among the stupid, superannuated bulls. These let the stratagem steal by them, and when at last in the south the violet column of the first smoke waved a signal above the traveling dust, the great attack began. Near at hand, the ignited shriveled grass flung up orange hands of astonished flame. And the herd caught the cruel laughter of it and the smell of man in the same instant. The straggling wolves became yelling humans, sprung up full height.

There was a buckling forward of the whole horde, driven on by

The Buffalo

flames from the rear, a wave of frantic flesh that was impacted by the return of the column's head. Between the two charges ran the naked human bodies. Through the dust and the uproar the arrows sped without a sound and stuck their taunts in flank and shoulder and chest. The bulls put down their heads and gored the earth up; they pawed defiance and glared about for the right thing to hate where everything was mounting, reddening waves of hate. But the arrows found them without an answer left to give; the knees buckled and the great forward weight unsteadily sank.

When the flames closed in, the goring began; the calves were trampled and the cows were killed by their lords. Then the herd milled in its death dance, till it had to turn and face the storm of arrows on the flank. So it rolled, a wave over its own dead, and charging blind with the blood in its eyes, broke through the Indian line and did not even see the yellow flight of its tormentors. Men fled like mice before the stampede, terror in the marrow of their brittle bones, and the tide of cresting hump and heaving rump hollows seethed westward, into cleaner air where the man stink and the smoke acid faded as they ran and their own snorting breath perfumed free air again.

South and north dashed the exultant flames. They too were loose now and would not stop till they had burned the prairie black and scorched the boughs of generous oak upon the farther shore of it. By their flickering light, in the gathering dusk, the men came back and began to claim their kill by the individual symbols on the arrows. There were seven hundred dead buffalo on the charred plain, and three dead men.

So they had their kill, the Illinois, and they paid their price. They took what they needed, like every tribe with hunting grounds in the range of the bison. They did not fracture the strength of the great bodily pyramid of Nature. Year after year and through the centuries the buffalo, like all the beasts of value to man, paid some toll to the cunning and the necessity of a fellow creature less strong than they. But there was no diminution in the great numbers. Save for our white men's coming, the bison would still blacken the plains, the passenger pigeons still cover the sun with the close net of their wings.

The Indian had no real greed because, except in a small way, he knew of no markets and had nothing so movable and disturbing and universal as money. I do not say that this was more than the innocence of his ignorance. Had his numbers been like ours, he would have had to lead a different life. But no estimate of his population has ever set his numbers north of Mexico at so high a figure as ten million mouths. For the higher the block in the pyramid, the smaller it must be. If you cut away the stones at the bottom, if you pile the weight upon the top, can a pyramid stand?

For ten days there was nothing but coming and going from the village to the place of the kill. It was a ragged procession of women and dogs, slaves, catamites and old men, going out to the slaughter where it lay mountainous on the prairie. They went out empty-handed and came back laden, like a defile of ants that has found a dead thing in the woods and brings it back by infinitesimal piecemeal to the nest.

Donald Culross Peattie

Out on the prairie the great hides came off under the knife, the mighty tongues were cut from the throats, enormous delicacy, and the steaks of the cows, always fattest at this season, were carved from the bones and tugged and staggered with back to the hundred fires. Around the feasting circle passed the tenderloin and fat, offered first to the old, to the visiting Osage and Mascouten and eaten in turn by the chiefs and the great warriors. The smell curled through the camp, into the bark and reed houses loose-woven for summer, suddenly chill and windy now, and the women were hungry and waited. They stole cuts and shreds of meat for the children, and kicked the leaping dogs. Out on the plain the slave captives were finishing the monstrous butchery, till the entrails and the bones were all that was left. Under night's cover the coyotes came for them.

When the steaks were jerked on the slow fires for the winter's use, and the last wild swan was pickled in brine, and the corn was dried and some of it warily buried, the tribe, like the bison, like the fowls of the air, were done with this hunting ground. They stood up and felt the cold wind at the roots of their hair, and how the sunlight on their limbs had little warmth in it. They gathered their weapons up, and mounted their medicine and their clan bundles on their hard male backs. The women took down the houses, collected and folded them; they piled the buffalo jerks and hides on the women slaves. The babies were strapped to their boards and shouldered; the children came running; even the fires were trodden out.

They moved from the grove by families, by groups with their dependents, the half-wild dogs running in and out between the steadily moving legs. Miles ahead already ran the stripped young scouts, but the least came last. The final figure in the deserted camp was a silent slave with three great cow jerks, two kettles, and a papoose, whose weight combined depended from the straps of buffalo skin passed round her forehead. As she straightened up from the last act of loading there was only the forest to see the sum of her burdens, great among them the curve of her pregnancy like the oblate ripeness of the pawpaw. But the tall trees were indifferent, and the squirrels bounded happily behind her back as she followed the last of the dogs into the charred prairie.

Now the rains came, and the dust was laid and the smells were washed out of the earth. Now was the season of great emptiness. A marvelous silence occupied the grove. The arriving winter birds settled their little clans without a word; they flickered through the trees like the leaves that blew off. The elk and the deer were at peace now, browsing on the last of the greenery. There was sleep in store for the one old he-bear that the red men had not caught; there was sleep for the woodchuck, obese as an old chief. The gophers and the chipmunks drowsed in their burrows.

Then the snow came, the white crystals spinning purely through the steely deciduous woods and falling on the bear's blowing fur to be speared or melted there. But storms overtook each other, and the snow flew as if the divinity of West were sending spirit arrow showers. So the drifts went over the head of the bear humped deep in the leaf bed with his back against the biggest fallen oak; they rose to the necks of the tallest weeds

The Buffalo

before they ceased. Then the crust was printed with the tracks of the foraging longspurs and snowflakes, and the field mice tunneled an intricate city of runways underneath the miles of prairie snow. Deep beneath the ground the muskrats worked their way toward the buried rootstocks of the water lily. More snow came, dry cold snow, and blew whispering across the glistening crust.

[1938]

THE PASSENGER PIGEONS

The last great flight of the passenger pigeons recorded from the island grove took place when Rhoda's child Flint was ten years old. I know this because there is Flint's letter written to his Uncle Timothy in California. They found it among Goodner's papers, and it says,

"DEAR UNCLE TIM——

You aught to of been here to see the pigeon we been having. Mother says there was more the first year they came here. I don't see how there could of been. Bird and I shot till our guns was all hot. We been eating pigeon pie till we are sick of it. Peple came from all around lots we never saw before. Some boys that did not have any gun but pertended they did would pick up my pigeons. Uncle Am said there was plenty for everybody but he is always so easy goin. Old Milerand drove in his hogs the third day to get fat on the dead birds. . . ."

The pigeons did not come every year to the grove, but only at rare and unforgettable intervals. They came when the mast in the Michigan forests gave out. Alexander Wilson calculated that a pigeon daily ate half a pint of acorns or beechnuts, and that a flock consumed seventeen million four hundred and twenty-four bushels in a day; Audubon makes it eighteen million. Wilson said that he saw a column a mile broad, every bird in it moving at the rate of a mile a minute. He watched it for four hours, which means that at his conservative estimate of three pigeons in a square yard, the ribbon of wings was two hundred and forty miles long and contained two thousand two hundred and thirty million, two hundred and seventy-two thousand passenger pigeons. This was but a single band, and of these birds not one today is living.

They are so gone that all we hear of them is fabulous. Alexander Wilson was standing one day at a pioneer's door when there was a tremendous roar out of the sky; the sun was so instantly darkened that he took this happening for a tornado and expected to see the trees torn up. "It is only the pigeons," said the frontiersman. Audubon saw a hawk pounce on a pigeon flight; the birds beneath it plummeted almost to earth like the funnel of a twister, and every bird coming after them executed the same figure, dashing into the vortex and by an unseen force shot out of it again. Everyone speaks of the roar of the wings; it plowed the forest boughs into billows. Their droppings fell like shot through the leaves till the ground was covered with them, and the voices forever called upon

Donald Culross Peattie

each other. Imagine the tender contented throaty plaint of the barnyard pigeon amplified by a million voices to a portentous crying thunder torn with the speed of flight. Imagine all your county under forest and all that forest one vast pigeon roost; in such quantities they nested or they rested.

If the evidence lay only on the word of a few, it might not be credible, but the agreement among the skeptical and the rivals is too telling. "The boughs of the trees were constantly breaking under the weight of the birds." "You could hear a pigeon roost miles away." "It was the grandest sight I ever saw to watch them streaming across the sky." "The sun was dark for hours when they went over."

They say that their wings flashed in the sun; the soft rose breasts, the delicate blue heads, the wings changeable green and blue and bronze all had pearl-like luster. The luster is gone from the sad museum specimen that looks at a curious public with a glass eye. But there is Audubon's plate, painted from the life with every nacreous gleam of a pinion, and the dour soul who is embarrassed by Audubon can read the testimony of the cautious Wilson, who makes the pigeon sound as though Audubon's brush had understated it. Such a head-shaker may not want to believe anything that a mere writer would write, like James Fenimore Cooper, but he will have to accept the numbers and the might of the passenger pigeon when told of them by those who suffered from them and so could not love or extol them. "The whole forest was like one vast chicken house; it smelled like it and sounded like it." "Sometimes they would be gone for years, and then they would come back when the nuts were plopping. They would clean up the woods of everything edible and turn their attention to the farmer's corn. In an hour they would ruin him."

I have just Flint's letter to go upon, and it would hardly make an item in a serious ornithological survey of Goodner's Grove, but Rhoda Goodner could not have heard the pigeons coming without feeling their shadow forecast upon her heart.

Hers was the last tragedy in a tragic summer. There was a saying that the first crops that grew so lushly from the virgin soil ran all to leaf, and that the grain was sick. At first the Goodners thought they had the "bread sick" from eating the unwholesome grain, but they saw at last that the prairie, outraged and angered, was shooting down these mortals with its final arrows. From ancient boggy sod it loosed its malarial and enteric fevers so that Asa was doubled up with an "ague cake" in his side. Patience was shaken with chills, and Timothy suffered then the injury to his heart that was to fell him suddenly in far-off foggy Humboldt County. There was a black mist on the horizon, and the wild sunflowers just beyond the broken land looked far away in the illusory shimmer of the heat. This the Indians had understood, how all things could drift apart on the prairie, dissolve under the sun and float in the day mist so that they seemed cut from earth.

The mornings would wake enchantingly, a little dew still in the shade, and though the birds were mostly silent now, the flickers and the bluejays did their best to be musical for an hour. But by eight o'clock the

The Passenger Pigeons

world was already blazing and intolerable. It was an era in which cool and scant clothing was unthinkable, and will and stoicism surmounted the tortures of the tight basque and the ample skirt. But the heat drew iron wires about the head; the arrows flew. Elizabeth Millerand was down, two of her children were ailing, and Mary Tramble came and went with broths and possets and cherry-bark infusions. Only Delia seemed somehow magically untouched, more than ever radiant, more than ever absent from the house. Much of her time was not accounted for, and amidst so much sickness her comings and goings were not watched. Only afterwards were they noticed and understood.

The prairie withered though the sky was humid. The sun got up and peered through the jaundiced blue where the dust began to gather. Far off, the grass was burning, and the smoke did not roll away but hung there in gloomy pillars; it smelled of burning humus, and somewhere in it there curled an odor of roasting ghostly and savage. A wind like a fever blew the mists away, and clear honest sunshine, flaming and terrible, scorched the clearing between the oaks. Now surely the last dampness was baked out of this unfathomed soil; surely the last arrow was shot. The ague melted away out of the weary bones of Asa; Patience got a little color. The twins played in the scant shade, for the hickory leaves were beginning to fall without ever having turned to gold. John Paul and Nancy came in looking both flushed and white and Mary Tramble felt their foreheads, no longer damp under the soft hair, but burning.

Eight days later John Paul was dead of bilious fever, and Nancy died the next morning. They were buried on the following day in terrific heat that made all eyes look scorched. Rhoda and Chance were there, and Rhoda stayed with her mother.

The second week in September a wind rose in the night and stripped the last of the hickories bare. In the morning the sky was blue and chill and warblers were being flung through the woods on the clear storm blowing from Lake Superior. The prairie, gone early to seed in the heat, was suddenly beautiful with the down of its numberless composites, and in the woods the haws turned color, it seemed almost overnight. You could hear the crows and jays and grackles and the big-crested flycatcher all shouting above the wind, but the young wind tore their calls away. It was a day for running, for letting the hair free. That was how they saw Delia for the last time, before the woods swallowed her.

It was Bird who came to tell Asa. He scraped and wept a little and vowed his own fidelity to Rhoda, and it was Asa who had to put the fact in words, in a question, to make sure of it. Yes, Randelman was gone and Miss Delia with him. Asa walked away from him and stood a long time looking at his fields before he found the strength to tell Rhoda.

He was telling her when the pigeons came. Without warning the cloud, not yet arrived, shook the air and passed over the sun like a shadow on the heart. Rhoda went to the door away from her father and looked up with blind eyes at the river in the sky. So wilderness had shaken and darkened her life; so it must pass. In that moment she was cut down, but

Donald Culross Peattie

she was hardy and the seed was in her. She would prevail like the little Rambo trees, when lawless flowering was frostbitten and blackened. Still the pigeons kept coming, a winged crying torrent, and, standing straight, she shaded glittering eyes with her hand to watch their passage. Her pain forecast our loss; we should have known that desire of it would drive the wilderness over the last border.

That year, that time when the pigeons went over, no one in the grove, out of some Goodner sense of fitness, fired a shot. The flying river shed no drop, though it was four days and nights in passing, thinning sometimes, coming again to flood. It went on into the autumn, south as the sun went, with the shortening days, and inevitably it ended; a sky meek now without death or portent in it was clear of the great horde. The last feathered arrow was spent and the last abundance vanished; the medicine bag is empty, and the year, the *annus mirabilis*, is over. The seed is in, fateful and indomitable; we have populated where we have slain. Still sometimes when in fall or spring the wind turns, coming from a fresh place, we smell wilderness on it, and this is heartbreak and delight.

[1938]

The Passenger Pigeons

John Steinbeck:
The Tractor Man

John Steinbeck (1902-1968), novelist, humanitarian, and winner of the Nobel Prize for literature (1962), is best known for his most important and most controversial work, *The Grapes
of Wrath* (1939). In all his writing his humanitarian partisanship emphasizes that meaning
and fulfillment in life can be found only through
realization of the ultimate kinship of all men
and all of nature.

The owners of the land came onto the land, or more often a spokesman for the owners came. They came in closed cars, and they felt the dry earth with their fingers, and sometimes they drove big earth augers into the ground for soil tests. The tenants, from their sun-beaten dooryards, watched uneasily when the closed cars drove along the fields. And at last the owner men drove into the dooryards and sat in their cars to talk out of the windows. The tenant men stood beside the cars for a while, and then squatted on their hams and found sticks with which to mark the dust.

In the open doors the women stood looking out, and behind them the children—corn-headed children, with wide eyes, one bare foot on top of the other bare foot, and the toes working. The women and the children watched their men talking to the owner men. They were silent.

Some of the owner men were kind because they hated what they had to do, and some of them were angry because they hated to be cruel, and some of them were cold because they had long ago found that one could not be an owner unless one were cold. And all of them were caught in something larger than themselves. Some of them hated the mathematics that drove them, and some were afraid, and some worshiped the mathematics because it provided a refuge from thought and from feeling. If a bank or a finance company owned the land, the owner man said, The Bank—or the Company—needs—wants—insists—must have—as though the Bank or the Company were a monster, with thought and feeling, which had ensnared them. These last would take no responsibility for the banks or the companies because they were men and slaves, while the banks were machines and masters all at the same time. Some of the owner men were a little proud to be slaves to such cold and powerful masters. The owner men sat in the cars and explained. You know the land is poor. You've scrabbled at it long enough, God knows.

The squatting tenant men nodded and wondered and drew figures in the dust, and yes, they knew, God knows. If the dust only wouldn't fly. If the top would only stay on the soil, it might not be so bad.

The owner men went on leading to their point: You know the land's getting poorer. You know what cotton does to the land; robs it, sucks all the blood out of it.

The squatters nodded—they knew, God knew. If they could only rotate the crops they might pump blood back into the land.

Well, it's too late. And the owner men explained the workings and the thinkings of the monster that was stronger than they were. A man can hold land if he can just eat and pay taxes; he can do that.

Yes, he can do that until his crops fail one day and he has to borrow money from the bank.

But—you see, a bank or a company can't do that, because those creatures don't breathe air, don't eat side-meat. They breathe profits; they eat the interest on money. If they don't get it, they die the way you die without air, without side-meat. It is a sad thing, but it is so. It is just so.

The squatting men raised their eyes to understand. Can't we just hang on? Maybe the next year will be a good year. God knows how much

John Steinbeck

cotton next year. And with all the wars—God knows what price cotton will bring. Don't they make explosives out of cotton? And uniforms? Get enough wars and cotton'll hit the ceiling. Next year, maybe. They looked up questioningly.

We can't depend on it. The bank—the monster has to have profits all the time. It can't wait. It'll die. No, taxes go on. When the monster stops growing, it dies. It can't stay one size.

Soft fingers began to tap the sill of the car window, and hard fingers tightened on the restless drawing sticks. In the doorways of the sun-beaten tenant houses, women sighed and then shifted feet so that the one that had been down was now on top, and the toes working. Dogs came sniffing near the owner cars and wetted on all four tires one after another. And chickens lay in the sunny dust and fluffed their feathers to get the cleansing dust down to the skin. In the little sties the pigs grunted inquiringly over the muddy remnants of the slops.

The squatting men looked down again. What do you want us to do? We can't take less share of the crop—we're half starved now. The kids are hungry all the time. We got no clothes, torn an' ragged. If all the neighbors weren't the same, we'd be ashamed to go to meeting.

And at last the owner men came to the point. The tenant system won't work any more. One man on a tractor can take the place of twelve or fourteen families. Pay him a wage and take all the crop. We have to do it. We don't like to do it. But the monster's sick. Something's happened to the monster.

But you'll kill the land with cotton.

We know. We've got to take cotton quick before the land dies. Then we'll sell the land. Lots of families in the East would like to own a piece of land.

The tenant men looked up alarmed. But what'll happen to us? How'll we eat?

You'll have to get off the land. The plows'll go through the dooryard.

And now the squatting men stood up angrily. Grampa took up the land, and he had to kill the Indians and drive them away. And Pa was born here, and he killed weeds and snakes. Then a bad year came and he had to borrow a little money. An' we was born here. There in the door—our children born here. And Pa had to borrow money. The bank owned the land then, but we stayed and we got a little bit of what we raised.

We know that—all that. It's not us, it's the bank. A bank isn't like a man. Or an owner with fifty thousand acres, he isn't like a man either. That's the monster.

Sure, cried the tenant men, but it's our land. We measured it and broke it up. We were born on it, and we got killed on it, died on it. Even if it's no good, it's still ours. That's what makes it ours—being born on it, working it, dying on it. That makes ownership, not a paper with numbers on it.

We're sorry. It's not us. It's the monster. The bank isn't like a man.

The Tractor Man

Yes, but the bank is only made of men.

No, you're wrong there—quite wrong there. The bank is something else than men. It happens that every man in a bank hates what the bank does, and yet the bank does it. The bank is something more than men, I tell you. It's the monster. Men made it, but they can't control it.

The tenants cried, Grampa killed Indians, Pa killed snakes for the land. Maybe we can kill banks—they're worse than Indians and snakes. Maybe we got to fight to keep our land, like Pa and Grampa did.

And now the owner men grew angry. You'll have to go.

But it's ours, the tenant men cried. We——

No. The bank, the monster owns it. You'll have to go.

We'll get our guns, like Grampa when the Indians came. What then?

Well—first the sheriff, and then the troops. You'll be stealing if you try to stay, you'll be murderers if you kill to stay. The monster isn't men, but it can make men do what it wants.

But if we go, where'll we go? How'll we go? We got no money.

We're sorry, said the owner men. The bank, the fifty-thousand-acre owner can't be responsible. You're on land that isn't yours. Once over the line maybe you can pick cotton in the fall. Maybe you can go on relief. Why don't you go on west to California? There's work there, and it never gets cold. Why, you can reach out anywhere and pick an orange. Why, there's always some kind of crop to work in. Why don't you go there? And the owner men started their cars and rolled away.

The tenant men squatted down on their hams again to mark the dust with a stick, to figure, to wonder. Their sun-burned faces were dark, and their sun-whipped eyes were light. The women moved cautiously out of the doorways toward their men, and the children crept behind the women, cautiously, ready to run. The bigger boys squatted beside their fathers, because that made them men. After a time the women asked, What did he want?

And the men looked up for a second, and the smolder of pain was in their eyes. We got to get off. A tractor and a superintendent. Like factories.

Where'll we go? the women asked.

We don't know. We don't know.

And the women went quickly, quietly back into the houses and herded the children ahead of them. They knew that a man so hurt and so perplexed may turn in anger, even on people he loves. They left the men alone to figure and to wonder in the dust.

After a time perhaps the tenant man looked about—at the pump put in ten years ago, with a goose-neck handle and iron flowers on the spout, at the chopping block where a thousand chickens had been killed, at the hand plow lying in the shed, and the patent crib hanging in the rafters over it.

The children crowded about the women in the houses. What we going to do, Ma? Where we going to go?

John Steinbeck

The women said, We don't know, yet. Go out and play. But don't go near your father. He might whale you if you go near him. And the women went on with the work, but all the time they watched the men squatting in the dust—perplexed and figuring.

The tractors came over the roads and into the fields, great crawlers moving like insects, having the incredible strength of insects. They crawled over the ground, laying the track and rolling on it and picking it up. Diesel tractors, puttering while they stood idle; they thundered when they moved, and then settled down to a droning roar. Snub-nosed monsters, raising the dust and sticking their snouts into it, straight down the country, across the country, through fences, through dooryards, in and out of gullies in straight lines. They did not run on the ground, but on their own roadbeds. They ignored hills and gulches, water courses, fences, houses.

The man sitting in the iron seat did not look like a man; gloved, goggled, rubber dust mask over nose and mouth, he was a part of the monster, a robot in the seat. The thunder of the cylinders sounded through the country, became one with the air and the earth, so that earth and air muttered in sympathetic vibration. The driver could not control it— straight across country it went, cutting through a dozen farms and straight back. A twitch at the controls could swerve the cat', but the driver's hands could not twitch because the monster that built the tractor, the monster that sent the tractor out, had somehow got into the driver's hands, into his brain and muscle, had goggled him and muzzled him—goggled his mind, muzzled his speech, goggled his perception, muzzled his protest. He could not see the land as it was, he could not smell the land as it smelled; his feet did not stamp the clods or feel the warmth and power of the earth. He sat in an iron seat and stepped on iron pedals. He could not cheer or beat or curse or encourage the extension of his power, and because of this he could not cheer or whip or curse or encourage himself. He did not know or own or trust or beseech the land. If a seed dropped did not germinate, it was nothing. If the young thrusting plant withered in drought or drowned in a flood of rain, it was no more to the driver than to the tractor.

He loved the land no more than the bank loved the land. He could admire the tractor—its machined surfaces, its surge of power, the roar of its detonating cylinders; but it was not his tractor. Behind the tractor rolled the shining disks, cutting the earth with blades—not plowing but surgery, pushing the cut earth to the right where the second row of disks cut it and pushed it to the left; slicing blades shining, polished by the cut earth. And pulled behind the disks, the harrows combing with iron teeth so that the little clods broke up and the earth lay smooth. Behind the harrows, the long seeders—twelve curved iron penes erected in the foundry, orgasms set by gears, raping methodically, raping without passion. The driver sat in his iron seat and he was proud of the straight lines he did not will, proud of the tractor he did not own or love, proud of the power he could not control. And when that crop grew, and was harvested, no man had crumbled a hot clod in his fingers and let the earth sift past his fingertips. No man had touched the seed, or lusted for the growth. Men ate what they had not

The Tractor Man

raised, had no connection with the bread. The land bore under iron, and under iron gradually died; for it was not loved or hated, it had no prayers or curses.

At noon the tractor driver stopped sometimes near a tenant house and opened his lunch: sandwiches wrapped in waxed paper, white bread, pickle, cheese, Spam, a piece of pie branded like an engine part. He ate without relish. And tenants not yet moved away came out to see him, looked curiously while the goggles were taken off, and the rubber dust mask, leaving white circles around the eyes and a large white circle around nose and mouth. The exhaust of the tractor puttered on, for fuel is so cheap it is more efficient to leave the engine running than to heat the Diesel nose for a new start. Curious children crowded close, ragged children who ate their fried dough as they watched. They watched hungrily the unwrapping of the sandwiches, and their hunger-sharpened noses smelled the pickle, cheese, and Spam. They didn't speak to the driver. They watched his hand as it carried food to his mouth. They did not watch him chewing; their eyes followed the hand that held the sandwich. After a while the tenant who could not leave the place came out and squatted in the shade beside the tractor.

"Why, you're Joe Davis's boy!"

"Sure," the driver said.

"Well, what you doing this kind of work for—against your own people?"

"Three dollars a day. I got damn sick of creeping for my dinner— and not getting it. I got a wife and kids. We got to eat. Three dollars a day, and it comes every day."

"That's right," the tenant said. "But for your three dollars a day fifteen or twenty families can't eat at all. Nearly a hundred people have to go out and wander on the roads for your three dollars a day. Is that right?"

And the driver said, "Can't think of that. Got to think of my own kids. Three dollars a day, and it comes every day. Times are changing, mister, don't you know? Can't make a living on the land unless you've got two, five, ten thousand acres and a tractor. Crop land isn't for little guys like us any more. You don't kick up a howl because you can't make Fords, or because you're not the telephone company. Well, crops are like that now. Nothing to do about it. You try to get three dollars a day someplace. That's the only way."

The tenant pondered. "Funny thing how it is. If a man owns a little property, that property is him, it's part of him, and it's like him. If he owns property only so he can walk on it and handle it and be sad when it isn't doing well, and feel fine when the rain falls on it, that property is him, and some way he's bigger because he owns it. Even if he isn't successful he's big with his property. That is so."

And the tenant pondered more. "But let a man get property he doesn't see, or can't take time to get his fingers in, or can't be there to walk on it—why, then the property is the man. He can't do what he wants, he can't think what he wants. The property is the man, stronger than he is.

John Steinbeck

And he is small, not big. Only his possessions are big—and he's the servant of his property. That is so, too."

The driver munched the branded pie and threw the crust away. "Times are changed, don't you know? Thinking about stuff like that don't feed the kids. Get your three dollars a day, feed your kids. You got no call to worry about anybody's kids but your own. You get a reputation for talking like that, and you'll never get three dollars a day. Big shots won't give you three dollars a day if you worry about anything but your three dollars a day."

"Nearly a hundred people on the road for your three dollars. Where will we go?"

"And that reminds me," the driver said, "you better get out soon. I'm going through the dooryard after dinner."

"You filled in the well this morning."

"I know. Had to keep the line straight. But I'm going through the dooryard after dinner. Got to keep the lines straight. And—well, you know Joe Davis, my old man, so I'll tell you this. I got orders wherever there's a family not moved out—if I have an accident—you know, get too close and cave the house in a little—well, I might get a couple of dollars. And my youngest kid never had no shoes yet."

"I built it with my hands. Straightened old nails to put the sheathing on. Rafters are wired to the stringers with baling wire. It's mine. I built it. You bump it down—I'll be in the window with a rifle. You even come too close and I'll pot you like a rabbit."

"It's not me. There's nothing I can do. I'll lose my job if I don't do it. And look—suppose you kill me? They'll just hang you, but long before you're hung there'll be another guy on the tractor, and he'll bump the house down. You're not killing the right guy."

"That's so," the tenant said. "Who gave you orders? I'll go after him. He's the one to kill."

"You're wrong. He got his orders from the bank. The bank told him, 'Clear those people out or it's your job.'"

"Well, there's a president of the bank. There's a board of directors. I'll fill up the magazine of the rifle and go into the bank."

The driver said, "Fellow was telling me the bank gets orders from the East. The orders were, 'Make the land show profit or we'll close you up.'"

"But where does it stop? Who can we shoot? I don't aim to starve to death before I kill the man that's starving me."

"I don't know. Maybe there's nobody to shoot. Maybe the thing isn't men at all. Maybe, like you said, the property's doing it. Anyway I told you my orders."

"I got to figure," the tenant said. "We all got to figure. There's some way to stop this. It's not like lightning or earthquakes. We've got a bad thing made by men, and by God that's something we can change."

The tenant sat in his doorway, and the driver thundered his engine and started off, tracks falling and curving, harrows combing, and the phalli of

The Tractor Man

the seeder slipping into the ground. Across the dooryard the tractor cut, and the hard, foot-beaten ground was seeded field, and the tractor cut through again; the uncut space was ten feet wide. And back he came. The iron guard bit into the house-corner, crumbled the wall, and wrenched the little house from its foundation so that it fell sideways, crushed like a bug. And the driver was goggled and a rubber mask covered his nose and mouth. The tractor cut a straight line on, and the air and the ground vibrated with its thunder. The tenant man stared after it, his rifle in his hand. His wife was beside him, and the quiet children behind. And all of them stared after the tractor.

[1939]

John Steinbeck

Louis Bromfield:
The Cycle of a Farm Pond

Louis Bromfield (1896-1956), popular novelist, was the Pulitzer Prize winner for *Early Autumn* in 1927. Bromfield's last years were spent as a scientific, experimental farmer near his birthplace of Mansfield, Ohio. A prolific writer and a man of deep faith in the natural order, he had a gift for nature writing, a characteristic unfortunately frequently overlooked by his critics.

> A useful contact with the earth places man not as superior to nature but as a superior intelligence working in nature as a conscious and therefore as a responsible part in a plan of evolution, which is a continuing creation.
> —Liberty Hyde Bailey, *The Holy Earth*

Of the three ponds at Malabar, the low, shallow one at the Fleming Place is the most productive of big fish. This is so because it is the oldest and the richest in vegetation. It was made out of an old ox-bow left when Switzer's Run was foolishly straightened by the County Commissioners before we came here. We raised the banks about two feet by a day's work with hand shovels and thus raised the water level by the same depth. It is fed by a big spring in the bottom which has increased its flow by at least 100 per cent since we began keeping the rainfall where it fell on our land, and by the flow of an abandoned gas well which has turned into a first-rate artesian well flowing hundreds of gallons a minute of ice-cold water. Drainage from the neighboring barnyard during heavy rain occasionally reaches the pond and fertilizes the heavy vegetation in it. It is a comparatively shallow pond with a gravel bottom long since stopped tight by layers of decaying water vegetation.

The natural balance and cycle of this pond is very nearly perfect. The population is made up of bass, bluegills, sunfish and innumerable hybrid variations of the sunfish family which occur in fish ponds. There is also a single large carp caught by the children in Switzer's Run as a small fish and dumped into the pond along with a miscellaneous assortment of minnows, shiners, suckers, etc. All but the carp have long since disappeared, devoured by the big bass. On the richness of the table set for him by nature beneath the surface of the water, the carp has grown to nearly three feet in length and must weigh in the neighborhood of thirty pounds. He is occasionally accompanied by a gigantic goldfish which seems to have for him a romantic attachment—a situation not unusual since carp and goldfish belong to the same family and in Lake Erie where huge goldfish, descended from a few which escaped from a pond in Cleveland years ago during flood times, are not uncommon and frequently breed with the big carp to create new crossbred strains puzzling of identification to the amateur and sometimes to the commercial fishermen who find them in their nets.

The goldfish also came into the Fleming pond through no design but through the zeal of the children who, six years ago, dumped into the pond a dozen fingerling-size goldfish bought at Woolworth's. On the rich diet of the pond they have grown to eighteen inches and more in length and to a weight of two or three pounds. They are very fat and lumbering and awkward beside the swift-moving streamlined bass and bluegills and have the appearance of red-gold galleons wallowing through the deep green-blue water moss and weeds. Some have the appearance of large luminous streamlined carp and others have long flowing tails and fins which trail behind them in the clear blue water like the veils of brides. Some have their red-gold scales variegated with silver. It is easy to see why the Japanese and Chinese long ago regarded goldfish as works of art, of high

Louis Bromfield

artistic value in their shallow ornamented pools, and made a science and an art of breeding them into fantastic almost artificial shapes and colors. A glimpse of these big, brilliantly colorful fish seen moving through the gently undulating weeds in the blue, clear water from the high bank of the Fleming pond gives the beholder the sudden delight that comes from the contemplation of an old Chinese painting or from the luminous beauty of Redon's flower pictures.

Neither the goldfish nor the great carp belong in a properly managed Ohio fish pond but all efforts to remove them have failed. The goldfish, fat and contented, will sometimes nose about a worm-baited hook but never take the worm. The great carp has refused all baits persistently and has even managed to escape the marksmanship of the boys who regularly attempt to shoot him with a twenty-two calibre rifle.

However, beyond consuming some of the food supply of the pond, neither goldfish nor carp do any serious harm. I am not at all sure that they are not an asset in the cycle of the pond and to the food supply of the big, small-mouthed bass. They have never succeeded in producing a single surviving descendant and there is consequently no way of knowing whether the romance of the great carp and his love-lorn accompanying goldfish has ever been fruitful. Each year the goldfish gather, after the fashion of carp, in a herd in the shallowest water and there thrash about in the ecstasy of reproduction for several days at a time. But apparently the big bass immediately devour the roe or any young goldfish which by chance have hatched out. Thus they continue—the great carp and his fleet of goldfish cousins—to lead, if not a sterile existence, a fruitless one, taking their place in the cycle of pond life and producing a perpetual supply of caviar for the bass.

I have seen literally acres of great carp spawning in the shallow waters of the big Pleasant Hill lake at the end of the farm in late May or June. In the late spring they gather from the deep holes of the Clear Fork and the deeper waters of the lake itself by some common and terrific urge and then move into the shallow waters where they indulge in a wild orgy of reproduction continuing for several days. At such times it is possible to walk in water up to one's knees among hundreds of thrashing, wallowing carp, which in their ecstasy pay little attention to one's presence—so little indeed that it is possible to knock them over with blows of a club. In Lake Erie at spawning time, the big carp put on a similar performance in the shallow waters along the beaches and boys amuse themselves by shooting at them with rifles.

The fresh-water shad which exist in great numbers in the waters of the lake and the Clear Fork have another way of spawning. They will gather in schools on the surface of fairly deep water and swarm and flash, jumping in and out of the water in the brilliant sunlight of June. They are prodigiously fecund and reproduce themselves by the hundred thousands and their offspring are devoured in great quantities by the big bass which fit into the cycle of life in the streams, ponds, and lakes of most of the Mississippi basin. So intent do the shad become during the season of

The Cycle of a Farm Pond

breeding that you can swim among them while they continue their gyrations and silvery leaps above the surface of the clear, blue water.

There are no shad in our ponds but their place is taken in the pond cycle by the bluegills and sunfish which also reproduce themselves in prodigious numbers. Tom Langlois of the Ohio Fish Laboratories, one of the great authorities on mid-American fresh-water fish, tells me that not only are there many distinct and identifiable members of the sunfish family, but that they have an indiscriminate way of crossbreeding an infinite number of variations. Many of these are sterile, like the mule, and each year go through the fiercely compulsive process of breeding and laying eggs without producing anything. It appears also that the urge to breed overtakes them earlier in the season than it does the accepted and recognized members of the sunfish family. Very often they will pre-empt the available nesting grounds on shallow gravel beds in their fruitless and sterile efforts and fiercely fight off the fertile members of their tribe when these attempt a little later to find nesting places, a fact that can upset the regular cycle of pond life and food supply within the pond.

The mating habits of many fish and of most of the sunfish family in particular are fascinating to observe. In our ponds, they begin to nest about the end of May and all along the edges of the ponds in shallow waters, you will find them in great numbers beginning to clear away the mud or the decayed vegetation that cover the clean gravel which they like for nesting purposes.

The bass, the bluegills and the other members of the sunfish family all follow a similar urge and procedure. Each one will select, not without considerable fighting, a chosen site and then begin to clear off the silt or decayed vegetation that has settled over the gravel during the year. Each one will take a place above his selected site and without moving either backward or forward will set up a fluttering motion with his fins which in turn creates a current in the water that washes the gravel clean. This procedure sometimes requires a day or two of work. When the gravel has been washed clean and a slight depression of from one to two inches deep has been created (similar in appearance beneath the water to the nest of the killdeer plover which lays its eggs and hatches its young on a nest of gravel on the adjoining dry ground), the female will deposit her eggs in the nest and the male will swim over them and fertilize them. From then on the duty of guarding the nest becomes that of the male and until the young are hatched he will remain over the nest, moving his fins very gently, unless another fish of any species comes within an eighteen-inch radius of the center of the nest. Then he will attack furiously until the molesting fish is driven off. The bluegills and some varieties of sunfish build their nests in clusters side by side, each with a male fish fiercely guarding his own nest and darting angrily at his nearest neighbors if they attempt to cross the invisible line which guards his nursery from that of his neighbors.

I am not certain that the male fish is aware of the exact moment when the tiny fish he has fathered hatch, nor of how long the period

Louis Bromfield

of gestation is but overnight the whole pond will become infested with millions of tiny fish no bigger than a pin which move about in schools of thousands and promptly seek refuge in very shallow water or among the algae which by the time they have hatched covers large areas of the pond. There would seem to be some purpose in the presence of the algae as a protection for the tiny fish not only because its fabric makes it impossible for the big bass to swallow the young fish in a single sweeping gulp but because the larger fish find the algae itself distasteful and unpalatable. I have observed that even the smallest filament of algae attached by accident to a baited hook or fly will prevent the bigger fish from swallowing or striking at the bait.

I doubt that the male fish is aware of the moment when the young fry hatch out and flee the nest for the safety of the very shallow waters or of the webbed, clinging algae. I suspect that very often, driven by an urge which covers a comparatively fixed period well overlapping the period of gestation, the male fish often remains on guard long after the roe have hatched and fled the nest.

In certain parts of the pond which the fish have chosen as nesting and spawning beds, the whole character of the pond bottom has changed over a period of years. On bottoms which once were clay and muddy, the clay-mud element has been entirely washed away by the motions of countless small fins season after season until they have become clean, gravel shelves, bars and beaches. If, as sometimes happens during the spawning season, which usually coincides with a season of rains and thundershowers, floodwaters cover the nests with a thin layer of silt, the male fish will immediately and frantically go to work washing away the deposit of silt to make the nests clean once more.

During the spawning season, the male becomes fierce and even the little male bluegill will stand by his particular nest and give battle to a stick or a finger thrust into the water near him. I have had my finger "bitten" by big male bass when I thrust my hand into the water above his nest. At other times when the fish are not nesting my mere presence on the bank or that shadow cast over the water will suffice to send them in a darting brilliant course into deeper water.

All of these elements play their part in the "balance" of a good fish pond. The algae and vegetation shelters and produces vast quantities of minute animal life upon which the fiercely fecund and reproductive small-mouthed, purse-lipped bluegills and sunfish largely feed along with the flies and insects which fall on the surface of the ponds during the long, hot, insect-breeding months on a fertile middle-western farm. In turn the small-mouthed sunfish produce millions of small fish which provide food for the big, predatory bass and trout and some of the larger-mouthed and predatory green sunfish.

Weather and flood conditions occasionally alter the nesting habits not only of fish but of marsh-nesting birds. During the disastrously wet spring and summer of 1947 the red-winged blackbirds provided a remarkable example of the effect of weather upon nesting habits. These lovely

The Cycle of a Farm Pond

birds which normally nest among the sedge grass and bullrushes of marshes, creek banks and ponds, abandoned their usual habits and took to nesting on the high ground in the alfalfa fields. When I began mowing alfalfa in mid-June I started up considerable numbers of fledglings just old enough to fly and found several old abandoned nests set into clumps of alfalfa exactly as the birds normally set their nests in a clump of sedge or marsh grass. The fact raises again the old question of whether birds by some instinct are aware in advance of weather or the exact time of changing seasons. The migration time of many birds varies a great deal. In this case I do not know whether the birds anticipated the floods which later inundated their usual low-ground nesting places or whether they took to the higher ground because the whole of the spring had produced continuously flooding rains and abnormally high water. In the same season of disturbed and turbulent water in the ponds, the sunfish and bass did not breed and nest until five or six weeks later than usual. Whether they attempted to do so earlier at the normal time and found their efforts thwarted or whether their later nesting and breeding period produced the usual results I do not know. In that same summer, the red-winged blackbirds developed or at least exhibited habits that in my observation were new and strange. They appeared in great numbers, indeed in flocks, following the mower and gorging themselves on the leafhoppers which infested the alfalfa. Except at migrating time the red-winged blackbirds had generally flown about in pairs or occasionally appeared in groups of five or six all of the same sex. It scarcely seems possible that the birds through nesting on high ground suddenly and for the first time discovered the leafhoppers as a rich source of food supply. The occurrence, however, was one more proof of the benefit to the farmer of supplying adequate cover in fence rows or isolated patches of undergrowth and marshland for the bird population.

In the same season the killdeer plovers, which also nest on low ground along creeks made no apparent change in their nesting habits. They are among the most careless of nest-builders, taking no trouble at all beyond hollowing out a shallow nest on a bare spot of gravel or sand in a low pasture by a creek. Presumably the eggs and the young killdeer which were not yet old enough to leave the nest were destroyed by the floods. Like quail, however, the young of the killdeer are extremely precocious and leave the nest very early, running about on the sandbanks and on the short bluegrass pasture even before they are able to fly. The young of the red-winged blackbird, on the other hand, must be fully feathered and well grown before they are able to leave the nest. They live almost entirely in the air or by clinging to high bullrushes and weeds, rarely making excursions on the ground as walking birds.

The green sunfish is the broad general name in our part of the country for a group of fish with varying characteristics. Although they rarely attain a length of more than six inches, there is no fish which fights more gamely. Indeed, if their size is taken into consideration, I know of no fresh- or salt-water fish which puts up so valiant a fight. They are, so far as I have been able to discover, the only group of the minor sunfish

Louis Bromfield

which feed upon the young of other fish. I have observed them greedily pursuing young bass which is a little like the fox turning upon the hounds. Naturally they are equipped with much bigger mouths than the other minor sunfish and some of them actually resemble closely small bass in appearance. When they get out of balance in a pond or lake they may become a menace even to the predatory bass population. The green sunfish is altogether a very aggressive little fish and a gallant fighter which will provide good sport on a light flyrod.

All will take a worm from a hook and, of course, artificial flies, but at times it is difficult to take the bluegills or some of the varieties of sunfish because of the extreme smallness of their mouths. The bass, even the small-mouth which is the variety which inhabits our ponds, has an immense mouth and gullet, sometimes making up very nearly half his length. The great mouth and gullet permits him to swallow a good-sized sunfish at a single gulp. In the case of the Fleming pond, the bass provide an absolute check or block upon the increase of carp or goldfish by devouring their roe or their young very soon after they are hatched.

This process and control and the operation of a natural cycle and balance of life is observable not only in ponds but in the free, open, fresh-water streams. In almost any clear running stream with abundant vegetation throughout most of the Mississippi basin, the balance and life-cycle will include some carp and catfish as well as bass, crappies and other members of the sunfish, game fish family. If the stream becomes polluted either by sewage or siltation or is swept clean of vegetation by periodic floods, the balance is upset and the game fish will gradually disappear and the mud-loving fish will presently dominate in overwhelming numbers until gradually and finally only coarse mud-loving fish—carp, catfish, et al.—alone exist.

This has been the history of many once fine fishing streams and lakes in the Mississippi basin where either sewage pollution from cities or steadily increasing siltation coming from ignorantly and poorly managed farm lands gradually produce conditions which exterminate all the game fish and leave only the coarse fish and finally exterminate all stream life save turtles and frogs.

This is what happened to countless streams in the South which were once famous for good sport fishing. Increasing erosion has turned many of them at certain times of the year into what is little more than a mass of viscous, thin, slow-flowing mud in which all fish life becomes impossible.

For the sportsmen this gives the problem of soil and water conservation and reckless deforestation an important place in the scheme of things. In the past, stream after stream, pond after pond, and bay after bay in the bigger lakes which were once famous fishing grounds for sportsmen have been reduced, by incessant floods and siltation coming from bare, poorly farmed fields, to the category of coarse, mud-fish territory or of no fish at all. In Lake Erie even the commercial fishing business, representing millions of dollars a year, is being threatened by the pollution of the big industrial cities and the siltation of spawning beds in its shallower waters.

The Cycle of a Farm Pond

On the other hand, in a few streams in limited areas where good soil, water, and forestry practices have come into existence, clean water and vegetation have come back into the streams, ponds, and lakes, and periodic floods have been largely eliminated with the result that in streams which only a few years ago had been reduced to the level of coarse-fish carp and catfish waters, the proper balance and cycle is being restored and the waters are becoming known again as fine places for game fishing.

In our own farm ponds every effort has been made to prevent siltation. The practice of proper forestry and soil conservation and a program of grass farming has reduced siltation virtually to zero, and after and even during the heaviest rainfall the excess water reaching at least two of the ponds is as clear as the rainwater itself. In one pond the water becomes discolored from the run-off of a neighboring gravel lane which cannot be controlled, but the siltation amounts to little more than discoloration and is mostly very fine sand which settles quickly leaving the water clear and blue after a short time. Under these conditions the balance of aquatic life quickly establishes itself and the ponds rapidly become filled with too many fish, so that fishing becomes not only a pleasure but a duty, for unfished ponds existing under proper conditions need no stocking; on the contrary it is necessary to fish them constantly in order to keep down the population. Otherwise the population exceeds the food supply and the pond becomes filled with innumerable fish which are too small either for good sport or for food.

The pond on the Fleming Place has long since reached the point of ideal balance and cycle. If fished steadily it goes on producing quantities of big game fish providing both unlimited sport and "fish for supper" for every family on the farm as often as they want it. Because the pond is a fertile one filled with vegetation, it produces a constant supply of food for small fish and small-mouthed sunfish which in turn provide food for the bass and the bigger fish. The cycle of production for sport and food is constant and prodigious despite the fact that the pond is little over an acre in size. Constant fishing is in itself a part of the cycle of abundance since the pond is land-locked and would quickly become overpopulated and the fish small and bony if a considerable poundage of fish were not removed from it annually.

The Fleming pond is an old pond. Those on the Anson and the Bailey Places are newer. The one on the Anson Place was constructed only seven years ago and the one on the Bailey Place only two years ago. In the Anson pond the perfect balance and cycle has not yet established itself. It is a deep pond with a comparatively small amount of shallow water. In the beginning no stocking was done, save the fish caught in other ponds or in neighboring streams and dumped into it. Two years ago about 500 fingerling rainbow trout were put in. The fish from local ponds and streams were largely bluegills and varieties of sunfish with a few suckers and minnows. Among them were a score and more of big small-mouth bass weighing from one to two pounds upward. These were taken out of the older Fleming pond which at the end of each

Louis Bromfield

summer is cleaned systematically by worm and hook fishing to eliminate the biggest fish which turn cannibal and devour not only the "food fish" within the pond cycle but also the young and half-grown bass.

Of all the fish put into the six-year-old pond on the Anson Place, the minnows and suckers very quickly were eliminated, either by being eaten or by going out of the outlet into the flowing streams which were much more their natural habitat than the still ponds. A heavy winter following the transplantation of the big bass kept the pond frozen over solidly and the lack of oxygen and sunlight was apparently too much for the bass for when the ice thawed in the spring all of them were floating dead on its surface. They never had a chance to nest or breed.

Fish ponds and even lakes of considerable size throughout Ohio suffered similar losses of the bass and some other fish during the same severe winter. Open streams did not suffer similar losses because the movement of water kept them open wherever there were ripples. Ponds, of course, are not the natural or ideal habitat for the small-mouthed bass which prefers streams, varied by deep pools and swift flowing water over steep gradients. The fish for which the pond is a natural habitat suffered much less from the shortage of oxygen and sunlight.

As it turned out, this worked into the plan of control on the six-year-old Anson pond. Its waters ran to a depth of twenty feet and it was spring fed both at the inlet and from springs in the bottom and even in the hottest days of August the deeper water remained cold, at a temperature of about fifty degrees. This depth and temperature made it a possibility as a trout pond. Trout could never have survived in the old shallow Fleming pond which was too warm and which already contained a flourishing population of bass. We found long ago that trout and bass cannot exist indefinitely in the same waters; the bass inevitably exterminate the trout, perhaps because they have much bigger mouths and can out-swallow the trout both in number and size of fish. Therefore, the elimination of the big bass by a severe winter left the deep, cold, six-year-old Anson pond ready for stocking by trout, especially since the food supply of the smaller fecund sunfish of all varieties was already well established.

Rainbow or brown trout were chosen as the most likely to flourish in the Anson pond and eventually we put in the 500 fingerlings not more than three of four inches in length. During the first summer there was no evidence of them whatever. They were never seen at all, either alive or floating dead upon the surface, and I came to the disappointing conclusion that they had all left the pond through the open outlet. When spring came the following year there was still no evidence of the rainbows. None of them were seen either dead or alive or in the shallow waters where the sunfish could be watched nesting.

During the six years of the pond's existence, following the "amateur" stocking of native fish from neighboring ponds and streams, the fish population increased immensely until this spring it became evident that there were far too many fish and that we should have to go to "work" fishing them out. There were thousands of them, mostly too small for table use. When we went to work, we made a remarkable discovery. Among the scores of fish which we took out as rapidly as the hook struck the water, more than 99 per cent were of two varieties—either long-eared or green sunfish with some odd unidentifiable hybrids. There being no big predatory fish in the pond, we came to the conclusion that these two varieties had survived and dominated and because the green sunfish had the biggest mouths. They could swallow the other varieties of smaller, purse-mouthed sunfish like the bluegill, the punkin-seed and even the long-eared sunfish. They had simply eaten the other fish out of existence, and themselves had no control placed upon them since the small-mouthed fish could not swallow them once they were above a certain size, even if they had been inclined to include other fish as legitimate articles of diet which, as a rule, the small-mouthed fish do not do.

In any case, we were made sharply aware of the vast population of green sunfish, which I suspect in our case, may have been a crossbred variety in that particular pond, for their mouths and gullets appear to be much larger than the ordinary green sunfish described and pictured in all books dealing with the fish of the Mississippi basin.

These voracious green sunfish, although they never attain much size even under favorable conditions and I have seen only a few that approached a pound in weight, make excellent sport with a flyrod. They take the fly with a rush and ounce for ounce put up a fiercer and longer fight than any trout or bass. That summer we did not look for sport in the Anson pond so much as to reduce the population of fish, so we used cane poles and worms to fish. Even with this steady tackle, I have seen the little fellows take a worm on the rush and bend the bamboo pole half way to double.

"Cleaning" a pond to reduce the fish population is a pleasurable procedure. Armed with cane pole and worms and with a big milk can at one's side we take fish after fish off the hook at half-minute intervals and throw them into the milk-can for transference to a new pond or to the neighboring streams, but there is not much real excitement in it. At times eight or ten of us will spend an evening simply "cleaning" a pond.

I began the "cleaning" process on the six-year-old Anson pond to cut down the population of green sunfish and I got my excitement, even with a bamboo pole and worm-baited hook, when after I had half-filled the milk can with fish, the bait was taken by a fish which behaved differently from the ones I had been catching. I brought him to the surface and the sight of his silvery speckled body gave me one of the thrills of a long fishing career. He was no sunfish. He was a rainbow trout, ten inches in length, one of the 500 I had put in a year earlier and bemoaned as lost. He was not only still in the pond but he had grown in the span of a year from three inches to ten. I raised him reverently from the water. I had hooked him through the cartilage around the mouth and he was unhurt. Reverently I threw him back into the pond to go on growing into a two or three pound big fellow who later on will make wonderful sport and wonderful eating.

Louis Bromfield

And about every tenth fish we took out in the process of "cleaning" was a handsome, silvery, speckled fellow, one of the rainbow fingerlings we had put in a year earlier. Most of them were uninjured and were put back to grow some more.

It is clear what happened. The trout fingerlings stayed in the clear, cold, deep water and never appeared in the warm shallow water where the sunfish nested, frolicked and ate. They are still staying most of the time in the deep, cold water but now the fingerlings are big enough to go foraging into the shallow haunts of the sunfish, clearly in search of food which meant that they were after the young sunfish. The latter are now having competition from predatory fish with as big or bigger mouths than their own and it is probable that a balance and cycle like that between bass and sunfish in the older Fleming pond will establish itself between trout and sunfish in the six-year-old Anson pond. In the evenings we see the trout foraging on the surface for insects.

The vegetation and life growing in the algae of the pond are clearly already sufficient to support considerable population of food sunfish, enough to give the rainbow trout as fat a diet as the bass already have in the older Fleming pond. Whether the trout whose breeding habits are different from those of the bass-sunfish family will manage to reproduce themselves as rapidly as the bass have done in the Fleming pond or even at all, remains to be seen. I am hopeful. If they do, the productivity and balance of the newer pond will be established and we shall, in order to maintain it at the maximum level of food and sport, have to fish it regularly, a hardship any fisherman is willing to suffer when it means that he is getting fish from a pound to four or five pounds, all fighters whether they are big bluegills and sunfish or bass or rainbow trout.

The life cycle of fish is a subject of some dispute among scientists and to be sure, varies greatly with the species. Legend has it that there are carp in the moats and ponds of Fontainebleau and Chantilly which were there at the time of François Premier and guides point to the rings set in the snouts of the huge, mangy old carp with the statement that they were thus ringed two hundred years ago. All this may be true for certainly the carp are immensely old and very large. Recently a female sturgeon weighing 175 pounds was taken in Lake Erie and the press attributed to it an age of over a hundred years. This particular fish was a female and yielded many pounds of caviar at the time of the catch. It is a sad fact that the sturgeon population of the Great Lakes like that of many other fish, has been steadily decreasing as siltation, sewage, and industrial pollution has increased.

Growth and size of fish and perhaps their age is determined largely by food supply. A green sunfish in the controlled Fleming pond will reach what is apparent maximum size much more rapidly than in the six-year-old Anson pond where the population of its own kind, feeding upon its own diet, is much too great at present. In the Fleming pond where its food is abundant, a bass will reach a weight of three or four pounds in approximately the same number of years. The largest bass

The Cycle of a Farm Pond

taken from the pond weighed a little over five pounds. I do not know its exact age. But because the Fleming pond is comparatively small and shallow it is possible to observe and check with a considerable degree of accuracy the age and growth of the fish. There always appears to be at least four sizes: (1) The newly hatched pin-sized fry. Those which survive apparently reach a length of three to four inches in one season. (2) The two-year-olds which at the end of the second season have grown from the four-inch length to a length of eight or more inches. (3) The three-year-old crop which runs a foot to eighteen inches. (4) Those fish of all sizes above eighteen inches which are the biggest ones and whose cannibalistic habits with regard to the five to eight inch bass lead us to clear them out of the pond at the end of each summer.

The newest of theories among fish experts is that if a pond or stream provides the proper conditions, and is not subject to violent periodic flooding, siltation or pollution and the food supply is adequate, there is no need for stocking and that, on the contrary, there is a need to fish the stream or pond constantly in order to control the population and secure bigger fish and better sport.

The Ohio State Conservation Commission, of which the author is a member, has opened several lakes and some streams where the food, and control conditions are right and pollution is virtually non-existent, to unrestricted fishing without season, size or bag limit, and the results tend to show over a short period of time that such wholesale fishing improves both the size and quality of the fish without diminishing the amount of the catch. Other states are making similar experiments and if the final results are in line with the early indication of the experiment it is likely that stocking fish in polluted or heavily silted streams where they cannot live or reproduce will be abandoned, together with bag and season restrictions, and the emphasis and expenditure of taxpayers' money will be diverted from expensive fish hatcheries and stocking programs to the cleaning up of streams and lakes and the establishment of conditions which permit and encourage almost unlimited fish populations which actually *demand* unrestricted fishing to keep their populations in control.

Among the great and beautiful artificial lakes created in the Tennessee Valley Authority area all restrictions as to season, bag and size limit have been removed. The result has been to create a veritable fisherman's paradise. The creation of proper conditions, clean water, vegetation, etc., has proven that legal rules on take, season, etc., are unnecessary and that actually the more fish taken the better the fishing becomes. This is both reasonable and scientific procedure since a single female bass will produce as many as a hundred thousand and upward of eggs which when fertilized become small fry. Sunfish, crappies and coarse fish reproduce themselves at an even more prodigious rate. Not long ago I happened along the shore of Pleasant Hill lake at the end of the farm when a Conservation Commission employee was dumping five thousand fingerling small-mouth bass into the lake. As he poured the bass into the lake he remarked cynically, "Each one of these fish cost a lot of money to produce

Louis Bromfield

and all this stocking is a lot of hooey. Maybe it makes some ignorant sportsmen feel they're getting something, but a couple of pairs of good bass could do the same job without any expense at all." The man was not a scientist. He was an unskilled laborer but he had learned a great deal of wisdom through observation. I am told that in Colorado where hatchery-raised trout are introduced into streams, the cost of each trout is about $4.75. This, of course, is paid out of the sportsman license fees which could be expended far more profitably in providing clean streams and proper habitat where the fish could reproduce themselves successfully by the million. The new belief that money expended upon clean streams and habitat is better spent than on hatcheries and stocking is growing among state fish and game commissions and sportsmen generally. The same theory is spreading to the realm of hatchery bred and stocked quail, pheasant, partridge, to raccoon "farms" and all fields of game conservation and propagation.

This is a revolutionary idea, but it is also a wise development in reason, science and common sense. If the streams and lakes of the country were cleaned of pollution and siltation and floods checked by proper agricultural and forestry methods, there would be fine fishing in unlimited quantity for the whole of the population which enjoys fishing. Certainly our own experience with both ponds and streams has proven that this is true and that fishing becomes not only a sport but at times a duty and occasionally a real job.

One of the most fascinating spectacles in the world is the fashion in which Nature herself will take over a naked, newly constructed pond and set to work to make it into an old fertile pond in which natural controls are set up throughout the whole cycle of its life.

We have had an opportunity during the past years to observe the process in the case of the new ponds constructed and particularly the one on the Bailey Place. The site chosen for this pond was the corner of a field which even in midsummer was too wet for use as cultivated ground. Nearby was a very fine, big spring and several smaller ones as a source of water. In two days' work with a big bull-dozer and scoop a pond was constructed of about three acres in size varying from under a foot to fourteen feet in depth. The shallow area is large and makes an ideal feeding and breeding ground for fish once aquatic life is fully established. The barrier was made by excavating the soil from the bottom of the pond and piling it up as a dam which also serves as a road way to and from adjoining fields.

Nearly seven weeks were required to fill the pond to its full depth for some of the water evaporated and much of it seeped through the bare, newly created bottom.

Watching the pond carefully, I observed a number of things. The first life to appear was the native killdeer, accompanied now and then by a dozen or more of their cousins, the rare golden plover. They waded about, crying and fluttering apparently in delight over the shallow rising water. They did not appear to feed but simply to wade about screaming

The Cycle of a Farm Pond

and flapping their wings. Then a few frogs appeared from the damp spots in the neighboring fields and numbers of water skaters and water beetles. In the water warmed by the sun a few thin strands of algae, possibly carried in on the feet of the killdeer and plovers, appeared and began to grow in long strands, like the green hair of mermaids, and presently as the frogs increased in number the smaller herons appeared, and at last the pair of great blue herons which has been with us winter and summer for six years and ranges the ponds and the shallows of the big lake at the end of the farm, acknowledged the existence of the new pond by visits to do a little frog hunting. What new life they brought to the pond clinging to their feet or in their excreta I do not know, but they too undoubtedly made their contribution to the growing, expanding life of the pond.

On the naked sides and on the newly constructed dam we put a layer of barnyard manure and sowed rye to bind the soil with its deep, wide-spreading fibrous roots and stop all erosion. In the manure there must have been millions of undigested seeds of ladino clover and other plants for there quickly grew up a carpet of vegetation which included rye-grass and bluegrass, white, sweet, red alsike and ladino clovers, and within a few weeks all danger of erosion or siltation from the naked soil surrounding the pond was eliminated. Even after a heavy rain the water remained clear. The apparent high rate of germination in the manure-sewn clover seeds could doubtless be traced back a season or two to the activities of thirty hives of bees which we keep on the farm to provide honey and pollenize the legumes. During all that first summer the level of the pond continued to rise and fall, varying according to the seepage in the pond bottom as it settled itself. By autumn there was a thick growth of algae over a considerable part of the surface. The winter came, the vegetation froze hard, the frogs and bettles disappeared, the killdeer and plover went south and the great blue herons abandoned visiting the pond for the richer, shallower, unfrozen waters of the big lake. Then the pond froze over and went dormant.

With the coming of spring, the ice melted and presently the crying of frogs and spring peepers were heard from along the shallow edges. The vegetation came back with a rush. Then in the shallows occurred the mating orgies of the hundreds of toads which appeared out of nowhere—accompanied by struggling and crying which put to rout the excesses of the Babylonians, and presently great strands of frog and toad spawn appeared in the shallow waters. In the same shallow waters the coarse hardy dock plants, submerged the summer before where they grew, thrust their tough heads up through the water and presently began to turn yellow and drown to slow death to be supplanted by the new growth of seedlings and water grasses brought in as seeds clinging to the feet of water birds. And the seepage problem seemed to have solved itself. The pond had settled, the weight of the water closing up the open places in the bottom. And the algae had done its part for with the coming of winter it had sunk to the bottom and laid a network of fine webbing over the whole of the pond bottom. The clay which had been squashy the season before so that when

Louis Bromfield

you waded into the pond you sank very nearly to your knees, became firm and hard under the weight of tons of water and remained only a little sticky on the top surface. What had once been a naked excavation walled in by a naked earthen dam had become within a year a watertight reservoir, its banks covered with protective vegetation, its shallow waters alive with vegetable and animal life.

The beetles and water skaters and water flies reappeared in vastly greater numbers and presently the shallow water was filled by millions of animated exclamation points that were tadpoles. And along the banks one came upon various kinds of water snakes which had discovered the new pond and taken up residence there to feed upon the young frogs and fish which their instinct told them would soon provide a rich source of food. But most curious of all, there appeared presently in a pond completely shut off from outside waters, among the myriad tadpoles, a few pin-sized fish. Where they came from I do not know unless the eggs became attached somehow to the feet of the plovers and herons as they waded over the nests of fish in the other ponds or in Switzer's Creek. They were, at the time, still too small to be identified as to species save through the use of a magnifying glass or microscope. The eggs may have remained wet, the germ still living during the flight of the birds from one pond to another or from the creek or the shallows of the big lake at Pleasant Hill dam. Those who live near to water know that in the business of carrying on life, nature can be incredibly tough and resistant and overwhelming. As the summer progressed all of these small fry turned into varieties of sunfish indicating that their origin probably lay in neighboring ponds.

In the case of the frogs and tadpoles which appeared early during the second year of life in the pond, we were indeed overwhelmed. The tadpoles appeared by the thousands in the shallow waters and presently were turned into myriads of small frogs, mostly of the handsome green and black spotted leopard varieties, none of them too big to sit comfortably on a silver half dollar. As we walked along the banks they went into a panic and leaped into the water like flights of grasshoppers in a grasshopper year. One could understand easily the Old Testament plague of frogs brought upon Egypt in Moses' time. One could understand too why nature produced tiny frogs in such vast quantities for their behavior during panic was idiotic and made them an easy victim of any predator, snake, fish, or raccoon. As one approached, they went into a panic-stricken hysterical flight, some jumping into the water some away from the water. The truth was that the new pond, still partly undeveloped by nature and with no natural balance established, contained not yet enough enemies and predators to cope with the prodigious fecundity of the frogs which produced in the scheme of things thousands of frogs in order that a few score might survive. There were in the waters of the pond no bass or trout or pike which would have made short work of the hysterical young frogs which leaped into the open water, and not yet enough snakes, raccoons and herons to devour the more foolish of their numbers on land or in the very shallow waters.

The Cycle of a Farm Pond

It is easy to see how the frogs of the world, unhampered by natural checks and predators, could soon increase to such numbers that they would overrun everything, fill the whole of the land, and leave no room for the rest of us.

The muskrats were certain to be the next settlers at the new pond. Always in the second year they make their appearance, coming up the narrow silver thread of overflow water in the moonlight from the marshes in the Jungle, a wild piece of wet land in the middle of the farm, and from the marshes about the big lake where they exist by the thousand. One rarely sees them save sometimes in the moonlight when the nose of a muskrat moves across the ponds leaving a long V-shaped wake behind it in the still, silvery waters. One rarely sees them but the evidence of their presence is all around the edges of the pond, in the holes they dig for dens in the banks, in the nibbled foliage of certain plants and in the runways they make along the edges of the streams that feed the ponds. Usually they migrate during the second winter of the life of a pond and once they are established they like the easy living and remain there. When their numbers exceed the food supply, the younger ones go back to the marshes about the big lakes which are a muskrat's paradise.

The ones which remain are an endless source of trouble. They devour the succulent roots of the water lilies and the bullrushes and the tender underwater shoots of the arrowleaf which we try to establish in a new pond, and they attack even the tubers of the irises in the flower garden only fifty feet from the house. Two years ago during a hard winter when the ponds were frozen over for three months they burrowed beneath a tree wistaria and ate off all its roots so that in the spring, it simply fell over, rootless and dead. They burrowed into the dams and threatened to destroy them until we discovered that twenty-four-inch chicken wire laid along the dam at the surface of the water, where they like to dig, prevented further burrowing. They are tough and shrewd and sly and prolific and no amount of trapping by the boys on the farm, who pick up a good many extra dollars that way during the winter, either intimidates or discourages them. Now and then one of the dogs catches a foolish young muskrat offside and ends his career, but the dogs do not serve as a sufficient check upon the fecundity of the water rodents. There are no more wolves in our country but there are an abundance of foxes which at night bark from the wooded ridge back and forth in the moonlight. Save for the dogs they are the only check upon the woodchucks and the muskrat and they get only the young and foolish ones. A big muskrat is too shrewd for a fox and a big, old woodchuck can outfight him. Without the dogs, the woodchuck would, like the frogs, eventually take us over.

It must be said, however, that one of the last things we should desire at Malabar is the total extermination of woodchucks. The holes they dig and their generous hospitality in sharing them with other animals make them a great asset in building game and wildlife populations. Their holes serve at all times, but particularly during the winter months, as shelter and refuge for rabbit, quail, possum, skunks, partridges and other

Louis Bromfield

animals and birds. Female raccoon, when natural tree dens are scarce or non-existent will house their litters in woodchuck holes. So valuable does the Ohio Conservation Commission consider the place of the woodchuck and the hole he digs in the whole cyclical balance of wildlife that in 1947 it established a closed season from March, when the woodchuck wakens to emerge from his hole, to August, by which time the young are able to take care of themselves. The ruling does not prevent a farmer from reducing the woodchuck population which gets out of control but it does put an end to the idiotic and unsportsmanlike habits of some city dwellers who go into the countryside merely to use the woodchuck for target practice. Among emigrant Southerners, both white and colored, woodchuck is considered a delicacy.

Rarely have I seen a muskrat by daylight and then only when lying very still among the sedge grass and weeds, I have been so well hidden that he was unaware of my presence. His habit is to travel in the shallow water of a creek close to the bank and even though the water is clear he is difficult to notice or to see. The concealment arises less from his fantastically protective coloring than from the undulations of his wet shining body which are like the movements of the flowing water itself. He moves, half-swimming, half-walking with a flowing motion and only a sharp eye can detect his presence where there is any current at all.

Perhaps the most beautiful newcomers to the pond during the second summer were the dragonflies. They appeared in prodigious numbers, looking like gaudily painted miniature planes. At least three varieties were noticeable. One variety, the largest, was about three to four inches long, with purple-black body and with bars of black on the widespread transparent wings. Another smaller dragonfly came in various shades of green with deep emerald green wings. The third, smallest and most beautiful was a fragile dragonfly all of one color, an iridescent turquoise blue with body which appeared to be almost transparent as they hovered over the surface of the water. All three varieties spend the whole of their brief lives in frantically eating and breeding. They dart and hover over the shallow water, the floating algae and the water weeds, devouring hosts of tiny gnats, mosquitoes and other insects which deposit their eggs in the water where they hatch into larvae to feed the sunfish as well. The prodigious number of dragonflies over the new pond probably arose from the fact that the fish population has not yet become established to devour the larvae and act as a check upon the almost unlimited increase of insects.

The great numbers of hatching insects brought not only hordes of the delicate dragonflies, but wild, soaring flights of deep, iridescent blue and red swifts and barn swallows which each year build their neat mud nests on the beams of the big Bailey barn beside the pond. In the evenings they circle, hover and dive-bomb the newly hatched insects, dipping their tiny, swift wings into the water, sending up tiny jets of spray in the evening light.

Of course, within the depths of the new pond there came quickly into existence trillions of amoebae, rotifers and tiny plants and animals

The Cycle of a Farm Pond

invisible to the naked eye which flourish in the warm shallow waters of ponds and in the form of fresh water plankton which makes up a large part of the food supply of the fish from the smallest pin-sized fry up through the larger sunfish. These animals and plants, seen under a microscope, reveal complicated and brilliantly beautiful patterns of life. Although invisible they comprise a vital part of the natural life-cycle of a pond. Doubtless they are carried there upon the feet of birds and muskrats or the damp skin of frogs and on the bellies of slithering water snakes from adjoining ponds and streams. Many already existed in the wet ground of the pond site. The Natural History Museum in New York City contains a truly wonderful exhibit of these organisms executed brilliantly in colored glass many thousands of times larger than life.

Nature has a million subtle ways of quickly converting a raw, new pond into an old pond, fertile and teeming with life, but in all our ponds we have helped her as much as possible to speed the rate of conversion. One thing which a good farmer quickly learns is that in fighting nature he will always be defeated but that in working with her, he can make remarkable and immensely profitable progress. Beside the barnyard manure and the seeding of the banks we have thrust young willow butts here and there along the banks and every three or four feet along the crest of the dam. Within two or three years the fast growing willows, the particularly beautiful and hardy, semi-weeping variety known as *Babylonica*, will grow twelve to fifteen feet and along the dam their roots create a solid mat which binds the earth together and makes it resistant to the waters of the most devastating cloudbursts. Along the edge they provide the shade which the big bass love and a resting place for insects which drop into the water and feed the hungry fish waiting below.

The Conservation Commissions of many states send out free to all farmers of the state bundles of shrubs and trees for planting around farm ponds. These hasten the efforts of nature to convert a new pond into an old one and provide food and shelter for small game. The bundles include native flowering wild crabapple, standing honeysuckle, fruit-bearing viburnums, hazelnuts, pines and many other shrubs and trees. These are now planted in the areas about the ponds and help to build up that balance and cycle in the pond and the area about it which is a part of any successful fish pond. The new ponds are treated with fertilizer along the edges in the shallow water to encourage the growing of vegetation which plays so large a part in the cycle of pond fertility and life. A little fertilizer—particularly phosphate—will increase the number and size of the fish enormously.[1]

During the first summer of the Bailey pond's existence we transplanted to its borders a few roots of arrowleaf and some of the water plants already growing in the older ponds. It was a simple enough process, simply that of thrusting the roots into the soil in the shallow water. These took hold immediately and increased prodigiously during the summer, as much

[1]At Georgia State Agricultural College experiments with the fertilizing of fish ponds achieved an increase in fish production of up to five hundred pounds to the acre.

Louis Bromfield

as many hundreds of times, joining the water and marsh vegetation already seeded there through visits of muskrats and water birds in providing shelter for all sorts of minute animal life as well as for the small fry which appeared mysteriously and those hatched out after the stocking of the new pond in the early spring with mature bass, bluegills and sunfish from the older ponds.

By the end of the second summer the first evidence of balance had become apparent. The plague of small frogs and toads had leveled off to a normal population, the number of dragonflies diminished and the whole cycle of birth, life, death, and rebirth had begun to operate.

At the end of the third year the new pond on the Bailey Place already took on the aspect of the older ponds. The shallow water had been invaded by thick growths of arrowhead, bulrush, water lilies and a great variety of water grasses and subaqueous vegetation. Within the refuge they provide against the attacks of the bigger fish, the water snakes and birds, there appeared in due course of time literally thousands of young bluegills, sunfish and young bass up to three or four inches in length. The fingerlings of the pound-size bluegills and the big bass which will make the sport of tomorrow.

A week ago we began seriously the annual "cleaning" of the older ponds with bamboo poles, worms, and a couple of big milk cans, transferring fish wholesale from the fertile older ponds into the newer ones. The task becomes a sport in which all the farm takes part. The boys, the older men and even some of the women join in, and in the crowded ponds every cast means a strike, and one never knows what one will get—a bluegill, a bass or any one of the varieties of sunfish and sometimes in the Anson pond, a nice-sized trout. Only the trout are thrown back because we want to establish in the Anson pond that cycle of trout and sunfish based upon the bass and sunfish cycle which has proven itself so productive in the old Fleming pond.

Fish after fish, the catch is tossed into the milk cans, kept aerated by changing the water and pouring in fresh bucketfuls constantly from the pond. There is a wide range of beauty in the catch from the lovely deep sea-green of the bass and the silvery-spotted beauty of the trout, through the whole range of sunfish up to the iridescent, fantastic beauty of the long-eared type with his brilliant yellow belly, his stripes and changeable colors and the jet-black spot behind his gills.

Last night we sat among the willows along the old Fleming pond, fishing, nine of us, as the sun went down and a virgin crescent moon appeared as the sky changed from scarlet and gold to pale mauve to deep blue. The women sat in the grass shelling the glut of peas from the garden for canning and the quick freeze and the small children yelled with excitement each time they managed to hook and bring in a fish. We fished until it was too dark to see the bobber, and then set out with a flashlight to transfer the fish to the new ponds. There was at least thirty pounds of fish ranging in size from a few baby sunfish to a fine big bass of about four pounds which somehow had eluded us in "cleaning" the pond of big fel-

The Cycle of a Farm Pond

lows the preceding autumn. And everyone had fresh fish for breakfast the next morning.

The farm pond is becoming rapidly not only a pleasure but a necessity. State Conservation Commissions are encouraging them. Ohio aids the individual farm without cost in their construction. Missouri plans to construct 200 thousand farm ponds during the next few years. They tend to catch and hold the precious rainfall on thousands of farms, to supply water for the livestock, swimming holes, and fish for the table. On our farm whenever a family wants fish for supper one has only to take a pole and a line and in a half hour or more get all the fish he wants.

But there are other advantages to farm ponds which are not wholly utilitarian. Our ponds are each one a spot of beauty, a small universe teeming with life. The big herons visit them and the lovely red-winged blackbirds build their nests in the rushes along the borders. They are the delight of the big fierce Toulouse geese and the tame mallards. They are the source of much music in the night from the peeping of new young frogs to the booming bass of the big Louisiana bullfrogs which we put in as tadpoles years ago and which now measure as much as eighteen to twenty inches when stretched out. In April their borders turn green and gold with the lush foliage and flowers of the marsh marigold, and later they are bordered with the blue of Siberian iris and the purple and gold of the native wild flags. At night the muskrats move across the surface in the moonlight and the raccoons and foxes and possum come down out of the thick woods to drink and catch unwary frogs, leaving the imprint of their small paws in the wet mud along the banks. And there are the scavenging mud-turtles and a few big destructive snapping-turtles which the mallards avoid by shrewdly never taking their young onto the ponds until they are well grown. And there are countless birds, the swifts and barn swallows which skim low over the ponds in the blue evenings, to catch the insects hatching from their depths, and the flocks of goldfinches which fianlly mate off and build their nests from the down of the purple thistles growing in the damp ground. And in spring and autumn there are the visits of the wild ducks which join our mallards and feast off the richness of the farm ponds and the neighboring fields for three or four weeks at a time. For a lonely farm a pond provides life and fascination.

Each year, spring and autumn, we have been accustomed to visits of wild ducks. Usually these were mallards and so-called shallow-water ducks, but with the establishment of the Bailey pond we began to receive visits from flocks of bluebills and other deep-water ducks. We discovered presently that they were attracted by the tender shoots of the fast spreading arrowleaf, spending hours diving and burrowing for the young growth. Wherever they burrowed their bills left tiny holes in the mud bottom of the pond. Dessie and Al often sit on the veranda of the big, old Bailey house in the evening watching the life on the pond until darkness comes down, the swallows take to the barn and the muskrat and raccoons come out to haunt the reeds and the shallow water.

In a way, a farm pond is a symbol of life itself. It is a bright spot on

Louis Bromfield

any farm, a whole universe in which the laws of nature operate under the close and intimate gaze of the interested. One can find in farm ponds and along their borders almost everything. They change with the season, awakening from the frozen, silent sleep of winter, going into the beginning of spring and the fierce breeding life of early summer. They provide skating in winter and swimming in summer and good fishing for three seasons of the year. For the children they are a source of inexhaustible delight. And like the fishponds of the abbeys and castles of medieval Europe and the Dark Ages, when all the world fell apart in anarchy and disorder, they provide not only food for the table but peace for the soul and an understanding of man's relationship to the universe.

[1948]

The Cycle of a Farm Pond

Joseph Wood Krutch:

Postscript

Joseph Wood Krutch (1893-1970), literary scholar and critic and naturalist, was led into his deep, lifelong appreciation of nature through literary and humanistic study. In his nature writing there is a keen awareness of natural beauty, a sense of awe, and a conviction that all of nature, including man, is ultimately one.

More than twenty-five years ago I first bought a house in the country. My motives were various, but as in the case of many another man who acquires something he never had before, the most compelling was the fact that my wife wanted it. Among the reasons I gave myself to explain my acquiescence, the possibility that I might some day be writing about nature was certainly not one. As a matter of fact I had been leading a double life, in the city and out of it, for almost a quarter of a century before it occurred to me. Then one evening when I was reading with delight about someone else's feeling for his countryside, I said to myself that it would be nice if I could do it too.

Until then I had never realized what had been happening to me. I still thought that I thought the country was a place where one went to get away from the fatigues of the city. Its virtues were still supposed to be largely negative and I had never realized how, in actual fact, I had long been regarding it as the principal scene of those activities for the sake of which I made a living elsewhere, how completely it had become the place where it seemed to me that I must live or have no being. Since then I have seen myself referred to somewhat condescendingly as a "nature writer," and though I did not mind it a bit, I was set to wondering just what a nature writer might be and just why or from just what he should be distinguished by his special label.

A great many people, I am afraid, do not even care to know. When they hear the phrase they think of "the birds and the bees"—a useful device in the sex education of children but hardly, they think, an occupation for a grown man. A biologist is all right and so is a sportsman. But a nature writer can hardly expect more than a shrug from the realistic or the robust.

The more literary quote Wordsworth: "Nature never did betray the heart that loved her" or "to me the meanest flower that blows can give thoughts that do often lie too deep for tears." But Darwin, they say, exploded such ideas nearly a century ago. Even Tennyson knew better: "Nature red in tooth and claw." We can't very well learn anything from all that. Ours are desperate times. The only hope for today lies in the study of politics, sociology, and economics. If a nature writer is someone who advocates a return to nature then he must be a sentimentalist and a very old-fashioned one at that.

But why, then, should I have discovered that my week ends and my summers in the country were becoming more and more important, that I spent more and more time looking at and thinking about plants and animals and birds, that I began to feel the necessity of writing about what I had seen and thought? Why, finally, when I saw fifteen free months ahead of me, should I have been sure that I wanted to go back to the southwestern desert to see what an entirely different, only half-known natural environment might have to say to me?

It was more than a mere casual interest in natural history as a hobby. Certainly it was also more than the mere fact that the out-of-doors is healthful and relaxing. I was not merely being soothed and refreshed by

Joseph Wood Krutch

an escape from the pressures of urban life. I was seeking for something, and I got at least the conviction that there was something I really was learning. I seemed to be getting a glimpse of some wisdom of which I had less than an inkling before.

Actually, of course, nature writing does flourish quite vigorously today as a separate department of literature even though it does remain to some extent a thing apart, addressed chiefly to a group of readers called "nature lovers" who are frequently referred to by outsiders in the same condescending tone they would use in speaking of prohibitionists, diet cranks, Holy Rollers, or the followers—if there still are any—of the late Mr. Coué. And that makes me sometimes wonder whether its very importance as a "department of literature" does not mean that what was once an almost inevitable motive in most imaginative writing has become something recognizably special, for the reason that most writers of novels and poems and plays no longer find the contemplation of nature relevant to their purposes—at least to the same extent they once did. And I wonder also whether that seeming fact is merely the result of urban living, or whether "merely" is not the wrong term to use in reference to a phenomenon which may mean a great deal more than the mere disappearance from fiction of apostrophes to the mountains.

A generation ago the first page of the epoch-making *Cambridge History of English Literature* listed among the enduring characteristics of the English people, "love of nature." That phrase covers something which has meant a good many different things at different times. But would it have suggested itself to a critic who was concerned only with the most esteemed English or American books of our time? Is there any love of nature—as distinguished from an intellectual approval of the processes of biology—in Bernard Shaw? Does T. S. Eliot find much gladness in contemplating nature? Does Joyce's apostrophe to a river count, and is Hemingway's enthusiasm for the slaughter of animals really to be considered as a modern expression of even that devotion to blood sports which, undoubtedly, really is a rather incongruous aspect of the Anglo-Saxon race's love of nature? In America Robert Frost is almost the only poet whose work is universally recognized as of major importance and in which the loving contemplation of natural phenomena seems a central activity from which the poetry springs.

All this is probably the result of something more than mere fashion. True, ridicule of conventional description in fiction is no new thing, and Mark Twain once tested his theory that readers always skip it by inserting a paragraph which told how a solitary esophagus might have been seen winging its way across the sky. It is true also that observations of natural phenomena do still sometimes get into fiction. *The Grapes of Wrath* begins with the symbolic use of a turtle crossing a highway and nearly everybody knows that at least one tree did grow in Brooklyn. But somewhere along the road they have traveled, most moderns have lost the sense that nature is the most significant background of human life. They see their characters as part of society or, more specifically, members of some profession or slaves at some industry, rather than as part of nature. Neither her appearances nor her ways any longer seem—to use a favorite modern term—as "relevant" as they once did. She is not often, nowadays, invoked to furnish the resolution of an emotional problem.

Whistler was probably the first English-speaking writer ever to say flatly "Nature is wrong." Of course he meant to be shocking and he also meant "artistically wrong"—unpictorial or badly composed. And goodness only knows most contemporary painting is the product of hearty agreement with this dictum. Either natural objects are so distorted in the effort to correct nature's wrongness that they are just barely recognizable, or the artist, refusing to look at nature at all, plays at being God by attempting to create a whole new universe of man-made shapes. In either case the assumption is that modern man is more at home and gets more emotional satisfaction in this world of his own making than in the world which nature gave him.

Only the most extreme forms of the most desperately "experimental" writing go anything like so far. Only the poets of the Dada produce literary analogies of abstract painting. But without being, for the most part, even aware of a theory about what they are doing, many novelists and poets have obviously ceased to feel that the significant physical setting for their characters or sentiments is the fields or woods, or that the intellectual and emotional context of their difficulties and problems is the natural world rather than that of exclusively human concepts. This amounts to a good deal more than a mere loss of faith in the dogma that nature never did betray the heart that loved her. It also amounts to a good deal more than the somewhat romantic Victorian distress in the face of her red tooth and red claw. It means that the writer finds neither God dwelling in the light of setting suns nor a very significant aspect of the problem of evil in nature's often careless cruelty. Faced with either her beauty or her ruthlessness, his reaction is more likely to be only, "so what?" Man's own achievements, follies, and crimes seem to him to lie in a different realm.

As cities grow and daily life becomes of necessity more and more mechanized, we inevitably come to have less to do with, even to see less often and to be less aware of, other things which live; and it comes to seem almost as though all the world outside ourselves were inanimate. In so far as the writer thinks of himself as a secretary of society he has that much justification for treating man as a creature whose most significant environment is that of the machines he has built and, to some small extent, the art which he has created. But in so far as the writer is more than a recorder, in so far as he should see deeper than a secretary is required to see, he might be expected to be aware both of the extent to which the fact that man is an animal sharing the earth with other animals is still significantly true, and of the consequences of the extent to which it has actually become less so. Those consequences, though difficult to assess, are certainly enormous and they did not begin to be fully felt until the twentieth century.

Joseph Wood Krutch

The nineteenth century was deeply concerned with what is called "man's place in nature," and as some of the writers pointed out, that had much more than merely scientific implications. It did not imply only, or even most importantly, that man was descended from the apes and was, therefore, still apelike in many of his characteristics. It meant also that animal life supplied the inescapable context of his life, spiritually as well as physically. It meant that life was an adventure which he shared with all living things, that the only clue to himself was in them. But of that fact many, perhaps most, of the most intelligent and cultivated people of our time are unaware. Having to do almost exclusively with other human beings and with machines, they tend to forget what we are and what we are like. Even the graphic arts are forsaking nature so that even on the walls of our apartments the wheel or the lever are more familiar than the flower or the leaf. And perhaps all this is the real reason why we have tended more and more to think about man and society as though they were machines, why we have mechanistic theories about consciousness and about human behavior in general, why we have begun to think that even the brain is something like an electronic calculating machine. After all, it is only with machines that most people are more than casually familiar. And perhaps it is trying to think in this way that makes us unhappy— nearly everybody seems to agree that we are—because we know in our hearts that we are not machines and grow lonesome in a universe where we are little aware of anything else which is not.

In so far then as nature writing has become a special department of literature, consciously concerned with an expression of the individual writer's awareness of something which most people are not aware of; in so far also as it finds readers other than those members of the small group to whom natural history and allied subjects is a hobby like any other unusual interest; then perhaps to that extent what the existence of this department of literature means is simply that it exists principally because works in other departments are no longer concerned with certain truths of fact and feeling which some part of even the general public recognizes as lacking. In any event, at least all of those nature writers who stem ultimately from Thoreau are concerned not only with the aesthetic and hedonistic aspects of the love of nature, but also with what can only be called its moral aspect.

Every now and then the average man looks at a kitten and thinks it is "cute." Or he looks at the stars and they make him feel small. When he thinks either of those things he is being aware of the context of nature, and that is good as far as it goes. But it does not go very far, and there is little in modern life or art to make him go further. What the nature writer is really asking him to do is to explore the meaning of such thoughts and feelings. He is asking him to open his heart and mind to nature as another kind of writer asks him to open them to art or music or literature. Nearly everyone admits that these have something to say that science and sociology cannot say. Nature has something to say that art and literature have not.

Postscript

But nature writing also implies something more fundamental than that. It also raises the question of the moral consequences of taking that opposite point of view which is now more usual. It raises the question of the effect which forgetting that he is alive may have upon man and his society.

Today the grandest of all disputes is that between those who are determined to manipulate man as though he were a machine and those who hope, on the contrary, to let him grow like an organism. Whether our future is to be totalitarian or free depends entirely upon which side wins the dispute, and the question which side we ourselves are on may in the end depend upon our conception of "man's place in nature." Nearly every taste we cultivate and nearly every choice we make, down to the very decoration of our wall, tends to proclaim where our sympathies lie. Do they suggest a preference for the world which lives and grows or for the world which obeys the laws of the machine? Do they remind us of the natural universe in which every individual things leads its own individual, unique and rebellious life? Of the universe where nothing, not even one of two leaves, is quite like anything else? Or do they accustom us instead to feel more at home in surroundings where everything suggests only machines and machine parts, which do as they are told and could never have known either joy or desire? In its direct, brutal way even official Marxism recognized that fact when it rested its hopes for a revolution not on the peasants but on the urban proletariat. It is certainly no accident that the totalitarian countries are those which have made mechanistic theories the official philosophy of the state. If man is nothing but a machine, if there are laws of psychology precisely analogous to the laws of physics, then he can be "conditioned" to do and to want whatever his masters decide. Society is then a machine composed of standard parts, and men can be ordered to become whatever cogs and levers the machine happens to require at the moment.

Our forefathers were in no danger of forgetting that they were dependent upon nature and were a part of it. No man who clears forests, grows crops, and tends cattle is. He sees his food coming up out of the ground, and when he would travel further than he can walk, he calls a living, four-footed creature for aid. But unless our civilization should be destroyed as completely as the gloomiest prophets of the atomic age sometimes predict, we shall never again be a rural people and probably we would not want to be. What tools can give us is very much worth having, and the machinery of an industrial society is merely a collection of tools. But our physical as well as our spiritual dependence upon nature is merely obscured, not abolished, and to be unaware of that fact is to be as naïvely obtuse as the child who supposes that cows are no longer necessary because we know get milk from bottles.

In the early stages of mechanized civilization no one thought of mechanics as a threat to the soul of man. The machine was too obviously an alien though useful contrivance. The threat did not arise until we began to be overawed by the lifeless things we had created and to worship, rather

Joseph Wood Krutch

than merely to use, our tools. Science and psychology began to talk about the "body machine" and the "brain machine" just about the time when we began to be more and more aware of the artificial rather than the natural environment. When men lived most intimately with things which were alive they thought of themselves as living. When they began, on the contrary, to live most intimately with dead things, they began to suppose that they, too, were dead. And once men were thought of as machines, governments began inevitably to be thought of as merely a method of making the machines operate productively. An engineer does not consider the tastes, the preferences, the desires, or the possible individual talents of the mechanical units he employs. Why should a government concerned with body machines and mechanically conditioned reflexes do so either?

It is highly improbable that we shall ever again lead what a Thoreau would be willing to call a "natural life." Moreover, since not every man has the temperament of a camper, it is not likely that most people will take even periodically to the woods. But there are other ways in which even the urban dweller not fortunate enough to have his country home can remain aware, at least in the important back of his mind, of the fact that his true place is somewhere in nature.

The more complicated life becomes, the more important is the part that symbols play, and all the arts, including the arts of architecture and decoration, are the products of symbolic acts. To plant a garden, a window box, or even to cultivate a house plant is to perform a sort of ritual and thereby to acknowledge, even in the middle of a city, one's awareness that our real kinship is with life, not with mechanism. To hang a picture or to choose a design or a color may be, only a little more remotely, the same thing.

It may be upon such rituals that our fate will ultimately depend. Organisms are rebellious, individual, and self-determining. It is the machine which is manageable and obedient, which always does the expected and behaves as it is told to behave. You can plan for it as you cannot plan for anything which is endowed with a life of its own, because nothing which is alive ever wholly surrenders its liberties. Man will not surrender his unless he forgets that he too belongs among living things.

This is not, in its emphasis at least, quite the same lesson which others at other times have deduced. From nature as from everything else worth studying one gets what at the moment one needs, sometimes perhaps only what at the moment one would like to have. The Wordsworthians, for instance, got the conviction that some pantheistic God who approved of the same thing that they approved of really did exist. Many of us who look back at them are inclined to suspect that what they were contemplating was only a projection of themselves and that Wordsworth might have profited by a little more objective observation—a little more of what he called the scientist's willingness to "botanize upon his mother's grave"—instead of devoting so much of his time to reading into clouds or mountains or sunsets what he liked to find there.

As for myself I settle for what Wordsworth would have considered

Postscript

a good deal less than what he managed to get. What I think I find myself most positively assured of is not that man is divine but only that he is at least not a machine, that he is like an animal, not like even the subtlest electronic contraption. Today in a good many different ways most of us are willing to settle for less than most men at most times got, and that less seems quite enough for me.

In other respects, also, the demands I make upon nature before I will call her sum total "good" are less exorbitant than those which others have made. I do not think that her every prospect pleases or that only man is vile. No one who actually looks at nature rather than at something his fancy reads into her can ever fail to realize that she represents some ultimate things-as-they-are, not some ideal of things-as-he-thinks-they-ought-to-be. There is in her what we call cruelty and also, even more conspicuously, what we call grotesqueness, even what we call comedy. If she warns the so-called realist how limited his conception of reality is, she is no less likely to bring the sentimentalist back, literally, to earth.

How much of the cruelty, the grotesqueness, or the sublimity any given man will see depends no doubt to some considerable extent upon his own temperament, and I suppose it is some indication of mine when I confess that what I see most often and relish the most is, first, the intricate marvel; second, the comedy. To be reminded that one is very much like other members of the animal kingdom is often funny enough, though it is never, like being compared to a machine, merely humiliating. I do not too much mind being somewhat like a cat, a dog, or even a frog, but I resent having it said that even an electronic calculator is like me.

Not very long ago I was pointing out to a friend the courtship of two spiders in a web just outside my door. Most people know that the male is often much smaller than his mate, and nearly everybody knows by now that the female of many species sometimes eats her husband. Both of these things were true of the common kind beside my door, and the insignificant male was quite obviously torn between ardor and caution. He danced forward and then darted back. He approached now from one side and now from the other. He would and he wouldn't.

My friend, no nature student and not much given to observing such creatures, was gratifyingly interested. Presently he could contain himself no longer. "You know," he said thoughtfully, "there is only one difference between that spider and a human male. The spider knows it's dangerous."

That, I maintain, both is and ought to be as much grist for a nature writer's mill as a sunset or a bird song.

[1953]

Joseph Wood Krutch

Maurice Stein:

Suburbia—A Walk on the Mild Side

Maurice Stein (b. 1926), contemporary sociologist and author, is concerned with the nature of the American environment as it affects the psychological development of its people. Here he examines the relationship between the modern phenomenon of suburbia and the problem of human identity.

I

Sociologists have traditionally approached communities by trying to identify the ways whereby the several aspects of life—family, occupation, politics, religion, education and recreation—are given order and meaning through coherent cultural values and networks of social roles. In the past this could be undertaken through interviews and observation: the assumption being that members of the community would thus reveal their true values and self-conceptions. But it is here that the suburb begins to present some unusual problems. Its residents are so accustomed to projecting images of themselves as supremely happy and successful that the researcher finds it extremely difficult to penetrate this façade. The problem seems partly to be that life in the suburb consists in a silent conspiracy directed toward mutual deception.

The authors of *Crestwood Heights* have succeeded in capturing the delicate interplay between appearances and reality as the two are woven together to form the fabric of suburban social life. Their very starting point, the problem of mental health, which forms a crucial means of getting past the façade of contented suburbia, forced them to pay attention to the underlying realities. By starting from the guidance clinic in the school, they were able to work back into those families where "unmentionable" life problems had cracked through the shell of appearances.

The social structure of Crestwood Heights is strangely paradoxical. On the one hand it arranges matters so that the daily life of the individual, not matter what his age or sex, is divided into many compelling tasks that leave little or no time for freely chosen activity. Like modern industrial life, which it fundamentally resembles, the suburb is frantically devoted to the rhythm of keeping busy. Even the playtime of the children is routinized, and many families find that the separate schedules of the various members leave no time for intimate moments with one another. On the other hand, while people are so desperately busy, they do not know or have forgotten how to perform some of the most elemental human tasks. The most glaring evidence for this is the genuine crisis in the American suburb over child rearing. Anxious mothers, uncertain as to how to raise their children, turn to scientific experts to find out if their children are normal or even more important, what the standard of normality might be.

We face a curious and probably unprecedented situation here: a society of material comfort and apparent security in which the most fundamental of human relationships, that between mother and child, has become at the very least problematical. No one is surprised to discover that businessmen treat each other in impersonal and manipulative terms; but surely it should be cause for some dismay to find it habitual, as the authors of *Crestwood Heights* report, that mothers regard suburban children as "cases" the moment they lag behind the highly formalized routines of their mates or show signs of distinctive individuality. The paradox between busyness and helplessness, between outer bustle and inner chaos, may now become easier to explain: "keeping on the go" is the prime way for

Maurice Stein

the suburbanite to avoid facing the socio-cultural vacuum in which he lives. Hence, the peculiarly painful fact that in suburbanite society, for all that it is so conspicuously child-centered and for all that parents habitually make sacrifices in order to get "the best things" for their children, it is an unusual mother who really knows her own child.

As Mr. Newman has shown, no one in the suburb really has to know anyone else as long as appearances are kept up. Housewives, taught to desire careers but trapped in the home, cannot lower their fixed grins for fear they will never be able to raise them again. Husbands, trapped in careers which drain their best energies can look forward to a fate that has become as dreaded as death—that of retirement and free time. Looking out to their own prospective life cycles, the children soon learn to submerge the spectre of a life that lacks rooted values and creative meanings by throwing themselves into the struggle for status. All of the vital roles wherein the human drama used to be played out—mother-son, father-daughter, worker-player, adult-child, male-female—have been levelled. Their specific contents making them channels for realizing a particular set of human possibilities have been bartered for an ephemeral and empty sense of status. Not to perform these roles is to lose one's place, but sadly enough, performing them can never give one a place.

Now it is true that all societies use status, the systematic allocation of prestige and esteem, as a way of motivating people to fill social roles. Those performing valued activities in a competent manner receive the awards of respect and approval. This presumes, however, that there *are* some stable roles which receive acclaim. Crestwood Heights, however, is distinguished by the absence of this kind of consensus. For not only does the suburbanite have to keep up with the Joneses; he also has to spend a tremendous amount of time and energy trying to find out which status models the Joneses are themselves currently keeping up with. Since no other activities are finally valued in and of themselves apart from this quest for status, it soon becomes obsessive. *Status becomes an autonomous motive and mode of life.* Human relationships are valued only as sources of status rather than status being the sign of having successfully become a valued kind of human being. We have reached here the result of that process within bourgeois society which, call it alienation with Marx or *anomie* with Durkheim, transforms the human being into an object—and this, strikingly enough, at the very moment when human beings in the suburb believe they have triumphantly won the battle to gain control over material objects.

II

The preoccupation with status as an end in itself has deep roots in the earlier experiences of the American community. Helen and Robert Lynd in their classic study, *Middletown*, reported on the effects of industrialization on a medium sized midwestern town between 1880 and 1924. During this interval a fairly coherent society premised on the continued functioning of a craft economy gave way to a much less coherent system shaped by the developing economy of mass production and consumption. The Lynds showed how this emerging economic system transformed every area of institutional life so that traditional relationships were badly disrupted. For example, the collapse of the craft hierarchy, and the emergence of industrial employment made it possible for sons, previously subordinate to their fathers, to assume higher paying and more valued jobs. Meanwhile, the craft skills of the older generation lost their market value and social meaning.

Within the framework of the old craft system, the new business classes had begun to assume a dominant role in the community; they were the carriers of the life style that was to emerge with industrialization. Their emphasis on the acquisition of property became the model to which workers turned when faced with the collapse of previous patterns of life. Though disturbed at the loss of the work satisfactions their crafts had provided them, the workers in Middletown had little choice but to assume the new industrial roles. It is important to note, however, that this assumption of industrial roles was itself rooted in the disintegration of a round of communal life. Wives and mothers formerly confined to the home now took jobs to augment the all-important purchasing power of the family. Church attendance declined as workers and businessmen alike acquired automobiles and elected to enjoy as well as display these on the day formerly reserved for religious services. The change symbolized an entire shift of values and assumptions.

It is impossible here to describe fully the institutional transformations taking place in Middletown during this period, but I would suggest that anyone turning to the Lynds' book will find a surprising number of resemblances to the contemporary suburb, perhaps more than he might expect. Family life had already begun to disintegrate, even though the full paraphernalia of status appearances was not yet available. The middle class had already adopted the Crestwood Heights pattern of projected happiness and success, while the working class was beginning to follow suit.

Ten years later, during the depression, the Lynds returned to Middletown and reported their findings in *Middletown in Transition*. Their most striking observation was that Middletowners had clung to the success formula in spite of the social crises brought about by the depression, largely because they were unable to question a basic premise which seemed to provide them with the only sense of place and continuity they possessed.

Yet the depression did expose Middletowners to new social experiences. They became aware of the fact that their destinies could be radically altered by forces that transcended local, regional and even national boundaries. They had to turn to the Federal government for help and thereby confirmed Middletown's dependent position. The mass media brought big-city cultural models into their lives, breaking down local boundaries and loyalties as it did so. Putting up a "front" became harder for both classes during the depression but this fact seems to have reinforced rather than weakened the need for doing so. As the depression furthered the transition

Maurice Stein

to an industrial economy, local bases for "belonginess" disappeared. Middletown became a city with all of the impersonality and atomization that this development implies in twentieth century America. Its citizens found themselves caught up in the workings of impersonal bureaucratic structures so that the intimacies of small town life soon became dim and possibly idealized memories.

Americans in larger cities experienced similar transitions. Immigrant families were exposed to special problems as the discontinuity between the generations was accentuated by cultural differences. Second generation children of immigrant fathers found themselves in even greater opposition to their parents' way of life than did the children of Middletown craftsmen. They coped with this by segregating themselves in their own up-to-date "second-generation ghettos" or losing themselves in the anonymous regions of the city. Here too the same process was at work. Families abandoned distinctive cultural life styles in order to pick up the American minimum package built entirely around acquiring and displaying commodities appropriately. Perhaps segments of the urban proletariat did develop some kind of "class consciousness," but hindsight suggests that even this was permeated by our perculiar brand of individualism. Trade unions and political parties remained for the most part instrumental "counter-bureaucracies" providing occasional protection against equally impersonal big business and big government without commanding any deeper loyalties than either of the latter.

In this context, the findings of the Research Branch of the United States Army during World War II, as reported in the several volumes of *The American Soldier*, are very important. The American soldier emerges from this collective portrait as a man without serious commitment. He fought because he *had* to; meanwhile he looked out for himself as much as he could. The resistance to ideology, stemming partly from the American dream of individual success which not even the depression had been able to destroy, was now reenforced by military experience. Soldiers fighting for democracy found themselves serving under a tremendously authoritarian military caste system which they justifiably despised. It is worth noting that many of the most vehement objections to the army were based on the fact that it violated the "American system" of competitive social display: officers had preferential access to consumer privileges which the ranks were inherently unable to match. Having already been deprived of a sense of relationship in regard to the factories where they worked, the communities in which they lived, and even the families to which they belonged, the soldiers' natural response to participation in a large-scale organization like the army was a deep-seated skepticism toward its larger purposes, together with an eye for their own prospects.

The experiences of Americans in military service during the forties were quite continuous with their experiences during the depression. Their life plans were for the most part, arbitrarily disrupted by vast social upheavals over which they had no control. They were moved to new locations and there forced to associate with people they had never seen before.

Suburbia—A Walk on the Mild Side

While all this was happening, sociologists were busy discovering the importance of "primary group relations" in such diverse contexts as the city neighborhood, the factory and the army. This discovery itself reflected the widespread breakdown in such relations.

Now in the fifties, our suburbs embody the most advanced forms of urban impersonality. There are no groups of buddies as in the army, nor does there seem to be that minimal sense of shared experience that Middletowners preserved out of their desperate struggle to survive the ravages of industrialization and economic depression. Gone too, is the shared sense of having jointly rejected certain old world life styles which the sons of immigrants held in common. In Crestwood Heights, as our authors describe it, even the family is no longer a primary group. Each member looks out for his own interests and the only shared value resides in their mutual concern with the impressions they make on their neighbors. This carefully manipulated public image rather than the human relationships sustaining it receives the bulk of attention.

III

Contemporary social psychiatric theory is just beginning to explore the many special problems raised by this kind of community. One looks to the suburb for the real life counterparts of such familiar conceptions as Erich Fromm's "marketing orientation," David Riesman's "other directed orientation," Harry Stack Sullivan's "exaggerated security operations," Erik Erikson's "identity diffusion" and even the thoroughly unsavory "authoritarian personality." There are broad convergences among these various concepts deriving at least in part from the fact that the personality configuration described by all of them emerges from what can conveniently be called "mass" society. And the suburb is a better place in which to study this human type than most other city neighborhoods, even though all of them contain some form of the species.

Mr. Newman has neatly summarized the authors' descriptions of personal relations in Crestwood Heights. There is massive covert competition, always with its thin veneer of friendliness in the relations between children in the school, women in their clubs and men at their businesses. Everybody is trained to deprecate his competitors without appearing to do so. As they rise through the complex status structures, careful manipulation of their own personalities remains the main stock-in-trade.

All social psychiatric descriptions of personality types finding their natural habitat in suburbia emphasize the central role played by anxiety. This anxiety is rarely recognized as such, although it governs the suburbanites' self-marketing operations. The children become aware of its sting when they discover that they are part of the status equipage of their parents and must comport themselves accordingly. They are loved for what they do rather than what they are and this becomes especially bewildering and devastating because their parents constantly insist that the opposite is the case. Small wonder that the child begins to see himself in depersonal-

Maurice Stein

ized, almost schizoid, terms even going so far as to develop paranoid attitudes toward his parents and the adult world.

It should be stressed, however, that such terms lose their specifically psychopathological implications when we deal with a community in which these responses can hardly be avoided. The anxieties that cue these responses must remain well below the threshold of awareness; otherwise, they would leave the individual in an unbearably agitated state. Children and adults alike develop standardized patterns for restoring some kind of inner balance when their security is threatened; however, it must be noted that the price paid for this restored equilibrium is an impoverished emotional life. Because they cannot face their own anxiety and its origin in their life routines, they are unable to visualize other solutions.

It is important to note the self-sealing character of this situation. Adults in the community, committed to precariously maintained status postures, must continually reiterate to each other and to their children their proclaimed success and happiness. Insofar as they do this efficiently, they are barred from comprehending their own true situation as well as the true situation of their audiences. Inevitably, however, it appears that children do gain some sort of insight into the real feelings and dissatisfactions of their parents. Furthermore, they sometimes even sense the complicated system of exploitative emotional relationships that under-cuts the apparently placid surfaces of their family life. Yet they cannot use this insight for growth because doing so would force them to repudiate the only basis for security, such as it is, that they have. The child cannot turn to his relative or to the more accessible families of his friends because they too are busy keeping the mask of happiness propped in front of their faces. If he decides that his own family is inadequate, or even worse, hypocritical, then he will carry a wound that might eventually mark him as a "problem child." Otherwise, his feelings are suppressed and the child inducted into the ways of responsible adulthood.

IV

At this point, we can clearly see the most grievous human loss that life in the suburbs entails. Dedication to a status-dominated life style deprives individuals of their capacity to establish more complicated identities encompassing a much broader range of human possibilities. It forces them to remain permanently juvenile, regardless of chronological aging. Everything is blurred, but above all perception of self.

Yet it would be a mistake to assume that the typical suburbanite's anxious preoccupation with status as well as his anxious avoidance of genuine experience insulate him completely from the real conflicts in his life. He may be able to postpone consciously facing these conflicts but he cannot permanently avoid their consequences. Women usually suffer from these contradictions more than men because they are confronted squarely with an insoluble role conflict. Whether they choose housekeeping, careers, or a combination of both, they must sacrifice something of themselves.

Suburbia—A Walk on the Mild Side

Their busy schedules prevent them from having too much time on their hands in which to feel dissatisfied or envious but when they do there is always one of the ubiquitous psychological experts to turn to. These professional "helpers" play an increasingly important role in Crestwood Heights. They begin to look like modern shamans exorcising the tribal ghosts so that the routines of living can be maintained without interference. But these shamans cannot remove the underlying causes of the anxiety they temporarily allay.

One suspects, or perhaps hopes, that even the career-driven men occasionally feel doubtful about the whole enterprise. The barrenness of their lives cannot be completely concealed and as they approach the "male menopause" this emptiness may even penetrate their own consciousness. As the age of obsolescence nears, the old compulsive preoccupations lose their power to divert attention from the realities of their existence. By then, it is usually too late to do much about it. There is nothing sadder than the face of an aging man who has gone through life with the emotional equipment of a juvenile.

It is important, however, to recognize that the "human material"—just because it is human—does not completely adapt to the pressures or embrace the substitutes. Continual distractions provided by busy schedules and supplemented by heavy doses of mass entertainment may turn attention away from the real problems of life, but the half dreaded, half desired moments of unavoidable reverie cannot be entirely suppressed. Sometimes these realities break through in the form of "problem" children, or "problem" marriages or even problems arising from loss of control over one's own organism or psyche. People can't sleep, or they sleep too much, or they overeat. Sometimes clear cut psychopathological or psychosomatic symptoms appear and justify expensive psychiatric treatment. This forces the disordered individual to assume a new identity: he becomes a patient. And for a time the patient-therapist relationship offers a real sense of new possibilities. But these new possibilities cannot be automatically carried over into the patient's everyday life. If he chooses to remain in the suburb where intimate emotional communication is precluded, then he must prolong his therapy, since it becomes the only place he can express his cure. The patient's life commitments undo any beneficial effects of the therapeutic relationship and this paradoxically renders the patient even more dependent on it. Perhaps this helps to explain why so many analyses drag on endlessly.

There is no reason to assume that the problem of identity stops at the boundaries of the suburb. Few people reared in modern America manage to escape the pressures toward acceptance of stereotyped self-identities that provide a temporary resting point in the status struggle but prevent further emotional or intellectual growth. The role conflicts described in *Crestwood Heights* wherein basic human identities are distorted by the quest for status, are not the exclusive prerogative of any social strata. The establishment of productive masculine identities covering the various phases of the life cycle is as precarious among workers as among managers,

Maurice Stein

and the wives of both groups struggle with the problems of femininity. Unfortunately, it is always easier to settle for the stereotyped juvenile patterns promulgated by the mass media and reinforced by the conditions of modern social life. Still, growth happens. Some people do find their way through the banalities of social life to something better. But before progress can be made, identity must first be seen as problematic and the growth anxieties as real.

Perhaps a glance at some difficulties in establishing radical identities will clarify the direct relevance of this viewpoint. Certainly radicals, if anyone, must stand against the ready-made identities, yet readers of DISSENT sometimes complain that too much space is devoted to discussion of the nature of radicalism and of mass society. One might argue in reply that clarification of a viable radical identity as well as of the pressures threatening to warp it is the main task facing this kind of magazine. Similarly, in a mass society that blurs all political distinctions, serious attempts have to be made to distinguish radical from liberal views, just because merging the two does justice to neither. Finally, radicals are by no means immune from the status panic and role conflicts that beset suburbia; but it can be hoped that they will consciously confront these anxieties differently.

But the people of Crestwood Heights are certainly not radicals: they can hardly search for cures as long as they take the symptoms of social illness as signs of personal health. One can still hope that some of them occasionally feel dissatisfied and lonely. In moments of special vulnerability, like most of us, they must yearn to be members of a genuine community. The only grain of truth in present day emphasis on "adjustment" lies in its implicit recognition that certain kinds of important human growth can only be achieved by playing major life roles within a community. Today's adjustment peddlers—whether they be theologians, psychologists, or novelists—seize on a perfectly legitimate impulse, and it is important to recognize this when criticizing them. That people should want to be a part of a community in which they encounter others in dignified human contexts—occupational, familial, political, aesthetic and perhaps even religious roles—is simply to say that people today want no more and no less than at any other time in history. When this demand, however, can only be expressed as a desire to fit into a way of life that is inherently incapable of satisfying it, then we have a truly tragic misdirection of human energies. The victim's cries may not necessarily name his disease properly, but they do indicate that he needs help.

[1958]

Suburbia—A Walk on the Mild Side

Norman Mailer:
Architectural Excerpts

Norman Mailer (b. 1923), novelist, essayist, and
social critic, first became known for *The Naked
and the Dead* (1948), a powerful novel of World
War II. In recent years he has become increasingly concerned with such aspects of American
life as the impact of war, prejudice, and the environment. A resident of New York, he is particularly concerned with the problems of the city.

A PIECE FOR THE NEW YORK TIMES

In Lyndon Johnson's book, *My Hope for America*, the fifth chapter is titled "Toward the Great Society." It contains this paragraph:

. . . fifty years from now, . . . there will be four hundred million Americans, four-fifths of them in urban areas. In the remainder of this century, . . . we will have to build homes, highways, and facilities equal to all those built since this country was first settled. In the next forty years we must rebuild the entire urban United States.

It is a staggering sentence. The city we inhabit at this moment is already close to a total reconstruction of the world our parents knew in their childhood. If there is no nuclear war, if we shift from cold war to some kind of peace, and there is a worldwide rise in the standard of living, then indeed we will build a huge new country. It is possible that not one in a thousand of the buildings put up by 1899 will still be standing in the year 2000.

But what will America look like? How will its architecture appear? Will it be the architecture of a Great Society, or continue to be the architecture of an empty promiscuous panorama where no one can distinguish between hospitals and housing projects, factories and colleges, concert halls, civic centers, and airport terminals? The mind recoils from the thought of an America rebuilt completely in the shape of those blank skyscrapers forty stories high, their walls dead as an empty television screen, their form as interesting as a box of cleansing tissue propped on end. They are buildings which reveal nothing so much as the deterioration in real value of the dollar bill. They are denuded of ornament (which costs money), their windows are not subtly recessed into the wall but are laid flush with the surface like a patch of collodion on the skin, there is no instance where a roof with a tower, a gable, a spire, a mansard, a ridge or even a mooring mast for a dirigible intrudes itself into the sky, reminding us that every previous culture of man attempted to engage the heavens.

No, our modern buildings go flat, flat at the top, flat as eternal monotony, flat as the last penny in a dollar. There is so much corruption in the building codes, overinflation in the value of land, featherbedding built into union rules, so much graft, so much waste, so much public relations, and so much emptiness inflated upon so much emptiness that no one tries to do more with the roof than leave it flat.

As one travels through the arbitrary new neighborhoods of the present, those high squat dormitories which imprison the rich as well as the poor, one is not surprised that the violence is greater than it used to be in the old slum, up are the statistics for juvenile delinquency and for dope addiction. To live in the old slum jungle left many half crippled, and others part savage, but it was at least an environment which asked for wit. In the prison vistas of urban renewal, the violence travels from without to within, there is no wit—one travels down a long empty corridor to reach one's door, long as the corridors in the public schools, long as the corridors in the hospitals at the end of the road; the landscape of modern man takes on a sense of endless empty communications.

Sterile as an operating table is the future vista of suburban spread,

Norman Mailer

invigorating as a whiff of deodorant is the sight of new office buildings. Small elation sits upon us as we contemplate the future, for the picturesque will be uprooted with the ugly, our populations will double, and in a city like New York, the brownstone will be replaced by a cube sixteen stories high with a huge park for parking cars and a little grass. The city will go up a little and it will go out, it will spread. We will live with glass walls in a cold climate. The entire world will come to look like Queens Boulevard. We will have been uprooted so many times that future man will come to bear the same relation to the past that a hydroponic plant bears to soil.

Yet some part of us is aware that to uproot the past too completely is a danger without measure. It must at the least produce a profound psychic discomfort. For we do not know how much our perception of the present and our estimate of the future depend upon our sense of what has gone before. To return to an old neighborhood and discover it has disappeared is a minor woe for some; it is close to a psychological catastrophe for others, an amputation where the lost nerves still feel pain. This century must appear at times like a great beast which has lost its tail, but who could argue that the amputation was not self-inflicted?

There seems at loose an impulse to uproot every vestige of the past, an urge so powerful one wonders if it is not with purpose, if it is not in the nature of twentieth-century man to uproot himself not only from his past, but from his planet. Perhaps we live on the edge of a great divide in history and so are divided ourselves between the desire for a gracious, intimate, detailed and highly particular landscape and an urge less articulate to voyage out on explorations not yet made. Perhaps the blank faceless abstract quality of our modern architecture is a reflection of the anxiety we feel before the void, a kind of visual static which emanates from the psyche of us all, as if we do not know which way to go.

If we are to spare the countryside, if we are to protect the style of the small town and of the exclusive suburb, keep the organic center of the metropolis and the old neighborhoods, maintain those few remaining streets where the tradition of the nineteenth century and the muse of the eighteenth century still linger on the mood in the summer cool of an evening, if we are to avoid a megalopolis five hundred miles long, a city without shape or exit, a nightmare of ranch houses, highways, suburbs and industrial sludge, if we are to save the dramatic edge of a city—that precise moment when we leave the outskirts and race into the country, the open country—if we are to have a keen acute sense of concentration and a breath of release, then there is only one solution: the cities must climb, they must not spread, they must build up, not by increments, but by leaps, up and up, up to the heavens.

We must be able to live in houses one hundred stories high, two hundred stories high, far above the height of buildings as we know them now. New cities with great towers must rise in the plain, cities higher than mountains, cities with room for 400,000,000 to live, or that part of 400,-000,000 who wish to live high in a landscape of peaks and spires, cliffs and

Architectural Excerpts

precipices. For the others, for those who wish to live on the ground and with the ground, there will then be new room to live—the traditional small town will be able to survive, as will the old neighborhoods in the cities. But first a way must be found to build upward, to triple and triple again the height of all buildings as we know them now.

Picture, if you please, an open space where twenty acrobats stand, each locking hands with two different partners. Conceive then of ten acrobats standing on the shoulders of these twenty, and five upon the ten acrobats, and three more in turn above them, then two, then one. We have a pyramid of figures: six thousand to eight thousand pounds is supported upon a base of twenty pairs of shoes.

It enables one to think of structures more complex, of pyramids of steel which rise to become towers. Imagine a tower half a mile high and stressed to bear a vast load. Think of six or eight such towers and of bridges built between them, even as huge vines tie the branches of one high tree to another; think of groups of apartments built above these bridges (like the shops on the Ponte Vecchio in Florence) and apartments suspended beneath each bridge, and smaller bridges running from one complex of apartments to another, and of apartments suspended from cables, apartments kept in harmonious stress to one another by cables between them.

One can now begin to conceive of a city, or a separate part of a city, which is as high as it is wide, a city which bends ever so subtly in a high wind with the most delicate flexing of its near-to-numberless parts even as the smallest strut in a great bridge reflects the passing of an automobile with some fine-tuned quiver. In the subtlety of its swayings the vertical city might seem to be ready to live itself. It might be agreeable to live there.

The real question, however, has not yet been posed. It is whether a large fraction of the population would find it reasonable to live one hundred or two hundred stories in the air. There is the dread of heights. Would that tiny pit of suicide, planted like the small seed of murder in civilized man, flower prematurely into breakdown, terror and dread? Would it demand too much of a tenant to stare down each morning on a flight of 2,000 feet? Or would it prove a deliverance for some? Would the juvenile delinquent festering in the violence of his monotonous corridors diminsh in his desire for brutality if he lived high in the air and found the intensity of his inexpressible vision matched by the intensity of the space through a fall?

That question returns us to the perspective of twentieth-century man. Caught between our desire to cling to the earth and to explore the stars, it is not impossible that a new life lived half a mile in the air, with streets in the clouds and chasms beyond each railing could prove nonetheless more intimate and more personal to us than the present congestions of the housing-project city. For that future man would be returned some individuality from his habitation. His apartment in the sky would be not so very different in its internal details from the apartments of his neighbors,

Norman Mailer

no more than one apartment is varied from another in Washington Square Village. But his situation would now be different from any other. His windows would look out on a view of massive constructions and airy bridges, of huge vaults and fine intricacies. The complexity of our culture could be captured again by the imagination of the architect: our buildings could begin to look a little less like armored tanks and more like clipper ships. Would we also then feel the dignity of sailors on a fourmaster at sea? Living so high, thrust into space, might we be returned to that mixture of awe and elation, of dignity and self-respect and a hint of dread, that sense of zest which a man must have known working his way out along a yard-arm in a stiff breeze at sea? Would the fatal monotony of mass culture dissolve a hint before the quiet swaying of a great and vertical city?

A STATEMENT FOR ARCHITECTURAL FORUM

The essence of totalitarianism is that it beheads. It beheads individuality, variety, dissent, extreme possibility, romantic faith; it blinds vision, deadens instinct; it obliterates the past. It makes factories look like college campuses or mental hospitals, where once factories had the specific beauty of revealing their huge and sometimes brutal function. It makes the new buildings on college campuses look like factories. It depresses the average American with the unconscious recognition that he is installed in a gelatin of totalitarian environment which is bound to deaden his most individual efforts. This new architecture, this totalitarian architecture, destroys the past. There is no trace of the forms which lived in the centuries before us, none of their arrogance, their privilege, their aspiration, their canniness, their creations, their vulgarities. We are left with less and less sense of the lives of men and women who came before us. So we are less able to judge the psychotic values of the present: overkill, fallout shelters, and adjurations . . . to drink a glass of milk each day. . . .

People who admire the new architecture find it of value because it obliterates the past. They are sufficiently totalitarian to wish to avoid the consequences of the past. Which of course is not to say that they see themselves as totalitarian. The totalitarian passion is an unconscious one. Which liberal, fighting for bigger housing and additional cubic feet of air space in elementary schools, does not see himself as a benefactor? Can he comprehend that the somewhat clammy pleasure he obtains from looking at the completion of the new school—that architectural horror!—is a reflection of a buried and ugly pleasure, a totalitarian glee that the Gothic knots and Romanesque oppressions which entered his psyche through the schoolhouses of his youth have now been excised? But those architectural wounds, those forms from his childhood, not only shamed him and scored him, but marked upon him as well a wound from culture itself—its buried message of the cruelty and horror which were rooted in the majesties of the past. Now the flat surfaces, blank ornamentation, and pastel colors of the new schoolhouses will maroon his children in an endless hallway of the present. A school is an *arena* to a child. Let it look like what it should be,

Architectural Excerpts

mysterious, even gladiatorial, rather than look like a reception center for war brides. The totalitarian impulse not only washes away distinctions but looks for a style in buildings, in clothing, and in the ornamentations of tools, appliances, and daily objects which will diminish one's sense of function and reduce one's sense of reality by reducing such emotions as awe, dread, beauty, pity, terror, calm, horror, and harmony. By dislocating us from the most powerful emotions of reality, totalitarianism leaves us further isolated in the empty landscapes of psychosis, precisely that inner landscape of void and dread which we flee by turning to totalitarian styles of life. The totalitarian liberal looks for new schools and more desks; the real liberal looks for more difficult books to force upon the curriculum. A good school can survive in a converted cow barn.

Yes, the people who admire the new architecture are looking to eject into their environment and landscape the same deadness and monotony life has put into them. A vast deadness and a huge monotony, a nausea without spasm, has been part of the profit of American life in the last fifteen years—we will pay in the next fifteen as this living death is disgorged into the buildings our totalitarian managers will manage to erect for us.

Our commodities are swollen in price by false, needless and useless labor. Modern architecture is the child of this fact. It works with a currency which (measured in terms of the skilled and/or useful labor going into a building) is worth half the real value of nineteenth-century money. The mechanical advances in construction hardly begin to make up for the wastes of advertising, public relations, building union covenants, city grafts, land costs, and the anemia of a dollar diminished by armaments and taxes. In this context the formulas of modern architecture have triumphed, and her bastards—those new office skyscrapers—proliferate everywhere: one suspects the best reason is that modern architecture offers a pretext to a large real-estate operator to stick up a skyscraper at a fraction of the money it should cost, so helps him to conceal the criminal fact that we are being given a stricken building, a denuded, aseptic, unfinished work, stripped of ornament, origins, prejudices, not even a peaked roof or spire to engage the heavens.

It is too cheap to separate Mafia architects with their Mussolini Modern (concrete dormitories on junior-college campuses) from serious modern architects. No, I think Le Corbusier and Wright and all the particular giants of the Bauhaus are the true villains; the Mafia architects are their proper sons; modern architecture at its best is even more anomalous than at its worst, for it tends to excite the Faustian and empty appetites of the architect's ego rather than reveal an artist's vision of our collective desire for shelter which is pleasurable, substantial, intricate, intimate, delicate, detailed, foibled, rich in gargoyle, guignol, false closet, secret stair, witch's hearth, attic, grandeur, kitsch, a world of buildings as diverse as the need within the eye. Beware: the ultimate promise of modern architecture is collective sightlessness for the species.

[1966]

Norman Mailer

Rachel Carson:
A Fable for Tomorrow

Rachel Carson (1907-1964), biologist, author of the best-selling *The Sea Around Us* (1951) and the prize-winning *Silent Spring* (1962), was the first to warn, in urgent terms, of the effects of environmental abuse. Her careful study and frightening conclusions are only now beginning to receive the popular and political recognition that conservationists and naturalists gave them upon publication.

There was once a town in the heart of America where all life seemed to live in harmony with its surroundings. The town lay in the midst of a checkerboard of prosperous farms, with fields of grain and hillsides of orchards where, in spring, white clouds of bloom drifted above the green fields. In autumn, oak and maple and birch set up a blaze of color that flamed and flickered across a backdrop of pines. Then foxes barked in the hills and deer silently crossed the fields, half hidden in the mists of the fall mornings.

Along the roads, laurel, viburnum and alder, great ferns and wildflowers delighted the traveler's eye through much of the year. Even in winter the roadsides were places of beauty, where countless birds came to feed on the berries and on the seed heads of the dried weeds rising above the snow. The countryside was, in fact, famous for the abundance and variety of its bird life, and when the flood of migrants was pouring through in spring and fall people traveled from great distances to observe them. Others came to fish the streams, which flowed clear and cold out of the hills and contained shady pools where trout lay. So it had been from the days many years ago when the first settlers raised their houses, sank their wells, and built their barns.

The a strange blight crept over the area and everything began to change. Some evil spell had settled on the community: mysterious maladies swept the flocks of chickens; the cattle and sheep sickened and died. Everywhere was a shadow of death. The farmers spoke of much illness among their families. In the town the doctors had become more and more puzzled by new kinds of sickness appearing among their patients. There had been several sudden and unexplained deaths, not only among adults but even among children, who would be stricken suddenly while at play and die within a few hours.

There was a strange stillness. The birds, for example—where had they gone? Many people spoke of them, puzzled and disturbed. The feeding stations in the backyards were deserted. The few birds seen anywhere were moribund; they trembled violently and could not fly. It was a spring without voices. On the mornings that had once throbbed with the dawn chorus of robins, catbirds, doves, jays, wrens, and scores of other bird voices there was now no sound; only silence lay over the fields and woods and marsh.

On the farms the hens brooded, but no chicks hatched. The farmers complained that they were unable to raise any pigs—the litters were small and the young survived only a few days. The apple trees were coming into bloom but no bees droned among the blossoms, so there was no pollination and there would be no fruit.

The roadsides, once so attractive, were now lined with browned and withered vegetation as though swept by fire. These, too, were silent, deserted by all living things. Even the streams were now lifeless. Anglers no longer visited them, for all the fish had died.

In the gutters under the eaves and between the shingles of the roofs, a white granular powder still showed a few patches; some weeks be-

Rachel Carson

fore it had fallen like snow upon the roofs and the lawns, the fields and streams.

No witchcraft, no enemy action had silenced the rebirth of new life in this stricken world. The people had done it themselves.

This town does not actually exist, but it might easily have a thousand counterparts in America or elsewhere in the world. I know of no community that has experienced all the misfortunes I describe. Yet every one of these disasters has actually happened somewhere, and many real communities have already suffered a substantial number of them. A grim specter has crept upon us almost unnoticed, and this imagined tragedy may easily become a stark reality we all shall know.

[1962]

A Fable for Tomorrow

Lynn White, Jr.:
The Historical Roots of Our Ecologic Crisis

Lynn White, Jr. (b. 1907), educator, former
president of Mills College, and social critic, is
active in the movement to understand and protect the total natural environment. He has been
important in defining the relationship between
man's spirit and his environment as he develops a rationale for ecological study and action.

A conversation with Aldous Huxley not infrequently put one at the receiving end of an unforgettable monologue. About a year before his lamented death he was discoursing on a favorite topic: Man's unnatural treatment of nature and its sad results. To illustrate his point he told how, during the previous summer, he had returned to a little valley in England where he had spent many happy months as a child. Once it had been composed of delightful grassy glades; now it was becoming overgrown with unsightly brush because the rabbits that formerly kept such growth under control had largely succumbed to a disease, myxomatosis, that was deliberately introduced by the local farmers to reduce the rabbits' destruction of crops. Being something of a Philistine, I could be silent no longer, even in the interests of great rhetoric. I interrupted to point out that the rabbit itself had been brought as a domestic animal to England in 1176, presumably to improve the protein diet of the peasantry.

All forms of life modify their contexts. The most spectacular and benign instance is doubtless the coral polyp. By serving its own ends, it has created a vast undersea world favorable to thousands of other kinds of animals and plants. Ever since man became a numerous species he has affected his environment notably. The hypothesis that his fire-drive method of hunting created the world's great grasslands and helped to exterminate the monster mammals of the Pleistocene from much of the globe is plausible, if not proved. For 6 millennia at least, the banks of the lower Nile have been a human artifact rather than the swampy African jungle which nature, apart from man, would have made it. The Aswan Dam, flooding 5000 square miles, is only the latest stage in a long process. In many regions terracing or irrigation, overgrazing, the cutting of forests by Romans to build ships to fight Carthaginians or by Crusaders to solve the logistics problems of their expeditions, have profoundly changed some ecologies. Observation that the French landscape falls into two basic types, the open fields of the north and the *bocage* of the south and west, inspired Marc Bloch to undertake his classic study of medieval agricultural methods. Quite unintentionally, changes in human ways often affect nonhuman nature. It has been noted, for example, that the advent of the automobile eliminated huge flocks of sparrows that once fed on the horse manure littering every street.

The history of ecologic change is still so rudimentary that we know little about what really happened, or what the results were. The extinction of the European aurochs as late as 1627 would seem to have been a simple case of overenthusiastic hunting. On more intricate matters it often is impossible to find solid information. For a thousand years or more the Frisians and Hollanders have been pushing back the North Sea, and the process is culminating in our own time in the reclamation of the Zuider Zee. What, if any, species of animals, birds, fish, shore life, or plants have died out in the process? In their epic combat with Neptune have the Netherlanders overlooked ecological values in such a way that the quality of human life in the Netherlands has suffered? I cannot discover that the questions have ever been asked, much less answered.

Lynn White, Jr.

People, then, have often been a dynamic element in their own environment, but in the present state of biological scholarship we usually do not know exactly when, where, or with what effects man-induced changes came. As we enter the last third of the twentieth century, however, concern for the problem of ecologic backlash is mounting feverishly. Natural science, conceived as the effort to understand the nature of things, had flourished in several eras and among several peoples. Similarly there had been an age-old accumulation of technological skills, sometimes growing rapidly, sometimes slowly. But it was not until about four generations ago that Western Europe and North America arranged a marriage between science and technology, a union of the theoretical and the empirical approaches to our natural environment. The emergence in widespread practice of the Baconian creed that scientific knowledge means technological power over nature can scarcely be dated before about 1850, save in the chemical industries, where it is anticipated in the eighteenth century. Its acceptance as a normal pattern of action may mark the greatest event in human history since the invention of agriculture, and perhaps in non-human terrestrial history as well.

Almost at once the new situation forced the crystallization of the novel concept of ecology; indeed, the word *ecology* first appeared in the English language in 1873. Today, less than a century later, the impact of our race upon the environment has so increased in force that it has changed in essence. When the first cannons were fired, in the early fourteenth century, they affected ecology by sending workers scrambling to the forests and mountains for more potash, sulfur, iron ore, and charcoal, with some resulting erosion and deforestation. Hydrogen bombs are of a different order: a war fought with them might alter the genetics of all life on this planet. By 1285 London had a smog problem arising from the burning of soft coal, but our present combustion of fossil fuels threatens to change the chemistry of the globe's atmosphere as a whole, with consequences which we are only beginning to guess. With the population explosion, the carcinoma of planless urbanism, the new geological deposits of sewage and garbage, surely no creature other than man has ever managed to foul its nest in such short order.

There are many calls to action, but specific proposals, however worthy as individual items, seem too partial, palliative, negative: ban the bomb, tear down the billboards, give the Hindus contraceptives and tell them to eat their sacred cows. The simplest solution to any suspect change is, of course, to stop it, or, better yet, to revert to a romanticized past: make those ugly gasoline stations look like Anne Hathaway's cottage or (in the Far West) like ghost-town saloons. The "wilderness area" mentality invariably advocates deep-freezing an ecology, wheher San Gimignano or the High Sierra, as it was before the first Kleenex was dropped. But neither atavism nor prettification will cope with the ecologic crisis of our time.

What shall we do? No one yet knows. Unless we think about fundamentals, our specific measures may produce new backlashes more serious than those they are designed to remedy.

The Historical Roots of Our Ecologic Crisis

As a beginning we should try to clarify our thinking by looking, in some historical depth, at the presuppositions that underlie modern technology and science. Science was traditionally aristocratic, speculative, intellectual in intent; technology was lower-class, empirical, action-oriented. The quite sudden fusion of these two, towards the middle of the nineteenth century, is surely related to the slightly prior and contemporary democratic revolutions which, by reducing social barriers, tended to assert a functional unity of brain and hand. Our ecologic crisis is the product of an emerging, entirely novel, democratic culture. The issue is whether a democratized world can survive its own implications. Presumably we cannot unless we rethink our axioms.

THE WESTERN TRADITIONS
OF TECHNOLOGY AND SCIENCE

One thing is so certain that it seems stupid to verbalize it: both modern technology and modern science are distinctively *Occidental*. Our technology has absorbed elements from all over the world, notably from China; yet everywhere today, whether in Japan or in Nigeria, successful technology is Western. Our science is the heir to all the sciences of the past, especially perhaps to the work of the great Islamic scientists of the Middle Ages, who so often outdid the ancient Greeks in skill and perspicacity: Al-Razi in medicine, for example; or ibn-al-Haytham in optics; or Omar Khayyám in mathematics. Indeed, not a few works of such geniuses seem to have vanished in the original Arabic and to survive only in medieval Latin translations that helped to lay the foundations for later Western developments. Today, around the globe, all significant science is Western in style and method, whatever the pigmentation or language of the scientists.

A second pair of facts is less well recognized because they result from quite recent historical scholarship. The leadership of the West, both in technology and in science, is far older than the so-called Scientific Revolution of the seventeenth century or the so-called Industrial Revolution of the eighteenth century. These terms are in fact outmoded and obscure the true nature of what they try to describe—significant stages in two long and separate developments. By A.D. 1000 at the latest—and perhaps, feebly, as much as 200 years earlier—the West began to apply water power to industrial processes other than milling grain. This was followed in the late twelfth century by the harnessing of wind power. From simple beginnings, but with remarkable consistency of style, the West rapidly expanded its skills in the development of power machinery, labor-saving devices, and automation. Those who doubt should contemplate that most monumental achievement in the history of automation: the weight-driven mechanical clock, which appeared in two forms in the early fourteenth century. Not in craftsmanship but in basic technological capacity, the Latin West of the later Middle Ages far outstripped its elaborate, sophisticated, and esthetically magnificent sister cultures, Byzantium and Islam. In 1444 a great

Lynn White, Jr.

Greek ecclesiastic, Bessarion, who had gone to Italy, wrote a letter to a prince in Greece. He is amazed by the superiority of Western ships, arms, textiles, glass. But above all he is astonished by the spectacle of water-wheels sawing timbers and pumping the bellows of blast furnaces. Clearly, he had seen nothing of the sort in the Near East.

By the end of the fifteenth century the technological superiority of Europe was such that its small, mutually hostile nations could spill out over all the rest of the world, conquering, looting, and colonizing. The symbol of this technological superiority is the fact that Portugal, one of the weakest states of the Occident, was able to become, and to remain for a century, mistress of the East Indies. And we must remember that the technology of Vasco da Gama and Albuquerque was built by pure empiricism, drawing remarkably little support or inspiration from science.

In the present-day vernacular understanding, modern science is supposed to have begun in 1543, when both Copernicus and Vesalius published their great works. It is no derogation of their accomplishments, however, to point out that such structures as the *Fabrica* and *De revolutionibus* do not appear overnight. The distinctive Western tradition of science, in fact, began in the late eleventh century with a massive movement of translation of Arabic and Greek scientific works into Latin. A few notable books—Theophrastus, for example—escaped the West's avid new appetite for science, but within less than 200 years effectively the entire corpus of Greek and Muslim science was available in Latin, and was being eagerly read and criticized in the new European universities. Out of criticism arose new observation, speculation, and increasing distrust of ancient authorities. By the late thirteenth century Europe had seized global scientific leadership from the faltering hands of Islam. It would be as absurd to deny the profound originality of Newton, Galileo, or Copernicus as to deny that of the fourteenth century scholastic scientists like Buridan or Oresme on whose work they built. Before the eleventh century, science scarcely existed in the Latin West, even in Roman times. From the eleventh century onward, the scientific sector of Occidental culture has increased in a steady crescendo.

Since both our technological and our scientific movements got their start, acquired their character, and achieved world dominance in the Middle Ages, it would seem that we cannot understand their nature or their present impact upon ecology without examining fundamental medieval assumptions and developments.

MEDIEVAL VIEW OF MAN AND NATURE

Until recently, agriculture has been the chief occupation even in "advanced" societies; hence, any change in methods of tillage has much importance. Early plows, drawn by two oxen, did not normally turn the sod but merely scratched it. Thus, cross-plowing was needed and fields tended to be squarish. In the fairly light soils and semiarid climates of the Near East and Mediterranean, this worked well. But such a plow was inappropriate to the wet climate and often sticky soils of northern Europe. By the latter part of the seventh century after Christ, however, following obscure beginnings, certain northern peasants were using an entirely new kind of plow, equipped with a vertical knife to cut the line of the furrow, a horizontal share to slice under the sod, and a moldboard to turn it over. The friction of this plow with the soil was so great that it normally required not two but eight oxen. It attacked the land with such violence that cross-plowing was not needed, and fields tended to be shaped in long strips.

In the days of the scratch-plow, fields were distributed generally in units capable of supporting a single family. Subsistence farming was the presupposition. But no peasant owned eight oxen: to use the new and more efficient plow, peasants pooled their oxen to form large plow-teams, originally receiving (it would appear) plowed strips in proportion to their contribution. Thus, distribution of land was based no longer on the needs of a family but, rather, on the capacity of a power machine to till the earth. Man's relation to the soil was profoundly changed. Formerly man had been part of nature; now he was the exploiter of nature. Nowhere else in the world did farmers develop any analogous agricultural implement. Is it coincidence that modern technology, with its ruthlessness toward nature, has so largely been produced by descendants of these peasants of northern Europe?

This same exploitive attitude appears slightly before A.D. 830 in Western illustrated calendars. In older calendars the months were shown as passive personifications. The new Frankish calendars, which set the style for the Middle Ages, are very different: they show men coercing the world around them—plowing, harvesting, chopping trees, butchering pigs. Man and nature are two things, and man is master.

These novelties seem to be in harmony with larger intellectual patterns. What people do about their ecology depends on what they think about themselves in relation to things around them. Human ecology is deeply conditioned by beliefs about our nature and destiny—that is, by religion. To Western eyes this is very evident in, say, India or Ceylon. It is equally true of ourselves and of our medieval ancestors.

The victory of Christianity over paganism was the greatest psychic revolution in the history of our culture. It has become fashionable today to say that, for better or worse, we live in "the post-Christian age." Certainly the forms of our thinking and language have largely ceased to be Christian, but to my eye the substance often remains amazingly akin to that of the past. Our daily habits of action, for example, are dominated by an implicit faith in perpetual progress which was unknown either to Greco-Roman antiquity or to the Orient. It is rooted in, and is indefensible apart from, Judeo-Christian teleology. The fact that Communists share it merely helps to show what can be demonstrated on many other grounds: that Marxism, like Islam, is a Judeo-Christian heresy. We continue today to live, as we have lived for about 1700 years, very largely in a context of Christian axioms.

Lynn White, Jr.

What did Christianity tell people about their relations with the environment?

While many of the world's mythologies provide stories of creation, Greco-Roman mythology was singularly incoherent in this respect. Like Aristotle, the intellectuals of the ancient West denied that the visible world had had a beginning. Indeed, the idea of a beginning was impossible in the framework of their cyclical notion of time. In sharp contrast, Christianity inherited from Judaism not only a concept of time as nonrepetitive and linear but also a striking story of creation. By gradual stages a loving and all-powerful God had created light and darkness, the heavenly bodies, the earth and all its plants, animals, birds, and fishes. Finally, God had created Adam and, as an afterthought, Eve to keep man from being lonely. Man named all the animals, thus establishing his dominance over them. God planned all of this explicitly for man's benefit and rule: no item in the physical creation had any purpose save to serve man's purposes. And, although man's body is made of clay, he is not simply part of nature: he is made in God's image.

Especially in its Western form, Christianity is the most anthropocentric religion the world has seen. As early as the second century both Tertullian and Saint Irenaeus of Lyons were insisting that when God shaped Adam he was foreshadowing the image of the Incarnate Christ, the Second Adam. Man shares, in great measure, God's transcendence of nature. Christianity, in absolute contrast to ancient paganism and Asia's religions (except, perhaps, Zoroastrianism), not only established a dualism of man and nature but also insisted that it is God's will that man exploit nature for his proper ends.

At the level of the common people this worked out in an interesting way. In Antiquity every tree, every spring, every stream, every hill had its own *genius loci*, its guardian spirit. These spirits were accessible to men, but were very unlike men; centaurs, fauns, and mermaids show their ambivalence. Before one cut a tree, mined a mountain, or dammed a brook, it was important to placate the spirit in charge of that particular situation, and to keep it placated. By destroying pagan animism, Christianity made it possible to exploit nature in a mood of indifference to the feelings of natural objects.

It is often said that for animism the Church substituted the cult of saints. True; but the cults of saints is functionally quite different from animism. The saint is not *in* natural objects; he may have special shrines, but his citizenship is in heaven. Moreover, a saint is entirely a man; he can be approached in human terms. In addition to saints, Christianity of course also had angels and demons inherited from Judaism and perhaps, at one remove, from Zoroastrianism. But these were all as mobile as the saints themselves. The spirits *in* natural objects, which formerly had protected nature from man, evaporated. Man's effective monopoly on spirit in this world was confirmed, and the old inhibitions to the exploitation of nature crumbled.

When one speaks in such sweeping terms, a note of caution is in

The Historical Roots of Our Ecologic Crisis

order. Christianity is a complex faith, and its consequences differ in differing contexts. What I have said may well apply to the medieval West, where in fact technology made spectacular advances. But the Greek East, a highly civilized realm of equal Christian devotion, seems to have produced no marked technological innovation after the late seventh century, when Greek fire was invented. The key to the contrast may perhaps be found in a difference in the tonality of piety and thought which students of comparative theology find between the Greek and the Latin Churches. The Greeks believed that sin was intellectual blindness, and that salvation was found in illumination, orthodoxy—that is, clear thinking. The Latins, on the other hand, felt that sin was moral evil, and that salvation was to be found in right conduct. Eastern theology has been intellectualist. Western theology has been voluntarist. The Greek saint contemplates; the Western saint acts. The implications of Christianity for the conquest of nature would emerge more easily in the Western atmosphere.

The Christian dogma of creation, which is found in the first clause of all the Creeds, has another meaning for our comprehension of today's ecologic crisis. By revelation, God had given man the Bible, the Book of Scripture. But since God had made nature, nature also must reveal the divine mentality. The religious study of nature for the better understanding of God was known as natural theology. In the early Church, and always in the Greek East, nature was conceived primarily as a symbolic system through which God speaks to men: the ant is a sermon to sluggards; rising flames are the symbol of the soul's aspiration. This view of nature was essentially artistic rather than scientific. While Byzantium preserved and copied great numbers of ancient Greek scientific texts, science as we conceive it could scarcely flourish in such an ambience.

However, in the Latin West by the early thirteenth century natural theology was following a very different bent. It was ceasing to be the decoding of the physical symbols of God's communication with man and was becoming the effort to understand God's mind by discovering how his creation operates. The rainbow was no longer simply a symbol of hope first sent to Noah after the Deluge: Robert Grosseteste, Friar Roger Bacon, and Theodoric of Freiberg produced startlingly sophisticated work on the optics of the rainbow, but they did it as a venture in religious understanding. From the thirteenth century onward, up to and including Leibnitz and Newton, every major scientist, in effect, explained his motivations in religious terms. Indeed, if Galileo had not been so expert an amateur theologian he would have got into far less trouble: the professionals resented his intrusion. And Newton seems to have regarded himself more as a theologian than as a scientist. It was not until the late eighteenth century that the hypothesis of God became unnecessary to many scientists.

It is often hard for the historian to judge, when men explain why they are doing what they want to do, whether they are offering real reasons or merely culturally acceptable reasons. The consistency with which scientists during the long formative centuries of Western science said that the task and the reward of the scientist was "to think God's thoughts after

Lynn White, Jr.

him" leads one to believe that this was their real motivation. If so, then modern Western science was cast in a matrix of Christian theology. The dynamism of religious devotion, shaped by the Judeo-Christian dogma of creation, gave it impetus.

AN ALTERNATIVE CHRISTIAN VIEW

We would seem to be headed toward conclusions unpalatable to many Christians. Since both *science* and *technology* are blessed words in our contemporary vocabulary, some may be happy at the notions, first, that, viewed historically, modern science is an extrapolation of natural theology and, second, that modern technology is at least partly to be explained as an Occidental, voluntarist realization of the Christian dogma of man's transcendence of, and rightful mastery over, nature. But, as we now recognize, somewhat over a century ago science and technology— hitherto quite separate activities—joined to give mankind powers which, to judge by many of the ecologic effects, are out of control. If so, Christianity bears a huge burden of guilt.

I personally doubt that disastrous ecologic backlash can be avoided simply by applying to our problems more science and more technology. Our science and technology have grown out of Christian attitudes toward man's relation to nature which are almost universally held not only by Christians and neo-Christians but also by those who fondly regard themselves as post-Christians. Despite Copernicus, all the cosmos rotates around our little globe. Despite Darwin, we are *not*, in our hearts, part of the natural process. We are superior to nature, contemptuous of it, willing to use it for our slightest whim. The newly elected Governor of California, like myself a churchman but less troubled than I, spoke for the Christian tradition when he said (as is alleged), "when you've seen one redwood tree, you've seen them all." To a Christian a tree can be no more than a physical fact. The whole concept of the sacred grove is alien to Christianity and to the ethos of the West. For nearly two millennia Christian missionaries have been chopping down sacred groves, which are idolatrous because they assume spirit in nature.

What we do about ecology depends on our ideas of the man-nature relationship. More science and more technology are not going to get us out of the present ecologic crisis until we find a new religion, or rethink our old one. The beatniks, who are the basic revolutionaries of our time, show a sound instinct in their affinity for Zen Buddhism, which conceives of the man-nature relationship as very nearly the mirror image of the Christian view. Zen, however, is as deeply conditioned by Asian history as Christianity is by the experience of the West, and I am dubious of its viability among us.

Possibly we should ponder the greatest radical in Christian history since Christ: Saint Francis of Assisi. The prime miracle of Saint Francis is the fact that he did not end at the stake, as many of his left-wing followers did. He was so clearly heretical that a General of the Franciscan Order,

The Historical Roots of Our Ecologic Crisis

Saint Bonaventura, a great and perceptive Christian, tried to suppress the early accounts of Franciscanism. The key to an understanding of Francis is his belief in the virtue of humility—not merely for the individual but for man as a species. Francis tried to depose man from his monarchy over creation and set up a democracy of all God's creatures. With him the ant is no longer simply a homily for the lazy, flames a sign of the thrust of the soul toward union with God; now they are Brother Ant and Sister Fire, praising the Creator in their own ways as Brother Man does in his.

Later commentators have said that Francis preached to the birds as a rebuke to men who would not listen. The records do not read so: he urged the little birds to praise God, and in spiritual ecstasy they flapped their wings and chirped rejoicing. Legends of saints, especially the Irish saints, had long told of their dealings with animals but always, I believe, to show their human dominance over creatures. With Francis it is different. The land around Gubbio in the Apennines was being ravaged by a fierce wolf. Saint Francis, says the legend, talked to the wolf and persuaded him of the error of his ways. The wolf repented, died in the odor of sanctity, and was buried in consecrated ground.

What Sir Steven Ruciman calls "the Franciscan doctrine of the animal soul" was quickly stamped out. Quite possibly it was in part inspired, consciously or unconsciously, by the belief in reincarnation held by the Cathar heretics who at that time teemed in Italy and southern France, and who presumably had got it originally from India. It is significant that at just the same moment, about 1200, traces of metempsychosis are found also in western Judaism, in the Provençal *Cabbala*. But Francis held neither to transmigration of souls nor to pantheism. His view of nature and of man rested on a unique sort of pan-psychism of all things animate and inanimate designed for the glorification of their transcendent Creator, who, in the ultimate gesture of cosmic humility, assumed flesh, lay helpless in a manger, and hung dying on a scaffold.

I am not suggesting that many contemporary Americans who are concerned about our ecologic crisis will be either able or willing to counsel with wolves or exhort birds. However, the present increasing disruption of the global environment is the product of a dynamic technology and science which were originating in the Western medieval world against which Saint Francis was rebelling in so original a way. Their growth cannot be understood historically apart from distinctive attitudes toward nature which are deeply grounded in Christian dogma. The fact that most people do not think of these attitudes as Christian is irrelevant. No new set of basic values has been accepted in our society to displace those of Christianity. Hence we shall continue to have a worsening ecologic crisis until we reject the Christian axiom that nature has no reason for existence save to serve man.

The greatest spiritual revolutionary in Western history, Saint Francis, proposed what he thought was an alternative Christian view of nature and man's relation to it: he tried to substitute the idea of the equality of all creatures, including man, for the idea of man's limitless rule

Lynn White, Jr.

of creation. He failed. Both our present science and our present technology are so tinctured with orthodox Christian arrogance toward nature that no solution for our ecologic crisis can be expected from them alone. Since the roots of our trouble are so largely religious, the remedy must also be essentially religious, whether we call it that or not. We must rethink and refeel our nature and destiny. The profoundly religious, but heretical, sense of the primitive Franciscans for the spiritual autonomy of all parts of nature may point a direction. I propose Francis as a patron saint for ecologists.

[1967]

The Historical Roots of Our Ecologic Crisis

Paul R. Ehrlich:

Eco-Catastrophe!

Paul R. Ehrlich (b. 1932), biologist and ecologist, examines the implications of environmental abuse for future decades. Though speculative and exaggerated, his emphasis on what could happen is based upon statistical possibility and is intended to be taken seriously.

The end of the ocean came late in the summer of 1979, and it came even more rapidly than the biologists had expected. There had been signs for more than a decade, commencing with the discovery in 1968 that DDT slows down photosynthesis in marine plant life. It was announced in a short paper in the technical journal, *Science,* but to ecologists it smacked of doomsday. They knew that all life in the sea depends on photosynthesis, the chemical process by which green plants bind the sun's energy and make it available to living things. And they knew that DDT and similar chlorinated hydrocarbons had polluted the entire surface of the earth, including the sea.

But that was only the first of many signs. There had been the final gasp of the whaling industry in 1973, and the end of the Peruvian anchovy fishery in 1975. Indeed, a score of other fisheries had disappeared quietly from overexploitation and various eco-catastrophes by 1977. The term "eco-catastrophe" was coined by a California ecologist in 1969 to describe the most spectacular of man's attacks on the systems which sustain his life. He drew his inspiration from the Santa Barbara offshore oil disaster of that year, and from the news which spread among naturalists that virtually all of the Golden State's seashore bird life was doomed because of chlorinated hydrocarbon interference with its reproduction. Eco-catastrophes in the sea became increasingly common in the early 1970's. Mysterious "blooms" of previously rare microorganisms began to appear in offshore waters. Red tides—killer outbreaks of a minute single-celled plant—returned to the Florida Gulf coast and were sometimes accompanied by tides of other exotic hues.

It was clear by 1975 that the entire ecology of the ocean was changing. A few types of phytoplankton were becoming resistant to chlorinated hydrocarbons and were gaining the upper hand. Changes in the phytoplankton community led inevitably to changes in the community of zooplankton, the tiny animals which eat the phytoplankton. These changes were passed on up the chains of life in the ocean to the herring, plaice, cod and tuna. As the diversity of life in the ocean diminished, its stability also decreased.

Other changes had taken place by 1975. Most ocean fishes that returned to freshwater to breed, like the salmon, had become extinct, their breeding streams so dammed up and polluted that their powerful homing instinct only resulted in suicide. Many fishes and shellfishes that bred in restricted areas along the coasts followed them as onshore pollution escalated.

By 1977 the annual yield of fish from the sea was down to 30 million metric tons, less than one-half the per capita catch of a decade earlier. This helped malnutrition to escalate sharply in a world where an estimated 50 million people per year were already dying of starvation. The United Nations attempted to get all chlorinated hydrocarbon insecticides banned on a worldwide basis, but the move was defeated by the United States. This opposition was generated primarily by the American petrochemical industry, operating hand in glove with its subsidiary, the United States

Paul R. Ehrlich

Department of Agriculture. Together they persuaded the government to oppose the U.N. move—which was not difficult since most Americans believed that Russia and China were more in need of fish products than was the United States. The United Nations also attempted to get fishing nations to adopt strict and enforced catch limits to preserve dwindling stocks. This move was blocked by Russia, who, with the most modern electronic equipment, was in the best position to glean what was left in the sea. It was, curiously, on the very day in 1977 when the Soviet Union announced its refusal that another ominous article appeared in *Science*. It announced that incident solar radiation had been so reduced by worldwide air pollution that serious effects on the world's vegetation could be expected.

Apparently it was a combination of ecosystem destabilization, sunlight reduction, and a rapid escalation in chlorinated hydrocarbon pollution from massive Thanodrin applications which triggered the ultimate catastrophe. Seventeen huge Soviet-financed Thanodrin plants were operating in underdeveloped countries by 1978. They had been part of a massive Russian "aid offensive" designed to fill the gap caused by the collapse of America's ballyhooed "Green Revolution."

It became apparent in the early '70s that the "Green Revolution" was more talk than substance. Distribution of high yield "miracle" grain seeds had caused temporary local spurts in agricultural production. Simultaneously, excellent weather had produced record harvests. The combination permitted bureaucrats, especially in the United States Department of Agriculture and the Agency for International Development (AID), to reverse their previous pessimism and indulge in an outburst of optimistic propaganda about staving off famine. They raved about the approaching transformation of agriculture in the underdeveloped countries (UDCs). The reason for the propaganda reversal was never made clear. Most historians agree that a combination of utter ignorance of ecology, a desire to justify past errors, and pressure from agro-industry (which was eager to sell pesticides, fertilizers, and farm machinery to the UDCs and agencies helping the UDCs) was behind the campaign. Whatever the motivation, the results were clear. Many concerned people, lacking the expertise to see through the Green Revolution drivel, relaxed. The population-food crisis was "solved."

But reality was not long in showing itself. Local famine persisted in northern India even after good weather brought an end to the ghastly Bihar famine of the mid-'60s. East Pakistan was next, followed by a resurgence of general famine in northern India. Other foci of famine rapidly developed in Indonesia, the Philippines, Malawi, the Congo, Egypt, Colombia, Ecuador, Honduras, the Dominican Republic, and Mexico.

Everywhere hard realities destroyed the illusion of the Green Revolution. Yields dropped as the progressive farmers who had first accepted the new seeds found that their higher yields brought lower prices—effective demand (hunger plus cash) was not sufficient in poor countries to keep prices up. Less progressive farmers, observing this, refused to make the extra

Eco-Catastrophe!

effort required to cultivate the "miracle" grains. Transport systems proved inadequate to bring the necessary fertilizer to the fields where the new and extremely fertilizer-sensitive grains were being grown. The same systems were also inadequate to move produce to markets. Fertilizer plants were not built fast enough, and most of the underdeveloped countries could not scrape together funds to purchase supplies, even on concessional terms. Finally, the inevitable happened, and pests began to reduce yields in even the most carefully cultivated fields. Among the first were the famous "miracle rats" which invaded Philippine "miracle rice" fields early in 1969. They were quickly followed by many insects and viruses, thriving on the relatively pest-susceptible new grains, encouraged by the vast and dense plantings, and rapidly acquiring resistance to the chemicals used against them. As chaos spread until even the most obtuse agriculturists and economists realized that the Green Revolution had turned brown, the Russians stepped in.

In retrospect it seems incredible that the Russians, with the American mistakes known to them, could launch an even more incompetent program of aid to the underdeveloped world. Indeed, in the early 1970's there were cynics in the United States who claimed that outdoing the stupidity of American foreign aid would be physically impossible. Those critics were, however, obviously unaware that the Russians had been busily destroying their own environment for many years. The virtual disappearance of sturgeon from Russian rivers caused a great shortage of caviar by 1970. A standard joke among Russian scientists at that time was that they had created an artificial caviar which was indistinguishable from the real thing—except by taste. At any rate the Soviet Union, observing with interest the progressive deterioration of relations between the UDCs and the United States, came up with a solution. It had recently developed what it claimed was the ideal insecticide, a highly lethal chlorinated hydrocarbon complexed with a special agent for penetrating the external skeletal armor of insects. Announcing that the new pesticide, called Thanodrin, would truly produce a Green Revolution, the Soviets entered into negotiations with various UDCs for the construction of massive Thanodrin factories. The USSR would bear all the costs; all it wanted in return were certain trade and military concessions.

It is interesting now, with the perspective of years, to examine in some detail the reasons why the UDCs welcomed the Thanodrin plan with such open arms. Government officials in these countries ignored the protests of their own scientists that Thanodrin would not solve the problems which plagued them. The governments now knew that the basic cause of their problems was overpopulation, and that these problems had been exacerbated by the dullness, daydreaming, and cupidity endemic to all governments. They knew that only population control and limited development aimed primarily at agriculture could have spared them the horrors they now faced. They knew it, but they were not about to admit it. How much easier it was simply to accuse the Americans of failing to give them proper aid; how much simpler to accept the Russian panacea.

Paul R. Ehrlich

And then there was the general worsening of relations between the United States and the UDCs. Many things had contributed to this. The situation in America in the first half of the 1970's deserves our close scrutiny. Being more dependent on imports for raw materials than the Soviet Union, the United States had, in the early 1970's, adopted more and more heavy-handed policies in order to insure continuing supplies. Military adventures in Asia and Latin America had further lessened the international credibility of the United States as a great defender of freedom —an image which had begun to deteriorate rapidly during the pointless and fruitless Viet Nam conflict. At home, acceptance of the carefully manufactured image lessened dramatically, as even the more romantic and chauvinistic citizens began to understand the role of the military and the industrial system in what John Kenneth Galbraith had aptly named "The New Industrial State."

At home in the USA the early '70s were traumatic times. Racial violence grew and the habitability of the cities diminished, as nothing substantial was done to ameliorate either racial inequities or urban blight. Welfare rolls grew as automation and general technological progress forced more and more people into the category of "unemployable." Simultaneously a taxpayers' revolt occurred. Although there was not enough money to build the schools, roads, water systems, sewage systems, jails, hospitals, urban transit lines, and all the other amenities needed to support a burgeoning population, Americans refused to tax themselves more heavily. Starting in Youngstown, Ohio, in 1969 and followed closely by Richmond, California, community after community was forced to close its schools or curtail educational operations for lack of funds. Water supplies, already marginal in quality and quantity in many places by 1970, deteriorated quickly. Water rationing occurred in 1,723 municipalities in the summer of 1974, and hepatitis and epidemic dysentery rates climbed about 500 percent between 1970 and 1974.

Air pollution continued to be the most obvious manifestation of environmental deterioration. It was, by 1972, quite literally in the eyes of all Americans. The year 1973 saw not only the New York and Los Angeles smog disasters, but also the publication of the surgeon general's massive report on air pollution and health. The public had been partially prepared for the worst by the publicity given to the U.N. pollution conference held in 1972. Deaths in the late '60s caused by smog were well known to scientists, but the public had ignored them because they mostly involved the early demise of the old and sick rather than people dropping dead on the freeways. But suddenly our citizens were faced with nearly 200,000 corpses and massive documentation that they could be the next to die from respiratory disease. They were not ready for that scale of disaster. After all, the U.N. conference had not predicted that accumulated air pollution would make the planet uninhabitable until almost 1990. The population was terrorized as TV screens became filled with scenes of horror from the disaster areas. Especially vivid was NBC's coverage of hundreds of unattended people choking out their lives outside of New York's hospitals.

Eco-Catastrophe!

Terms like nitrogen oxide, acute bronchitis and cardiac arrest began to have real meaning for most Americans.

The ultimate horror was the announcement that chlorinated hydrocarbons were now a major constituent of air pollution in all American cities. Autopsies of smog disaster victims revealed an average chlorinated hydrocarbon load in fatty tissue equivalent to 26 parts per million of DDT. In October, 1973, the Department of Health, Education and Welfare announced studies which showed unequivocally that increasing death rates from hypertension, cirrhosis of the liver, liver cancer and a series of other diseases had resulted from the chlorinated hydrocarbon load. They estimated that Americans born since 1946 (when DDT usage began) now had a life expectancy of only 49 years, and predicted that if current patterns continued, this expectancy would reach 42 years by 1980, when it might level out. Plunging insurance stocks triggered a stock market panic. The president of Vesicoll, Inc., a major pesticide producer, went on television to "publicly eat a teaspoonful of DDT" (it was really powdered milk) and announce that HEW had been infiltrated by Communists. Other giants of the petro-chemical industry, attempting to dispute the indisputable evidence, launched a massive pressure campaign on Congress to force HEW to "get out of agriculture's business." They were aided by the agro-chemical journals, which had decades of experience in misleading the public about the benefits and dangers of pesticides. But by now the public realized that it had been duped. The Nobel Prize for medicine and physiology was given to Drs. J. L. Radomski and W. B. Deichmann, who in the late 1960's had pioneered in the documentation of the long-term lethal effects of chlorinated hydrocarbons. A presidential commission with unimpeachable credentials directly accused the agro-chemical complex of "condemning many millions of Americans to an early death." The year 1973 was the year in which Americans finally came to understand the direct threat to their existence posed by environmental deterioration.

And 1973 was also the year in which most people finally comprehended the indirect threat. Even the president of Union Oil Company and several other industrialists publicly stated their concern over the reduction of bird populations which had resulted from pollution by DDT and other chlorinated hydrocarbons. Insect populations boomed because they were resistant to most pesticides and had been freed, by the incompetent use of those pesticides, from most of their natural enemies. Rodents swarmed over crops, multiplying rapidly in the absence of predatory birds. The effect of pests on the wheat crop was especially disastrous in the summer of 1973, since that was also the year of the great drought. Most of us can remember the shock which greeted the announcement by atmospheric physicists that the shift of the jet stream which had caused the drought was probably permanent. It signalled the birth of the Mid-western desert. Man's air-polluting activities had by then caused gross changes in climatic patterns. The news, of course, played hell with commodity and stock markets. Food prices skyrocketed, as savings were poured into hoarded canned goods. Official assurances that food supplies would remain ample

Paul R. Ehrlich

fell on deaf ears, and even the government showed signs of nervousness when California migrant field workers went out on strike again in protest against the continued use of pesticides by growers. The strike burgeoned into farm burning and riots. The workers, calling themselves "The Walking Dead," demanded immediate compensation for their shortened lives, and crash research programs to attempt to lengthen them.

It was in the same speech in which President Edward Kennedy, after much delay, finally declared a national emergency and called out the National Guard to harvest California's crops, that the first mention of population control was made. Kennedy pointed out that the United States would no longer be able to offer any food aid to other nations and was likely to suffer food shortages herself. He suggested that, in view of the manifest failure of the Green Revolution, the only hope of the UDCs lay in population control. His statement, you will recall, created an uproar in the underdeveloped countries. Newspaper editorials accused the United States of wishing to prevent small countries from becoming large nations and thus threatening American hegemony. Politicians asserted that President Kennedy was a "creature of the giant drug combine" that wished to shove its pills down every woman's throat.

Among Americans, religious opposition to population control was very slight. Industry in general also backed the idea. Increasing poverty in the UDCs was both destroying markets and threatening supplies of raw materials. The seriousness of the raw material situation had been brought home during the congressional hard resources hearings in 1971. The exposure of the ignorance of the cornucopian economists had been quite a spectacle—a spectacle brought into virtually every American's home in living color. Few would forget the distinguished geologist from the University of California who suggested that economists be legally required to learn at least the most elementary facts of geology. Fewer still would forget that an equally distinguished Harvard economist added that they might be required to learn some economics, too. The overall message was clear: America's resource situation was bad and bound to get worse. The hearings had led to a bill requiring the Departments of State, Interior, and Commerce to set up a joint resource procurement council with the express purpose of "insuring that proper consideration of American resource needs be an integral part of American foreign policy."

Suddenly the United States discovered that it had a national consensus: population control was the only possible salvation of the underdeveloped world. But that same consensus led to heated debate. How could the UDCs be persuaded to limit their populations, and should not the United States lead the way by limiting its own? Members of the intellectual community wanted America to set an example. They pointed out that the United States was in the midst of a new baby boom: her birth rate, well over 20 per thousand per year, and her growth rate of over one percent per annum were among the very highest of the developed countries. They detailed the deterioration of the American physical and psychic environments, the growing health threats, the impending food shortages,

Eco-Catastrophe!

and the insufficiency of funds for desperately needed public works. They contended that the nation was clearly unable or unwilling to properly care for the people it already had. What possible reason could there be, they queried, for adding any more? Besides, who would listen to requests by the United States for population control when that nation did not control her own profligate reproduction?

Those who opposed population controls for the U.S. were equally vociferous. The military-industrial complex, with its all-too-human mixture of ignorance and avarice, still saw strength and prosperity in numbers. Baby food magnates, already worried by the growing nitrate pollution of their products, saw their market disappearing. Steel manufacturers saw a decrease in aggregate demand and slippage for that holy of holies, the Gross National Product. And military men saw, in the growing population-food-environment crisis, a serious threat to their carefully nurtured Cold War. In the end, of course, economic arguments held sway, and the "inalienable right of every American couple to determine the size of its family," a freedom invented for the occasion in the early '70s, was not compromised.

The population control bill, which was passed by Congress early in 1974, as quite a document, nevertheless. On the domestic front, it authorized an increase from 100 to 150 million dollars in funds for "family planning" activities. This was made possible by a general feeling in the country that the growing army on welfare needed family planning. But the gist of the bill was a series of measures designed to impress the need for population control on the UDCs. All American aid to countries with overpopulation problems was required by law to consist in part of population control assistance. In order to receive any assistance each nation was required not only to accept the population control aid, but also to match it according to a complex formula. "Overpopulation" itself was defined by a formula based on U.N. statistics, and the UDCs were required not only to accept aid, but also to show progress in reducing birth rates. Every five years the status of the aid program for each nation was to be re-evaluated.

The reaction to the announcement of this program dwarfed the response to President Kennedy's speech. A coalition of UDCs attempted to get the U.N. General Assembly to condemn the United States as a "genetic aggressor." Most damaging of all to the American cause was the famous "25 Indians and a dog" speech by Mr. Shankarnarayan, Indian Ambassador to the U.N. Shankarnarayan pointed out that for several decades the United States, with less than six percent of the people of the world, had consumed roughly 50 percent of the raw materials used every year. He described vividly America's contribution to worldwide environmental deterioration, and he scathingly denounced the miserly record of United States foreign aid as "unworthy of a fourth-rate power, let alone the most powerful nation on earth."

It was the climax of his speech, however, which most historians claim once and for all destroyed the image of the United States. Shankarnarayan informed the assembly that the average American family dog

Paul R. Ehrlich

was fed more animal protein per week than the average Indian got in a month. "How do you justify taking fish from protein-starved Peruvians and feeding them to your animals?" he asked. "I contend," he concluded, "that the birth of an American baby is a greater disaster for the world than that of 25 Indian babies." When the applause had died away, Mr. Sorensen, the American representative, made a speech which said essentially that "other countries look after their own self-interest, too." When the vote came, the United States was condemned.

This condemnation set the tone of U.S.-UDC relations at the time the Russian Thanodrin proposal was made. The proposal seemed to offer the masses in the UDCs an opportunity to save themselves and humiliate the United States at the same time; and in human affairs, as we all know, biological realities could never interfere with such an opportunity. The scientists were silenced, the politicians said yes, the Thanodrin plants were built, and the results were what any beginning ecology student could have predicted. At first Thanodrin seemed to offer excellent control of many pests. True, there was a rash of human fatalities from improper use of the lethal chemical, but, as Russian technical advisors were prone to note, these were more than compensated for by increased yields. Thanodrin use skyrocketed throughout the underdeveloped world. The Mikoyan design group developed a dependable, cheap agricultural aircraft which the Soviets donated to the effort in large numbers. MIG sprayers became even more common in UDCs than MIG interceptors.

Then the troubles began. Insect strains with cuticles resistant to Thanodrin penetration began to appear. And as streams, rivers, fish culture ponds and onshore waters became rich in Thanodrin, more fisheries began to disappear. Bird populations were decimated. The sequence of events was standard for broadcast use of a synthetic pesticide: great success at first, followed by removal of natural enemies and development of resistance by the pest. Populations of crop-eating insects in areas treated with Thanodrin made steady comebacks and soon became more abundant than ever. Yields plunged, while farmers in their desperation increased the Thanodrin dose and shortened the time between treatments. Death from Thanodrin poisoning became common. The first violent incident occurred in the Canete Valley of Peru, where farmers had suffered a similar chlorinated hydrocarbon disaster in the mid-'50s. A Russian advisor serving as an agricultural pilot was assaulted and killed by a mob of enraged farmers in January, 1978. Trouble spread rapidly during 1978, especially after the word got out that two years earlier Russia herself had banned the use of Thanodrin at home because of its serious effects on ecological systems. Suddenly Russia, and not the United States, was the *bête noir* in the UDCs. "Thanodrin parties" became epidemic, with farmers, in their ignorance, dumping carloads of Thanodrin concentrate into the sea. Russian advisors fled, and four of the Thanodrin plants were leveled to the ground. Destruction of the plants in Rio and Calcutta led to hundreds of thousands of gallons of Thanodrin concentrate being dumped directly into the sea.

Eco-Catastrophe!

Mr. Shankarnarayan again rose to address the U.N., but this time it was Mr. Potemkin, representative of the Soviet Union, who was on the hot seat. Mr. Potemkin heard his nation described as the greatest mass killer of all time as Shankarnarayan predicted at least 30 million deaths from crop failures due to overdependence on Thanodrin. Russia was accused of "chemical aggression," and the General Assembly, after a weak reply by Potemkin, passed a vote of censure.

It was in January, 1979, that huge blooms of a previously unknown variety of diatom were reported off the coast of Peru. The blooms were accompanied by a massive die-off of sea life and of the pathetic remainder of the birds which had once feasted on the anchovies of the area. Almost immediately another huge bloom was reported in the Indian Ocean, centering around the Seychelles, and then a third in the South Atlantic off the African coast. Both of these were accompanied by spectacular die-offs of marine animals. Even more ominous were growing reports of fish and bird kills at oceanic points where there were no spectacular blooms. Biologists were soon able to explain the phenomenon: the diatom had evolved an enzyme which broke down Thanodrin; that enzyme also produced a breakdown product which interfered with the transmission of nerve impulses, and was therefore lethal to animals. Unfortunately, the biologists could suggest no way of repressing the poisonous diatom bloom in time. By September, 1979, all important animal life in the sea was extinct. Large areas of coastline had to be evacuated, as windrows of dead fish created a monumental stench.

But stench was the least of man's problems. Japan and China were faced with almost instant starvation from a total loss of the seafood on which they were so dependent. Both blamed Russia for their situation and demanded immediate mass shipments of food. Russia had none to send. On October 13, Chinese armies attacked Russia on a broad front. . . .

A pretty grim scenario. Unfortunately, we're a long way into it already. Everything mentioned as happening before 1970 has actually occurred; much of the rest is based on projections of trends already appearing. Evidence that pesticides have long-term lethal effects on human beings has started to accumulate, and recently Robert Finch, Secretary of the Department of Health, Education and Welfare, expressed his extreme apprehension about the pesticide situation. Simultaneously the petrochemical industry continues its unconscionable poison-peddling. For instance, Shell Chemical has been carrying on a high-pressure campaign to sell the insecticide Azodrin to farmers as a killer of cotton pests. They continue their program even though they know that Azodrin is not only ineffective, but often *increases* the pest density. They've covered themselves nicely in an advertisement which states, "Even if an overpowering migration [sic] develops, the flexibility of Azodrin lets you regain control fast. Just increase the dosage according to label recommendations." It's a great game—get people to apply the poison and kill the natural enemies of the pests. Then blame the increased pests on "migration" and sell even more pesticide!

Paul R. Ehrlich

Right now fisheries are being wiped out by overexploitation, made easy by modern electronic equipment. The companies producing the equipment know this. They even boast in advertising that only their equipment will keep fishermen in business until the final kill. Profits must obviously be maximized in the short run. Indeed, Western society is in the process of completing the rape and murder of the planet for economic gain. And, sadly, most of the rest of the world is eager for the opportunity to emulate our behavior. But the underdeveloped peoples will be denied that opportunity—the days of plunder are drawing inexorably to a close.

Most of the people who are going to die in the greatest cataclysm in the history of man have already been born. More than three and a half billion people already populate our moribund globe, and about half of them are hungry. Some 10 to 20 million will starve to death *this year*. In spite of this, the population of the earth will have increased by 70 million in 1969. For mankind has artificially lowered the death rate of the human population, while in general, birth rates have remained high. With the input side of the population system in high gear and the output side slowed down, our fragile planet has filled with people at an incredible rate. It took several million years for the population to reach a total of two billion people in 1930, while a *second two billion will have been added by 1975!* By that time some experts feel that food shortages will have escalated the present level of world hunger and starvation into famines of unbelievable proportions. Other experts, more optimistic, think the ultimate food-population collision will not occur until the decade of the 1980's. Of course more massive famine may be avoided if other events cause a prior rise in the human death rate.

Both worldwide plague and thermonuclear war are made more probable as population growth continues. These, along with famine, make up the trio of potential "death rate solutions" to the population problem—solutions in which the birth rate-death rate imbalance is redressed by a rise in the death rate rather than by a lowering of the birth rate. Make no mistake about it, *the imbalance will be redressed*. The shape of the population-growth curve is one familiar to the biologist. It is the outbreak part of an outbreak-crash sequence. A population grows rapidly in the presence of abundant resources, finally runs out of food or some other necessity, and crashes to a low level or extinction. Man is not only running out of food, he is also destroying the life support systems of the Spaceship Earth. The situation was recently summarized very succinctly: "It is the top of the ninth inning. Man, always a threat at the plate, has been hitting Nature hard. It is important to remember, however, that NATURE BATS LAST."

[1969]

Eco-Catastrophe!

Norman Cousins:

Needed: A New Dream

Norman Cousins (b. 1912), critic, humanitarian,
and editor of the *Saturday Review,* is perceptive in his comments on the nature of twentieth-
century civilization and on the proper course for
the future. Here he questions the continued va-
lidity of a major motivating force in modern life.

For more than two hundred years, the sense of a Promised Land has imparted a glow to the whole of American history and served as a charmed magnet for the rest of the world. Despite all its ordeals, errors, and flaws, the United States has never lost this enchantment, nor have the world's peoples ever ceased to regard us with wonder and envy. For America is a country that has readily lent itself to dreams. It has offered the promise of growth, space, mobility, confidence, recognizable paths to glory, and liberation from ancestral rigidities. An individual might be overwhelmed by the size and magnificence of America, but he has always known, somehow, he would not be lost.

In country after country, the pursuit of a workable national design has had its inspiration in the American dream. Even in the Soviet Union, the attempt to catch up with or surpass the United States in industrial and agricultural production has long been a national obsession. Throughout the world, most of the yardsticks for measuring progress and well-being in the world are notched with American units. What is the per capita income? What is the per capita production? What is the per capita food consumption? What is the average life expectancy? How many automobiles, television sets, refrigerators, pianos, electric hair curlers, electronic computers?

But the dream is dated. For nothing would be more dangerous today to the human future than if the American standard were to be achieved in country after country. Consider what would happen if the present level of American industrialization, electrification, transportation, and consumption were extended to the rest of the world. A tidal wave of prosperity would sweep across the globe, but within a very few years the Earth would become uninhabitable. For it is not just affluence but the things that go with it that must be taken into account. If the American way of life were to be universalized, the world's atmosphere would have to sustain 200 times more sulphur dioxide and sulphur trioxide than it does now, 750 times more carbon monoxide, carbon dioxide, and benzopyrene, 10,000 times more asbestos. The streams, lakes, and oceans would be burdened with 175 times more chemical poisons. The Earth's forest areas would be reduced by two-thirds. Thirty million acres would be taken out of cultivation each year to make way for spreading cities and highways.

The total result would be the onset of another Ice Age. For the massive increase of smoke and dust in the air would diminish sunlight and produce a significant lowering of the Earth's temperature. Even without respect to the cooling off of the Earth, an even greater danger would be the depletion of the world's oxygen supply caused by the chemical poisoning of the oceans and the consequent impairment of the process of photosynthesis.

What gives grim point to all this is that most of the world's nations, not excluding the Soviet Union and Communist China, are now resolutely bent on a program of intensive and massive industrialization as the best means of serving their peoples. Thus, whether with respect to the United States or other governments, there is little sense of global responsibility,

Norman Cousins

little awareness of the need for planetary planning or of the fact that the most important questions and problems of our time are worldwide in scope, requiring a world philosophy to deal with them.

For years many Americans had no hesitation in prescribing their way of life as a comprehensive remedy for the ills of mankind. Terms such as "the American Century" or "the American Mission" reflected their conviction that we had created a design for living within the reach of all men who were ready to accept our institutions, and who were bold and ingenious enough to apply them. But now we must confront the stark fact that this design is contrary to the human interest.

The implications will of course be viewed differently by different people. Some Americans may find it difficult to adjust to the realization that the American dream no longer fits the generality of men. Some of them may feel that a freeze ought to be imposed on further development elsewhere, now that the adverse consequences of a high degree of industrialization are measurable in global terms. Other Americans, however, will recognize that the most useful thing we can do right now is not to try to shut everyone else off from the largesse we have enjoyed, but to bring our dominant energies to bear on the need to bring life into balance in our own land. What is required are not only new methods and programs for preventing and controlling pollution, but new ideas and values directed to a future made safe for man. In such a future, the good life would be measured more in terms of an improvement in human relationships than in any increase of the gross national product. Satisfactions would be reckoned more in terms of the full creative and moral development of the individual than in the pleasures made possible by generating vast quantities of electric power. There would be genuine joy in being able to draw a deep breath of clean air, scoop up a handful of rich loam, or put one's mouth to a cool brook. The restoration of the natural environment and the discovery of how to live at peace with it would become a national purpose. It is possible that the rest of the world would find this new purpose even more compelling and worthy of emulation than the present one.

Maybe this is what our young people are trying to tell us.

[1970]

Needed: A New Dream

Robert Frost:

Birches

Robert Frost (1874-1963), poet, primarily of
New England, was a master of his technique,
often obscured by a myth that threatens to over-
whelm his life and his work. Part of that myth,
encouraged by himself, stems from the fact that
he was constantly and reverently aware of
man's relationship to nature. Beyond this relationship, however, Frost saw the source of
modern man's despair to be a refusal or an inability to understand the nature of that relationship.

When I see birches bend to left and right
Across the lines of straighter darker trees,
I like to think some boy's been swinging them.
But swinging doesn't bend them down to stay
As ice storms do. Often you must have seen them
Loaded with ice a sunny winter morning
After a rain. They click upon themselves
As the breeze rises, and turn many-colored
As the stir cracks and crazes their enamel.
Soon the sun's warmth makes them shed crystal shells
Shattering and avalanching on the snow crust—
Such heaps of broken glass to sweep away
You'd think the inner dome of heaven had fallen.
They are dragged to the withered bracken by the load,
And they seem not to break; though once they are bowed
So low for long, they never right themselves:
You may see their trunks arching in the woods
Years afterwards, trailing their leaves on the ground
Like girls on hands and knees that throw their hair
Before them over their heads to dry in the sun.
But I was going to say when Truth broke in
With all her matter of fact about the ice-storm,
I should prefer to have some boy bend them
As he went out and in to fetch the cows—
Some boy too far from town to learn baseball,
Whose only play was what he found himself,
Summer or winter, and could play alone.
One by one he subdued his father's trees
By riding them down over and over again
Until he took the stiffness out of them,
And not one but hung limp, not one was left
For him to conquer. He learned all there was
To learn about not launching out too soon
And so not carrying the tree away
Clear to the ground. He always kept his poise
To the top branches, climbing carefully
With the same pains you use to fill a cup
Up to the brim, and even above the brim.
Then he flung outward, feet first, with a swish,
Kicking his way down through the air to the ground.
So was I once myself a swinger of birches.
And so I dream of going back to be.
It's when I'm weary of considerations,
And life is too much like a pathless wood
Where your face burns and tickles with the cobwebs
Broken across it, and one eye is weeping
From a twig's having lashed across it open.

Robert Frost

I'd like to get away from earth awhile
And then come back to it and begin over.
May no fate willfully misunderstand me
And half grant what I wish and snatch me away
Not to return. Earth's the right place for love:
I don't know where it's likely to go better.
I'd like to go by climbing a birch tree,
And climb black branches up a snow-white trunk
Toward heaven, till the tree could bear no more,
But dipped its top and set me down again.
That would be good both going and coming back.
One could do worse than be a swinger of birches.

[1916]

Birches

T. S. Eliot:

The Hollow Men

Thomas Stearns Eliot (1888-1965), pessimistic modern American poet who found permanence in conservative British institutions, captures in his early work the bafflement, frustration, and horror of modern man in a modern post-Darwinian, post-Marxian, post-Freudian universe. A pure poet, his statements are metaphysical rather than naturalistic as they probe the meaning of existence.

Mistah Kurtz—he dead.

A penny for the Old Guy

I

We are the hollow men
We are the stuffed men
Leaning together
Headpiece filled with straw. Alas!
Our dried voices, when
We whisper together
Are quiet and meaningless
As wind in dry grass
Or rats' feet over broken glass
In our dry cellar

Shape without form, shade without color,
Paralyzed force, gesture without motion;

Those who have crossed
With direct eyes, to death's other Kingdom
Remember us—if at all—not as lost
Violent souls, but only
As the hollow men
The stuffed men.

II

Eyes I dare not meet in dreams
In death's dream kingdom
These do not appear:
There, the eyes are
Sunlight on a broken column
There, is a tree swinging
And voices are
In the wind's singing
More distant and more solemn
Than a fading star.

Let me be no nearer
In death's dream kingdom
Let me also wear
Such deliberate disguises
Rat's coat, crowskin, crossed staves
In a field
Behaving as the wind behaves
No nearer—

T. S. Eliot

Not that final meeting
In the twilight kingdom

III

This is the dead land
This is cactus land
Here the stony images
Are raised, here they receive
The supplication of a dead man's hand
Under the twinkle of a fading star.

Is it like this
In death's other kingdom
Waking alone
At the hour when we are
Trembling with tenderness
Lips that would kiss
From prayers to broken stone.

IV

The eyes are not here
There are no eyes here
In this valley of dying stars
In this hollow valley
This broken jaw of our lost kingdoms

In this last of meeting places
We grope together
And avoid speech
Gathered on this beach of the tumid river

Sightless, unless
The eyes reappear
As the perpetual star
Multifoliate rose
Of death's twilight kingdom
The hope only
Of empty men

V

Here we go round the prickly pear
Prickly pear prickly pear
Here we go round the prickly pear
At five o'clock in the morning.

The Hollow Men

Between the idea
And the reality
Between the motion
And the act
Falls the Shadow
  For Thine is the Kingdom

Between the conception
And the creation
Between the emotion
And the response
Falls the Shadow
  Life is very long

Between the desire
And the spasm
Between the potency
And the existence
Between the essence
And the descent
Falls the Shadow
  For Thine is the Kingdom

For Thine is
Life is
For Thine is the

This is the way the world ends
This is the way the world ends
This is the way the world ends
Not with a bang but a whimper.

[1925]

T. S. Eliot

Hart Crane:

The River

Hart Crane (1899-1932), a gifted poet, attempted to define the essence of America in his work, particularly in *The Bridge* (1930), but was inhibited by inner torment that ultimately destroyed him. Though the spiritual quality of America he sought to proclaim ultimately eluded him, in "The River" he demonstrates a deep faith in and feeling for the American natural reality.

Stick your patent name on a signboard
brother—all over—going west—young man
Tintex—Japalac—Certain-teed Overalls ads
and lands sakes! under the new playbill ripped
in the guaranteed corner—see Bert Williams what?
Minstrels when you steal a chicken just
save me the wing, for if it isn't
Erie it ain't for miles around a
Mazda—and the telegraphic night coming on Thomas

a Ediford—and whistling down the tracks
a headlight rushing with the sound—can you
imagine—while an EXPRESS makes time like

SCIENCE—COMMERCE and the HOLYGHOST
RADIO ROARS IN EVERY HOME WE HAVE THE NORTHPOLE
WALLSTREET AND VIRGINBIRTH WITHOUT STONES OR
WIRES OR EVEN RUNning brooks connecting ears
and no more sermons windows flashing roar
Breathtaking—as you like it . . . eh?

                    So the 20th Century—so
whizzed the Limited—roared by and left
three men, still hungry on the tracks, ploddingly
watching the tail lights wizen and converge,
slipping gimleted and neatly out of sight.
The last bear, shot drinking in the Dakotas,
Loped under wires that span the mountain stream.
Keen instruments, strung to a vast precision
Bind town to town and dream to ticking dream.
But some men take their liquor slow—and count—
Though they'll confess no rosary nor clue—
The river's minute by the far brook's year.
Under a world of whistles, wires and steam
Caboose-like they go ruminating through
Ohio, Indiana—blind baggage—
To Cheyenne tagging . . . Maybe Kalamazoo.

Time's renderings, time's blendings they construe
As final reckonings of fire and snow;
Strange bird-wit, like the elemental gist
Of unwalled winds they offer, singing low
My Old Kentucky Home and Casey Jones,
Some Sunny Day. I heard a road-gang chanting so.
And afterwards, who had a colt's eyes—one said,
"Jesus! Oh I remember watermelon days!" And sped
High in a cloud of merriment, recalled

Hart Crane

"—And when my Aunt Sally Simpson smiled," he drawled—
"It was almost Louisiana, long ago."

"There's no place like Booneville though, Buddy,"
One said, excising a last burr from his vest,
"—For early trouting." Then peering in the can,
"—But I kept on the tracks." Possessed, resigned,
He trod the fire down pensively and grinned,
Spreading dry shingles of a beard. . . .

               Behind
My father's cannery works I used to see
Rail-squatters ranged in nomad raillery,
The ancient men—wifeless or runaway
Hobo-trekkers that forever search
An empire wilderness of freight and rails.
Each seemed a child, like me, on a loose perch,
Holding to childhood like some termless play.
John, Jake, or Charley, hopping the slow freight
—Memphis to Tallahassee—riding the rods,
Blind fists of nothing, humpty-dumpty clods.

Yet they touch something like a key perhaps.
From pole to pole across the hills, the states
—They know a body under the wide rain;
Youngsters with eyes like fjords, old reprobates
With racetrack jargon,—dotting immensity
They lurk across her, knowing her yonder breast
Snow-silvered, sumac-stained or smoky blue,
Is past the valley-sleepers, south or west.
—As I have trod the rumorous midnights, too.

And past the circuit of the lamp's thin flame
(O Nights that brought me to her body bare!)
Have dreamed beyond the print that bound her name.
Trains sounding the long blizzards out—I heard
Wail into distances I knew were hers.
Papooses crying on the wind's long mane
Screamed redskin dynasties that fled the brain,
—Dead echoes! But I knew her body there,
Time like a serpent down her shoulder dark,
And space, an eaglet's wing, laid on her hair.

Under the Ozarks, domed by Iron Mountain,
The old gods of the rain lie wrapped in pools
Where eyeless fish curvet a sunken fountain
And re-descend with corn from querulous crows.

The River

Such pilferings make up their timeless eatage,
Propitiate them for their timber torn
By iron, iron—always the iron dealt cleavage!
They doze now, below axe and powder horn.

And Pullman breakfasters glide glistening steel
From tunnel into field—iron strides the dew—
Straddles the hill, a dance of wheel on wheel.
You have a half-hour's wait at Siskiyou,
Or stay the night and take the next train through.
Southward, near Cairo passing, you can see
The Ohio merging,—borne down Tennessee;
And if it's summer and the sun's in dusk
Maybe the breeze will lift the River's musk
—As though the waters breathed that you might know
Memphis Johnny, Steamboat Bill, Missouri Joe.
Oh, lean from the window, if the train slows down,
As though you touched hands with some ancient clown,
—A little while gaze absently below
And hum *Deep River* with them while they go.

Yes, turn again and sniff once more—look see,
O Sheriff, Brakeman and Authority—
Hitch up your pants and crunch another quid,
For you, too, feed the River timelessly.
And few evade full measure of their fate;
Always they smile out eerily what they seem.
I could believe he joked at heaven's gate—
Dan Midland —jolted from the cold brake-beam.

Down, down—born pioneers in time's despite,
Grimed tributaries to an ancient flow—
They win no frontier by their wayward plight,
But drift in stillness, as from Jordan's brow.

You will not hear it as the sea; even stone
Is not more hushed by gravity . . . But slow,
As loth to take more tribute—sliding prone
Like one whose eyes were buried long ago

The River, spreading, flows—and spends your dream.
What are you, lost within this tideless spell?
You are your father's father, and the stream—
A liquid theme that floating niggers swell.

Damp tonnage and alluvial march of days—
Nights turbid, vascular with silted shale

Hart Crane

And roots surrendered down of moraine clays:
The Mississippi drinks the farthest dale.

O quarrying passion, undertowed sunlight!
The basalt surface drags a jungle grace
Ochreous and lynx-barred in lengthening might;
Patience! and you shall reach the biding place!

Over De Soto's bones the freighted floors
Throb past the City storied of three thrones.
Down two more turns the Mississippi pours
(Anon tall ironsides up from salt lagoons)

And flows within itself, heaps itself free.
All fades but one thin skyline 'round . . . Ahead
No embrace opens but the stinging sea;
The River lifts itself from its long bed,

Poised wholly on its dream, a mustard glow,
Tortured with history, its one will—flow!
—The Passion spreads in wide tongues, chocked and slow,
Meeting the Gulf, hosannas silently below.

[1930]

The River

Robinson Jeffers:

Hurt Hawks

November Surf

Robinson Jeffers (1887-1962), poet, primarily of the California coast, saw little hope for man's redemption in the evidence around him. Like Mark Twain, he believed that man was flawed in the making, and that man's inability to perceive that flaw ensures corruption.

HURT HAWKS

1

The broken pillar of the wing jags from the clotted shoulder,
The wing trails like a banner in defeat,
No more to use the sky forever but live with famine
And pain a few days: cat nor coyote
Will shorten the week of waiting for death, there is game without talons.
He stands under the oak-bush and waits
The lame feet of salvation; at night he remembers freedom
And flies in a dream, the dawns ruin it.
He is strong and pain is worse to the strong, incapacity is worse.
The curs of the day come and torment him
At distance, no one but death the redeemer will humble that head,
The intrepid readiness, the terrible eyes.
The wild God of the world is sometimes merciful to those
That ask mercy, not often to the arrogant.
You do not know him, you communal people, or you have forgotten him;
Intemperate and savage, the hawk remembers him;
Beautiful and wild, the hawks, and men that are dying, remember him.

2

I'd sooner, except the penalties, kill a man than a hawk; but the great
    redtail
Had nothing left but unable misery
From the bone too shattered for mending, the wing that trailed under his
    talons when he moved.
We had fed him six weeks, I gave him freedom,
He wandered over the foreland hill and returned in the evening, asking
    for death,
Not like a beggar, still eyed with the old
Implacable arrogance. I gave him the lead gift in the twilight. What fell
    was relaxed,
Owl-downy, soft feminine feathers; but what
Soared: the fierce rush: the night-herons by the flooded river cried fear
    at its rising
Before it was quite unsheathed from reality.

[1928]

NOVEMBER SURF

Some lucky day each November great waves awake and are drawn
Like smoking mountains bright from the west
And come and cover the cliff with white violent cleanness: then suddenly
The old granite forgets half a year's filth:

Robinson Jeffers

The orange-peel, eggshells, papers, pieces of clothing, the clots
Of dung in corners of the rock, and used
Sheaths that make light love safe in the evenings: all the droppings of
    the summer
Idlers washed off in a winter ecstasy:
I think this cumbered continent envies its cliff then. . . . But all seasons
The earth, in her childlike prophetic sleep,
Keeps dreaming of the bath of a storm that prepares up the long coast
Of the future to scour more than her sea-lines:
The cities gone down, the people fewer and the hawks more numerous,
The rivers mouth to source pure; when the two-footed
Mammal, being someways one of the nobler animals, regains
The dignity of room, the value of rareness.

[1932]

November Surf

Denise Levertov:

Merritt Parkway

Denise Levertov (b. 1923), contemporary poet, attempts in her work to crystallize and examine everyday aspects of American life. In "Merritt Parkway" (1958), she reveals much about the significance of what she observes.

As if it were
forever that they move, that we
keep moving—

Under a wan sky where
as the lights went on a star
pierced the haze and now
follows steadily
a constant
above our six lanes
the dreamlike continuum . . .

And the people—ourselves!
the humans from inside the
cars, apparent
only at gasoline stops

unsure,
eyeing each other

drink coffee hastily at the
slot machines and hurry
back to the cars
vanish
into them forever, to
keep moving—

Houses now and then beyond the
sealed road, the trees/trees, bushes
passing by, passing
the cars that
keep moving ahead of

us, past us, pressing behind us

and
over left, those that come

in six lanes, gliding
north and south, speeding with
a slurred sound—

toward us shining too brightly
moving relentlessly

[1958]

Denise Levertov

Lawrence Ferlinghetti:
A Coney Island of the Mind

Lawrence Ferlinghetti (b. 1919), poet of the beat movement, seeks to unite poetry and music, particularly jazz. Technically and rhythmically an experimenter, he has dedicated himself and his work to social criticism typical of the movement and to improving the social climate for artists and the arts.

1

In Goya's greatest scenes we seem to see
                              the people of the world
exactly at the moment when
  they first attained the title of
                              'suffering humanity'
They writhe upon the page
            in a veritable rage
                              of adversity

Heaped up
            groaning with babies and bayonets
                              under cement skies
  in an abstract landscape of blasted trees
      bent statues bats wings and beaks
              slippery gibbets
      cadavers and carnivorous cocks
  and all the final hollering monsters
  of the
              'imagination of disaster'
  they are so bloody real
                  it is as if they really still existed

And they do

          Only the landscape is changed

They are still ranged along the roads
  plagued by legionaires
              false windmills and demented roosters

They are the same people
              only further from home
  on freeways fifty lanes wide
  on a concrete continent
                  spaced with bland billboards
    illustrating imbecile illusions of happiness
The scene shows fewer tumbrils
      but more maimed citizens
                  in painted cars
    and they have strange license plates
    and engines
            that devour America

Lawrence Ferlinghetti

3

The poet's eye obscenely seeing
sees the surface of the round world
with its drunk rooftops
and wooden oiseaux on clotheslines
and its clay males and females
with hot legs and rosebud breasts
in rollaway beds
and its trees full of mysteries
and its Sunday parks and speechless statues
and its America
with its ghost towns and empty Ellis Islands
and its surrealist landscape of
mindless prairies
supermarket suburbs
steamheated cemeteries
cinerama holy days
and protesting cathedrals
a kissproof world of plastic toiletseats tampax and taxis
drugged store cowboys and las vegas virgins
disowned indians and cinemad matrons
unroman senators and conscientious non-objec-
tors
and all other fatal shorn-up fragments
of the immigrant's dream come too true
and mislaid
among the sunbathers

[1958]

A Coney Island of the Mind

Allen Ginsberg:
A Supermarket in California

Allen Ginsberg (b. 1926), poet who first gained prominence in the beat movement of the 1950s, was, like many in the movement, a frustrated idealist and a caustic social critic. His most ambitious and controversial poem is "Howl" (1955). "A Supermarket in California" (1956) reveals much of the antimaterialistic protest that dominates his work and motivates his life.

What thoughts I have of you tonight, Walt Whitman, for I walked down the sidestreets under the trees with a headache self-conscious looking at the full moon.

In my hungry fatigue, and shopping for images, I went into the neon fruit supermarket, dreaming of your enumerations!

What peaches and what penumbras! Whole families shopping at night! Aisles full of husbands! Wives in the avocados, babies in the to-matoes!—and you, Garcia Lorca, what were you doing down by the water-melons?

I saw you, Walt Whitman, childless, lonely old grubber, poking among the meats in the refrigerator and eyeing the grocery boys.

I heard you asking questions of each: Who killed the pork chops? What price bananas? Are you my Angel?

I wandered in and out of the brilliant stacks of cans following you, and followed in my imagination by the store detective.

We strode down the open corridors together in our solitary fancy tasting artichokes, possessing every frozen delicacy, and never passing the cashier.

Where are we going, Walt Whitman? The doors close in an hour. Which way does your beard point tonight?

(I touch your book and dream of our odyssey in the supermarket and feel absurd.)

Will we walk all night through solitary streets? The trees add shade to shade, lights out in the houses, we'll both be lonely.

Will we stroll dreaming of the lost America of love past blue auto-mobiles in driveways, home to our silent cottage?

Ah, dear father, graybeard, lonely old courage-teacher, what America did you have when Charon quit poling his ferry and you got out on a smoking bank and stood watching the boat disappear on the black waters of Lethe?

[1956]

Allen Ginsberg

Galway Kinnell:
The River That Is East

Galway Kinnell (b. 1927), contemporary poet, examines the American natural environment in a search for spiritual meaning. However, in looking at the East River, which suggested so much hope to Walt Whitman and Hart Crane, he sees that it carries the debris of human life as it symbolizes a different ultimate meaning.

1

Buoys begin clanging like churches
And peter out. Sunk to the gunwhales
In their shapes tugs push upstream.
A carfloat booms down, sweeping past
Illusory suns that blaze in puddles
On the shores where it rained, past the Navy Yard,
Under the Williamsburg Bridge
That hangs facedown from its strings
Over which the Jamaica Local crawls,
Through white-winged gulls which shriek
And flap from the water and sideslip in
Over the chaos of illusions, dangling
Limp red hands, and screaming as they touch.

2

A boy swings his legs from the pier,
His days go by, tugs and carfloats go by,
Each prow pushing a whitecap. On his deathbed
Kane remembered the abrupt, missed Grail
Called Rosebud, Gatsby must have thought back
On his days digging clams in Little Girl Bay
In Minnesota, Nick fished in dreamy Michigan,
Gant had his memories, Griffeths, those
Who went baying after the immaterial
And whiffed its strange dazzle in a blonde
In a canary convertible, who died
Thinking of the Huck Finns of themselves
On the old afternoons, themselves like this boy
Swinging his legs, who sees the *Ile de France*
Come in, and wonders if in some stateroom
There is not a sick-hearted heiress sitting
Drink in hand, saying to herself his name.

3

A man stands on the pier.
He has long since stopped wishing his heart were full
Or his life dear to him.
He watches the snowfall hitting the dirty water.
He thinks: Beautiful. Beautiful.
If I were a gull I would be one with white wings,
I would fly out over the water, explode, and
Be beautiful snow hitting the dirty water.

Galway Kinnell

4

And thou, River of Tomorrow, flowing . . .
We stand on the shore, which is mist beneath us,
And regard the onflowing river. Sometimes
It seems the river stops and the shore
Flows into the past. Nevertheless, its leaked promises
Hopping in the bloodstream, we strain for the future,
Sometimes even glimpse it, a vague, scummed thing
We dare not recognize, and peer again
At the cabled shroud out of which it came,
We who have no roots but the shifts of our pain,
No flowering but our own strange lives.

What is this river but the one
Which drags the things we love,
Processions of debris like floating lamps,
Towards the radiance in which they go out?

No, it is the River that is East, known once
From a high window in Brooklyn, in agony—river
On which a door locked to the water floats,
A window sash paned with brown water, a whisky crate,
Barrel staves, sun spokes, feathers of the birds,
A breadcrust, a rat, spittle, butts, and peels,
The immaculate stream, heavy, and swinging home again.

[1964]

The River That Is East

LeRoi Jones:
A Contract for the Destruction and Rebuilding of Paterson

LeRoi Jones (b. 1934), contemporary poet, views the modern American scene from the vantage point given him by his experience as a black. But in his verse the race problem gives way to the human problem as he faces the dehumanizing, destructive effects of a mass, depersonalized, materialistic society.

Flesh, and cars, tar, dug holes beneath stone
a rude hierarchy of money, band saws cross out
music, feeling. Even speech, corrodes.
                                        I came here
from where I sat boiling in my veins, cold fear
at the death of men, the death of learning, in
cold fear, at my own. Romantic vests of same death
blank at the corner, blank when they raise their fingers

Criss the hearts, in dark flesh staggered so marvelous
are their lies. So complete, their mastery, of these
stupid niggers. Loud spics kill each other, and will not

make the simple trip to Tiffany's. Will not smash their stainless
heads, against the simpler effrontery of so callous a code as gain.

You are no brothers, dirty woogies, dying under dried rinds, in massa's
droopy tuxedos. Cab Calloways of the soul, at the soul's juncture, a
music, they think will save them from our eyes. (In back of the
    terminal

where the circus will not go. At the backs of crowds, stooped and vulgar
breathing hate syllables, unintelligible rapes of all that linger in
our new world. Killed in white fedora hats, they stand so mute at what
whiter slaves did to my fathers. They muster silence. They pray at the
steps of abstract prisons, to be kings, when all is silence, when all
is stone. When even the stupid fruit of their loins is gold, or something
else they cannot eat.

[1964]

LeRoi Jones

Index of Authors

Index of Titles

Acknowledgments

EDWIN ARLINGTON ROBINSON: *Sonnet*
"Sonnet" is reprinted by permission of Charles Scribner's Sons from *The Children of the Night* by Edwin Arlington Robinson (1897).

VACHEL LINDSAY: *A Gospel of Beauty*
Reprinted with permission of The Macmillan Company from *Collected Poems* by Vachel Lindsay. Copyright 1914 by The Macmillan Company, renewed 1942 by Elizabeth C. Lindsay.

VACHEL LINDSAY: *Factory Windows Are Always Broken*
Reprinted with permission of The Macmillan Company from *Collected Poems* by Vachel Lindsay. Copyright 1914 by The Macmillan Company, renewed 1942 by Elizabeth C. Lindsay.

CARL SANDBURG: *Chicago*
From *Chicago Poems* by Carl Sandburg. Copyright 1916 by Holt, Rinehart and Winston, Inc. Copyright 1944 by Carl Sandburg. Reprinted by permission of Holt, Rinehart and Winston, Inc.

FRANKLIN D. ROOSEVELT: *State Planning for Land Utilization*
Reprinted with permission of the Franklin D. Roosevelt Library from *Looking Forward* by Franklin D. Roosevelt.

HENRY A. WALLACE: *Putting Our Lands in Order*
From *New Frontiers*, copyright, 1934, renewed, 1962, by Henry A. Wallace. Reprinted by permission of Harcourt Brace Jovanovich, Inc.

THOMAS WOLFE: *The Train in the Night*
Reprinted with the permission of Charles Scribner's Sons from *Of Time and the River*, pages 25-35, by Thomas Wolfe. Copyright 1935 by Charles Scribner's Sons; renewal copyright © 1963 Paul Gitlin, Administrator, C.T.A.

SHERWOOD ANDERSON: *I'll Say We've Done Well*
Reprinted by permission of Harold Ober Associates Incorporated. Copyright 1922 by The Nation, Inc. Copyright 1926 by Eleanor Copenhaver Anderson. Copyright renewed 1949 by Eleanor Copenhaver Anderson.

SHERWOOD ANDERSON: *The TVA*
Reprinted by permission of Harold Ober Associates Incorporated. Copyright 1935 by Charles Scribner's Sons. Copyright renewed 1962 by Eleanor Copenhaver Anderson.

DONALD CULROSS PEATTIE: *The Buffalo*
Reprinted by permission of Simon and Schuster, Inc. Copyright 1938 by Donald Culross Peattie.

DONALD CULROSS PEATTIE: *The Passenger Pigeons*
Reprinted by permission of Simon and Schuster, Inc. Copyright 1938 by Donald Culross Peattie.